INVENTING THE DREAM

AMERICANS AND THE CALIFORNIA DREAM

Americans and the California Dream, 1850–1915

Inventing the Dream

California Through the Progressive Era

INVENTING THE DREAM

California Through the Progressive Era

KEVIN STARR

New York   *Oxford*

OXFORD UNIVERSITY PRESS

1985

OXFORD UNIVERSITY PRESS

Oxford   London   New York   Toronto
Delhi   Bombay   Calcutta   Madras   Karachi
Kuala Lumpur   Singapore   Hong Kong   Tokyo
Nairobi   Dar es Salaam   Cape Town
Melbourne   Auckland

and associated companies
Beirut   Berlin   Ibadan   Mexico City   Nicosia

Published by Oxford University Press, 200 Madison Avenue
New York, New York 10016

LIBRARY OF CONGRESS CATALOGING IN PUBLICATION DATA

Starr, Kevin.
Inventing the dream.

Bibliography: p.
Includes index.

1. California, Southern—History.   2. California,
Southern—Social life and customs.   I. Title.
F867.S8   1985   979.4'9   84-19093
ISBN 0-19-503489-9

Printing (last digit): 9 8 7 6 5 4 3 2
Printed in the United States of America

FOR
Oscar Lewis, Lawrence Clark Powell, and
Albert Shumate
a triumvirate of beloved Californians

Preface

With the exception of certain deliberate excursions to the north, this narrative is more than half concerned with the rise of Southern California in the nineteenth and early twentieth centuries. As such, it both supplements the Northern California focus of my previous study and carries forward the larger narrative of the rise of California as a regional society. My focus remains, as usual, the imaginative and symbolic aspects of experience as the imagination impinges upon social and psychological realities and in turn transforms the materials of experience into the building blocks of identity. The process is circular, or perhaps even dialectical, as the California of fact and the California of imagination shape and reshape each other. In this narrative an attempt has been made to move beyond overtly imaginative material, most noticeably the literary and artistic record, and to seek in such enterprises as politics, business, banking, and agriculture comparable dramas of imaginative experience. In terms of methodology or the absence thereof, the procedures at work in this narrative are simple, self-evident, and totally personal. After extensive investigation, I have isolated to my tentative satisfaction the story line I believe is most expressive of those elusive inner realities—in a person or a social moment—that can be glimpsed through a glass darkly (or brightly, for that matter, this being California) but never fully quantified. This narrative, then, exists in the borderlands between history and literary criticism. While it is neither of those in a pure form, my method (such as it is) depends upon each: upon history for the establishment of the record, and upon literary criticism for ways of disclosing how imagination and experience can transform each other. As suggested, my technique is story, narrative—suggestion rather than explanation, the elusive over the quantifiable. As a professional librarian, I relish information. As a working journalist, I respect story line as a way of getting one's point across. As an Americanist, I love American materials in all their variety and promise.

Here, then, is a narrative that with certain omissions (such as the story of irrigation, reserved for further study) tells how certain Californians, Southern Californians especially, defined their region to themselves and to others in the 1850–1920 period. Totally dependent upon a rich body of extant scholarship, this narrative builds upon the work of others, but breaks new ground in both scholarship and interpretation when necessary. How hauntingly beautiful, how replete with lost possibilities, seems that Southern California of two and three generations ago, now that a dramatically different society has emerged in its place. What possible connections, one can legitimately ask, can there be between that lost world, with its arroyo cabins and Spanish imagery, its daydreams of Malibu sunsets and orange groves, and today's megasuburbia extending from Mexico to Kern County? This is a good question, and it cannot be answered by mere pieties regarding the usable past, for few American regions have experienced accelerations and quantum leaps comparable to those experienced by Southern California in the years that followed the period of this narrative. That older Southern California, however—that Southern California dream, if you will—is, I believe, primarily of value in and of itself as a past creation of American society as it found itself on the Pacific Coast south of the Tehachapi Mountains in the decades before and after 1900. Here flourished for fifty years or so a unique interaction of Protestant high-mindedness (frequently clothing itself in Latin Catholic imagery), the genteel tradition, the booster spirit, conformity, eccentricity and rebellion, Progressive reform, naturalism, and agrarian myth, all at work, primarily, among the American middle classes as they settled into a unique, semi-arid landscape fronting a spectacular seashore and graced by perhaps the finest weather on the planet. From this rich, often eccentric mixture of orthodoxy and innovation emerged a regional society that in its future developments and transformations would set national standards of American identity, as the attitudes and style of Southern California were exported via the film industry to the rest of the nation. In an elusive but compelling manner, Southern California was destined to secure for itself a fixed place in the collective daydream of America. The story of the emergence of this part of California as a regional society is therefore of more than passing significance.

San Francisco   K.S.
September 1984

Contents

bohemians of the Arroyo, the genteel was enriched by semi-arid California and by the desert. There, amidst mesa and arroyo, communing with the Indian past, they found a borderland, a backcountry, that spoke directly to their desire to challenge the genteel with the severities of a less complicated, more integrated way of life.

5   Works, Days, Georgic Beginnings   128

In the late nineteenth century, Californians envisioned a glorious new work for their state, the transformation of California into the Garden of America. Just exactly who would own this garden, however, and who would live amidst its bounty remained unanswered and deeply troubling questions. In the meantime, amidst pressing social and economic problems, the ancient tasks of clearing, tilling, planting, and harvesting were pursued on an increasingly unprecedented scale. In these decades California won for itself an enduring reputation as a land of orange groves and vineyards, of sunshine, fruits, and flowers.

6   Arthur Page Brown and the Dream of San Francisco   176

Meanwhile, up in San Francisco, a young New York City architect was tutoring an emerging city in the proprieties of the American Renaissance style. Through the work of Brown and the young men he recruited into his firm, San Francisco experienced its first systematic program of architecture and public works. In building after building, Brown and his design team encouraged the premier American city on the Pacific Coast first to envision and second to display itself as an urban culture possessed of solidity and self-confidence.

7   Reforming California   199

Turn-of-the-century California was alive with reformist ambitions on a number of fronts. Some programs had for their goal nothing less than the reform of California itself. Whether in politics or education, however, labor or the women's movement, the crusade for kindergarten care or the founding of chambers of commerce or the invention of branch banking, these reform efforts took energy and direction from their common California context. Seeking to upgrade their society, Californians reinforced the utopian possibilities of their state.

8   Progressivism and After   235

In 1910 a band of young reformers captured the political and governmental machinery of California. In the brief years of their power, they sought and partially achieved the recreation of California governmentally. Beginning as rebels and reformers, these young men, as they grew older, generally moved to the right. In this conservative tendency some observers beheld a representative California pattern—a taste, that is, for radical reactions of various sorts.

9   Stories and Dreams: The Movies Come to Southern California   283

By 1920 yet another California was in the process of defining itself, this time through the medium of the nascent film industry. For a half-century Southern California had been a land of dreams, and now these dreams were finding a way to multiply themselves with an intensity and a lavishness beyond measure. It was no accident that motion pictures, a medium speaking so powerfully, so directly to the subliminal self, found such an appropriate environment in Southern California.

INVENTING THE DREAM

I

Place, Patterns, Premises

Southern California, where the search for the California dream attained significant intensity at century's turn, was a land that rushed to the sea as if to an eager lover. No wonder: some five hundred million years ago the sea possessed the Southland in its entirety. It had been pushed back to the present coastline only at the cost of eons of struggle. Burnt off by an angry sun, the sea surrendered its embrace, leaving the land to the formative work of weather and geology. Volcanic action convulsed the earth into great mountain ranges. Slippages born of catastrophic subterranean shifts carved out canyons, valleys, and arroyos of every size. Glacial movement cleared the lowlands, and in the eastern deserts left behind a giant's garden of heroic sculpture. This carving and shaping was a work of time, an earth dance of ages. Its gestures and stored music kept their tense strength in earthquake faults beneath the land's surface, giving testimony to the fact that the task of arranging the continents was not yet through.

Mountains, a coastal plain, desert: Southern California is not difficult to understand, unless the human factor be considered. The Coast Range and certain spur lines—the Santa Lucia, the San Rafael—sweep down from the north and in the area of Point Conception turn eastwards. That lateral sweep, the Tehachapis, meets the westward curving of the southern Sierra Nevada, forming a northern barrier to Southern California. South of the Tehachapis, the Transverse Ranges—the Santa Ynez, the Topatopa, the Santa Susana, the Santa Monica, the San Gabriel, the San Bernardino—continue the downward drift of the Coast Range but also tend to run off in an east-west direction. Beneath these the Santa Ana, the San Jacinto, the Santa Rosa, the so-called Peninsular Ranges, begin their southeastern run down to Baja California. Another downward range, the Panamint, guards Southern California's northeastern flank. Three

3

peaks—Mount San Bernardino, Mount San Jacinto, and Mount San Antonio—surpass ten thousand feet. This indeed is mountain country, judging itself, dividing itself by its ranges: cismontane, from sea to mountains, where most settlement—Indian, Spanish, Mexican-American—would occur; montane, the mountainous centerlands; transmontane, the desert beyond.

The desert, called Mojave, and south of this called Colorado, extends along the entire southeast flank of Southern California. Immediately east of the Peninsular Ranges runs the Salton Trough, a sink reaching to the head of the Gulf of California, formed by subsidence along the San Andreas Fault. Much of Southern California is rugged country. Human habitation held itself mainly to the coastal areas, especially the Los Angeles Basin, to this day the center of the state's population. Valleys later named Santa Maria, Lompoc, Santa Ynez, or, south of these, San Gabriel, San Fernando, Santa Clara of the South, mitigate the harshness of the interior, as does the great coastline itself. So much of immediately habitable Southern California lies in earshot of rolling surf. Few coastlines in the world can match the grandeur of this littoral, with its expanse of sea, its foaming surf, white beaches, and saline marshes, its tidepools teeming with life. The presence of so much seacoast mitigates the basic semi-aridity of the interior, or at least provides a dramatic contrast, for Southern California is not naturally blessed with water. No great river courses through its center, and those that do run are problematic, drying to a trickle, or to even drier riverbeds, in the summer months.

Climate varies from coastal plain to mountains to interior regions. Snow falls on mountaintops in sight of deserts whose only moisture is stored three feet beneath the surface. Death Valley has but two inches of rain a year, while the coastal regions experience seventeen inches (Santa Barbara), fourteen inches (Los Angeles), eleven inches (San Diego). Rain falls between October and March, especially in the December-to-February season. The rest of the year is dry— and filled with sunshine: the bold, direct rays of the desert, the luminous sunlight of the mountains, the riviera of golden warmth that floods the coast from Santa Barbara to San Diego, making of it a new Mediterranean shore. In terms of its weather, Southern California brings the Sunbelt to perfection: that arc of sunny regions running from Florida and the South across Texas and the Southwest to the Pacific Ocean, lands of long dry seasons and easy winters.

Nothing is perfect, even weather. The rains of Southern California can be unleashed in blinding sheets. Once-dry riverbeds can overnight become engorged torrents, and in October or so, hot winds beginning in the scorched deserts of southern Utah sweep down along the coast, the dreaded Santa Ana sirocco, driving temperatures to over a hundred, humidity down to 30 percent, making men mad with lust or killing rage.

In the ages before human habitation, much life was here: flora and fauna, differentiated by landform and region, rich in webs of interdependent complexity. Flora varied with elevation: from coastal chaparral to upper woodlands, mountain forests, and the desert beyond. Flora was native—and touched by migration. After the Pleistocene, the flora of Mexico migrated northwards, giving an exotic richness to the flowers and plants of the foothills. Eurasian varieties, delphinium and crepis for instance, made their way down across the Bering Strait. With the European presence, diversification intensified, especially in flowering plants and trees: the Old World palms and peppers, the Australian eucalyptus, among others, now so much a part of the Southern Californian scene. Washed up on shore, kelp and seaweed brought landwards the vegetation of the sea. Succulent plants anchored the shifting sands. Sturdy beach grass held the more solid dunes overhanging the shore.

Because the Southern California foothills run close to the sea, coastal sagebrush commences soon after the giving out of beach plants. Sagebrush grows below three thousand feet, mixing at its farthest reaches with the lower chaparral. From one to four thousand feet coastal Southern California is chaparral country. A mini-forest of dense, tangled trees and shrubbery runs from Santa Barbara to San Diego along the mid-regions of the coastline. Then come the mountains, and with the mountains, trees; for in its natural state the coastal lowland of Southern California, like the Mediterranean region it resembles in topography and weather, suffers a scarcity of trees. They are there, but not in abundance, for rainfalls are greater in the heights. Straggly stands of Monterey pine had, windborne, made it over a longtime ago to the offshore islands—Santa Rosa, Santa Cruz, San Nicolás, Santa Catalina, San Clemente, the above-water peaks of certain submerged mountains of the Transverse chain. The redwoods of California have their origins in the Santa Lucia Range, running northwards along the coast to Oregon. The live oak survives on the semi-arid plains, for it is the sturdiest of trees. Poplars, willows, sycamores, and cottonwoods have a genius for finding moist places, in semi-dry riverbeds or in arroyos which run with water but once a year. The pioneers, in fact, dug for water when they saw clumps of these trees gathered in depressions or standing sentry along canyon beds. The foothill woodlands below twenty-five hundred feet support these trees also, together with box elder, buckeye, laurel, and wild walnut. The middle heights below five thousand feet abound in madrone, mountain maple, aspen, cypress, mountain dogwood (red-leaved in autumn, white-flowering in the spring), and incense cedar, which is not a true cedar yet seemed to European settlers Old Worldly in stateliness, worthy of standing in the hill forests of Lebanon, in the Apennines, or in the Campagna. Above five thousand feet, where the rainfall runs as high as fifty inches a year, the ponderosa pine forests begin. On the windswept passes of these heights, centuries of prevailing winds have flattened certain pine trees into grotesque shapes so that they resemble the Dantesque cypresses facing the Pacific from the headlands of Monterey.

The eastern slopes of the mountains of Southern California lead down to the desert. The trees here take up a desert motif. Piñon pine, the fork-trunked digger pine, the juniper, the Joshua tree, whose speary leaves ward off animal predators: these are rugged desert trees, capable of getting by on very little. They are joined on the desert floor by the yucca, which can take a thousand contorted shapes; the honey mesquite, which sinks a labyrinthine root system into the parched soil and once fed the Indians with its ripened beans; the leafless smoke tree, whose fullness of branches defies the aridity; the fan palm, the only indigenous palm tree of the desert, rising to more than sixty feet, lining the canyon bottoms like soldiers waiting to go over the top; the desert apricot, found near Palm Springs; the palo verde, blooming in yellow.

Desert country is cactus country. Cacti are everywhere and in every variety: barrel cactus, deerhorn cactus, the prickly pear (the most widespread), and the giant cactus, which fed and sheltered the desert tribes. Creosote bush shares the desert dominion of the cacti; so does greasewood, gnarled and tough and continuous. Here and there stands a century plant, a strange, gongoristic instance of vegetation, lying quiet for decades, then, with no discernible regularity or cycle, breaking forth into outrageous hue. Each spring the sand verbena blooms, carpeting the desert floor in pink. Desert lavender flowers in violet-blue, and the cacti in saffron, red, and yellow-gold.

Desert, mountain, coast: Southern California used to be a Shakespearean riot of wildflowers. April through June was wildflower time. Near the coast, great fields of poppies, orange-gold in the sun, would run for twenty miles in length, as would varieties of flowering mustard—lemon, canary, burnt orange—which rose man-high on the inland plains. On the seashore, purple ice plant blossomed, together with pink abronia and blue larkspur. Sturdy wild roses guarded the bluffs above the coastline, while behind them, in a falling away of pale red bus-mallow, wetted canyon floors supported ferns, wild lilies, tangled honeysuckle. In the foothills, after rain, was the scent of wild mint.

One hundred and twenty-seven species of mammal occupied the region, part of the Upper Sonoran life zone. These were isolated animals, relatively secure in their environment. The desert and the Sierra Nevada kept to a minimum any westward migration of predators. In the Pleistocene, mammoths, giant bison, great ground sloths, and saber-toothed tigers roamed the Los Angeles Basin—camels and tapirs also; and back in some dawn time before this were giant reptiles which walked or swam or flew. All these had been replaced by elk and mule deer, by raccoons, badgers, kit foxes, grizzly bears (to the Indian a fierce deity), and the universal coyote, first citizen of the Far West.

As in everything else Southern Californian, mountain and ocean differentiated biological provinces. Offshore was its own teeming life zone. Shrimp, prawns, abalone, clams, mussels, scallops, starfish, squid: the teeming fertility of the Pacific banked itself against the Southern California coast. Sea otters sported on their backs like playful mermaids. Dolphins cavorted, and in the autumn gray whales moved southward, their spoutings visible in the distance. There were seals, sea lions, and elephant seals.

Bighorn sheep picked their way through the mountains, where also were the grizzly and the black bear. Mountain lions, or cougars, roamed some fifty square miles a day in search of prey. Pronghorn antelope ranged the desert backcountry, sharing that environment with a host of sturdy mammals and reptiles. Owls, doves, swallow, finches, bluejays, hawks, eagles, vultures, ducks, sparrows of every sort: seashore, mountain, desert, the bird life of Southern California, like its display of wildflowers, was a riot of profusion. Five hundred and eighty species or subspecies inhabited the state, most of them making it south of the Tehachapis to Southern California. Birds of the starling family were found in abundance. Pheasants, partridges, quail, and grouse nested in the woodlands and beneath the chaparral. Falcons, hawks, eagles, and vultures held the high places, the mighty condor—the largest bird in creation—soaring above them all on triumphant wings. Ducks, geese, and swans dominated the fens and marshes, while birds of coast and sea—gulls, terns, cranes, puffins, pelicans, shearwaters, herons, egrets—brought the life zones of air, land, and water into harmony.

Southern California sustained the birds of familiar perception, wrens, larks, thrashers, thrushes, doves, plovers: the birds, that is, of classical European art and poetry. Yet the region also supported indigenous varieties of Far Western birds: the western crow, for instance, lustrously black, a scrappy survivor like the coyote below; the piñon jay, also called the blue crow or the pine jay, Tyrian blue mingled with bluish gray, whose mewing calls disturbed the silence of desert slopes; the California finch, musical, given to elaborate mating rituals, running through ranges of flecked red; and, of course, the California blue jay, cadet to Venetian blue, a sturdy, feisty bird, loving the oak-covered hillsides but capable also of survival in the plains.

The cliff swallows, like the jay, were ordinary citizens, but ones touched by elegance. Experts in mud masonry, they built pueblo colonies along the protected crevices of the seacoast. Later, in the time of Spanish habitation, their annual nestings in the bell tower of Mission San Juan Capistrano signaled the return of spring.

This land, then, awaited human habitation in the dawn time before Indian migration. It had much to recommend it: its seacoast, the attractiveness of its coastal plains, its superb climate. Its semi-aridity, however, or the outright aridity of its inland desert, severely restricted its ability to support life. Only the technology of the twentieth century could satisfy this thirst, could make the dry soil of the inland valleys bloom. The drama of water would long remain the essential metaphor of the struggle in Southern California for a regional civilization.

The Indian, who drifted into Southern California some eight thousand years ago, had less defiant ways of dealing with the possibilities and deficiencies of the land. The Indian conformed himself to Southern California in its natural state, or adjusted to it with minimal technology. Indian culture stabilized in Southern California some three thousand years ago, remaining intact until disturbed by the whites.

It was a Stone Age culture, devoid of the wheel or the ax, dependent upon the hunting of small game with bow and arrow and, even more, upon the granary and pharmacopoeia of nature itself. The Yuma to the southeast practiced agriculture, but in the main the Southern California Indian, like his counterparts to the north, dug in the earth or gathered from shrubs, trees, and cacti that which was needed for nourishment. Acorns and pine nuts were the staff of life, augmented by edible roots, berries, and thistle sage made into a mush. Animal protein came from fish, rabbits, lizards, insects, and, when fortune smiled, a fleet-footed deer downed by a rudimentary bow.

Tribal distinctions among Southern California's Indians had neither the anthropological sophistication nor the Homeric sense of kinship of Indian civilizations to the east. A common culture obtained, differentiated by more than twenty linguistic families supporting 135 languages. Complexions were dark; hair, black and thick. Women dressed in short skirts. Men went naked, or in skimpy breechclouts. A fur cloak was worn for warmth. Social organization was rudimentary, the chieftainship not having evolved into much more than a *primus inter pares*. The shaman function was frequently shared by the entire community.

The Southern California Indian used shell money. He smoked tobacco in clay pipes. He avoided war when he could, although once on the warpath he did take scalps. The sweat house was a universal institution, a closed hut heated by fire or hot coals, used daily as a ritual device for maintaining health, a club, even a sort of sauna therapy, relaxing tension and getting rid of ill humors. The Southern California Indian had no drums, but danced to rattles and rhythmically beaten gourds. He did not write, although earlier desert Indians left pictographs on stone. Basketry was his highest art form: intricately woven baskets, waterproof, decorated with a multiplicity of patterns which took their varying themes from differing environments. There was also pottery, influenced by the vigorous tradition of the Southwest.

Anthropology (functioning as archeology and history, for the Indian cultures of Southern California did not survive the coming of the whites) makes many distinctions in what to the lay observer appears to be a uniform way of life. There were groupings among the Indians of Southern California, and differing characteristics, if not coherent convictions of tribe or nationhood.

The Chumash, for instance, a coastal people living in shoreside villages from Point Conception to Malibu, were considered by the Spanish a superior tribe.

The Chumash were a maritime people, who took to the Santa Barbara Channel in well-wrought twenty-five-foot canoes, plank-built and caulked in asphalt, driven by crews of up to a dozen, using a double-bladed paddle known only to them and the Eskimos of the Far North. Skilled fishermen, employing a unique no-slip hook of their own design, the Chumash colonized the offshore islands in a manner suggestive of the Polynesian migrations of the South Pacific. Also Polynesian were their large hemispherical houses, fifty feet in diameter, where some forty or fifty Chumash might live in a dozen or so separate rooms, lying on comfortable beds, the only Southern California Indians to sleep this way. The Chumash buried their dead, another rare practice. Their baskets were the best in California. They invented a spear-throwing device of rather effective technology. There was a touch of elegance to Chumash life—their woven caps, their blankets of interlaced feathers and rabbit fur—and much industry. The Spaniards, who encountered them first in 1542–43, during the Cabrillo-Ferrelo expedition, praised the Chumash for their innate sense of courtesy.

Little is known of the people south of the Chumash, the Gabrieleño, who occupied the area now designated as Los Angeles and Orange counties and who also reached the offshore islands of Santa Catalina and San Clemente. They resembled the Chumash most likely, partaking in their higher culture. A charming belief of theirs survives: that porpoises guard the world, swimming around it to keep the earth safe from cosmic harm.

The Gabrieleño and their neighbors to the south, the Luiseño-Cahuilla, who lived inland from the sea across parts of Orange, Riverside, San Diego, and Imperial counties, practiced a jimsonweed cult. This semi-narcotic plant was taken as part of an initiation ritual by young men and by adults at certain times of the liturgical year. Luiseño-Cahuilla life revolved much around religion. Chungichnish was their principal god, and a rather theologized, nonanthropomorphic god at that: a Jehovian figure, powerful, personal, transcendent, who through revelation laid down the conduct of daily life. Luiseño-Cahuilla culture was rich in all that pertained to the mythological and the shamanistic. They practiced a cult of esoteric names, for instance, by which secret words conveyed hidden identities and revealed the unseen order of things. In their initiation ceremonies, young men of the Luiseño-Cahuilla drank a jimsonweed brew until they reached a state of narcosis. They dreamed dreams that would become the secret pattern of their lives, and beheld animals that would forever more be sacred.

The Luiseño-Cahuilla practiced astronomy through ritualistic ground paintings. These sacred cosmographies depicted the earth and the heavens through symbol, especially the Milky Way, which held these mystic people entranced. To the wonder and beauty of the Milky Way they returned again and again in their calendars and in their chants. The Luiseño-Cahuilla liturgy teemed with various songs, dances, and ceremonial addresses, such as the homily given to boys and girls at the completion of the initiation rites urging good behavior. Songs told of birth, death, season cycles, the creation of the universe. There were songs in which eagle and deer appear, fleeing the hunter. There were drinking songs and a fire dance in which a blaze was stomped out by bare feet.

The Yuma, their neighbors to the south, living in what is now San Diego and Imperial counties, were one division of a larger group which included the Diegueno and the Mohave, with whom the Yuma were virtually identical. Yuma-Mohave culture extended from the coast through the backcountry, across the Colorado River and into Arizona. The inner life of these people revolved around the dream, their central psychological event and the basis of their cults and shamanistic practices. Interestingly enough, their dreams frequently involved prenatal events. ("Before I was born," claimed one medicine man, "I would sometimes steal out of my mother's womb while she was sleeping, but it was dark and I did not go far.") Dreams for the Yuma-Mohave were the absolute facts of history. The past was known solely through dreams. Dreams guided conduct, and through dreams one generation passed on its knowledge to the next.

For all their dreaminess, however, the Yuma-Mohave loved the warpath, in sharp contrast to the laissez-faire attitude of their coastal neighbors. They also practiced agriculture and had a strong tribal sense, all very un-Californian. With them, in one sense, began the Indian cultures of the inland Southwest. Their neighbors to the north, the Serrano and the Ute-Chemehuevi, dwelling in Kern, San Bernardino, and Riverside counties, also showed signs of being influenced by the stronger Indian cultures of the Southwest. The baskets of the Ute-Chemehuevi, for instance, had the decorative patterns of the interior. Many Ute-Chemehuevi wore Apache-style dress. Affected strongly by the powerful Shoshonean culture of the interior and by the Yuma-Mohave culture to their south, the Ute-Chemehuevi were an eclectic, culturally colonized people, like certain nations in Eastern Europe, incapable of bringing into focus their regional identity.

The Shoshoneans were not a Southern Californian tribe at all, although they had spilled into its southeastern flank some fifteen hundred years ago from the Great Basin of Utah-Nevada. The Shoshoneans belonged to the Ute-Aztecan family, a huge conglomerate of affiliated peoples which stretched from the Great Basin down through Mexico. As such, the Shoshoneans of eastern Southern California were remote cousins of the mighty Aztecs.

And if the mighty Aztecs had fallen before the Spanish, then it was no wonder that the weaker tribes of Southern California succumbed with but a few gestures of organized resistance. Spain's conquistadors conquered an empire, South and Central America, Mexico and the Caribbean, although it took the Crown some time to settle Southern California with colonists: some 227 years to be exact, between the coastal explorations of Juan Rodríguez Cabrillo in 1542 and the raising of the cross at Mission San Diego de Alcalá on 16 July 1769 by a group of Franciscans headed by Father Junípero Serra and soldiers commanded by Captain Gaspar de Portolá.

The colonization of Upper California was the last venture of imperial Spain. For two centuries the Crown knew that it must eventually secure this northwestern flank of its Latin American empire, but the energy and right circumstances had not been there. There is a good chance that Hernando Cortés himself, conqueror of Mexico and founding father of the Spanish empire, gave California its name in May of 1535 when he landed on Baja, the lower peninsula. Cortés thought that California was an island, most likely getting that idea—together with the name "California"—from a popular romance of the period, *Las sergas de Esplandían* (The Deeds of Esplandían) by Garcí Ordóñez de Montalvo. Montalvo described California as an island kingdom near the Terrestrial Paradise to the right of the Indies, inhabited by Amazons and ruled by Queen Calafía. In the novel, Esplandían conquers California and converts the Amazons to Christianity, a rather clear-cut parable of Spanish ambitions for romantic California's actual counterpart.

The mission system, brought into Southern California in 1769 with the founding of Mission San Diego de Alcalá, extended itself to the north of San Francisco Bay by 1823, the year the last mission was founded. Combining elements of church, cloister, and plantation, the missions ran up the coast at intervals of a day's journey along El Camino Real, the king's highway. Each mission had a presidial or military garrison to insure order. In Southern California civilian towns were established at San Diego, Los Angeles, and Santa Barbara, together with a number of ranchos granted by the Spanish Crown or by the Republic of Mexico, which held California after 1822. Sprawling establishments, run by their owners along feudal lines, the central haciendas of these Southern California ranchos might support scores of people bound to each other in various relationships of servitude and kinship. Their vaqueros were said to be among the most skilled riders ever to take to horse. Their herds of innumerable longhorns, raised for the hide and tallow trade with the United States, constituted the backbone of the region's economy.

II

California by the end of the 1850s was, like Caesar's Gaul, divided into three parts. In the mountainous north, forested in redwood and pine, watered by wild rivers, and in the oak-dotted Sacramento Valley, fertile, hazy from the sun, the Gold Rush had with ferocious midwifery induced the birth pangs of a society recognizably American. Stockton, Sacramento, Marysville—the towns of the northern interior were Yankee towns: wood and brick houses huddled along main streets, church, general store, jail, schoolhouse, all not so very different, save in stages of development, from settlements in the East.

Port and emporium for this vast northern region, the City of San Francisco was a city in the fullest sense of the term. Organized as a Vigilance Committee, energetic American businessmen fought for, and attained, public order and improved government. As yet San Francisco had few stable civic symbols by which to know itself (a ripe self-consciousness not coming until the late 1860s), but already there were churches, libraries, and signs of art.

Monterey, in contrast, the capital as it were of Central California, was a shabby little town of mingled Mexican and American associations. The rugged, unsettled Big Sur coast stretched to the south, and fanning eastward to the Sierra was an inland sea of undeveloped prairie, teeming with wheat in the 1870s, but in the 1850s remaining as it had been for ages past: a primal, empty vastness of condor and elk. A few mining towns in the Central Sierra foothills attested to American occupation, but even here associations were vague, for Sonora had a large French colony, and Mariposa showed more Indians than whites.

Invaded in 1846, annexed in 1848, taken into the Union in 1850: Southern California was never Americanized. No Gold Rush overwhelmed the Southland with Yankees; rather, the Spanish-speaking culture held its own. A visitor to San Francisco in, say, 1860 encountered a bustling American city. *El Pueblo de Nuestra Señora la Reina de los Angeles de Porciúncula* offered a Mexican contrast. The pueblo—a random collection of adobes rimmed by sandy wastes, wild mustard, and willow trees—rested on an inland plain watered by the Los Angeles River. To the north, the snowy peaks of the San Gabriel Mountains blocked off an otherwise limitless horizon. In the city itself, open irrigation ditches crisscrossed the unpaved streets. The city had its drinking water from these canals, and at their edge Indian women were frequently seen rinsing garments and beating them clean on flat rocks. Pigs, chickens, stray dogs fed upon rotting refuse. A particularly superb sycamore asserted itself against the city's interior treelessness, while on the indeterminate outskirts of the settlement a few small vineyards and citrus groves attested to the beginnings of industry.

If it were early in the day, our American visitor might see a line of shawl-draped Mexican women, and an Anglo lady or two, making their way across the plaza for morning mass at the Church of Our Lady Queen of the Angels.

By midmorning a number of loungers, having taken up their stations in various spots of shade on the Calle Principal, would begin the day's work of watching life pass by. There is little to see. The hours slowly pass. A ranchero rides into town, a don of mixed ancestry (but calling himself Spanish), swathed in serape and sash, saddle and bridle glittering with metalwork. The *zanjero*, an Indian charged with keeping the irrigation ditches flowing freely, makes his rounds. At six o'clock the angelus ring. Later, from the Calle de los Negros, a row of saloons and bordellos off the plaza, come the sounds of banjo music, curses, and gunfire.

Los Angeles was founded in 1781 as an agricultural supply center for Alta California. By 1791, 139 settlers lived in twenty-nine adobes. By 1830, the population reached 650. Until 1820 the pueblo remained under the jurisdiction of the Presidio at Santa Barbara, but by 1845, the final year of uninterrupted Mexican rule, it reached such importance in the scheme of things that it succeeded Monterey as capital of the department.

American occupation brought little change. First of all, Frenchmen, not Yankees, were for some time the dominant non-Spanish element, so much so that the French government maintained a vice-consul in the city. Americans did not pour in from the north. The Butterfield Company took until 1858 to connect Los Angeles with St. Louis by stagecoach. Telegraph connection with San Francisco came in 1860. The first American census of Los Angeles County, taken in 1850, presented a portrait of nondevelopment. The county had 8,329 inhabitants, half of whom were Indian and most of whom were illiterate. There were no schools or libraries—and no newspaper.

On 17 May 1851 the first edition of the *Los Angeles Star* appeared, and in its pages for the ensuing two decades is chronicled the establishing of an American city. Los Angeles the Mexican colony became, successively, an American garrison during the Mexican War; a violent cow town during the 1850s, when Northern California lived off Southern California beef; a crossroads in the 1860s, with the arrival of the Butterfield Stage; and finally, in the mid-1870s, with the coming of the Southern Pacific and the influx of immigrants, the capital city of an agricultural empire.

Cowboys, gamblers, bandits, and desperados of every description brought to the Los Angeles of the 1850s a tone of border-town mayhem. Rough statistics indicate that in 1850 a murder occurred for every day of the year. The Reverend James Woods, a scholarly Massachusetts Presbyterian, arrived in October 1854, hoping to bring the gospel and social order. Despite the beauty of surrounding vineyards and orange trees, he noted, Los Angeles was a hellhole, a valley of dry bones, a city not of angels but of demons. An orgy of murder fills the diary Reverend Woods kept during his desperate ministry of six months. In his first two weeks alone, ten Angelenos met violent ends. Ordinary citizens walked the streets armed with pistols, bowie knives, and shotguns. Cruelty was everywhere. He was horrified to find an Indian servant girl dying in the street, abandoned by a household wishing to avoid burial expenses. A young cowboy, David Brown, sentenced to hang for the shooting of Pinckney Clifford, refused to see Woods, telling the sheriff he would rather have a bear in his cell than a minister. Shortly after, Brown was dragged from the jailhouse and lynched. The mob was led by Stephen Clark Foster, mayor of Los Angeles and a Yale man. Woods felt himself fortunate if, out of a population of a thousand Americans, more than a dozen—mainly women—attended the services he held in the courthouse. Mocked in his efforts, Woods began to show signs of stress. A man of scholarly habits, used to systematic study, he feared that his powers of concentration were on the wane. Reading seemed impossible, and in any event, why should he prepare his sermons? So very few in this violent, shabby town seemed willing to listen to what he had to say. He began to fret about his health and to worry over the safety of his wife and children. Broodingly, he preached to his tiny congregation about the destruction of Sodom and Gomorrah.

Woods's final entry in his Los Angeles diary is that of a man wrestling with demons without and demons within: "April 29: 1855 Sabbath—Between four and five oclock in the afternoon. And all around my house near the head of main Street, are hundreds of Spaniards in all sorts of revelry and noise—men on horse back—women on foot—children crying—and such a constant gibber jabber, as would remind one of bedlam. Horse racing is the object calling the crowd together. Several races have already occured this afternoon and also a fight or two. Sam got alarmed and went away and I would have left the house, but was afraid of its being broken open thefts committed. Boys, both Spaniards and many americans are among the crowd and many American men—what a spectacle for a country laying claims to christianity & Here in this Sunday horse racing is seen the fruits of popery—the only form of religion known among the Spaniards of this region—A poor child with its wretched mother I suppose, is crying constantly with cold—And now the dogs are in a fight. Just now a row was raised by one man trying to ride over another. . . . I hear every few minutes the voices and conversation of Americans, betting, cursing, and blaspheming as they stand leaning against my window blind—this is nominally a christian town, but in reality heathen. If it had been God's will I should have like to have contended for the truth in this place, this retreat of Satan, but God by his Providence has otherwise decided. My right arm is broken. Whether it will ever be restored to strength the future will develope. It seems a plain indication of Providence that I leave this place, and the wicked will rejoice at it I have no doubt."

In September of 1855 Reverend Woods and family departed north for a parish in Santa Rosa, Sonoma County.

Woods's distaste for everything Mexican—religion, customs, even physical appearance—was, unfortunately, not untypical. Secure in comparison to their compadres to the north, the Californios of the South were nevertheless in the long run doomed to give way before Yankee numbers, economic power, and intolerance. They were, after all, a straightforward pastoral people, the part-Indian, part-African, part-Spanish descendants of soldiers who had received land grants after service in the ranks, like Corporal José Vicente Félix of Santa Barbara, for instance, or the three privates who provided military protection for the first forty-four settlers of Los Angeles, or Juan José Domínguez, another soldier, granted the Rancho San Pedro by Governor Fages in the late 1780s, the estate staying in the family for a hundred years. Many of them were barely literate, but capable of knowing a good piece of Southern Californian land when it was given to them, capable of herding stock, building adobe homes of unpretentious beauty, marrying daughters of the country, Indian or part-Indian like themselves, and raising ten, fifteen, twenty children who succeeded to the same rugged but dignified ranch life—the rounding up and branding of great herds (disputes settled by Judges of the Plain, whose word was law), riding league upon league to neighboring ranchos or into Los Angeles for days of dancing at festival time, staking what currency was available on horse races and spending the winnings on a silver-studded saddle—a prodigal, unheeding life, cruel and seedy upon occasion and in the main unfatigued by reflection or the more complicated apparatus of civilization. If one needed a horse, one took it from a corral, then let it go at one's destination for someone else's use. If beef was needed, one slaughtered the animal nearest the adobe, rarely bothering to remove the refuse. Religion provided mystery; the sun, warmth; and the days slipped by.

The Americanization of Southern California occurred in four stages. In the immediate post-annexation stage, first of all, the old Mexican elites held their own, a hegemony they shared with such gringos as Abel Stearns, Benjamin Davis Wilson, Juan Warner, and William Wolfskill, among others, who had come to Southern California before the Conquest. The drought of the early 1860s, together with a number of other factors—the inability of the dons to do business Yankee style, for instance—ended this first stage of Hispanic reconsolidation. The 1870s witnessed the falling into American hands of the Mexican land-grant ranchos. In the 1880s many of these American held ranchos, especially those of Los Angeles County, were subdivided and sold as residential property. In the 1890s these subdivisions grew into towns and cities.

Thus the Rancho San Pedro and the Rancho Los Palos Verdes passed through successive stages into the port towns of Wilmington and San Pedro. The Rancho Los Alamitos and the Rancho Los Cerritos became the American city of Long Beach. The beach resort of Santa Monica grew up on portions of Malibu Rancho, northwest of the Topanga Canyon, granted in 1805 to José Bartolomé Tapia, and the Rancho San Vicente y Santa Monica, granted in 1828 to Francisco Sepúlveda. Rancho San José became the town of Pomona. Rancho Rodeo de las Aguas (bought in 1854 for a mere $500 cash by two Americans) became the city of Beverly Hills. In 1887 a colony of Quakers established Whittier on the site of the Rancho Paso de Bartolo Viejo. Glendale occupied part of the 36,000 acres granted in 1784 to José María Verdugo, a corporal in the Spanish army, who retired there in 1798 to raise children and cattle. Juan Mariné, a Catalonian artillery lieutenant, acquired the Rancho San Pasqual in 1835. The Sepúlvedas held it briefly before it became the property of Manuel Garfias, a

Mexican army officer intent upon a Southern California retirement. (Garfias's adobe, the scene of forty years of life and hospitality, was demolished in the 1880s to make way for an expanding Pasadena.)

A myriad of American names—Sherman Oaks, Encino, Tarzana, Canoga Park, Northridge, Van Nuys, North Hollywood—now dot the landscape where once roamed the herds of Mission San Fernando. These ranchos passed, and with them a way of life, but not before a generation of Americans had the chance to live the life of the dons. Even after the ranchos had collapsed as viable modes of economic organization, and the rancheros themselves lay mingled in the dust, their names—the lovely, liquid Spanish names of acreages and people—held to the landscape of Southern California like a litany refusing to be hushed. For the rancho was the underlying mode of social organization. The Spanish Californians had come north from Mexico first and foremost because they had hungered after land. It was by rancho and by occupying family group that they identified themselves: the Ticos of Ojai, the Danas of Nipomo, the Sepúlvedas of Palos Verdes; in Orange County, the Vejars of Boca de la Playa and the Serranos of Cañada de los Alisos; in Santa Barbara, the de la Guerras of Rancho Alamos, the Carillos of Punta de la Concepción; the Palomares and Vejars of Azusa; the Aguirres and del Valles of Tejón; the Alvarados of Rancho Cañada Larga y Verde in Ventura. This litany of names now has a remote, feudal texture, as is proper, for in many ways early Southern California was a semi-barbaric society struggling toward feudal order. The land conferred identity and stability upon a rather haphazard, genetically diverse band of colonists who had only the Spanish language in common, and whose social experience vacillated between pastoral somnolence and comic-opera civil war.

Ever since Mexico broke with Spain in the 1820s, certain Californios had been working toward the establishment of a secular liberal republic. Taken at its best, the secularization of the missions in the 1830s was a gesture in that direction, as well as the chance to confiscate some choice church property. Californios of ideas and some acquaintance with the wider world flirted with the notion of an American connection, either as a state or as a client territory, believing that only Yankee civil institutions and Yankee capital could bring progress. After 1848 they had their American association: they had been conquered. In Southern California they resisted the invasion with great courage. At dawn on 6 December 1846, near the Indian village of San Pasqual, a company of them serving under Captain Andrés Pico wheeled their horses about, leveled their lances, and faced the charge of American dragoons. Ten minutes of hand-to-hand combat followed, willow lance against cavalry saber. Losing no one themselves, the Californios left eighteen American dead on the field. Three more dragoons died later, and nineteen were wounded. Some American corpses were pierced with as may as ten lance thrusts. For all their courage, however, the Californios were so many Don Quixotes. The Americans whom in brief resistance they lanced from their horses would, like fruit shaken from a tree, be the seed of future growth.

It had not always been this way. Yankees had once come in peace, eager to be one of them, to learn their language, marry their daughters, and become true *hijos del pais*, sons of the country. Such Americans had prospered: Don Abel Stearns, for instance, a Massachusetts man who by the time of his death in 1871 was the most important landowner in the Southland. Arriving in Southern California in 1829, Stearns became a Mexican citizen, then went into trade, dealing in pelts, hides, and tallow for shipment to the United States, and in turn selling American goods to the Californians. In 1842 he purchased the Rancho Los Alamitos, which an 1850 survey showed as covering 28,512 acres and possessing cattle 10,000, sheep 1,100, horses 700. Marrying the daughter of a prominent ranchero, Arcadia Bandini (she was fourteen and he was forty), Don Abel built an elegant adobe in Los Angeles for his bride, El Palacio, which served as the social center of the city until the Civil War. In 1858 he spent nearly $85,000 building a two-story brick business block in Los Angeles, the Arcadia Block, named after his wife. It had an iron balcony, iron doors, and iron shutters, and it lasted well into the twentieth century, when, like a lot of other things in Southern California, it was torn down to make way for a parking lot.

If even a shrewd Yankee like Abel Stearns of Massachusetts found it difficult to adjust to the new conditions (his San Francisco partners in a land syndicate complained that Stearns was lackadaisical, spending too much time with his horses), then it is not surprising that many a hidalgo went under. Used to a world of barter and simple credit, they succumbed to the seductions of compound interest. Law had once been a matter of custom, usages, and commonsense interpretation; now they were forced to negotiate their way through a labyrinth of deceptive legislation. The Land Act of 1851, which placed upon them the burden of proving title to their holdings, ensnared them in the courts for years, and they sold off acre after acre to pay legal fees.

Some coped, especially the younger ones who learned the new ways. Elected lieutenant governor in 1871, Romualdo Pacheco held the governorship for a few months in 1875 when Newton Booth resigned to go to the United States Senate. Born in Santa Barbara in 1831, Pacheco, the son of a military officer, was sent to the Hawaiian Islands as a boy to be educated by New England schoolmasters. He was later admitted to the California bar. Brigadier commanding the Native Californian Cavalry in the Southwest during the Civil War, and after the war an active Republican, Pacheco served as a California assemblyman and state senator, and for two terms in the House of Representatives.

Young Ygnacio Sepúlveda, born in Los Angeles in 1842, went east for his education, proper in frock coat and flowing cravat. He returned and took the bar, served in the legislature, and sat on the superior bench. President Grover

Cleveland sent him to Mexico City as first secretary of the American legation. Wells Fargo and Company kept him there for some years as chief counsel. An ample man, given to a Vandyke beard and mustache, Judge Sepúlveda died full of years and honors in 1916 at Los Angeles, city of his birth.

Others were not so capable, or so lucky. The most wretched *paisanos* lost everything, seeing in their old age themselves and their children eat the bitter bread of strangers. Others carried on in a twilight world of defiance and partial coping, perhaps the most sadly representative being Juan Bandini and Pío Pico. Coming to California from Peru in the early 1820s, Juan Bandini made himself one of the three or four most powerful rancheros in Southern California. Like Mariano Vallejo in the North, Bandini—a thin, slightly nervous man, frequently sarcastic—felt himself confined by life in a backward Mexican province, which is ironic, in that Richard Henry Dana, Jr., in *Two Years Before the Mast* described Bandini as the embodiment of that heedless prodigality at the core of California's backwardness. Educated in the law, an advocate of *liberalismo*, Bandini believed he could play a larger part in life once a progressive order came to Pacific shores. Pío Pico, the last Mexican governor, wanted progress but felt that California should seek it on its own. His father, a sergeant in the San Diego garrison, had in the days of Spanish rule been jailed for republican leanings. During the American invasion, Pío's brother Andrés led the lances at San Pasqual, while Pío briefly maintained in Sonora a government in exile. Bandini, on the other hand, welcomed the Yankees, and especially enjoyed entertaining the officers. Lieutenant William T. Sherman frequently dropped by, as did Lieutenant Cave J. Couts, who married Bandini's daughter Ysidora and whose cousin Ulysses S. Grant also served in California.

Throughout the 1840s and 1850s Bandini and his wife Doña Refugia managed to maintain the grand style. They could afford it. Their holdings stretched across an empire, from Baja California to the San Bernardino Mountains. Their fandangos and fiestas went on for days at a time, with Don Juan, an accomplished dancer, leading over a hundred guests in the *jota* or the waltz, and the evening ending in the hilarity of the *cascaron*, eggshells filled with confetti and cologne which the men and women broke flirtatiously upon one another's heads.

Pío Pico went in for horse racing. In 1852 he rode his Sarco, a California horse, against Black Swan, an Australian mare owned and ridden by José Sepúlveda, in a nine-mile race. Sarco lost by seventy-five yards. Over $50,000 in money and property had been bet. Pico himself lost $1,600 in cash and three hundred head of cattle.

Once an admirer of the United States Constitution, Bandini, forced to defend his property against the Land Act, learned to fear American law and to hate American lawyers. Taking out disastrous loans, he was ruined by the interest. Abel Stearns made an effort to guide his father-in-law's affairs but was rebuffed. Bandini was suspicious of his three Yankee sons-in-law, feeling that they were taking advantage of him. Unable to repay the $24,000 he had borrowed from Stearns, he deeded over to his son-in-law the marvelous Rancho La Jurupa.

Pico lost the Rancho Los Coyotes to Stearns in default of a $15,000 note. Because of a bad investment, he also lost the Rancho Santa Margarita, the Rancho Los Flores, and the Paso de Bartolo. He and his brother Andrés ruined themselves and a score of others when a mortgage scheme collapsed.

In 1859, the year Don Juan Bandini died at his son-in-law's Los Angeles home El Palacio after a long and painful illness, Andrés Pico, then a state senator, succeeded in getting a bill passed by the legislature calling for the separation of Northern and Southern California. It was not a new idea. As early as August of 1851 the *Los Angeles Star* editorialized that Southern California would be better off as a territory dependent upon the federal government than as six counties neglected by the state. The South, it said, received next to nothing for its tax dollar. That October a convention met in Santa Barbara and called for the separation of the southern counties into the Territory of Colorado. Not surprisingly, Old Californians were in the vanguard of this movement. Territorial status would give them breathing space. Free from the domination of the Yankee North, they might more gradually approach the new conditions, achieving in the long run something which would be theirs, Spanish, and part of the Union. Pico's bill was approved by popular vote and sent to Congress for consideration. The outbreak of the Civil War destroyed its chances.

Taken as a gesture of cultural consciousness, the idea of separation indicated that the Californios knew they were in trouble. Francisco P. Ramirez, editor of *El Clamor Público*, the Spanish-language newspaper published in Los Angeles in the mid-1850s, sustained a brave front in the matter of his people's future. The legislature published its proceedings in Spanish. The races intermarried and socialized and gave signs of good humour. But the gringos were getting everything, even in the South, and the Californios knew it.

Separation implied legality and due process for the Spanish establishment. A good many young men took to the hills, and some of these justified their banditry, or had it justified for them, as an act of politics—as revolution. The level of articulation in this regard was not high. No ideologue appeared on the scene capable of focusing Spanish resentment, nor did the Californios find an effective political leader capable of directing their energies, inside or outside of the system. What happened was more simple: young Spanish men (a number of them already of criminal disposition), kept from money and women, their society in a state of disintegration, formed outlaw gangs and marauded the countryside. Their depredations fanned ethnic hatred—and tore away the veil obscuring the murderous rage already seething between the races.

Take, for instance, the Flores incident of 1857. Escaping from San Quentin Prison, where he was doing time for horse stealing, Juan Flores, twenty-one, headed south to San Juan Capistrano. With the assistance of one Pancho Daniel, Flores assembled the largest gang ever to operate in California, fifty or so, and began a career of robbery and murder. When the Flores gang ambushed and killed Sheriff Jim Barton and two deputies in the Santiago Canyon, Los Angeles County panicked. A Committee of Public Safety was formed and the city was declared under martial law. The army was summoned from San Diego and Fort Tejón. A company of mounted rangers went on patrol.

Most importantly, lynch law went into effect. Fifty-two Mexicans were herded into the Los Angeles jail as suspected collaborators. Eleven of these were lynched. A Vigilance Committee, chaired by Judge Jonathan R. Scott, sat in open judgment of suspects. The verdict was given by voice vote of the assembled citizens. Lynchings outside of Los Angeles were carried on with less formality. The Texas boys from El Monte, a town near Los Angeles, showed themselves especially greedy for a pound of Mexican flesh. They lynched bandits as they captured them. In the case of three innocent farmers whom they strung up, the El Monte boys confessed that in a pinch any Mexican would do. The rope around Diego Navarro's neck broke before he strangled to death, so the El Monte boys shot him and rode off, leaving Navarro to expire in his wife's arms. At Santa Barbara a patrol of gringos broke into the home of Encarnación Berreyesa, accused him—vaguely—of murder, and strung him up. All told, the Berreyesa family, north and south, lost eight of its clan to the lynchman's noose.

Flores himself was hanged with some ceremony in Los Angeles before a crowd of three thousand on 14 February 1857. A handsome man, he conducted himself with dignity on the scaffold, telling the crowd he bore no malice, was dying justly, and that he hoped those he had wronged would forgive him. The hangman, however, was not in a forgiving mood. He kept Flores's noose short, so that his neck would not break as the body fell. Flores died a long and horrible death.

The Flores uprising deeply divided the Spanish-speaking community. The upper class went out of its way to disassociate itself from it. General Andrés Pico, having led the resistance of 1846, knew from first hand the political symbolism of armed Mexicans riding the Southern California hills. He took a force of more than a hundred, gringo and Californio alike, into the field in hot pursuit, and he lynched two captured bandidos as readily as any gringo vigilante. Usurping the Yankee in intensity of outrage, Pico's class protected its own. One bandit, connected to the Sepúlveda and del Valle families, was quietly freed.

The *paisanos* in the countryside had more ambivalent feelings toward Flores. They resented him for bringing down a reign of terror, but they also aided the gang as it moved through the backcountry. They acted from fear, no doubt, but some perhaps did what they did out of baffled patriotism. In Mexico it was a time of civil war, liberal against conservative, mestizo against Spaniard. Who knows, some of those riding with Flores may have thought that they were joining the reforming patriots to the south, men like Juárez and Díaz, in an effort to better the lot of the lower classes. There was talk of some five hundred possible guerrillas in the hills, awaiting a leader and a course of action. When it was over, there was bitterness. Various classes of Spanish-speaking Californians had been divided against each other, the upper classes recognizing they had been used against their own people, the *paisanos* in the countryside bitter that their own hidalgos had turned against them in indiscriminate suppression. The hatred between the two races had surfaced, and the relationship between the races, conqueror and conquered, dispossessor and dispossessed, stood clear.

III

No single place provides a better case study in the successive social evolutions and displacements of this first American era than Rancho El Tejón, a vast tract of land straddling the Tehachapi Mountains dividing Southern California from the San Joaquin Valley. Explored intermittently by the Spanish but never settled, the Tejón took its name from the Spanish *el tejón*, the badger, because in 1806, Lieutenant Francisco Ruiz encountered a badger when he led a troop of soldiers up Cañada de las Uvas, Grapevine Canyon, so named because of the wild cimarron grapes growing there, en route to the site of the present-day city of Bakersfield. The Tejón was a pass through the Techachapis—Tejón Pass, to the east of Grapevine Canyon—but also the designation for one of the Mexican land grant ranchos in the area, Rancho El Tejón, awarded to José Antonio Aguirre and Ygnacio del Valle of Santa Barbara by Governor Manuel Micheltorena on 11 November 1843.

Born in Spain of Basque parentage, José Antonio Aguirre had emigrated to Mexico as a young man and established himself as a shipper and merchant on the Mexican Pacific coast, operating out of the port of Guaymas. Aguirre would buy the products of Mexican ranchos—hides, tallow, olive oil—and in turn sell the rancheros manufactured goods from around the world. In 1838 Aguirre moved his business north to Santa Barbara, consolidating his position there by marriage into the prominent Estudillo family. His business partner Ygnacio del Valle was the son of a Spanish soldier, Antonio del Valle, who upon his retirement from active service had been granted the famous Rancho Camulos near Ventura, later made famous as the site of Helen Hunt Jackson's novel *Ramona* (1884). Ygnacio del Valle himself followed his father into the Spanish service, being commissioned *alferez*, or ensign, in 1831. In 1841 del Valle left the Mexican army to devote the rest of his career to ranching and to politics. Both the historian Hubert Howe Bancroft and the novelist Helen Hunt Jackson considered Don Ygnacio del Valle the very essence of the Old Californian gentleman, a polished and courteous hidalgo, a feudal lord of land and cattle, possessed of the manners and courtesy of Old Spain. Del Valle would later serve as an *al-*

calde, or judge, in the American administration of Los Angeles and in the state legislature in Sacramento.

The War of Conquest brought to California a young man whose destiny, whose forty-seven years of remaining life, would be inextricably bound up with the Tejón: Edward Fitzgerald Beale. It is no exaggeration to say that for all practical purposes Edward Fitzgerald Beale *was* the Tejón, and the Tejón was Edward Fitzgerald Beale for the remaining decades of the nineteenth century. Born in the District of Columbia to a navy family, Beale attended Georgetown College before being commissioned a midshipman in the United States Navy by President Andrew Jackson, a family friend. Graduating from the naval school in 1842, Beale went on active service with the rank of passed midshipman, and it was as a midshipman on the frigate *Congress* that Beale sailed for California in 1845. Before his ship reached California, however, Beale was sent back to Washington by Commodore Robert Field Stockton with important dispatches. In Washington, Beale was promoted to lieutenant and ordered to rejoin the *Congress* at Callao, Peru. In the first months of the war, Beale operated ashore under the command of Marine Lieutenant Archibald Gillespie, who seconded him to ride with General Stephen Watts Kearney and his ill-fated dragoons. Drawing his defeated troops into a circle after the debacle of San Pasqual, Kearney ordered Beale, along with his chief scout, Lieutenant Kit Carson, and an Indian guide, to penetrate the territory held by the Californios and bring word to Commodore Stockton in San Diego that the army was cut off and needed rescue. Beale, Carson, and the Indian guide crawled past the Californio sentries in the early hours of the morning, passing within twenty yards of their camp fires. The next evening they reached San Diego and reported to Commodore Stockton, who immediately sent 170 men out to Kearney's relief. Two months later, on 9 February 1847, Beale and Carson were brought together for another mission, this time to bring dispatches overland to Washington.

Within the next two years, Lieutenant Edward Fitzgerald Beale crossed and recrossed the continent an incredible six times as the bearer of military dispatches. On the second of these journeys, in the course of which he cut across northern Mexico, in danger of losing his life at every moment at the hands of vengeful soldiers and bandits in this just-defeated country, Beale brought along a bag of gold, newly discovered in Northern California. Resting from his fourth journey, he married Mary Edwards, the daughter of a Pennsylvania congressman. When next back in Washington, in August 1850, Beale was promoted to full lieutenant, but even this promotion, and Beale's own naval family background, could not keep him in the service. The thoughts of the young navy lieutenant returned again and again to California, where he knew his destiny awaited him. His good friend, the American poet Bayard Taylor, himself a California adventurer in the year 1849, called Beale "a pioneer in the path of empire." An intelligent, well-read man, later to serve with great distinction in the Grant administration as minister to the court of the Austro-Hungarian empire in Vienna, Edward Fitzgerald Beale had a vision of what California could and should become. Beale wanted to play a part in that impending development. Interestingly enough, the man who had brought the first California gold back to Washington did not seek his fortune in the gold mines but on the land. Beale spent two years managing the California properties acquired by New York shipper W. H. Aspinwal and Commodore Robert Field Stockton, the American military governor of California from 1846 to 1847, who retired from the navy in 1850, prior to being sent to the United States Senate by the legislature of his native New Jersey. Managing the land of others gave rise to landowning ambitions in the recently resigned navy lieutenant, yet actual ownership was a number of years away.

The years 1850, 1851, and 1852 witnessed a series of Indian uprisings in Central and Southern California. The Indians were protesting violations of their rights to farm the land or to live in the free-roaming ways of their ancestors. They were also angry at being cheated by dishonest Indian agents. The state legislature authorized the formation of a volunteer Mariposa Batallion to deal with instances of armed insurrection. President Fillmore, however, wanted the government's Indian programs in Nevada and California thoroughly reformed and reorganized, and so he appointed Beale superintendent of Indian affairs for California and Nevada and got through Congress on 3 March 1853 a budget of $250,000 to back Beale's efforts. Beale had rather advanced ideas regarding the treatment of Indians. He believed that they should be encouraged to develop themselves as farmers and ranchers, gathered together into cooperatives based upon tribal groupings. For this purpose he chose the Tejón, which he had revisited in early 1854 with twelve army dragoons and Judge Benjamin Hayes of Los Angeles. As of 1854, two other white men had lived on the Tejón. Dr. E. D. French, a one-time army surgeon, had been with Kearney at the Battle of San Pasqual. Building an adobe on the Tejón in the spring of 1850, Dr. French had run cattle there for about a year before being driven off by hostile Indians. Alonzo Ridley was also on the Tejón by 1852, trading with the Indians and siring a daughter by his Indian mistress. Ridley later left Los Angeles with the units mustered there by Albert Sidney Johnston for service in the Confederacy. Refusing to take an oath of allegiance to the federal government after the Civil War, Alonzo Ridley went off with other unreconstructed Confederates to help on the construction of the Vera Cruz railroad in Mexico. Returning years later to the Rancho Camulos, Ridley discovered that his Tejón Indian mistress had borne him a daughter, Guadalupe, whom he instantly adored. The story of Guadalupe partially inspired the novel *Ramona*.

As the site of his model reservation Beale chose the lower portion of the Tulare Valley near Tejón Pass, where he eventually gathered more than twenty-five hundred Indians, who built adobes for themselves and planted the land in wheat, barley, and corn. Beale also employed twelve white men, including his superintendent of farming, Alexander Godey, who had first come west with John Charles Frémont in 1843, later serving as a lieutenant in Frémont's Mounted California Volunteers, and had fought at the Battle of San Pasqual with Beale and Kit Carson in December 1846. Beale also brought his wife with him in June 1854, and so Mary Beale became the first American woman to live on the Tejón. While it lasted, Beale's Indian colony was a model of its kind. A reporter for the *Los Angeles Star* wrote up his visit to the Tejón on 24 June 1854. The reporter praised the neat, orderly farms run by the Indians under Beale's supervision. When one considered the brief time that the Indians had been working the Tejón, the reporter wrote, this transformation of a remote wilderness into a productive agricultural preserve was nothing short of miraculous. That same month the *Alta California* reported that Beale and his Indians had put 2,800 acres into productive use—wheat, barley, corn, pumpkins, potatoes, beans, and a vineyard—watered by ten miles of irrigation ditches.

The establishment of the Sebastian Indian Reserve, as Beale's colony was called, also involved the opening of an army outpost, Fort Tejón. Constructed in 1854, Fort Tejón consisted of a series of one- and two-story adobes arranged neatly around an open plaza. What a colorful sight it must have been that spring day in 1855 when Company A of the First United States Dragoons rode into the Tejón—more than a hundred men in blue coats with stiff, high-necked collars, brass buttons, gold insignia, and sky-blue trousers, with orange piping on collars and cuffs and an orange stripe running down the side of each dragoon's trousers. The dragoons, each armed with a percussion lock carbine, a Colt six-shooter, and a curved saber, topped their flamboyant uniform off with a dark blue shako in the French style, held in place by a chin strap and crested with an orange pom-pom. An elite regiment, the First United States Dragoons had been on continuous frontier service since 1836. Companies C and K of the First Dragoons had been involved in the ill-fated charge at San Pasqual, one of the regiment's few defeats. Commanded by Lieutenant Colonel Benjamin L. Beall, the dragoons first established themselves against the Tehachapi foothills before shifting their headquarters a few months later to Grapevine Canyon. There they built a fort universally praised for its dignity and orderliness, its mixed ambience of military spit-and-polish and adobe charm. A visitor to Fort Tejón in November 1857 praised its fifteen adobe buildings, situated adjacent to a stream of water running through the canyon, with fine grazing land nearby. "All the quarters are furnished in the best style," the visitor reported, "and it is generally acknowledged to be one of the finest, if not the best, on the Pacific Coast . . . and with the exception of Fort Kelly, Kentucky, the finest in the Army." Operating out of Fort Tejón, the First Dragoons patroled as far east as Owens Valley and, in certain cases, offered escorts all the way to

Salt Lake City. Their major mission was to keep the peace and to keep the newly established road to Los Angeles open.

Bringing an ambience of American purpose to the Tejón, Fort Tejón was the first American community on the Tejón and, as such, must be considered an important development in the creation of American society in this region. The officers of the First Dragoons brought their wives out to live at the fort, and when William Ingraham Kip, the first Episcopal bishop of California, visited Fort Tejón in 1855 (a mural in the Grace Cathedral of San Francisco depicts this visit) he praised the atmosphere of gracious civility that the officers and their wives had established in this remote frontier outpost. Bishop Kip preached to the officers and men (Episcopalianism was a strong tradition in the American officer corps at that time), confirmed a number of officers as lay readers, and was entertained at dinner by the officers and ladies of the fort, who were pleased by the visit of this polished Yale-educated prelate. The New England-born scholar also attended a nighttime ceremonial dance at a nearby Indian camp, and declared himself fascinated by the spectacle of dancing Indians moving rhythmically to chants and songs by the flickering firelight. A civilian population grew up around Fort Tejón—tradesmen, storekeepers, civilian employees, people connected with the transportation and shipping business between Los Angeles and the San Joaquin Valley made possible in 1854 when the citizens of Los Angeles subscribed $2,900 to make the road from Los Angeles to Fort Tejón and beyond passable by heavy wagons. As the Tejón became more and more settled with a civilian population, it became unnecessary to maintain an army unit in the Grapevine Canyon. On 2 August 1864 the San Francisco headquarters of the United States Army, Department of the Pacific, issued Special Order No. 168 reassigning the dragoons at Fort Tejón to Los Angeles and closing down the fort.

In 1861 President Abraham Lincoln appointed Beale surveyor general for California and Nevada. At the outbreak of hostilities, Beale had asked Lincoln to be ordered to active military service, but Lincoln wanted a knowledgeable and influential Californian administering the public lands in this area. A false story was later circulated that Lincoln refused to reappoint Beale to this position because the Tejón rancher, so Lincoln was supposed to have said, "became the monarch of all that he surveyed." The story is amusing but untrue; while Beale did consolidate himself in the ownership of the Tejón land grants, he did this before and after his tenure as surveyor general, and not while he held office. All in all, Beale consolidated over 150,000 acres of land by 1866. A few years before this final consolidation, Beale had already entered into various partnerships for the raising of sheep and cattle. For more than fifteen years his partner in the sheep business was Colonel Robert S. Baker, a Rhode Islander who came to California to mine for gold in 1849 before turning his hand to business and

ranching in the Southland. Baker and Beale entered jointly into the sheep business in 1854, and after Don Abel Stearns, the leading gentleman of Los Angeles, died in 1861, Baker married his widow, Arcadia Bandini de Stearns, the
daughter of Don Juan Bandini. This marriage consolidated Baker's position as
one of the leading landowners of Southern California, for with the buxom widow,
who had been married to Stearns when she was barely into her teens, came
leagues of land and herds of cattle in dowry. The assessment rolls for 1868
show Beale and Baker grazing 20,000 head of sheep. By 1871, the figure had
increased to 37,000.

The next year, 1872, the New York journalist Charles Nordhoff stopped off
at the Tejón in the course of researching his 1872 best-seller *California for Health,
Wealth, and Residence,* a book which painted life on the Tejón and in California in general in such roseate colors that it single-handedly stimulated significant migration from the East and from Europe. Nordhoff depicted the Tejón as possessed of the grandeur and the spaciousness of a medieval barony,
with General Edward Fitzgerald Beale its feudal lord. (Beale had upped his rank
by becoming a general in the California state militia.) "The rancho from which
I write this—the Tejón it is called—" Nordhoff reported, "seems to me . . .
the finest property in the United States in a single hand. . . . You may ride
for eighty miles on the country roads of this great estate. It supports this year
over 100,000 sheep; and it has a peasantry of its own." Nordhoff was referring
to the three hundred Indians whom Beale had allowed to settle on the Tejón
as tenant farmers after the Sebastian Indian Reserve was discontinued in 1862.
Nordhoff praised the Indian farmers of the Tejón, finding them a "happy, tol-
erably thrifty and very comfortable people." He lauded Beale for buying off their
surplus products at good prices and for paying them fair wages when he needed
their labor. Nordhoff noted that the Indian farmers of the Tejón had snug houses
and good horses, which Beale allowed them to pasture on the general field. He
praised their abilities as farmers and sheepherders. The Indians of the Tejón,
he noted, had a better standard of living than the majority of Irish peasants.
Their wives and daughters dressed neatly and cooked good meals in the American manner. Vineyards and fruit trees surrounded their cottages. The Indians
of the Tejón, Nordhoff wrote, were "as civilized as a good many who came in
emigrant ships from Europe to New York."

On Beale's immediate staff, Nordhoff noted, was a general superintendent,
a bookkeeper, and a storekeeper. There were also teamsters, ploughmen, gardeners, a blacksmith, and a number of Chinese house servants. "The gardeners
and servants are Chinese, as they usually are in this State," Nordhoff observed,
"and very good men they are—civil, obliging, and competent." With a reporter's eye for detail, Nordhoff observed the management of sheep on the Tejón—
their assignment to bands of from thirteen hundred to two thousand sheep per
band, each band under the responsibility of a different shepherd team. These

shepherds, Nordhoff noted, led a remote and lonely existence in their mountain huts. Each night, the shepherds performed the arduous task of gathering the flocks into corrals as protection against the puma, the wildcat, the fox, the coyote, and the dreaded grizzly bear. To protect himself in the open, the shepherd slept by night on a *tepestra*, a platform raised twelve feet off the ground by stout poles. Most of the shepherds, Nordhoff reported, were Indian, Spanish, Chinese, or Scots in ethnic origin. They reported to one of the ranch's *mayordomos*. Each *mayordomo* had charge of a certain number of sheep vans. "To one who likes a free outdoor life," Nordhoff exulted, "I think nothing can be more delightful than the life of a farmer of sheep or cattle in Southern California. The weather is almost always fine; neither heat nor cold ever goes to extremes; you ride everywhere across country, for there are no fences; game is abundant in the seasons; and to one who has been accustomed to the busy life of a great city like New York, the work of a sheep or cattle *rancho* seems to be mere play."

A remote wilderness into the early 1850s, the Tejón becomes from the mid-1850s onward a more and more humanized place. Two of the most famous pioneers of Southern California, Phineas Banning and Remi Nadeau, were associated with the Tejón because of the transportation business. From the late 1850s onward Banning, then later Nadeau, operated a mule-drawn freight-hauling service along the Los Angeles–Fort Tejón road, a road made more easily passable by heavily loaded wagons thanks to the passageway General Beale cut through a sandstone hill three miles below Newhall. The general stationed two yoke of oxen and a drover at the Beale Cut to help pull wagons up the incline. Banning also carried passengers. It cost twelve dollars to travel between Los Angeles and Fort Tejón, a journey of fourteen hours. Remi Nadeau got into the business a few years later. Nadeau designed a special freight wagon named in his honor, which was pulled by an overlong line of strong mules. Eventually Nadeau extended his business out to the Owens Valley and to the settlements along the Colorado River as far as Arizona. The Nadeau wagons are today considered some of the best haulers ever to have operated in the West. Starting in 1858, service was also provided by the Butterfield Overland Mail Company, which linked Los Angeles, Fort Tejón, San Francisco, and St. Louis, the first extensive commercial stagecoach operation in Central and Southern California.

The first *mayordomo* of the Tejón was Francisco (Chico) de Acuña, a young man from Mexico whom General Beale first met during the War of Conquest. In 1859 Beale placed Chico Acuña in charge of his sheep operation; in 1874 the general promoted him to the majordomoship of the Tejón, and put José Jesús López in charge of the sheep. Beale built for Acuña and his wife a lovely adobe home, and it was there on 17 October 1886, one year after his retirement, that Majordomo Chico Acuña died in the arms of General Beale. "This has been the saddest day I have passed on the rancho," the general wrote his wife that evening. "When I got here, as soon as I had washed off the dust, I went to see my old friend Chico. He knew I was coming and had been waiting for me all day most anxiously. When I came into the room, he struggled to put his arms around my neck, but was too weak, and I had to raise his hands up to my shoulders. He looked so pleased for a moment, but the excitement of my coming soon left him, and he began to sink rapidly. I sat at his bedside with his hands in mine until they stiffened in Death."

Born in Los Angeles in 1852 and living on until 1939, Don José Jesús López had an incredibly long tenure as majordomo—from 1874, when General Beale bought out López's sheep herd and employed him as head shepherd for the Tejón, to 1885, when General Beale placed López over the entire ranch, to the very year of his death, when the aged yet energetic López was still functioning as a consultant to the ranch's management in his sixty-fifth year of active service.

Educated in the old Spanish State Normal School of Los Angeles, Majordomo López was a proficient reader and writer. Throughout his life he kept a massive diary recording the day-to-day events of the ranch, together with the stories General Beale would tell him as the two of them camped overnight on the Tejón on one of their many journeys of inspection. Unfortunately, these records were all lost in the fire that destroyed General Beale's home (then serving as ranch headquarters) in April 1917. What a loss to history! Vanished were the minutely recorded details of more than fifty years of Tejón life. López especially rued the loss of the diary he kept during the six months' overland trek with sixteen thousand sheep to Green River, Wyoming, in 1879. General Beale decided that year to get out of the sheep business and into the cattle business, and so he sold his herd to a Wyoming sheep rancher. Gone also were details of the long cattle drive from Tejón to Butchertown in San Francisco County, a journey of 350 miles, another spectacular feat of droving. Majordomo López governed the vaqueros of the Tejón with the authority of a regimental cavalry officer. At noontime, when the vaqueros were at headquarters, Don José would sit down to the midday meal with thirty or forty vaqueros, seated at long tables. No one dared lift a fork until the majordomo had said a quiet grace and had himself begun to eat. The cuisine of Tejón was like Tejón itself, ample and abundant and without pretense. For more than forty years, Mrs. Refugia Garcia Tirado cooked sustaining meals for the vaqueros of beef and chile, potatoes and vegetables, homemade pies and Mexican pastries.

Tejón vaqueros were second to no cattlemen in the world. Many had Indian blood in their veins, and were descendants of the first citizens of the Tejón. They worked long, hard hours for weeks without interruption, tending the innumerable herds of longhorn cattle grazing the vast domain of the Tejón. Many vaqueros were married, and the ranch provided them with adobe cottages. Single vaqueros were housed in a central bunkhouse. They were steady men for the most part, although when they were drinking some of them could be trouble, as Don José found out on a number of occasions. He also discovered that a judicious administration of fisticuffs worked marvels on a drink-befuddled vaquero, who the next day held no grudge as he reported to the majordomo for assignment, a swollen eye or a discolored nose attesting to yesterday's misbehavior. Don José never brought the matter up; he merely sent the men back to their jobs. Occasionally there was a murder or a rape, and then the guilty vaquero would take to the hills in flight, never to be seen again on the Tejón. At branding time the vaqueros branded Tejón cattle with the ancient mark of the crescent and the cross, one of the oldest brands in continuous use in the Old World and the New, traceable to frontier Spain, where Moorish and Christian Spaniards lived side by side.

Many of the Indian field-workers on the Tejón had first been settled there in the 1850s by Beale when he was an Indian agent. Chief Francisco Cota, for instance, who brought his people to the Tejón in 1851, remained a lifelong friend of the general. Educated at Mission San Fernando by the padres, Chief Cota could read and write Spanish and Latin and could sing the ancient Gregorian chants of the church. The general made a point of visiting Chief Cota at least once a year. The two of them, so López reports, would stand before each other in an attitude of respectful attention, both of them approximately of the same age and height and weight. It was as if they were still on the frontier, and the young American officer were negotiating with the young Indian chieftain. At the end of each visit General Beale would ask Chief Cota if he wanted anything. Once the general was wearing a sleek top hat during the interview. The chief said matter-of-factly, "General, I want that hat." General Beale took the hat from his head and placed it on the chief. The general knew that the plug hat would confer enormous prestige upon Francisco Cota, and help him govern his people.

When Edward Fitzgerald Beale died in 1893, Rancho El Tejón passed to his son Truxton, who spent most of his time in the family's Decatur Mansion on Lafayette Square in Washington, D.C., which he also inherited from his father, while Majordomo López ran the ranch out in California. In 1912, deciding upon a permanent Washington residence, Truxton Beale sold the Tejón to a Los Angeles land syndicate headed by Harry Chandler of the *Los Angeles Times* and Moses H. Sherman, a prominent Los Angeles land developer. Even in its new era of corporate ownership, however, Rancho El Tejón preserved into the twentieth century its assertive amalgamation of Indian, Spanish, Mexican, and American elements. In the crucible of the Tejón were mixed and suspended into relatively stable relationships the genetic and social materials of Southern California, from the dawn age of Indian occupation down to the impending era of corporate Los Angeles. Isolated, sealed off by the Tehachapis from the development occurring in the Los Angeles Basin, the Tejón sustained its quasi-feudal society of Indian farm hands, part-Indian vaqueros, Hispanic supervisors, and Yankee owner long after such arrangements had disappeared elsewhere in the Southland. The Tejón fulfilled the law of history that genres, social or artistic, often possess their greatest energy and significance just before they disappear entirely. As a social experiment, feudal and generally benevolent, the Tejón suggested the best possibilities of Southern California's frontier American period. The Indians of the Tejón were not slaughtered or exploited into slavery. Far from it: they became accomplished and self-subsistent agriculturalists and cattlemen. Nor did the Hispanics fade away in bitterness. Losing ownership, they survived in dignity as managers respected for their skills, living on the land, raising their families in the simple style of their forebears. As Mary Austin, who encountered Edward Fitzgerald Beale in the late 1880s, later wrote of him in her autobiography *Earth Horizon* (1932), the general embodied the best possibilities of the American establishment: an Easterner of education and family, an officer and a gentleman, a pioneer distinguished by ambassadorial service in Vienna. For thirty years and more, Beale kept vital on the Tejón an American recapitulation of the previous social order. Given the rapidity of change, Southern California had need of this reminder of how it had been in the days of Hispanic possession and the early American frontier.

2

Early Sojourners and Formulations

Among the many distinctions to be made between Northern and Southern California in the first phase of American settlement is that of literature. In the North, letters flourished; indeed, for a brief period following the Civil War, San Francisco was the literary capital of the nation, the city of Mark Twain, Bret Harte, the *Overland Monthly*, and young Henry George. The decades of San Francisco's literary frontier, 1849–79, witnessed a prodigious outpouring of poetry, memoirs, sermons, histories, short stories, promotional treatises, and legal prose. Only the novel languished, dependent as it is upon a more developed state of society.

Southern California, nonurban, underpopulated, remained a literary wasteland until the 1890s. The terrain is even more arid, in fact, if the Spanish memoirs prepared by Old Californians for the archives of historian Hubert Howe Bancroft are excluded from consideration. Here, at least, the work of memory and imagination went on. American literature in Southern California begins, appropriately, with the first book published in Los Angeles: *Reminiscences of a Ranger; or, Early Times in Southern California* (1881) by Major Horace Bell. This, taken together with the 138 volumes of historical material assembled between 1850 and 1877 by Judge Benjamin Hayes, asserts the fact that some struggle for symbolic expression did occur. Lawyers of literary inclination, both Bell and Hayes stand like cactus plants in the desert of early expression in the Southland: thorny, thriving, giving forth little nourishment but now and then erupting into bloom.

Choleric, quick to take and to avenge an insult, a man living close to the substance and symbols of violence and retribution, Horace Bell was a hard-drinking attorney of florid style, the profane veteran of the Nicaraguan civil war, the War Between the States, and innumerable face-offs, brawls, and horse-whippings. As a type, Horace Bell betokened the presence in Southern California of a frontier reminiscent of Andrew Jackson's Tennessee, a frontier of patriarchal law, an eye for an eye and a tooth for a tooth, the smiting down of one's enemies with the Cromwellian conviction that it was the Lord's work. Horace Bell knew (and relished, it must be said) violence. As an officer with General William Walker's filibustering government in Nicaragua, 1856–57, he witnessed, and took part in, prodigious slaughter. He served as a Union scout in the Civil War. He had been in Northern California during its most unsettled period, and in the thick of the quarrels of Southern California from the late 1850s onwards.

Written in the late 1870s on Sunday mornings before church in Bell's more subdued middle age, *Reminiscences of a Ranger* is the first narrative history in English of Southern California's founding time. Bell read and spoke Spanish fluently, and one of his favorite books, read again and again, was Bernal Díaz's lively and idiomatic *Historia verdadera de la conquista de la Nueva Espanña* (True History of the Conquest of New Spain) (1632), in which the old veteran tells the tale of how Cortés conquered Mexico. Major Bell casts himself similarly, as an old soldier having his say at last.

The military metaphor is important, part of the title itself. Mustered together in 1853 in the El Dorado Saloon, the Los Angeles Rangers were a mounted vigilante group of more than a hundred men organized along paramilitary lines. They wore a uniform inspired by the costume of the Californian caballero; indeed, a number of the members—Agustín Olvera, for instance, and Juan Sepúlveda—were from the Spanish-speaking upper class. Men like John Downey belonged, the future governor of the state, together with professionals like Dr. Alexander Hope, who was the battalion commander, and the attorney Benjamin Hayes. The group enjoyed itself, but it also meant business, claiming the capture and execution of about twenty-two criminals in the period 1853–54.

Speaking haphazardly, colloquially, in the manner of Bernal Díaz, Major Horace Bell, the "Old Ranger," tells a similar story of conquest: of how order was brought to the frontier, and at what price. As in Díaz's *True History*, a monumental squandering of human life occurs. The building blocks of Bell's narrative are acts of mayhem; the movement is from anarchy to civilization, and the end result is the founding of Southern California. In *California, From the Conquest in 1846 to the Second Vigilance Committee in San Francisco: A Study of American Character* (1886), Josiah Royce of Grass Valley, serving in the 1880s as assistant professor of philosophy at Harvard, presented a classic study of this frontier process. Bell had neither Royce's mental power nor his dialectical perspective. He could barely make sense of what occurred, but he knew that it had led to some good because, looking around himself in the late 1870s, he could see that what the Rangers stood for had triumphed.

Why, then, Bell's hyperbole and heavy-handed humor? Why does he glory so much in the brutality of yesteryear? Part of the answer is simple human nature: a middle-aged man's nostalgia for the past, taking the form of exuberant affirmation. Part of the answer, however, is a more complex blend of memory, literary convention, and social interpretation. If only two-thirds of the violent events narrated by Bell are true (and they are), then he must have had to seek some form of psychological control over such essentially chaotic memories. From his reading in Spanish he knew the picaresque tradition, and so, when he sought for a genre—an imaginative structure, that is to say, with which to order and signify events—he adopted the strategy and speaking voice of the *pícaro*. Living on the edge of the apocalyptic, devoid of social role, consoled by neither law nor predictability, the *pícaro* fends off threats to his existence by audacious counterattack. Filling the dark night with bold talk, he disarms terror by embracing it as a constant in the human condition. He meets violence with parody, aping with mock gusto that which terrifies him most. Challenging reality, he makes the world seem even more cruel and absurd than it is.

This, then, is what Horace Bell does with the frontier decades 1850–70, when life was so often less than nasty, brutal, and short. He makes the violent past grotesquely funny; he exaggerates it, so that its legacy of seedy violence and shabby pathos might take on some aura of the heroic, if only the mock-heroic. Bell parodies everyone and everything. His Hudibrastic approach allows him to sustain a complex response toward his memories. The founding time is evoked, judged terrifying, then defensively burlesqued; it is nevertheless put forward as something of a usable past.

Even before Yankee Southern California had a past, however, Bell's colleague in the Los Angeles Rangers, Benjamin Hayes, was determined to see that its materials would not be lost. By the time of his death in 1877, Hayes had collected 138 scrapbooks of printed and manuscript material. Born in Baltimore of Irish Catholic ancestry, educated there at Saint Mary's College and admitted to the Maryland bar, Hayes practiced for a while in St. Louis before traveling overland to Southern California in 1850. Twice elected judge of the southern district of California, an area comprising all counties below the Tehachapis, Hayes rode the circuit between 1852 and 1864, when he was defeated for reelection for allegedly being a pro-Confederate Copperhead. He died in his rooms at the Lafayette Hotel in Los Angeles on 4 August 1877.

Hayes lived a Southern California life of personal complexity and cultural association. He was gentle, religious (he had seriously considered the Roman Catholic priesthood), deeply learned, and in many ways tormented by his imagination. He loved the bottle with an Irish ardor. Now and then court had to be adjourned when the judge was in his cups. Hayes was interested in seeing to it that culture and memory were brought to the frontier. His was the South-

ern California of schoolroom, pulpit, and newspaper office, of books carted across
the continent in saddlebag and trunk, read and reread by rude fireplaces in hours
snatched from the work of getting a society underway.

Major Horace Bell, the frontier as patriarchal rectitude, was over six feet tall,
had a great walrus mustache, carried a gun, and strolled the streets of Los Angeles in an Inverness cape, carrying a stout walking stick with which he now
and then pummeled an adversary. His courtroom outbursts earned him frequent admonitions from the bench. Hayes, smallish, stooping, heard his cases
with patience and with a lack of egocentricity, although he did carry along a
shotgun when he rode on circuit. He read law constantly, devoted as he was to
bringing order to the brawling Southland. His legal papers still survive, in their
economical and scholarly script: a point of research relating to the law of title,
notes in Spanish transcribed from a mission archive, a compassionate address
to a prisoner about to be sentenced to San Quentin or the hangman. For Horace Bell the law was a staff with which to smite one's enemies, hip and thigh.
For Benjamin Hayes the law was a staff of life, a rod plunged into the dry
Southern California earth to point the way away from barbarism.

Attuned to religion and reflection, Hayes was ever in search of sustaining
orthodoxies, sacred and profane. A mood of Vergilian adventure pervades the
notebook he kept on his overland journey, a sense of *condere urbem inferreque
deos Latio*; for Hayes was, after all, seeking more than his fortune in the West.
Like Aeneas, he was voyaging outward to found a new commonwealth, and
along with hopes for personal advancement he was bringing the hopes of religion, literature, and law.

The works and days of Benjamin Hayes, recorded in his diaries, suggest that
here and there on the frontier another and new Southern California was beginning its process of development. Hayes and his wife Emily Martha (she arrived
in 1852 after a sea voyage of forty-three days) take to the countryside in an open
carriage to enjoy the scenery. On holiday, Hayes works long hours in his garden, planting roses and lemon trees. Emily joins him there in the late afternoon, reading aloud from a book of poetry as her husband finishes his garden-
ing and as their son Chauncey, wearing his second-best Fauntleroy suit, rocks
back and forth on a hobbyhorse. They attend Easter mass at the Plaza Church,
a supper party at a nearby ranch, a reception aboard ship in San Diego Harbor,
for which the officers and wives from the garrison turn out in force.

It all has a certain antebellum charm, a responsiveness to California as South,
but without slavery. On 11 September 1857 the judge and his wife took a long
walk among the fruit trees surrounding Los Angeles. They returned home with
a basket of figs and peaches. After dining on crayfish and treating themselves
to figs in milk and sugar, they talked together about the upcoming judicial elections, Emily having her doubts as to whether or not the judge should seek re-
election. She died the next day, at evening, of a sudden sickness. Fathers Raho

and Garibaldi of Our Lady Queen of the Angels chanted a high mass of requiem.

Major Horace Bell was totally Protestant in attitude and tone, although piety did not come to him until late in life. Benjamin Hayes was thoroughly Catholic, as a matter of both piety and culture. He collected a number of volumes of religious material which reveal the catholicity of his Catholicism: dispatches relating to Pio Nono's resistance to Italian unification; essays by John Henry Newman, Orestes Brownson, and others; articles on ecclesiastical affairs in Europe, the Eastern United States, and California; temperance sermons (a warning to himself); religious poetry; lives of the saints; descriptions of great monasteries, shrines, and cathedrals. These volumes (*Memoriae Catholicae*, he called them) bespoke a man sustaining an inner richness of intellectual reference and imaginative extension amidst external cultural scarcity. Hayes's learned Catholicism, his reading of Newman and Wiseman and Alphonse Liquori, his near-obsession with the politics of the church, afforded him something very much like a palace of art, a way of upgrading the meager Catholic suggestions of Southern California and hence of keeping alive his hopes for the development of a society there which one day might also be fertile in utterance and significant in event.

He attempted to found the archives of that coming society in his scrapbook collection, which must be considered, in content and design, a proto-history of Southern California. In two decades of patient effort, Hayes gathered and arranged the raw materials of the Southern California story: the geography and history of the Spanish Southwest, of which Southern California was the Pacific extension; the geography of Southern California itself, together with that of Baja California—the climate, the birds, the animals, the plants and flowers and trees; the Indian tribes; the mission system; the folklore and folk songs of Spanish California; the Conquest; the Civil War in Southern California and in the American Southwest; railways; minerals and mines; agriculture; literary history; data concerning the great Pacific Basin, Australasia and the Far East, the source of California's future economic greatness. Hayes also made certain that the human story would not be lost. Births, deaths, marriages, hangings: the details of early Southern California are all there, mainly in the form of clippings from the *Los Angeles Star*.

The Hayes scrapbooks are the half-written history of a region whose history was but half underway. They constitute Hayes's act of prophecy. Assured that Southern California would have a future, Hayes gathered the materials of its present and past, so that they would be there one day when they were needed. It had all, finally, eluded the hardworking judge's ability to put it together into narrative, as he had intended to do. He sensed, but could not write, the epic. Dragging great stones out onto a grassy plain, he left them there for someone else to set upright and build a temple with. His collection, however, constitutes

American Southern California's first act of self-consciousness. Hayes stored up the signs and symbols by which Southern California would one day know itself. His importance to literature, in the end, was this work of heroic and lavish harvest.

II

By 1877, the year of Judge Hayes's death, Southern California had shed its prevalent Mexican tone, although the rancho economy yet held sway. In the early 1860s a long drought dealt the cattle industry a devastating blow. Bleached bones dotted the hillsides of the South for years afterwards, at countless spots where an animal had dropped in an agony of thirst, or where a ranchero, desperate to salvage a few cents' worth of hide, had slaughtered what remained of his stock. Then the sheepmen came, and with them a more developed order; sheep, grazing intensely, wander less widely than cattle and take more care. Slaughtering time gave way to shearing time, and the mildness of sheepshearing, immemorial in association (like beekeeping, also underway), brought beauty and civility to the semi-barbaric Southland.

Obtaining land grants in the lingering days of Mexican rule, Jonathan Trumbull Warner and Benjamin Davis Wilson lived on well into the American era, their experiences typical of the transitional generation. Warner was of New England stock, born in Connecticut in 1807, Wilson a Tennesseean, born in Nashville in 1811. Warner had the advantage of a good public school education; he was, in fact, one of the most literate of the Americans who made their way into Southern California before the Conquest. Benjamin Davis Wilson, a son of the less developed Tennessee border country, received but a skimpy education. He made it, however, well over the threshold of literacy.

Both men went west for their health. As a storekeeper on the Yazoo River above Vicksburg, trading with Choctaws and Chickasaws (he went to work at age fifteen), B. D. Wilson had some sort of physical breakdown. J. T. Warner experienced similar difficulties in his early twenties. His doctor advised him to go west. Warner went to St. Louis and presented himself to the greatest mountain man of them all, Jedediah Strong Smith, himself then barely into his thirties but already a legend in his own time. Since taking to the field in 1822, Jedediah Smith had encircled the Far West twice, including two trips to California. He now headed his own Rocky Mountain Fur Company, along with two other partners. Smith told Warner, then about the same age Smith had been when he presented himself to General William Ashley for a three-year expedition into the upper Missouri and the Yellowstone, that the life of a mountain man was no way to recover one's health. It was a better way to lose it—permanently. Had he to do it over again, Smith told Warner, he would have stayed home in Ohio. Young Warner persisted, and because he was an educated man, Smith took him on as clerk to an expedition he was fitting up to trap and trade down along the Santa Fe Trail. Smith was killed by the Comanches, and the expedition lost its momentum when it reached Santa Fe. In December 1831 Jonathan Trumbull Warner reached Los Angeles as part of a party led by Smith's partner David Jackson. He spent the next two years in the interior of California, trapping beaver.

B. D. Wilson spent eight years operating out of Santa Fe as a trapper and a trader in the employ of Josiah Gregg, the Southwestern entrepreneur whose *Commerce on the Prairies* (1855) is a classic narrative of Far Western travel and trade. The natural drift of trapping, pushing further and further West in search of scarcer and scarcer beaver, brought Wilson to Southern California in 1841.

In 1833 Jonathan Warner returned from the field and began work as a storekeeper for Abel Stearns in Los Angeles. He opened a store of his own in 1836, and in 1837, at Mission San Luis Rey, he married Anita Gale, an English girl left as a child by her sea captain father with the Pico family to be raised as their ward. In 1843 Warner became a Mexican citizen and was baptized a Roman Catholic, taking the name Juan José, although the Californians called him Juan Largo (Big John) because of his six-foot-three-inch frame. In 1844 Warner acquired a large land grant in the Valle de San José, near Hot Springs in San Diego County. He built a hacienda there and a trading post, staffing his establishment with Yuma Indians, with whom he had good rapport.

Juan José Warner was a sensitive, educated, somewhat visionary man, not destined for business success. He never made much money from his rancho, having to eke out his income as a Southern California correspondent for East Coast and San Francisco newspapers. He moved back to Los Angeles in 1855 and in 1858 began his own newspaper, the *Southern Vineyard*. As early as 1840, while on a trip to the East, he gave a speech calling for the annexation of California and the building of a transcontinental railroad. Secretary of War Jefferson Davis heard of the speech and was impressed. As editor of the short-lived *Southern Vineyard*, Warner continued the work of local promotion. He envisioned a prosperous future for Southern California agriculture once the railroad arrived and the irrigation problem was solved.

Warner was a man more of vision than of action. He had lost all his ranch property by 1861. The less educated, more shrewd Benjamin Davis Wilson put Warner's dreams into practice. Warner became, in 1883, the first president of the Historical Society of Southern California, a beloved figure from Southern California's founding time. Benjamin Davis Wilson became rich. His rise to Southern California prominence in the 1846–76 period is an epic of ordinary talent and extraordinary aspiration: a Southern California story typical of the generation which inherited and inhabited the land-grant ranchos and made them work in American terms.

In 1844 Benjamin Davis Wilson married into a rancho family, the Yorbas of Rancho Santa Ana, although he did not become either a Mexican citizen or a Roman Catholic, as had Warner. He bought part of the Rancho La Jurupa in Riverside. In the early 1850s he acquired interest in Rancho San José de Buenos Aires (now Westwood and the campus of UCLA), where he raised cattle and sheep, and the Huerta de Cuati, where he located Lake Vineyard, his county seat. By the time of his death in 1878, B. D. Wilson owned ranchos occupying the present sites of Pasadena, San Marino, Alhambra, and San Gabriel.

Wilson lived a life combining the feudal spaciousness of the early cattle era with the developmental urges of the American mid–nineteenth century. He made the transition from cattle to sheep, and then, with the coming of the 1870s, went on to wheat, fruit, and citrus. He helped pioneer the wine industry in Southern California, worked for the coming of the railroad, and in the mid-1860s was associated with early efforts to drill for oil. He served once as mayor of Los Angeles and three terms as state senator.

Both Warner and Wilson fit into a landscape of regional transition and developing regional identity. Both began their careers in Southern California before the Conquest. Wilson married a Yorba; Warner married a ward of the Pico family. Their friends, their tastes, their interests were partly Mexican. During the war, in fact, Lieutenant Archibald Gillespie of the Marine Corps placed both Warner and Wilson under arrest as enemy sympathizers. As a state senator, Wilson fought to have Southern California separated from the rest of the state as the Territory of Colorado. A states'-rights, anti-slavery Democrat, Wilson had Confederate sympathies during the Civil War, and Southern sympathies long after the defeat of the South. His daughter by a second marriage married Virginia-born George Smith Patton, the son of a Confederate colonel killed while serving with the Twenty-second Virginia Infantry. Wilson's grandson, George Smith Patton III, attended his father's alma mater, the Virginia Military Institute, then went on to West Point and a career in the regular army.

Wilson was, in short, a developed provincial type, representative of Southern California's first American phase. Whatever his other interests—interests prophetic in the long run of Southern California's urban-industrial future—he himself stayed primarily on the land, as did so many others: Thomas Hope, for instance, Irish-born, coming to Santa Barbara County in 1849 after a sojourn in Texas and eventually acquiring Los Ranchos de las Positas y la Calera, which he renamed (after himself, no doubt) Hope Ranch. Hope built himself an elegant mansion in 1875, at the cost of $10,000, as did Elias Jackson Baldwin ("Lucky Jim," his friends called him), who acquired the Rancho Santa Anita in 1873, a 13,000-acre spread in Los Angeles County, which he expanded to 54,000 acres around the San Gabriel Valley, making it the largest single rancho in Southern California. Baldwin grazed 20,000 head of sheep and 2,000 dairy cows. He planted wheat, almonds, olives, figs, prunes, pears, walnuts, apricots, oranges, and lemons. His vineyards produced 100,000 gallons of wine yearly, and 30,000 gallons of brandy. A sporting man, Lucky Jim paid $28,000 in 1874 for two Kentucky-bred stallions. From them he bred prize-winning race horses. He sent the first Southern California horses East to compete. Baldwin's stable of winners eventually brought in $100,000 a year.

The size of Santa Anita, 54,000 acres, indicated a trend in Southern California ranchos of the period—indeed, in the ranchos of Central California and the North as well. They were vast. Rarely in the history of the United States was so much acreage consolidated into so few hands. Senator George Hearst, for instance, acquired some 240,000 acres in San Luis Obispo and Monterey counties: the San Simeon Ranch, built up out of annexations of Ranchos Piedra Blanca and Santa Rosa, San Miguel Mission lands, and other holdings. In the 1870s and '80s two European immigrants, a German butcher named Heinrich Kereiser (changed to Henry Miller in America) and an Alsatian named Charles Lux, put together over 700,000 acres in the San Joaquin Valley alone. Their total acreage in California: one million. Their total holdings in California, Nevada, Oregon: three million acres. Northern California capitalists—Henry Mayo Newhall and James Irvine of San Francisco among the most prominent—sought outlets for their money in Southern California land in the 1870s. The relationship of this second generation of American landholders to the land differed from that of the 1845–75 era. The Newhall and the Irvine holdings, and others like them, were implicitly enterprises of agribusiness, owned and directed by men who had made their first money in sophisticated urban circumstances and who by temperament and style of operation were more venture capitalists than rancheros. The Mayo and Newhall holdings in Los Angeles County grew like modern conglomerates. To the north, the Kern County Land Company, financed by San Francisco banker Lloyd Tevis, showed similar growing power.

And yet even conglomeration could not dispel completely the Spanish styles of the past. Beale, Newhall, Mayo, Irvine, Miller, Hearst, capitalists all, nevertheless felt the hold of the land upon them as more than a commercial venture. As landowners, they became more than businessmen. They felt again the baronial, feudal land pride of the dons whom they had displaced. Their children, growing up on the land (albeit with expensive educations as well), grew even closer to it. Take Sarah Bixby Smith, for instance. Her father, Llewellyn Bixby; his brother Jotham; a cousin, John William Bixby; and two other cousins, Thomas and Benjamin Flint, formed the Flint-Bixby Company in 1855. By the mid-1880s they had put together a huge empire: the San Justo Rancho near San Juan Bautista, the Rancho Los Cerritos and the Rancho Los Alamitos at Long Beach, large parts of the Rancho Los Palos Verdes and the Rancho Cajón de Santa Ana. Sarah was born in the early 1870s on the San Justo Rancho. The Bixbys were Maine people. In 1852 the brothers and cousins had driven a herd of sheep across country from the East into Southern California, a ten-month

journey. On the Rancho San Justo the entire clan lived together in a New England–style ranch house, where Sarah spent the first years of her life before
removing to Southern California.

Adobe Days (1925), Sarah Bixby Smith's account of her girlhood on the San
Justo, Los Cerritos, and Los Alamitos, is deservedly a classic of California autobiography. Bixby Smith captures perfectly that intersection of civilization and
frontier, New Englandism and Spanish Southwest, which turn-of-the-century
Southern California defined as its own special heritage. In the meridian of middle
age, Sarah Bixby Smith put on record a vanished way of life: the constant sunshine and fresh air; shearing time, when some fifty to sixty Mexican shearers
rode en masse to the rancho, attired in their best finery—black broadcloth suits
tailored Spanish style, white ruffled shirts, silver-brimmed sombreros—riding
in so flamboyantly, as if this were yet the age of the dons and vaqueros and
they yet the lords of their own land, then changing into brown overalls and
encircling their thick black hair with red bandanas to catch the sweat, getting
to work in the shearing pens. Dipping time followed shearing time, the shorn
sheep thrown one by one into foul-smelling vats, whose sulphurous soup sealed
their nicked, naked skins and forestalled the diseases of the open range.

Sarah Bixby Smith remembered the Maine books in the parlor, the Bible,
Scott, Dickens, *Two Years before the Mast*. She remembered the parlor concerts of singing, fiddle, and piano—"Arkansas Traveler," "Money Musk," "Turkey
in the Straw"—or, more solemnly of a Sunday, "Shall We Gather at the River?"
and "Pass under the Rod." Out front before the ranch house was a solitary orange tree whose white springtime blossoms and summer fruit promised a Southern
California yet to come. In from the range, the workingmen ate at long outdoor
tables: mutton stew, boiled onions, frijoles, heavy black coffee, prepared by
Mexican and Chinese cooks. For a picnic on the empty shores of Long Beach
the Bixbys grilled chops over a driftwood fire. It was, she remembered, a fine,
vigorous life, a frontier sort of life, yet touched by civilization. The Basque
shepherds fascinated her. They seemed figures dropped from time past, shepherds in bas-relief from an excavated Etruscan tomb. One was found dead in
his remote shack, hanging from a timber beam, she recalled, the victim of some
impenetrable despair, dying alone, far from his Pyrenean homeland.

It was a good life, a semi-heroic life, and like all bronze ages it gave way to
an age of iron. In the late 1860s Mexican vaqueros used to race their horses
against the locomotive which ran between Los Angeles and the harbor town of
Wilmington. They would win for a while, but the locomotive had more staying
power, and after a few minutes of being beaten it would pull out ahead.

The railroads settled Southern California: first the Southern Pacific, blasting
its way through the San Fernando Mountains in 1876 to link Los Angeles with
San Francisco and the East, and then, in 1885, the Atchison, Topeka and Santa
Fe, arriving overland through the deserts and gorges of the Southwest. The rail-

roads brought new varieties of Americans to the Southland: the homesteader, the urban immigrant, the health seeker, the tourist. The Southern Pacific subdivided and sold off its vast holdings. It and the Santa Fe maintained elaborate publicity operations to promote travel to the Southland. Single-handedly, in fact, the Southern Pacific, under the direction of publicity agent Jerome Madden, waged a campaign in the 1870s to domesticate the image of Southern California. The company brought out the experienced journalist Charles Nordhoff, then an editor with the *New York Evening Post*, whose report *California for Health, Pleasure, and Residence* (1872) put forth Southern California's new identity. Now began the new age, Nordhoff asserted: a time not of gold and speculation and disorder, but of plantings, harvests, and domestic life.

Certainly Los Angeles fulfilled Nordhoff's prophecy. In the decade of the 1870s it became an American city. Adobe gave way to brick and wood, candles and kerosene to gas. The streets were paved and tracks laid for horse-drawn streetcars. Police and fire departments were organized on a permanent basis and a lending library was established. A city hall was built, together with a train station, a county hospital, an opera house, and a theater seating four hundred. In 1878 the Methodist Church founded the University of Southern California. By that time there also existed in Los Angeles a public high school; a normal school for the training of teachers; a Catholic men's college, St. Vincent's (now Loyola University); and two finishing schools for young ladies, one run by the Sisters of Charity and the other conducted by Miss Anne W. Chapman and Miss Josephine Cole. There were several newspapers and a racetrack.

Interestingly enough, Pío Pico, the last Mexican governor, financed the construction of the first modern hotel, the Pico House, built in 1869 and opened in 1870. The Pico House was a grand affair, the finest hotel in the entire Southwest for a decade or so. A sturdy three-story pile of massed arches, described as American Romanesque, the hotel enclosed a richly planted central court and fountain. Furnished in the heavy, sumptuous style of the period, the rooms of the Pico House were gas lit and connected to the central desk by speaking tubes. Cuisine and dining room appointments were of the finest, while the lobby and upstairs corridors were made fragrant with daily displays of fresh flowers and enlivened by the singing of caged birds. Hotels, of course, are symbolic enterprises, condensing and displaying as they do a city's or a region's flavor. Here, then, suggested the Pico House to travelers arriving by stage from the North or overland from across the arid and empty Southwest, here was a land of present plenty and incipient taste, and of beauty made more provocative by a touch of the exotic.

The clock atop the Temple Block tower said in no uncertain terms that Los Angeles now ran on American time. A chamber of commerce formed, and a number of business buildings were constructed, the most elaborate being the Baker Block at the corner of Main and Acadia. A wedding cake of arches and columns, its three stories surmounted by a mansard roof and a gazebo-like tower, the Baker Block expressed perfectly the taste and values of what was in the East called the Gilded Age. It was a temple to business conducted in the Yankee manner. Again, however, as in the case of the Pico House, there was an Old Californian connection. Colonel R. S. Baker, the owner, had married Arcadia, widow of Abel Stearns and daughter of Don Juan Bandini, who then became Doña Arcadia Bandini de Baker. The couple maintained a luxurious suite in the Baker Block, and from there reigned over Los Angeles social life: the colonel the very embodiment of Yankee business energy, and Doña Arcadia, daughter of Old California, widow of the transition, now mistress of an American present.

She was, of course, a Roman Catholic, as was a majority of Los Angeles' population until the influx of Midwesterners which began in the mid-1880s changed the nature of the city. In 1876 Los Angeles consecrated a monument to the Spanish Catholic tradition which yet remained a reality, Saint Vibiana's Cathedral, a massive building for the time and the place, seating three thousand and based upon the Puerto de San Miguel in Barcelona, Spain.

Saint Vibiana's, the Baker Block, the Pico House: the city of Los Angeles had these and other public places (the Merced Theatre, for instance, called Wood's Opera House after 1876) which served certain social needs—travel, business, entertainment, religion—but which also suggested a developing civic maturity in the once heedless town. The quality of life in Los Angeles as a whole improved. Citizens no longer bathed, washed, and drank from the same open ditches. Private dwellings, done in East Lake, General Grant, or Queen Anne, began to show signs of elegance, especially in the matter of gardens. In 1878 Los Angeles staged an elaborate and successful Horticultural Fair, building a special pavilion for the purpose.

Violence abated, at least the violence of the mob—but not before one last horrible orgy which outdid anything that had happened in the previous two decades. On Tuesday morning, 24 October 1871, two rival Chinese companies, the Nin Yung and the Hong Chow, got into a gun battle over Ya Hit, a disputed female. When the law arrived, the Chinese barricaded themselves in the Coronel Block, an adobe building in the notorious Negro Alley. Robert Thompson, a former saloon keeper who volunteered to help the police, was shot and critically wounded as he tried to enter a room where some of the Chinese were holed up. It took a few hours for Thompson to die, and as he lay expiring at Wollweber's Drug Store on Main Street a mob formed. At its height the mob numbered about five hundred, 5 percent of the population of Los Angeles—which is to say that 5 percent of the population of Los Angeles was the worst sort of rabble, about whom the law could do, or wanted to do, nothing. Racial hatred seethed, and blood lust, and there was talk of $6,000 in gold coin stashed away in one of the besieged rooms. Part of the mob chopped holes into the roofs of the block and fired in indiscriminately. Wong Tuck made a run for it, was seized, tortured, then strung up. The rope broke, and he fell to the ground. He begged for mercy, but was hanged a second time. The mob amused itself by bashing his head against the posts from which he had been hanged. Before the day was over, seventeen other Chinese males, including a boy of fourteen, died equally horrible deaths, tortured by the mob in the open street before being lynched. One man, the possessor of a diamond ring, had his finger pulled from his hand before the end came. Some Chinese, already dead from gunfire, were dragged out and hanged anyway, for the sake of the spectacle. The Chinese quarter was looted.

The grand jury examined more than a hundred citizens, but only a handful were ever sentenced to San Quentin, and they were released shortly after on a technicality. It must be admitted that certain Angelenos risked their lives resisting the mob, and that others offered their homes as havens to the Chinese during the massacre. It must be admitted also, however, that the city government was helpless during the blood orgy (the mayor took one look at the situation and then disappeared) and that the police, all political appointees, were not very active in resisting the mob. The official interpretation had it that only the riff raff of Los Angeles was involved, the denizens of the sixty-two saloons which served the city of ten thousand. Horace Bell had another opinion. An atmosphere of city-wide complicity surrounded the massacre, he claimed. The mob grew bold because it knew that it had the approval of the community at large. In fact in subsequent investigations and trials the prosecution showed no vigor in bringing the guilty to justice.

The massacre of the Chinese points out the transitional nature of the early 1870s. The final barbarity after two decades of frontier violence: nothing like it would ever—or could ever—happen again (racism would find more subtle outlets). But when it happened it sent a shudder through proper Southern Californians, shocked to find that so much of the old ferocity remained. Perhaps this is why three years later, in 1874, when they captured the bandit Tiburcio Vásquez, they made such a show of behaving so well. Having such distinguished colleagues as Joaquín Murieta and Juan Flores as predecessors, Tiburcio Vásquez was the last of a generation of bandits to lead marauding bands through the backcountry of Southern California. Had his capture occurred ten years earlier, Vásquez would have been dragged from the Los Angeles jail and lynched. In 1874, however, the captured Vásquez found himself a celebrity. A physician treated his wounds. His cell was made as comfortable as possible. The ladies of Los Angeles paid the jail house solicitous visits to see how Vásquez was getting along. He was interviewed by reporters, who praised him for his courtesy. A formal portrait was photographed, a suit being provided for the occasion.

In a wily effort to save his neck, Vásquez played out the role demanded of him, more than half believing it himself. In interviews he depicted himself as a figure in a romantic tragedy. His dramatized himself as a young man bullied by Americans for defending the honor of his countrywomen. Vásquez knew exactly what he would have to say if he were to have a chance at clemency. Instinctively, he played to the incipient self-consciousness of the society which had captured him. He was the last of his kind, he claimed, the symbol of a vanishing order, a cabellero, with the courage of a cabellero. *("Yo soy un ca-ballero, con el corazón de un caballero!")* He was a patriot, he told the Associated Press, whose goal had been to raise an army and sweep Southern California free of the gringo.

It was all very ambiguous on both sides. History will never know how much Vásquez believed of what he was saying, how much was a shrewd attempt to win favor with his captors. Despite their willingness to make him a folk hero, the Americans, on their part, had no intention of treating Vásquez other than as a criminal. They hanged him on 19 March 1875. And yet frontier Southern California had reached the stage of development where it wanted to feel good about itself, and an essential part of feeling good about Southern California was believing that Southern California had a past it could romanticize. Southern Californians encouraged Vásquez's self-mythologization because they knew the bandit's experience had a representative quality. It said something about what had been, what was passing away, and what was coming about. A softening had arrived with self-consciousness, a mitigation of frontier ferocity. The violent edges of Vásquez's career were blurred, the question of his murders held as much as possible in abeyance. In 1871 eighteen Chinese had been tortured and killed most foully by a raging mob. In 1875 Californians sent Tiburcio Vásquez to the hangman with flowers, a photograph, a new suit, and their most sincere best wishes.

III

Major Benjamin Truman, a Los Angeles journalist, interviewed Vásquez extensively in 1874 and published the results. He also published that year a promotional treatise, *Semi-Tropical California*, which both expressed and solidified Southern California's post-frontier hopes. Truman belonged to a breed of writer common in California journalism, although much more so in the North than in the South: a variously learned, Tory bohemian jack-of-literary-trades, possessed of a good Civil War record and excellent political connections, and very much the gentleman. (Ambrose Bierce brought the type to perfection.) Rhode Island born and bred, Truman made rank in the Civil War and served for a while as private secretary to the ill-fated President Andrew Johnson. He arrived in Los Angeles in 1866, charged with the supervision of the postal service in Southern California and Arizona. In the early 1870s he resigned his post to found, publish, and edit the *Los Angeles Daily Star*.

Learned, loquacious, well traveled, a connoisseur of wine and a gastronome known in gourmet circles from Paris to Paraguay, Truman promoted Southern California as a place for the good life, by which he meant a balanced interplay of outdoor industries in congenial surroundings and the subtle social satisfactions of urban life. For Truman, the impending Southern California would fulfill the dream of pastoral, Horatian America: rural but not countrified, hardworking but not too hard-working, knowing in some measure the consolations of civility, art, speculation, and society. The railroad paid him to say this because saying it sold real estate and brought hundreds of thousands to the Southland. Paid or not, however, Truman believed in the ideal, for it arose naturally out of the nineteenth-century American agrarian experience. Not surprisingly, Southern California's first self-image after the passing of the frontier was that of the American farm perfected, saved from loneliness and back-breaking labor, graced with some degree of aesthetic satisfaction.

"Semi-tropical," the rubric beneath which Truman massed his data, had its problems, both as a fact and as a controlling metaphor. One side of the American imagination had always been South-seeking, in search of the sun and all the sun symbolized: warmth, color, fertility, radiance of spirit and flesh. In Southern California, the sun was dramatically there, shining for more than 240 days a year, abundant of nurture and light. The semi-tropical comparison, however, drove the metaphor of California as South, as land of the sun, to an extreme. South of the Tehachapis one could grow bananas, pineapples, orchids, and guavas—true, but only as an act of botanical showmanship, not sound agronomy.

The semi-tropical comparison eventually collapsed under scientific scrutiny, but more than this—from its first appearance it did not sit well with the American imagination. It allowed nature a wild, defiant luxuriance which could never be subdued by industry. It made the sun too hot, a scorching sun or, more frighteningly, a sun that would sap the Northern European sources of the American will, turning industrious immigrants into loafers. Truman invokes the semi-tropical metaphor, is uneasy with it, and midway through his treatise replaces it with a Mediterranean comparison. "Semi-tropicalism" would leave its traces in the chemistry of Southern California, however. An element of the exotic, of undisciplined luxuriance, had been introduced, and it stayed, taking many forms: ostrich farms, riotous planting, extravagances of architecture and design, and, most importantly, displaced semi-tropicalisms of thought and behavior which would in time make Southern California a place where anything and everything could take hold, and usually did.

In the meanwhile, the more civilized Mediterranean comparison won the battle of metaphor. Even Truman, despite the title of his treatise, finds the Mediterranean comparison more comfortable. Southern California is not so much the semi-tropics as it is Spain, Italy, Greece, Corsica, Corfu, the Levant; not an Edenic rain forest teeming with guavas and wild orchids but a sunny, mellow garden of Southern civility, planted patiently with vines, dates, olives, and oranges. At its core, the semi-tropical metaphor had an element of chaos. The Mediterranean comparison invoked values of responsible order and conveyed a sense of impending civilization. It did so because the Mediterranean was rich in both nature and history, and Southern Californians wanted both blessings. Abundance, sun, aesthetic surroundings, a measure of ease and social discourse: they wanted a bourgeois utopia, with an emphasis on outdoor living and domestic pleasures. Eventually, in Pasadena, Santa Barbara, and elsewhere, architecture would incorporate these ideals into superb spatial expression. In the 1870–90 phase of Southern California development, however, the dream attached itself to agriculture.

The farmer in Southern California, promotional writers promised, would be a middle-class horticulturist. The agricultural industries proper to the region—citrus, fruit, vineyards—were not back-breaking efforts, once the initial work of planting and irrigation had been accomplished, nor was much acreage needed to yield a comfortable income. Freed from the back-breaking ordeal of the New England and Midwestern farm, the Southern Californian horticulturist had time and means for the finer things. There would be books, a rose garden, a piano in the parlor. Fuchsia and heliotrope would smother his gabled cottage. Because holdings were small, he would have neighbors, and together they could support a variety of amenities: schools, churches, concert halls.

The colony system in Southern California agriculture was founded on this ideal. Each cooperative was, in effect, a quasi-utopian experiment, in which a homogeneous group jointly purchased a tract, subdivided it amongst themselves, then lived in social and economic cooperation. In various ways and with various degrees of communality, Riverside, Long Beach, Westminster, San Fernando, Alhambra, San Bernardino, Anaheim, Pomona, Ontario, Lompoc, and Pasadena all had their starts as settlements in this manner. San Bernardino, Southern California's first American colony (for the Franciscan missions were cooperatives of an enforced sort), was knit tightly together by Mormonism. Indianans settled Pasadena in the early 1870s. The English gathered at El Toro, the Germans at Anaheim, the Danes at Solvang, near Santa Barbara.

These settlements kept their coherence and flavor long after the first agricultural colonies broke down and incorporated townships took their place. In their first phase, colonies dispelled the terrible isolation of nineteenth-century life on the land. They also brought about stable translations of values and styles of living. For some time to come, for instance, Pasadena kept its tone of Protestant high-mindedness. The English at El Toro celebrated the Queen's birthday, had drinks at sundown, and organized one of America's first polo teams. Southern California developed in the 1870–90 period as a confederation of transitional colonies, each with a quasi-utopian impulse. Like hothouse plants, these subcultures only flowered for the moment, yet they cast seeds of utopian eclecticism into the humus from which grew modern Southern California.

The Polish colony near Anaheim had the brief life of a mayfly, but was a charming case in point. The venture began in Warsaw, where in the mid-1870s a coterie of upper-middle-class and aristocratic liberals gathered itself around Count Karol Bozenta Chlapowski, who had fought in the anti-tsarist, anti-German insurrection of 1863, been wounded and imprisoned, and now edited a journal of enlightened patriotic opinion, *Kraj* (The Country). Among the group were Henryk Sienkiewicz, a dreamy young aspirant writer of about thirty, destined to win fame for his novel *Quo Vadis?*; Jules Sypniewski, another young idealist, who had been in prison with the count; and the count's wife, Helena Modrzejewski, then in her early thirties and already a distinguished actress on the Polish stage. Despite the revolutionary background of the count, the Chalapowski-Modrzejewski salon was not explicitly political; it was united, rather, by a deep vein of romanticism, a vague but compelling yearning for a better time and a better place, far from either Russian or German rule. Amidst the clatter of tea cups, or in the heady hours of early morning conversation, their thoughts turned to Southern California. An ambition consolidated itself from all the dreamy talk: they would establish a colony in Southern California modeled upon Brook Farm, where they would till the soil and lead lives of heightened purpose. Helena Modrzejewski reserved for herself the especially poetic task of bleaching linen by a riverbank, like a maiden in the *Iliad*.

Madame Modrzejewski herself did the cooking the first morning of the colony's actual existence, slightly annoyed that everyone ordered something different, including one colonist who would break his fast on nothing less than an elaborate wine soup. In any event, the men left for the citrus groves well nourished and eager to begin. There was less spring in their step when they walked away from luncheon. By the end of the week nobody was going to the fields, preferring riding, hunting, fishing, swimming, and loafing in the sun to caring for the chickens and the orange trees. Sienkiewicz read a lot, began some sketches, and tamed a badger. Helena devoted less and less time to cooking and more and more time to preparing for the evening recitals. Cattle wandered in and ate their barley. The dog ate the fresh eggs. Passersby helped themselves to the muscat grapes. No one knew how to milk a cow, so they had to buy their dairy products from a neighboring ranch. All in all, Count Chlapowski (who in Southern California preferred to be addressed as Mr. Bozenta) lost about $15,000 in the experiment.

The count and his wife, however, were destined to thrive in the United States. Helena learned English, shortened her last name to Modjeska, and, under her husband Mr. Bozenta's management, embarked in San Francisco upon a legendary stage career. In 1885 they returned to Southern California, buying, this time, a working ranch in the Santiago Canyon of the Santa Ana Mountains, twenty miles east of Orange. They called it Arden, after the enchanted forest in *As You Like It*. The Brook Farm expectations of 1876 had ceded to elegant *villegiatura*. They hired professionals to run the ranch. Stanford White designed a rambling bungalow, placed back beneath the trees, and in front a little lake, across which glided swans. Modjeska and the count loved to ride about the estate after breakfast on the veranda, inspecting the vineyards and the orange groves, inhaling the springtime fragrance of the blossoms or hearing the drowsy hum of the apiary. Afternoons were spent reading in the library, or sitting in conversation on the lawn, under great oak trees. Evenings were musical (Ignace Jan Paderewski once visited) or given to recitals by Modjeska from one or other of her favorite parts—Maria Stuart, Camille, Portia, Cleopatra, Viola, Rosalind, Lady Macbeth.

Arden, obviously, was not Brook Farm, nor was it a working Southern California ranch. The agricultural expectations of the 1870s gave way in the 1880s to a more self-consciously aesthetic ideal (for those who could afford it): Southern California as a place apart, a land of sunny afternoons. In Arden's enchanted forest, fantasy and fact commingled, and the American Southern Californian dreamed a dream of beauty and ease.

A new institution, the tourist hotel, sprang up to accommodate this ideal. By 1900 more than a hundred such hostelries were operating in Southern California. The Arlington in Santa Barbara established the genre in 1876, followed by the Hotel Del Monte in Monterey, opened in 1880 by the Southern Pacific and rebuilt in 1887 in such a way as to set standards of elegance for all hotels to come. The Raymond in Pasadena was owned and managed by the same company, Raymond-Whitcomb Tours, which operated the famous Crawford House in the White Mountains of New Hampshire. Opening its doors in 1886, the Raymond deliberately sustained a tone of proper Boston, of which, indeed, it was an outpost. Even President Charles Eliot of Harvard found the Raymond respectable.

The archetypal Southern Californian tourist hotel, the Del Coronado at Coronado Beach in San Diego County, advertised itself when it opened in 1889 as the largest resort hotel in the world. Built of redwood in architect James W. Reid's own version of Queen Anne, the Del Coronado, 399 rooms, rambled over seven and a half acres of the narrow peninsula dividing the Pacific Ocean from the Bay of San Diego, a sun-drenched setting of sea and sky. The hotel boasted electric lighting, a main dining room of ten thousand square feet uninterrupted by pillar or post, an interior court lushly planted in tropical fruits and flowers, and views of both garden and sea from the well-decorated suites. The routine at the Del Coronado was elegant and stately, in the manner of the unhurried late nineteenth century. An orchestra played at luncheon and dinner. Mornings and afternoons were lazed away on the sunny glass-covered verandas facing the bay, or more strenuously filled with sailing, golf, tennis, riding to hounds, or swimming in the hot or cold indoor plunges. Dances, receptions, recitals, and the like occupied the evenings. The management was especially proud of its Ladies' Billiard Parlor.

As deliberate assertions of a romanticized Southern Californianism, tourist hotels like the Del Coronado had utopian overtones. Like the agricultural colonies, they were statements of an ideal, in the hotels' case something about Eastern elegance being brought to Southern Californian shores. Henry James, who felt that the blood of Southern California's civilization ran thin, enjoyed the Del Coronado, finding it an idealized garden of the South. The tourist hotel brought the East and Easterners to Santa Barbara, to Pasadena, San Diego, and Long Beach, setting a tone, creating an ambience, for developing communities. Many Eastern immigrants to these cities had their first exposure to Southern California as tourists—a fact conferring on the hotel the role of colonizing agent. As symbolic or idealizing statements, tourist hotels upgraded the possibilities of Southern California, bringing new cultural associations to the region, showing what social patterns might be established, pointing out an aesthetic relationship to environment. They were, obviously, for the few, not the many; but because the immigrant of the 1880s and 1890s was quintessentially middle class—and thus capable of being impressed by the habits and styles of privilege—the tourist hotel did more than pleasure its wealthy clientele.

The decade of hotel construction, the 1880s, is Southern California's founding time from the point of view of population increase. When the Santa Fe reached Los Angeles in 1885, a rate war broke out between it and the Southern Pacific, bringing the price of a ticket to Southern California down to as low as fifteen dollars. By 1890 more than 130,000 people had come to Southern California, many from the Midwest. Los Angeles alone grew by 500 percent, reaching a population of 50,000 by 1889. The three years between the coming of the Santa Fe in 1885 and the collapse of the boom in 1888 was a time of furious speculation in real estate. Subdivision followed subdivision. Entire towns were planned, auctioned off, and abandoned without there being a single act of construction.

And so Southern California was no longer a frontier, but a province awaiting the subtle and complex developments of urbanization and art it would experience in the 1890–1915 period. An age of iron, of nonreflective foundation, surrendered to an age of bronze, an age of thought and craftsmanship and city making, during which the pliant alloys of Southern California—the land, the people, the hopes—would be subsumed into categories and symbolic forms.

From the point of view of the national experience, the epigenesis of provincial Southern California from its frontier had been a nearly anonymous act. Even local history, motivated by piety and a desire for usable myths, found it difficult to distinguish any heroes. The lives of the pioneers were, in the main, ordinary lives, lived out on a frontier that was ordinary in almost everything save its setting. Yet they had done their work and, looking back, they had found their works and days good.

Some had come overland: like Eli Rundell of Cayuga County, New York, who arrived by covered wagon in 1846, fought with Frémont's California Battalion, panned for gold in the North, and then went south to set himself up in the harness business (Alice, his daughter by a second marriage, married a physician in Ukiah); or like A. W. Buell of Santa Barbara County, who made the trek in 1857, raised sheep and cattle, and voted Republican.

They acquired, lived on, and worked the land. Penniless, newly arrived in Southern California, Stephen Rutherford slept under an oak tree one night on the Hill Ranch near Santa Barbara. He vowed to himself that he would one day own the property. Eventually he did. Ellwood Cooper, of Quaker descent, after living ten years in the West Indies, began growing olives in Santa Barbara County in 1872. By the 1890s he was producing some of the best olive oil in the world. A onetime president of the state board of horticulture, Cooper wrote a treatise on olive growing which won the praise of a visiting English agronomist, the Marquis of Lorne.

Lucy Toland Glassell, born in South Carolina, bore her husband Andrew nine children and died at the age of thirty-one. Anna M. Davis, who supported her children, served for nine years as the postmistress of Norwalk. She also managed real estate and wrote articles on literature and art for the Los Angeles newspapers. Ella Whipple Marsh took the M.D. degree from Willamette University and entered practice in Pasadena, where she also headed the Women's Christian Temperance Union. Mrs. Caroline Seymour Severance got a public library system under way in Los Angeles. An advocate of Christian Socialism and the kindergarten movement, she sent her sons back east to Harvard for their educations.

Ferdinand Nieman of Los Angeles served in the Hanoverian Guards during the Franco-Prussian war. Lazard Kahn, a French Jew from Lorraine, married Josephine Ortega of Santa Barbara in 1875, then went into the wine and distilled spirits business in Los Alamos. As a youth in Darmstadt, Germany, Frank Lindenfeld learned the paving trade. Arriving in San Diego in 1874, he opened a brewery because the town needed one. During the Danish-German war, Lorenz P. Hansen of North Schleswig, Denmark, was shot in the neck and slashed by a saber over the right eye. Oak Villa, his Pasadena home, was adjacent to an orange grove. Laurina, his daughter, went north to San Francisco to study at the Irving Institute. John B. Procter, English born and a longtime resident of Santa Monica, served as captain of the Southern California Polo Club.

Frontier Southern Californians devoted themselves to the work of economic development. These were years of building, planting, drayage, and investment, which had to be done well in their first phase; unlike the North, the Southland possessed no excesses of capital enabling it to lay aside projects and begin in different directions. Phineas Banning—teamster, harbor master, contractor, banker, speculator in oil and land—perhaps best embodies this first phase of economic entrepreneurship in Southern California, with its diversity and optimism, its unambiguous satisfaction in fulfilling obvious and necessary needs.

A bold leonine man, massive of frame and booming of voice, Banning had not at first intended a Southern Californian career. On his way to Mexico in 1851 he was stranded in San Diego when the ship on which he had passage was seized for debt. He was twenty-one, so he made the best of it—just as he had eight years earlier when as a lad of thirteen he had walked from his native Delaware to Philadelphia in search of a clerkship, which he had found and made much of. Moving to Los Angeles, he put together the odds and ends of a business. Jobbing, wholesaling, retailing, hauling: Phineas Banning turned his hand to anything and everything that might in turn turn over a dollar. Sweating profusely as he worked alongside his hired help in heavy brogans and canvas pants held up by wide braces, his collarless shirt open at his massive neck, the very figure of the worker-entrepreneur, Banning set about the task of making a fortune and building up an American commonwealth.

Banning realized that Los Angeles would need a harbor if the city were ever to amount to much, so in 1857 he purchased a tract of seaside land from the Domínguez family for development as a harbor town, which he named Wilmington, after the capital of his home state. He subdivided and encouraged settlement. He had warehouses and wharves constructed. Because the harbor was too shallow for direct approach, he assembled a fleet of five small steamers to ferry passengers and freight from ship to shore. (On 27 April 1863 one of these, the *Ada Hancock*, exploded, killing twenty-six. Banning himself was blown twenty feet into the air but, miraculously, survived.) The United States Army selected Wilmington for a key installation, Drum Barracks, and spent over a million dollars developing the site. In 1858 Banning subcontracted the telegraph line being built between Los Angeles and San Francisco. In 1869 he put through the Los Angeles and San Pedro Railroad, connecting city and port.

Frontier Southern California needed people and things moved, so Banning went into the drayage and transportation business. The Wilmington Transportation Company hauled passengers and freight throughout an area of the Southwest triangulated by Los Angeles, Santa Fe, and Salt Lake City. He designed and built wagons specially suited for rugged desert travel, and in 1860 experimented with a self-propelled steam wagon with which he hoped to haul freight between Wilmington–San Pedro and Los Angeles. He bought and shipped twenty-one thousand crates of Southern California table grapes to San Francisco. He went into lumber and meat packing. He speculated in land. He sank wells and sold water commercially. In 1865 he was founding president of the Pioneer Oil Company. Very much a man of his time, Banning rode with the Los Angeles Rangers in the 1850s. In 1863 he led a lynch mob into the Los

Angeles jail to string up a certain Charles Wilkins, who had murdered his brother-in-law.

In 1864 Banning moved into a three-story mansion in Wilmington, built in the colonial style he remembered from his Delaware boyhood, when he had glimpsed, from the outside, how the First Families lived. He had a lawn laid out, and formal gardens, and a eucalyptus-lined driveway, the first of its kind. By now he was General Banning, brigadier of militia for the great State of California during the rebellion of the Southern states; like another militia officer in an earlier mansion on an earlier frontier—Andrew Jackson at the Hermitage—Phineas Banning, having wrestled with the frontier and won, now wanted some measure of elegance, as he remembered them having in the Eastern states.

Nothing is perfect, not even boyhood dreams come true. Illness marred Banning's last years (he died in 1885, age fifty-five). He lost his first wife and five of his eleven children. Yet a certain cocksure exuberance, expressing itself in hospitality, marked his career, as if Banning felt himself charged with acting out the myth of Southern California as land of plenty and promise for poor boys from the East. Even before he was firmly established, in 1853, he hosted a gargantuan three-day barbecue for the Fourth of July, in which wine flowed and whole carcasses turned in the spit. He celebrated the opening of Wilmington harbor in 1858 with a parade of his steamers and champagne for all on board. In June of 1859 he brought sixty friends along on a day trip to the island of Santa Catalina. The party began with a champagne breakfast at dawn, followed by a sail out of Wilmington aboard Banning's steamer *Comet*, decorated in flags and bunting for the occasion. Around noon the party transferred to a Coast Survey ship for a champagne luncheon and the voyage out to Santa Catalina, where they spent the afternoon exploring the pristine beaches. Champagne eased the voyage homeward, and all found themselves back in Los Angeles by midnight that evening. Banning was rumored to have spent a quarter of a million dollars over the years on dinner parties.

Others also achieved fortune, and that degree of fame possible in such a remote region. John Gately Downey, an Irish-born druggist, reached the governor's chair in 1859, the first Southern Californian to do so. Like Banning, Downey plunged himself into a diversity of enterprises: his drugstore, land (Warner's Ranch and the Santa Gertrudis Rancho, which he subdivided and where he established the town of Downey), real property (the Downey Block on Temple and Spring streets), and banking (founding president of Farmers and Merchants Bank of Los Angeles, established in 1871). He promoted public improvements: a railroad connection with San Francisco, horse-drawn streetcars for Los Angeles (this in 1873), a public library system, the chamber of commerce, the University of Southern California, a historical society.

Dr. John Strother Griffin, a physician-entrepreneur, joined with Downey in 1868 to help found the Los Angeles City Water Company. In 1873 they financed the laying of iron water pipes throughout East Los Angeles. Griffin, a Virginian who had taken his medical degree at the University of Pennsylvania, arrived in Southern California in 1848 as ranking surgeon with Kearney's dragoons. In 1854 he resigned his commission to settle permanently in Southern California, where for the ensuing forty-four years he practiced medicine, business, and land speculation. Griffin's Rancho San Pasqual, purchased from the Garfias family in 1858, when its patriarch, Don Manuel, had overextended himself to the point of bankruptcy, was sold to the Indiana Colony in the 1870s and became in the 1880s the city of Pasadena.

There were varieties of connections bringing these pioneers together: civic connections (the Los Angeles Rangers at first, then later less ferocious associations, like the Southern District Agricultural Society) and business connections (almost everyone, for instance, seemed to have a piece of the Pioneer Oil Company). When Dr. Griffin served as superintendent of schools in Los Angeles in the mid-1850s, he courted and married the city's sole teacher, Louisa Hayes, Benjamin Hayes's sister.

Griffin's own sister, Eliza, married the Confederate general from Los Angeles, Albert Sidney Johnston, a match which emphasized an even more important link among these early Southern Californians (Banning and Horace Bell being notable exceptions): their Successionist sympathies. Hayes, Griffin, Downey, Davis, Johnston, and many others in the Southland favored the Confederacy. Their efforts in 1859 to have Southern California separated from the North had strong states' rights overtones, and even suggestions of a pro-slavery posture.

Elected lieutenant governor in 1859 as a Lecompton Democrat, Downey succeeded to the governorship when the legislature sent Governor Milton S. Latham to the United States Senate. Downey performed well as governor, vetoing one particularly disastrous bill which would have put the Port of San Francisco into private hands, but his sympathetic attitude toward the Southern states precluded his re-election in a state that was largely Unionist. Leland Stanford and the Republicans swept Downey from office in 1861.

Recruiting a force of about a hundred in the Los Angeles area (including a number of hell-raising Texans from El Monte), Albert Sidney Johnston led them overland to fight for the Confederacy. Commissioned a brigadier general, Johnston fell at Shiloh. His widow, John Strother Griffin's sister, returned to Southern California after the war and built Fair Oaks, a mansion in the antebellum manner of her Virginia plantation girlhood, to which she retired. Dr. Griffin himself, Virginia gentleman and scholar of the classics, in a rare display of bad taste yahooed in approval when word reached Los Angeles that Abraham Lincoln had been assassinated.

Newspaper clippings, coroners' reports, the proceedings of courts, the records of hospitals, prisons, and institutions for the insane and feebleminded attest that life in Southern California offered no exemption from the inevitable human experience of vice, crime, disease, self-destructiveness, and undeserved suffering. On the night of 24 March 1877 a masked gunman assassinated John F. More's older brother, T. Wallace More of the Rancho Sespe, and set fire to the ranch buildings. John More sent his daughter north to Mills Seminary in Oakland for her education. She graduated with class honors, but died (of natural causes) not long after her return to Sespe. The mangled body of María Jesús Guirado Downey, wife of the former governor, was pulled from the wreckage of a Southern Pacific passenger train on 20 January 1881. Twenty died and scores of others were injured when the runaway train plunged into a ravine in the Tehachapis. Governor Downey himself never fully recovered, physically or psychologically, from the accident.

Devoid, in the main, of heroes, Southern California excelled in ordinary Americans. In a very special way, this became their place. As an Iowa farm boy in the 1860s, James A. Hill, a Los Angeles contractor, received but six months of formal education. At age thirteen he was drawing journeyman wages as a bricklayer. Coming to Southern California during the boom of the 1880s, he got into the construction business and married Nellie Fillburn, originally of Santa Rosa. A. L. Jenness of Santa Monica, a schoolteacher who turned to real estate, was throughout the 1890s active in the Ancient Order of United Workmen, the Independent Order of Odd Fellows, and the vestry of the Santa Monica Episcopal Church. José Dolores Palmoares, a rancher in San Diego County, married Sarafina Macias, and they had nine children: Porfirio, Maggie, Chonita, Francisco, Arturo, Emilia, Rosa, Issavel, and Ernestine.

There were, of course, more elaborate families, especially in Pasadena and Santa Barbara. Miss Myra Fithian of Santa Barbara, for instance, married Chester Allan Arthur, son of the president of the United States. Miss Myra's father, Major Joel Adams Fithian, founded the Montecito Country Club. Her two brothers, Barrett and Joel, were excellent polo players. Fannie Fithian, Myra's sister, married the Comte Arthur de Gabriac and moved to Paris. The major died in 1898 while returning from the Continent, and his wife died there in 1901, visiting Fannie.

IV

In the 1880s emerges a consolidated myth of Southern California. Its two most important elements are health and romantic nostalgia. Southern California was a healthy place, it was felt, because of the climate. Nineteenth-century medicine had great faith in the curative powers of climate, most obviously in the case of tuberculosis and other pulmonary disorders. In his now classic *Climatology of the United States* (1857), Lorin Blodget gave the climate of California the equivalent of three Michelin stars. He compared it to the climates of Italy,

Spain, and Portugal. Linking climate with healthfulness, Blodget claimed that Southern Californians seemed especially free from lung disease. During the decades 1860 to 1880 Blodget's judgment ticked away like a time bomb, tinkered with by others but never broadly acted upon because Southern California was so remote. The arrival of the railroads, however, together with the ensuing drastic reduction of fares, precipitated a health rush. Consumptives flocked to the region, hoping (often against hope) for a cure. Sanitariums and boardinghouses catering to consumptives sprang up, and a diverse literature promoting Southern California as a health resort found its way into print.

The promise, of course, outran the reality. Some found restoration, but many more coughed away what little life remained, alone and lonely in a faraway land, mocked by the sunshine they thought would save them. The effect on Southern California's developing culture of so many desperate Americans fleeing there only to die is easy to imagine. A paradoxical morbidity, an anger against defeated expectations of healthfulness and other hopes, subtly pervaded the civilization of the Southland. In Los Angeles during these years, death seemed everywhere, and a mood of death, strange and sinister, like flowers rotting from too much sunshine, remained with the city.

This amalgam of death and sunshine, morbidity and romance, went into the making of Helen Hunt Jackson's best-selling novel *Ramona* (1884). No other act of symbolic expression affected the imagination of nineteenth-century Southern California so forcibly. This tale of star-crossed Indian lovers and Spanish ranch life as it lingered on into the 1870s cast a spell on Southern Californians. They appropriated the characters, mood, and plot of *Ramona* as the basis of a public myth which conferred romance upon a new American region.

First of all, Southern California in the 1880s was more than ready for nostalgia. Subdivision and the growth of cities had shifted the emphasis of society away from the ranchos. Psychologically, the urban immigrant, caught in the throes of a rapidly expanding American present, wanted some emotional and imaginative connection to the Southern Californian past. The gargantuan annals issued throughout the 1880s by the Bancroft Company in San Francisco answered one aspect of this need, chronicling the story of California with a narrative breadth and a massiveness of detail which attested to the need in Californians to shore up a sense of present identity by searching out a usable historical myth. Attitudes toward the missions began to change. Once the neglected vestiges of a justly displaced theocracy, they became the objects first of scrutiny, then of romantic veneration.

Helen Hunt Jackson came to Southern California in 1881 as an investigative reporter for *Century* magazine. By background and temperament she was an ideal mythmaker. She and Southern California had a confluence of needs.

First of all, Southern California needed promotion as a region of beauty, peace, and healthfulness. No one sought such values of place with greater ap-

petite than Helen Hunt Jackson. Ever since her first husband, an army engineer, was killed in an ordnance accident during the Civil War, she had wandered the world in search of a place where she could feel at home. Even when
she remarried, she spent long periods of time away from her second husband.
Sudden voyages to Europe, dashes by train across the United States, movement
from city to city at home or abroad, and—once she finally chose a city—re-
movals from hotels to lodging houses to private rooms to the homes of friends:
Helen Hunt Jackson's search for a place to be at peace with herself was an obsession—and also an income, for she supported herself as a travel writer. She
was neurotic and difficult to be around. Orphaned as a teenager, widowed as a
young woman after losing two children, she fell frequently into despondency.
Periods of overwork alternated with periods of physical and emotional collapse.

Southern California calmed her. She did not get along with everyone there,
but her quarrels were fewer. Traveling about in a hired open carriage, she gathered data for an article on the outdoor industries of Southern California. Bees,
sheep, citrus, olives: the sunny Mediterraneanism of it all soothed her ever restless nerves. She was especially impressed by the Rancho Camulos in the Santa
Clara Valley of Ventura County, forty-five miles northwest of Los Angeles. Here,
under the watchful supervision of Doña Ysabel del Valle, the widowed mistress
of the estate, the old ways held on as fact and as recoverable poetry. Fountain,
patio, orange grove, winery, the private chapel near an arbor smothered in
grapevines, the excitement of sheep-shearing time, the retinue of relatives and
retainers: the observant Mrs. Jackson stored up the details.

She made her living by the picturesque, yet here, at Rancho Camulos and
a few other places—Mission Santa Barbara and the home of Don Antonio de
Coronel in Los Angeles, for instance—she felt the presence of something more
compelling than mere prettiness. She felt a connection with the Latin Catholic
past of Southern California. By the early 1880s relics of this Spanish past—a
past not yet intensified by romantic myth—were few indeed. Of twenty-one
missions, only Mission Santa Barbara remained in Franciscan hands. Many of
the rest—their roofs collapsed, their protective cover of lime plaster long since
flaked away—were being washed back into the adobe hills from which they first
came by the swift, devastating rains of Southern California. In the course of
two Southern California visits Mrs. Jackson managed to visit most of the California missions. At the Bancroft Library in San Francisco she did her own sort
of haphazard, intuitive research into the mission era. At Mission Santa Barbara
in January 1882, charmed by its mood of monastic tranquillity and by the beauty
of its site overlooking the sea, she browsed in the library and chatted with the
friars. One old padre, Francisco de Jesús Sánchez, especially intrigued her. Born
in Mexico in 1813, Padre Sánchez had been in California since 1841. Pious,
benevolent, rotund—the old friar seemed to Mrs. Jackson the last of his kind,

the last to experience that peculiar blend of energies, religious and secular, which had brought the Spanish north from Mexico.

In Los Angeles, Bishop Francisco Mora of the Roman Catholic Diocese of Los Angeles, to whom she had a letter of introduction, referred Mrs. Jackson to Don Antonio de Coronel and his young wife Mariana. The Coronels lived in an adobe just outside Los Angeles, where the family had resided since 1834. Brought to Southern California as a teenager in 1834, Don Antonio, in semi-retirement when Mrs. Jackson met him, had had a varied career in both Mexican and American California. In 1846, during the resistance, he had been commissioned by the embattled Californian government to ride to Mexico City with American flags captured in battle. In the new regime, Don Antonio served as mayor of Los Angeles in 1853 and state treasurer in 1867. Turning to antiquarianism in middle life, he filled his home with the artifacts of Old California. Dressed in Mexican costume, he and Mariana (decades younger than Don Antonio, and a very handsome woman) would perform the old dances and sing the old Spanish songs. It was Don Antonio de Coronel who suggested that Mrs. Jackson visit Rancho Camulos to see how Californians had lived in times gone by, and it was he who most imbued her with a feel for the flavor and physical texture of the Spanish past.

All this proved a heady wine. The daughter of a Calvinist theologian teaching at Amherst, Mrs. Jackson had grown up with a derogatory view of Mediterranean Catholic culture. Her earlier printed remarks regarding the Church of Rome ran in the Whore of Babylon vein, the staple expression of Yankee Protestant distaste. As a travel writer she reported on Italy with caustic scorn, preferring Bavaria. The New England culture, however, of which she was a protagonist (Emerson went out of his way to praise her now forgotten poetry) had been for some decades effecting a rapprochement—on the level of the imagination, at least—with the Latin Catholic South. The monumental histories of Ticknor and Prescott, the scholarship and poetry of Longfellow, the marvelous landscapes of Hawthorne's fiction: the pre–Civil War phases of this meditation had resulted in an energetic harvest of Mediterranean thoughts, symbols, feelings, and heroic figures (Dante, above all others) into the granaries of New England culture, then dangerously depleted by a constriction of sympathy and association endemic to a self-obsessed people for too long feeding on what their forefathers had planted and gathered. The dialogue had religious dimensions. An assortment of New Englanders—George Ripley, Orestes Brownson, Isaac Hecker, for instance, veterans of transcendentalism and Brook Farm—left the stony ground of unbelief for the lush meadows of Rome or Canterbury. Hawthorne's daughter Rose founded an order of Catholic nursing nuns dedicated to the care of terminally ill patients.

Helen Hunt Jackson's developing interest in things Catholic lacked such depth and magnitude. She knew, however, that she despised the orthodox Calvinism of her youth. For a while, in a period of near insane grief after the death of her husband and son, she, along with so many others in the late 1860s and 1870s, had turned to spiritualism, but only as a desperate flirtation. Spiritualism was a form of therapy, only half believed in. It could never take the place of a mature creed. A feeling of baffled religious longing pervaded many of her poems, a hunger for some act of assent that might assuage her existential loneliness. Such faith never came, but in Southern California she felt warmed vicariously by its banked fires. Her long essay, "Father Junípero [Serra] and His Work," published in the May and June 1883 issues of *Century* magazine, shows a total sympathy with the context and purposes of Spanish Catholicism. Already for her—and because of her, eventually for all of Southern California—the days of the padres shimmered in a golden haze of mingled myth and memory, free of fanaticism and injustice, their cruelty and pain forgotten.

No matter that the mission system itself was founded on ambiguity: the enforced enclosure of the Indians. No matter that the Spanish soldiers hunted them in the hills like so much prey and drove them down into the mission compounds like so much cattle. There, in churchly captivity, the majority of them declined—from the syphilis the soldiers gave their women, from the alien work the padres made them do, from the trauma of having their way of life and their tribal places so cruelly taken away. In Helen Hunt Jackson's version of it all (and by the 1890s it was official myth), grateful Indians, happy as peasants in an Italian opera, knelt dutifully before the Franciscans to receive the baptism of a superior culture, while in the background the angelus tolled from a swallow-guarded campanile and a choir of friars intoned the *Te Deum*.

Strangely enough, although she accepted the myth in its historical dimensions, she had no illusions regarding the present plight of the Mission Indians. *Ramona*, in fact, was intended as an act not of romance but of social protest. Among her set in Boston after the Civil War, the crusade for Indian rights had replaced abolitionism as a fashionable concern. Mrs. Jackson herself devoted the last six years of her life to Indian philanthropy (she died of cancer in San Francisco on 12 August 1885). After extensive research in the Astor Library of New York, she assembled what was in effect a massive legal brief regarding violated Indian rights, *A Century of Dishonor* (1881), and sent it at her own expense to government officials and members of Congress. So well known was Mrs. Jackson as an expert on Indian affairs that in 1883, while she was in Southern California, she received a commission from the Department of the Interior to investigate the condition of the Mission Indians.

Accompanied by Abbot Kinney (about whom more later) and a driver, she toured the Indian villages of the southern counties in an open trap. Temecula, Agua Caliente, Saboba, Cahuilla Valley, Santa Ysabel: everywhere, Mrs. Jackson wrote in the August 1883 issue of *Century* magazine and in the official

Report (1883) she and Kinney filed in Washington, everywhere Mission Indians were in grave decline. The Spanish had kidnapped and then abandoned them. The Americans completed the process of destruction, exploiting their labor, bullying them, removing them from what little land they possessed.

Two incidents stood in Mrs. Jackson's mind as representative of the entire tragedy. Near San Jacinto, she heard how in 1877 Sam Temple, a drunken, wife-beating teamster, frequently afoul of the law, had shot and killed a Cahuilla Indian, Juan Diego, allegedly in self-defense. Juan Diego, the story ran, was given to periods of partial insanity. During the last of these, he took a horse belonging to Temple and hitched it before his own hut, where he lived with his wife. As a piece of theft, it was so obvious that it underscored Juan Diego's insanity. Temple, nevertheless, rode over to Diego's hut in a state of rage. He later told the court (which acquitted him) that Juan Diego attacked him with a knife. Others said that Temple had summarily executed the unarmed, half-crazed Indian on the spot, leaving the bullet-ridden corpse in the arms of Juan Diego's Indian wife.

From Don Antonio de Coronel and from Father Anthony Ubach—a tall, bearded diocesan priest in San Diego, devoted to the Mission Indians (as well as to snipe hunting, buttermilk, and doughnuts)—Mrs. Jackson heard how in 1869 a sheriff's posse had, under orders from the district court, physically removed an entire Indian village, Temecula in San Diego County, from lands which the Indians thought the government had granted them but which whites had won in a legal action. They and their belongings were carted off to an inferior site nearby, Temecula remaining (Mrs. Jackson visited it in 1883) nothing but an abandoned burial ground.

Out of all this, then—the impressions of her Southern California sojourn, her frustration at having the recommendations of her and Kinney's *Report* ignored (they called for a survey of Indian lands, the removal of white squatters, a program of medical and educational assistance)—Mrs. Jackson, back in New York City, resolved to write an *Uncle Tom's Cabin* for the Mission Indian, which she did, in her rooms at the Berkeley Hotel: *Ramona*, first appearing as a serial in the *Christian Union* on 15 May 1884.

It was a tale of love and death, race and religion, the passing of a social order, and the spirit of time and place. On the Moreno ranch, founded by the late General Moreno in the 1820s, the ways and values of Old California are jealously preserved into the late 1860s by his widow and son, despite the loss of many acres to the Yankee courts. Among the dependents of Señora Gonzaga Moreno is Ramona Ortegna, nineteen, a half-breed orphan raised to think of herself as Spanish. Falling in love with Alessandro Assis, an Indian, captain of the sheep-shearing band from Temecula, Ramona rediscovers her suppressed Indianhood. Señora Moreno opposes the match, and so the couple flee to San Diego, where they are married. They cannot settle in Temecula because the

Indian lands have been confiscated by the American courts. After a year and a half of struggle, Alessandro manages to establish himself as a small farmer near San Pasqual, where a colony of Temecula refugees scratch meager livings from the arid soil. In desperation over his infant daughter's illness, he enrolls his name with the Indian Agency as a dependent, hoping for medical assistance. The white doctor, however, refuses to make a crucial house call. Their daughter dies. The government orders all agency Indians removed to a reservation. Once again Ramona and Alessandro take flight, settling this time in the backcountry near Mount San Jacinto, where another daughter, Majella, is born.

Alessandro, however, loses his mental balance. He becomes obsessed with Americans, who by now have taken two farms from him. He suffers lapses of memory, and his will to begin again is feeble. In a dispute over a horse he is gunned down by a white, Jim Farrar, and dies in Ramona's arms. Felipe Moreno, heir to the Moreno ranch now that Señora Moreno is dead, seeks out Ramona and her daughter Majella. They are eventually married but decide to live in Old Mexico, because for both Indian and Spaniard Southern California is now an alien place.

Attempting a parable, Helen Hunt Jackson offered a symbolic anatomy of the Southern California experience as she encountered it in the early 1880s. Every character and detail of *Ramona* was based on fact, or composites of facts. The Moreno estate was based upon Rancho Camulos in Ventura County. Into the delineation of Ramona and Alessandro went a number of observed or heard-of people. Juan Diego, the Cahuilla Indian shot by Sam Temple in 1877, and Juan's widow Ramona Lubo (who lived until 1924) provided the factual beginnings of her central characters, their histories augmented by elements from the lives of Rojerio Rocha, another Indian, skilled like Alessandro in the church music of the missions; Blanca Yndart, a Spanish orphan raised on Rancho Camulos; and Guadalupe, daughter of a Piru chief, also part of the crowded Camulos retinue. Señora Moreno can be traced to Doña Ysabel del Valle, the widowed owner of Camulos, and Felipe to her son Reginald. Father Salvierderra, the saintly Franciscan who takes a special interest in Ramona's education and who represents the finest possibilities of the mission protectorate, is Padre Francisco de Jesús Sánchez, the old Mexican missionary who so impressed Mrs. Jackson when she visited Mission Santa Barbara. Father Ubach, the secular priest who championed the cause of the Temecula Indians, became Father Gaspara, the parish priest who marries Ramona and Alessandro.

The source of *Ramona*'s popular appeal, however—why it ranks with Harold Bell Wright's *The Winning of Barbara Worth* (1911) and Margaret Mitchell's *Gone with the Wind* (1936) as one of American's persistent best-sellers—is not that it translates fact into fiction, but that it translates fact into romantic myth. Despite its exaggerated, sometimes shrill sentimentalism, its awkward character development and occasional hysteria, *Ramona* spoke to Southern California with the direct and compelling power of culture-defining romance. Gathering to herself the scattered, fragile, inert materials of the Southern Californian experience, Helen Hunt Jackson enlivened them, as best she could (she had a minor but lively talent), with the repairing touch of significant associations: religion, the twilight days of a race, the spirit of time and place, and the yearning for present possession of a healing past.

In *Ramona* Helen Hunt Jackson collapsed American Southern California back onto the Spanish past. There, she suggested, in the days of the Franciscan missions, Southern California could find spiritual foundations with which to upgrade the crass vacuity of the present. The protagonists of *Ramona* defy the Americans by their piety. Each religious observance is part of a continuing act of self-definition in which they remind themselves who they are as a people. Señora Moreno, who dresses in black like a nun, veiled and with a rosary around her waist, goes so far as to have high wooden crosses erected on the hills of the Moreno estate so as to remind Americans that they are passing through Old California, whose occupants yet remember their religion and their past. The yearly arrival of Father Salvierderra at shearing time brings even closer the feel of the old days. Based in Mission Santa Barbara, Father Salvierderra walks El Camino Real as three generations of Franciscans have trod it before him. Pushing his way through the blooming mustard fields outside the Moreno ranch, he chants the Canticle of the Sun by Saint Francis of Assisi. At the ranch, the sacred vessels, smuggled out of Mission San Luis Rey by the sacristan during the Conquest to prevent them from falling into Yankee hands, are brought from their cases, and the old Franciscan celebrates mass for the household in the estate's private chapel.

None of this is to suggest that *Ramona* sustains any significant spiritual drama or offers much in the way of theological reflection. What does occur, however—and this is why the Ramona myth took such hold of the popular imagination in Southern California—is that through literature a representative Protestant sensibility, Mrs. Jackson's, deracinated from place and dogma, feels the comforts of a local Catholic tradition. *Ramona* was a Pacific Coast extension of the larger process of the New England mind Mediterraneanizing. Amherst and Calvinism she had abandoned, but here in Southern California, in mid–middle age, Helen Hunt Jackson experienced and expressed lingering, comforting traces of faith and place. Through *Ramona*, in turn, Americans of Mrs. Jackson's time, fearful about themselves and what they had wrought in Southern California, took some warmth from the banked fires of the culture they had displaced.

A paradox, obviously, was involved in turning into a founding fable a story whose central characters either hated or were being destroyed by Americans—unless, of course, the fable was being appropriated partly as a corrective. *Ramona* made some atonement to Spanish California by acknowledging what had been done; meanwhile, it availed itself of the Spanish past for its own purposes. Henceforth the mission era was part of American history.

Social protest, Mrs. Jackson's original intent, was suppressed in the savoring of *Ramona*'s celebration of Southern California as a sunny Arcadia. On the Moreno rancho the myth of Southern California attained a local habitation and a name. *Ramona* exudes enchantment. Here indeed, Mrs. Jackson suggested, was the poetry and the color of this new American region and the arcadia which had once obtained—and might again, when American energies were properly directed: the arroyos, lined with willow and sycamore, so mysterious by evening, in whose chiaroscuro of shadow and moonlight the Indian lovers met for stolen moments; the long, low hacienda of whitewashed adobe and red tile, bulwarked on its eastern side by a veranda where ancient Juanita, now senile, earned her keep by shelling beans in the midmorning sun, where Anita and Mary, twins born on the ranch forty years previously, gossiped at noon, and where Juan Capito, the head shepherd, cajoled more food from Marda the cook; sheep-shearing time, when the Indians came in from the villages, organized into competing bands; the work of the ranch in feeding so many; the sanctuary light burning in the chapel; the great oaken furniture in the thick-walled, cool rooms within the main house; the patio garden planted in cactus, carnations, geraniums, and musk; the finches, the swallows; the days of quiet content; the orange grove; the orchards fragrant with the springtime blossoms of almond, peach, apricot, and pear.

It was, obviously, a mythical time and place, a garden of earthly delight which in truth had never existed with such sensuous and imaginative fullness, although its inspiration, Rancho Camulos, was among the most beautiful places in Southern California. As a myth, however, *Ramona*'s ideal Southland gave expression to a yearning that Southern California be a land of beauty and memory and sunny afternoons. The pastel ideality of *Ramona*'s locale was a way of suggesting that the frontier was over, that aesthetic self-consciousness had come to *California del Sur*. From now on—from the 1880s on, that is—Southern California would pay attention to more than getting and spending.

Contemporary critics made the point that, while Mrs. Jackson idealized her subject, she had captured the spirit of the Southland taken at its best. Well into the 1930s the *Ramona* myth remained one of the essential elements by which Southern California identified itself, to itself and to others. For years a massive public pageant based on Helen Hunt Jackson's novel was produced annually at Hemet, in a natural amphitheater at the base of Mount San Jacinto, where much of *Ramona*'s story takes place. Garnet Holme, who had written and produced a number of pageants in the Greek Theater in Berkeley, directed a cast of nearly two hundred players, most of them volunteers from nearby towns. The Ramona Pageant was compared to the Passion Play at Oberammergau. Mrs.

Jackson herself became something of a cult figure. Nearly every hour of her Southern California sojourn was the object of painstaking scrutiny and hagiological documentation. She had, after all, coaxed Southern California along toward self-consciousness. She had given it a myth by which to know itself.

3

Art and Life in the
Turn-of-the-Century Southland

After decades of obscure lethargy, the city of Los Angeles began to grow during the boom of the 1880s. Its population multiplied fivefold in that decade, reaching 50,395. By 1910 Los Angeles had 319,198 residents, a more than sixfold increase since 1890. By then, Los Angeles spread out over some sixty-two square miles. One by one, communities adjacent to Los Angeles succumbed to incorporation: Wilmington and San Pedro in 1906, Colegrave in 1909, Hollywood in 1910, Arroyo Seco in 1912, and finally the extensive sun-baked San Fernando Valley in 1915—Los Angeles's Louisiana Purchase, increasing the city's size geometrically in terms of land mass and, more importantly (when water came in from the Owens Valley), offering infinite possibilities for an expansion that was at once metropolitan and suburban.

The year 1900 found Los Angeles an eclectic, patchwork sort of a place, combining elements of the Spanish Southwest and the American Midwest. The plaza itself, together with its adjacent Chinese and Mexican quarters, still suggested the sleepy Mexican frontier, although the city's commercial section had by then moved uptown. In the hushed early morning hours, shawl-draped women still crossed the plaza for mass, and thrice daily the angelus tolled from the belfry of La Iglesia de Nuestra Señora la Reina de Los Angeles as it had since 1822. The dominant music of Los Angeles was not Spanish bells, however, but American ragtime: the clang-clang and rattle-rattle of electric streetcars along Broadway, Spring, and Main streets; the clippety-clop clippety-clop of horse-drawn buggies and wagons; the staccato beat of swiftly passing hansom cabs; the occasional whir of electric buggies; and even now and then the cough and sputter of a combustion engine. The grainy black-and-white photographs of Los Angeles during this era bespeak the city's new ambience of American bustle and enterprise. Downtown streets teem with people: the men in high starched collars, multibuttoned coats, derbies and boaters; the women in long dresses and lavishly feathered hats. These distinctly American crowds move along streets which are sunny by day and lit up at night by electric lights mounted on ornate ironwork.

Architecturally, the Los Angeles of this era was not a distinguished city, yet certain of its larger buildings—the seven-story headquarters of the Pacific Electric Company, for instance, or the elaborately fenestrated Chamber of Commerce Building on Main, between First and Second—proclaimed solid satisfaction with the present and confidence regarding the future. Like the rest of America, Los Angeles had recently undergone a love affair with Richardsonian Romanesque. In Los Angeles's case, the result of this love affair was a grandly castellated City Hall and County Court House, dedicated in 1888. In one sense too grand for a city of fifty thousand, the Los Angeles City Hall asserted a conviction of impending development—a faith more than fulfilled by 1910. Besides, the Mediterraneanism of the Romanesque City Hall (as in the case of the Romanesque quadrangles of Stanford University, then under construction in the North) reinforced California's turn-of-the century conviction that it was America's Mediterranean littoral, its Latin shore, sunny and palm-guarded. Los Angeles did, in fact, suggest here and there a Mediterranean town: not a city of the first order, mind you, but something leisurely, provincial, picturesque, such as Toulouse or Nice. Palm and pepper trees were everywhere. (By the 1930s the palms, grown to monstrous heights, nodded over Los Angeles like wise giraffes.) Flowering shrubs and trees blazed in the sunlight, their colors augmented by the brightly striped canvas canopies which arched out over many windows, keeping the interiors shaded and cool at midday. The dominant style of domestic architecture, the bungalow, was in fact sun-oriented. Much of Los Angeles's domestic living was carried on outdoors, in the garden by day and on the porch in the evening. All this Mediterranean flavor—sunlight, color, an operatic flora, a picturesque domestic architecture—helped offset the dominant no-nonsense bourgeois tone of the city, which for all its Mediterranean suggestions was in its essential life a colony of Iowa, Kansas, and Illinois.

To be frank, turn-of-the-century Los Angeles had little in the way of formal culture in comparison with, say, fin-de-siècle San Francisco, then in the throes of its era of greatest artistic activity; but there were signs of developing urbanism that fought against the unsophisticated boom-town tone that dominated. In 1896, for example, Colonel Griffith J. Griffith donated thirty-five hundred acres of the old Rancho Los Feliz to the city for use as a public park, although it took a number of decades for the acreage to be properly developed. For a while, the trees of Griffith Park were cut for firewood! Eventually, however, with the development of Griffith Park, together with the establishment of Hollenbeck Park, Eastlake Park, Westlake Park, Echo Park, and Exposition Park, Los Angeles enjoyed an excellent network of open spaces.

A Museum of Art, Science, and History was dedicated at Exposition Park in 1915, although Los Angeles would wait for nearly another half century before it had an adequate center for the performing arts. Len Behymer, a pioneer movie impresario, did what he could to get serious music into the city. The Metropolitan of New York and other opera companies sporadically played Los Angeles, and in 1898 a newly organized Los Angeles Symphony began giving six to eight concerts a year at twenty-five cents per ticket.

Club life made its appearance: the Jonathan Club, devoted, like the Bohemian Club of San Francisco, to epicurean sociability; the Los Angeles Athletic Club, modeled on another San Francisco institution, the Olympic Club; the California Club, like the Pacific Union of San Francisco a bastion of banking privilege; and the Concordia Club at the corner of Sixteenth and Figueroa streets, founded by the city's Jewish community, which was beginning to feel for the first time in its long Los Angeles sojourn the sting of anti-Semitism, an unwelcome by-product of Midwestern migration.

Los Angelenos loved the seaside. On weekends and holidays they flocked by electric trolley to the seashore. Manhattan Beach, Hermosa Beach, Redondo Beach, Playa Del Rey, Huntington Beach, Newport Beach—one by one seaside resorts grew up, Long Beach and Santa Monica becoming the city's favorites. The plunge bath at Long Beach was said to be the finest in the country. Beginning in the late 1890s, Santa Monica sponsored an annual tennis tournament, followed by a ball at the Arcadia Hotel. In 1892 William and Hancock Banning, sons of the great Southland entrepreneur Phineas, after purchasing Santa Catalina Island for about $150,000, developed the island as a summer resort. Their first move was to build the Hotel Metropole on the shore of Avalon Bay. Looking back at those summers in Avalon, Marshal Stimson, a prominent Los Angeles attorney and Progressive reformer, remembered the elegiac vacations he and his friends enjoyed on Santa Catalina in the 1890s when he was a young man about town. The young men would set up elaborate encampments under colorfully striped canvas some distance from the Hotel Metropole, where, on Saturday evenings, they would join the girls for outdoor dancing at the pavilion under softly glowing Japanese lanterns. On other evenings there would be camp fire songfests to the accompaniment of someone or other's collegiate mandolin. Deep-sea fishing for yellowtail, barracuda, and bass occupied the day, or hiking in the hills toward a promontory that offered a view of the Capri-like blueness of Avalon Bay. And of course there was always swimming, which the young crowd loved, even the girls, who despite the proprieties of the 1890s joined the men in challenging the breakers: the Winston girls, for instance, Marguerite and Carolina, who could keep up with the best of the male swimmers and got as tan as their bathing costumes would allow during those languid summer idylls at Avalon.

Stimson and his young friends all knew each other from their time together at Los Angeles High School, founded in 1873 and located since 1891 in a great red brick building downtown. For twenty-five years it was the only high school in Los Angeles. Miss Katherine Carr, a Vassar graduate, began teaching there in 1892, drilling generations of students in Latin and English composition until her retirement in 1941. Principal William Harvey Housh arrived in 1895 and served for thirty years. Staffed by such dedicated pedagogues as Miss Carr and Mr. Housh, Los Angeles High School nurtured young Los Angelenos with serious-minded fare: Latin, mathematics, English grammar and composition, the sciences, literature, and history—all of it, so teachers and students alike believed, leading to an assured future in a rising city. Marshal Stimson, for instance, nurtured his dream of a legal and political career with bouts of reading in American history. He studied the speeches of Webster, Calhoun, and Clay, dreaming of the day when he too would sway men and shape events through forceful utterance on a grand stage. In later years, graduates of Los Angeles High School looked back upon this period in their lives with Booth Tarkington–like nostalgia. They remembered the football games, the baseball games, the track meets. They remembered how earnestly they had prepared their speeches for the Lyceum, the school's debating and literary club; how avidly they had sought membership in Greek letter societies, or had written for the school paper, the *Star and Crescent,* and the yearbook, *The Blue and the White.* Graduation time filled Los Angeles with excitement. The graduation ceremonies themselves were held in the downtown opera house, and an alumni ball was held that evening, to be reported upon extensively in the next day's newspaper. Many a Los Angeleno began to keep serious company during these high school years, and at graduation time boys and girls who were interested in each other were encouraged to sit side by side during the diploma ceremonies, as a sort of formal declaration.

Stimson's chronicle of his late adolescence and young manhood in Los Angeles before he went east to Harvard suggests to us reading it today that by the early 1890s a certain coherence had come to the upper middle class of Los Angeles: which is to say that Los Angeles was by the turn of the century settling into sociological patterns analogous to those of other American cities. An elite had established itself, for instance, as evidenced by the elegant open carriages, handled by uniformed liverymen, which whizzed in and out of the developing districts of fashion and wealth—West Adams Park, Westchester Gardens, Fremont Place, Windsor Square, Hancock Park—where Chandlers, McCreas, the Van Nuys clan, and the O'Melvenys had ensconced themselves. The widow of Phineas T. Banning presided over Los Angeles social life, assisted by her two daughters, Mary and Lucy. Mark Sibley Severance, author of *Hammersmith, His Harvard Days* (1876), the first novel written by a Los Angeleno, married the niece of railroad magnate Mark Hopkins and then proceeded to make money in his own right as a real estate speculator. In 1889 Severance built Los Angeles's first distinguished mansion, which he furnished with the chinoiserie and japonaiserie beloved by the period. Edward L. Doheny, a graduate not of Harvard but of the school of hard knocks who struck it rich in oil, had a private Roman Catholic chapel installed in his mansion, built in 1892, where he established himself like a pious Irish squire: not a bad ending for a rugged, self-educated former Indian fighter, prospector, and self-made oil millionaire.

Doheny knew firsthand the often brutal Western frontier. The men rising to prominence in turn-of-the-century Los Angeles, however, were mostly of another sort: lawyers and businessmen of education, like Henry William O'Melveny and Jackson A. Graves, attorneys both, and dominant in the establishment by 1910 or so. Henry O'Melveny was born and raised as a member of the Los Angeles elite. His father, an attorney and insurance man who had sat as a judge on the Illinois bench, had done very well since bringing his family to Los Angeles in 1869, where he worked as an attorney before becoming a judge in the superior court. Henry O'Melveny graduated from the University of California, then went into law practice. By 1910 he had become a partner in his own very successful firm—O'Melveny, Stevens, and Millikin—while also serving as vice-president and general counsel of the Farmers and Merchants Bank, the Securities Savings Bank, the Azusa Ice and Cold Storage Company, and the Industrial Realty. His sometime law partner, Jackson A. Graves, came to Los Angeles in 1875 after taking his degree from St. Mary's College in San Francisco. At one time the firm of Graves, O'Melveny, and Shankland handled the legal business of literally every bank in Los Angeles. In 1887 Graves, O'Melveny, and associates formed the Abstract and Title Insurance Company, later reorganized as Title Insurance and Trust Company, one of the most powerful corporations in Southern California.

Conspicuous among Los Angeles entrepreneurs was the Yankee émigré Frederick Hastings Rindge, a Cambridge, Massachusetts–born scion of more than two hundred years of New England history. His ancestors had taken arms against the Narragansett Indians during King Philip's War, had held high positions in the Massachusetts Bay Colony's administration, and had commanded troops at Concord and Lexington when the rebellion broke out. Rooted in the Boston area, especially Cambridge, where he was born and raised and where he entered Harvard College in 1875, Rindge—despite his robust physique, the apparently healthy floridity of his bearded face—fought ill health all his life; and what better place to do this than in Southern California, which he first visited in 1870 when he was sent there as a thirteen-year-old to improve his constitution. Plunging himself into a round of business activities in the Boston area, upon reaching adulthood, Frederick Rindge substantially improved the fortune he inherited. He made a gift to his native Cambridge of a city hall, two land tracts to be used for sites for the Cambridge English High School, the Cambridge Latin School, and the Rindge Manual Training School (the first such technical school in Massachusetts, which Rindge supported out of his own pocket for nineteen years) and, later, a handsome public library in the Romanesque style, designed by H. H. Richardson. Psychologically, this philanthropy, spread out over a period of years, helped Frederick Rindge say good-bye to the wintry land of his ancestors. He made another trip out to Southern California in 1880, again for health reasons, and in 1887 he moved permanently to Southern California, setting himself up in three sites: a townhouse in Los Angeles, a seaside residence overlooking the Santa Monica Bay, and most importantly, the historic Rancho Topanga Malibu y Sequit, a vast holding extending northwards along the Pacific coast from Santa Monica. Plunging himself once again into business, as he had in Boston—life insurance, banking, manufacturing, public utilities, water systems, transportation—Rindge expanded Rancho Topanga Malibu until it extended along twenty-four uninterrupted miles of seacoast. There, in a baronial ranch house, Frederick Hastings Rindge, the Boston Brahmin turned Los Angeles entrepreneur, lived a third life as well, one which he prized above his other lives, for it restored to him his health: that of the American heir to the Spanish ranchero José Bartolomé Tapia, who first ran cattle on these acres in 1804. Rindge's account of these Malibu days, *Happy Days in Southern California* (1898), is a book soaked through with the satisfactions of living on the shores of the sundown sea. We encounter Rindge riding after cattle like a Spanish vaquero through the Malibu hills, down through wooded canyons, through fields ablaze with red columbine and carpeted in wild tiger lilies growing five feet tall. Of a fresh morning, Rindge rides out to inspect his walnut trees, his citrus groves, his apiaries—all within sound of the ceaseless Malibu surf. That evening, at sunset, he walks along the seashore, his playful Saint Bernard loping at his side. In Rindge's life and in *Happy Days in Southern California* coalesce themes of business, health, the outdoors, and the overwhelming promise of the Southland, intended, so it seemed to Rindge and his generation, for such bold entrepreneurs as themselves, Eastern men, educated and energetic, seeking the satisfactions of building in Southern California a new commercial empire, while at the same time staying sensitive to sunsets and mountains and the music of the surf at Malibu.

To represent their interests in the United States Senate, these Southern Californians sent Stephen Mallory White to Washington, the first native-born Californian to represent California in the upper chamber. The story of White's rise to the Senate is typical of a generation of Northern Californians who went south in the 1870s to seek their fortunes. As was the case with so many who rose to prominence in Southern California, Stephen Mallory White was a college man (A.B., Santa Clara College 1871) and a well-connected scion of the bourgeoisie (his father served as state banking commissioner). Steadily and surely, young White mounted the local political ladder: district attorney of Los Angeles County (1883), state senator (1886), then on to the United States Senate in 1893. Eloquent and learned, loving good liquor and good conversation, White transcended the fact that he was Irish, a Catholic, and a Democrat to win the approval of the Southland's Republican party establishment. Stephen Mallory White, after all, was a conservative, pro-business Democrat, in the manner of Mayor James Duval Phelan of San Francisco, and like Mayor Phelan, Senator White was also a fierce urban patriot, passionately identified with the rise of Los Angeles as a center of commerce and industry.

In the case of Henry Edwards Huntington and the Pacific Electric Company, entrepreneurial energy made possible an entire way of life. Turn-of-the-century Southern California grew because it had a remarkable rapid transit system. The electric streetcar or trolley, perfected in the late 1880s by Frank J. Sprague of New Jersey, an assistant of Thomas Edison's, came to Los Angeles in 1887. Throughout the 1890s the electric streetcar replaced the horse-drawn streetcar in downtown Los Angeles. Two venture capitalists, Eli P. Clark and Moses H. Sherman, excited by the possibilities of an interurban electric system, formed the Los Angeles and Pasadena Railway, which reached Pasadena in 1895 and Santa Monica in 1896. Their company collapsed in 1898, however, due to bad management, and Henry Edwards Huntington, the first vice-president of the Southern Pacific, stepped in. Huntington was the nephew of Southern Pacific president Collis P. Huntington, one of the original Big Four who had linked the nation by rail in 1869. When Collis P. died in 1900, Henry Edwards lost out in his effort to succeed his uncle as president of SP. Blocked in this ambition, the heir of Collis P. turned elsewhere. Selling his Southern Pacific stock, he concentrated his energies upon mass transit and real estate. The two enterprises went hand in hand. Huntington would link his trolleys with undeveloped areas he had invested in as the principal in one or another real estate syndicate, most noticeably the Los Angeles Pacific Boulevard and Development Company (among other investors: Harrison Gray Otis, publisher of the *Times*). He and his associates would then sell the land, whose value skyrocketed once it became accessible to downtown Los Angeles. These developments were helped along by favorable publicity in the *Los Angeles Times*.

Incorporated in 1901 with Huntington as president, the Pacific Electric Company extended rail service to Long Beach in 1902. By 1910, the year Huntington stepped down as president and, ironically, the Southern Pacific acquired control of the company, Pacific Electric linked over fifty communities in four counties—Los Angeles, Orange, Riverside, and San Bernardino—into one suburban whole. The system pushed as far south as Newport, as far east as Redlands, San Bernardino, and Riverside, and as far north as San Fernando: 1,164 miles of track in all, the largest such electrical transit system in the world. Six hundred trains a day passed through the Los Angeles Terminal alone, which was the largest building west of the Mississippi. Electrical mass transit had made a new sort of urbanscape possible: a network of communities, separate yet joined at fifty miles per hour into a suburbanized conglomerate. Alhambra, Arcadia, Glendale, Whittier, Inglewood, San Fernando—there might yet be acres and acres of farmland between stops, but suburbanization had begun in the Southland. The automobile, and then the freeways, completed what Huntington's big red cars started.

Aside from its rapid transit system, the growth of Los Angeles was also served by the development of a deep-water harbor at San Pedro and by the acquisition of water from the Owens Valley some two hundred and fifty miles to the east. Both projects were feats of engineering that were also complex achievements of civic will.

As early as 1888, the Los Angeles Board of Trade petitioned Congress for a $200,000 grant to dredge a deep-water harbor at Wilmington–San Pedro. From the start, the project was controversial. The Los Angeles Chamber of Commerce and the Southern Pacific fought for more than a decade over where this harbor should be situated. Los Angeles interests, most noticeably the chamber of commerce but also a number of other groups, organized themselves in 1895 as the Free Harbor League and came out in favor of the Wilmington–San Pedro site. The Free Harbor League also wanted the harbor to be municipally owned and operated. Collis P. Huntington and the Southern Pacific lobbied for a privately owned and operated port at Santa Monica. Throughout the 1890s Huntington began developing the Santa Monica site, which, with characteristic effrontery, he called Port Los Angeles. The question was: where would federal money be spent to do the necessary dredging and to construct a breakwater? Senator William B. Frye of Maine, chairman of the Senate Commerce Committee, which had the power to authorize the funds, favored the Santa Monica site being developed by his good friend Collis P. Huntington. Senator Stephen Mallory White favored Wilmington–San Pedro. The senator from California broke the stranglehold held by the senator from Maine on federal funding by getting the Senate to agree to a compromise. Three million dollars in harbor improvement funds were authorized, to be used either at Wilmington–San Pedro or at Santa Monica, depending upon what an impartial board of engineers should determine to be the best site. In 1897 the committee, headed by Rear Admiral John G. Walker, decided in favor of Wilmington–San Pedro. The secretary of war, Russell A. Alger, another friend of Collis P. Huntington, sat on the appropriation for nearly a year before putting the project out to bid. By April 1899, however, all delays had been exhausted. Construction at last began on a 9,250-foot breakwater, 200 feet wide at its base, 64 feet high, which, together with dredging, at last gave Los Angeles a deep-water capacity. Los Angelenos were so grateful to Senator Stephen White that, after his early death in 1901, they erected an oversized bronze statue (sculpted by the great deaf-mute artist Douglas Tilden) to his memory in the Civic Center.

The arrival in Los Angeles of Owens Valley water via an overland aqueduct on 5 November 1913 climaxed an unparalleled feat of politics, engineering and finance. To state the matter briefly: by 1913 Los Angeles had its sine qua non for further growth—an adequate water supply. With the arrival of water, the city's destiny stood assured.

Were one to single out a single figure whose life might, as fact and symbol, incarnate the energies of Los Angeles's rise to prominence as an American city— its essential, albeit sun-soaked Midwesternism, its unequivocal and unembarrassed acquisitiveness—that figure would be Harrison Gray Otis, publisher of the *Los Angeles Times* and the city's ultimate booster. Otis arrived in Los Angeles in 1882, forty-five and nearly penniless. He died there thirty-five years later a multimillionaire. As editor and publisher of the *Los Angeles Times*, Harrison Gray Otis promoted the growth of the city. As a real estate speculator, he profited from the growth the *Times* promoted. The *Times*, for instance, spearheaded the drive to bring Owens Valley water into Los Angeles. Otis headed a real estate syndicate known as the Los Angeles Suburban Homes Company. Among other shareholders were Southern Pacific president E. H. Harriman and Henry E. Huntington of Pacific Electric. The Los Angeles Suburban Homes Company held options on huge acreages in the San Fernando Valley. The process was clear and simple. The *Times* urged the public to pass bond issues to bring in the water. The voters complied. Pacific Electric then ran tracks into the area. Both water and transit made the San Fernando Valley attractive to home-seekers. Land prices soared. Otis, Huntington, and associates got rich. A similar process occurred in the development of Hollywood. A small oligarchy, in other words, put together press, transit, water, and politics in the service of real estate speculation. Los Angeles grew, and they prospered.

It had not always been so clear-cut or so profitable for Harrison Gray Otis. His pre–Los Angeles career, with the exception of his Civil War service, had been spotty and inconclusive. Born in a Marietta, Ohio, log cabin in 1837, the youngest of sixteen children, Otis received a sketchy education before going to work at fourteen as a printer's apprentice. In one sense, Otis typified the sort of journalist entrepreneur who drifted west in search of better opportunities: self-educated and more than a little defensive as to background, hence sarcastic, even vitriolic in manner. After the war, Otis returned to Marietta and for a while published a small paper, then drifted down to Washington, D.C., where from 1871 to 1875 he was employed as foreman of the Government Printing Office. In 1876 Otis moved to Santa Barbara, California, where he struggled along for three years as the owner-editor of a failing newspaper that eventually went bankrupt. Left without means of support, Otis besieged President Rutherford B. Hayes, who had been his commanding officer in the Ohio Volunteer Infantry, with pleas for a federal appointment, and after months of pestering the president, Otis was at last dispatched to the Seal Islands in the Bering Sea as a Treasury agent. Otis spent sixteen very cold, very isolated months monitoring customs payments on seal pelts: hardly a distinguished post for a self-regarding, highly decorated veteran of Second Bull Run and Antietam, then into his forties and beginning to grow bitter that life was passing him by while slouches who had safely sat out the carnage of the Rebellion got ahead.

Los Angeles, then, specifically the *Los Angeles Times*, was Harrison Gray Otis's last chance; and although he recovered his fortunes in Los Angeles, scar tissue had formed around the early failure. Harrison Gray Otis was defensive, even paranoid about possible betrayal or failure, and ever ruthless in pursuit of money and power, as if his Yankee Calvinist imagination, deprived of faith or any sustaining memories of a fulfilled early manhood, now fastened relentlessly upon every facet of his middle-aged success as atonement for early humiliation and failure: the minor editorships; the obscurity of his foreman's job in Washington, when he, a former commissioned officer, wore a leather apron and ate his lunch from a satchel; the cruel and humiliating exile to Alaska after the Santa Barbara failure, all that the president of the United States, his former companion on bivouac, would—or worse, could—offer him.

Only the memory of the war offered any comfort to Harrison Gray Otis. In the conflict, Otis had fought long and well with Ohio regiments, and of equal importance, he had been recognized for his efforts, emerging from the war as a brevet lieutenant colonel of volunteers. Four years in the field, fifteen engagements, two wounds, the command of a scout company operating behind Confederate lines, promotion from private to lieutenant colonel: Harrison Gray Otis was known and respected among veterans of the Grand Army of the Republic. He edited, in fact, the *Grand Army Journal* for a while after the war and was instrumental in getting veteran support for Grant's bid for the presidency, although no important federal offices came his way from a grateful president. As time went on, the military metaphor became more and more important to Otis. The war had offered him a cause and a campaign in which he had triumphed unambiguously over lesser men. The Grand Army on the march became his metaphor for the good society, an America responsive to ennobling Republican values and, most importantly, responsive to command from above. Otis affected a military cut to his tailoring and an aggressive imperial goatee. He avidly collected guns. He enshrined a great bronze eagle on top of *Times* headquarters and named his neo-Moorish mansion on Wilshire Boulevard the Bivouac. He ran the *Times* like a field officer, calling his staff "the phalanx." When war broke out with Spain, Otis angled a brigadier's commission through Senator Stephen Mallory White and, despite his sixty-two years, took to the field in the Philippines as an active combat commander, leaving active service this second time as brevet major general of volunteers.

A man who envisions himself as a soldier on campaign needs an enemy. Harrison Gray Otis hated labor unions with a bitter passion. He began his political career as a Frémont Republican in 1856 and had been a delegate to the

Chicago Convention that nominated Abraham Lincoln in 1860. After the war, however, Otis's reformist Republicanism veered rightward. He especially loathed the rise of unionism. Ironically, as a working printer he had once carried a union card himself. In 1856, in fact, he had been fired for trying to organize a shop. The collapse of the boom in the late 1880s, however, ended all sympathy for unions among Otis and his fellow oligarchs. They believed with passion and ruthlessness that Los Angeles must be kept an open-shop city with a plentiful supply of cheap industrial labor if it were to have any chance whatsoever of competing with San Francisco and the Eastern United States as a manufacturing center. Anti-unionism was therefore essential to Los Angeles's booster program. Rather than remain passive, Otis took to the attack—like a good soldier. He cut his printers' salaries by 20 percent, thereby provoking a strike, which he won by bringing in non-union printers from Kansas City. Thoughout the 1890s he waged bitter war against the Los Angeles chapter of the International Typographers Union. After 1896 the Los Angeles Merchants and Manufacturers Association, a businessmen's group dedicated to keeping Los Angeles an open-shop city, came to his assistance.

The assassination of Otis's good friend and one-time house guest, President William McKinley, threw "the General" (so he was called, and so he called himself, after returning from the Philippines) into an attitude of total war reminiscent of Sherman's march to the sea. The open shop, once merely a tenet of boosterism, now became for General Otis a holy crusade like the war against slavery in days gone by, a cancer to be cut from the body of the Republic. Unionism, the general believed, was the main weapon of radical foreign ideologies committed to the subversion of the Republic and all it stood for. Whatever went on elsewhere, the general would see to it that a stand was made in Los Angeles. Matters came to a head on the morning of 1 October 1910. A horrendous blast destroyed the *Times* building. Twenty employees were killed, a number of them horribly burned alive after surviving the initial explosion. (It was later learned that eighty sticks of dynamite were used.) The sabotage occurred in the midst of a mayoral election in which the Socialist candidate, Job Harriman, a labor lawyer, was showing surprising strength.

The events following the *Times* sabotage have been told and retold countless times and need only be summarized here. William J. Burns, a detective hired by the City of Los Angeles, investigated the case and eventually fingered two brothers, John J. and James B. McNamara, both of them associated with the International Association of Bridge and Structural Iron Workers, and an accomplice, Ortie McManigal, who was skilled in dynamite demolition and, it was later learned, had been engaged in dynamite terrorism for a number of years. Without benefit of formal extradition, Burns got McManigal and the McNamaras back to Los Angeles from Indianapolis, where they were arrested. Labor rallied to the McNamaras' cause, charging a frame-up. Clarence Darrow was retained for their defense. American Federation of Labor president Samuel Gompers himself visited the men in the Los Angeles County jail.

Through the agency of muckraker-journalist Lincoln Steffens, a deal was worked out among Darrow, the McNamaras, city officials—and Harrison Gray Otis of the *Los Angeles Times*. Pleading guilty, the McNamaras avoided the death penalty. But no matter: General Otis had what he wanted. The Mc-Namara brothers and Ortie McManigal went to prison, convicted of heinous mass murder. Job Harriman, the Socialist candidate, was defeated, and the union movement in Los Angeles was broken for thirty years. Had the McNamaras been hanged for their crime, Otis gloated in a *Times* editorial, they would have become martyrs, believed innocent by labor and perhaps by the general public as well. As it turned out, there were no martyrs except the twenty *Times* employees. "Viewed fundamentally," Otis editorialized, "the stupendous climax of the case was in essential particulars the most consequential event that has occurred in this country since the close of the Civil War."

II

A great city needs symbols and myths with which to establish its identity. Until the turn of the century, Los Angelenos had little time for mythmaking. Los Angeles was all about making money in the mid-1880s during the boom, and all about losing money in the late 1880s, when the boom collapsed. The oligarchs of Los Angeles, however, eventually needed more refined goals than the naked dollar bill. They felt the need of culture, of civilization. Los Angeles and Southern California in general was to be celebrated and embellished. Its growth was to be justified by being put into a context of higher purpose. In this work of justifying the development of Los Angeles and the Southland in the name of Higher Things, no one did yeoman service more than Charles Fletcher Lummis.

Colonel Harrison Gray Otis first met Charles Fletcher Lummis under an oak tree at Mission San Gabriel in the late afternoon of 4 December 1885. Lummis had just walked in from Cincinnati, Ohio, having hiked 3,000 miles in 143 days. Otis and Lummis enjoyed a picnic supper together, then hiked the remaining ten miles into town. The next morning at 10:00, Charles Fletcher Lummis, age twenty-five, reported to work as city editor of the *Los Angeles Times*. Lummis was one of thousands of health-seekers pouring into Southern California in the mid-1880s. While serving as editor of the *Scioto Gazette* in Chillicothe, Ohio, Lummis had come down with malaria. It left him weakened. Desperate to regain his strength, Lummis conceived of the idea of walking overland to Los Angeles. He wrote to Otis and offered to do a series of travel reports for the *Times*, based on his journey. Not only did Otis agree, he offered Lummis a job on the *Times* once he arrived.

Despite a broken arm, self-set in the desert and cradled in a colorful bandana, Lummis was the picture of health—lean, tanned, fit from 143 days of walking—the day he joined Harrison Gray Otis at Mission San Gabriel for a picnic supper under an ancient oak tree. At five feet seven inches, weighing 135 pounds, Charles Fletcher Lummis was a bantam cock of paradox. He came to Los Angeles to regain his health, yet in the course of four years at the city desk of the *Times*—years of coffee, cigarettes, whiskey, compulsive womanizing, and twenty-hour work days—Lummis worked himself into a paralytic stroke before he was thirty. It took him three years of slow recuperation in New Mexico to regain his health (he suffered two more minor strokes before his recovery was final), yet immediately upon his return to Los Angeles he threw himself into countless new projects: books on the Spanish Southwest, photography, an encyclopedia of Spain in America, the founding of the Southwest Museum, the city librarianship of Los Angeles, the preservation and restoration of the Franciscan missions, the fight for Indian rights, the promotion of local art and literature, and—above all else—the editorship of *Land of Sunshine* (later *Out West*) from 1895 to 1909. Under Lummis's guidance, *Land of Sunshine/Out West* spearheaded Southern California's turn-of-the-century search for a sustaining ideology: for, that is, a dramatization of what it was—or rather, what it daydreamed it could be.

A Harvard man (though he never graduated), widely read in Latin, Greek, and contemporary literature, Charles Fletcher Lummis was perhaps the brightest, and certainly the most eccentric, of the journalists Harrison Gray Otis gathered around himself at the *Times*. Lummis, Harry Carr, Robert J. Burdette, John Steven McGroarty—through the talents of such men Otis promoted an image of Southern California that dominated the popular imagination at the turn of the century and is alive to this day: a mélange of mission myth (originating in Helen Hunt Jackson's *Ramona*), obsession with climate, political conservatism (symbolized by the open shop), and a thinly veiled radicalism, all put to the service of boosterism and oligarchy.

The mission myth was the keystone of this booster ideology. Much of the Mediterranean metaphor subsumed by the Southern California mission myth originated in a genuine, complex cultural response on the part of the upper-middle-class Protestant American imagination in its Mediterraneanizing mode. It partook of the Italianizing impulse that pervaded genteel America in the 1880s and 1890s, a sensibility characterized in its finer moments by certain novels of William Dean Howells and Henry James, the fledgling connoisseurship of young Bernard Berenson, the founding of the Isabella Stewart Gardner Museum in Boston, the architectural creations of McKim, Mead, and White, and other instances of what is now known as the American Renaissance style. *Our Italy* (1891) by Charles Dudley Warner of Hartford, Connecticut—a friend of Lummis's, to whom Lummis dedicated his own *A Tramp Across the Continent* (1892), his compilation of *Times* pieces—represents the most elegant sortie of genteel Eastern American Mediterraneanizing into Southern California. Warner encouraged Southern Californians to develop a regional culture based upon the implications of its Mediterranean topography and climate: to become, that is, a society that mediated between American efficiency and Latin *dolce far niente*, a society having time for both productivity and leisure, the indoor life of manufacture and the outdoor life of the sun.

Another transplanted Easterner, Grace Ellery Channing, also a friend of Lummis's, and featured prominently in his *Land of Sunshine*, took up Warner's campaign in the early 1900s, but with an edge of disappointment in her voice. Grace Ellery Channing emigrated to Southern California in the late 1880s from Providence, Rhode Island. Like Lummis, she was a health seeker, in her case because of lung trouble, which was cured. A descendant of the famous Channing clan of Unitarian ministers and men of letters, Grace Ellery Channing, the bluest of bluestockings, was typical of a generation of New England expatriates then settling into Pasadena outside Los Angeles, a group determined to maintain Eastern gentility under the Southern California sun. She adored Italy, where she had lived for three years in the early 1890s, writing about it most charmingly in a series of short stories pervaded by a dreamy sense of Italy as a land of everlasting afternoon. Her poetry employed both Mediterranean and Southern Californian settings and imagery in the service of passionate aesthetic fervor and high moral purpose. This was very much the style of many writing women of that era, this juxtaposition of aesthetic luxuriance, moralism, and bluestocking intellectuality: very Isabel Archerish indeed! In 1898 Grace Ellery Channing joined Lummis as associate editor of *Land of Sunshine*, bringing with her what Lummis truly wanted for his Southern Californian magazine—the right sort of New England tone. In two essays, "Italy and Our Italy" (1899) and "What We Can Learn from Rome" (1903)—this written in Rome itself—the sun-loving New Englander encouraged Southern California's Italian metaphor, but also brought it into question. For all the talk of Southern California being an American Mediterranean, Miss Channing chided, there had been little true adaptation on the part of Americans living there to the fact that they were living with the sun. Architecture, city planning, dress, living habits all showed little regional modification, because the underlying cultural values in question had not been Southern Californianized. The aesthetic and moral values of neo-Mediterranean living, Miss Channing complained, had not yet penetrated the crass American soul. The pace of living, for one thing, was too mindlessly frenetic. Americans behaved as if they were still in the East or the Midwest. Men wore derby hats, stiff collars, and dark broadcloth in the bright sunshine. Women wore furs or clumsy coats. Colonial New England mansions were built next to orange groves.

Rome, Grace Ellery Channing argued, not New York, offered Los Angeles its proper model of urbanity and urbanism. Rome and Los Angeles had similar topographical situations and similar semi-arid climates. Rome offered Los Angeles a wealth of suggestions as to how growth could occur without loss of civility. First of all, the Roman habit of living outdoors translated easily to Southern California. Los Angeles homes, like Roman homes, should be built around a central patio, and the homes themselves clustered around open squares. The transition, then, from private open spaces to public open spaces would be natural and continuous. Landscaping should also be of one piece: from landscaped patios to public gardens to more ambitious public parks. Like Rome, Los Angeles should favor the pine, the cypress, and the laurel. Since water, as in Rome, was a semi-precious commodity, it should be used as frequently as possible in public display—in pools and recycling fountains—for water thus displayed was a symbolic evocation of civilization, of man's proper reordering of nature for his own ends. Dependent, like Rome, upon aqueducts, Los Angeles should glory in water as an essential symbol of the city, of what man had wrought. Above all else, Grace Ellery Channing argued, Los Angelenos and Southern Californians in general should learn to live happily in the sun, and not fight it or ignore it, as they had been doing. Since the maintenance of body heat was not a problem in Southern California, cuisine should shy away from the American staples of steak, potatoes, and gravy, toward a greater reliance on vegetables and fruit. A moderate but daily use of wine should be fostered, and perhaps even the midday siesta introduced. Life in the sun, she argued, properly pursued, might introduce into American life, Southern California style, a certain lightness and grace lacking in the climatically rigorous American Northeast and Midwest: a Southern neo-Mediterranean style, possessed of sunny charm yet having also a strong streak of serious Yankee purpose.

Grace Ellery Channing's dreams of an Italianized Southern California were given local habitation and a name by another Italianizing Easterner in Southern California, Abbot Kinney. Born in Brookside, New Jersey, in 1850 and raised in Washington, D.C., by his uncle, a United States senator, Abbot Kinney is perhaps the most conspicuous Southern Californian of his type and generation (among others were Gaylord Wilshire and Joseph Pomeroy Widney): the entrepreneur-philanthropist in whom self-serving sagacity and an otherworldly, slightly eccentric humanitarianism coexisted in creative tension. In Abbot Kinney merged strains of mysticism and practicality, nostalgia and inventiveness. Educated in France and at Heidelberg University, Kinney made a walking tour of the European continent upon the completion of his studies. When he returned to the United States, he went into the family's cigarette business with his brother. The Kinney brothers manufactured the very popular Sweet Caporal brand of cigarettes. Then the tobacco trust bought out the firm of Kinney Brothers of New York, makers of Sweet Caporal cigarettes. The sale left Abbot Kinney wealthy for life. While in the tobacco business Kinney had traveled throughout Turkey, Macedonia, and the Levant in search of new tobacco strains. Upon becoming a gentleman of leisure, he went abroad for another three years, which included a long period of residence in Egypt. Kinney first visited Southern California in 1873, and for a while he hesitated between there and Florida as a place to establish himself.

Abbot Kinney appeared on the Southern California scene, then, as a rather developed specimen: well traveled, well read, well languaged (he translated from the French a history of the civil war by the Comte de Paris), well intended, and well endowed. Purchasing a 530-acre ranch near Claremont, next to the Sierra Madre, the newly enthusiastic Southern Californian built himself a mansion which he named Kinneloa. Planting orange and lemon trees on his estate, Kinney became an early advocate of citrus culture as the agricultural hope of the Southland. He joined Helen Hunt Jackson as a special federal commissioner investigating the status of the scattered and defrauded Mission Indians. A crack rifle shot, he secured a major's commission in the California National Guard, responsible for riflery instruction. Interested in forestry, he became chairman of the State Board of Forestry, where he worked to establish a systematic program of conservation for the state's forest reserves, to include the replanting of burnt-out areas and the maintenance of watersheds. As presiding officer of the Yosemite Commission in the late 1890s, Abbot Kinney worked to put the park exclusively in the public domain. He led the Eucalyptus Crusade, which covered huge portions of treeless Southern California with that sturdy, stately native tree of Australia, so capable of thriving in semi-arid conditions. He helped get the Australian ballot adopted in California (ballots cast in secret, candidates and issues printed up at public expense), and he assisted in the founding of three public libraries. As if all this were not enough, Abbot Kinney wrote a number of high-minded Emersonian essays on topics as diverse as eugenics, diet, women's dress (he favored a loosening of stays and corsets), sex education (including a frank discussion of venereal disease), nervous disorders, aesthetics, botany, and forest management. Abbot Kinney was, in short, a jack-of-all-trades in tweeds and a well-trimmed beard (he reminds one of George Bernard Shaw), very much in the late-nineteenth-century American manner, a dreamer and an energetic pragmatist, capable of crossing continually back and forth between theory and practice, animated by a slightly eccentric but ultimately effective muscular Christianity which drove him to do the world's work. He was also a promoter and a shrewd businessman. The establishment of Venice, California, crowned Kinney's efforts to combine moral uplift with entrepreneurial ambition. The Venice project, begun in 1892 and completed in 1904, also expressed the most dramatic version possible of Southern California's Mediterranean metaphor. Venice combined elements of do-goodism and old-fashioned real estate speculation.

In 1892 Kinney acquired a tract of marshy tidelands favored by duck hunt-ers, about fifteen miles from downtown Los Angeles, on the site of the old Rancho La Ballona. In 1900 Huntington ran a trolley line out there, and Abbot Kinney began the development of Venice, a residential community and a fantasy resort, the first of the many theme developments in Southern California culminating in Disneyland. Alongside a winding Grand Canal—a half mile long, seventy feet wide, four feet deep—Kinney had lots surveyed and commenced the building of homes connected to the canal by fifteen miles of smaller waterways and palm-planted lagoons. A series of gates controlled the flow of seawater. For a while, singing gondoliers were employed to punt gondolas along the Grand Canal. Kinney spent an estimated $1.4 million improving Venice's harbor and waterfront, including construction of a five-hundred-foot-long breakwater to protect the piers of Venice from the pounding Pacific. This breakwater nearly bankrupted him. The largest pier supported a recreational arcade. There was also the St. Mark's Hotel, elaborate in the Venetian manner, with columns, archways, and decorative banners. Kinney envisioned Venice as an upper-middlebrow Italianate chautauqua resort for greater Los Angeles. He offered free trolley transportation to and from the resort. He built a 2,500-seat auditorium near the wharf, complete with a great pipe organ and high glass windows with a breathtaking view of the ocean. There, Abbot Kinney dreamed, Southern Californians would flock to enjoy lectures, recitals, opera, and theatrical performances. He brought in Sarah Bernhardt to perform *Camille* and made plans for the founding of a university-level research institute where humanistic and philosophical questions might be pondered.

Kinney's dream, alas, outran the realities of Southern California. Sarah Bernhardt performed for an indifferent audience, and for six months a full orchestra played nightly to a near empty auditorium. Southern Californians, it seemed, were not interested en masse in Culture. Ever resilient, Kinney turned Venice into Coney Island West. The Ferris wheel from the Chicago World's Fair was purchased, shipped to Venice, and reassembled there, and a shoot-the-chutes constructed. On the Great Wharf a skating rink opened, together with a dance pavilion, a bowling alley, a shooting gallery, an aquacade, and a bathhouse. Kinney's canals never worked, however: the water never circulated properly, and they grew stagnant and slimy. In 1912 the state board of health stepped in to declare the canals a menace to public health. Filled in, they were paved as ordinary streets in 1927, when Venice was developing as an ordinary Los Angeles suburb.

The story of Abbot Kinney and Venice underscores the essential naiveté of the Southern California Italian metaphor. No amount of dreamy genteel Mediterraneanism could massively induce the picturesque or subdue to gentility the exuberantly vernacular American culture growing up there. Most Southern Californians found the Ferris wheel more fun than Sarah Bernhardt and would always prefer the aquacade to opera, the shoot-the-chutes to *Camille*. Southern California might have sunshine and laurel trees, but it was definitely not Italy.

Charles Fletcher Lummis's metaphor was Spanish, not Italian, but it was doomed to the same ultimate discontinuity. Lummis, however, made a forceful case that Southern California had a usable Spanish past that was historically verifiable. As an undergraduate at Harvard, Lummis had studied under the renowned Charles Eliot Norton, the professor of art history who imbued generations of Harvard students with a feel for the ethos of art: the ability of art, that is, to shape and sustain emerging social patterns and institutions through moral uplift. For Charles Eliot Norton, art was the most important recoverable fact of history because art idealized the best energies of a given social period, then kept those energies from waning by holding forth that ideal to ensuing generations. Art, if you will, was the genetic code of history. Europe-oriented in his scholarship and Bostonian in his culture, Norton, in the best manner of Harvard, nevertheless looked out to the great American continent as well. He helped preserve the Niagara Falls from commercial exploitation and was one of the founders of the Archaeological Institute of America, an organization that pioneered the recovery and preservation of American antiquities. Norton encouraged his students to cherish and preserve whatever evidences of an art past were contained in their region.

Walking across the Southwest in 1885, young Charles Fletcher Lummis encountered the tangible signs of a past equal to Professor Norton's exhortations: the Indian and Spanish past. His second Southwest sojourn, made while covering for the *Los Angeles Times* the Apache revolt led by Geronimo in the Arizona badlands, intensified Lummis's appreciation of this austerely beautiful region. Resting briefly at the Santa Fe hacienda of Don Manuel Antonio Chaves, Lummis found himself enchanted by the personal civility and dignified lifestyle of this borderland patriarch. Lummis felt that there yet survived in the Chaves household much of the tone and feeling of Old Spain, modified by a three-century sojourn in the Southwestern borderlands, where Spain had encountered, and to a certain extent intermingled with, highly developed Indian cultures—Hopi, Navaho, Zuñi. As a student of Charles Eliot Norton, whose hold on Lummis's imagination had not lessened in the years since Lummis had left Harvard, Lummis felt himself in the palpable presence of the Past in Santa Fe, an Art Past surviving in objets d'art (altar paintings; *santos* statues of saints; silver candlesticks mule-packed up from Mexico City two centuries earlier) and in a thousand daily objects as well—plates, bowls, combs, saddlery, all demonstrating an inner coherence of culture, an internal sense of identity that graced life with ritual and touched all that was said or done with the transforming touch of tradition. As an undergraduate, Lummis had thrown himself headlong into the Latin and Greek classics (his Latin and Greek were excellent); in New Mexico he encountered something with a nearly classical ambience and ethos—something chaste, severe, morally heroic, yet touched also by romance and imagination.

In 1887 Lummis returned to stay once again with the Chaves family at their ranch in San Mateo. This time, however, Lummis came not as a dashing reporter for the *Times*, eager to cover the clash of bluecoats and Apache, but as a paralyzed cripple, felled by the stroke he had courted through dissipation. When he first arrived, Lummis had to be pushed around the ranch in a wheelbarrow. For three long and painful years of recovery, Lummis limped about Rancho San Mateo, supported by Don Manuel and befriended by his son Amado Chaves, back in New Mexico after taking a law degree in Washington, D.C. Encountered first as an imaginative ideal, Spanish New Mexico now became for Lummis the scene and the occasion of his miraculous physical recovery. At first he limped embarrassingly about the ranch, making feeble efforts to help with the work. In time he managed to hold himself on a horse. Once able to do that, he spent hours riding ferociously across the mesas and canyons in pursuit of his lost vigor. After three years of such strenuous therapy, he regained it.

No wonder, then, that Lummis enthusiastically identified with Spanish civilization as an heroic and sustaining ideal. Like the conquistadores of old, Lummis had marched against adversity and won.

In *The Spanish Pioneers* (1893), his single best sustained performance as a scholar, before journalism and social activism diffused his literary and intellectual energies, Lummis celebrated the saga of the Spanish borderlands. The austerity of Spanish frontier civilization—its internalization of complex ideals, together with its sparseness of external detail—especially attracted him. Personally, Charles Fletcher Lummis could never keep his house in order. Moderation in anything he enjoyed never came easily. Even after his stroke, he continued to smoke and to drink heavily. Until his fires banked in later years, a compulsive love life made him notorious. Lummis kept a private record of his frequent conquests, using a Spanish vocabulary and Greek characters. He had three wives (one divorced him when she found the Greco-Spanish diary) and a procession of "secretaries" who accompanied him into the field on archeological expeditions so that he might not miss his accustomed postprandial relaxations. (On one field expedition, another researcher complained that his siesta had been ruined by all the noise emanating from Lummis's tent!) Lummis tried to counter these exuberant impulses with what he took to be the Spanish imperatives of restraint and purpose. Out of the confusion of his personal life, he had once fled to work as to a narcotic, and it had left him a bedridden invalid. Now he returned to Los Angeles to preach the pace of the land of *poco tiempo*, where things occurred in stride and where there was a time and a place for everything. Characteristically, he celebrated this modified work ethic by plunging remorselessly into work on its behalf. He contemplated and began work on a comprehensive *Dictionary, Concordance, and Encyclopedia of Spain in America, 1492–1900.* Had it been completed, it would have been the size of the *Encyclopaedia Britannica.* Lummis worked at it for years, gathering over ten thousand index cards of information. It was never completed because he had so much else to do.

As editor of and frequent contributor to *Land of Sunshine/Out West,* Lummis advanced something similar to the Sunbelt theory of today. He predicted a shift of social, cultural, and economic vigor away from the Atlantic East to the Southwest, or Sunbelt, states. Los Angeles, he exulted, would become the capital city of this emerging American empire, the Pacific port and the cultural center of a region stretching from California to Texas. Two key symbols of identification for this emerging region were the sun and the Spanish past. The effects of the sun, Lummis argued, were physical and psychological. Southern Californians and Southwesterners were, and would continue to be, more healthy than Easterners. He ran a series of photographs of Southern Californian children in *Land of Sunshine* to prove his point. On the psychological level, as the motto of his magazine put it, "the lands of the sun expand the soul." Life in Southern California could be freer, more joyous, and more expansive than life in the East or Midwest because it was a life lived with the sun. Lummis was sensitive to the counterargument that the sun could also debilitate, could induce torpidity and languor. He ran articles by Charlotte Perkins Gilman of Pasadena and by Charles Dudley Warner arguing that, before arriving in Southern California, the Anglo-Saxon race had never before truly had a chance to develop a society in a Mediterranean climate, so that the enervating effect of the sun on Anglo-Saxons was yet to be proved. Mrs. Gilman, a leading feminist writer, said that she had been in Southern California for eight years and had never been more productive in her life. Charles Dudley Warner asserted that there was no contradiction between strength and energy and "the less anxious and more contented spirit" of the South. Besides, Lummis retorted in an editorial, "California has the climate of the lands which have given the world its noblest religion, its soundest philosophy, its highest art, its greatest poets and painters and sculptors and musicians. There does not seem to be anything bad for the intellect or the heart in the sort of climate that has mothered Jesus of Nazareth, and Homer and Socrates, and Praxiteles, Plato, Virgil, Michelangelo, Titian, Correggio, Velásquez, Saavedra, and all the interminable list—even to Napoleon."

In his own books and throughout thousands of pages of journalism, Lummis exhorted Americans first to acknowledge their Spanish heritage, next to respect it, and finally to make a deeper act of appropriation. The epic of the Spanish frontier, he argued, was part of the colonial heritage of the states and territories stretching from Texas to the Pacific. The citizen of the Southwest, he insisted, should live a life touched by this Spanish heritage. Lummis carried his own suggestion to an extreme that was partly histrionic but also partly a sincere effort at symbolic statement. Styling himself "Don Carlos," Lummis lived on Southwestern food—chili, tamales, frijoles, olives—and wore a green corduroy suit cut in the Spanish style, set off by boots, a brightly colored cummerbund, a frilled shirt, a broad-brimmed hat, and Navaho jewelry. When he traveled he carried his shaving gear and clean linen in a buckskin saddlebag slung across his shoulder. He rolled his own cigarettes, lighting them with a flint and a rag treated with gunpowder, as did the Spanish vaqueros of old.

In 1898 Lummis began the construction of the mansion he called El Alisal (The Alder Grove) after a nearby grove on the west bank of the Arroyo Seco, the generally dry river running from the San Gabriel Mountains through West Pasadena, toward Los Angeles. Lummis laid stones for the house himself with the assistance of Indian artisans. On and off, he worked on El Alisal for about fifteen years. Consisting of thirteen rooms, faced with granite boulders, surmounted by a campanile modeled on that of San Gabriel Mission, El Alisal was a home, a museum of the Southwest, and a Spanish fantasy. Built as a four-wing structure around a patio, its walls hung with Indian rugs and California paintings, its ceilings crossed by beams showing the rough cut of an ancient adze, El Alisal dramatized perhaps better than anything he had written Lummis's feeling for the rugged romance of Southern California as a subregion of New Spain. At El Alisal, wearing his "party buckskins" and (later) the Grand Cross of the Order of Isabel the Catholic (King Alfonso XIII of Spain knighted Lummis in 1915 for *The Spanish Pioneers*), Don Carlos entertained the great, the near great, the merely colorful, and assorted hangers-on for twenty-five years. His El Alisal "noises," or Saturday night soirees, were famous: bohemian evenings of food, music, and talk attended by such personalities as Sarah Bernhardt, John Muir, Madame Modjeska, the Duke of Alba, Senator William Gibbs McAdoo, David Starr Jordan (the president of Stanford University and a very close friend), together with aspiring writers, painters, and actors such as Maynard Dixon, Eugene Manlove Rhodes, Douglas Fairbanks, Will Rogers, Nora May French, and Mary Austin.

For all his histrionics, however, Charles Fletcher Lummis was a Charles Eliot Norton–trained Harvard scholar, ultimately genteel and possessed of a reverence for formal institutions. An ardent bookman, he devoted six years of his life to serving as city librarian of Los Angeles, leaving the Los Angeles Public Library with a well-developed local history collection. He helped found the Southwest Museum, built near his home on the Arroyo Seco. As editor of *Land of Sunshine/Out West*, Lummis commissioned and ran numerous articles on Old Californian and Southwest culture by leading authorities. He was himself a more than amateur archeologist, having worked in the field with the great Adolph F. Bandelier from 1888 to 1890 as part of his recuperative program.

Helping to pioneer the use of photography in the service of cultural anthropology, Lummis once photographed the Holy Week rites of the Penitentes of New Mexico, who literally reenact the Crucifixion, and was seriously wounded by shotgun fire in retaliation. He used color photography in the field, and recorded hundreds of old Spanish songs, Indian war chants, folk songs, and the like on an early Edison wax cylinder machine. These recordings are now part of the collection of the Southwest Museum he founded. As founding president of the Landmarks Club, Lummis led a successful effort to restore many of the Franciscan missions, then falling into ruins. Although he despised the sort of fake mission romance engendered by *Ramona*, Lummis campaigned for both the preservation of the missions and proper interpretation of mission history. Contrary to what the mission myth would have Americans believe, Lummis roared from the pages of "The Lion's Den" (his monthly column in *Land of Sunshine*), Southern California had never supported the pastel, pseudo-Castilian mise-en-scène the myth extolled. It had been a much more rugged frontier than the mission myth would have it—yet one touched withal by beauty. The Californian need not turn the mission into a fantasy resembling a La Scala production of *La Forza del Destino* in order to feel its ideality and charm. These frontier churches strung along the California coast like so many beads in a rosary stood for spiritual foundations as impressive as those suggested by the rooster-vaned spires of Massachusetts. One need not be a Catholic, Lummis asserted, to feel the power of the missions as historical monuments or to internalize them as symbolic elements of great use to the present.

Besides, as Lummis also pointed out, "the Missions are, next to our climate and its consequences, the best capital Southern California has." There was a strong streak of boosterism in Lummis. Although he himself made little money, and died broke, the veil of Spanish romance he helped throw over Southern California, together with his vigorous advocacy of its climate and the possibilities of its culture, helped to sell the Southland, and the selling of Southern California made its oligarchy rich. The *Land of Sunshine*, after all, began as a publication subsidized by the Los Angeles Chamber of Commerce. It was sent into the Midwest and the East as promotional literature, and no doubt helped to stimulate migration into the Southland. In advertising terms, Lummis was giving Southern California an image, a brand name, to promote sales. His commitment to Spanishness might have had its origins in his education under Charles Eliot Norton or in his personal experiences while crossing the Southwest or recovering there when sick, but as a myth the Spanish comparison served development. In more ways than one, Lummis's life and point of view were shot through with paradox. His Spanish myth, for instance, was incipiently pastoral; it celebrated a simple, feudal society. Yet as a promotional device, the Spanish myth fostered the opposite: mass society and industrialization. No wonder Harrison Gray Otis and Henry Edwards Huntington solidly backed Lummis,

lending financial support to his enterprises; and no wonder the core group be-
hind the anti-union open-shop movement, the Merchants and Manufacturers
Association, promoted a Fiesta de Los Angeles modeled upon the New Orleans
Mardi Gras the very same year, 1894, that Los Angeles was threatened with
the possibility that the railroad strike might erupt locally into a general walkout.
The Spanish myth said that all was well in Arcadia. The same year, however,
as the railroad strike, when fiesta floral floats paraded through downtown Los
Angeles and a masked ball was held in the evening, Pío Pico, the last Mexican
governor of California, an authentic survivor from the supposedly arcadian era,
died broke and alone in Los Angeles and was buried in a pauper's grave.

Both architecturally and in terms of boosterism, Frank Miller's Mission Inn
in Riverside pushed Lummis's Spanish myth about as far as it could go, which
in Southern California was very far indeed. A Midwestern lad of strong Protestant piety, Frank Miller took over his family's hostelry in the early 1880s,
when it was still an unpretentious roadside inn called the Glenwood Tavern.
Business was poor; at one point Miller tried to sell the place. Miller struggled
through the early 1890s, and then Lummis's Spanish myth hit him with the
force of a religious conversion. By temperament pious, Miller conceived of a
hotel that would be a shrine to California's Spanish past—a past, of course,
that never existed with the luxuriance Miller imagined for it. Beginning in the
late 1890s, he embarked upon twenty-five years of architectural fantasizing,
creating a Spanish Revival Oz: a neo-Franciscan fantasy of courts, patios, halls,
archways, and domes, which he furnished with the statuary, stained glass windows, and religious artifacts of Spain, Italy, and Mexico, gathered on pilgrim-
ages abroad. Architect Myron Hunt provided Miller with his first design, and
he was later assisted by the architect-antiquarian G. Stanley Wilson, an expert
in Southern European ecclesiastical architecture. But the Mission Inn was basically Frank Miller's creation, an imagined palace of Spanish dreams, giving
spatial expression to a California that never really existed. The Cloister Wing,
the Carmel Mission Wing, the Spanish Art Gallery, the Catacombs under the
inn, the Music Room of the Spanish Renaissance, the tile-domed Alhambra
Suite, the stained glass, hundreds of statues of saints, religious banners, medals, and tapestries, and (this for visitors to the Panama-California Exposition of
1915 in San Diego) a life-sized Tussadesque tableau of the papal court of Pius
X: it was as if the Midwest Protestant American imagination, disordered with
suppressed longing for the luxuriant bosom of the repudiated Mother Church,
now indulged itself in any orgy of aesthetic hyperdulia. Riverside, California,
which had not even had a mission in the days of the padres, now became the
Southern Californian center of the mission cult. In 1907 Miller had a cross
erected in honor of Junípero Serra atop Mount Rubidoux. It was blessed by the
Roman Catholic bishop of Los Angeles as Huntington and Otis stood nearby.

Two years later, the first annual Easter sunrise service was held, attracting thousands to Riverside—and to the Mission Inn.

Frank Miller of Mission Inn was a booster par excellence, and a power in the local Republican establishment which ran Riverside County. President Theodore Roosevelt stayed at the inn on 7 May 1903, accompanied by his fellow Harvardian in love with the West, Charles Fletcher Lummis. The next morning Theodore Roosevelt planted a parent navel orange in front of the inn, one of the two Brazilian navel orange trees that had been sent to Riverside in 1873, from which were derived all the orange trees of the region. President William Howard Taft visited Riverside on 11 October 1909 and sat splendidly at a banquet held in the Mission Inn that evening in a huge Mission Revival chair Miller had especially designed and built to accommodate Taft's 350 pounds of presidential presence. The Mission Inn, in other words, put Riverside—and Frank Miller—on the map, which was where every good booster wanted to be.

Harrison Gray Otis was quite impressed that morning of 26 April 1909 atop Mount Rubidoux as he watched the Most Reverend Thomas J. Conaty bless the great cross erected in honor of the founder of California's missions. The mission myth, Otis realized, together with its Spanish Revival variation, promoted a sense of stability in the Southland. When Miller approached General Otis to ask that *Times*man John Steven McGroarty be given a leave of absence from his duties so he could write a historical pageant celebrating the mission era, Otis readily agreed. Frank Miller conceived of the idea while watching the Passion Play in Oberammergau, Bavaria. He talked to David Starr Jordan of Stanford about it, and the towering walrus-mustached educator said that *Times* writer John Steven McGroarty was the right man for the job. Miller took McGroarty to the cross atop Mount Rubidoux and fired him up with enthusiasm.

A genial journalist and a dreamy poet of the lo! hark! school, John Steven McGroarty had come to Southern California in his late thirties after qualifying for the bar in his native Pennsylvania. As a type, McGroarty was typical of the sort of journalists Otis attracted to the *Times* and dominated once they got there: intelligent but not overly critical, politically conservative, genial, genteel, appreciative—and most importantly, a booster, someone who wanted into the fast-forming oligarchy of Southern California. McGroarty wrote for the *Los Angeles Times* for forty years: Sunday essays of chitchat, poetry, and Emersonian encouragement, penned in his house in the Verdugo Hills. (He was known popularly as "the Poet of the Verdugo Hills.") A facile writer, McGroarty compiled a number of official histories of the Southland; his *California of the South* (1933), in fact, five volumes fat, is perhaps the last of the great commissioned mugbooks glorifying local worthies willing to underwrite the cost of publication. Reveling in Southern California's growth, McGroarty looked forward to the day when the Southland would be the most densely populated region on earth. Like his chief on the *Times*, the General, he invested heavily in real estate so that he might profit by the growth he promoted through speaking, journalism, poetry and his *Mission Play*.

Early twentieth-century California supported a number of outdoor drama-pageants: at the Forest Theater in Carmel, the Greek Theater in Berkeley, the Bohemian Grove in Sonoma County, the Ramona Pageant at Hemet, and the Pasadena Festival of Roses. *The Mission Play*, however, outdrew them all. It cost $1.5 million to mount. Seeing its promotional possibilities, Henry E. Huntington helped underwrite the production. After founding the Mission Play Association as an umbrella organization, McGroarty and his backers built a playhouse near Mission San Gabriel outside Los Angeles. Costing $750,000 and done, naturally, in the Mission Revival style, the Mission Playhouse seated 1,450. Its giant pipe organ was a wonder to hear. A cast of 300 players was hired, together with a director, Henry Kabierske, who had had extensive experience with historical pageants on the East Coast and in Europe. A local girl, the actress Eleanor Calhoun, then married to a Serbian prince and acting in Europe under her married name, Princess Lazarovich-Hrebelianovich, returned to Southern California to take the female lead. On 29 April 1912 *The Mission Play* opened to a full and enthusiastic house. Front and center were Otis, Huntington, and Bishop Conaty. McGroarty's play combined music, mime, drama, pageant, choral singing, and dance to celebrate the work of the Franciscans in Alta California. The dialogue was spotty and sententious (Father Junípero Serra, to a Spaniard casting lustful glances at an Indian maiden: "If you shall but so much as touch this young creature with your vile polluting hands, upon your head shall I hurl the curse of the Church!"), but spectacle carried the day. Even the sophisticated and acerbic Willard Huntington Wright, soon to damn the provinciality of Los Angeles in the cynical and glittering pages of *The Smart Set*, confessed himself moved on opening night by *The Mission Play*'s direct power of romantic myth.

The Mission Play became a Southern California institution. It played to an estimated 2.5 million people between 1912 and 1929. In recognition of his services to the Spanish myth of Southern California, McGroarty was named poet laureate of California, knighted by the pope and the king of Spain, and twice elected to Congress.

The levels of appeal tapped by McGroarty's *Mission Play*—and the mission myth in general—were multiple. Like Frank Miller of Mission Inn, and somewhat like Charles Fletcher Lummis of *Land of Sunshine*, John Steven McGroarty provided Southern California with a usable past, a revered founding time, at once escapist and assuring, linking a parvenu society with the rich ecclesiastical cultures of Mediterranean Europe. A Presbyterian, McGroarty fell so much under the spell of Franciscan California that he converted to Catholicism—which is a paradox, because the mission myth was an essentially Protestant creation for an essentially Protestant Southern California. McGroarty, for instance, used to give speeches in Protestant churches extolling the padres. For all its luxuriant imagery, the mission myth fundamentally celebrated the Protestant virtues of order, acquisition, and the work ethic. "They took an idle race," claimed McGroarty of the Franciscans' work with the Indians, "and put it to work—a useless race that they made useful in the world." The mission myth depicted Spanish California as a busy utopia, with no labor troubles and with Father Junípero Serra as the original booster. If, as McGroarty claimed, Spanish California "was the happiest land the world has ever known," and if the chamber of commerce approved (which it did) of McGroarty's estimation, then we have the paradox of Americans promoting their growth in Southern California via a mythic perception of a time and place that had been destroyed by the arrival of Americans. The first version of McGroarty's play cast the conquering Americans as villains. The second version pushed the last act back a bit, to a time before the Yankees arrived, and made the secularization of the missions by the secularist republican government of Mexico responsible for California's social decline. In the final moments of the revised *Mission Play*, the dying Spanish heroine, shot accidentally by Indians, tells an American that California's glory will return only at such time as the Americans restore a cross to every hill. *The Mission Play*, then, is a rather obvious but effective parable of Protestant piety and the work ethic. The mission myth baptized boosterism. The new Franciscans were the members of the chamber of commerce; the workers of Southern California were their Indians—needing tutelage and occasional chastisement, but capable of productivity when carefully supervised. As in the mission days, Southern California was being put to use in the Lord's name. A better order—productive, stable, conservative, pious—was in the making. Harrison Gray Otis's long blue line of Union skirmishers now wore sandals and gray Franciscan homespun.

III

A racial myth underlay all this, a conviction on the part of many that Southern California was the Anglo-Saxons' destined place. Charles Fletcher Lummis pushed the notion of Southern California as "the new Eden of the Saxon homeseeker" continually in *Land of Sunshine/Out West*. He predicted the rise of a Sunbelt Anglo-Saxon culture in the Southland just as the declining East was filling up with undesirable foreigners. "The ignorant, hopelessly un-American type of foreigner which infests and largely controls Eastern cities is almost unknown here," he boasted of Los Angeles in 1895. An actual physical and social

process of evolution was underway, Lummis claimed, the result of the intersection of Anglo-Saxon physical vigor with the healthfulness of the sun regions.
The Anglo-Saxon stock was improving.

A Southern California physician, Joseph Pomeroy Widney, provided Southern California with the full implications of Lummis's suggestions. Until his death
at ninety-seven in 1938, Widney—physician, educator, polymath, and visionary—played a conspicuous role in local affairs as mystic seer in residence and
prophet of Southern Californian Anglo-Saxonism. Joseph Pomeroy Widney
studied Latin and Greek at Miami University of Ohio just before the Civil War
and took an M.D. degree just after the war at the Toland Medical School in
San Francisco (later absorbed by the University of California). All his life, Dr.
Widney read voraciously in classics, medicine, and world history. Arriving in
Los Angeles in 1868, he entered private practice. In 1871 he helped found the
Los Angeles Medical Association, and in 1885 he was part of the group of ministers and physicians who established the Methodist-affiliated University of
Southern California in Los Angeles. Widney served USC as dean of the medical school, and from 1892 to 1895 he led the institution as president, getting
the university through the depression of 1893, when it nearly foundered. Like
nearly everybody of any ambition during this period of Southern California's
growth, Widney speculated in real estate, making enough money to retire at
age fifty-five and devote the next forty-two years of his long life to writing. Like
so many of the Southern Californian protagonists of this period—Abbot Kinney, H. Gaylord Wilshire, Charles Fletcher Lummis—Joseph Pomeroy Widney came dangerously close to being a crank, yet as in the case of these others,
a streak of hardheaded practicality and a flair for entrepreneurial success qualified his utopianism. Widney administered a university, dabbled in real estate,
hobnobbed with men of affairs. He was, like everyone else, a booster—and his
California of the South (1888) is one of the finest promotional books of the
period.

Like so many others also, Joseph Pomeroy Widney came to California for
his health. As a medical corpsman in the Union army during the Civil War,
he suffered a physical and nervous collapse after a year in the field working
with casualties. Discharged in 1862, he came to California and spent three rather
mysterious years wandering about the state before doing a quick medical degree
in San Francisco. Widney reentered the army in 1867 as a surgeon and was
sent to Arizona, where the Apaches were causing trouble. There, in the desert,
Widney experienced a series of mystical encounters with the Almighty Himself,
who, as Widney later described it, spoke directly to him in a way that left Widney marked for life. For the next twenty-five years, Widney later tells us, he
carried on an externally busy life while internally pondering these desert revelations. After years of prayer, thought, and research, he embarked upon the
writing of *Race Life of the Aryan Peoples*, which was finally published in 1907,

following it with a steady stream of books, pamphlets, and poetry which amplified his theories.

The Engle people, Widney argued (by which he meant the Angles or Anglo-Saxons), were destined by divine providence to flourish in Southern California and the American Southwest. Civilization, he asserted, advanced through a series of breakdowns and reconsolidations. When in some lost dawn time the proto-Aryans of the highlands of Mid-Asia began their westward trek, they commenced a folk migration now reaching its fulfillment on the Pacific Basin: in Southern California, Australia, and New Zealand, where the most vigorous of the Aryans, the Engles or North Sea peoples of Europe, were rebuilding a civilization that had been weakened by an overlong confinement on the crowded and chilly British Isles. In America, the westward frontier had reinvigorated and reinforced the health and spirit of the Engle race. As an army doctor in the Southwest, Widney wrote, he had treated the Engles as they followed the sun. Pioneer life had been a racial testing, a process of natural selection. The Engle had passed the test. He had conquered the land and vanquished the Indian. "It is Law," he writes, "the Law of the survival of the fittest. We may pity the weak: but we cannot change the workings of the Law." Now, in the post-frontier era, the Engle people stood ready to move upward to a higher civilization.

The fundamental characteristics and energies of this Sunbelt Engle empire, Widney asserted, would be healthfulness and monotheism, both gifts of the sun. A lifelong health faddist and physical culturist (no liquor, no tobacco, a raw onion in the morning to get the gastric juices flowing), Widney envisioned Los Angeles as developing into the health capital of the world, a heliopolis of holistic health culture, highly technological (Widney called for freeways some thirty years before they were built) but also devoted to natural living. Los Angeles and Istanbul, he claimed, were the point cities of the arch of Aryan civilization that extended from the Bosporus to the Pacific. The true destiny of Los Angeles was to become an Aryan city of the sun.

Committed to a non-trinitarian but biblically inspired universalism, Widney built a church on his property, Beth-El, where he conducted services in worship of the All Father, the universal god of mankind. A racialist, Widney nevertheless did not espouse the belief that non-Aryan peoples were inferior. They were just different. Each race, Widney felt, had a special place on the planet where it flourished—the black man, for instance, had an affinity for tropical climates—and it would be best if nations, in acknowledgment of this principle, were to regroup and rebuild themselves along racial lines. All peoples have the same god, Widney insisted, the All Father; yet if the All Father Himself had a special place, it was the desert, especially the desert of the Southwest, where the All Father had spoken to Widney forty years before. Here, in the desert, where monotheism had arisen in ancient times, the Engle folk would embrace its mystic destiny.

Joseph Pomeroy Widney took to extremes a notion implicit in much of Southern California's turn-of-the-century self-reflection: the notion of Anglo-Saxon superiority and its special relationship to the Southland. Widney's religion was not orthodox (he even favored polygamy), but it was evangelical in its intense biblicism and in the fervid temper of its piety. Perceived from one point of view, he was a harmless eccentric; from another angle, however, he can be considered an incipient fascist. Dr. Widney personally viewed himself as an Oelderman, or elder, of the Engle folk. Yet whatever Widney was, his day-dreams of a rejuvenated white Anglo-Saxon Protestant culture were shared by many in Southern California.

This hope took many forms. In Charles Fletcher Lummis's case, for instance, it took the form of an aggressive, albeit ambivalent, Easternism. Lummis' sombrero, sash, and Spanish-cut corduroy were, after all, a little outré, as if he were protesting too much. Despite the costume and the Southwestern pose, Charles Fletcher Lummis was basically a Harvard-trained Yankee from Lynn, Massachusetts, who as an undergraduate had sent autographed copies of his first book of poetry, *Birch Bark Poems* (bound in birch bark) to Oliver Wendell Holmes, James Russell Lowell, Henry Wadsworth Longfellow, and John Greenleaf Whittier. At sixteen he had had a poem published in the *Atlantic Monthly*, which magazine always stood in his mind as the model of what he wanted the *Land of Sunshine/Out West* to be. He admired the *Nation*, the *Century*, and the *Dial* also: solid, respected journals of commentary, conducted beyond the necessities of boosterism. Deliberately, Lummis gathered to his coterie as many writers of New England origin as he could find, Grace Ellery Channing, Charlotte Perkins Gilman, and Margaret Collier Graham among them. He insisted on the Eastern tone of Southern California ("We are Easterners—just lucky ones who got away"), and described Los Angeles as "a city of lovely homes, of cultured, well-to-do people with Eastern education and Western coridality." Yet he sent his daughter Turbese east to the National Cathedral School in Washington, D.C., so that she could have contact with what he called "the Right People"; apparently not enough of the Right People resided in Southern California. Lummis, ultimately, was caught on the horns of a dilemma of his own making. A displaced New Englander compensating for what had been lost, he overplayed the genteel aspects of Southern California, making of it a new New England with a Spanish past. In the long run, Lummis's myth of Southern California—East Coast Anglo-Saxonism with a Spanish accent—worked against itself, for he was forced to assert the superiority of Southern California by claiming that the Southland was better than what made it good in the first place—its Eastern associations. He was forced to posture, to play the booster against certain of his better instincts, because he only two-thirds believed what he was saying. Apostle of the genteel, he found himself attacking the genteel tradition in favor of Western vigor. Advocate of Western vigor, he found himself extolling the arrival of Eastern refinement to the Pacific Coast. When an Eastern paper cirticized Lummis for wearing his Spanish buckskins and corduroys on a visit to certain Eastern cities, he roared like a wounded lion in his column "The Lion's Den." Easterners—his own sort—had called his bluff. The paradox of his masquerade, the contradictions of his Southern Californianism, stood revealed.

No wonder, then, Lummis made much of Eastern women writers who shared his exile, who like him loved (and felt uneasy about) the Southland. The genteel tradition, after all, was largely feminine in tone and personnel. The greatest lady of them all, Jessie Benton Frémont, widow of the Pathfinder, received especial reverence from Lummis. In the 1850s and 1860s Mrs. Frémont had brought to the founding of American California virtues which Lummis intensely admired: vigor, culture, political courage, and social cachet—all of which she also brought to her retirement years in Los Angeles. The Frémonts settled in Los Angeles, in a cottage on Oak Street, in 1888. The Pathfinder had been in failing health before that, although with Jessie's help the general did manage to complete the first volume of his *Memoirs*. The couple skirted poverty before Congress restored Frémont to major-general's rank on the retired list, with a pension of $6,000 a year. Jessie went personally to Collis P. Huntington, president of the Southern Pacific, for the courtesy of a railroad pass to Los Angeles. Revisiting the East in 1890, General Frémont fell ill and died. On his deathbed he talked of returning home to California. He was buried in a simple coffin, wearing a plain black suit and holding in his hands a miniature of Jessie, carried overland to him in 1845 by Kit Carson as a gift from his wife.

Theirs was one of the great romances of the nineteenth century: that between a dazzling handsome young lieutenant of Topographical Engineers, born in Charleston, South Carolina, of French ancestry and made doubly ambitious by the stigma of his illegitimacy, and the spirited bluestocking daughter of Senator Thomas Hart Benton of Missouri. All her life Jessie Benton Frémont remembered how splendid John Charles looked that day in 1841 in Washington, D.C., when she first saw him, resplendent in his blue uniform. He seemed to her a Greek hero, stepping forth from the sunlight. She began to nurture his legend almost before he gave her cause—and never more so than in the decade of her Los Angeles widowhood. To Lummis's way of thinking, Jessie Benton Frémont embodied all that was splendid in the drama of manifest destiny that had brought California into the Union. He praised her continually in *Land of Sunshine* as the founding mother of California, the paragon of Anglo-Saxon civilization and fortitude. He did a photographic study of her in 1895: still handsome in her late seventies, the daughter and consort of history makers, a woman whose energy, Lummis claimed, had made California possible. He fumed at Josiah Royce (calling him "a megalocephalic Harvard professor") when Royce claimed that Frémont had exceeded his orders in 1846 by taking up arms against the Californios. But Lummis himself wrote glowingly of Jessie Benton (and this, paradoxically, only underscored Royce's point) that she "defied the War Department and sent her Young Man to find and conquer and make new national boundaries, in defiance of the provincialism of his superiors." Mrs. Frémont herself was less assertive, claiming only that she had been personally present when her father, in the name of the Senate War Committee, authorized Captain Frémont to enter California at the head of an invading army. Of course, that also would have been illegal, further reinforcing Royce's point, but no matter: what was relevant was the symbolic assertion of America's right by conquest to the continent, especially its Californian coast. "From the ashes of his campfires," Mrs. Frémont once wrote of the general, "cities have sprung." This remark is the best summary of the Pathfinder's spotty career.

In 1892 the women of Los Angeles presented Mrs. Frémont with a two-story shingled home on West Twenty-eighth Street called The Retreat, where Jessie lived on a major-general's widow's pension of $2,000 a year. No wonder Lummis so revered her! No wonder John Gutzon Borglum sculptured her in bronze! In her amalgam of caste, strength, and genteel civility, in her ambience of the great world and the style of the Republic, Jessie Benton Frémont confirmed for Los Angelenos her own stated opinion of their community. "This is not a narrow atmosphere with taint of village or a raw community," she had written upon her arrival, praising Los Angeles's people, climate, parks, libraries, and tennis courts. She spoke and read French and Spanish, had lived in Europe and traveled extensively, and loved a hero and helped to create a legend; she had dominated San Francisco in the 1850s and 1860s, had helped her husband run for president in 1856—and now she was here, in Los Angeles, providing a continuity, setting a tone. A gifted writer, she had helped to support herself and her husband over the years when money was scarce as an essayist; now, at Lummis's urging, she began her autobiography, to be serialized in *Land of Sunshine*. She read and discussed books with him: such recent novels as George Moore's *Esther Waters* and Thomas Hardy's *Tess of the D'Urbervilles*, but also old books as well, the books of her bluestocking girlhood, books which had accompanied her back and forth across the continent and down to Arizona when the general served there as territorial governor: a rare edition of Montaigne's *Essays*, for example, or a two-volume French prose translation of the *Odyssey*, printed in Paris in 1819, from which in days long ago her father the senator would read to her in the course of a picnic outing, the two of them sitting under a tree, as Jessie listened wide-eyed to the senator's stentorian tones, she munching apples and biscuits with youthful appetite. President McKinley called on her at The Retreat in 1901 (by then she was confined to a wheelchair), accompanied by his secretary of state, John Hay, whom Jessie had petted and spoiled as a boy. "My goodness, John, how you have grown," she remarked to the secretary of state. In the autumn of 1902, Mrs. Frémont took to her bed, asking only that her favorite portrait of the general be placed near her bed so that she could gaze on it when the end came. On Christmas Eve 1902 her presents were opened for her. "I am very happy over such attention from *mes enfants*," she said, "but I am very tired. Now I will sleep." She never awoke, dying peacefully on the morning of the twenty-seventh.

Thus ended a career animated by an intense devotion to the role of wife, as the nineteenth century envisioned it. For Lummis, Jessie Benton Frémont was, symbolically, the Mother of the Race in Southern California, as well as "the Isabella of our overland Columbus." *Land of Sunshine*, remember, was a highly female magazine, written in the main by women for women under Lummis's guidance. Lummis surrounded himself with high-minded women bent on a better Southern California. (Sexually, he sought less cerebral companionship.) The Landmarks Club, for instance, founded in 1896 with Lummis as president and dedicated to the restoration of the California missions, was largely feminine in support and staffing. *Land of Sunshine* featured a feminist column by Margaret Collier Graham of South Pasadena, "The Angle of Reflection," which encouraged and guided the emergence and development of high-minded Southern California women—who were also featured frequently by Lummis in chatty profiles, suggestive of today's "people" journalism, of women such as Rose T. Bullard, a gynecologist who graduated from medical school at Northwestern in 1886, took her postgraduate training at Gottingen and Vienna, and was then teaching at USC; Elizabeth Kenney, an attorney at law admitted to practice before the Supreme Court of California; Kate Douglas Wiggin, active in the kindergarten movement; and Belle Reynolds of Santa Barbara, president of the Woman's Parliament of Southern California, also a physician, who became interested in medicine during the Civil War, when she served as a field nurse with the Seventeenth Illinois so she could be near her husband. Such women, Lummis asserted, together with thousands of others, less visible but similarly accomplished, were in the process of bringing high Anglo-Saxon culture to Southern Caifornia, as had Jessie Benton Frémont a half century earlier.

Clubwoman and social activist Caroline Seymour Severance led the way. For twenty years, before coming to Los Angeles in 1876, Mrs. Severance had been active in a number of reform movements in the Boston area: women's rights, abolitionism, liberal Christianity, hospital reform, diet reform, the reform of women's dress. She assisted at the foundation of the New England Hospital for Women and Children, the Girls' Latin High School, and the New England Women's Club of Boston. Her friends included the who's who of New England transcendentalism and social reform: Ralph Waldo Emerson, Margaret Fuller, Elizabeth Cody Stanton, O. B. Frothingham, Bronson Alcott, Louisa May Alcott, Julia Ward Howe, Lucy Stone, Susan B. Anthony, Horace Mann (her brother-in-law), and many others. Her husband, a Boston banker, came to California to restore his health by working in the outdoors as an orange grower.

Caroline Severance, then fifty-five, at once threw herself into a variety of projects. She helped found Unity Church, one of Los Angeles's early Protestant congregations. She persuaded the German-born kindergarten pioneer Emma Marwedel to establish a training school for kindergarten teachers, which Mrs. Severance sponsored. She brought the New England women's club movement to Southern California. She worked tirelessly for woman's suffrage. In 1911, in recognition of her efforts, she was the first woman to register to vote in the entire state. For over thirty years the Severance home, El Nido, was the center of progressive, reformist thought in Los Angeles, to include a flirtation with Fabian socialism, concerning which conservative Republican Lummis kept his counsel. The Friday Morning Club of Los Angeles, as Caroline Severance ran it during the time she served as president, brought the earnest, energetic mood of Boston reform out to lackadaisical Los Angeles. Among women of a certain class, the Friday Morning Club promoted discussion of diet, universal suffrage, feminism, the single standard in sexual conduct, and the economic independence of women. "Constricting Corsets" was the subject of the Friday morning talk of 18 December 1891, for instance. The women who had abandoned the excruciating Victorian corset were asked by the chair to stand. Thirty-five women out of the hundred or so present sprang to their feet.

Such clubs were essentially conservative organizations, although the energies and frustrations that seethed beneath the surface of womanly uplift and high-mindedness foretold a more overt conflict to come. Even Charles Fletcher Lummis could not fully persuade his female colleagues to play out with passive acceptance his scenario of woman as agent of Anglo-Saxon cultural uplift. Too many things were wrong between men and women, in all classes and conditions, as the thrice-married Lummis himself well knew. Behind *Land of Sunshine* columnist Margaret Collier Graham's placid exterior, for example, there seethed a discernible anger over the subjugation of females. "A woman kisses the fist that fells her," she wrote in her feminist tract *Do They Really Respect Us?*, "if that same fist is to her the only source of supply; but as for loving it— do not deceive yourselves, my brothers, and do not wonder that she is restless under dependence which would gall you beyond endurance, for she is made of the same stuff as yourselves."

Another *Land of Sunshine* staff writer, Charlotte Perkins Gilman of Pasadena, became perhaps the most prominent, and certainly the most prolific, feminist writer in America. Like Lummis and so many others of his circle, Gilman was a New Englander who had moved to Southern California for her health. Born in Hartford, Connecticut, in 1860, Charlotte Anna Perkins was descended from the great preacher-theologian Lyman Beecher (her great-grandfather) and was also related to Henry Ward Beecher, the prominent minister, and to Harriet Beecher Stowe, the author of *Uncle Tom's Cabin*. Her father, a librarian and magazine editor, abandoned his family and subsequently lent it little support—but did find the time to send his daughter lists of books to read from San Francisco, where he worked as city librarian. Charlotte grew up a lonely, introspective, very intellectual child. Within a year of her marriage in 1884 to Charles Walter Stetson, a Providence, Rhode Island, artist, and the birth of a daughter, she suffered a nervous breakdown. In 1885 she went alone to Pasadena and recovered. Returning to Providence, and to her marriage, she suffered a relapse. She cried continually. She hid under beds and in closets. She played distractedly with rag dolls. The fictional version of her experience, the novella *The Yellow Wall Paper*, now a minor classic, was rejected by Horace Scudder of the *Atlantic* because, as he put it, it would make too many women readers too miserable! Charlotte was treated by S. Wier Mitchell, the famous Philadelphia psychiatrist, but Mitchell's "rest cure" (a long period of total bed rest) did her no good. Marriage itself was her problem. In 1887 she left her husband, and in 1888 she left for Pasadena with a train ticket, a packed lunch, and ten dollars in her pocket. Caroline Severance, whom she had met on her first trip to Southern California, helped her to get established.

Charlotte Perkins Stetson credited Southern California with her recovery. "Everywhere," she recalled, "there was beauty, and the nerve-rest of steady windless weather." And again: "Never before had my passion for beauty been satisfied. This place did not seem like earth; it was paradise." Leaving her husband also helped. They were divorced in 1894, very amicably. Charles Stetson then married another Pasadenan, Grace Ellery Channing, the *Land of Sunshine* writer and Charlotte's closest friend. Katharine Beecher Stetson, Charlotte's daughter, went to live with her father and his new bride.

Charlotte's stay in Southern California was brief. In 1891 she moved north to Oakland, where she supported herself as a writer and a lecturer. In 1894 she left California altogether, chafing at its provinciality and especially distressed by the sensational play the San Francisco newspapers had given her decision to give up her daughter. In 1900 she married her cousin George Houghton Gilman, a New York attorney. She finally returned to Pasadena in 1934, suffering from a malignancy. She committed suicide the next year, leaving a note reading, "I have preferred chloroform to cancer." Southern California, however, had earlier been the scene of her recovery and reconsolidation—and also the place where her developing feminist thought found support from a large number of similarly oriented women, many of whom were also rebuilding broken lives in the Southland. Charlotte Perkins Gilman eventually developed into the dominant intellectual voice in the women's rights movement of her era. Her analysis of the socioeconomic forces subjugating women in industrial societies, made in the early 1900s, still has cogency and force. The androcentric nature of our social institutions, the economic basis of marriage, the exclusion of women from self-support, their oversexualization, their imprisonment in housework, the double standard in sexual morality, the question of equal rights: the issues addressed by Charlotte Perkins Gilman are to this day the pertinent issues of feminist debate.

Was there any continuity or pattern to all this eclecticism of definition? The Spanish borderlands, the mission myth, the Engle people, Venice, Rome, a new opportunity for the American woman to reform society and liberate her own condition: Southern California of this era might appear a magic lantern screen onto which any fantasy might indiscriminately be projected. Was Southern California the austerity of Lummis's borderlands or the lush, exaggerated romanticism of Miller's Mission Inn? Was Widney's theory of racial migration a harmless delusion or an extreme version of an underlying belief that Southern California somehow offered Protestant America a long-desired place in the sun? Through all this eclecticism and miscellaneousness of purpose, however, a pattern does assert itself: that of the American imagination, especially in its white Protestant dimensions, seeking to reassert itself in new surroundings with a new and luxuriant symbol system. Whether it be the women's movement, the search for a usable prehistory, academic eclecticism in architecture, or white xenophobia, each Southern California formulation intensifed, often naively, a notion or pursuit from elsewhere in America, reexpressing it in vivid new imagery. What was Abbot Kinney's Venice, after all, but an exotic chautauqua resort, based upon the same premises of convivial camp meeting and self-improvement? And whereas the women of Southern California might feel special possibilities in their new environment for an expansion of opportunity and an enlarged freedom of movement, the fundamental energies of their crusade had their origins in the New England of a generation earlier, and was running parallel to the contemporary suffragette movement in the East. A colony of the Eastern and Midwestern states, Southern California offered the longings and dreams of older American regions enhancement and recycling on the shores of the sundown sea. For all its surface exoticism, however, turn-of-the-century Southern California remained a recognizably American place.

4

Pasadena and the Arroyo:
Two Modes of Bohemia

Located twenty-five miles inland, Pasadena lies on the site of the Rancho San Pasqual at the head of the San Gabriel Valley. The San Gabriel Mountains flank its eastern edge. Along its western border runs the Arroyo Seco, a deep cut running part of the year with water, making its way westward from the Sierra Madre down along to the sea. In the 1880s the lower areas of the Arroyo Seco were still thick with sycamores, oak, willows, alder, tangled thickets of wild grapes, clematis, and other flowering plants, providing Pasadenans with a ready-made wilderness retreat. The name Pasadena itself, some claimed, was Chippewa for "crown of the valley." Pasadena was certainly that, the crown of the valley, as it developed in the 1880s from its original foundation in 1875 as an agricultural cooperative owned and managed by the San Gabriel Orange Grove Association. Incorporated as a city in 1886, Pasadena grew into a charming town of ten thousand by century's turn (thirty thousand by 1907), with a church for every thousand residents (including a massive Romanesque Universalist Church at Raymond and Chestnut), a neo-Moorish opera house seating fifteen hundred (Madame Modjeska brought *Mary Stuart* and *Camille* there in 1889), and a large number of distinguished homes facing broad, well-planted boulevards. Pasadena's balmy climate nurtured its growth as a health resort and a retirement community.

Mrs. James Garfield, the former president's widow, settled in, as did the children of abolitionist martyr John Brown. Visiting Pasadena in 1882, Walter Raymond, the owner of the Boston travel firm Raymond and Whitcomb, saw the possibilities of a resort hotel there for Easterners in search of escape from the rigors of an Atlantic winter. In November 1886 the luxuriant and vast Hotel Raymond (a subsidiary of Raymond and Whitcomb) opened on a great knoll overlooking South Pasadena. In an era of lavish hotels, the Raymond was one of the best—two hundred rooms, elegant service, catering exclusively to Raymond and Whitcomb tours, which introduced a large number of wealthy Easterners to the delights of Southern California. Many tourists returned to Pasadena as permanent residents. The Raymond burned to the ground on 14 April 1895, but by then a thriving hotel culture of Eastern visitors had been established as part of the Pasadena scene. Well into the 1920s, at places like the Hotel Maryland, the Wentworth (later the Hotel Huntington), and the Hotel Green, rich America lazed in the sun, played polo, and held teas and masquerade balls while the East Coast lay under a mantle of snow.

The resort aspects of Pasadena were accentuated by the Mount Lowe Incline Railway, completed in 1893. Electrically powered trolleys defied gravity as they lifted passengers up five thousand feet into the San Gabriel Mountains, where atop Mount Lowe, whatever the time of year, tourists could frolic in the snow or enjoy the hospitality of the Alpine Tavern. The brainchild of Thaddeus S. C. Lowe, a self-taught engineer, inventor, and aeronaut (he commanded the Union army's balloon observation forces during the Civil War), the incline railway cost Lowe his fortune to finance, but won him the respect of Southern Pacific president Collis P. Huntington, who said that the Pasadena incline was better than anything he had ever seen in Switzerland. In 1894 a three-million-candlepower searchlight recently in use at the just-completed Columbian Exposition in Chicago was emplaced atop Mount Lowe. Nightly the giant beam swept the skies over Pasadena, or played about prominent places in the plain below.

Like most Southern Californians of this period, Pasadenans vigorously nurtured the domestic ideal. *Land of Sunshine*, for instance, featured a continuous array of photographs depicting the joys of domestic life in the Southland: a woman seated, book in lap, by a window opening out on a spacious garden; a young girl, in the lavish starched white pinafores and oversized floppy hair bows of the period, petting her dog in the shade of a palm tree; a family gathered in late afternoon on a veranda, enjoying the sunset scent of blooming orange trees; an elderly gentleman trimming a rosebush. Horticulture—gardens, lawns, rosebushes—was the special glory of Pasadena. "It is the land of the afternoon," wrote Pasadenan Charles Frederick Holder; "people live out of doors, and have an inherent love of flowers." Beginning as an agricultural colony, Pasadena mingled at its outskirts with still extant orchards. March and April were especially lovely times of year. Then, Pasadena rioted in flowering trees—peach, almond, apricot; the vineyards grew leafy; poppy fields ran right into the city; and blossoming orange trees filled the region with a languorous perfume. Starting in 1876, the agronomist Ezra S. Carr and his wife Jeanne made a special project of developing the gardens of their Pasadena estate, Carmelita, as a paradigm of botanical possibilities. Carmelita eventually became a public park, but not before it helped establish a lavish landscaping tradition which made Pasadena the premier garden and floral city of Southern California. When President Benjamin Harrison stayed overnight in Pasadena on 10 March 1891, his open coach was showered with roses as it passed through an arch of calla lilies and pampas plumes extended over Marengo Avenue. Cherokee roses decorated the curtains and bureaus of his room in the presidential suite at the Hotel Green. Wisteria hung from the chandeliers, and a monogram BH in red and white roses on a background of calla lilies sat in the fireplace.

To experience Pasadena at century's turn was to encounter a mixed ambience of languor and energy, rusticity and Eastern tone. Stately homes of shingle and stone—bristling with upper-middle-class pride, encircled by verandas, lawns, and rosebushes—lined wide boulevards (South Orange Grove, Buena Vista) planted in palm, oak, and eucalyptus. Interiors and home furnishings showed the influence of the aesthetic movement in a certain simplification of taste: a preference for shiny hardwood floors, for instance, and a dramatic use of throw rugs; Arts and Crafts furniture; an overall absence of clutter and bric-a-brac. No one knew or expressed this design ideal better than the Pasadena firm of Greene and Greene, whose Pasadena homes were poems of wood and light. Like their clients—indeed, like Charles Fletcher Lummis himself—Charles Sumner Greene and Henry Mather Greene were Midwesterners (Ohio) touched by New England (architectural study at the Massachusetts Institute of Technology, followed by work with various Boston firms), who were transformed in 1893 into ardent Southern Californians when they joined their health-seeking parents in Pasadena. There, like their fellow Pasadenans, the Greene brothers pursued the pleasures of the genteel tradition—art, music, poetry, painting, history, literature—and, of course, the outdoors, taken as domesticated landscape, taken, that is, as the garden enlivened by a lingering element of original wilderness, the so-called middle landscape, which allowed American nature and the European art past to blend in harmony: the landscape, in short, of Pasadena. Like their clients, the Greene brothers favored simplicity and solid thought, touched by the aesthetic. For architects and clients alike, Pasadena was a liberal Protestant upper-middle-class daydream—a daydream occurring in the Edwardian Tiffany years before the First World War when money and fantasy, for the upper middle class at least, still sustained a direct rate of exchange.

Influences on the Greenes were eclectic, but all influences led them in the direction of aesthetic functionalism. "I seek till I find what is truly useful," said Charles Sumner Greene, "and then I try to make it beautiful." From John Ruskin, William Morris, and the English Arts and Crafts Movement in general, the Greenes absorbed a sense of architecture as deliberate social statement. Their homes, like Pasadena, were metaphors of an America brought to liberality, simplicity, and taste. The vernacular traditions of Northern Europe, Switzerland and Norway especially, taught the Greenes how to use wood with bold simplicity and sculptured playfulness. At the 1893 Columbian Exposition in Chicago, they found themselves enchanted by the airy modernity of Japanese design. Something Japanese, some severity of line and abstraction of space, also pervaded their Pasadena creations.

By the early 1900s their style had matured to the level evident in their acknowledged masterpiece, the house they designed and built in 1908 for David B. Gamble of Procter and Gamble (who retired to Pasadena in 1895) at 4 Westmoreland Place.

The Gamble House is a poem of wood, texture, and light. The inner essence of the building is boldly apparent in great open beams, crossed and recrossed both in the function and as the symbol of weight and stress. Skylights and leaded windows of stained glass let in the soft Southern Californian light in a daily cycle of sunshine and shadow that plays across the brightly colored hand-woven throw rugs, the interior brickwork, the pillows and polished benches and shelves of books. At night, the glow of Tiffany lamps adds opal luster to the stained glass windows or quickens the subtle colors of a Japanese vase. Always and everywhere, by day or by night, there is wood, wood, wood: boldly used as support beams, fitted as joints, sculptured in an astonishing staircase, glistening in hardwood floors, taking on quiet weathering as outside shingles. Here, indeed, in architectural terms, is the upper-middle-class Pasadenan daydream come true— a realized suggestion of the good life, Pasadena style.

The Greenes, of course, built for a rather restricted range of financially affluent clients. One of the most noticeable traits of a Greene and Greene home, as Brendan Gill points out, is the cunning concealment of servant staircases and house service areas. Yet despite the class bias of their work (or was it because of it?), the Greene brothers did hope that their creations would set a pattern usable in mass housing. In this sense also, the sense of setting an example, Pasadenans envisioned themselves establishing standards of lifestyle for the rest of Southern California. Through all the variations of their middle-class life— from the Valley Hunt Club to the Arroyo Culture—Pasadenans sought the emblematically genteel. In 1887, for example, Pasadena outlawed saloons. Just about the same time, librarian Mrs. S. E. Merritt proudly announced that "Ouida's passionate French immorality is never found on these shelves." Pasadena, Charles Frederick Holder claimed in the early 1890s, "has been built up by wealthy, refined, and cultivated people from the great cities of the East; and, while without maturity in years, she possesses all that time can bring, especially as regards the social ties that bind and mould communities." Organizations such as the Social Purity Club, the Chautauqua Literary and Scientific Circle, and the Shakespeare Club upheld a sense of heritage braced by a conviction of white upper-middle-class Protestant caste, raised at the time to a high level of defensive self-consciousness because of the wave of European immigrants arriving in the East, Catholic and Jewish, and labor troubles in Los Angeles, Catholic and Jewish also. *Pasadena Daily News* editor Lon Chapin, editorializing in 1907, took pride in "the high character of citizenship that has made the city what it is: Beautiful, Clean, Cultured, Moral, and Esthetic." When the opera or symphony played in Los Angeles, the Pacific Electric Railway ran special cars to and from Pasadena. Writers like Frank Pixley, Bronson Howard, Thomas Nelson Page, Gertrude Potter Daniels, Ella Wheeler Wilcox—forgotten today, but in their time the rage of middlebrow America—made their homes in this "Western clearing house for Eastern genius." Local figures in the Pasadena landscape such as Charles Frederick Holder and Perry Worden did their best to describe and to act out a representative Pasadena style.

Charles Frederick Holder, Southern California's leading gentleman sportsman, devoted a lifetime to the practice and aesthetics of sport in California. Ironically, the aristocratic Pasadena club Holder helped to found, the Valley Hunt Club, itself spawned the more democratic Pasadena Tournament of Roses. Organized by Holder in the late 1880s, the Valley Hunt Club grew into a socially prestigious organization, devoted to the chase: horses and greyhounds after rabbits in its simpler beginnings, fox hunting in full regalia in later years. On New Year's day the Valley Hunt Club held a great outdoor picnic, followed in the evening by a hunt ball. In 1890 a Tournament of Roses, consisting of riding contests in the style of Spanish California, followed the picnic. The Tournament of Roses grew more and more formalized and elaborate through the 1890s. By 1907 it had grown to a floral parade in the morning, chariot races and other riding contests in the afternoon, and a ball at the Hotel Green in the evening. A Tournament of Roses Association, formed to run the annual event, made it a more and more extended civic celebration over the years, turning the floral pageant into a full-scale downtown parade and replacing the riding competitions with a college football game.

The tournament went democratic, but the Valley Hunt Club and all that it stood for kept its tone. Miss Olive Percival, for instance, tended her garden, wrote poetry, read, and collected a library of over ten thousand books. Active in the Friday Morning Club, the Daughters of the American Revolution, and the Society of Mayflower Descendants, Olive Percival lived the old-style genteel life, Southern California style, until her death in 1945, assisting in her own support with articles for the magazine *House and Garden*. From the vantage point of lawn and library, she viewed the world and fashioned her delicate, sensitive poems of garden living: the roses, lilacs, and chrysanthemums which were her major company; the seasons in their subtle Southern Californian passages; reading by firelight in February, when there was a hint of cold in the air; sitting outside in the lilac mist of an April twilight, Eden-scented with orange blossoms, something in the air recalling *la primavera*, the springtime of Botticelli's Italy.

In 1900 Perry Worden returned from nine years of study in Europe, having finished and published a doctoral dissertation on Longfellow for the University of Halle. He settled in an orange grove in nearby Altadena, lecturing on topics

European and literary: a scholar, antiquarian, and editor, who did most of the research and the writing for Harris Newmark's *Sixty Years in Southern California* (1916), which Lummis called the Pepys's diary of Los Angeles. Perry Worden embodied the Pasadenan as high-minded savant and litterateur. For nine years he had drunk deep at the well of European learning, yet his doctoral dissertation for a German university had been on the American poet Longfellow. Longfellow-like was Worden's own taste for learned retirement, for a Horatian mode of rustic scholarship and writing in orchard-rich Altadena.

The presence in and around Pasadena of such Cassiodorian figures as Olive Percival and Perry Worden should not obscure the fact that Pasadena also had its life of *Our Town*, its daily round of birth, growth, and death in the style and mood of turn-of-the-century small-town America. Wilson High School, in the manner of public high schools of the period, brought the various social strata of Pasadena together in one institution. James D. Graham, principal and professor of mathematics (high school teachers were frequently called "professor" at this time, following the custom of the European *gymnasium* and *lycée*), ran a tight ship. Latin, Greek, German, French, music, biology, mathematics, chemistry, trigonometry, history, and composition were all solidly taught. There was also football, baseball, basketball (this for women as well), track, tennis, debating, a literary quarterly, and a glee club.

The less egalitarianly inclined attended the Classical School for Boys, a private Episcopalian institution, where George Smith Patton, Jr., studied between 1897 and 1903 before going on to the Virginia Military Institute, his father's alma mater. As the grandson of Benjamin Davis Wilson (who once owned the Rancho San Pasqual, where Pasadena now stood) and the son of George Smith Patton, Sr., one-time district attorney for Los Angeles County, United States Senate candidate, manager of the Huntington Land and Improvement Company, and landowner in his own right, young George S. Patton, Jr., approached adolescence with a complicated and representatively Southern California heritage. His father's father, also a VMI graduate and a colonel in the Confederate army, died in the battle of Fredericksburg. The memory of Grandfather Patton's last gallant charge hung about his son with a suggestion of subtle reproach, for try as hard as he might, marry as well as he did, George Smith Patton could do nothing equal to the glorious sacrifice of his Virginian father on the field of honor. Southern Californian and Virginian strains converged in young George Junior. Born on 11 June 1885 at Lake Vineyard, the San Gabriel estate which his grandfather Benjamin Davis Wilson had owned back when it included all that the eye could see, George Smith Patton, Jr., possessed in the Southern Californian side of his nature the assurances of social caste. The Virginia side, equally aristocratic, had suffered an interruption when George Smith Patton, Sr., had been brought to Los Angeles in 1866 by his widowed mother. The son of the fallen Confederate colonel now raised his own son to be a soldier like the boy's grandfather. Patton Senior read the *Iliad* and the *Odyssey* aloud to his son, whom he dressed in a soldier's suit. The son's adeptness at riding and riflery delighted the father.

Towheaded, handsome, with more than a suggestion of feminine refinement in his nature, George S. Patton, Jr., grew up in a mixed atmosphere of pampering and challenge. He rode the family estates on horseback, or went on rugged pack trips into the Sierra Madre. He also enjoyed leisurely, upper-class summer sojourns on Santa Catalina Island, where he met his future wife, a Beverly, Massachusetts, patrician. (Like his father, George S. Patton, Jr., married well, and also like his father, in later years he dressed for dinner whenever possible.) By age seventeen George S. Patton, Jr., had decided upon a military career, which was no surprise. George's notebooks from the Classical School of Pasadena are filled with references to ancient captains and great battles—and pervaded by a sense of himself as a cut above the ordinary, a boy born to command. Admitted to Princeton, he chose the Virginia Military Institute instead and transferred a year later to West Point.

A photograph taken some time in the summer of 1903, now in the Huntington Library, shows the Patton family on the porch of Lake Vineyard. George, Jr., wearing his cadet's uniform, leans languidly against a wall and regards his father, his mother, and a walrus-mustached Henry Edwards Huntington, who is in grand repose in a rocking chair. At the time Huntington was in the midst of making his second fortune as president of Pacific Electric. In 1892, on his first visit to Southern California, Huntington, then vice-president of the Southern Pacific, visited the San Marino Ranch of J. de Barth Shorb adjacent to Pasadena. He fell in love with the site, a plateau surmounted by a gentle knoll which afforded a view across the San Gabriel Valley to Los Angeles and the sea. In 1903, the year he sat with his neighbors, the Patton family, on their Lake Vineyard porch, Huntington bought the San Marino Ranch and began to make plans for its development. Money, obviously, was no barrier. His uncle Collis P. Huntington had left him something like $40 million in 1900, to which he was in the process of adding another $30 million from real estate investment and the Pacific Electric. It was an era—the last era, in fact—of scarcely taxed fortunes and heroic spending: a possibility compounded in Huntington's case by the fact that his wife Arabella had been his Uncle Collis's other heir. Married to Collis P. Huntington in 1884 after a long liaison, Arabella Huntington kept her money in the family, as it were, when in 1913, age sixty-three, she married her sixty-four-year-old nephew by marriage and fellow heir, Henry Edwards Huntington.

Arabella Huntington was a strange, imperious woman, whose aristocratic hauteur (so evident in the portrait of her painted by Sir Oswald Birley in 1924, the year of her death) masked a continued fear of discovery. She hid her tracks skillfully—no birth certificate, no baptismal record, no marriage license—but it is very probable that before she met Collis P. Huntington she lived in war-time Richmond, Virginia, as the mistress of a gambler and faro banker, one John Archer Worsham, who, after the war, abandoned her (most likely pregnant) in New York City. In any event, like Scarlett O'Hara, Arabella was a survivor. A few years later she resurfaced as the mistress, lobbyist, and business advisor of Collis P. Huntington, president of the Central Pacific. She eventually became his second wife. Her son Archer was either Huntington's or the result of her early liaison with John Archer Worsham. By 1900 Arabella Huntington had not only survived, she was one of the richest women in the world—and she acted like it, especially in the international art market, where she spent millions. Arabella detested Southern California, preferring Paris instead; so in order to lure her to California, Henry Huntington set about to transform his San Marino estate into a utopia of high culture.

Henry Edwards Huntington took the formula of genteel Pasadena and multiplied it by ten. Pasadena architect Myron Hunt designed in the French classical style and built for Huntington the most lavish private house in Southern California before the construction of the Hearst Castle at San Simeon. Botanist and landscape architect William Hertrich turned the ranch grounds adjacent to the house into the most elaborate private garden in America. Huntington had always loved books. Now he began to collect them with a vengeance, empowered by the second fortune he attained in 1910 when he sold Pacific Electric to the Southern Pacific. He paid $50,000 for a Gutenberg Bible. In December of 1919 he broke the one-day record for sales at Sotheby's of London, spending 110,356 British pounds sterling for English Renaissance materials. Whole libraries were purchased, crated, and shipped to San Marino: the library of Robert Hoe of New York, the Beverly Chen library, the library of the Duke of Devonshire, the E. Dwight Church library (2,133 volumes of rare British and American materials, including the manuscript of Benjamin Franklin's *Autobiography*, the whole selling at $1 million), the F. R. Halsey library ($750,000 for 20,000 items), the MacDonald library of Californiana. In the early 1920s Huntington put his book-buying affairs into the hands of the great bibliographer A. S. W. Rosenbach. By the mid-1920s only the British Museum and the Bodleian Library of Oxford University surpassed Huntington's collection of English Renaissance materials.

Arabella Huntington collected art, and so her husband turned to that field as well, under the guidance of the premier English art dealer, Sir Joseph Duveen. Between 1907 and 1909 Huntington spent $2 million on paintings, tapestries, furniture, and statuary. Gainsborough's "Blue Boy" found its way to San Marino, as well as Reynolds's "Duchess of Devonshire" and Constable's "View on the Stour near Dedham." In 1919 the Huntington Library, Art Gallery, and Botanical Gardens were incorporated as a trust, with George S. Patton, Sr., sitting as one of the founding trustees. A splendid library building was completed in 1919. After the Huntingtons' deaths, their home became the art gallery. The Huntington Library, Art Gallery, and Botanical Gardens eventually became an international mecca for scholars of American history, the English Renaissance, and eighteenth-century art.

II

In contrast to the Huntingtons and others of their ilk, Pasadenans of the Arroyo Seco Culture felt more at home in local circumstances. The Arroyo Culture is the collective designation now given a loosely defined, scattered movement, many of whose protagonists lived, like Charles Fletcher Lummis at El Alisal, along the Arroyo Seco. Although it was touched by the genteel, Arroyo Culture gloried in local circumstances: in Indians and Mexicans, in the blankets, pottery, jewelry, colors, and physical textures of Southern California as desert Spanish Southwest. Orange Grove Avenue Pasadena, the Pasadena of the Valley Hunt Club, kept nature in the middle distance. Arroyo Pasadena—symbolically and to a certain extent in fact—lived on the edge of the wilderness; for the rocks and chaparral of the Arroyo Seco brought the ecology of the untamed interior right into the suburbs. To build homes on the Arroyo, as did these bohemians, was to embrace the symbol of desert wilderness and to glory in Southern California's resistant, elemental texture. On Orange Grove Avenue, the Pasadenan looked out on a lawn and a trimmed hedge. On the Arroyo Seco, he looked out on jackrabbits and chaparral.

Not that the Arroyo Culture was purely nativist in origins. Very few American aesthetic movements are. The Arts and Crafts Movement, of which the Arroyo Culture was a Southern California variation, came to America from England, having in its background the thought of Thomas Carlyle, John Ruskin, and, most importantly, William Morris. The Arts and Crafts Movement sought communality, rusticity, and a neo-medieval appreciation of handicraft: ideas advanced in America by Gustav Stickley's *Craftsman* magazine, but reaching Southern Californians also through such magazines as *House Beautiful, Ladies' Home Journal,* and *Architectural Record.* The houses of the Arroyo—Swiss, Bavarian, semi-Tudor, Shingle in inspiration—were less elaborate than those of Orange Grove Avenue. Home furnishings tended to be in the Mission Revival style popularized by Gustav Stickley, with a generous use of leather, dyed burlap, stained glass, colored tile, and inlaid wood. Pasadenans of the Arroyo Culture loved crafts: bookbinding, stone laying, woodworking, leather, pottery, metalwork. They surrounded themselves with beautiful handmade things. Between 1891 and 1911 a Pasadena institution, Throop Polytechnic Institute, founded in 1891 by Amos G. Throop, a retired Chicago businessman with a passion for crafts, offered instruction in the practical arts. Amos Throop felt that the American middle class was becoming too theoretical and bookish, so he endowed a school to offset this tendency at the same time that Senator Leland Stanford, who held similar ideas, directed that crafts instruction be a mandatory part of the curriculum at his new Palo Alto university. Throop Polytechnic Institute eventually developed into a much different sort of institution, the theory- and research-oriented California Institute of Technology. But while it lasted, its crafts and manual training program gave focus and direction to the Arroyo Culture spirit.

With one exception—George Wharton James's short-lived Arroyo Craftsman Guild—Arroyo Culture was not so much an organized movement as it was a shared lifestyle signifying a related variety of local values. For South Pasadena nurseryman Horatio Nelson Rust, for instance, the style involved a passionate interest in Indian antiquities. A native of Amherst, Massachusetts, who migrated to Chicago after the Civil War, in which he served as a volunteer medical corpsman, Rust was a lifelong antiquarian and amateur archeologist. Coming to South Pasadena in the early 1880s and setting himself up as a wholesale nurseryman, Rust devoted himself to the problem of Indian welfare and the collection of Indian artifacts. (His detractors said he cared more about Indian antiquities than he did about Indians.) Rust played the Yankee to the hilt. He let it slip around town that he had ridden with John Brown in Kansas during the 1850s. He grew a great beard, which made him resemble his mentor, and took an abolitionist-like posture toward the Mission Indians. In the early 1890s he served as United States Indian Agent for the Mission Consolidated Agency.

Rust's friend Adam Clark Vroman ran a bookstore and Kodak agency in Pasadena. An employee of the Burlington Railroad, Vroman came to Southern California in a vain effort to cure his wife's tuberculosis. Widowed, he stayed on, advancing the Arroyo sensibility through photography. He photographed the Arroyo itself in 1900, his camera picking up every detail of its tangled lower reaches. Vroman's photographic essays present to us the world as envisioned through the selective eye of the Arroyo Culture: a Hopi mother nurses her child in an Arizona pueblo, stark and simple and vital with classical dignity; the Very Reverend Father O'Keefe stands in the inner courtyard of Mission San Juan Capistrano sometime in the year 1900, rotund and serene in his friar's robes, his eyes wise with remembrances of things past; boats lie at anchor in Avalon Harbor, Catalina Island, 1895, suggestive of Capri in its curve and bluest of blue water; the Old Mill in Pasadena; the bells of Mission San Gabriel; the forming up of the Pickwick Club for the Tournament of Roses parade of 1900, the men in Dickensian attire, a flower-draped wagon of white-gowned girls in the background.

For the printer Clyde Browne, Arroyo Culture signified something a little more recherché. Architectural scholarship and neo-Franciscan fantasy pervade the Abbey San Encino that Clyde Browne built for himself near Lummis's El Alisal on the Arroyo. Like Lummis at El Alisal, Clyde Browne had the Abbey

San Encino constructed from dressed boulders taken from the Arroyo itself. In the abbey's great hall Browne built a marvelous pipe organ, on which he played for his guests. A stained glass window depicted a Franciscan printer working a handpress with the help of an Indian boy, which was historically untrue (no Franciscan in California ever ran a printing press), but suggestive nevertheless of Browne's conception of himself as a master printer in the early Renaissance tradition of Aldus Manutius: a craftsman-patron of learning, religion, and the arts. Wanting San Encino to develop into a lay monastery of creative artisans, Browne had a series of workshops and studios built near the abbey. There he hoped to gather the best printers, bookbinders, and graphic artists of his day, all of them living and working together under the benevolent sponsorship of Abbot Clyde Browne.

The tile fireplace of Abbey San Encino was designed by another prominent Arroyon, the tile maker Ernest Batchelder, onetime director of art at the Throop Polytechnic Institute, now the owner of a Pasadena kiln where he designed and produced a breathtakingly lovely series of ceramic tiles used in home decoration. Whenever possible, Batchelder employed Southern Californian motifs on his creations (an art nouveau swirl of vines, flowers, oak trees) and bright Southern Californian colors (brown, blue, apricot, yellow). Trained in England at various Arts and Crafts centers and the author of two published treatises on design, Ernest Batchelder ensconced himself in a lovely Swiss-style chalet perched over the Arroyo, where he embodied both the theory and the practice of Arroyo Culture.

The most vocal protagonist and most tireless promoter of Arroyo Culture was George Wharton James, an English-born former Methodist minister who supported himself by a ceaseless round of lecturing and journalism. Born in 1858 in Lincolnshire, England, on the North Sea Coast, James survived a sickly youth and a sparse education to grow up into a booming, virile, self-taught polymath, the author of more than forty books and hundreds of pamphlets and articles. From 1881 to 1887 the Reverend Mr. James served as a Methodist minister in western Nevada, before accepting a pulpit in Long Beach. In 1895 he settled in Pasadena with his second wife and stepdaughter at 1098 North Raymond, a two-story shingle house surrounded by two dozen orange trees. There, in his spacious library, seated in his Craftsman's chair before a walnut rolltop desk, brightly colored Indian baskets and blankets adorning the wall, James did his writing, or, on Tuesday evenings when he was home from his many journeys, held meetings of the Pasadena Browning Society, followed by an open house. Like everyone else, George Wharton James dabbled in real estate and was a booster. He served as social director of the Echo Mountain House, the alpine hotel atop Echo Mountain run by the Mount Lowe Railway. He conducted guided tours for Eastern groups and compiled a still usable series of travel guides to Southern California, Lake Tahoe, Arizona, and Utah. He lectured across the country on an amazing variety of topics—astronomy, ancient history, Indian lore, the literary history of California, the ecology of the Southwest—illustrating his talks with colored slides projected by a Malden Trinopticon, which allowed for the fading in and out of three photographs for dramatic effect. George Wharton James always had a project in hand. Bitten by a rattlesnake in Phoenix, Arizona, he recovered—then marketed his own rattlesnake bite kit. He possessed an excellent baritone voice, having trained himself as a youth in elocution. This onetime Methodist minister preached marvelously and sang well, accompanying himself on the piano or the organ. From 1912 to 1914 he edited *Out West* magazine, the successor to *Land of Sunshine.*

All of this suggests a certain late-nineteenth-early-twentieth-century type: the bluff, hearty, bearded "professor" in a black frock coat (James, incidentally, did use this title, self-awarded), preacher, booster, salesman, huckster, a Wizard of Oz mesmerizing his audiences with words. George Wharton James was all of this, with all the suggestions of hearty confidence; but he was also a hopeless neurotic. As a boy he endured morbid fears—of heights, blood, drunkenness, eternal damnation—all of which he coped with in some way. Fearful of the razor, he never shaved, growing a luxuriant black beard. Frightened by excess, he became a vegetarian, a temperance advocate, and a proselytizing non-smoker. Sickly, he threw himself into a lifetime orgy of bicycling, hiking, swimming, and sunbathing (the latter two in the nude whenever possible). Fearful of heights, he became a skilled mountain climber. Bothered by his interrupted education (a few years of common school), he read heroically, trained his memory, wrote volumes, angled for and attained election to various English learned societies, and proudly called himself Doctor James after Santa Clara University honored him with this title in 1907.

Yet it all did not quite work out. An element of instability, of suppressed hysteria, remained. James overworked himself to the verge of collapse, then was forced to go to sanitariums for recovery. (In 1923 he died in a Seventh-Day Adventist sanitarium at St. Helena in the Napa Valley of pneumonia compounded by exhaustion.) In the spring of 1889 his first wife, herself unstable, threw him out of their Long Beach home, accusing him of threatened violence and gross sexual misconduct, including incest and the multiple seduction of a sixtyish lady and her three daughters. James leveled a countercharge of adultery, committed (and later admitted, he claimed) when his wife had returned home to England for a visit. It was a messy divorce. James pounded on the door of his home, threatening suicide if he could not see his children. Mrs. James called the police. She leveled awful charges against him during the court proceedings. Panicked, the Methodist elders removed James from his Long Beach pastorate, then defrocked him. (He was later reinstated by the church and cleared of all charges.) In the spring of 1889 George Wharton James, not surprisingly, suffered a nervous collapse.

Like Charles Fletcher Lummis, James went to the Southwest to recover. He lived with Indians, explored the Grand Canyon, spent time in small towns, hiking or riding in the desert. There in the Southwest, he later wrote, he recovered his health and nervous equilibrium. As a spokesman for Arroyo Culture, George Wharton James could vigorously and unambivalently advocate the aesthetic Southwesternism which the Arroyo Culture nurtured as one of its main tenets of faith. Like Lummis, James had been born again in the Southwest. Ever a health faddist, James especially approved of the desert Indians' manner of natural living: their diet, their lack of nervous instability, their unselfconscious sex lives, their rapport with their environment. He became interested in Indian crafts, basketry and blanket weaving especially, writing books on the subject in which, among other things, he praised the psychologically therapeutic value of these handicrafts when practiced by whites. As a protagonist of the Arroyo Culture, James consolidated an eclectic but workable philosophy which he felt had value for all of Southern California. It consisted of a liberal Protestant base laced with New Thought high-mindedness and a dash of Browningesque optimism, the whole flavored by the semi-mysticism of Swedenborg and an attraction to Hindu thought. The outdoor life, in the desert and the Southwest particularly, and the Arts and Crafts Movement (James became associate editor of the *Craftsman* in 1904), together with an interest in the Indian crafts of the Southwest, were fixed by James as essential elements of the Southern Californian style. James brought this sensibility to the editorship of the *Arroyo Craftsman* (1909)—"a quarterly magazine," so he described it, "of simple living, high thinking, pure democracy, genuine art, honest craftsmanship, natural inspiration, and exalted aspiration." The *Arroyo Craftsman* spoke for the Arroyo Guild, an association of Arroyo artisans who hoped to plan, build, and furnish homes for new Southern Californians in the Arroyo style. "They will plan your home," James promised, "whether it be a palace or a bungalow, they will design its every detail; the stained glass, the wall and ceiling decorations, the hangings of every description, the carpets, the furniture, the mantles, the gas and electric fixtures, the vases, the pictures—and all will be done with that rational, systematic harmony which comes of experience and expert knowledge."

This ambitious program was more dream than fact. The *Arroyo Craftsman* folded after one issue, and to this day scholars are still trying to find out just how coherent or effective a group the Arroyo Guild ever really was. It had a president, apparently, the artist Walter Judson, dean of the USC School of Fine Arts. James served as secretary—but that seems to be the extent of it. James, most likely, was trying (unsuccessfully, as it turned out) to call the guild into fuller being by providing it with the journal that folded after one issue. What is important, however, about the *Arroyo Craftsman*, volume one, number one (and only!) is its expression of the Arroyoan ideal: the spiritualization of daily life through an aestheticism tied to crafts and local materials. Like the ethos of

Pasadena in particular and Southern California culture as a whole, this was a strongly domestic ideal. The impending era of simplicity, health, peace, content (James's categories), "of pure, simple, democratic art," would begin at home, so James and the other Arroyoans believed, and would be expressed primarily through the home. Southern California, James asserted, was destined to become the great center of aesthetic expression in America. In that rise to aesthetic preeminence, no art would be more important to Southern California than the art of domestic living.

Southern Californians were doing their best to live well along the Arroyo, led by Charles Fletcher Lummis at El Alisal, who could not stand George Wharton James. The Englishman crowded Lummis's territory. The Arroyo had room but for one prophet of place. In September 1901, James, ever rushed, made the mistake of publishing a faked article in a London magazine, in which he falsely claimed to have witnessed the sacred fire dance of the Navaho. He had lifted the information about the ceremony from an essay by Dr. Washington Matthews (a friend of Lummis and a *Land of Sunshine* contributor) published in the fifth annual report of the American Bureau of Ethnology. Gleefully, Lummis crucified James in the *Land of Sunshine*. Although it was of no relevance, he even brought up the matter of the Long Beach scandal of twelve years earlier. Showing no mercy, Lummis kept up the attack for the next twenty years, until James's death in 1923. James's indiscretion in the Navaho article, however, together with a half dozen other examples of hasty workmanship, cannot detract from his accomplishments as a writer on the Southwest. James's books— *In and Around the Grand Canyon* (1900), *Indian Basketry* (1901), *Indians of the Painted Desert Region* (1903), *The Wonders of the Colorado Desert* (1906), *What the White Race May Learn from the Indian* (1908), among others—are classics of Southwestern writing. Only one book of Lummis's, *The Spanish Pioneers* (1893), shows comparable achievement; Lummis himself most likely suspected this, and this rekindled his animus.

As brutal as he was to George Wharton James, however, Lummis could be generous to fledgling young writers, many of whom he published in *Land of Sunshine*. Contemporaneously with Hamlin Garland's *Crumbling Idols* (1894), Lummis did his best to promote the local-color movement. He pointed out that most great literature was in one way or another regional. As a region, Southern California and the Southwest possessed all the raw materials of art. All that was needed was imagination, effort—and talent. Theoretically, at least, Lummis had no use for the second-rate. He wanted writers committed to Southern Californian and Southwestern themes and materials, and not New York dropouts choosing the Southland as a second-best place. "Here," he claimed of Southern California, "is no asylum of failures; no conspiracy of literary soreheads to beprint us with whatever thing Eastern editors have refused; no summoning of strangers to make or manage our literature. We are nearly all graduate Easterners. We know and respect and love the old home; we have chosen the new simply because it is so much better worth living in. We read the Eastern magazines, and help to make them, and have no desire to compete with them—but merely to fulfill a certain special need which they do not and cannot quench."

The masthead of *Land of Sunshine* reads like a who's who of turn-of-the-century California letters. Organizing what he called "a syndicate of western writers," Lummis tried to promote upcoming California talent in his book review column, "That Which Is Written." He immediately recognized Frank Norris's *McTeague* (1899) and *The Octopus* (1901), for instance, as California classics, praising their sweep and energy. He welcomed the collected short stories of a twenty-five-year-old Oakland roustabout-turned-writer, Jack London, predicting a great future for him. As an Arroyoan, Lummis favored writers who dealt directly with Southern Californian and Southwestern themes: the poet Sharlott Hall, for instance, of Prescott, Arizona, or Eugene Manlove Rhodes, a cowboy poet from New Mexico. One of his writers, the stylish, doe-eyed Gwendolen Overton of Los Angeles, had been raised in the army forts of Arizona and New Mexico by her officer father, then sent to France for a little polishing. Lummis praised her first novel, *The Heritage of Unrest* (1901), a tale of Arizona during the Apache uprisings of the 1870s, for its vivid depiction of locale and its firsthand knowledge of Apache and Mexican life. He also ran a photograph of the superbly handsome Miss Overton, which he himself took, catching her flattered but quizzical look as—who knows?—she half suspiciously sorted out the full range and implications of Lummis's approval. He published short stories of West Coast Chinese life by Sui Sin Fah, a half-English, half-Chinese Los Angeles stenographer, and ran *A Soul in Bronze*, an Indian novel by Constance Goddard DuBois, in which the Indian hero not only does not get the white heroine but is condemned to life in prison, a fate which he accepts with stoical resignation.

Near Lummis lived Ida Meacham Strobridge, a Mills College graduate who had put in twenty years as a rancher's wife in Nevada before moving to the Arroyo in about 1900, after her husband had died and her sons were grown. Opening the Artemesia Bindery, Strobridge did bookbinding and set up exhibitions of local painting. She also kept a salon, competition that made Lummis a little nervous. In any event, he began publishing Strobridge's desert stories when she was still in Nevada and continued to do so after her arrival on the Arroyo. Two of Ida Meacham Strobridge's books, *The Loom of the Desert* (1907) and *The Land of Purple Shadows* (1909), remain classic descriptions of desert living.

Gwendolen Overton, Sui Sin Fah, Constance Goddard DuBois, Ida Meacham Strobridge—Lummis favored women writers, and none more so than a hauntingly beautiful Occidental College undergraduate, Nora May French. A spirited horsewoman and lover of the sea, Nora May French wrote poems bristling with realized Southern California imagery—the sundown Pacific, the Arroyo itself, a mission garden, sagebrush, desert flowers—all of it put in service to a pervasive plaintiveness, a sadness she felt at the heart of things, as if she foresaw her own fate. Or was this sadness a self-fulfilling prophecy? After all, she would later claim that "all sensible people will ultimately be damned." In any event, she of the curly hair and the soft eyes was dead from cyanide of potassium in the early hours of 14 November 1907 on George Sterling's porch in Carmel: done in by her vulnerability to eros (a succession of affairs, a number of abortions), sick with confusion over having loved unwisely and not well. At the funeral services on Point Lobos, a quarrel broke out among a number of men as to who would have the right to cast her ashes into the sea.

Robinson Jeffers, another Occidental College poet published in *Out West*, was destined to go the distance as both man and poet. Then in his late teens, Jeffers contributed two poems to Lummis, neither of which showed any hint of his future powers. Although Robinson Jeffers had another decade of apprenticeship to serve, he was taking his first steps in poetry as part of the Arroyo scene, and the characteristics of an Arroyoan—learning, a love of the outdoors, a certain refinement of perception and diction—were well rooted in him. As befitted even this shirttail Arroyoan, Robinson Jeffers was of upper-middle-class stock, his father being a well-off Old Testament scholar who in 1903 moved to Highland Park on the Arroyo west of Pasadena, where Lummis built El Alisal. Professor Jeffers had left Pittsburgh for Southern California in the hopes of improving his health. At sixteen his son Robinson entered Occidental College, a Presbyterian school in Highland Park. Already an accomplished scholar, fluent in Italian, French, and German (mastered during boyhood sojourns in Continental boarding schools), Jeffers continued at Occidental the studies in Latin and Greek he had begun at home under his father, who started his son off in Greek when the boy was only five. By virtue of this devoted bookishness, Robinson Jeffers was already an Arroyoan. While in boarding schools in Zurich and Leipzig, Jeffers had become an accomplished alpinist. In one school, in fact, he was known as "the little spartan" because of his strength and skill at mountaineering. Moving to the West Coast, Jeffers fell in love with the mountains of Southern California. He made innumerable trips into various ranges by foot or on horseback, defying the mountainous silence (so one college friend remembered) with lusty quotations from Homer in the original Greek and from Tennyson. He also was an excellent swimmer, a long-distance runner, and a championship wrestler in the heavyweight class.

Bookish, genteel, a Presbyterian of New England stock, an avid outdoorsman, Robinson Jeffers fit easily into the Arroyoan landscape. His passion for learning was to continue through graduate studies in literature and medicine at USC (he entered medical school solely for the scientific education, never intending to practice) and a semester's study of forestry at the University of Washington in Seattle. With proper Arroyoan foresight (for all its assumed simplicity, the Arroyoan lifestyle depended upon a ready supply of cash), Jeffers also had a small but adequate legacy, which he eventually used to support a life of semi-reclusive rusticity on the Big Sur coast south of Carmel. With his own money he subsidized the publication of his first book of poems, *Flagons and Apples* (1912), paying for so many copies they were a glut on the market for years after. The appearance of *Californians* (1916), published by Macmillan— no subsidy was necessary—proved that Robinson Jeffers, then near thirty, was the finest poet at work in California. He remained such for the next forty years.

Californians is a collection of Wordsworthian pastorals set mainly in Southern California's coastal and hill country. The San Bernardino Range, Old Baldy (Mount San Antonio), Grayback (Mount San Gorgonio), Mount San Gabriel, La Jolla, Redondo Beach, the Santa Lucia Range, the Santa Ynez Valley—like an Arroyoan, Jeffers constructed his house of poetry from local materials. Much of the poetry of *Californians* is derivative, as if Wordsworth had come to the Southland, yet its conjunction of vividly specific locale and symbolic drama boded well for the future. By the time of the volume's publication Jeffers had left for Big Sur, but *Californians* made its major contribution through its Arroyoan commitment to Southern Californian materials. In the work of his apprenticeship, Robinson Jeffers showed what could be done with the life and landscape of Southern California. Robinson Jeffers, however, could never remain content with a merely descriptive mode. He was meant for better—and more bitterly tragic—things. The Arroyo, after all, banished tragedy in favor of an arts-and-crafts conception of the good life, and certainly there are moments in even the early *Flagons and Apples* which no proper Arroyoan could approve of: moments such as when the poet, hearing a drinking Mexican couple quarreling at twilight near the old plaza church, says to his beloved:

> How simple were life—how human
> If I were a drunken cholo,
> And you my dark-skinned woman!

No, no indeed: the Arroyo would never approve!

Charles Fletcher Lummis published Jeffers. Ultimately, however, Robinson Jeffers followed the star of his own superior talent. So did Mary Austin, the greatest Arroyoan of them all—if Arroyoan she ever truly was; for, although committed to the spirit of the Arroyo, Mary Austin, like Jeffers, sustained an independent vision. She came to El Alisal from Independence in the Owens Valley to see Lummis in the late summer of 1899—a shortish, slightly dumpy woman, unfavored by beauty and already, in her early thirties, touched by tragedy: a retarded child and a marriage that was not working out. She unloaded on Lummis all her hopes for a writing career, talking (he noted in his diary) some four hours straight, even while he barbecued a beefsteak. She had moved to Los Angeles, Austin told Lummis, on a trial separation from her husband, Stafford Austin—by turns a vineyardist, irrigationist, schoolteacher, and civil servant—and was supporting herself as a teacher of pedagogy at the State Normal School in the city (later UCLA). Lummis had already published some of her poetry and would eventually run four short stories, more poetry, and a novella in five installments. He found a house on the Arroyo for her use and invited her to his "noises," where she met and became friendly with such other Arroyoans as Ida Strobridge (another desert dweller) and Dr. Frederick Webb Hodge, the authority on Indian anthropology from whom she learned much that would later prove of use to her writing. Back in Independence, a remote agricultural community, she had suffered severe criticism for her bohemian ways; now, at El Alisal, the provincial woman aspiring to the life of art encountered such dynamic personalities as the naturalist John Burroughs, the opera singer Mary Gordon, and Helena Modjeska, the actress, all so electric with the ambience of life lived for art and the great world beyond Los Angeles. Lummis's sickly son Amado, who died soon after, played with Mary Austin's retarded child Ruth, destined herself to die in an institution as a young adult.

When she returned to Independence in 1900, her problems with her shaky marriage still unresolved, Mary Austin wrote Lummis requesting a handwritten copy of something he had written in his *Land of Sunshine* column, "In the Lion's Den," so that she could frame it and hang it over her writing desk. "Man is made to be bigger than anything that can happen to him," Lummis had written. "He was made to master first himself, and then whatever he runs against— obstacles, perplexities, dangers, sorrows. He *can* if he will; and the man who will is educated." A trifle bromidic perhaps, and who knows?—Mary Austin might have only been trying to flatter Lummis by asking for it in the first place. But then again, she could have been sincere, for when she returned to Independence, given her unresolved personal situation, the way to art was not yet clear. That year, however, she placed her daughter in a private home and began selling her stories to magazines more distinguished than the *Land of Sunshine*—to the *Atlantic Monthly, Cosmopolitan*, and *St. Nicholas*. "Another voice crying out in the wilderness," Lummis had written of her, "and not in vain." Now the East heard this voice also, and Lummis was a little miffed. He criticized her inaccurate use of Spanish. He said that she had talent and industry, but little genius. She, for her part, detected in him the poseur, the pseudoromantic, and, worse, the exploiter of women. She felt, so she later reminisced in her autobiography, *Earth Horizon* (1932), that Lummis "rested too much on the lesser achievement; on working too many hours a day; on sleeping too little; on drinking too much; on his wife's translations of Spanish manuscripts." Mary Austin was referring to Lummis's second wife, Eva Douglas, an accomplished Hispanicist whom he met in New Mexico when he was recovering from his stroke and whom he married in 1891. Lummis had secretly married his first wife, Dorothea Rhodes, a Boston University medical student, in 1880 when a junior at Harvard. He was, so Mary Austin claimed, embroiled in a paternity suit at the time (true) and used Dorothea as an escape (debatable; however, Lummis's illegitimate daughter did eventually join his household). Personally, Mary Austin liked both of the Mrs. Charles Fletcher Lummises. Feminist to the core, she accused Lummis of having asked too much of both women—which, of course, reflected her anger at her own ne'er-do-well husband, who had asked her to content herself with the career of a dutiful ranch wife, bound to his unstable career and the exhausting, heartbreaking demands of caring for a retarded child.

And this, Mary Austin continued with sharp tongue and with a pen dipped in the terrible gall of spurned protégéeship, brought up another point. Lummis loved to go on and on about the land, the desert, the Southwest, yet at heart, Mary Austin chided, he was a Los Angeles booster. He had never made his living off the land, as she had, and it was the water-hoggery of Los Angeles, promoted by Harrison Gray Otis, the *Los Angeles Times*, Lummis and company, that destroyed the Owens Valley, thereby destroying the Austins—or at least Mr. Stafford Austin, Mary's former husband; for by that time (1906) Mary was living upcountry in Carmel, working full time as a writer. In short, to Mary's way of thinking, Lummis was a Grade A phony—playing the Harvard man when he had never taken his degree there (he flunked trigonometry and analytical geometry); making much of his Spanish scholarship and his friendships with academics like David Starr Jordan, president of Stanford, but never really possessing the willpower and the concentration of mind necessary for substantive scholarly achievement.

But no matter: whatever their differences, Lummis and Austin, flawed and quarreling personalities, were partially reconciled by the spirit of the Arroyo. Whatever opinions she came to hold regarding Lummis, Mary Austin had in fact been pointed by Don Carlos in a direction which he knew that he himself could never fully follow: the direction of dedication to art. To his credit, Lummis welcomed Mary Austin's first book, *The Land of Little Rain* (1903), as the masterpiece it was. Over the years, Mary Austin was to produce some skilled and interesting fiction: *Isidro* (1905), for instance, a novel of the California missions; *Santa Lucia* (1908), a love story set in a small California college town; *Outland* (1910), a fantasy narrative dealing with Carmel; the pioneering feminist novels *A Woman of Genius* (1912), *The Lovely Lady* (1913), and *26 Jayne Street* (1920); and *The Ford* (1917), a novel dealing with the Owens Valley–Los Angeles controversy over water rights. But she reached her greatest creativity as an essayist, as a literary landscapist and master of style. Her evocative poetic portraits of California and the Southwest—*The Land of Little Rain* (1903), *The Flock* (1906), *Lost Borders* (1909), *California, Land of the Sun* (1914), *The Land of Journeys' Ending* (1924)—together with her autobiography, *Earth Ho-*

rizon (1932), are one and all tours de force: prose poems of vision and grace, in which perception, intuition, and mystical insight are realized and presented through metaphor, cadenced language, and exquisite precision of detail. These books evoke Southern California and the Southwest as regions of dramatic beauty and immemorial mystery, akin to the classic landscapes of the ancient world.

III

Mary Austin's literary landscapes resembled the landscapes of painting in their line and color and in their studied arrangements of topographical features. The effort to discern pattern and to celebrate the landscape of Southern California through painting proceeded apace with the other arts. Like every other phase of Southland life, the great leap forward occurred in the mid-1800s. Initially, artists were slow to take up permanent residence south of the Tehachapis. A certain Mrs. C. P. Bradfield arrived in 1874 from New York, losing all her previously completed paintings in a steamer shipwreck. Supporting herself as an art teacher at the Los Angeles Catholic girls' school run by the Sisters of Mary, Mrs. Bradfield turned out an astonishingly vivid series of wildflower still lifes which were awarded a medal at the World's Fair in London. Another New Yorker, Paul Petrovits, a sixty-five-year-old artist married to an attractive but flirtatious twenty-three-year-old woman, arrived in Los Angeles in 1876, thinking the climate would be good for his health. Petrovits set himself up briefly in the Pico House as a portrait painter and experienced great success. A year in South America followed this brief stint in Los Angeles, whereupon the restless Petrovits (fleeing his wife's suitors, perhaps) moved back to the North American West—this time Virginia City, Nevada—before sailing to Australia, where he at last murdered his wife in a fit of jealous rage, and was hanged.

With such fitful beginnings as these, it is not surprising that a taste for painting was slow to develop in Los Angeles. In 1878 a painting entitled "The Morning Bath" was exhibited in the front window of Pruess's Drug Store in downtown Los Angeles and caused controversy because of its depiction of female flesh. It was finally removed. In 1891 the Los Angeles police chief ordered optician M. H. Alter to remove "Sale of Circassian Girls at the Base of the Pyramids" from his front window for similar reasons.

Despite such setbacks, matters artistic eventually showed signs of improvement. Founded in 1888 by culture-starved Los Angelenos, the Ruskin Art Club of Los Angeles two years later opened an informal museum and art gallery in rented rooms. In January 1891 the club began a series of annual exhibitions with an impressive display of 341 etchings and prints, including 18 prints by Albrecht Durer, 11 Rembrandts, and works by Claude Lorraine, Millet, Meissonier, and Whistler. An artists' league, the Society of Fine Arts of Southern California, was incorporated in February 1895. That November, eighty-four paintings by twenty-five Southern Californian artists were exhibited by the society in rooms made available by the Los Angeles Chamber of Commerce. This show announced the solid beginnings of a regional school. No artist was more instrumental in getting this regional tradition underway than the well-traveled, well-educated bon vivant, outdoorsman, painter, and violinist John Bond Francisco.

A bluff, hearty Theodore Roosevelt sort of person, given to outdoorsiness and Tory bohemianism, John Bond Francisco grew up in Los Angeles before leaving for European study (Berlin, Munich, Paris) of painting and the violin. In addition to his painting, Francisco served as concertmaster of the Los Angeles Symphony Orchestra, which he helped found. He also taught both painting and the violin, in between bouts of hunting, fishing, and socializing, which he loved with a passion and carried on in the grand manner he had acquired on the Continent. To do his work and to entertain his guests, Francisco built for himself a marvelous home on the outskirts of Los Angeles. It boasted a sixty-five-foot-long combination studio, music room, and art gallery, done in polished redwood, where Francisco exhibited his own considerable private collection of European art, played chamber music with local string players, painted pictures, and entertained lavishly the visiting great or near great, especially the theatrical and musical people whom Francisco adored. Victor Herbert came, and so did Sarah Bernhardt and Lillian Russell, and once an entire opera company, which partied throughout a long musical night. "He was made for big things," said Francisco's good friend George Wharton James, "—big mountains, big trees, big outlook." He also lived big and had big expenses.

Francisco did for the landscape of Southern California what Albert Bierstadt, another high-living Tory bohemian, did for the landscape of the North: painted it in the Barbizon style for wealthy Easterners willing to pay well to possess romantic landscapes. Francisco's success—his home, his parties, his upper-class associations (good clubs, an excellent wine cellar, social prestige), his well-heeled safaris into the hinterlands and mountains of Southern California, which he loved to paint, and painted well—conferred respectability on the artist's calling in Los Angeles. More importantly, however, John Bond Francisco showed that it could be done: that life could be lived for art in Los Angeles and Southern California with panache and financial success. A community leader and a social lion, John Bond Francisco was also a devoted practitioner of the arts. The very Toryness of the man—his physical vigor, his skills at hunting and fishing, his delight in playing the lavish paterfamilias to his large family, his upper-class demeanor and associations, his skills as a host and social lion—now seem in retrospect very much part of what is coming to be called the American Renaissance era: the turn-of-the-century time of hearty men with imperial ambitions, exuberantly bestriding the stage of Teddy Roosevelt's and Stanford White's America. For provincial Los Angeles, moreover, John Bond Francisco bespoke

Art. His German, his French, his celebrity friends from music and the theater dazzled contemporary Los Angelenos and filled them with pride that Culture was at last coming to the Southland.

Other turn-of-the-century Southern California painters—William Lees Judson, Elmer Wachtel, John Gutzon Borglum, and Maynard Dixon, for instance—carried on less flamboyantly than John Bond Francisco, but with a parallel pioneering earnestness. Many of them lived out along the Arroyo, and together they constituted an informal but discernible Arroyo School. William Lee Judson, in fact, served as the one and only president of the Arroyo Craftsman Guild. English-born, New York- and Paris-trained (the Julian Academy), a Civil War veteran and a seventeen-year resident of London, William Lee Judson came to Southern California from Chicago in 1893 in very bad health. Like a lot of people then arriving in the Southland, Judson expected to die. Unlike so many others, he survived, living on until 1928, professor, later dean, at the University of Southern California College of Fine Arts, which he deliberately built not at the downtown campus but out on the Arroyo Seco at Garvanza (now Highland Park). While a student in Paris, Judson had fallen in love with the "sunkissed, light-emblazoned and color-illumined canvases" of Manet. To the perception and painting of Southern California in all its various modes, Judson imported Manet's palette together with his own local brand of impressionism tempered by realism. Seascapes, the missions, and the Arroyo Seco were Judson's favorite subjects. Laguna, San Pedro, Santa Catalina, La Jolla, the Arroyo Seco—Judson worked steadily and well at his landscapes and seascapes. His influence as a teacher was enormous. If John Bond Francisco brought bravado and dash to the Southern California scene, William Lee Judson brought patience and technique. Painting in Southern California throughout the 1895–1915 period shows his pervasive influence, his uneasy impressionism above all else: uneasy because Judson was constantly tempted to document the Southland, to fix it for the record, as if it had never been seen or painted before, which was partially the case.

Stimulated by the colors of Manet, Judson rediscovered these colors in the land and sea and sky of the Southland. Watercolorist Elmer Wachtel also employed an exciting palette of the special colors he saw throughout Southern California country. Elmer Wachtel lived on the Arroyo Seco with his wife, Marian Kavanagh, also an artist, in a rustic house at the foot of the Sierra Madre. He had arrived in Southern California in the early 1890s at age eighteen, an Illinois farm boy, virtually self-taught in painting and the violin, out west to get a job at the Sunnyslope Ranch in San Gabriel, which his older brother managed. There Elmer Wachtel fell in love with the landscape of the Southland. Saving his earnings as a ranch hand and, later, a furniture store clerk, Wachtel studied at the Art Students' League in New York, then at the Lambeth Art School in London, where he also improved his abilities as a violinist to the point that, like John Bond Francisco, he played professionally in Los Angeles.

Possessed thoroughly by the spirit of the Arroyo, Wachtel wooed the wild landscape of his region, realizing it through a range of subtle but strong colors: the brown-green of the grass in the Santa Anita Canyon at midwinter; the golden browns and yellows of October sunshine in the Santa Paula Valley; violet and purple, discerned in the distant hills from the floor of Ojai Valley; sycamores, yellow-pink to tender green at various seasons; the summertime russet settling over Monrovia Canyon; the pale amethyst in the sky over La Canada Hills; the opalescent mists over the wild, unsettled San Fernando Valley; a brook dashing laterally across Topanga Canyon. Wachtel celebrated Southern California as a landscape not of semi-arid monotony but of shifting and dramatic variations, and occasional luxuriance. Working exclusively in watercolor—a medium that makes its point simply through color itself—Wachtel sometimes verged upon abstraction, so vivid were the color-dramas of his landscapes. For John Bond Francisco the landscape of Southern California nurtured a robust romanticism; for William Lee Judson it was possessed of a lyrical luminosity, conditioned by a haze of outline. Elmer Wachtel saw color, color, color everywhere around him, persistent, assertive color, and he painted Southern California accordingly.

As an art student in London, Elmer Wachtel shared *la vie bohème* in the studio of another art-obsessed Los Angeleno, a Danish-American raised on the Nebraskan frontier and brought to Los Angeles in 1884 by his physician father, who had grown tired of winters on the Great Plains. Even at this early date, the mid-1890s, John Gutzon Borglum was doing rather well. Borglum would always do rather well. He achieved, in fact, the greatest degree of personal fame of all these early Southern California artists. Apprenticed to a Los Angeles lithographer, Borglum began painting on his own. Charles Fletcher Lummis first met him at this time, and saw in the teenaged Borglum's rude, self-taught canvases the promise of better things. Encouraged by Lummis, a group of Los Angeles businessmen got up a purse to send Borglum north to San Francisco to study under Virgil Williams and William Keith at the Art Institute. Upon his return to Los Angeles, Mrs. Jessie Benton Frémont, who had played the patroness fifty years before in San Francisco to the likes of Thomas Starr King, Charles Warren Stoddard, and Bret Harte, now took John Gutzon Borglum under her wing. Borglum did a portrait of General Frémont just before the Pathfinder's death, and a commanding bronze bust of Mrs. Frémont herself. She, in turn, secured for him introductions to the great—the Huntingtons, the Stanfords, even Theodore Roosevelt—which blossomed eventually into commissions.

By 1890, in fact, Borglum had made enough money from the sale of his paintings to go to Paris to study at the Academie Julian and L'École des Beaux Arts. The recessive feminism of impressionism, however, turned Borglum off. He believed that a more assertive art was appropriate to the American West, so he switched to an informal apprenticeship under the sculptor Rodin. Borglum's later medallion, "Father Throop," commemorative of the founder of the Throop Institute, would be very much in the Rodin manner. In letters home to the *Los Angeles Times*, Borglum insisted that he was in Paris to learn technique and technique only. His strength and his inspiration, he claimed, came from Southern California and the West. Practicing what he preached, Borglum exhibited two Western sculptures in Paris exhibitions: "Mort du Chef" in 1891 (horse comforting a dying Indian war chief), and "Scouts" in 1892. Both won medals, and Borglum was elected an associate of the Société Nationale des Beaux Arts. After travel in Spain (1891–92), Borglum returned to Southern California and set himself up in a Sierra Madre cottage tucked amid grapevines and orange and lemon trees. "There is," he remarked at the time, "enough beauty in nature here to keep me painting for a lifetime."

Borglum helped Lummis give *Land of Sunshine* its "look," to use a modern graphic term. He designed its cover and its logo, a mountain lion framed by a setting Southwestern sun. He published a personal testament in the magazine entitled "An Artist's Paradise," in which he praised the color, texture, and general paintability of the Southern California landscape. "We have only begun," he exulted, "our artists are thoroughly in earnest, and as independent of the prevailing eccentricities of Impressionism as if we lived on another planet. In fact in California we are quite in another world. The art influence here is so direct and so pure, that Benjamin Constant remarked in 1892 that the young men from California came better prepared for the deeper studies than those from New York."

Shortly after offering this paean to Southern California as a painter's paradise, Borglum returned to Europe, dissatisfied with what he considered the mean-minded provinciality of Southern Californians. In November 1894 some wretch poisoned all four of Borglum's Great Danes. The incident angered him because he loved the dogs but also because Borglum considered the poisonings a personal warning to get out of town, which he did. After a short period of struggle, Borglum took London by storm. His paintings sold, and solid rewards soon followed: a suburban villa in St. John's Wood, for instance, the city's upperbrow bohemia; membership in the Royal Society of British Artists; the notice of Queen Victoria herself; weekends at country estates, painting the portraits of the rich and the titled; lavish parties for his friends, at which Isadora Duncan, another Californian expatriate, danced for the guests. In 1902 Borglum returned to the United States and pursued a successful national career. He is best known today as the sculptor of Mount Rushmore.

Charles Fletcher Lummis's closest friend among the artists he promoted in *Land of Sunshine* was Lafayette Maynard Dixon. Dixon was not an easy man to know. There was an aloofness, an essential reserve, to his personality—a sardonic detachment masking the passionate, raging life within. Born in 1875 in

Fresno of Southern stock, Maynard Dixon grew up an asthmatic, lonely boy, possessed of a sense of caste. His father, Harry St. John Dixon, a Mississippi plantation owner, acquitted himself bravely in the Confederate cavalry during the War Between the States, only to lose everything during Reconstruction. Migrating to the San Joaquin Valley in Central California, the one time plantation owner and cavalryman began anew as a lawyer-rancher. Maynard Dixon's maternal grandfather, Lafayette Maynard, who had resigned his naval commission in 1846 in protest against what he felt was an unjust war against Mexico, settled in San Francisco as a venture capitalist and leader of the fashionable Southern set. In Fresno, young Maynard Dixon had status. Until he suffered a nervous breakdown, Maynard's father took the lead in local political and civic affairs. When the Veterans of the Blue and Gray (organized by his father) marched down Fresno's main thoroughfare, young Maynard Dixon led the parade as drummer boy. Frail, high-strung, asthmatic, Maynard Dixon nevertheless knew from boyhood that he was destined to be an artist. He began drawing at the age of seven. As a young teenager he studied the illustrations in *Harper's, Scribner's*, the *Art Journal*, developing a quick, direct sketching style of his own. At sixteen he sent a portfolio of his work to the great Western illustrator Frederic Remington, who responded with warm encouragement, telling the young Fresnan that he sketched better than Remington himself had at a comparable age. Dixon quit high school soon after, preferring to educate himself. This pattern of inner-directed independence, in matters of both life and art, would be a lifelong characteristic. "So live," Maynard Dixon would be saying by 1896 (he was actually quoting Charles Fletcher Lummis), "that you can look every damn man in the eye and tell him to go to hell."

After spending a mere three months at the San Francisco Art Institute in 1893, Dixon, age nineteen, quit art school to support himself as a free-lance illustrator. In 1895 he joined the *San Francisco Morning Call* as a staff artist, transferring later to William Randolph Hearst's *Examiner* when he got a better offer. At the *Examiner*, Dixon designed and illustrated the Sunday supplement, working with such *Examiner*-connected worthies as Frank Norris, Jack London (whose stories Dixon illustrated for the *Overland Monthly*), Ambrose Bierce, Edwin Markham, and Kathleen Norris. He hated being chained to a desk, however, or being at the beck and call of an editor, so in early 1900 he left full-time newspaper work and began supporting himself as a free-lancer for the *Chronicle*, the *Bulletin, Sunset*, and the *Pacific Monthly*.

In the December 1898 *Land of Sunshine*, Charles Fletcher Lummis gave Maynard Dixon his first public critical recognition. Dixon and Lummis soon became friends and began a twenty-year correspondence. Dixon came down to Los Angeles to do the decorative metal work for El Alisal, where Dixon and his first wife were married. "Pop Lummis," Dixon later said, "was in effect my foster father over those years. Lummis gave me new confidence in my ideals of truthfulness in my work, and fortitude in facing the commercial world." Lummis also turned Dixon in the direction of the subject matter of his major creativity, the Spanish Southwest, including Southern California. In 1900 Lummis offered to arrange a tour of the Southwest for Dixon, who financed the expedition with a thousand dollars he had saved while working on the *Examiner*. A trip to the Southwest, Lummis wrote Dixon in San Francisco, would alleviate the nervous strain Dixon was suffering from and help him give focus to his developing talent. Lummis introduced Dixon to the Indians of Isleta Pueblo in New Mexico. The head man of the pueblo, Juan Rey Albeita, took Lummis and Dixon in for a stay of several weeks.

Seeing the Indians going about their daily lives, reverberating to the drama of desert color, the cloud-architecture of the sky, Dixon found his life's work as a painter—or at least the subject of his life's work, for it would be twelve years before he was financially able to devote himself full time to painting. He returned to Arizona in 1902, staying this time at Ganado with Indian trader J. L. Hubbell, who lived like an old Spanish hidalgo, surrounded by Navaho retainers. During this second trip Dixon made the first of many extensive stays with the Hopi and the Navaho, whom he considered a noble people, Homeric in dignity. Eventually, Maynard Dixon would fill hundreds of canvases with Hopi and Navaho subjects in various guises and attitudes—craftsman, shaman, shepherd, weaver, warrior, worshipper—caught in bright color, rivaling that of the desert itself, and presented with the bold, direct technique of Dixon's mature style. Like another *Land of Sunshine* artist, Mary Austin, Maynard Dixon found in the Spanish Southwest, land and people, the anti-type of, and the antidote for, the soul sickness of hyper-self-conscious modernism. The Indian, Dixon believed, lived and moved and had his being in an older, better way of knowledge and behavior.

IV

Meanwhile, as the Arroyans daydreamed of Indians and the desert and lined the walls of their rustic cottages with Navaho blankets, another Los Angeles was in the making: a city that by 1905 had 350 miles of graded streets, more automobiles and telephones (40,000) than any comparably sized city in the United States, and a new sort of eating place, a cafeteria, where you could serve yourself and save time. The first theater in the United States to show motion pictures opened in Los Angeles in 1902. It seated two hundred and cost ten cents a ticket. Four years later two Los Angelenos, George Van Guysling and Otis M. Grove, opened a studio in Los Angeles for film production. They did their outdoor filming on a ranch outside the city, in an area soon to be known as Hollywood. In 1908 a film version of *The Count of Monte Cristo* became the first feature-length film completed in California. The next year its producer,

Colonel William Selig, owner of the Selig Polyscope Company of Chicago, filmed a second feature-length film, *The Heart of a Race Horse Tout*, in and around the Santa Anita race track in the San Gabriel Valley in downtown Los Angeles.

Taking off from an air field on the Dominguez Rancho, aviator Paul Paulhan of the Signal Corps of the French Army flew out over the Santa Anita race track on 18 January 1910, circled it, then returned after a one-hour, two-minute flight of forty-five miles, the longest flight thus far in aviation's six-year history. Sponsored by the Merchants and Manufacturers Association of Los Angeles, the Los Angeles International Air Meet ran from 10 to 20 January 1910 and was the first such international event in aviation history. A total of 176,466 tickets were sold for the ten-day Dominguez Rancho affair, intended to show to the just-born world of aviation that Southern California had a climate and a terrain ideal for flying. At Dominguez Field Frenchman Paul Paulhan stole the show: taking actress Florence Stone aloft on the 11th (she thus became the first woman on the Pacific Coast to conquer the fear of flying); attaining an altitude of 4,165 feet on the 12th, a new world's record; establishing a time and distance record on the 18th with his flight out to Santa Anita; and finally, on the 19th, taking his charming wife with him for a flight out to the seacoast, where the two of them gaily buzzed Redondo Beach and Hermosa Beach as Southern Californians on the ground tilted their heads upwards and beheld, the more perspicacious of them, the future.

That future, alas, was not to be Charles Fletcher Lummis's future—although Don Carlos did not exactly wave his sombrero and ride off into the sunset at the first fly-by of Paulhan's aeroplane. Lummis's decline was more gradual. The descending arc of his waning physical strength and cultural influence plotted the decline of a generation's dreams as well.

Lummis's influence had been primarily exercised through his magazine *Land of Sunshine*, later *Out West*, which he took over as a chamber of commerce handout and transformed into a dynamic force for regional identity. Even at its most influential, however, *Land of Sunshine/Out West* was always on shaky ground financially. Lummis kept it going month to month through the sheer force of his personality. He took from it a seventy-five-dollar-a-month salary and a third of the year-end profits. As he became more and more involved with his work as city librarian of Los Angeles, however, his editorial influence on the magazine waned. He sold his stock in the magazine in November 1909 and resigned as editor. His hated rival, George Wharton James, took his place.

In the old days, the 1890s and early 1900s, Lummis would have had no trouble holding down the *Out West* editorship while serving as city librarian, and doing a half dozen other things as well; but as often is the case with the overextended and the overworked, Lummis's energy left him suddenly, all in a rush, as if an overdue account had peremptorily come due. It had happened before, this rhythm of ferocious activity followed by total collapse, only now there was no recovery. Some of his friends felt that Lummis had never really recovered from the shock of losing his six-year-old son Amado (named for Lummis's New Mexican friend Amado Chavez), who died of meningitis in 1900. Lummis ran a photograph in *Land of Sunshine* of Amado in his long curls and sailor suit, sharing his grief with his readers. He went gray soon after. In 1912 he suffered a temporary loss of eyesight as a result of contracting a fever in Guatemala, where he had gone to explore Mayan ruins. He recovered his eyesight, but his vision grew dimmer and dimmer in the ensuing decade. In the end he was blind. The *Los Angeles Times* dropped his column "I Guess So" in 1915, ostensibly because of a news-print shortage; although he had spearheaded the foundation of the Southwest Museum in 1914, he was voted out of his paying secretaryship there shortly after he had been dropped by the *Times*. Stripped of the editorship of *Out West*, the secretaryship of the museum, and his column, his lack of energy apparent to everyone, Charles Fletcher Lummis seemed a shrunken figure, a premature ghost from the immediate past.

By 1922 his yearly income had shrunk to $255.06, a devastating condition for this lover of travel and parties, this builder of the stone mansion El Alisal, which he hoped would house a dynasty, the children and grandchildren of Don Carlos. On the night of Saturday, 16 January 1925, an enfeebled Lummis eased himself into his green corduroy Spanish charro suit, tied his sash around his waist, draped his Grand Cross of Isabella around his neck, and gathered his friends about him at the refectory table at El Alisal for one of his old-fashioned "noises." After simple fare and an apple cobbler dessert, Spanish song books were passed around, and everyone joined in the singing of Old California songs. At the request of one guest, Mrs. Edward MacDowell, the wife of the noted American composer, Lummis moderated a lively discussion of the topic "nationalism in music."

The next day, Lummis lamented in his *Journal* that his children did not seem to care for the artistic, scholarly guests their father brought to El Alisal, nor, by extension, did they show signs of internalizing his overall vision of life and culture. ". . . I have worked constructively for 40 years," he brooded, "and have won the world's respect, and a host of ardent friends, all of whom have something to give—and I cannot seem to make it hereditary. In a sense it is very much like being childless—there is a comparable failure to project in the latter case your own life and blood, and in the former, your own mental wealth and accumulation. . . . If I had had such a chance, at any time between my 8th and 30th years, I would have felt myself the luckiest person in the world. But I had imagination, also respect. . . ."

He still possessed these gifts, imagination and reverence; but alas, he also nurtured a cancer in his brain that brought him close to total enfeeblement and caused him intermittent pain when in 1928 (when he was sixty-nine) the end drew near and he took to his bed, which was by a great open window looking out upon the Arroyo and the sycamores. When he could, he strummed his guitar and sang some of the old Spanish songs. It was a time of memory and assessment, of sweet-sad savoring of the last of the Southern California sunlight as it slanted through the lead-lined glass. What had he accomplished, he asked himself, across all these busy, busy years? Defiantly, as if to answer his own question, he directed the gathering of his best fugitive essays into one last volume, the posthumously published *Flowers of Our Lost Romance* (1929), and he refused to die until he held the page proofs in his hands. He held them in his hands, and he died, and to a certain extent his vision—the vision of his provincial generation—died with him.

5

Works, Days, Georgic Beginnings

In the beginning, and always, was the land; and from the land, the first and last premise of the California experience, Californians sought with increasing success to feed themselves, and then the nation, and then the world. In California's third American decade, agriculture succeeded mining as the primary industry of the state, a precedence that has lasted a hundred years and more. An era of cattle had already yielded to an era of sheep, and then the wheat had come, a quick dry-land crop, needing no irrigation or intensive care; and when the wheat had exhausted itself and the land as well, there began in the 1880s an era of patient georgic nurture that eventually covered the hillsides and valleys of California, its Central Valley flatlands and foothill fields, with orchards, vineyards, citrus groves, and vegetable and cereal crops of every description.

The Gold Rush made it necessary for California to feed itself. Soil, climate, and the availability of river-borne transportation made such self-sufficiency immediately possible. Within a year after the Forty-niners had begun to arrive, farms and ranches within a hundred-mile radius of San Francisco were shipping enough meat and produce, cereals and fruit up the Sacramento River by barge and paddlewheel steamer to sustain thousands of hungry men at work on the Mother Lode. The unforested lands of the Bay Area counties offered no resistance to the pioneer plow, and in the delta country between the Sacramento and the San Joaquin rivers, immediately adjacent to shipping points, the flooded earth resembled the banks of the Nile in ancient times: rich, loamy, dark, teeming with fertility. In September 1851, a mere year after statehood, the first agricultural fair was held in San Francisco. Fairgoers delighted in the gigantic strawberries on display, the oversized cabbages, the potatoes, beets, and melons weighing three to four times their weight in the East.

John Horner of Santa Clara County was producing that year from his 130-

acre ranch outside San Jose 35,000 bushels of potatoes, together with onions, cabbages, and tomatoes, for a cash gross of $175,000. The next year Horner added wheat, oats, and barley to his repertoire. By the end of the decade, in 1859, the 1,866-acre Napa County ranch of George C. Yount was producing 17,800 bushels of wheat annually, 2,400 bushels of corn, and 1,500 gallons of wine, all of it for the Bay Area market. No wonder James LaFayette Warren was urging as early as 1852 the establishment of a state agricultural society. A Massachusetts merchant and nurseryman, Warren had arrived in California in 1849 at age forty-four and headed with the others up to the mines. Observing the scurvy there, the result of a diet of whisky and hardtack, Warren determined that what California needed promptly was agriculture and agricultural institutions. Setting himself up in the seed business in Sacramento, Warren organized the city's first agricultural fair in 1852. By 1854 Warren was issuing his *California Farmer and Journal of Useful Sciences*, the first agricultural journal on the Pacific Coast. On 13 May 1854 Warren was on hand to witness the signing by Governor John Bigler of a bill establishing the State Agricultural Society of California.

Unlike other frontier Americans, Californians had little doubt that their environment seethed with agricultural promise. The state, first of all, was characterized by clear divisions between forests and open rangeland, but lacked the intermittently wooded areas of the East, so back-breakingly difficult to clear of stumps and stones. As a legacy of its crowded and varied geological past, the soils of California were astonishingly diverse. One ranch might contain side by side soil varieties found hundreds of miles apart in the East, thus making possible an equal diversity of crops. California soil ran deep, moreover; so the pioneers found as they sank wells into the earth, delighted that the fertile soil, rich and dark and durable, ran down, down, down before rock was reached. Warmed on its Pacific edge by the Japanese Current, which brought with it the temperature of the Indian Ocean, and protected north and east by great mountain ranges—the Cascades deflecting the polar winds of the north, the Sierra Nevada stabilizing the interior—California boasted a climate unspoiled by either heavy frost or low humidity. It was, moreover, a stable climate, running north and south across distances that in the East would support scores of climate variations. From Shasta to San Diego, a distance equivalent to that between Georgia and New York, sat one vast Sunbelt, stabilized by the Pacific on one side and the mighty Sierra Nevada to the east. The traversing ranges of the coast, moreover, acted as windbreakers against whatever cold air did manage to sweep down over the Cascades. These traversing formations also created a series of coastal valleys—Alexander, Santa Clara, Salinas, Santa Ynez, Santa Clara of the South—where cooling sea weather played off against inland sunshine.

All in all, California offered five major regions suitable for planting: three coastal regions, north, central, and south; a mountain and plateau region on the edge of the Sierra Nevada; and in the center of the state the mighty Central Valley, one-fifth of California's total area and 60 percent of its irrigatable land, an endless plain between the Pacific and the Sierra, first explored in the fall of 1808 by Ensign Gabriel Moraga and his soldiers from the garrison of San Francisco, the young officer noting in his journal the great rivers and plains, the oak groves, arroyos, and grass-covered hills, and speculating that the areas flooded by rivers were good plains for sown crops. Not for another thirteen years, however, would the Spanish again venture inland; for most of the time of Spain and Mexico's dominance, the great interior valley remained terra incognita, crossed only occasionally by a military expedition. During these years of neglect, the Franciscan missionaries dreamed of one day establishing an inland chain of missions in the San Joaquin (so the great valley was named), paralleling those of the coast, and turning its soil with Indian labor; but the moment of the missions was past by the late 1820s, and as the fathers died off or returned to Spain, dispirited by the secularist hostility of the newly established Republic of Mexico, the Central Valley receded for another forty years from the consciousness of the white man.

The Americans at first tilled the coastal lands around the Bay of San Francisco or established ranches near their Hispanic neighbors on the plain of Los Angeles. During this first era, beginnings were made in the more than two hundred crops that would eventually flourish throughout California. Dairy farming, a middle ground between the cattle economy of Old California and the agricultural future, also took hold. In this pre-railroad era, California was too remote from Eastern markets to compete with Texas and the Great Plains as a cattle producer, but the dairy cattle which crossed the plains with the pioneers at once proved profitable enterprises, as Philip Lynch of Ophir in Placer County discovered in 1851. Each of Lynch's cows, which cost him less than $50 a month to maintain, provided twelve quarts of milk a day, selling for fifty cents a quart or $6 a day, or $180 a month per cow, for a net profit of $130.

As San Francisco grew into the fourteenth largest city in the United States by 1870, the dairy industry, centered across the bay in Marin and Alameda counties, or down the peninsula in San Mateo County, kept apace, its herds improved by the stud services of such imported bulls as the Fourth Duke of Northumberland, a shorthorn sire brought around the Horn in the late 1850s to improve the resident California stock. Visiting the dairy farms of Marin County in the early 1860s, John Quincy Adams Warren, James LaFayette Warren's son and Boston-based business partner, confessed his astonishment at finding dairy farms of up to three thousand cattle, larger than any comparable farms in the East, all of them geared to the San Francisco market. Portuguese, Dutch, Danish, and Swiss immigrants, familiar with the dairying operations of their native countries, entered the industry, attracted by the prospect of earning good livings from modest-sized herds. Other dairymen moved north to Sonoma County and created in and around the town of Petaluma the largest poultry and egg-producing region on the planet.

All these early pioneers lived on the land that supported them, in fulfilled dialogue with the basic American myth of self-sufficiency on the soil. Clustered in the coastal valleys surrounding San Francisco Bay or spread across the Los Angeles plain, these early farms brought to California landscapes of settled civility reminiscent of the older settlements of the East. But this agriculture of the 1850s was exclusively local, committed to the feeding of the 380,000-odd Californians of that time and place. In the ensuing era of wheat, another and more persistent pattern emerged: corporate agriculture. Wheat, first of all, required no irrigation; hence the interior rangelands of the Central Valley, beginning in the 1860s, could be planted with wheat by the hundreds of square miles, six hundred square miles of wheatland between Sacramento and Fresno alone. The wheat fields of California were so vast that a plowing section might work all day to reach the end of one field, camp there overnight, then plow its way back all the next day, repeating this process for days on end until the work was complete. Wheat, secondly, was an export crop, capable of being shipped long distances via California's excellent network of railroads and Bay Area ports. By 1868 California was producing 20 million bushels a year, almost all of it for export: the figure grew to 29 million bushels by 1880 and 40 million bushels by 1890, a productivity second only to that of Minnesota. Not until 1894, when wheat bottomed out at eighty cents a cental, a price below the cost of production, did wheat recede as an important California crop.

In contrast to the snug family farms of the first phase of California agriculture, wheat was a big business, owned by a handful of wheat barons who ran their fiefdoms through hired hands possessed of little regard for the land from which for over fifteen years they extracted two, even three, wheat crops a year for the world market, driving the soil into dangerous depletion. Capitalists such as Isaac Friedlander, the Grain King of San Francisco (at six feet seven inches and three-hundred pounds, a figure as imposing as his holdings), William S. Chapman (the Grain King's sometime partner), Isaac Lankershim (German-born, as was Friedlander, but operating out of Los Angeles, not San Francisco), and Dr. Hugh Glenn (a dentist from Missouri who after his death had a county named in his honor) each controlled huge wheat baronies. Glenn's operation, the largest of these, ran to 60,000 acres and employed six hundred workers. (One of them, a bookkeeper discharged for drinking, dispatched the doctor with a shotgun in February 1883.) Moreover, Friedlander not only owned land, he controlled the shipping. At one point in the 1870s Friedlander's agents were buying and exporting to Europe and Asia on their own or leased ships three-quarters of all the wheat grown in California.

In every phase of its finances and operation, wheat was an industry based in the bonanza attitudes of its predecessor industry, mining. As in the case of mining, wheat employed advanced technology (the steam-powered combine, capable of cutting, threshing, and sacking a hundred acres a day, came into use in the mid-1870s) to extract wealth from the soil with no thought whatsoever for the renurturing of the land after it had been used up. Wheat workers, moreover, were single men, as were most of the miners, and when they returned from the fields they lived, as did the miners, in shacks or bunkhouses devoid of domesticity. Coming into railheads—Willows, Turlock, Modesto, Hanford—or the shipping towns of the Carquinez Straits on the North Bay, they drank, fought, gambled, and whored as had the miners in Marysville and Sacramento a generation earlier.

This using up of rural California by capitalists and great machines and rowdy men was obviously no Hesiodic idyll, no Vergilian or Jeffersonian georgic of men and women living lovingly on the land from which they took their living. But even as the wheat industry gathered momentum, a transition was occurring. In 1869 more Californians, 47,863 of them, for the first time made their living in agriculture, including wheat, than the 36,339 who made their living from mining. Throughout the 1860s and 1870s wheat provided a transition economy to agriculture. Drawing upon the existing infrastructure of the mining era—its financial resources, its foundries and iron works, its labor pool, its inclination toward an innovative, labor-saving technology—wheat brought these structures and operational patterns into the next era of agricultural growth, establishing a direct link between mining and agriculture that, along with other factors, land monopoly most importantly, would orient agriculture in the direction of a dominant corporate industrial model from which it would never free itself. "The time will yet come," Colonel E. D. Baker orated at the State Fair of 1859, "when the ditches which traverse the whole mineral regions of California will be more valuable for agriculture than they ever have been for gold finding." That year, California was grossing some $50 million a year from its mining operations. The figure dropped to $18 million by 1870. By 1880, when mining accounted for less than $15 million in gross revenue, the time had drawn near for Baker's prediction to come true.

II

In the year 1880 mining leveled off in Northern California and a worldwide drop in wool prices threatened the sheep industry of Central and Southern California, thus encouraging sheep raisers to look for another use for their rangelands. That year thus provides a convenient point of demarcation between the two economies of California, mining and agricultural. Two interrelated factors made possible this new era of California agriculture: a national market and the refrigerated railroad car. Although California increased its population in the 1880s from 864,694 to 1.2 million, even this larger population might have been fed by a minimally expanded local agriculture, given the high productivity of the California farm. Without Eastern markets, however, overproduction and a consequently fluctuating price structure would always remain a problem. But if California could ship its fruit and produce to the rest of the country, as it was shipping its nonperishable wheat to the world, then an expanded agriculture would be possible. Urbanizing Americans in the Midwest and the East, moreover, were growing restive with the meat-and-potatoes diet of an earlier era. The newly rising urban middle classes of American cities could be expected to welcome fresh fruit and produce into their diet, if available. The cramped farmlands and short growing seasons of the East could never meet this need, but California could, provided Californians could safely move these perishables to market.

In 1870, a year after the transcontinental railroad opened, seventy ice-cooled, air-ventilated railroad carloads of pears, apples, grapes, and plums, seventy tons in all, left California for the East. Since it took a month for such shipments to reach Eastern retail markets, much of the fruit arrived in a spoiled condition. Still, Californians persisted. In 1877 the first shipment of oranges left the Wolfskill groves of Los Angeles for St. Louis. Meanwhile, Gustavus F. Swift, a Chicago meat packer, was pushing ahead with a much improved system of air-and-ice railroad refrigeration. In this new technology, intake scoops atop each car funneled a steady stream of air across a bunker of salted ice, then circulated it through the moving car. When the Swift system was modified for fruit shipment, a whole new era became possible.

In June 1888 the first trainload of California fruit using this new refrigeration technology left for the East, cherries and apricots from Suisun Valley. In 1892 five carloads of California oranges reached London via refrigerated railroad cars and a fourteen-day voyage in the storage locker of a steamship. Queen Victoria herself tasted one of the oranges. Back in California, Her Majesty's judgment ("palatable") was interpreted as a ringing endorsement. This new refrigeration technology was clumsy and expensive. Up to eight thousand pounds of ice was necessary in each railroad to cool ten to fifteen tons of fruit, which often had to be unloaded en route and recooled in trackside ice houses. But improvements came: precooling, for instance, in massive indoor plants which used ice, fans, and ammonia pipelines to bring the air down to thirty-eight degrees before pumping it into each fruit-filled railroad car via canvas tubes, then packing the car with ice for the trip east. With each improvement in refrigeration technology, the amount of California fruit leaving for the East increased: the 30 tons of 1869 becoming the 70 tons of 1870, the 1,571 tons of 1880 becoming the 81,976 carloads of 1906. Thus the optimism of these years, as Californians leveled, drained, and irrigated the land, planted orchards and groves of fruit trees and laid out endless rows of vegetables, all in response to this growing national market.

A half century earlier the gold of California, reaching the East, had restruc-
tured the nation's finances; now the nation's diet—starchy, oleaginous, salty from
the use of pickling as a primary mode of preservation—would be affected by
California as well. An entire American generation would now encounter California in its urban or village markets as a crate of oranges, a lug of figs or
mountain pears, an exotic display of desert-grown palm dates or walnuts from
the Central Valley. Broadening the diet of America, giving it naturalness and
variety, California was also saying something about itself to the rest of the nation, now consuming its fruits and produce or drinking its wine. In the color
of a plum or an apricot, in the luxuriance of a bowl of grapes set out in ritual
display, in a bottle of wine, the soil and sunshine of California reached millions of Americans for whom that distant place would henceforth be envisioned
as a sun-graced land resplendent with the goodness of the fruitful earth.

But before all this could come about, a work of planting, tilling, and harvest
was necessary. Between 1880 and 1920 California recreated itself into an agricultural empire. Fruit culture, including citrus and viticulture, led the way.
No agricultural endeavor stood in greater contrast to the get-rich-quick, land-
hungry exploitations of wheat. Fruit culture was a work of time and patience.
Capable of generating livable incomes from smaller land plots, fruit culture encouraged families to live on the land. Fruit culture nurtured values of responsible land use, prudent capitalization, cooperation among growers in the matter
of packing, shipping, and marketing. Above all else, fruit culture encouraged a
level of rural civility in the care of homes, the founding of schools, churches,
and libraries, the nurturing of social and recreational amenities which stood in
complete contrast to the Wild West attitudes of wheat. The wild fruits of California, to begin with, on which the Indians had fed, provided autochthonous
suggestions of what might be effected through the horticultural arts. Runtish,
sour, scarce—nevertheless the wild apples, plums, cherries, peaches, almonds,
filberts, acorns, blackberries, gooseberries, raspberries, cranberries, and cur-
rants of California were already spontaneously nourishing more than a quarter
of a million First Californians when the Spanish arrived: a legacy improved
upon by the Franciscans, who planted their mission gardens with the fruit trees
of Mexico and Spain, five thousand bearing trees by 1792, including (at a later
date) six hundred pear trees at Mission San Jose alone.

After the Gold Rush, after the wheat, Californians now reached back to this
mission legacy and planted anew. By 1920 a vast fruitbelt—eight-hundred miles
in length, two hundred miles in width—extended down the state. Within this
belt, fruit culture varied according to topography and climate. On the coast,
with its sea fogs and sunshine, its broken terrain of valleys and passes, orchards
of apples, pears, cherries, plums, and apricots were planted. The apple orchards came first, clustered in the hilly coastlands of Sonoma County or in
similar terrain around Santa Cruz. By 1880 California had more apple trees

than all other deciduous fruit trees combined. Hardy and resilient, apples needed a minimum of care and were unaffected by sudden frosts. Not so the apricot, whose very name, derived from the Latin *apricus* (loving the sun) suggested its fickle temperament. California eventually developed a monopoly on the apricot, whose color, together with that of the orange, found its way so evocatively into the palette of California art. But this dominance did not come easily, for the apricot needed just the right amount of the sun it so loved and thus would not grow above fifteen hundred feet. Too green for the harvest one day, the apricot could with a sudden warming of the weather need to be picked within a fortnight or be lost. Like the vine, the apricot thrived in the Mediterranean foothills of the Bay Area, in Santa Clara County especially, whose hillsides in spring were radiant with the speckled white of blossoming fruit. Sharing this Santa Clara Valley terrain were prune and plum trees descended from cuttings from the Ville Neuve d'Agen which Louis Pellier, a San Jose nurseryman, brought back from his native France in 1856 when he returned there to find a wife. Spreading out from Pellier's nursery, the California prune, as the *petite prune d'Argen* was renamed, was planted around San Jose, Cupertino, and Saratoga in Santa Clara County. By 1886 California had more than a million trees, producing forty million pounds of prunes annually, most of it for shipment East. Not faced with the same necessities of refrigeration as other fruits, prunes had immediate access to Eastern markets, where the fruit already possessed a reputation for healthfulness. In their hardy fecundity, moreover, prune trees mocked the fickle apricot. Each Santa Clara prune tree averaged an annual yield of 300 pounds. Yields of 600 to 800 pounds were not uncommon. One six-year-old tree yielded 1,102 pounds of fruit in a single season.

Other crops spreading southwards from strong bases in the San Francisco Bay Area included olives, walnuts, and almonds. As suggestive as the vine was of civilization itself, the olive came to California with the Franciscans. Mission San Jose supported the most successful olive grove of that early era, ancient and gnarled trees which remained on into the American period (some are still bearing today) as symbolic connections between the American present and the Spanish past. By 1900 a million and a half bearing olive trees, their leaves glimmering silver-green in the sunlight, were growing in the state. Walnut and almond trees thrived in comparable numbers: the walnut in the outer East Bay region extended around Walnut Creek, where the heat of the interior valley began to assert itself; and the almond, 1.6 million trees by 1900, clustering there as well and also flourishing in the Chico area, the Santa Clara Valley, and the Los Angeles plain. By the late 1880s almonds from California were dominating almonds imported from Spain and North Africa in the Eastern market. By 1920 imported almonds were a thing of the past.

In the Central Valley, ranchers favored fruit and nut crops that ripened before the long hot summer of the interior. Peaches and pear trees proved ideal for valley cultivation and were planted by the tens of thousands. In Fresno County, in the very center of the valley, the California raisin industry developed, the largest in the world by 1920, when 350,000 San Joaquin Valley acres, most of them in Fresno County, were producing 115,521 tons of raisins each year, or half the world's total output. Other hot-weather crops, figs (190,000 trees by 1900) and melons especially, flourished on the flat irrigated fields of the San Joaquin, along with the peaches, nectarines, pears, prunes, walnuts, and almonds that had also proven so suitable, once problems of irrigation were solved. Later, after the turn of the century, another hot-weather crop, the date, was introduced into the Imperial Valley by Dr. Walter T. Swingle, a Department of Agriculture scientist who found conditions for date growing in the Salton Basin analogous to those in the best date-growing regions of North Africa.

Vegetable and cereal crops, meanwhile, kept apace. By 1919 California led the nation in barley and alfalfa and was second only to Louisiana in the production of rice. The cultivation of vegetables languished during the wheat years as everyone went into wheat or similar quick-cash crops. Asians restored vegetable farming to the forefront of the agricultural economy, the Chinese and Japanese in particular, who brought to California their ancient arts of making a few carefully tended acres yield a significant harvest. In the 1870s and 1880s the Chinese established vegetable farms catering to the urban markets of Marysville, Sacramento, Stockton, and San Francisco. From the 1890s onward the Japanese predominated. Meanwhile, the non-Asian growers of Southern California were diversifying into vegetables on a major scale as new farming acres, many opened for the first time by irrigation, became available. In 1894, for instance, a former Kansan, D. E. Smeltzer, discovered wild celery growing in the low-lying peat lands of Orange County. Smeltzer threw himself into large-scale celery growing. By the early 1900s, only Michigan produced more celery than Southern California. Similar stories can be told regarding sugar beets (only Colorado could compete), beans (by 1920 the largest vegetable crop in the state), onions, peas, artichokes (the Salinas Valley dominated the national market), lettuce (a late crop, introduced in 1910 into the Salinas and Imperial valleys but soon supplying a third of the nation's needs), carrots (again, California became the nation's leading producer), asparagus (the loamy Sacramento–San Joaquin river delta lands pushed this crop to national dominance), cauliflower (a Monterey area crop, also commanding the national market), tomatoes (another latecomer, soon outshipping the production of other states), potatoes (improved by one Californian, Luther Burbank, and controlled by another, George Shima), peas and spinach (two other national dominants), together with cucumbers, pumpkins, rhubarb, cabbage, Swiss chard, peppers, and eggplant, in which California, while not dominating the national market, commanded a considerable share. Only with one crop, corn, did the California magic fail to work its wondrous way. By 1919 California was producing only one two-hundredth of the corn grown in Iowa.

Presiding over this turn-of-the-century era of expanding horticulture in fruits, nuts, grains, cereals, and vegetables, agronomist Edward James Wickson, the leading agricultural writer of his day, sought to convince the ranchers and farmers of California that they were embarked upon a work not only of economic importance, but of social and cultural significance as well. An 1869 graduate of Hamilton College in upstate New York, a region leading the rest of the country in agricultural sophistication, Wickson studied classics and chemistry as an undergraduate. By temperament and training Wickson preferred to live his life, imaginatively and professionally, at the point of intersection between literature and science, language and the practical arts. Like his beloved Hesiod, the ancient Greek author of the agricultural poem *Works and Days*, and the Roman poet Vergil, author of the *Georgics*, a poem similarly inspired by agriculture (each poem studied at Hamilton College in the original and remembered throughout a lifetime), Wickson was enamored of agriculture as an archetypal act of culture building, an enterprise in which all the details, all the prudent choices coalesced to create a landscape and a way of life that promoted civility, prosperity, and good order. Trained through the master's level in the agricultural sciences, Wickson did not desire a research career. His humanistic vision of what a proper rural society could and should be extended beyond the borders of scientific analysis. Wanting to promote agriculture as a humanistic enterprise, Wickson joined the staff of the *Utica Morning Herald* in 1872 as that newspaper's dairy correspondent. Three years later he moved to San Francisco, where he assumed the editorship of the *Pacific Rural Press*.

Agricultural journalism had been launched in California in a grand manner in 1854 by the Warrens, father and son, whose *California Farmer* ranked in range and excellence with such Eastern counterparts as *Rural New Yorker*, *Country Gentleman*, and the *American Agriculturist*. From the start, the ranchers and farmers of California, living and working a continent away from the established agricultural society of the East, wanted a connection to the best research and techniques of the older states, which the Boston-based John Quincy Adams Warren was only too happy to provide them. Under Warren's editorship, the *California Farmer* set standards in rural journalism which over the years such periodicals as the *California Rural Home Journal*, the *California Fruit Grower*, the *California Citrograph*, and Wickson's own *Pacific Rural Press* sustained: a journalism aimed at a largely middle-class, literate clientele, many of whom had turned to the land after urban careers in the East and were hence accustomed to taking advice from the printed page.

"How can I tell when a watermelon is fully ripe?" Wickson's readers wrote in. "What is the value of grape pomace as a hog feed? How can I distinguish the sex of Toulouse geese? In what direction shall I face open-front poultry houses? How shall I plant and handle a crop of Niles peas? Advise me what to do for a bull that masturbates." In his forty-eight years, 1875 to 1923, as editor of the *Pacific Rural Press* ("The Leading Agricultural Home Newspaper and Standard Authority on All Branches of California Agriculture," it advertised itself), Wickson answered thousands of such questions from readers, ranging from the prosaic to the exotic ("Kindly tell me of anyone who is working upon the application of electricity to stimulating agricultural growth"): questions dealing with the storing of apples, the pruning of almond trees, the propagation of apricots, the ripening of walnuts ("I send you two walnuts. I am in doubt if they will mature"), the interaction between bees and pear blight. Sharing such questions among themselves, reading Wickson's well-researched and pithy replies, rural Californians created a community among themselves extending throughout the state. Each question, after all, had behind it the weight of individual economies, if not the actual survival of a random farm. With Wickson's help, an entire generation of newcomers to farming struggled with that special mosaic of interdependent details, that skein of organic and socioeconomic dependencies that is agriculture. Sensing Wickson's talents as a teacher, Professor Eugene W. Hilgard of the University of California appointed him a lecturer in dairy husbandry in 1879. Throughout his long career in agricultural journalism, Wickson pursued an equally effective career as a pioneering educator in agricultural science, with specialities in horticulture and dairying. Along with his editorial and teaching duties, Wickson ran the university extension program, taking the latest in agricultural research out to the farmers of the state. In 1887 he assumed direction of all agricultural lands owned by the university. In 1905 Wickson succeeded his mentor Hilgard as dean of the College of Agriculture.

Like Hesiod and Vergil, though obviously lacking these poets' depth of imagination and force of verbal power, Wickson sought as a writer and teacher the promotion of civility on the land. Wickson's best-known book, for instance, *The California Fruits and How to Grow Them* (1889), is pervaded throughout its abundant detail by the sustaining vision of the new way of life that intensive farming will bring to California. So many Americans were entering fruit farming, Wickson wrote in his preface, and European and American treatises were so devoid of specifics relating to California, that this manual was necessary to serve the needs of basic practical instruction. Exuberantly and with that style of straightforward writing that Americans like to believe is peculiarly their own, Wickson provided the city dwellers turned California fruit growers with a creation catalogue and practical georgic of the fruits that challenged to new nurture on the California land, each fruit with its special poetry, each with its distinct needs.

Yet readers of Wickson's guide were presented with something else as well—

the building blocks, in terms of orchard management, of what they had come out to California to become: Americans grafted onto new root stock, taking strength from a new sun and soil. Each step in establishing an orchard—budding and grafting, the laying out of trees in double or alternating squares, planting, pruning, weeding, watering, draining, fertilizing—bespoke a metaphor for life and society as well. Roots stood in special danger of damage, Wickson wrote, when the tree made the transition from one soil to another. Too much California sun, too little or too much water, and a young tree would not survive to bear fruit in its new surroundings. The social metaphor for California was obvious. In later books, Wickson approached the growing of vegetables and flowers with the same Hesiodic and Vergilian blend of practical advice and implied metaphor. In *The California Vegetables in Garden and Field* (1913), for instance, Wickson promoted the small-to-medium-sized vegetable garden as a means of health and self-sufficiency. A diet based primarily on vegetables, Wickson wrote, promoted low blood pressure and longevity. Through the rotation of crops, such a garden remained productive twelve months a year. Ideally, most California rural families and many suburban and even urban ones might meet their own nutritional needs from a relatively small-sized vegetable plot, as so many Asians in California were already doing. Health, self-reliance, a chance to compete on the land with the threateningly successful Asian farmers: vegetables meant more than vegetables for Edward James Wickson. And so did flowers. The work of creating California as the garden of America, Wickson wrote in *California Garden* (1915), had come a long way since the days when only a shack or two broke the monotony of the wheat fields; but much work yet remained to be done if California was ever to enjoy rural aesthetics worthy of its natural circumstances. Advocating the planting of flowers, shrubs, trees (palm and eucalyptus especially), and vines around the ranch houses of the state, Wickson urged rural Californians to create a landscape worthy of the assertion that "California stands clear in the eyes of the world as the point most desirable to attain for the fullest joys of living."

Over the years, Wickson's books sold nearly forty-six thousand copies. *California Fruits* alone went through nine editions. Wickson's six books and his numerous pamphlets and research papers, together with his forty-eight years of journalism on the *Pacific Rural Press*, constituted a promotional, developmental georgic of great importance to California's evolving rural society. Student of the classics, Wickson sought what Hesiod and Vergil had sought before him: the promotion of rural virtue and civility based upon an ethos of steady work and prudent use. Wickson believed that with the proper attention to detail Californians might flourish as an educated yeomanry on the land, self-supporting, living amidst beauty, having the means to enjoy the amenities of life as well as to turn the earth and make it yield its welcomed and necessary harvest.

III

No agricultural enterprise, Wickson believed, expressed immemorial values of usefulness and beauty more successfully than did the citrus culture of Southern California. The orange, Wickson wrote, was the premier fruit of California, in itself a symbol of California's call to civilized rural life. Citrus culture brought aesthetics to agriculture and made possible for citrus growers a lifestyle blending the best of outdoor living with civilized amenities. The orange, first of all (and to a lesser extent the lemon, tangerine, and grapefruit), was a fruit of romantic lineage, appearing in Greek myth as the Golden Apples of the Hesperides and known in classical times to travelers to Asia. In medieval times the Arabs reintroduced the orange to Spain, North Africa, and the Levant. From Damascus to Granada, orange groves ringed the cities of the medieval Mediterranean Arab crescent or grew more singly in the enclosed courtyards of sumptuous homes, filling each hidden garden with fragrance and color. From Spain, citrus came to the New World, arriving with Columbus's second voyage in 1493. Spreading with the Spanish empire through Mexico and the Caribbean, including Florida, citrus was brought to Baja California by Jesuit missionaries around 1739, then introduced by Franciscans to Alta California in 1769. At San Gabriel Mission outside the Pueblo of Los Angeles, a six-acre orange grove was planted in 1804. The orange tree and the lemon tree, then, implied for Californians a connection, a continuity with fabled Asia, ancient Greece, medieval Islam, Arab Spain, and the Spanish translation to the New World, all of which reverberated with romantic suggestion for a society in search of metaphors. As a tree (dark-leaved, white with flowers in springtime, golden with fruit in the summer), or as a fruit itself (so close to the gold which the Golden State took as its primary symbol), the orange bespoke heritage and aesthetics with an intensity that would render it by the early twentieth century a key image of regional identity.

Unlike other fruits, citrus had languished as a minor crop throughout the mission era. It remained for an American, William Wolfskill, a Kentucky-born trapper and trader who had arrived in Los Angeles in 1831 on the Old Spanish Trail, to establish citrus commercially. In 1841, using seedlings from the citrus orchard at San Gabriel, Wolfskill planted a twenty-eight-acre orange grove near the Pueblo of Los Angeles. By 1862 an estimated twenty-five thousand citrus trees were bearing fruit in Southern California, most of them in and around Los Angeles. By 1870 Wolfskill's original orange grove, now expanded, was earning a thousand dollars an acre from the San Francisco market. Earnings as high as this were not lost on the sheep ranchers of Los Angeles County, faced with the falling off of their industry. Throughout the 1870s sheep ranges gave way to orange groves, and by 1881 Los Angeles County supported a half million orange trees. In 1877, a year after the railroad reached Southern California, the first boxcarload of oranges—from the Wolfskill orchard, appropriately—left for the East via San Francisco. A few years later, in 1885, the completion of the Atchison, Topeka and Santa Fe Railroad gave Southern California its own direct connection to the East, thus making orange shipments possible in large quantities; and California oranges, competing against the citrus of Florida, won twenty medals at the New Orleans World Fair, creating a demand for California oranges on the Eastern Seaboard. On 14 February 1886 a Santa Fe train, loaded exclusively with oranges, left Los Angeles for the East Coast. By 1914 some thirty thousand railroad carloads, or approximately twelve million orange crates, valued at $20 million, were steaming East each year.

Two varieties of orange, the Valencia and the Washington navel, dominated Southern California citrus, with the Mediterranean sweet running a far third. Sometime in 1810, in the vicinity of São Salvador de Bahia in the state of Bahia, Brazil, an orange tree of the Selecta variety mutated a new orange type. This new type, which remained local for more than half a century, was large, solid, heavy, and smooth-skinned. Within, it was pulpy, juicy, and virtually seedless. In 1870 an American Presbyterian missionary with an interest in horticulture, the Rev. F. Schneider, then serving in Bahia, sent twelve newly budded trees of this superior Brazilian orange to William Saunders, superintendent of gardens and grounds for the United States Department of Agriculture in Washington, D.C. Schneider had previously been in correspondence with Saunders regarding the magnificent variety of orange he had discovered in Bahia. Receiving the budded trees in Washington, Saunders transferred the buds to some sturdy rootstalks, and when the graft had taken, he described the new orange in departmental literature, calling it the Washington navel.

Out in Riverside, then a struggling agricultural colony in San Bernardino County, Luther Tibbets, a Maine man with a scholarly interest in citrus culture (he had brought a considerable horticultural library out to Southern California), read Saunder's descriptions of the Washington navel and sent for two trees. When they arrived, Tibbets made the sixty-five-mile round trip to the Los Angeles train station by buckboard. Returning to Riverside, he planted the Washington navels in his front yard sometime in December 1873. Legend has it that his wife Eliza watered these parent navel orange trees (so they became) with her dirty dishwater. In any event, these two Bahia trees, sent from Brazil to Washington and from Washington to Riverside, bore their first fruit in 1878: two oranges per tree (so again does legend have it), each orange over a pound in weight. Successfully transplanted, the Washington navel proved itself a sturdy, resilient tree, capable of flourishing in the drier heat and uplands of inland San Bernardino and Riverside counties. The Valencia orange, by contrast, a summer-ripening tree introduced in 1876 from a Long Island nursery by Judge A. B. Chapman of San Gabriel, thrived best in the fog-cooled coastal regions. Together the summer-ripening coastal Valencia and the winter-ripening inland navel enabled Southern California citrus growers to challenge Florida's dominance of the American market. Two varieties—the Lisbon, a European import, and the Eureka, a local fruit developed in 1858 by C. R. Workman of Los Angeles—likewise dominated the lemon groves of the Southland, although the California lemon did not rise to prominence as rapidly as did the California orange. By 1900 fully 70 percent of the lemons used by Americans and Canadians were still being imported from Italy. By 1921 California had captured 85 percent of the market. The California grapefruit, a dry-lands citrus tree, proved itself an even later crop, not arriving from Florida until the late 1880s, when a grove of Marsh seedless grapefruit was planted in Riverside. California would share the production of grapefruit, a fruit slow to win its way into the American diet, with Arizona, Texas, and Florida, its first American home.

To prepare for, guide, and encourage this agriculture of citrus, Southern Californians produced a series of promotional georgics comparable to Wickson's more generalized efforts on behalf of fruit and vegetable culture. Writers such as Thomas A. Garey, in *Orange Culture in California* (1882); L. M. Holt, in *The Great Interior Fruit Belt and Sanitarium of Southern California* (1885); William Andrew Spalding, in *The Orange, Its Culture in California* (1885); and Byron Martin Lelong, in *A Treatise on Citrus Culture in California* (1888), sought to provide useful information regarding the developing citrus industry but also to evoke its charm as a new way for Americans to find fulfillment in rural living. Themselves journalists and growers from the area (Thomas Garey had sixteen years of experience as a grower; Byron Martin Lelong was secretary to the Board of Horticulture of the State of California), each writer wrote from his long knowledge of the subject and a belief—promotional in its motivation but possessed as well of strong elements of sincerity—that citrus culture would bring to Southern California a mode of agriculture totally suitable to refined middle-class growers. Citrus culture, first of all, was intensive farming at its most intense. Every acre might support many trees; each tree, once it had come of age, bore much fruit and might be expected to continue bearing for three to four hundred years. A newcomer to Southern California might therefore get into citrus culture with a minimum of capital, promotional writers claimed, without the necessity of acquiring a large acreage, providing that he had the means to see himself through the start-up phase. Once trees began to yield, within three to five years of planting, a grower might enjoy a lifetime income with a minimum of effort. Such a life would be at once healthful and refined. One writer, William Andrew Spalding, described how he had personally regained his health, broken from newspaper work, as a citrus grower. Another, L. M. Holt, described the citrus groves of San Bernardino County as one vast sanitarium, where an entire generation of middle-class Americans was recovering from the fatigues of city life. "Orange culture," wrote Spalding, "must continue as it has begun, an industry suited to the most intelligent and refined people. It is better adapted to small farms than large. It produces better results under the eye and hand of the master than when delegated to hired labor. As it requires both skill and industry, it gives healthful occupation to the mind as well as the body." As if to reinforce his point, Spalding's manual included an illustration of a grower inspecting his trees, attired in suit, vest, cravat, and homburg hat, the very essence of the gentleman citrus farmer, Southern California style. Aesthetics, these writers urged, were everywhere: in the snug houses of citrus growers, filled with the amenities of urban culture; in the groves themselves, gardens of blossoming trees and golden fruit; in the snow-capped mountain ranges that marked off the distant horizon; in the rows of palm or eucalyptus trees that differentiated properties; and above it all, in the blue sky and golden sun of Southern California, whose warmth and nurture might be returned to the Eastern states as citrus, for the profit and benefit of both sides of the American continent.

Lest such evocations be dismissed as mere ballyhoo, it must be said that in the thirty years that followed these predictions, much of what was envisioned came true. Rarely, if ever (save in the vineyards of the North), has such beauty and civility, such luxuriance and orderly repose been achieved on an American landscape as that brought about by citrus on the landscape of Southern California in the coastal belt running up through the counties of San Diego, Orange, Ventura, and Santa Barbara, with their alluvial, sedimentary soils derived from the sandstone and shale formations of the nearby hills; or inland from the San Gabriel Valley along the foothills from Pasadena to Redlands in the counties of Los Angeles, San Bernardino, and Riverside, on soil of decomposed granite, with excellent drainage in that necessarily irrigated inland area; or in the lemon groves clustering around Azusa, San Dimas, Ontario, Rialto, Arlington Heights, Corona, Whittier, and Hollywood, or growing in coastal groves outside San Diego, Santa Paula, and Santa Barbara. Groves such as these, broken intermittently by gingerbread cottages or Spanish-style haciendas, conferred on parts of Southern California an ambience of Mediterranean idyll, a visual poetry of leaf, blossom, or fruit (depending on the season) that offset the realities of the American present with a charm that was enthusiastically exported on the orange crate labels sent East as the very image of Southern California and was largely believed in by an entire generation of Americans, for whom Southern California would always be orange groves flowering on a sun-splashed plain, with the blue Pacific and the snowcapped peaks of the San Gabriel or San Bernardino range in the distance.

Today, a half century since citrus culture passed its peak, surviving evidence—old photographs especially—come forward to justify that orange crate label pastoralism: the groves themselves first and foremost, extending from seashore to mountain range, and the great packing sheds adjacent to them, sweeping, open structures, forcefully aesthetic in their utility, banked by stands of eucalyptus trees which channeled the breezes to an advantageous angle as the fruit remained piled high in storage preparatory to packing; and within these sheds, the work of sorting, washing, wrapping each fruit in specially decorated tissue paper, tasks performed in the main by young women, who regard us today from the pages of old magazines, their hands folded atop white aprons in a moment's repose as the photographer asked them to cease work so that he might record the scene. These orange and lemon workers are, in one sense, the direct descendants of the New England mill girls of forty years earlier. One sees in their surroundings the same toil of piecework, but softened somewhat by the absence of heavy machinery and the much lighter nature of their task. These women, and the men who supervised them and oversaw the machinery that helped sort and crate the fruit, then moved it by conveyor belt to a loading dock where a railroad car awaited, lived in such nearby towns as Ontario, Pomona, Claremont, Cucamonga, San Bernardino, Pasadena, San Gabriel, Orange, San Diego, Anaheim in the heart of the Valencia district, Ventura, and Santa Paula in the Santa Clara Valley of the South, set in the very center of the lemon region which ran past Santa Barbara to Montecito and the sea. Each of these citrus towns had experienced a similar pattern of development: from agricultural colony with a diversified crop, through early years of uncertainty as one or another dominant crop was experimented with, and then in the '80s and '90s the conversion to citrus, followed by the transformation of these once dusty, unpretentious farm towns into more civil modes of urbanism, adorned with neo-Mission train stations and Romanesque public buildings that added their own version of Southern California Mediterraneanism to the suggestions of the surrounding landscape.

Redlands, San Bernardino County, shared honors with Riverside, Riverside County, as premier city of the citrus belt. Founded in March 1887 on the sloping hillside that formed the southern edge of the San Bernardino Valley, eighty miles inland from the sea, Redlands had become by the early 1900s a city of distinctive public buildings in Mission Revival or Romanesque—library, high school, denominational college, municipal swimming pool and bathhouse, two train stations (Southern Pacific and Santa Fe)—and gracious bungalows on broad streets shaded by pepper and palm, possessed on its western edge of a view across the orange-grove-carpeted San Bernardino Valley and to the east, the snow-capped peaks of the Sierra Madre, dominated by hoary Mount San Bernardino, looming over all like the protective alpine peak, at once grand and terrible, of a romantic painting. Riverside, by contrast, was situated on flat land alongside the Santa Ana River on lands of the former Rancho La Jurupa belonging to Don Juan Bandini; yet here also a peak, Mount Rubidoux, and a mountain range, the San Jacinto, marked the middle distance in a configuration typical of Southern California.

In every aspect of its history and developed circumstances, Riverside epitomized the Southern California citrus town. The Southern California Colony Association, formed in late 1869 in Knoxville, Tennessee, by John W. North, who had already been out to Southern California to survey the possibilities for an agricultural colony there, acquired the Riverside site in 1870. Previously these lands on the Santa Ana River had been owned by a silkworm-raising colony which had failed. Twenty-five families settled in Riverside in 1871, all of them middle-class, few with any previous agricultural experience, but all anxious to find a new way of life as intensive farmers living together in the township which John W. North had laid out in the style of Philadelphia, with all streets at right angles.

Before leaving for California, North and his fellow colonist Luther Tibbets had already done research at the Smithsonian in Washington, looking for the right varieties of semi-tropical fruits for the colony to grow once it was established. Because Tibbets brought the first two Washington navel orange trees to Riverside and harvested their fruit a few years later, he assumed a place alongside North as Riverside's founder: in later years, that is, after his death as an impoverished public charge in 1902. For Luther Tibbets—quarrelsome, improvident, a spiritualist verging on quackery, twice married before marrying Eliza, formerly the wife of his personal physician back in Maine—was not an easy man to get along with, not even for Riversiders, grateful to him though they were for their citrus economy, nor for Eliza for that matter, the quarrels between the couple becoming legendary. By the time he died in the charity ward of the Riverside County Hospital, Luther Tibbets had quarreled with just about everyone.

The colony's third founding figure, by contrast, the Irish-born Canadian Matthew Gage, who developed Riverside's extraordinary network of irrigation canals—including a twenty-mile waterway named the Gage Canal in his honor— was as revered as Tibbets was despised. As feeble a solace as this was, Riversiders rushed to Gage's consolation when he lost five of his eight children in an epidemic. A rancher, an irrigationist, an entrepreneur capable of attracting British financing to his canal project, which brought the waters of the Santa Ana to citrus groves, Matthew Gage made economically feasible in the 1880s the colony founded by North in 1870 and given its premier crop in 1878 by the testy Tibbets.

With the British investment attracted by Gage in the 1880s came an actual British presence after 1890, when a British syndicate, the Riverside Trust Company Ltd. (later the Riverside Orange Company), bought out Gage's canals and properties, then commenced the development of further canals and groves in the Arlington Heights area adjacent to the original colony. A considerable British community settled into Arlington Heights through the 1890s—the usual expatriate mélange of remittance men, second or third sons, failures looking for opportunity in a colonial situation, and the sort of solid, hardworking British entrepreneurs who were establishing themselves in Argentina, Africa, the Malay States, Singapore, and Hong Kong during the same period. In later years, legend exaggerated (as legend always does) the British tone of Arlington Heights, with talk of ruined peers seeking redemption in the orange groves, but even without such embellishments an intriguing British milieu did take hold in the Arlington Heights district of Riverside. In March 1892, for example, the Riverside Polo Club, a joint Anglo-American venture, brought polo to California for the first time. Four years later an expanded institution, the Riverside Polo and Golf Club, brought the concept of a full-service country club to the area. Tennis had been played in Riverside since 1883. As part of the Southern California Lawn Tennis Association, organized in 1887, the Riverside Tennis Club played the tennis clubs of Pasadena, San Gabriel, and Santa Monica in a yearly tournament held in Riverside. Nor were music and the drama unknown. As early as 1879, in the infancy of the colony, a choral society and orchestra had given the first live concert in Riverside. (Alas, four of the principals—Miss Lily Eastman, pianist; her father, Dr. Sanford Eastman, an original director of the colony; and two musician members of the Riverside Philharmonic Society, Johann F. Dietze and George Leach, each so happy that concert day of 4 June 1879—all died within a few years from tuberculosis, the white plague which even the sunshine of Riverside could not vanquish.) The Loring Opera House opened in Riverside on 8 January 1890 with a performance of Gilbert and Sullivan's *Iolanthe*. Over the next two decades, Helena Modjeska, Otis Skinner, Sarah Bernhardt, James O'Neill, John Philip Sousa and his band, John Drew, the Isadora Duncan dancers, and the Ruth St. Denis dance troupe all played Riverside.

In addition to the all-important Mission Inn, Riverside's self-esteem showed itself in an opulent array of General Grant, Queen Anne, Mission Revival, and Romanesque buildings, impressively if grandiloquently topped off by the Riverside County Courthouse, which celebrated Riverside's position as the county seat of Riverside County, formed in 1893 from parts of San Bernardino and San Diego—a full-scale replication of the Grand Palace of Fine Arts of the Paris Exposition of 1900, a Roman Imperial wedding cake of columns, towers, and pediments, which, while lacking regional reference, at least underscored Riverside's exuberant self-confidence little more than thirty years after the first twenty-five pioneering families had built their homes on empty streets set out at right angles from the Santa Ana River.

Citrus, citrus, citrus was the ambience and raison d'être of Riverside, especially after the Santa Fe inaugurated direct shipments East in 1886. By 1909 Riverside was shipping 2.3 million crates of oranges and lemons East. Each spring Riverside was awash with the scent of orange blossoms. Tourists from the Eastern states came out to see and smell the blossoms in much the same manner that others toured New England to enjoy the foliage of autumn. In tribute to both the economics and aesthetics citrus had brought to the region, Riversiders invited President Theodore Roosevelt on 8 May 1903 to transplant one of the two surviving parent navel orange trees to the cloister garden of the Mission Inn. This parent navel died in 1922. Today, the sole surviving parent navel, the very same grafted cutting brought out by buckboard from Los Angeles by Luther Tibbets in 1873, still survives at the corner of Magnolia and Arlington avenues.

IV

In terms of social and cultural heritage and aesthetic ordering of landscape, grapes were the crop most comparable to citrus. Viticulture brought with it, moreover, an ancient industry, winemaking, which embellished the agriculture of California with an art verging upon vocation and upgraded the culture of the state. The Franciscans brought *Vitis vinifera*, the wine vine, to California to produce wine for sacramental purposes and some limited table use. Through the 1830s most wine vines in California grew either in the mission gardens or in the private vineyards of the Los Angeles area, where as early as 1831 there were more than a hundred thousand vines planted. Throughout both the mission era of viticulture (1769–1834) and the pioneer era (1835–61) the Los Angeles region dominated the viticulture of Hispanic California and the early American commonwealth. Los Angeles County, for instance, was producing a million gallons of wine a year as early as 1865. An 1860 census of California winegrowers shows a pattern that would obtain even through the refounding of the wine industry after 1880, the *annus mirabilis* of California wine: that of wine as a cottage industry, dominated by owners of small cellars and surrounding vineyards, producing for a local market or for shipment to San Francisco. What few big producers there were, moreover—Benjamin Davis Wilson, William Wolfskill, William Workman, all of Los Angeles—were not the highly skilled and motivated Europeans of the next generation, but American ranchers for whom wine was but one aspect of a diversified agricultural operation. Even the smaller producers, so the 1860 census reveals, were in the main of Yankee or Irish stock, with only a few Mediterranean surnames appearing among their number.

The entrance of the Hungarian-born Agoston Haraszthy into the winemaking business in the 1850s anticipated a later generation of Europeans, to include Haraszthy's son Arpad, who would refound and systematize the industry. After service as a guards officer and administrative secretary in Vienna, Haraszthy fled to the United States in 1840 as a political refugee. As Haraszthy's *Travels in North America* (1844) attests, the Hungarian émigré, a member of the lesser nobility, fell in love with the United States, especially its opportunities for land ownership. Buying land in Wisconsin, Haraszthy grew hops, but the harsh winters of that region bothered the officer-turned-agriculturalist, ever dreaming of one day seeing the Haraszthy family reestablished in a fine home on a high hill overlooking well-tended fields which would be handed down through the Haraszthy generations. Taking his family overland in 1849, Haraszthy grew fruit trees and vineyards in the San Diego area, in addition to serving as a wholesale vintner for the small wine producers of the region. Elected sheriff, then state legislator, Haraszthy wangled himself an appointment in 1852 to the United States Mint in San Francisco, where he moved his family. His real ambition, however, was to grow grapes and to make wine as fine as the vintages of Europe.

Remaining with the mint, Haraszthy began purchasing land in San Mateo and Sonoma counties, planting his San Mateo properties with six varieties of grapes imported from Hungary. Happily for the future of the wine industry in California, but to his immediate distress, Haraszthy's career as a federal official collapsed in the mid-1850s, when $130,000 worth of gold dust was discovered to have disappeared from his jurisdiction. Charged with embezzlement, Haraszthy was forced to endure a humiliating inquiry—until it was discovered that the gold dust had not been stolen after all, but had disappeared up a faulty smelter flue and been sprinkled irretrievably over the rooftops of San Francisco. When it was over, Haraszthy, shaking the lesser dust of San Francisco from his feet, retired to his Sonoma properties in 1857, where he planted four hundred acres of vineyards that swept up from the Sonoma Valley floor to the well-drained, gravelly hillsides so perfect for viticulture at the base of the Mayacamas Mountains separating the Sonoma Valley from the Napa Valley to the east. On the highest portion of his six-thousand-acre property Haraszthy built Buena Vista, a neoclassical Pompeian villa perfectly expressive of his long-held dream of living on the land with the feudal expansiveness of his Hungarian ancestors.

The wines which Haraszthy produced under the Buena Vista label, pioneering the use of redwood for wine casks, attracted immediate attention. In 1858 they were judged best in the state. The State Agricultural Society commissioners who had awarded Haraszthy first prize then asked him to write the pioneering *Report on Grapes and Wines in California* (1859), the first such manual produced in California. On 11 June 1861, this time at the request of the legislature, Haraszthy sailed for Europe, where he traveled for the rest of the year through various wine regions, seeking grape stocks that might flourish in California. All in all, Haraszthy sent back some two hundred thousand cuttings, representing more than fourteen hundred varieties, thus singlehandedly effecting a mass migration of vines from Europe to California. This work of transplantation, together with the example of his own Buena Vista Vineyards and the influence of his two manuals, the *Report* and the classic *Grape Culture, Wines and Wine-Making, with Notes upon Agriculture and Horticulture* (1862), which he wrote upon his return from Europe, earned Agoston Haraszthy the designation "Father of California Viticulture."

As a viticulturalist, winemaker, and wine writer, Agoston Haraszthy ushered in the involvement of Europeans in California wine which would, ultimately, raise standards and thus provide California with its most complex, most symbolically associative agricultural product. Unfortunately, the Father of Viticulture would not live to see his heirs, including his own son Arpad, flourish as winemakers. In 1869, crossing a river in Nicaragua en route to the Eastern United States, Agoston Haraszthy fell from his canoe and was devoured by caiman alligators, a grotesque, horrible end, irrational and perversely ludicrous, to say the least, unworthy of such a civilizing spirit.

In later years, a belief grew up that among the cuttings Haraszthy sent back from Europe was a Hungarian red grape which, when grafted onto the hardy mission grape stock, made for a new red wine, Zinfandel, which combined the smooth finish of the Old World with the robust fullness of California. Recent scholarship has debunked this long-held belief. Zinfandel was actually developed from a Massachusetts table grape (ultimately Hungarian in origin, however), grown under hothouse conditions and first brought to California in the early 1850s by Frederick W. Macondray, a New England ship captain with an interest in horticulture who served as first president of the California Agricultural Society. As the wine industry of California expanded, it looked to Zinfandel, grafted onto mission stock and capable of thriving without irrigation, as the basis of its dry red wine production. That Californians wished to believe that this wine had been personally introduced by Agoston Haraszthy from Europe testifies to the fact that by the 1880s the wine industry was on the lookout for symbols of its emerging identity as the matrix of an all-important Europe-California connection. Haraszthy led off this procession of Europeans into the vineyards of California, and throughout the period of foundation and refoundation, from the 1860s through the passage of the Volstead Act in 1919, the migration of Europeans into this sector of California agriculture continued.

Haraszthy's contemporary, Pierre Pellier, arriving in San Jose in 1853 from his native La Rochelle, returned to France in 1856 on the busy expedition which netted him a wife as well as prune, plum, and vine cuttings, which he inserted into raw potatoes for safekeeping on the six-month voyage back from Europe. Pellier's vineyards and cellar, which he commenced operating in 1859, were left to his son-in-law, Pierre Mirassou, who inaugurated a five-generation wine dynasty in the Santa Clara and Monterey counties. Haraszthy himself sold Charles Krug, a German-language journalist on the staff of the Oakland-based *Staatszeitung*, his first vineyard in Sonoma in 1858. Moving to the Napa Valley in 1860 after his marriage to one of General Vallejo's nieces, Krug spent the remaining thirty years of his life as the Napa Valley's leading winemaker. Another German, Jacob Schram, a Rhinelander who arrived in the Napa Valley in 1862, supported himself as a barber until his vines matured. It was Schram's winery that Robert Louis Stevenson visited in 1880 while on his honeymoon. In *Silverado Squatters* (1883) Stevenson praised Schram's wine as proof positive that the ancient craft of winemaking could be successfully translated to California. Carl Heinrich Wente, a Hanoverian immigrant, apprenticed himself to Charles Krug in Napa after his arrival in California in 1880. Three years later Wente moved to the Livermore Valley on the eastern side of San Francisco Bay and bought fifty acres, which he planted with Semillon and Sauvignon Blanc. By the end of the century Wente was producing the finest white wines in California. Two more Rhinelanders, the brothers Jacob and Frederick Beringer, born to an old winemaking family in Mainz, opened a Napa winery in 1876, which they headquartered in Rhine House, an elaborate recreation of a Rhineland vineyard villa. A Finn in his early forties, Gustave Niebaum turned to Napa winemaking in 1879 after making a fortune as a partner in the Alaska Commercial Company. Captain Niebaum (he began his career in the seal fur trade) graced his thousand-acre Inglenook estate with an ambitious three-story stone winery in semi-Gothic style. Georges de Latour, meanwhile, a French-born Sonoma County businessman with a background in chemistry, was scouting around Napa for possible vineyard properties. It took de Latour until 1899 to make the transition from his business in Healdsburg to wine growing in the Napa Valley. His wife, Fernande de Latour, named their property just north of Inglenook, Beaulieu, or beautiful place; the de Latours planted it with vines brought back personally from France. Also at work in Napa by this time were Samuele Sebastiani, a Tuscan who had saved his wages as a laborer in San Francisco to buy property, and Antonio Foni, a Lombardian whose Lambarda Cellars (later Freemark Abbey) was situated in a charming ecclesiastical-style stone winery. Across the Mayacamas Mountains in Sonoma, a colony of northern Italian and Swiss immigrants at Asti had been busy producing wine since the late 1880s, while a few miles east on the Russian River the three Korbel brothers from Bohemia, joined by the widely experienced winemaker Franz Hazek of Prague, were turning out a dry sparkling wine in the style of Central Europe.

In the design of their homes and cellars, in the way they lived on the land or celebrated a harvest, and most obviously in the wines they cellared in oaken casks in the stony recesses of their wineries or produced in bulk for an immediate market, these Euro-Californians brought to their immediate agricultural environments an element of translated heritage, of patience and care for the land, and frequently of exuberant joy in life that added itself to the accumulating maturity of agricultural society in California. It would take time for their wine to win a wider American acceptance, but from the beginning these Euro-Californian vineyardists and winemakers held up to California agriculture an example of individual fulfillment in vital connection with the land and the cycles of season, of developed patterns of daily living, that was sorely needed by Californians seeking to return, against odds, to rural living.

Paul Masson provides a larger-than-life example of how the values and life-styles of Europe were transplanted to the wine country of California along with viticultural cuttings. Perhaps no other figure, certainly not the beleaguered Agoston Haraszthy, epitomized the joy of life that could come from wine as did this gargantuan Burgundian: shrewd, heroically hedonistic, by turns his-trionic and sincere—a character, in short, whom another Burgundian, Rabe-lais, would have instantly recognized as one of his own. As a boy in the town of Beaune in the Cote d'Or of Burgundy, Paul Masson grew up with wine, which was from his earliest years his chosen calling. After a local apprentice-ship and studies at the Sorbonne, Masson traveled to California in 1878 at the age of nineteen, on the lookout for wider prospects than were available in his own region, where an entrenched wine elite made new ventures difficult and where the phylloxera epidemic had severely damaged the Masson family vine-yards. Visiting Charles Lefranc, a French friend who was growing grapes near the town of Saratoga in the Santa Clara Valley, Masson discovered the place where he was to pursue his life's work. Going to work for Lefranc, Masson, with a shrewd Gallic sense of family, married his employer's daughter. Lefranc, on his part, brought his son-in-law into the winery, which was reconstituted as Lefranc and Masson. Feeling the need of further study, Masson returned to France in 1884 to study the production of champagne, which he believed he could make in the hillside vineyards of Saratoga. Buying out his father-in-law in 1892, Masson launched the Paul Masson Champagne Company. Eight years later he had the satisfaction of an honorable mention at the Paris Exposition of 1900, followed by a *grand prix* at the Louisiana Purchase Exposition of 1904.

As prosperity came, Paul Masson established himself as the grand man of California wine, a tireless traveler, salesman, and propagandist for his own products and for the California wine industry in general. At La Cresta, a hilltop cloister dominated by a Spanish Romanesque portal overlooking a sweeping panorama of vineyards, Masson lived an aggressively Burgundian version of the good life, reachieved amidst California circumstances. His gastronomic incli-nations were legendary. Masson raised his own prize squab and guinea hens, which he roasted wrapped in strips of pork on spits in an open hearth in his villa kitchen. Live lobster and crayfish were kept readily available in a garden pool. Not surprisingly, Masson's crayfish and lobster salads were legendary. Shrewdly, Masson knew the value of a good dinner and an array of fine wines presented to prospective clients at La Cresta or down in San Jose at the Sainte Claire Club; for while Paul Masson was ever in pursuit of the good life—wine, food, women (scholarship must reject as mere hearsay, however, the story that he personally bathed actress Anna Held in champagne when she visited him at La Cresta in 1917)—he was first and foremost an ardent businessman, anxious to develop his own winery and to advance California winemaking in general. His villa, his gardens, his supper parties, the lavish luncheons on the terrace overlooking his vineyards were in great part intended as a marketing device. Paul Masson wanted to sell champagne, and he also wanted to sell a concept: that viticulture had brought more expansive, more exuberant possibilities to American culture in California. Having come to the United States at nineteen, Masson occasionally overplayed the Frenchman, and certain of his amorous indiscretions infuriated his long-suffering wife, yet Masson did serve for decades as the premier spokesman for an emergent agricultural industry, the living embodiment of California wine as a total way of life.

The decade of the 1880s, in the midst of which Paul Masson returned to France for further study, witnessed much progress in California wine. Lecturing on California wine in London in 1894, wine importer C. F. Oldham later described 1880 as an *annus mirabilis*, a year of decision. After heroically more than doubling its vines in the 1860s, from 10.5 million to 26.5 million, the wine industry of California should have consolidated itself in the 1870s, putting emphasis upon the technology of production. Instead, a bonanza mentality similar to that of the wheat industry kept vineyards expanding. By 1876 overexpansion had led to a depression. There were too many grapes, so many, in fact, that vineyardists, threatened with foreclosure, leased their properties to pig farmers, whose animals browsed happily on ripe grapes that had been intended for quality vintages. Much of the wine that was made, furthermore, was rushed through production in an effort to maintain an endangered cash flow. Haste, poor cooperage, and sloppy cellaring all took their toll, and inferior California wine went out on the market, creating a reputation that further depressed the industry. Then the destructive parasite phylloxera struck Napa and Sonoma, not as brutally as in France, where an age-old industry was threatened with virtual extinction, but significantly enough to retard the recovery process under way between 1876 and 1880. That year, Arpad Haraszthy, who had followed his father into the wine business and was then serving as president of the state Viticultural Society, joined such other wine growers as Charles Wetmore and Charles Krug and Professor Eugene Hilgard of the University of California department of agriculture to persuade the legislature to create a publicly funded Board of State Viticultural Commissioners, authorized to promote the industry and set standards for California wine, fight phylloxera and other viticultural diseases, and advance viticultural and enological research and education. A pure wine law was also passed to prevent (it was hoped) the disastrous practices that had led to the abominable vintages of the mid-1870s.

At their first meeting on 24 May 1880 the commissioners elected as their chairman and executive officer Charles Wetmore, a San Francisco journalist who had become interested in wine in the course of investigating the collapse of 1876. To better inform himself, Wetmore had traveled to France in 1879 as an unpaid agent of the state Viticultural Society. There he made a thorough study of French viticultural and winemaking practices, which he described in a series of articles for the San Francisco press. These articles were not uniformly adulatory. While finding much to admire in French wine, Wetmore despised the French practice of sending less-than-ordinary *vin ordinaire* to the United States in bottles with fancy labels, wine which Americans preferred over superior Californian vintages. Even the finest restaurants of San Francisco, the capital city of the California wine country, Wetmore lamented, were guilty of pouring California wine into bottles with French labels: a distressing sign of both the deservedly inferior reputation of California wine and the American reluctance to consider wine a domestic agricultural product. Entering the wine business himself in 1882 at his Cresta Blanca Vineyard in the Livermore Valley, Wetmore returned to France to obtain Semillon and Sauvignon Blanc cuttings from Chateau d'Yquem. In 1889, five years after his first vintage, this onetime journalist, a native-born American of Protestant origins, thrilled the California wine world by winning two gold medals at the Paris Exposition.

Meanwhile, Wetmore had also busied himself with the commission's work of promoting standards and sponsoring research. Unfortunately, the bonanza mentality still remained. More than forty thousand new vines were planted between 1880 and 1882 alone. In a mere three years, 1881–83, Leland Stanford planted a prodigious million vines on his Tehama County properties. By 1889 Senator Stanford was growing more than three million vines on 3,825 acres in Tehama. By 1890 some 120 million vines covered 150,000 acres, hillside and valley, in the wine regions of the state. This rapid recovery involved an overexpansion similar to that of the 1870s, and in 1886, exactly ten years after the first major bust, the wine market once again collapsed. A large but poor crop and the withdrawal of Eastern wholesale vintners from the California market threw the previously improving industry into a recession lasting another six years. These repeated cycles of boom and bust suggest the underlying immaturity of California wine. Although millions of vines covered the hills and valleys of California and some internationally acknowledged vintages were being produced, together with much passable *vin ordinaire*, California wine had a long way to go before it could calibrate its production to its market, improve its general standards, and win a measure of critical acceptance among connoisseurs; and just as this was being accomplished, Prohibition descended like a long dark night.

Yet despite the problem of an erratically expanding and contracting industry, wine did achieve during these years a level of self-awareness that was absolutely necessary if this most important sector of California agriculture were ever to reach full maturity. As in the case of citrus, promotional writers, beginning with Agoston Haraszthy, helped in this evolution toward self-consciousness. Five years after Haraszthy's pioneering *Grape Culture, Wines and Wine-Making* appeared, Thomas Hart Hyatt, proprietor of the Mount Glenwood Winery in Napa, issued the very influential *Handbook of Grape Culture* (1867). A career diplomat before his arrival in California, with service as consul general in Morocco and China, Hyatt had in the course of his career traveled extensively throughout the wine regions of the Mediterranean with an eye toward wine as his second career. Leaving the consular corps, he chose California, he said, because it showed every prospect of flourishing as the land of the vine, the fig, the orange, the palm, and the olive. Ensconced as editor of the *California Rural Home Journal*, Hyatt made a thorough survey of the extant viticultural literature in preparation for his handbook, which he dedicated to the great Ezra Cornell of New York. Hyatt's *Handbook of Grape Culture* sold out within the year because it was a model of self-instruction, allowing the novice to proceed step by patient step with the diplomat-turned-vineyardist through the entire process of wine, from cutting to cooperage.

Reissued in 1876 by A. L. Bancroft, Hyatt's *Handbook* was soon supplemented by E. Rixford's *The Wine Press* (1883) and George Husmann's *Grape Culture and Wine-Making in California* (1888). The entrance of Professor Husmann, America's greatest viticultural expert, into the field of manual writing for California wine attested to the expectations for the industry. Along with an array of useful detail, these georgic manuals also suggested an ideality, a conception of life on the land, which permeated the most successful and intriguing wine book from this period, Frona Eunice Wait's *Wines and Vines of California* (1889). In fact, this *San Francisco Examiner* reporter, a native-born Californian then in her late twenties, with no practical experience in wine, wrote one of California wine's half dozen most signficant books: a summary statement subsuming nearly a half century's effort, a vivid description of the present state of the industry and a call for sophisticated and responsible future growth. Prior to joining William Randolph Hearst's *Examiner* as its first female reporter, Wait had worked as a staff researcher and writer in Hubert Howe Bancroft's San Francisco history factory. *Wines and Vines of California*, not surprisingly, is informed by historical perspective as well as enlivened by abundant detail. Wait spent months in the field, visiting wineries and interviewing wine growers. Beyond the immediate coloring of her portraits, as charming as they are, was a program for the future as well as a depiction of the present. California wine, Wait argued, should raise its standards and promote the national consumption of wine as a temperance beverage.

To debate the quality of California wine was by implication to debate the quality of California itself, for if Californians diluted their wine, or laced it with sugar, or falsely labeled their best vintages as French, were they not suggesting shabby deception in other aspects of California as well? Wait correctly credited Arpad Haraszthy with leading the fight to put California wine on an honest basis. Sent by his father to Paris in 1857 to study civil engineering, Arpad Haraszthy had spent two additional years as an intern in the champagne-producing House of De Venoge at Épernay. While there, he sent back articles on viticulture to the *California Farmer* which revealed that Arpad was following in his father's footsteps as a wine observer and propagandist. Rejoining his father in California in 1862 as cellar-master at Buena Vista, Arpad Haraszthy spent the next twenty years in pursuit of an elusive but compelling dream, the production of world-class champagne. In a series of articles published in the *Overland Monthly* (then at the height of its influence) in December 1871 and January and February 1872, Haraszthy argued that only the highest European standards would suffice for California wine, if the industry was to have even the remotest chance of capturing the Eastern American market from the European imports: standards which Haraszthy himself pursued as a winemaker and as a San Francisco–based vinter, buying bulk wine from California cellars for blending and shipment to the East. On the other hand, Frona Wait in *Wines and Vines of California* challenged Americans to give California wine a try—and not associate good wine only with French labels. The question remained complex and unresolved, suggestive, in fact, of the larger American lack of self-confidence in the matter of taste and the corroboration of taste in the high arts, including the art of wine. Local standards did improve, however, helped by the research programs of the state board of viticulture commissioners, which established a four-hundred-volume library, the best such collection in the country. The board also published an English translation of a treatise on wine classification by Professor G. Grazzi-Soncini, director of the Royal School of Viticulture at Alba, Italy, and cooperated with the research efforts of the Department of Agriculture of the University of California, to whom the legislature assigned primary responsibility for viticultural and enological research in 1895, after Charles Wetmore of the board and Eugene Hilgard of the university broke on the question of the value of primary research to the industry.

After 1886, moreover, the better European grapes began to be planted in increasing numbers, and Californians learned to reduce grape sugar through, in part, a better use of irrigation, thus producing drier varieties of wine that helped offset the reputation for sweetness that plagued California wine. A survey of menus from the better restaurants of San Francisco reveals that by the turn of the century the best California wines were now appearing under their own labels. But it was European recognition that counted most: the initial honorable mentions from Paris, and then the more gratifying silver and gold awards won by Italian Swiss Colony, Paul Masson, Charles Wetmore, and the others. Here was recognition indeed (even if boasting of such recognition underscored a persistent provincialism) that the wine of Europe had an aspiring offshoot on the other side of the planet.

As welcome as the recognition of connoisseurs might be, however, the primary need facing California wine, as Frona Wait saw so clearly in *Wines and*

Vines of California, was the creation of a national market similar to that being forged by citrus. If California wine was to develop beyond the status of an exotic provincial industry, Wait argued, Americans must be persuaded to drink wine as part of their daily diet. It was one thing, however, to win medals in Paris, another to win America—a rural Protestant nation—to an agricultural product which the evangelical mind considered exotic, if not downright sinful. The first priority for the winning of America, George Husmann believed, was an adjustment of the price structure. "How," he asked, "can we ever expect to see wine what it ought to be, the daily beverage of our people, enlivening and strengthening them, and making them truly temperate, when it is retailed at such enormous profit, the retailer charging six to eight dollars per gallon, for what costs him thirty cents?" Like citrus, California wine had to develop its own national marketing and shipping system, independent of exploitative middlemen. Secondly, wine had to be Americanized, which meant that both its snobbish associations and, paradoxically, its reputation as a cheap drink for Southern European immigrants had to be readjusted. In her influential book, Frona Wait included a chapter by Arpad Haraszthy entitled "How to Drink Wine," in which Haraszthy set forth in simple detail the whys and wherefores of wine service. In *See How It Sparkles* (1896) another Californian, journalist, and Southern Pacific publicist, Benjamin Cummings Truman, produced one of the finest American essays in wine connoisseurship of the turn-of-the-century era: a robust and affirming description of the interrelationships between wine and food, unmarred by provincial promotionalism. By linking Californian and European vintages together throughout his essay, Truman took for granted that California wine had come of age. Truman's international outlook underscored the dawning desire of California vintners to compete directly with Europe for Europe's own business and for that of other foreign markets. California, vintner D. W. C. Nesfield pointed out in 1883, had five to eight times more possible wine areas than France. Should these regions be developed, California wine could become a force on the international market. Even as Nesfield wrote, California vintners were beginning to compete with their European and New York–based counterparts for the considerable wine business of Mexico and Latin America. A few years later, on the evening of 31 January 1894, Charles Furley Oldham of the London firm of Grierson, Oldham and Company, 11 Regent Street, shippers of California wine to Great Britain, was telling the Society of Arts that not far into the twentieth century the wine regions of far-off California (he began his talk by pointing to California on the map, so that all might know where it was) would compete directly with France for the English market.

Back in the United States, California wine men, directly assaulting the core of evangelical Protestant objection, sought to sell their product as a temperance beverage. The temperance argument had its origins with Thomas Jefferson, the first important wine apologist in America. The argument, intact since Jefferson first made it ("No nation is drunken where wine is cheap, and none sober where dearness of wine substitutes ardent spirits as its common beverage"), ran thusly: In contradistinction to hard liquor, wine was a food as well as a mildly alcoholic beverage. Wine drinking, in conjunction with eating, promoted moderation. Hard liquor, by contrast, was consumed strictly for its exhilarating effects. Whereas wine promoted health and good order, hard liquor, especially as abused by American working men and women, destroyed health and family life. For Andrea Sbarboro, founder of the Italian Swiss Colony Winery at Asti in Sonoma County, the promotion of wine as a temperance agent became an all-consuming crusade. In the course of his ceaseless lecturing and pamphleteering, Sbarboro, speaking as an Italian-American and as a Californian, took his message right to President Theodore Roosevelt himself, who listened politely. How could wine be immoral, Sbarboro asked with an eye toward his fundamentalist antagonists, when Jesus himself turned water into wine at Cana? In contrast to France, Spain, Italy, Portugal, and South Germany, moreover, the United States had a collective drinking problem that related directly to its addiction to hard liquor. Served wine with dinner, Sbarboro argued, the American husband would avoid the saloon. A light wine ration for soldiers and sailors might help put an end to such incidents as the terrible deaths and blindings a few years earlier of those sailors stationed in San Francisco—ported ships after they had drunk wood alcohol when they could not get ashore to do their boozing. Taught to use wine at meals, Stanford undergraduates might not be so prone to the outbursts of drunken rioting which had recently disgraced the university.

For Sbarboro's generation of wine growers, the Volstead Act, ratified on 16 January 1919, came as a personal repudiation as well as an economic shock. From Jefferson onwards, the argument for wine, taken up so forcefully by the Californians, was an argument on the level of metaphor on behalf of American civility, for the attainment of the golden mean. Alcoholism, on the other hand, with its suggestions of a crushing industrial society, and Prohibition, with its prescriptive fundamentalism, were equally foreign to the Euro-Californians who made, used, and promoted wine. Defending wine, they were defending themselves as Mediterranean Americans and California as a society in which Mediterranean vines and values had been successfully transplanted. Certainly there was much to corroborate their belief and thus to justify their outrage when in 1919 America ordered them to make no more wine. Wine had brought civility to rural California: in stone cellars nestled amidst oak trees; in vineyard homes, each with their suggestion of dynastic hopes; in the heritages and lives of the European wine families, with their religion (including the religion of wine) and their memories of a way of life whose origins ran to antiquity; and most obviously in the vineyards themselves, leafy from March to mid-May, then graced with fruit buds bursting into bloom in June, the fruit ripening through summer for a September harvest, and then in October, the harvest complete, flaming out in an orgy of color—yellow for Chardonnay, bright crimson for Cabernet Sauvignon, purple for Petite Sirah, the older the vineyard the richer the color— until the vines stood empty in December and were pruned, to wait nakedly for March and the repetition of the cycle. And now Prohibition, fought so vigorously for all these years, put an end to the georgic splendor, and for over a decade the vineyards ran wild and unattended. For a span of years, however, from 1880 to 1919, wine had graced the hillsides of California with workaday prose and Vergilian poetry.

V

Between 1848 and 1869 the pioneer nurserymen of California, importing seeds and cuttings over vast distances, experimenting with what would grow, were more than purveyors of trees and plants. They were botanists and market researchers as well, for as a rash of exotic (and failed) crops would eventually show, the fact that nearly everything could grow in California did not necessarily mean that everything would grow well or that everything should be grown. A work of sorting and experiment, culminating in the career of Luther Burbank, was necessary. In 1848 California's first commercial nurseryman, A. P. Smith, purchased sixty-five acres from Captain Sutter on the banks of the American River just north of Sacramento and there established a Pomological Gardens, which by 1857 had grown to three greenhouses, each over a hundred feet in length, where Smith maintained 1,109 varieties of fruit trees while at the same time experimenting with grape stocks, including the progenitor of Zinfandel. By 1857 Smith was netting $40,000 from a $150,000 gross, a staggering income for that era. Others soon joined Smith in the nursery business: James Hutchison and George Lee of Oakland, Wilson Flint of Alameda (considered by 1856 the finest nurseryman in the state), and San Franciscans H. A. Sontag, James O'Donnell, W. C. Walker, and R. W. Washburn, all of them meeting together for the first time in San Francisco in 1858 to declare war upon the itinerant tree peddlers who were going from ranch to ranch hawking inferior seeds and cuttings.

Not every crop introduced by these experimenters met with success, nor did every agriculturalist who took their advice. Quite frequently, agricultural metaphors ran out ahead of agricultural realities. Why, for instance, should H. H. Messenger, a former missionary in West Africa, attempt in the late 1860s to grow plaintains, bananas, pineapples, cacao, coconuts, coffee, mangos, and avocados on his San Gabriel property? Or why should the state legislature offer bounties to anyone successfully growing cane sugar, sorghum, flax, hemp, tobacco, cotton, indigo, or rice? In each case, a metaphor—semi-tropical California, California as South—was dominating practical agriculture. The Mediterranean comparison led to a cultivation of dates, figs, and olives, which thrived together with many biblically mentioned fruits, which struck a deep chord among Protestants. Pursued after the Civil War by agriculturalists from the defeated Confederacy, the "California as South" metaphor led to many crops that failed—tobacco, sugarcane—but also to cotton and rice, in which California, after some difficulties, became a national leader. More exotically, the guava, medlar, persimmon, and pomegranate were brought to California with varying degrees of success because of the region's far-fetched associations with the spice islands of the East Indies and the Levant. Sensing California's affinities with Japan, Japanese immigrant T. A. Kendo proposed the cultivation of silk and tea, and a number of agriculturalists went broke taking his advice. The tangerine, however, did make a successful migration across the Pacific.

The symbolic significance of Luther Burbank—why he became such a cult figure—proceeded directly from this matrix of metaphor and practical agriculture. Living simply in his Santa Rosa cottage with his wife and elderly mother, Burbank, the wizard with plants, the creator of new fruits and flowers, absorbed and then projected onto the level of social myth that primary relationship to nature as garden, as horticulture, plastic and inventive, that so appealed to the American imagination in California. Just as Burbank's contemporary John Muir dramatized nature as transcendence, as a pathway to incipiently religious meaning, Burbank, a religious skeptic and a Darwinist by conviction and professional practice, dramatized nature as protean possibility awaiting the guiding hand of man. Burbank lacked the systematic approach of his colleague Carl Purdy of Ukiah, a former school teacher turned horticultural experimentalist who kept extensive observations and published his research in scholarly journals; nor did he possess the academic background of Dr. F. Franceschi, who was responsible for introducing so many new crops and flowering plants to California. Working, rather, with intuitive haphazardness—a gardener touched by genius, as he was later described—Burbank kept few notes, destroyed his unsuccessful experiments, kept his counsel regarding his methods, and in the end created astonishingly improved strains of vegetables, fruits, and flowers.

Since so many Californians considered evolutionism a key premise of California thought and practice, it was not surprising that Burbank was hailed as a hero. In this shy, retiring Santa Rosa nurseryman, living simply in a rose-covered cottage, Californians beheld an idealized image of themselves as scientific horticulturalists, coaxing nature to new harvests. Improving the fruits, flowers, melons, and vegetables of California or creating entirely new floral forms, such as his famed Shasta daisy, Burbank seemed to be speaking directly to nature and hearing nature's voice in return, then returning from this dialogue with new beauty and usefulness. Burbank seemed almost priestly in his ascetic, contemplative refusal to capitalize his nursery operation into a full-scale business venture. For San Francisco journalist Charles Howard Shinn, Luther Burbank was California's great civilizer, the embodiment of horticulture as "the great conservative force underlying our modern life and keeping us from destruction." As important as Burbank's achievement was, however, it did not perpetuate itself institutionally. Like so many inventive Americans of his era (his friends Thomas Alva Edison and Henry Ford, for instance), Luther Burbank was not a university man. His fellow agricultural researcher Eugene W. Hilgard, however, a university-trained soils scientist appointed to the chair of agriculture at the University of California in 1874, founded an Agricultural Experiment Station the year of his arrival. By 1890 Hilgard had a fully staffed College of Agriculture, which Hilgard's successor E. J. Wickson, augmented with a university farm at Davisville near Sacramento and a Citrus Experiment Station in Riverside, on the eastern slope of Mount Rubidoux.

California agriculture thus learned to think systematically about itself and to plan for its future. It also learned to cooperate. This cooperative impulse, of unquestioned value as a socioeconomic model for American agriculture as a whole, was also, as E. J. Wickson wrote in 1923, "unquestionably the most powerful agency for advancement in the quality of rural life in California during the last two decades." By 1920 one-half of California's total crop—honey, olives, lima beans, onions, asparagus, and sweet potatoes, together with such commanding crops as citrus, raisins, apples, walnuts, and rice—was harvested, processed, shipped, and marketed by nearly sixty voluntary cooperatives in which growers organized themselves to do together what none could do separately. In certain cases—walnuts, almonds, raisins, and citrus, most conspicuously—cooperatives literally created a national demand for their product. In 1890, for instance, walnuts and almonds were considered a luxury item among Americans, perhaps tasted once a year in a Christmas cake. Despite its vast potential for growing walnuts and almonds, California was producing a mere seventeen hundred tons or so of either crop. By the second decade of the twentieth century, however, two statewide cooperatives, the California Walnut Growers Association and the California Almond Growers Exchange, each formed at the turn of the century, had made Diamond Brand Walnuts and Fancy Brand Almonds a staple in millions of middle-class households.

In the late 1880s raisins were such an exotic food that, in a manner similar to the French labeling of California wine, the raisin growers of Fresno packaged their product in spurious Spanish labels. Organized in 1911, the California Raisin Exchange sought to sell a raisin crop that since 1892 had been exceeding Spain's but had yet to find a secure niche in the American diet. Happening upon a young woman drying her curly jet-black hair under a red bonnet in the front yard of her Fresno home one sunny Sunday morning in 1915, raisin cooperative executive Leroy Rayne glimpsed what would eventually be one of the most famous trademarks in history. Painted in her red bonnet, holding a basket of grapes, young Lorraine Collett was transformed into the Sun Maid, a marketing image so successful in its suggestions of health, abundance, and rural charm that in 1920 the cooperative took Sun-Maid as its formal name. Pouring $2.5 million and more each year into advertising and promotion throughout the 1920s, and hitting upon the idea of Little Sun-Maids, small packages selling for a nickel and designed as a snack for school lunches, the Sun-Maid Raisin Growers' Association tripled the consumption of raisins in America through the 1920s, while at the same time opening up new markets in Europe, Asia, and Latin America.

Nowhere was the cooperative ideal more fully enacted than in citrus, where the California Fruit Growers Exchange and its *Sunkist* trademark made marketing history. Through the Florida Fruit Exchange, founded in February 1885, the Florida citrus industry pioneered the cooperative as a means of collectively processing and marketing citrus fruit. That year in California, an Orange Growers Protective Union was formed as a trade association, together with a California Fruit Union, which sent agents east to represent California citrus, but a fully integrated cooperative was another decade on the horizon. The early 1890s were red-ink years for Southern California citrus, as speculators beat down prices and growers, having no means to get their citrus to Eastern wholesalers, found themselves at the speculators' mercy. Growers from the Riverside area led by T. H. B. Chamblin decided during this depressed period that they must put the means of packing, shipping, and marketing into their own hands, as had their Florida counterparts. The organization they formed in 1892, the Pachappa Orange Growers' Association of Riverside, brought the cooperative idea to Southern California. The very next year, in a meeting held in the Los Angeles Chamber of Commerce on 4 April 1893, the major orange growers of Southern California agreed to stimulate a federation of local associations and exchanges modeled upon the Pachappa cooperative, each agency reporting to a centralized board of control under the presidency of A. H. Naftzger, a Riverside banker. A year later the lemon growers of the citrus belt joined the Southern California Fruit Exchange, as it was called until its expansion and further reorganization on 27 March 1905 into the California Fruit Growers Exchange, an umbrella organization encompassing 15,000 individual citrus growers, organized into 201 local packing associations, which reported in turn to 25 district exchanges under the control of the governing board of the central exchange.

Aside from putting the means of packaging and shipping into the growers' hands, the exchange's major contribution was to convince Americans, millions of them, to eat oranges—by the millions. In the early 1880s, when most Americans had never laid eyes on an orange, the practice grew up of wrapping each piece of fruit in specially decorated tissue paper, so that it reached the Eastern market as a luxury item. Even then, however, many Southern Californians, such as Dr. O. P. Chubb of Orange County, who toured the East and Midwest in 1886 on behalf of the Orange Growers Protective Union of Southern California, were urging growers to bring oranges to the East as a staple food, not a luxury. Such a shift in perception did not come easily. Rather it had to be created by an emerging American medium, national advertising.

In 1904 the Lord and Thomas advertising agency of Chicago presented the board of the exchange with a citrus promotion campaign for the state of Iowa budgeted at $30,000. The board rejected the proposal as too expensive. Three years later, however, when Southern Pacific agreed to finance a joint campaign, the exchange allocated $10,000 toward the sending of a special Orange Train to Iowa, promoting "Oranges for Health—California for Wealth." Significantly, the selling of oranges and California were conjoined. That year, moreover, the exchange's trademark *Sunkist*, a refined version of the originally proposed *Sunkissed*, came into use, with its dual statement regarding the orange and the sunny land where oranges came from. Later stamped on each piece of fruit, the trademark *Sunkist* replaced the more than two hundred individual brand names in use in 1901, and eventually became, like Sun-Maid, one of the most successful trademarks in history.

In the years that followed the sending of the Orange Train to Iowa, Lord and Thomas's budget, together with the sophistication of its marketing and advertising techniques, grew tenfold, to include direct mailing, which Lord and Thomas pioneered as a promotional technique. By 1914—the year that Sun-Maid, impressed with *Sunkist*'s success, took its account to Lord and Thomas as well—consumption of oranges by Americans had increased by 79.6 percent, from the next-to-no-oranges of 1885 to approximately forty oranges per American per year. After 1916 the team of Don Francisco, the young advertising manager of the exchange, and Robert P. Crane, the Lord and Thomas copywriter with primary responsibility for the *Sunkist* account, hit upon a cluster of advertising themes—health, domestic happiness, prosperity, respectability—that would eventually make the eating of a California orange or the drinking of a glass of California orange juice a ritual of proper American intent. The invention of an efficient juice extractor the year Francisco took over the promotion desk at the exchange opened up further vistas. *Sunkist*'s "Drink an Orange" campaign, begun that year, soon brought fresh orange juice into the drugstores and soda fountains of America. Whether promoting oranges or orange juice, however, the campaign inaugurated by Francisco and carried on by Crane and others at Lord and Thomas aimed itself directly at middle-class hopes for the good life, and by so doing further linked these aspirations by subliminal association to Orangeland California.

In the inventive labels pasted upon each orange crate, moreover, the selling of California along with oranges as an image in the national imagination became even more explicit. So appealing in its color, the orange inspired graphic ambitions as early as the publication in 1888 of B. M. Lelong's citrus treatise by the state printing office. On the verso of the title page of Lelong's study was printed a color plate of a whole orange and a sectioned half fruit, luxuriantly rich in color. Even today, nearly a hundred years later, when the rest of the publication has faded with age, these bright orange illustrations fairly leap from the page, as full of assertive color as they were on the day of publication. In the 1890s the custom grew up of individual packing houses labeling their orange crates with a specific brand name and trademark. Initially these staid labels had little, if any, California reference: "Victoria Brand," for instance (a portrait of the queen herself), or "Gypsy Queen," "Elk Brand," and "Our Pride" (a battleship under full steam). But then Max Schmidt, a San Francisco printer, got into the business of designing, printing, and selling orange crate labels. With the help of such staff artists as Othello Michetti, an Italian-born San Franciscan, and Archie Vazques, a Los Angeles Basque, Schmidt created a significant genre of folk art, the orange crate label. Produced through a process call zincography, the orange crate labels issuing from Schmidt Lithograph glowed with the colors later made famous by Maxfield Parrish, colors that went beyond nature and spoke directly to fantasy: apricot, purple, cobalt blue, sea green, cinnamon, cinnabar, mauve, yellow, orange. Sending a force of salesmen into the citrus groves of Southern California, Schmidt encouraged each grower to collaborate in the creation of an individualized label.

Evolving as a genre through the art deco era, orange crate labels reached a special intensity of perfection in the teens and twenties, when they were also conveying their most explicit image of California. Literally hundreds of these designs, seen daily by millions in the grocery stores of America, involved an idealized California landscape. An even larger number involved one or another allegorical or symbolic image suggestive of California as a place apart, a land of fantasy and dreams. One such label—two luxuriant peacocks lazing in a grove near a fairy-tale castle, their expanded tail feathers radiant with color—bore the explicit title "California Dream," but the dream was everywhere else as well. It was the dream of Spanish California, in such label designs as "La Paloma" (1915), a Spanish dancer against a backdrop of cactus; "Wheeler's Choice" (1920), Ramona feeding doves beneath an orange tree; "Mission Bridge" (1925), a bridge in the Spanish style soaring across a blue river, joining an orange grove with a modern roadway; "Paisano" (1930), a Spanish guitarist; or "Orange Queen" (1939), a Spanish woman holding a basket of oranges. Many labels depicted the California lifestyle in images intended to speak directly to middle-class America's desire for a home and a happy marriage and healthy children. "Suburban" (1915), for instance, depicted a snug bungalow in an orange grove. In "Sea Side" (1919) a happy family enjoys a day at the beach. In "Nightcap" (1925) a suburban California couple enjoys orange juice before retiring, and in "Windermere" (1925) a similar pair drive in an open-air roadster through a sunny

orange grove. Health, especially healthy children, and sport, especially tennis—as in "Ventura Vital" (1930), a female tennis player—were frequent motifs, as were days at the beach, garden imagery, or, in the 1930s, imagery relating to Hollywood, including W. C. Fields's face on "It's a Gift" brand (1934),
inspired by the film in which an Easterner played by Fields inherits an orange
grove. It is impossible, obviously, to gauge the influence of these orange crate
labels with any precision, yet these highly stylized images, with their message
of California as an *outremer* of vibrancy, color, healthfulness, and lush repose,
verging on the fantastic, seen by millions of Americans over a twenty-year period in moments of uncensored perception—strolling down a grocery store aisle,
coming in from a bleak farm to a country store—must have contributed in part
to California's image of itself and the nation's collective image of California.

VI

The georgic idyll depicted on so many orange crate labels of the happy outdoor
life being enjoyed by Americans in California was sadly far from the truth. From
pioneer days onwards, agriculture in California suffered from a single dynamic,
land monopoly, that thwarted Jeffersonian hopes for a yeoman life on the land
for many Californians who wished to pursue that dream. During the Spanish
and Mexican eras, the Crown and later the Republic granted land in gargantuan quantities. Many of these land grant ranchos passed into American hands
in the 1860s and 1870s. Even subdivided, such land holdings were formidable.
The federal government, meanwhile, anxious to promote the growth of railroads, was making generous grants of California land to the Central Pacific.
Much of the subdivided land that did come up for sale to individuals, moreover, was clouded in title. Small farmers or ranchers were understandably reluctant to give years of labor to improving property that could turn out, after
long and expensive adjudication, to be not theirs at all. Nor did the federal
government vigorously enact the Homestead Act of 1862 on its California properties. Between 1863 and 1869, for instance, California reported 2,848 claims
for homesteads totaling 414,861 acres. Minnesota had these many claims for
1867 alone.

Thus by the 1870s much of the land of California had fallen into the hands
of a few individuals or corporations. By 1866, as an example, Edward Fitzger-
ald Beale had consolidated ownership of four Mexican land grants in southern
Kern County for a total of 150,000 acres—a figure up to 200,000 by 1870.
Beale also controlled 300,000 acres of publicly owned grazing land, making his
Rancho Tejón a half-million-acre enterprise, approaching the size of Rhode
Island. The lands consolidated by Henry Miller and Charles Lux in the San
Joaquin Valley equaled the size of Belgium. The Southern Pacific, meanwhile,

successor company to the Central Pacific, controlled ten million California acres by 1882. If all this were not monopolistic enough, the laws enacted by the federal government to promote smaller units of land ownership were used to bring about the very opposite condition. A manipulator such as William S. Chapman cleverly managed to use various laws and lawmakers to his advantage and eventually gobbled up a million acres of public domain. Even the well-intended Reclamation Act of 1902, which sought to impose a 160-acre-per-person limit (320 acres for a married couple) on lands irrigated by federal water projects, was in the long run thwarted of its purpose.

Such a pattern of monopoly, together with high interest rates, made it extremely difficult for individual Californians to gain ownership of a self-supporting family farm. By 1890, 17.9 percent of California's farmers were tenants, a figure that climbed to 23.1 percent in 1900 and 35.6 percent in 1925. And whether a family farm be owned or rented, small-scale farming, especially before the rise of cooperatives, was an uncertain, arduous enterprise. Orchards and vineyards took years to reach productivity. A farmer might double-crop to insure an income during these years, planting rows of carrots or lima beans in the rows between growing walnut trees, but even with such expedients it took plenty of cash or a long line of credit to bring an orange grove (seven years) or a vineyard (four to five years) into full production. Thus while a good percentage of the smaller ranches and farms of California were rented, an average of a third to a half of those which were nominally owned by the resident farmer actually belonged to the bank. Many small farmers worked full time for the large ranchers or for the Southern Pacific during the years they were struggling to bring their properties productively on line; far from making available a life of bourgeois leisure, as the myth and promotional literature promised, a return to the land often involved exhausting years of double employment, as the farmers who lined up in front of the Southern Pacific pay car each month (the SP paid in gold coin) could very well testify.

In the midst of these difficulties, there were those who still found the courage and the hope to work for improved self-esteem and quality of life among the farm people of California. Professor Ezra Slocum Carr, for example, who taught agriculture at the University of California in the early 1870s, wanted special programs in domestic economy inaugurated to train young women to manage farming households properly. Believing that the condition of agricultural life reflected upon the condition of culture in general, rural and urban, Carr deplored the lack of domestic amenities among the small farmers of California: the shabby houses, the absence of nearby schools, churches, or community centers, the undeveloped social life. Would the farm children of California, Carr asked the state agricultural society in 1875, themselves choose to remain on the land as adults if farm life remained so constrained and shabby?

A generation of healthy, happy, well-educated children, Carr argued, would in turn devote itself to the land as adults and was therefore in the long run the most important agricultural crop the farmers of California could produce.

Fortunately, another option, the agricultural colony, was working against the narrow isolation Carr so deplored. Conspicuous in Southern California and spreading to Central California as well, agricultural colonies allowed Californians to pool financial and social resources in pursuit of economic survival and that more elusive but equally American ambition of community, an end to the loneliness of an isolated farmhouse in the center of a vast and empty plain. Possessed perhaps of a greater desire to preserve the amenities of life amidst their new and challenging surroundings, Euro-Californians pioneered the colony system in California agriculture, the French in the San Jose area in the early 1850s and the Germans in Anaheim in the south.

Two German-born San Francisco musicians-turned-vintners, John Frohling and Charles Kahler, had already purchased twenty thousand acres of vineyards in Southern California by 1857 when the notion struck them to organize a colony of German vineyardists on a tract they owned on the Rancho San Juan Cajón de Santa Ana in what was later known as Orange County. The cooperative they established, the Los Angeles Vineyard Society, later the colony of Anaheim, recreated some of the flavor and gemütlichkeit of South Germany. In any event, the Anaheim colonists, whatever their problems, at least had each other, as later did the Alabamans fleeing the devastations of the Civil War who established a colony in Fresno County in 1868.

All in all, nine separate colony ventures took root in Fresno County during the 1870s and early 1880s, the most notable being the Central California Colony, established in 1875 by a group of middle-class San Franciscans, many of them educated Americans from the East or immigrants from England, Scotland, Sweden, and Denmark. Consisting of 192 twenty-acre farms intended for intensive fruit culture, the Central California Colony was no utopia. Irrigation problems and encroachments by neighboring sheep and cattle plagued the colony's early years. Yet by the late 1870s these dairy farmers and growers of raisins, peaches, and figs had managed to create a reasonably civil life for themselves, including the construction of a schoolhouse and a Grange Hall, where the Histrionic and Literary Society put on monthly plays. Other Fresno County colonies—the Washington Irrigated Colony (1878), the Scandinavian Home Colony (1879), the Fresno Colony (1881)—expanded and amplified this genre of bourgeois agricultural settlement organized as a semi-cooperative. Situated on two thousand acres near Cloverdale in the Russian River Valley of Sonoma County, a site chosen precisely because the landscape so resembled the Monferrato area in Northern Italy, the Italian Swiss Colony, established in 1881 by Andrea Sbarboro, offered a mirror image of the earlier German foundation at Anaheim. Some one hundred Italian Swiss got to work at Asti planting the rolling hills of the area in Barbera, Nebiolo, and Chianti, as well as oranges, olives, and figs. By 1889, so one visitor observed, the area's original resemblance to Monferrato had become even more pronounced. Germans, Alabamans, Danes, Italian Swiss: the agricultural colonists of California struggled to create a rural culture for themselves that would not be lacking in schools, churches, meeting halls, picnics, dances, festivals, and fellowship.

Raised on a farm in Alameda County, where his father earned a reputation as the most scholarly horticulturist in the state, San Francisco journalist and former rural school teacher Charles Howard Shinn believed that he and his equally literary sister, Milicent, later to revive and edit the *Overland Monthly*, had enjoyed a model blending of rural and refined values as they were growing up. In 1879, the year he left farming and country schoolteaching for a job on the *San Francisco Bulletin*, Shinn published his *Pacific Rural Handbook*, a guide to a more gracious mode of rural life. Rural California, Shinn wrote, "is a land for vines, fruits, and flowers. It is a land whose glowing future nerves us to renewed labors as we plant our vacant hillsides, and re-claim our miles of tidelands. My thoughts go out towards California as a region of many homes, and of boundless hopes." There was no need, Shinn wrote, for rural life in California to be barbaric. With a minimum outlay of capital, homes might be tastefully furnished, hung with framed engravings and garnished with displays of dried flowers and grasses. Rural Californians should establish a home library replete not just with agricultural monographs and reference books, but with works in general literature as well. With a little effort, the surrounding area might be tastefully landscaped with a garden and shade trees.

Shinn's prescriptions for each aspect of rural life—cooking, domestic management, family life, the education of children, leisure activities—anticipated the more important work of Wickson in this same crusade. In their call for civility, Shinn, Wickson, and others were fighting against the lingering atmosphere of shabby frontier that clung to so many rural California communities, such as Willows, the seat of Glenn County and the capital of California's wheat empire, where, as one resident later remembered, in the 1880s there were no lawns or shade trees and only a wretched sewer system that filled the main street with stench, and flies everywhere; where twenty-five saloons each evening dispensed raw whiskey from a barrel to wheat workers who, their bellies filled with liquor, returned to their boardinghouses, where a quarter bought them dinner and a night's sleep. Even in many of the more developed communities, the rural California of the 1870s and 1880s (with the notable exception of viticulture and citrus) offered little that was different from rural life elsewhere in the United States: long hours and a repetitive diet, ramshackle housing, few schools, inadequate medical care, little in the way of entertainment. A tough, lonely life, in short, from which the more venturesome of the young fled as soon as they were able to do so, including Charles Howard Shinn, who left for graduate school at John Hopkins and a journalist's career in New York City, and Eleanor Calhoun of Kern County, who, moving to San Francisco, caught the attention of Phoebe Apperson Hearst, who paid for her education. Properly educated, Miss Calhoun went on the stage and later married a Serbian prince, who took her as far away from Kern County as possible.

And yet, as Shinn pointed out in the *Pacific Rural Handbook*, the lack of civility could be fought against, as it was by many of the women agriculturalists of the era. The time had come, Shinn urged, for women to enter ranch life as independent entrepreneurs, not just as homemakers, schoolteachers, or hired help. Rural life offered women as well as men a chance at financial independence and a healthy life in the outdoors. Four former schoolteachers, for instance, established the Hedgerow Vineyard near Fresno in 1878, so named because they bordered their one hundred acres of Gordo Blanco vines with a hedge of pomegranate, osage, and cypress trees. In addition to Gordo Blanco raisins, the women also grew pears, apricots, peaches, prunes, and nectarines. One of their number, Miss M. F. Austin, pioneered new sulfuring techniques. Another female Fresno agriculturist, Minna Eshleman Sherman, a graduate of the University of Pennsylvania, turned 640 undeveloped acres into Minnewawa Vineyard, where the most luxuriant table grapes in the state were grown, together with subsidiary enterprises in dairy farming and olives. Mrs. Kate F. Warfield of Sonoma won a reputation in viticulture and winemaking, while further north in Marysville Mrs. Freda Ehmann, a clergyman's daughter and physician's wife with no previous ranching experience, made herself by 1911 one of the leading olive growers in the state. These and other women-run ranches, while not exactly constituting a movement, did fulfill some of Shinn's hopes for a better, more gracious mode of rural living.

Over the years, moreover, the search for community and civility on the land continued. Sometimes, as in the case of the Socialist Llano del Rio colony, the premises of community could be explicitly ideological. In other instances— the efforts of the state commission on land colonization to settle families on the land, as an example—private and public cooperation was involved. Other advances on the level of both fact and imaginative perception—the work, for instance, of *Sunset* magazine in promoting rural California as a place to live— proceeded out of old-fashioned promotional and developmental ambitions. In all instances, however, a persistent California dream of life on the land without loss of civility was being pursued and, intermittently, attained.

Established in 1914 in the Antelope Valley of northern Los Angeles County, the Llano del Rio cooperative brought to a final, brief flowering a generation of Socialist dreaming in Southern California. Its founder, lawyer Job Harriman, first turned his thoughts to the land in 1910 after the bombing of the *Los Angeles Times* denied him an all but certain victory in the mayor's race. Deprived of Los Angeles, Harriman (his face above his Gladstone collar, so Aldous Huxley described him, resembling that "of a revivalist or a Shakespearean actor") envisioned an even better Socialist experiment, a self-sufficient agricultural cooperative that would prove to America that Socialism had a message for agriculturalists as well as for industrial workers. It took Harriman four years to organize the enterprise, but by 1914 a community of Socialists, their numbers peaking at a thousand in August 1917, were working together to make their ten thousand acres of the Antelope Valley, much of it semi-arid, covered with brush and Joshua trees, bloom in Socialist vindication.

At its peak Llano del Rio—a hundred homes and utility buildings, a thousand men, women, and children, producing 95 percent of what they needed to live—seemed destined for long-range success. With all work borne equally, the work week was shortened for Llano del Rio residents, who organized an orchestra to play Saturday night concerts and dances and established a sports program for Sundays. The cooperative established a school, a hospital, and a library of good quality. Printing was taught in the cooperative's printing shop, where issues of the *Western Comrade*, noticeable for their fine lettering, illustrations, and graphics, were produced.

Photographs from these all-too-brief years depict residents of Llano del Rio pursuing life on the land in much the same style as the later (and equally Socialist-inspired) kibbutzim of Israel. Residents read a bulletin board for the day's work assignment; a group gathers for choral singing; young women sit together, preparing freshly harvested apples for applesauce and canning, their starched aprons and well-scrubbed faces betokening the overall cleanliness and order of the colony. Here indeed would seem to be proof positive that the colony system of nineteenth-century California, with its special ability to promote community and forestall loneliness and alienation, might very well make a successful transition into the modern era.

Alas, the *Los Angeles Times*, believing otherwise, thundered away at Llano del Rio as a dangerously radical experiment, going so far as to suggest wholesale domestic improprieties in what was actually a rather conventional citizenry. The *Times*'s hostility hurt the colony's credit, and credit is the lifeline of agriculture, whether pursued singly or in groups. In the first euphoric years, collective hope was sufficient to iron out difficulties, together with Job Harriman's presence as founder, which gave the colony a mode of arbitration. By 1917, however, problems with authority, the Achilles' heel of all cooperative ventures, were surfacing. With Harriman absent raising money, no one stepped in to organize the alfalfa harvest, and a valuable crop was lost. A year later the colony was foreclosed.

The de-socialized idea behind Llano del Rio, however, the clustering of farm families into cooperative structures, had already been picked up by California Progressives busy with the transformation of the state. Elwood Mead, professor of rural institutions in the University of California School of Agriculture, spearheaded the Progressives' foray into the reform and development of California's rural life. An irrigation engineer by training, with wide experience in water administration in Wyoming, Australia, and (later) Palestine, Elwood Mead had made a specialty of California rural life as early as the late 1890s while serving with the United States Department of Agriculture. Mead's technical specialty was irrigation (he later served in the 1930s as United States commissioner of reclamation); but beyond this specialty, as his book *Helping Men Own Farms* (1920) clearly demonstrated, Mead was at heart an agrarian reformer, animated by a Progressivist distrust of monopoly and a dream of Jeffersonian rural life. A mere 310 individuals or corporations, Mead pointed out, owned over four million acres of the farm land in California, the direct result of the fact that more than three-fourths of publicly held lands in California had fallen into the hands of the railroads, corporations, or individual speculators. As a result, much of the rural life of the state was based upon tenancy, especially among the Japanese, and a tenant economy bred a tenant society, devoid of permanent institutions. Individual ownership, the family farm, was the only way to combat the impending feudalization (feudal in ownership, but without the mediating institutions of feudalism) of rural California. Now that the private colony system had passed its peak, only government had the wherewithal to stimulate new patterns of land settlement.

When in 1915 the Johnson administration established a commission on Land Colonization and Rural Credit, Elwood Mead was the logical chairman. With consummate political skill, Mead used the patriotic prospect of returning California veterans to the land to secure the passage in 1917 of the California Land Settlement Act, modeled on similar settlement acts in Australia and New Zealand. The act established a state land settlement board to work with private banks to help qualified candidates finance family farms. In a sense, the circle was being circled, for in 1886 Alfread Deakin, then minister of agriculture for Australia's state of Victoria, later prime minister of Australia, in the course of visiting California had found himself strongly impressed by the colony organization of Riverside, especially its communally owned irrigation system. Deakin brought this organizational idea back to Australia, from whence it returned to California in 1917.

Mead, who had administered similar projects in Australia, astutely began to buy up unimproved land for settlement and to set in motion the construction of roads and other improvements, preparatory to the launching in 1920 of a full-fledged cooperative, the Durham Settlement, which Mead hoped would be a model of how government could stimulate land ownership. With $260,000 loaned it by the state for fifty years at 4 percent, the Land Settlement Board purchased 6,300 acres in Durham Station, Butte County, just outside Chico. Empowered by a second loan, $125,000 from the Federal Land Bank for thirty-five years at 5 ½ percent, the board began to make loans of $3,000 for fifty years at 4 percent interest to carefully screened applicants, who were expected to match this financing. The expectation was that having at least $3,000 of the start-up costs privately financed would eliminate ne'er-do-wells and potential deadbeats. By 1921, 120 families had settled on farms in the Durham Colony. Scores of farm workers, moreover, empowered by loans from the board, were able to build homes with adjacent vegetable gardens, a favorite project of Mead's, who believed that a stable work force with a stake in its own future was essential to the well-being of California agriculture. Another 130 families were similarly established on the 86,000 acres of the Delhi Colony in the San Joaquin Valley. All in all, some 3,000 applicants were screened before these 250 Durham and Delhi families were selected.

Buying into Durham or Delhi, an agriculturalist automatically joined a set-tlers' cooperative, which owned and operated certain common facilities—from a cream separator to King Morco Alcartra VIII, the herd sire at Durham—made common purchases, and jointly marketed the settlers' products, and also main-tained such joint facilities as a school, a community hall, gardens, tennis courts, a swimming pool, and a sports field. At Durham the cooperative owned a twenty-two acre grove of oak trees, where on Saturday evenings during the summer community dances and songfests occurred. "The best jazz orchestra in the country performs," wrote one *Sunset* reporter of these gatherings, "and everybody in the community for miles around attends the festivities. On the average night a hundred and fifty men pay a dollar each for the privilege of letting their collars melt to the strains of *Dardenella*, and scores of others, out of tune with modern jazz, come to look or to talk of prunes and pigs and Democrats. This weekly dance in the oak grove is the symbol of the new order in the rural life of the West. On this dance floor farmers and farm laborers, freeholders all, meet on a footing of social equality."

The mythology at work here is pure Jeffersonian agrarianism with overtones of that middle-class respectability so beloved by the Progressives. As in the case of other aspects of the Progressive program, moreover, a strong racial philoso-phy was at work as well. Elwood Mead and his supporters feared what they considered the Southern Europeanization and Japanization of California rural life. "If they intermarry," Mead asked, regarding the Italian, Portuguese, and Japanese farmers of California, "what will the mongrel descendants be like? What they are in South America we know. . . . If they do not intermarry, then each of our great valleys will be the home of racial friction which will make the Balkans seem like a prayer meeting." Immigrant agriculturalists, Mead be-lieved, could never be expected to develop American-style social institutions. "As citizens and as builders of rural society," Mead wrote of immigrants in *Helping Men Own Farms*, "these aliens were in sorry contrast to the State's first settlers, who were the finest type of American citizen this nation had produced. The California pioneer had been a citizen first, a moneymaker second. He was generous and public spirited to a fault. In contrast, the alien renter had no interest in rural welfare. He had a racial aloofness and he farmed the land to get all he could out of it in the period of his lease. Wherever he displaced the American, he put rural life on the down grade."

Professor Mead was not telling the truth. As has already been suggested, Euro-Californians, so active in wine and fruit, had long since brought to rural life the rich cultures and social organizations of the Mediterranean, enriching California immeasurably; as far as the Japanese were concerned, by the end of the first decade of the 1900s they had shown themselves eminently capable of the Jeffersonian ideal of the self-subsistent family farm, to such a degree, in fact, that they were exciting the envy of many whites.

The Chinese had preceded the Japanese into the fields of California. By 1880 fully one-third of the state's agricultural labor force was Chinese. As the Chinese presence in agriculture increased in the 1870s with the fall-off of mining, so did violence against them. On 15 March 1877, for instance, an organization of white gunmen calling itself the Order of Caucasians broke into a cabin of Chinese workers near Chico, robbed the inhabitants, then set fire to the cabin, killing four Chinese men. After the Chinese Exclusion Act of 1882 cut off Chinese immigration to California entirely, the Chinese held their own in rural California for a while but tended in the 1890s to drift back into cities and towns. At first, as the Chinese left the countryside in search of better opportunities, the large-scale farmers and ranchers of California gave serious consideration to importing blacks from the South to replace them, but by the 1890s not blacks but Italians, Portuguese, Japanese, and later Mexicans began to replace the Chinese in the fields.

By 1909 nearly half, 45 percent, of California's total farm labor force was Japanese. At first the Japanese underbid their competition, including the lingering Chinese work force, in order to gain a foothold. They entered the fields strongly organized, hiring themselves out through *kieyaku-nin*, trusted middlemen who negotiated contracts and guaranteed living arrangements, including smoothly functioning eating and boarding clubs and other support services. Once they had eliminated the competition through low bidding and efficiency, the Japanese began to behave just like union labor: controlling their numbers to keep wages high, negotiating one grower against another, organizing quick strikes when they felt exploited, boycotting farmers they did not like. They also began to rent land wherever they could and eventually to buy their own farms. Skilled in intensive farming (their California farms averaged 54.7 acres), Japanese agriculturalists were capable of paying higher rents or paying more to own marginal land ($15 an acre in 1910, when the going rate was $10) because they could coax a higher yield from the soil once it was theirs.

By 1910 some 1,816 California farms, for a total of 99,254 acres in Los An-

geles, Orange, Fresno, and Sacramento counties, most of it in vegetables, potatoes, fruit, berries, grapes, sugar beets, and other intensive crops, were controlled by Japanese. By 1913, 281,687 acres were in Japanese hands, either owned
or leased; 383,287 acres by 1920. One San Joaquin Delta farmer, George Shima,
who arrived in California in 1889 as a young laborer, controlled 28,000 acres
by 1913, from which came 85 percent of California's potato crop, earning Shima
the undisputed title of Potato King. Not only did the Japanese outdistance all
other groups in farm ownership, they also established an interlocking network
of marketing cooperatives and protective associations, presided over by the United
Japanese Deliberative Council in Northern California and the Central Japanese
Association in the South.

Bested in farm ownership, outproduced, outmarketed, excluded from employment (only George Shima showed any willingness to hire non-Japanese labor), white California grew envious, then angry, then overtly anti-Japanese,
complaining, as did Elwood Mead, of the impending Asiaticization of California agriculture. The major offense offered by Japanese success was that it cut
to the core of a dream that just was not working: small family farms for white
California. A state in which by 1900 7 percent of the farm owners controlled
63 percent of the agricultural land was finding its Jeffersonian self-image under
assault. As Berkeley economist L. H. Fisher would later write, in California
farming was a business, not a way of life: a business owned either by corporations in San Francisco or Los Angeles, or by local elites who from the 1920s
onwards appear in county histories as prosperous businessmen in suits and ties,
their well-furnished residences listed in the county seat, their offspring studying
in Berkeley or Palo Alto.

Throughout the year, meanwhile, hired hands did the agricultural work of
California: standing in cold muddy fields to pick broccoli in the winter, or in
the summer bending down under a blistering sun over a short-handle hoe to
clear weeds from endless rows of lettuce, cabbage, asparagus, and beets. Sunstroke, aching backs, tired muscles, cut hands, lost thumbs and fingers, a fall
from a ladder, lung trouble from pesticides and powdery soil, a crushed body
from an overturned load of hay: these, as well as the Saturday night dances at
Durham, were the daily scars of life on the land, and most of those who endured them did so for wages only (and poor wages at that), with no stake in the
future of the enterprise which momentarily required their bent backs.

That need, moreover, was inconstant, sometimes even cruel in its brevity.
As early as the Constitutional Convention of 1849, some Californians were arguing that only black slavery could provide California with a stable agricultural
workforce capable of this onerous but intermittent work. (Ironically, when cotton planters from the South brought blacks with them to Kern County after the
War Between the States, the blacks, discovering that they could do better else-

where, left the cotton fields almost immediately.) In its importation of Chinese workers, California flirted with the possibilities of a permanent servile caste, a fact not lost upon the state senate special committee convened in 1878 to look into the question of Chinese immigration. While some of the energies behind this inquiry were racist, the committee's report, *Chinese Immigration: Its Social, Moral and Political Effect*, as Paul Taylor has pointed out, crystallized for California a question that would take nearly another century even to half answer: What sort of rural society did Californians want for themselves, family farms or vast plantations worked by a rural helotry? The committee correctly saw that without the possibility of obtaining their own farms (for some unstated reason this prospect seemed out of the question), the Chinese, arriving in great numbers and living outside family structures in a ratio (in 1880) of eighteen men to one woman, were providing the land monopolists with precisely the cast of seasonally employed agricultural workers they needed to make their baronies profitable.

With the departure of the Chinese, other seasonal workers arrived, many of them contracted for through farm labor contractors who negotiated for their non-English-speaking clients, received payment, and in turn paid the workers after deducting fees and expenses: the Portuguese, Italians, and Japanese already mentioned, arriving in the 1890s; then the Hindustani, ten thousand of them, arriving between 1900 and 1906; followed by the Filipinos and Mexicans, who migrated after the First World War. Like the Japanese, the Filipinos—nearly 30,000 of them arriving through the 1920s—banded together in union-like guilds, which were also housing, eating, and recreational associations. With their population growing from 121,000 in 1920 to 368,000 in 1930, Mexican farm workers eventually dominated the agricultural work force of California. These Mexican immigrants were especially vulnerable to the contract system. Farmers grew accustomed to withholding up to a quarter of wages due their Mexican workers, pending a successful completion of the harvest—a success over which the workers had next to no control. Contractors, meanwhile, were notorious for defrauding and exploiting. "I have left the best of my life and my strength here," said one Mexican worker of his years in the fields of California, "sprinkling with the sweat of my brow the fields and factories of these gringos, who only know how to make one sweat and don't even pay any attention to one when they see that one is old."

For the nomadic farm workers of California, moving from place to place, harvest to harvest, living in shacks or tents or just throwing bedrolls out under the stars, taking their children into the fields in forfeit for their education, working outside the benefits and protections of a union system—no medical care or hospitalization, no pension or insurance, no unemployment in the off season— standing in the most impersonal relationship to employers, who paid them exactingly by unit of production rather than by time, the farm workers of California were hardly experiencing a georgic idyll of bourgeois civility on the land, much less Jeffersonian independence. They were, however, bearing these myths on their backs, and within the decade, during the ordeal of the Depression, major strife would flare forth in the fields of California.

6

Arthur Page Brown and
the Dream of San Francisco

For three and half months of agony in the fall of 1896, the architect Arthur Page Brown lay dying in his Burlingame home. His arms, legs, and skull were fractured. His brain reeled from concussion. He could barely whisper a coherent sentence, and most times when he spoke he made no sense at all. Brown's spine was so severely damaged that he could only lie on one side. If he tried to move, even the morphine his physicians were liberally administering could not cancel the pain. A horse-and-buggy accident had put Arthur Page Brown, a socially prominent New Yorker turned San Franciscan, into this terminal condition at age thirty-five, at the height of his career. On the morning of 7 October 1896 Brown had stepped into a light buggy which his groom had harnessed to Nipper, a onetime steeplechaser Brown wanted to try out as a carriage horse before buying. Rearing in panic as soon as Brown got behind the reins, Nipper bolted off. Brown might have jumped from the carriage immediately, but he chose to try to bring the frightened horse under control—which he was unable to do. Nipper ran wildly down the road adjacent to the newly established Burlingame Country Club, Brown desperately trying to bring the frightened steeplechaser to a halt. Horribly, man and horse and carriage careened off a bridge, down fifteen feet to a riverbed below. When Brown's groom and other stable attendants from the club reached the scene of the accident (so they later reported), they found Brown's broken, bloody body crushed under the mangled horse. The doctors did what they could to set his fractures, and his wife put out reports that Brown would recover, but as the weeks went by it became more and more obvious that Arthur Page Brown would not be able to go up to San Francisco to supervise (as his contract with the harbor commissioners called for) the construction of the Union Depot and Ferry House then underway on the Embarcadero at the foot of Market Street. At the time the largest single construction project ever undertaken in San Francisco, the Ferry Building had capped the second (and San Franciscan) phase of Brown's hurriedly accomplished architectural career, promising even grander achievements in the years to come. And now that vista of promising years-to-be was dwindling down to a handful of pain-wracked days.

The life that was so agonizingly ebbing away in the fall of 1896 had been filled with study, action, and achievement. Born in December 1859 in Ellisburg, New York, Brown left the Cornell School of Architecture after one year to enter the newly opened New York firm of McKim, Mead, and White. In later life Brown let it be thought that he was an honors graduate of Cornell—a minor transgression, to be sure, and rather understandable in a man who was ever reaching beyond himself, beyond his talents, in fact, on behalf of his adopted city, San Francisco, whose new architecture he wished to establish.

Brown spent three years as a draftsman with McKim, Mead and White before embarking upon a European study tour. Private study and routine work with this great firm, not Cornell, gave Arthur Page Brown his initial training in architecture. It was just as well, for American architectural education was in those years in its infancy, and no experience could be more valuable than working as a draftsman on projects underway with a dynamic New York City firm, just established in 1879 and destined to develop by the end of the decade into America's premier architectural firm, whose dominance would last well into the twentieth century. All three partners—the business-getting Charles Follen McKim, a student of H. H. Richardson; the design-oriented William Rutherford Mead; and Stanford White, the flamboyantly talented Renaissance man destined to be shot dead by an outraged husband—had something to teach the young ex-freshman from Cornell. From McKim, Arthur Page Brown learned the value of social and political contacts in securing commissions. From Mead, Brown learned the importance of scholarly design work, of bookish study in the search for establishment architecture. From White, Brown absorbed a certain playfulness, a taste for the learnedly fanciful that added an element of lightness, of fantasy even, to his otherwise scholarly buildings. All three partners, moreover, were grand men of the American Renaissance style, bold and establishment-oriented, and with the assistance of establishment money, dreaming of monumental buildings in the classical mode: such as their Boston Public Library (1888), perhaps the single most important building of its era, whose vastness and erudite taste perfectly expressed a dawning era of patronage and public works in the manner (self-consciously so) of the high Italian Renaissance on the part of the newly consolidated American rich. All these things Arthur Page Brown saw from the vantage point of his drawing board and dreamed of one day doing himself—on his own.

Brown went to Europe for two years of travel and study. He spent a period of time in Paris, informally connected (so it seems) to the École des Beaux Arts, and a longer period in Italy, musing over the great buildings of Venice, Florence, and Rome, sketchbook in hand, with that sense of studious leisure and assured expectations that aspiring Americans of this era all seemed so miraculously to possess. He visited London as well. By December 1884 we find Arthur Page Brown, architect, established in an independent practice in New York City, with offices at 57 Broadway. Not for Brown, however, was there to be a patient, steady rise in his profession. Then in his mid-twenties, Arthur Page Brown began his independent career busy, astonishingly busy, and ended it that way—very, very busy—a hurried, productive decade later.

Social connections helped. Brown married into the socially prominent and politically powerful Pryor family. His father-in-law, Justice Roger A. Pryor of the New York State Supreme Court, had lived the first half of his life in Virginia. After election to the United States House of Representatives (the secession of Virginia prevented him from taking his seat) and service in the Confederate army during the War Between the States (he rose to the rank of brigadier general) Pryor moved north to New York City after Appomattox, bringing with him his first-family-of-Virginia wife and their daughter Lucy, whom Arthur Page Brown eventually married. Qualifying for the bar, General Pryor cut a dashing figure in social New York, which savored the chivalric brigadier turned attorney, so eager to charm his former enemies. Pryor also established solid links to Tammany Hall, the New York Democratic political society which controlled the politics of New York, a relationship which eventually eased him onto the Supreme Court bench.

In addition to his well-connected in-laws, Brown was also befriended by another Virginian, Nettie Fowler McCormick, the wealthy widow of inventor-industrialist Cyrus Hall McCormick of Chicago. Taking Brown under her sponsorship, Mrs. McCormick secured for the young New Yorker a series of commissions connected with McCormick philanthropies in South Carolina and Tennessee—college and school buildings, an orphanage—together with at least one commercial commission and a number of private residences for her friends. This work, in turn, led to a number of major commissions for Princeton University (the Class of '77 Biological Laboratory, Clio and Whig halls, the Museum of Historic Art), a series of Princeton residences, Fowler Hall of the McCormick Theological Seminary in Chicago, a number of residences in New Jersey, New York, Massachusetts, and Ontario, and a series of ecclesiastical assignments in New York, beginning with the enlargements and restoration of Bethesda Church in Saratoga Springs, for which Brown also designed an exquisite reredos and altar (1887); and the design of the elegant English Gothic St. Peter's Church in Portchester (1887), which the *Churchman* on 3 September 1887 described as the finest church in Westchester County, praising its scholarship and restrained taste, all so appropriate to an Episcopalian parish church set picturesquely in the upstate countryside. Moving from Gothic Revival to Richardsonian Romanesque, Brown designed a luxuriantly fenestrated twin-towered residence for Mr. S. H. James of Toronto (1889), a massive (110 by 73 feet) gray stone, red-slate-roofed mansion that at once became the talk of the city.

Arthur Page Brown, then, burst onto the architectural scene possessed of an extraordinary ability to please upper-class clients by providing them with designs that, in the general manner of the academic eclecticism in vogue during the American Renaissance, corroborated their view of themselves as an emergent caste through a tasteful, scholarly orchestration of historical styles. In this Brown was imitating his first mentors, McKim, Mead and White. Brown's method of operation, moreover, followed the McKim, Mead and White principle of dividing labor. In terms of sheer design talent, Arthur Page Brown was not a great architect. He had, however, a good eye, a ready sense of the appropriate design solution, and a more than passable mastery of a wide range of historical styles. In the McKim, Mead and White formula, Brown paralleled Charles Rollen McKim, the getter of business. An entrepreneur par excellence, deeply social in his instincts, polished and charming, Brown, like McKim, moved with ease in an upper-class world in which friendships and social contacts generated new business, and new business, in turn, widened the social sphere. A commission secured, the preliminary design agreed upon, Brown turned his projects over to one of his talented assistants, then went on to secure further work. Only thus, as a cooperative partnership in all but name, can the astonishing productivity of Brown's brief career be understood.

Brown's chief designer—his silent partner, according to architectural historian Richard W. Longstreth—was the Boston-born A. C. Schweinfurth (1864–1900), a brilliant, high-strung, introspective designer of great virtuosity, whose personal reserve, verging upon reclusiveness, stood in total contrast to Brown's sociability. Schweinfurth's impatience (ineptitude even) with the process of securing contracts made it nearly impossible for him during his brief career (pneumonia felled him at thirty-six, finishing him off, like Brown, in the fullness of manhood) to secure commissions on his own. Joining Brown's New York office in 1885, Schweinfurth left the next year to try to make a go of it on his own. Failing, he rejoined Brown in San Francisco, remaining with him until Brown's death in 1896—with the exception of another attempt, in 1894, to launch his own practice. Much of the work that issued from Brown's New York office and virtually all of the major California commissions must, in terms of design, be seen as bearing A. C. Schweinfurth's imprint. The securing of projects, however, without which Schweinfurth's creativity would have remained dormant—the sensing of opportunities, the charming of clients, the positioning of an architectural practice so that it might be energized by emergent ambitions— was strictly the work of Arthur Page Brown.

As early as 1886 Brown was openly acknowledging in a letter to Mrs. Mc-

Cormick that he could never compete against McKim, Mead and White as long as he remained in New York City. If he were ever to become an architect of major importance, Brown recognized, he would have to take the grand manner of McKim, Mead and White out to another city anxious to express its evolving urbanism through ambitious design. Brown at first thought that Chicago might be the proper place, but some time in the later 1880s (1887 seems the most likely year) Henry Alexander, the friend of Mrs. McCormick's who had secured for Brown the Princeton commissions, introduced the thirty-year-old architect to the Charles Crockers of San Franciso, whose daughter Harriet had married Alexander's son Charles. The Crockers were impressed by young Brown, and the next year, 1888, when the formidable Charles Crocker, president of the Southern Pacific Railroad, died in San Francisco, his widow invited Brown to come west and design a granite mausoleum to be emplaced atop a hill in the Mountain View Cemetery in Oakland overlooking the Bay of San Francisco. With $100,000 to work with, Brown designed an *erectheum*, a terraced temple in the Greek style, sad and reposeful. It was intended for Charles Crocker alone, but on the afternoon of 29 October 1889 Mrs. Mary Crocker, who had personally supervised the construction of the monument, took to her bed for a predinner nap (an evening out with friends was planned) from which she never awoke; and so both Charles and Mary Crocker were laid side by side in Brown's first California construction.

What sort of a city—architecturally and otherwise—had Arthur Page Brown come to, bringing with him the message and style of McKim, Mead and White together with the architectural ambitions of Boston, Chicago, and New York? It was a city, first of all, that had become in the mere forty-odd years of its American existence the seventh largest city in the United States; yet it was also a ramshackle, incomplete city, haphazardly developed, devoid in the main of the distinguished architecture called for by its spectacular setting on the edge of a hilly peninsula surrounded on three sides by a great bay and on its western edge by the Pacific Ocean itself. Some fine architecture had been achieved— the Montgomery Block (1853), for instance, a downtown office complex; the Lick House (1862), a hotel; the Colton House (1872), a gracious neoclassical private residence; an equally successful Greek Revival United States Mint (1873)— but in general the San Francisco of the late 1880s awaited an architecture commensurate with its setting and its conception of itself as the American capital of the Pacific. Throughout the 1880s San Franciscans had been struggling toward such an architectural corroboration of San Francisco as a coming city through the construction of elaborately decorated wooden townhouses, many of them in the newly opened Western Addition district west of Van Ness Avenue.

Wood was a material convenient to San Francisco; its plasticity allowed it to be molded quickly and cheaply into a thousand ornamental shapes, most of them in some way or another reminiscent of Italian villa design. Known today as Victorians, these wooden villas—with their fanciful facades, their classical columns and inventive fenestration (including bay windows that reached out to catch the ever evanescent San Francisco sun), their generally narrow town-house lots—are prized as picturesque survivors of San Francisco's first system-atic effort at expressive architecture, despite the fact that for the newly arrived Arthur Page Brown, as well as for his sometime assistant Willis Polk, the Vic-torian townhouses seemed drearily repetitive and laden with unscholarly, dis-honest wood-as-stone decoration. The Victorians, moreover, were not the re-sults of an architect-client relationship, but were built en masse, block by block, by speculators guiding themselves by no more than a half dozen prefabricated designs.

Nor did the public sector offer much contrast. Under construction since 1871, the City Hall of San Francisco constituted the sole major civic public work to date. Mired in controversy and corruption, the building inched toward com-pletion over two decades of on-again-off-again construction. By the early 1890s, City Hall stood ready for its tower: "a bastard combination," so young Willis Polk described local architect Frank O'Shea's proposal, "of a Spanish clerestory crowned by an English cupola resting on a Franco-Roman base," all of it going to prove, Polk believed, "that while San Francisco is a city that really discrim-inates between fake articles and genuine merit, it usually accepts the fake."

The Establishment of San Francisco, meanwhile—so much of it in the sec-ond generation of its wealth, hence generally better educated and discriminat-ing than the first generation, which had made its fortune in the hurly-burly of the frontier—was beginning to want more than gingerbread fantasies or turreted wedding cakes in its architecture. Even before Brown's arrival in 1889, Senator and Mrs. Leland Stanford had engaged Frederick Law Olmsted in 1885 to lay out the Palo Alto campus of the newly established Leland Stanford Junior Uni-versity, and the formidable H. H. Richardson of Boston himself had been working on the preliminary sketches for the Stanford University quadrangles at the time of his death, a work continued by the successor firm of Shepley, Rutan and Coolidge. When in 1887 *Chronicle* publisher Michael de Young wished to build a new downtown headquarters, he went to the prestigious firm of Burnham and Root of Chicago, who in turn presented San Francisco with its first skyscraper.

The Stanfords and the de Youngs had their origins in the frontier elite. Their predilection for the architecture of the Eastern states, however, was locally reinforced by an influx of Eastern-educated professionals who began establish-ing themselves in San Francisco in the 1880s, attracted to the California city by its developing social and economic infrastructure. Educated Easterners turned San Franciscans and native San Franciscans educated in the East would for the next quarter century be commissioning the most architecturally significant residences in the city and helping to create as well a climate favorable to the undertaking of ambitious, architecturally important public works.

That is why Arthur Page Brown was so welcomed: he was formally establishing the McKim, Mead and White connection for the Pacific Coast metropolis. He was bringing to San Francisco the mood of 57 Broadway, where he had maintained his New York offices adjacent to and in association with the great firm where he himself had begun his career: absorbing the philosophy and practice of academic eclecticism at its very fount, discussing with the flamboyantly brilliant Stanford White the architecture of the Italian Renaissance, or sharing with other visitors to the McKim, Mead and White offices—John La Farge, Augustus Saint-Gaudens, John Singer Sargent—mutual hopes for a new American art and architecture, inspired by an assimilation to American purposes of the best of the European past, an academic eclecticism that would repossess and reenergize the high forms of the classical and Renaissance past with new American energy.

It was this studio mood, this atmosphere of an architectural atelier animated by bright prospects, that Arthur Page Brown brought to his San Francisco offices in the Benson Building at 318 Pine Street. Never before had so many brilliant young architects been gathered into one place in San Francisco and set to work on such challenging projects: the mercurial Willis Polk, for instance, whose design influence was felt so strongly during Brown's first two San Francisco years; the dreamy, mystical Bernard Maybeck, his talent sui generis, a solidly built young German, haunted by an architecture (inspired by the Gothic and by the wood-building traditions of Norway, Switzerland, and Japan) that would respiritualize American building design; the ever-present (after his return to Brown in 1890) A. C. Schweinfurth, patient, scholarly, his taste and inventiveness destined to dominate the major work of the Brown office in San Francisco; and the other aspiring young men—Alexander Oakey, Charles Rousseau, Joachim Mathisen, William Knowles, Sylvain Schnaittacher, Frank Van Trees, James R. Miller—who would first school themselves in Brown's technique of collaborative creation and aggressive commission seeking before leaving to establish firms of their own. Before all these young men, led with such energetic urbanity by their equally young mentor, lay no less a challenge than the creation of a regional architecture that would begin in San Francisco (effectively the capital city of California), then spread itself outwards to the suburbs, then on to the towns of the interior and, finally, down to Los Angeles and all of Southern California.

The seriousness and scope of Arthur Page Brown's architectural response to San Francisco is evidenced in an article he wrote for the *Chronicle* for Sunday, 30 December 1894. By then Brown was well into his San Francisco career, with a number of major achievements behind him, but the sentiments he expressed in 1894 can be safely backdated a few years, for they exhibit the psychology of an architect who knew New York and the great cities of Europe from firsthand experience and who now found himself in a remote provincial city which, for all its distance from the East and from Europe and for all its unfinished ambience, still emanated possibilities of civic maturity and grand architecture. San Francisco, Brown wrote, was comprised in general "of possibly the most uninteresting collection of wooden structures ever erected." What the city needed, Brown ventured (he would not live to see this half-serious suggestion come true, to the ruination of so much of his own work), was an earthquake and a sweeping fire ("if we could have it without loss of life") that would clear San Francisco of its hasty frontierish wooden structures ("buildings which were erected for immediate use and revenue") and allow the city to rise, phoenix-like, as the most architecturally distinguished seaport in the United States. Good building materials and skilled labor were abundant in San Francisco, Brown reported, and the topography was unparalleled. Anticipating the critical observations of Daniel Hudson Burnham by more than a decade, Brown described the unimaginative grid layout of San Francisco's streets, so indifferent, so defiant even, of the city's magnificent hills. As Burnham would do in his famous plan of 1906, Brown called for a replatting of many of the city's streets, if and when they could be cleared, so that they would ascend and descend in graceful circularity up and down the heights. Like Burnham also, he called for a spectacular civic center in and around the City Hall, one that would take the Ringstrasse of Vienna as its model.

Contemporary preservationists might wince at Brown's dismissal of that eclectic building style now known as San Francisco Victorian. "The imitation of chateaux and copies of fragments of palaces, carried out in thin, wooden, boxlike structures, with bay windows and small corner towers and turrets"—thus did Brown dismiss a style revered today. Despite the historical nature of much of his own work, moreover, Brown put himself on record as favoring experimentation and fresh ideas ("we must free ourselves from narrow-minded views and not condemn every new piece of work because it surprises us") in the search for a San Francisco style. That new city style, that new architecture, Brown asserted, should shift away from the prevalent wood construction ("the supply of redwood and pine is far from inexhaustible") in favor of brick, sandstone, marble, and cement, which would lend a more permanent air to the city and would also lend itself to the bold simplicity and sculptured effects of the best modern architecture. Citing the pale yellow light of San Francisco, its Mediterranean color, Brown called for a corresponding lightness of color in the city's buildings. San Francisco's special color, he wrote, was white—as in the whiteness of a sun-drenched Greek island village rising up steep hillsides from blue water below—and this whiteness was to be topped with red-tiled roofs: carmine, cinnabar, rose, and burnt orange against hills and sky.

The architectural challenge to San Francisco, Brown believed, was part and parcel of a larger challenge as well—the coming of age of the city. As of yet, he believed, San Franciscans did not have the proper regard for architecture and the aesthetics of the cityscape because the city had not yet collectively made up its mind to aspire to civic greatness. A city, Brown chided, that would fill every vacant lot and wall with a hodgepodge of crudely lettered signs, even doing this at the entrance to Golden Gate Park (where Brown wanted a marble arch), was not a city that took itself seriously. Indiscriminate billboarding should be made a criminal offense. Architecture was not everything, Brown admitted, but good architecture and good planning were at once causes and effects of civic sophistication. "There is no doubt in my mind," Brown wrote, "that the architectural abominations of San Francisco are the cause of much of our lack of progress in other directions."

II

By this time, late 1894, Brown had nearly five years of solid San Francisco work behind him. Through Charles Crocker's son, William H. Crocker (1861–1937), a young man of Brown's own age who soon became a close personal friend, the New York architect received in October 1889 a commission to complete the first Grace Cathedral, where William Crocker served on the building committee. Designed in 1860 by William Patton, later the architect of Thomas Starr King's First Unitarian Church (1863), an English Gothic edifice seating fifteen hundred and the most ambitious building in San Francisco at that time, and San Francisco's long-abuilding City Hall, Grace Cathedral stood incomplete and towerless on the corner of Stockton and California. Local architects were furious that a non-San Franciscan should receive the commission (the complaint that he was an outsider plagued Brown for the first few years of his San Francisco career), and certain newspaper critics found fault with the 190-foot English Gothic tower and all-new entrance and vestibule Brown designed to finish, quite successfully, the three-decade-old church. Critics might cavil and local architects might feel resentment over this smart-set New Yorker's instant acceptance by the beau monde, but with Crocker patronage, which he never lost, Arthur Page Brown was launched irrevocably into a San Francisco career.

Before her sudden death, Mrs. Mary Crocker, pleased with Brown's designs for her husband's mausoleum, engaged him to draw up plans for a new Old People's Home, an institution organized in 1874 for retired gentlefolk of refined tastes and minimal means, which Mrs. Crocker planned to expand in her husband's memory to accommodate 150 residents. Brown had two full fifty-vara lots on the southeast corner of Pine and Pierce streets and a princely quarter of a million dollars to work with. Drawing up plans in the late spring and early summer of 1889, Brown presented Mrs. Crocker with an eclectic blend of shingle-style American Colonial and medieval French for the hostelry. (Brown had developed a taste for the architecture of Brittany from Stanford White.) In the intervening years 2507 Pine Street (part of the St. Rose Academy, a girls' high school run by the Dominican Sisters) has been shorn of its upper story because of the danger of falling parapets, but much of Brown's intention remains evident in this still useful, still busy building: a cloisterlike mood appropriate to the retirement years of San Franciscans of a certain class, achieved through an interplay of arched windows and curved brick walls on the lower floor reminiscent of Brittany; an interior garden, monastic in tranquillity; a refectory-like dining room, high of ceiling; and a chapel wherein all 150 residents might offer an occasional prayer for the repose of the souls of Charles and Mary Crocker. Built of redwood and San Jose brick, the Old People's Home, subsequently known as the Crocker Home, was dedicated on 22 August 1890. Mayor Edward B. Pond himself was on hand for the dedication in honor of the late Charles and Mary Crocker, together with a gathering of local notables, gathered, in part, to see what the Crocker family's young New York architect had wrought.

Evidently these San Franciscans liked what they saw, for a series of residential commissions followed, on which Arthur Page Brown, whatever else he was doing at the time, would be busy for the rest of his life. Most of these homes were in the Queen Anne style derived from the work of English architect Norman Shaw. The Queen Anne style featured rounded corner towers attached to a mélange of late-nineteenth-century revivalist fashions. Among the first of these San Francisco Queen Annes—and undisputedly one of the finest private residences ever built in San Francisco—was the home Brown designed for Alban Nelson Towne at 1101 California Street, at Taylor atop Nob Hill (1890). Again there is the Crocker connection; Alban Nelson Towne, second vice-president and general manager of the Pacific system for the Southern Pacific Railway, was a professional colleague of Charles Crocker's and a close friend of the entire Crocker Family. Arthur Page Brown, then but a year in San Francisco, working with a budget of $125,000, created a home for the wealthy railroad man that in turn created a rage for Queen Anne. Set atop the symbolic crest of the city, the Towne residence, a daring combination of American Colonial and Classic Revival, became the talk of San Francisco even while it was under construction in late 1890. Praising its restrained luxuriance—the serene repose of the six Ionic columns of California marble gracing the portico, the bold oversized window dominating the paneling within, the omnipresence of marble, the Louis XIV drawing room, and the foyer frescos designed by Brown in the Venetian style—local observers proclaimed the Towne residence proof positive that the best taste of the East had at last arrived in San Francisco.

Brown's first commercial commission in San Francisco, the eleven-story Crocker Building—located at the intersection of Market, Post, and Montgomery and conceived of as a monument to Charles Crocker—was built at the then stupendous cost of $1.4 million and was the largest single commercial building erected in the State of California up to that time. It was literally and symbolically a blockbuster: an evocation in steel and brick, marble and terra-cotta, of San Francisco's future as the metropolis of the Pacific. More than $190,000 worth of structural steel, forged at the Phoenix Iron Works of San Francisco, went into the framework of the building, the first such major use of structural steel in San Francisco, and this modernity of construction was seized upon as a symbol of the new order of things to come on the Pacific Coast. *American Architect and Building News* might cavil at the top two stories of Brown's design, finding them redundant and top-heavy; most commentary, however, praised the Crocker Building's dramatic ground-floor arches and its imaginative fenestration, in which Brown's draftsman Bernard Maybeck assisted. As a corner building, set where three of the busiest streets in the city intersected, situated across Market Street from San Francisco's busiest hostelry, the Palace Hotel, Arthur Page Brown's Crocker Building was at the very center of downtown San Francisco, and remained so until it was demolished in 1966. Brown himself moved his offices into Room 238 of the Crocker Building, where for the few remaining years of his life he was busier than he really should have been (so he later lamented) with a score of projects commissioned by his carriage clientele, eager to have something from the hand of the young man who was bringing the best of academic eclecticism to San Francisco.

Designed in 1892 and dedicated in 1893, and along with the Ferry Building one of the few major Brown buildings to survive the catastrophe of April 1906, Trinity Episcopal Church on the corner of Bush and Gough streets manifests most dramatically the heightened mode of historically based architectural style that the Brown office was bringing to California. Modeled on Durham Cathedral in England, Trinity Episcopal is an archeologically exact recreation of Norman ecclesiastical architecture. To enter this wondrous church, passing from rough-hewn granite-gray Colusa sandstone without to a cool-finished surface within, is to experience a number of things at once: the Oxford Movement historicism of late-nineteenth-century Episcopalianism, with its special reverence for the medieval English tradition; the prosperity and taste of Brown's clientele, in this case the oldest (1849) Episcopal congregation in California; and, most gratifyingly for a city deprived of so much of its pre-1906 past, a perfect example of the taste of pre-earthquake San Francisco, when a passion for historical analogy came to a provincial Pacific metropolis eager to see itself in the context of world history. Its cornerstone was laid on 18 September 1892 by the Right Reverend William Ford Nichols, assistant bishop of the Diocese of California. Brown's Trinity church—with its erudite architecture, its great bronze angel by Louis Tiffany (added after Brown's death) which supports the reading

In 1857 when this view (the earliest thus far discovered) was taken, El Pueblo de Nuestra Señora la Reina de los Angeles de Porciúncula stood in dramatic contrast to the City of San Francisco in the north. Not for another twenty years would Los Angeles lose its ambience of frontier Mexico, and only in the twentieth century would it emerge as an important American city. *(The Department of Special Collections, University Research Library, University of California, Los Angeles)*

Three of the daughters of the Peruvian-born Don Juan Bandini of San Diego married Americans. Arcadia Bandini (shown above with her father) married Don Abel Stearns, a Yankee from Massachusetts flourishing since 1829 as a Southern Californian hildago. Linking as it did Latin America, New England, and Hispanic California, the Bandini-Stearns alliance—centered in *El Palacio*, the mansion Don Abel built for Arcadia in Los Angeles after their marriage—underscored the fleeting Yankee/Hispanic accommodation that persisted in Southern California through the 1870s. *(The Bancroft Library, University of California, Berkeley)*

[Opposite] Opening in 1870, the Pico House of Los Angeles was named in honor of Pío Pico, the last governor of Mexican California and a principal investor in the finest hotel in the Southwest. For more than a decade, the Pico House served as the best-known destination point in the region. Each room was gaslit and connected to the front desk by a speaking tube. Enjoying hot baths, sumptuous rooms, good cuisine, lavish floral displays, and choral birdsong from omnipresent birdcages, travelers recuperated from the long stagecoach journey across the desert. *(The Bancroft Library, University of California, Berkeley)*

Born in San Diego where his father was serving in the Spanish Army, Pío Pico served as the last governor of Mexican California. Returning to Los Angeles from exile in Mexico, Pico plunged into a business career. Gambling and business failures cost him four major properties and much cash. His brother Andres, who had led the lances of California to victory at San Pasqual, fared equally poorly. In 1894, the year of the first Fiesta de Los Angeles celebrating the Hispanic roots of the Southland, Pío Pico died broke and alone in Los Angeles and was buried in a pauper's grave. (*The Bancroft Library, University of California, Berkeley*)

To Helen Hunt Jackson's way of thinking, Rancho Camulos in the Santa Clara Valley of Ventura County preserved into the 1880s the recoverable poetry of Old California. Using Rancho Camulos as her setting, Jackson wrote a novel that affixed Southern California to a myth of identity that nurtured it through the turn-of-the-century period. *(The Southwest Museum, Los Angeles, neg. no. 24,276)*

[Opposite left] A Harvard dropout and hometown failure in Ohio, Henry Gaylord Wilshire prospered in Southern California. He grew oranges, grapefruits, and walnuts on his ranch at Fullerton, invented billboard advertising, and developed a boulevard linking Los Angeles and Santa Monica. Wilshire's passion, however, was social reform. His efforts as a Fabian gadfly in the style of his hero George Bernard Shaw helped create a climate of acceptance for the Progressive reforms of the early 1900s. *(The Department of Special Collections, University Research Library, University of California, Los Angeles)*

[Opposite right] The Almighty Himself, claimed Dr. Joseph Pomeroy Widney, had revealed to him the special destiny of the Southland. Here on the shores of the Pacific, the white race—fixed for so long in northern climes—would come into possession of the sun, and from the sun would come a higher era of white civilization. Los Angeles, Widney predicted, would reconcile values of natural living and technology. Mystic, health faddist, physician, a founder of USC, Widney prospered in real estate. He ate a raw onion each morning to get his gastric juices flowing and lived to be nearly one hundred. *(The Huntington Library, San Marino, Calif.)*

Harrison Gray Otis arrived in Southern California middle-aged and a near failure. Within a decade, he controlled the region. Otis involved himself in land, water, politics, and newspapers. Distinguishing himself as a field commander in both the War between the States and the War with Spain, he found in the image of an army on the march his most compelling metaphor for social order and disciplined progress. In the Southern California of the turn-of-the-century period, Otis more than successfully held down his flank on the far right. (*Copyright*, Los Angeles Times)

In 1907 B. Gamble—a founder of Procter and Gamble, retired in Pasadena since 1895—commissioned the Greene brothers, Charles Sumner and Henry Mather, to design a residence in an appropriate regional style. The Gamble House has since served as a primary icon of Southern California. Although they were working for a wealthy client, the Greene brothers hoped that the style they were pioneering would eventually find its way into the popular domestic architecture of the Southland. (*Photograph by Wayne Andrews, California Historical Society Library, San Francisco*)

In the summer of 1903 Henry Edwards Huntington, then busy linking the Los Angeles Basin with a network of high-speed electric streetcars, paused for a moment's repose on the porch of his Lake Vineyard estate in San Marino. Also on hand was the family of Huntington's land manager, George S. Patton, Sr., onetime district attorney of Los Angeles County. Languidly regarding the scene is George S. Patton, Jr., then in the process of transferring from VMI to West Point. On his mother's side, young George was a descendant of Spanish California; on his father's side, he was a Virginian. *(The Huntington Library, San Marino, Calif.)*

[Opposite] In its blend of genteel domesticity and garden richness, the Pasadena bungalow, guarded by palm trees, evoked the lure of Southern California in the turn-of-the-century period. Pasadena promised refinement and informality, civility and luxuriance. The promise of such a lifestyle, pursued amidst roses blooming in January, brought thousands of upper-middle-class immigrants to Southern California in general and Pasadena in particular, transforming the Southland into a special variation of the genteel tradition. *(Photograph by Munsey, California Historical Society Library, San Francisco)*

[*Opposite*] Tourist hotels such as the Del Coronado at Coronado Beach in San Diego County introduced a generation of genteel Eastern tourists to Southern California. Arriving on packaged tours, many affluent visitors later returned as permanent residents. As a young girl growing up in reduced circumstances in San Diego, Anita Loos vowed that she would one day swish proudly into the Del Coronado, a famous writer. Happily, her dream came true. *(The Southwest Museum, Los Angeles, neg. no. 24,236)*

The Mediterranean comparison encouraged much fanciful architecture in the turn-of-the-century Southland, such as this recreation of the Venetian Rialto constructed by Abbott Kinney on the tidal flats twenty-five miles east of Los Angeles. Kinney envisioned Venice as a serious-minded theme park devoted to the performing arts. Southern Californians preferred a Coney Island West. Rather than go broke, Kinney modified his program. *(California Historical Society/Ticor Title Insurance, Los Angeles)*

Like a medieval cathedral, The Mission Inn at Riverside was continually under construction as owner Frank Miller sought to give local habitation and a name in wing after wing to an imagined Spanish past. Thanks to the Inn, Riverside, although founded long after the end of the mission era, became the headquarters of the Southern California mission cult. *(The Southwest Museum, Los Angeles, neg. no. 24,278)*

The traffic on Spring Street proved beyond a doubt that by 1905, the one hundred twenty-fourth year of its existence, Los Angeles had at long last cast off its lethargy and was marching to the music of ragtime America. Within two decades, Los Angeles would reach the one million mark and become, in the words of one local journalist, America's premier City of Dreams. (*California Historical Society/Ticor Title Insurance, Los Angeles*)

[*Opposite above*] Wheat was vast fields of inland prairies covered with wheat as far as the eye could see. Wheat was mechanical harvesters, belching smoke in assertion of the technology that would eventually transform agriculture into agribusiness. Wheat was land used up in the bonanza decades 1870–1890, crop after crop, up to three crops a year. Wheat was California's transitional economy between mining and agribusiness. Wheat was abstract, remorseless, resistive of sentiment and metaphorical associations. (*The California Historical Society Library, San Francisco*)

[*Opposite below*] Nestled amidst the orange groves beneath hoary Mount San Bernardino and the other snowcapped peaks of the Sierra Madre, Redlands epitomized the civil charm of so many citrus-belt cities in early-twentieth-century Southern California. (*The Southwest Museum, Los Angeles, neg. no. 24,277*)

Orange and lemon crate labels brought an idyllic image of Southern California to millions of Americans living elsewhere. The selling of citrus involved the selling of Southern California as well. As a form of mass-distributed commercial art, citrus labels contributed to California's image of itself and the nation's collective image of California. Happily, much of the idyllic imagery was justified. Few American landscapes have ever attained the sumptuous civility of the citrus groves of the Southland. *(The Huntington Library, San Marino, Calif.)*

Arriving in California in 1889 after completing distinguished commissions in New York, Chicago, and Princeton University, Arthur Page Brown brought to the West Coast the robust *élan* of McKim, Mead and White, architects *par excellence* of the American Renaissance. In the style of his mentor Stanford White, Brown pursued a design philosophy of eclecticism, while expending major personal energies on social life. As in the case of another mentor, Charles Follen McKim, social connections engendered business. Before his tragic death at age thirty-seven in 1896, Arthur Page Brown had succeeded in bringing serious systematic architecture to California. *(California Historical Society Library, San Francisco)*

At its opening in 1891, the eleven-story Crocker Building in San Francisco was the single largest structure thus far built in California. Its architect, Arthur Page Brown, intended the Crocker Building as a gesture in the direction of San Francisco's future. In the brief seven years of its existence, the office of Arthur Page Brown—staffed by such brilliant young talents as Bernard Maybeck, Willis Polk, and A.C. Schwienfurth—created building after building for San Francisco and its suburbs as San Francisco sought to create an urban environment worthy of America's capital city on the Pacific. *(San Francisco Archives)*

hotograph of Dinner Party given to
JAMES N. GILLETT

Republican Nominee for Governor, and his friends on the day that he was nominated, to celebrate his nomination.

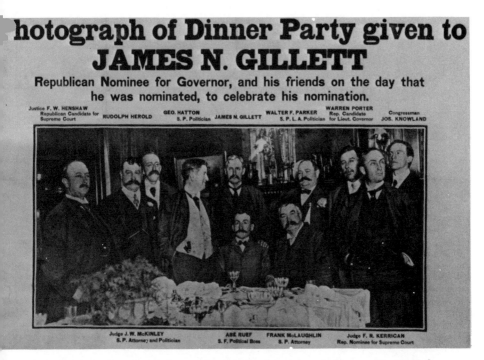

Justice F. W. HENSHAW
Republican Candidate for
Supreme Court
RUDOLPH HEROLD
GEO. HATTON
S. P. Politician
JAMES N. GILLETT
WALTER F. PARKER
S. P. L. A. Politician
WARREN PORTER
Rep. Candidate
for Lieut. Governor
Congressman
JOS. KNOWLAND

Judge J. W. McKINLEY
S. P. Attorney; and Politician
ABE RUEF
S. F. Political Boss
FRANK McLAUGHLIN
S. P. Attorney
Judge F. R. KERRICAN
Rep. Nominee for Supreme Court

On the evening of 10 September 1906, a bunch of the boys—judges, aspiring judges, a congressman, the bosses of Los Angeles and San Francisco, the Republican nominee for governor—foregathered at the home of Mayor Frank Laughlin of Santa Cruz. Boss Ruef of San Francisco had just that week brokered the nomination for Gillett, for a slight financial consideration. After dinner, the guests assembled for their portrait, Governor-to-be Gillett's hand planted appreciatively on Abe Ruef's shoulder. A few years later, the photograph, now entitled "The Shame of California," was on billboards up and down the State. (*The Bancroft Library, University of California, Berkeley*)

[*Opposite above*] As patroness and reformer, Phoebe Apperson Hearst brought intelligence and great presence to pre-Progressive California. Among her many causes, she advanced scholarship, museums, libraries, early childhood education, the women's movement, and the University of California, which she served as a virtual second founder after the State itself. In sifting through the record of pre-Progressive reform, one finds her corrective presence everywhere. History, however, has virtually forgotten her in favor of her more flamboyant son. (*The Bancroft Library, University of California, Berkeley*)

[*Opposite below*] Governor-elect and Mrs. Hiram Johnson relax at Lake Tahoe after the election of 1910. Minerva Johnson loathed the prospect of returning to Sacramento, where she grew up; but Hiram promised her Washington after four years as governor. It took Johnson eight years to make good on his promise—although he did try to take the Potomac by storm in 1912 as Theodore Roosevelt's running mate on the Bull Moose ticket. Offered the vice presidential spot on Harding's ticket, Senator Johnson, angry that he was not the candidate, refused and thus lost the presidency for a second and final time. (*The Bancroft Library, University of California, Berkeley*)

Encountering William Randolph Hearst in Chicago in late 1906, journalist Lincoln Steffens came away from his interview vaguely disturbed by the ambiguous presence of the newspaper magnate turned Democratic congressman. There was in Hearst, Steffens later suggested, a conjunction of resentments, opportunities, and power to communicate to the masses that made the fiercely ambitious Californian/New Yorker a new factor in American public life. Was Hearst—the Man of Mystery as Steffens described him—awaiting in the wings a casting call to play Tribune of the People? *(The Bancroft Library, University of California, Berkeley)*

Cycling was all the rage in the 1890s, and for residents of Los Angeles there was no better destination for a cycling excursion than the nearby village of Hollywood, where this group posed for its photograph on 18 March 1899 in front of the Sackett Store, Hotel, and Post Office on the southwest corner of Hollywood and Cahuenga. Horace and Daeida Wilcot, the founders of Hollywood, had hoped to create a Christian utopia. History had other plans. *(California Historical Society/Ticor Title Insurance, Los Angeles)*

Arriving in Southern California in the winter of 1910, Biograph director D.W. Griffith and his cameraman Billy Bitzer chose for their first all-Californian film *The Thread of Destiny*, a story of Old California starring Mary Pickford. Six years later, Griffith and Bitzer were ensconced on a platform on the corner of Sunset and Hollywood Boulevards filming *Intolerance*, the Ur-epic of the emerging Hollywood film industry. "He was the teacher of us all," Cecil B. De Mille later remarked of Griffith. *(The Bison Archives, Los Angeles)*

With the assistance of English stage designer Walter Hall, D.W.
Griffith recreated a daydream Babylon on the corner of Sunset and
Hollywood Boulevards. Looming three hundred feet above the sleepy
Los Angeles suburb, Babylon conferred upon Hollywood its most
enduring of future metaphors. Like Babylon, Hollywood would soon
become a temple to permissive gods and easy ways. (*The Bison Archives, Los Angeles*)

When opera diva Geraldine Farrar arrived in Hollywood in the fall of 1915, Cecil B. De Mille and Jesse L. Lasky were on hand, along with a welcoming crowd of five thousand, to greet their investment. For three films, Farrar received $20,000, plus the guarantee of a mansion, a chauffeur-driven limousine, a bungalow-sized dressing studio with a grand piano, and a full-sized orchestra to create the proper mood on the set. Miss Farrar, opined Sam Goldfish (later Goldwyn), was bringing class, real class to Hollywood. *(The Bison Archives, Los Angeles)*

Intense on the set with his protégé, actor Wallace Reid, Cecil B. De Mille needed only the sketchiest of scenarios to create films speaking directly to the dream life of mass America. When Reid died at age thirty of drug-related complications, CB turned to the Bible (enlivened by an orgy or two) in a successful effort to regain Hollywood's reputation in mid-America. *(The Bison Archives, Los Angeles)*

An entire generation of aspiring middle-class Americans took its cues in the matter of domestic living from what Mary Pickford and Douglas Fairbanks were up to at Pickfair, their Beverly Hills estate. Thanks in large part to Douglas and Mary, the Hollywood movie star—which was to say, the Hollywood movie star as representative Southern Californian—became the representative mid-American. Douglas, Mary, and their Hollywood peers took the message of Southern California to the rest of the nation. Not even orange crate labels had a comparable influence. *(Security Pacific National Bank Photograph Collection/Los Angeles Public Library)*

lectern, its exquisite stained glass windows (two of them by Louis Tiffany as well), with their suggestions of Pre-Raphaelitism and the dawning art nouveau—bespeaks the ethos of upper-class San Francisco of that era: a concern that San Francisco begin to express itself in perfect taste through an architecture heralding the arrival of the best art from past ages on Pacific shores.

The Brown office's other surviving San Francisco church—the Swedenborgian Church of the New Jerusalem at 2107 Lyon, at the northeast corner of Washington (1894)—vies with the Ferry Building and the Sainte Claire Club in San Jose for the honor of being considered the most architecturally significant extant work to have come from Brown and his colleagues. Taken as a collaborative effort, in fact—incorporating the talents of Brown, architects Bernard Maybeck and A. C. Schweinfurth, architect and pastor Joseph Worcester, and artists Bruce Porter and William Keith—the Church of the New Jerusalem emerges as the central text of fin-de-siècle San Francisco: not so much architecture, so Brown himself later said, as the poetry of architecture, an incipiently utopian memorialization of religion, culture, and nature harmonized through architecture and art. First of all, the Church of the New Jerusalem can be ascribed to the Brown office only in that Brown was formally responsible for the project. The church is, in reality, an Arts-and-Crafts collaboration of artists, each contributing to the whole. The chief demiurge behind the project was the Reverend Joseph Worcester, pastor of the Church of the New Jerusalem and an architect in his own right, whose simplified shingled homes on Russian Hill helped to create an idiom of domestic architecture known today as the Bay Region style. The Boston-born Worcester was at once a Swedenborgian mystic and a Telegraph Hill bohemian, a worshipper of nature (as a revelation of the mind of God) and a lover of history, human culture, and the art past. All in all, Worcester stood in delightful contrast to most of Brown's clients from the haute bourgeoisie. Under the pastor architect's guidance, Brown assembled a talented group of collaborators who in turn produced a building that, like any successful art, was a simple thing—yet a score of other things as well. To sort out the intentions and influences that went into the making of the Lyon Street church, in fact, is to unravel the skein of avant-garde aesthetic consciousness in fin-de-siècle San Francisco.

Take the matter of Mediterraneanism, that persistent belief that California should take as its aesthetic model the art, architecture, and lifestyles of Southern Europe. The first formal inspiration behind the Church of the New Jerusalem is from this movement. Returned from Italy, Bruce Porter showed Worcester a sketch he had done of a hillside church in the Po Valley near Verona. Worcester wanted this sketch to be the basis of the design, but with an element of Mission Revival thrown in, because the Franciscans had first brought Mediterranean architecture to California. Hence arose the brick-and-concrete church's orchestration of arch, grillwork, and wall, tower and tiled roof. To complete the link with the missions, a cross from Mission San Miguel in the Salinas Valley was emplaced in the garden.

Worcester also wanted the Church of the New Jerusalem to be a mini-cathedral of Swedenborgianism, suggesting the interpenetrations of spirit and nature, of the seen with the unseen. To do this, Brown and his collaborators drew upon that fascination with japonaisierie that was also characteristic of the fin-de-siècle: in this case, the appropriate Shinto tradition of the walled-off garden shrine, in which subtle but deliberate landscaping makes a symbolic statement. Around a serene pool in the center of the garden of the Church of the New Jerusalem was planted a rich array of trees—cedar of Lebanon, olive, sequoia, elm, pine, myrtle, hawthorne, maple, plum, crabapple, Irish yew—intended as an allegory of the worlds of the Bible, Europe, America, and the Far East (there was also a Japanese vase and gong on the premises) finding confluence and resolution in this one quiet spot, this *hortus conclusus* in San Francisco. For the interior of the church, Bruce Porter designed two circular stained glass windows—a dove alighting on a fountain, against a background of apple blossoms, and St. Christopher carrying the Christ child across a swollen river—and William Keith painted four murals depicting the subtle changing of the California seasons.

In lieu of pews and conventional church appointments, there was an atmosphere of Arts-and-Crafts domesticity, including an off-center fireplace in the rear of the church and eighty handmade maple chairs, with seats woven from tule reeds from the Sacramento Delta. Madrone tree trunks—selected and cut on the Glenn Ranch in the Santa Cruz Mountains, wrapped in burlap, and shipped up to San Francisco by wagon so as to avoid damage—arched overhead in support of the ceiling, an effect at once Gothic and Californian. The madrone arches were the idea of the young Bay Area architect Bernard Maybeck, the woodcarver's son who would himself do such wonderful things with wood in the course of his career. Maybeck's madrone arches are declarations of intent, a gesture in the direction of the half century of wood building ahead. It is to Arthur Page Brown's credit that he welcomed Maybeck's naturalism, and their arches of California madrone found a perfect setting in an Italian hillside church recreated in San Francisco.

As artistically successful as the Church of the New Jerusalem was, however, it remained an exception in the Brown canon. Brown's personal fortunes and dominant interests were centered in a more traditional mode of establishment architecture. Like so many of his social set, Brown was turning his attention down the Peninsula in the early 1890s to the oak-dotted meadows and softly rolling hills of Burlingame Park. Reachable by a brief train ride from downtown San Francisco, the Burlingame area was seen by Brown and others of the upper class as a perfect site for summer villas and estates or even for year-round suburban residence. Joining with Richard P. Hammond, a wealthy San Francisco park commissioner, and John McLaren, the Scots-born Golden Gate Park landscapist, Brown developed five small estates in Burlingame Park as a speculative venture. While McLaren did the landscaping, Brown designed five English half-timber country houses (1893) on El Camino Real between Bellvue and Floribunda, three of which yet survive. Eager to play the country squire, Brown reserved one of these estates for himself, and it was most likely here, on 5 September 1893, that the Burlingame Country Club was incorporated, with Brown's friend Will Crocker serving as the first president. Naturally, Brown was commissioned the next year to do the club's first clubhouse, a rustically gabled English half-timber set amidst tennis courts, golf links, a full race track, and a polo field judged superior to that of Newport, Rhode Island. The clubhouse was dedicated on Saturday, 26 May 1894, with day-long festivities that began with luncheon, continued through an afternoon steeplechase race, and ended with an evening ball and buffet supper.

That same year, Brown designed for the Crockers on a nearby site a French Renaissance palace based on Le Petit Trianon at Versailles, which the Crockers furnished sumptuously with the harvests of a number of European buying sprees. Burlingame, where Brown lived after 1893, and the Burlingame Country Club, where Brown and his wife, founding members, were the liveliest of the lively young set, perfectly embodied the aspirations and style of Arthur Page Brown. Social connections, moreover, continued to account for his livelihood and for his best work: the Spanish Revival villa he designed in 1893 for Mr. and Mrs. Hermann Oelrichs of Newport, Rhode Island, for instance—Mrs. Oelrichs being the former Virginia Fair, daughter of the Irish-born "Silver King," James Fair, onetime United States senator from Nevada (1881–87) and one of the wealthiest men in America. A close friend of Brown's wife, Virginia Fair caused a sensation when she debuted in Newport in 1891, being possessed of beauty, brains, and enormous wealth—in addition to being a Californian, which for Newport was sensation enough. In 1907 Virginia Oelrichs built the Fairmont Hotel in San Francisco in her father's honor. Had Arthur Page Brown been alive, he would no doubt have received this commission.

Spanish Revival—with some Midwest Prairie style surprisingly thrown in—characterizes another of Brown's social projects, the Sainte Claire Club (1894) in San Jose. Brown's good friend James Duval Phelan, the patrician future mayor of San Francisco and future United States senator from California, was at the time very active in Santa Clara County banking and real estate, and hence was spending much of his time in San Jose, whose amenities he wished to improve. There was talk, moreover, of moving the state capital back to San Jose from Sacramento, and so for both reasons—Phelan's desire to improve social life in the agricultural town, and San Jose's impending importance as state capital—Phelan and others of the local oligarchy decided that what San Jose needed, among other things, was a good men's club. The case can be made that the Sainte Claire Club is the most intriguing creation of the Brown office that has survived. So many of his truly distinguished buildings—the Princeton Art Museum, the Ferry Building—were in a historical mode; in the Sainte Claire Club, however, Brown's designer A. C. Schweinfurth (with Brown's guidance and approval) operated in the outer foyer of the avant-garde. Taking the nearby Mission Santa Clara as his motif, Schweinfurth fused Mission, Spanish Revival, and Prairie Modern, arriving at a brick, stucco, and tile style at once historical and progressive.

The greatest achievement of the Brown office in the Mission Revival mode was the monumental California State Building at the World's Columbian Exposition held in Chicago from May to November 1893. When the California commissioners for the Columbia Exposition announced an architectural competition for the California building in January 1892, they specified that the exhibition hall had to be in the Mission or Moorish style, then in its first phase of revival. The *Wave*, an influential San Francisco magazine which had previously criticized Brown's work and had not yet fully made its peace with Brown at the time, stated in its issue of 13 October 1892 that many young architects were not even entering the competition, since one and all knew that Arthur Page Brown had a number of close friends among the commissioners, including its president, Irving M. Scott of the Union Iron Works, and vice-president, James Duval Phelan. Bernard Maybeck, in fact, submitted a proposal which failed to place; but when Brown was awarded the contract, to no one's surprise, he brought Maybeck aboard as assistant architect. In 1886, Maybeck, then with John Mervyn Carrere and Thomas Hastings in New York City, had worked on that firm's designs for the Hotel Ponce de Leon in St. Augustine, Florida (1888); and the California State Building at Chicago, thanks to Maybeck's influence, showed a unifying of diverse elements through a great central dome similar to that of the Ponce de Leon. Brown sent Maybeck out to Chicago to supervise construction of what turned out to be one of the most popular buildings at the exposition.

At Chicago, Brown's building rose alongside the work of Daniel Hudson Burnham, Frederick Law Olmsted, the innovative Louis Sullivan, and Brown's former bosses, Charles Follen McKim and Stanford White, all of whom were designing a Great White City that would, as Frank Lloyd Wright later lamented, obsess American architects with neoclassical monumentality for the next quarter century. With the exception of the Illinois State Building, Brown's neo-Mission exhibition hall was—at 435 feet by 144 feet, rising 113 feet from the ground—the largest exhibition hall at Chicago, which was no mean feat, in that the Columbian Exposition abounded in heroic public spaces. The California State Building shows that the Brown office was capable at once of fantasy informed by scholarship and a structuralist passion for vast open interior public spaces. Externally, the California State Building evoked a never-never land of a Spanish Californian arcadia, a dreamy suggestion of whitewashed missions set against rolling hills, their red-tiled roofs glowing carmine in the sunset. Within the state building, however, there soared an accomplished instance of ferro-vitreous structuralism, steel and glass flying high overhead in futurist poetry. Staff (fiber mixed with rough cement) covered the outside of the California State Building in an effort to create a theatrical effect of adobe; within the more honest interior, however, great steel girders arched openly and massive skylights let in the spring and summer sunshine as hundreds of thousands of visitors moved from exhibit to exhibit announcing the wondrously plentiful commonwealth of California: great pyramids of fresh oranges (still a rarity in the Midwest), piles of dates, produce, and preserves of every sort, and in the art gallery ample evidence that a California School of painters was in the process of finding itself.

Designed at the beginning of the Mission Revival movement in California, the California State Building helped to fix Mission Revival as the semi-official public style in the state, especially in Southern California, where train depots, hotels, schools, hospitals, post offices, city halls, and other public places were soon designed in the elaborate Franciscan ecclesiastical style pioneered by the Brown office at Chicago. Some critics resented this imposition. They considered Mission Revival a pseudo-historical, pseudo-romantic appropriation for public purposes of the architecturally undistinguished California missions, which after all, so they argued, represented a backward feudal society at odds with a dynamic, forward-looking commonwealth. The California State Building, wrote one outraged Californian in the *Oakland Enquirer* of 15 February 1892, "should represent the California of 1892 and not the California of 1792." As awkward as pure Mission Revival could be, however, it was destined to prevail through the 1920s.

So successful was the World's Columbian Exposition that *Chronicle* publisher Michael H. de Young, one of the California commissioners, launched a successful drive to bring part of the fair out to San Francisco. Designated the California Midwinter International Exposition and held in Golden Gate Park from 1 January to 4 July 1894, De Young's brainchild attracted 2.5 million visitors. San Francisco was then in the throes of a massive recession, and de Young envisioned the Midwinter Fair as a temporary public works project that would create employment, stimulate business, and attract outside capital to the city. Raising $344,319 from the private sector, de Young and his associates from the downtown business establishment accomplished what had at first seemed impossible: the transporting of major exhibits from Chicago to the Golden Gate Park of San Francisco, where nearly two hundred acres were developed in less than five months as the Midwinter Fair site. Again there occurred the inevitable architectural competition, with many of Arthur Page Brown's friends sitting in judgment. Five major buildings were planned for the Midwinter Exposition. Brown submitted designs for all five, including two separate proposals for the Fine Arts Building, and was awarded two commissions, the Administration Building and the Manufacturers' and Liberal Arts Building.

For the Administration Building at the south end of the Grand Concourse, Brown and his colleagues designed a castellated fantasy variously described as Moorish, Byzantine-Gothic, Central Indian, and Siamese—and probably one or another motif justified all those designations. Like Xanadu, the fabled palace of Kubla Khan, Brown's Administration Building ascended upward through four hexagonal towers flanking a 135-foot dome crowned by a great flagpole. Banners, pennants, and flags flew everywhere, brightly flapping in the breeze, playing off the highly colored Arabic and Moorish patterns decorating the staff-covered walls of the temporary structure. Again, there was repeated the inside-outside counterpoint of the California Building in Chicago, for despite the fantasy without, Brown provided the Administration Building with a crisply efficient interior office structure. The Manufacturers' and Liberal Arts Building shows the same dichotomy. The working purpose of the building was to provide the Midwinter Fair with its central exhibition hall, which it did magnificently. At 237 feet by 462 feet, covering more than 100,000 square feet, and with a raised gallery area within that measured 47,000 square feet, the Manufacturers' and Liberal Arts Building, temporary though it might have been, was as of the year 1894 the largest single building constructed in the State of California. Nineteen gigantic wood and iron trusses, weighing nine tons each, soared 92 feet up from the exhibition hall floor to support the main roof, which featured 14,000 square feet of glass skylight. Brown used an adaptation of a Roman basilica for his floor plan, believing that this ancient model provided one of the most effective possible designs for the accommodation of large crowds, which circulated through the exhibits on the main floor, then took one of five staircases leading up to a 35-foot-wide gallery that rimmed the interior, adding 47,000 more square feet of exhibition space, but also working against the cavernous effect the great building might otherwise have had. The grand staircases leading to the galleries allowed for an ingenious two-way system of pedestrian circulation, as did the arrangement of exhibitions on the floor.

The interior of the Manufacturers' and Liberal Arts Building, then, was an intricate organization of swirling human movement, variegated but orderly beneath soaring trusses and vast expanses of skylight. Never before had the people of California beheld such a public space; never before had it been possible for Californians to experience themselves spatially, architecturally, as a collective entity whose exuberant variety had found the civilizing influences of orderly public promenade.

The color scheme of both these buildings, incidentally, was the work of artist Charles S. Graham, director of color for the Midwinter Fair. Graham also joined

Brown's office as an artist and colorist, responsible for producing the lavish renderings that helped Brown win his numerous contracts. Portly, flamboyant, and, like his mentor, socially ambitious, Charles S. Graham was introduced by Brown around town. With Brown as sponsor, Graham joined the Bohemian Club and the Burlingame Country Club, where he soon became a familiar figure, especially on racing or polo days, when he watched from the sidelines in a Yorkshire suit of checked tweed and a deerstalker hat. Everyone, including Arthur Page Brown, loved the amusing, anecdotal, fun-loving Charley Graham—until the day, that is, that Graham disappeared from San Francisco, and clubmen around town began to compare notes as to just how much money Charley had borrowed and what were the chances (slim, they admitted) that Charley would ever return to San Francisco and settle accounts. Scoundrelly as his behavior had been, Charley Graham did, however, leave his friend Brown with a revivified sense of the role color could play in enlivening architecture. Perhaps it was Graham himself who suggested the dramatic use of colored tile mosaics and sweeping colored banners in the Ferry Building, ideas which Brown was developing at the time of his fatal accident.

III

Awarded the Ferry Building commission in late September 1892, the Brown office was engaged in one way or another with this monumental project throughout the 1892–96 period. The construction of a grand new passenger terminal for San Francisco was very much a piece of 1890s business. During this decade, when the United States came of age as an internal empire, the drama of transportation took on symbolic significance. Witness the great railroad stations undertaken or completed in this era. Transportation symbolized the emergent unity of an America that had put the fratricidal sectionalism of the Civil War behind it and was now ready to march in unity onto the world's stage. San Franciscans felt this surge of ambition—but were without the possibility of a railroad station to express it. The transcontinental railroads ended or began their journeys in Oakland, across the Bay. In most instances of serious travel, passengers came to or departed from San Francisco by ferryboat. The ferry depot was thus San Francisco's actual and symbolic point of linkage with the outside world. Ever since 1877 San Francisco had served its commuters and its arriving and departing travelers through a dockside wooden shed and tower called the Central Terminal Building. Unpretentious and serviceable, the Central Terminal Building perfectly expressed the ramshackle frontier building style of mid-nineteenth-century San Francisco. The ambitions of the 1890s, however, extended in grander directions. A new depot was necessary, but it must also be a building that would serve as a citywide point of reference, an architectural expression of San Francisco's dawning ambition to become a center of world trade and a busy point of arrival and departure for international traffic. And besides, as the *California Architect* chided in its issue for 18 February 1890, San Francisco was a city virtually devoid of distinguished public works—or public buildings of any kind, for that matter. The city's haltingly progressing City Hall, twenty years in the building, announced to the rest of the nation the civic immaturity of San Francisco. A monumental bayside passenger terminal at the foot of Market Street seemed the logical project with which to inaugurate an era of public works.

The process of constructing a new Ferry Building began in Sacramento with the passage on 17 March 1891 of legislation authorizing the Harbor Commission of California to issue bonds for a new depot. The voters of California approved this measure in the statewide election of 8 November 1892. Even before this approval, on 29 September 1892, Arthur Page Brown, thanks to his Southern Pacific connections (the railroad's San Francisco Bay ferry system being the major tenant of the proposed terminal), was awarded the contract for what then promised to be the largest single piece of construction ever undertaken in California, even surpassing Brown's recently completed Crocker Building.

Brown spent the month of October 1892 in the East, making a study of major railroad stations and port facilities. Returning to San Francisco, he spent the next three months at work with Schweinfurth and the rest of his staff on a ferry building design that was formally unveiled to the harbor commissioners on 19 January 1893 as a beautifully rendered twelve-by-eight-foot colored sketch. On 9 February 1893 the commissioners, after three weeks of public and private discussion, voted to accept the proposal. Newspaper commentary, meanwhile, was unequivocally favorable, save in the matter of Brown's initial design for the tower, which, it was pointed out, was a rather uninspired copy of Stanford White's tower atop Madison Square Garden in New York City, a recently completed McKim, Mead and White project (1890).

Brown's general conception, however—a Roman Revival pavilion with flanking wings, surmounted by a 240-foot tower, the whole to be constructed of steel and concrete with a covering of gray Colusa sandstone—won instant acceptance. San Franciscans were delighted that in the near future, instead of a wooden shed anchoring the place where Market Street ran into the Bay, there would soon be a Roman Revival building of massivity and strength running for 661 feet down the Embarcadero, surmounted by a tower rising 240 feet above the San Francisco skyline. Modeled upon the Giralda Tower of the Cathedral of Seville, the Ferry Building tower bespoke Brown and Schweinfurth's early fascination with things Spanish. The powerfully arched facade and the light, fairytale-like tower went well together, critics agreed; the Roman Revival pavillion expressed the massivity and strength essential to a major American city, and the Spanish tower asserted an element of imagination, of lightness and grace, which San Francisco also had need of in its skyline.

The structure and interior of the Ferry Building were planned to be as modern as its outside was historical. As in the case of the Crocker Building, Brown used structural steel and self-supporting stone walls, reinforced with concrete. He worked closely with San Francisco engineer Ernest L. Ransome to devise the arched and vaulted concrete piles that would pierce the shifting sands of the bay floor and anchor the building onto more solid foundations of bedrock. For the interior of the building, Brown wanted an aerial pageant of steel and skylight and space, intended to sweep above a continuous pageant of human activity. Brown called for giant potted palms and other plants to be lavishly used, to give the terminal a gardenlike effect as greenery played off the open steel structure and the massive sandstone walls, the whole to be bathed in light from the skylights overhead or illumined at night by arc lights and incandescent lamps. With his usual extravagance, Brown called for marble, tile, colored mosaics, and lavish sculpted decorative motifs to be used throughout the building.

All of this added up to an estimated $1 million in cost, which started the project in controversy. The Ferry Building bond issue had only authorized $600,000. Both Brown and the harbor commissioners (most of whom, Brown later admitted, were his personal friends) came under attack for planning on too expensive a scale. For a while, in April 1893, there was talk of eliminating the tower altogether to cut expenses. Despite their personal friendships with Brown, certain commissioners had already tried to halve Brown's initial fee from $12,000 to $6,250, which the architect naturally resisted, going so far as to threaten a lawsuit. Controversy continued through the bidding process. In April 1893 Bateman Brothers Construction Company brought suit against the harbor commission in superior court, claiming that although its bid of $328,000 was the lowest bid on the job of building the Ferry Building foundations, the commission had awarded the contract to the San Francisco Bridge Company. Brown testified in court that $328,000 would not be enough to complete the foundations, no matter what the bond issue specified, and the court upheld the right of the commission to revise its estimate of expenses upwards to a true figure and award the foundation contract accordingly. Work on the foundations, delayed again and again as new techniques for working beneath the water were devised, continued for nearly two years.

The year 1895 proved to be one of special controversy, as both Arthur Page Brown and his foundations came under attack. Certain civil engineers put it about that the reinforced concrete pier foundations devised by Brown and engineer Ernest L. Ransome would be unable to support the weight of the proposed Ferry Building safely. The harbor commissioners appointed a group of engineering consultants to look into the matter, and Governor James Budd of California, an engineer by profession, entered a longboat and personally inspected the foundations from the bay side on 2 February 1895. At the end of his watery inspection, Governor Budd pronounced the foundations totally satisfactory. Four days later, however, on 6 February 1895, a new crisis arose. The *San Francisco Call*, rather belatedly it would seem, charged that no formal architectural competition had ever been held, that Brown was an inside appointment. Other architects had not even been able to discuss their ideas with the commission. Thus if the commission was having doubts as to the soundness of the foundations, it might very well use this occasion to open up the entire matter of Brown's contract before proceeding any further. Despite the favorable judgment of Governor Budd, the foundation controversy continued through the next two months.

As is always the case with political commissions under fire, the harbor commissioners began to grow edgy under the constant criticism—and in their edginess they began to take a second look at Arthur Page Brown. Brown's contract, for instance, stipulated that he serve as an on-site supervisory architect for the construction of the Ferry Building. The prodigious architectural output of the Brown office for the years 1893, 1894, and 1895 shows just how casually Brown took this supervisory obligation, despite the fact that he had drawn more than $20,000 in fees from the harbor commissioners for services rendered, including on-site supervision. The *Chronicle* reported on 23 April 1895 that the harbor commissioners were hopping mad over the disclosure that Brown had merely sauntered through the construction site a half dozen times since 1893, and were seriously considering firing him. Confronted in his office by a reporter with these charges, Brown thrust his hands into his well-tailored pockets, put his tongue into his cheek, and denied that he was Arthur Page Brown at all, no matter what the name on the door might say. The reporter was more charmed than offended by Brown's sangfroid. Called personally before the commission, Brown admitted his desultoriness and promised to do better. The commissioners backed off from sacking him, and for the remaining half year of his active life Brown did show up at the construction site. One suspects, however, that he also managed side trips of inspection to his other projects as well, such as the Macdonough Building (1895), an Italian Renaissance business block on the northeast corner of Sutter and Grant, his final downtown office building.

Brown's opposition, however, also rallied. The grand jury summoned him to appear on 3 May 1895 for a review of the entire affair: the initial cost estimate, the soundness of the foundations, construction delays, his own desultory supervision. The grand jury made no recommendations against Brown, but in July State Attorney General E. L. Fitzgerald said that he believed that Brown's contract with the harbor commission was illegal because of the lack of an open competition. Architect John C. Felton, Jr., then came forward with a competitive design. Brown's lawyer beat back this last assault. On the morning of his fateful accident, Arthur Page Brown was secure in his hopes of seeing the Ferry Building through to completion.

Arthur Page Brown died at 8:30 on the morning of Tuesday, 21 January 1896. He was thirty-five, and he left a wife and three children. When word of his death reached San Francisco that day, scores of friends and colleagues rushed to Brown's offices in the Crocker Building. Somberly, they talked to each other in disbelief. How could such a charming, totally alive man be gone so soon! Episcopalian funeral services were held two days later in Brown's home adjacent to the Burlingame Country Club. William H. Crocker and James Duval Phelan were among the pallbearers. In Brown's honor, his friend and Bohemian Club confrere William Keith added another mural, depicting a melancholy moonlight forest, to the murals in the Church of the New Jerusalem.

"Mr. Brown," remarked one obituary writer, "was not a rich man because he spent his income right royally. He gave his family the best that was to be had and was never so happy as when entertaining his friends." Brown left his widow an estate (including a valuable parcel of Burlingame real estate) valued at $43,869. Arthur Page Brown, however, had always loved the fast track, whether it be a matter of horses, social connections, or the good things of life. Not expecting to die at age thirty-five, and fully confident that his practice would eventually make him a wealthy man, he also left behind debts and obligations surpassing the value of his assets. This is not to say that Arthur Page Brown died broke. Gentlemen do not die broke; gentlemen die bankrupt. After the banks had finished with the Brown estate, there was nothing left for the family, except for two insurance policies valued at $50,000, one of which had already been eaten up by pressing obligations. Mrs. Brown had to go to court to protect the remaining money.

"How I wish I had remained in McKim, Mead, and White's office in New York after I came back from Europe," Arthur Page Brown wearily remarked just before his death. "I've got too much work to 'digest' here, and how I should like to simply carry out one idea at a time!" It was not, however, Brown's task to carry out one idea at a time. His work, rather, lay in the lavish scattering of ideas throughout San Francisco and the Bay Area, in the presentation of academic eclectic historical styles adapted to local purposes that might in turn instruct and improve an emergent California taste and thus assist in the establishment of a significant regional architecture. This he did with amazing vigor: bring history to the Pacific Coast. "California is positive," Willis Polk wrote in *The Wave* in 1893, "it is individual, it is great in opportunity, and when the ages have lent it dignity, it will go down in history with Egypt, with Greece, with Rome and with France. It will be the inheritor of all their greatness, but the projector of its own!" Arthur Page Brown brought to California the means whereby California might establish itself as an architectural heir to the ages while at the same time, in Polk's phrase, project its own possible greatness. The academic eclecticism of the American Renaissance was, after all, not so much a fixed style as it was an encouraging attitude of scholarly responsiveness to the challenge of memorializing the newfound power of America. Critics correctly chastize the style for its frequently overblown rhetoric, its elitism, and its obliviousness to the true processes and conditions of the urban industrial society which America had actually become, with all its suppressions and inequities. And yet academic eclecticism—as practiced by McKim, Mead and White and as brought to the San Francisco Bay area by Arthur Page Brown in July 1889—did enable a building California generation to invoke and evoke architecturally the values of civility and order, public culture and graciousness, it so ardently sought for itself. San Franciscans might think of Rome, Corinth, Naples, Geneva, Florence, or Constantinople when they searched for metaphors of what their city should seek to become. The buildings produced by the Brown office made such daydreams come partially true.

7

Reforming California

In the early 1900s California, along with a number of other states of the Union, reformed itself. Historians group this work of reformation—political and governmental in the main, but touching also upon other aspects of public life—under the general rubric of "the Progressive movement." Progressivism, we are told, helped to transform the United States from an agricultural nation, owned by an omnipotent oligarchy and governed by the corrupt party machines which the oligarchy subsidized, into an urban industrial society that had begun to put its political house in good order. Progressivism brought system and benevolence to a haphazard, frequently cruel and capricious Republic. Intense to the point of evangelism, by turns visionary and pragmatic, Progressivism was energized by forces bubbling up from deep within the collective Protestant bourgeois psyche. All this—external reform and an inner drama of search and meaning—flourished most intensely in California. By 1912, in fact, when Hiram Johnson, the Progressive governor of California, was chosen by Theodore Roosevelt as his vice-presidential candidate on the Progressive (Bull Moose) ticket, the claim was made that out of all the states of the Union to show signs of Progressive transformation, California had experienced the most profound and extensive upheaval and reform.

The reform and restructuring of California was no easy matter. Despite the fact that most major reforms were pushed through during a five-year period, 1910 to 1915, the gestation period was long and arduous. Early attempts at reform usually took the form of revolts against the all-encompassing power of the Southern Pacific Railroad, or as Californians were wont to call it, the SP. The SP offered the most obvious instance of what was grossly wrong with California: a very few of the super-rich virtually owned the state—its land, its economy, its government—and were running it as a private preserve. As a creation of the frontier era, the SP epitomized as a corporation all the ruthless energy, the scheming flexibility, the iron will to wealth and power that had characterized the Gold Rush and first frontier era of California through the 1870s.

The ownership of the SP, the Big Four, was a Gilded Age plutocracy, California style. Of relatively simple Eastern backgrounds (three from upstate New York, one from Connecticut), Leland Stanford, Mark Hopkins, Charles Crocker, and Collis P. Huntington all came to California during the Gold Rush, went into retailing in Sacramento, then by sheer cunning and will forged a railroad across half a continent, enriching themselves in the process beyond their wildest boyhood dreams: in railroads, steamship companies, land holdings (vast acres were granted by the federal government as a subsidy and spur to railroad construction), irrigation projects, hotels, and urban real estate.

When Leland Stanford served as governor of California during the Civil War, he served railroad interests as well. From the start, the SP respected politics. Politics, after all, in the form of massive federal loans and land grants, had created the company. Beginning in the 1870s, the SP systematically began to gain as much influence over the politics of California as possible. Between 1870 and 1900 the population of California grew from 560,247 to 1,485,053, and the SP grew from the third party of California politics to the only party, holding Democrats and Republicans alike in receivership. The reformist Constitution of 1879 created a three-man railroad commission, intended to regulate the SP. Stacked with genial retainers, the commission soon became waggishly known as the Southern Pacific Literary Bureau. Few adverse regulations came from this enfeebled commission in its thirty-year existence.

Nor did the courts set an opposite example. The SP, for one thing, had a very good friend on the national Supreme Court, Justice Stephen Field, a former California supreme court justice appointed to the Court in 1863 by Abraham Lincoln at the urging of the Big Four. Locally, the state supreme court could usually be counted on. (Years later, Fremont Older remembered the shock he felt when as a young San Francisco reporter in the late 1880s he first saw a California supreme court justice shamelessly display his annual pass to a SP railroad conductor.) Between 1895 and 1910, 57 out of 79 rate cases to come before the California Supreme Court were ruled in favor of the SP. No wonder the railroad was able to adjust rates to suit its purposes, favoring some freight shippers (especially those in which it held partial interest) and driving the uncooperative out of business. Needing oil for its trains, the railroad gained controlling interest in Associated Oil, a subsidiary of Standard, then gave rebates to both companies, which is to say to itself. Whatever was lost on oil shipments could be made up elsewhere.

Established in 1893 and headquartered in offices at Fourth and Townsend streets in San Francisco, the unambiguously named Political Bureau of the Southern Pacific, presided over by a skilled corporate attorney, William Franklin Herrin, chief counsel to the railroad between 1893 and 1910, coordinated the affairs of a statewide, indeed nationwide, political network. Experienced in the service of the oligarchy from his former service on the staffs of the William Sharon estate and the vast Miller and Lux holdings in the San Joaquin Valley, Herrin exercised control over local party organizations through the simple technique of placing key individuals on retainer. Elected legislators received free passes and hotel rooms, campaign contributions, special rates for their business friends. Since Republican party nominating conventions were SP-controlled, a steady supply of favorable legislators—such as Grove Johnson of Sacramento, father of the future reform governor—was insured. There were a few exceptions, but in the main the governors and United States senators of California were equally friendly. "From the village constable to the governor of the state," observed the reform-minded Dr. John R. Haynes of Los Angeles, "the final selection of the people's officials lay with Mr. Herrin or his subordinates in the railroad machine." Since by 1900 half of California's population resided in four urban centers, the control of city machines was crucial to the preservation of SP interests. The SP initially exercised its influence in San Francisco through Christopher Buckley, a blind saloon keeper turned Democratic boss, but when Buckley sided with Leland Stanford when Stanford broke with Huntington and ran for the Senate against Huntington's wishes (Huntington had another candidate in mind), Buckley rather precipitously found himself facing indictment, and fled the country. Later the SP dealt with Buckley's more cooperative successor, the dapper, persistently charming Abraham Ruef, a brilliant attorney of French-Jewish ancestry who ran San Francisco from 1902 onwards as boss of the Union Labor party.

The SP's man in Los Angeles, land agent and lobbyist Walter Parker, was the perfect political boss for Ragtime America: a portly, mustachioed man surveying life through a haze of cigar smoke, by turns ruthless or genial, depending upon whether or not he was getting his way. Parker ran the Republican party in Southern California, keeping a close eye on Los Angeles affairs. Controlling the wards, Parker put his men on the city council. In 1906 Parker blatantly bribed City Clerk Harry J. Lelande (who succumbed for a mere $1,000) to expedite an ordinance granting the railroad right of way on a dry riverbed running through the center of Los Angeles. Despite outraged protests when the bribe was discovered, a thoroughly domesticated city council passed the ordinance anyway.

This was not the first time that the railroad had brazened out adverse public opinion. In 1880 the SP raised prices on land it owned in Tulare County near the Kings River from the "$2.50 upward" it had promised to from $17 to $40 an acre. The settlers who had moved onto the land, building homes and barns and planting in expectation of the $2.50-an-acre price, were understandably enraged. They refused to pay the new price, and they refused to move. The SP

went to court and of course won its case. When the United States marshal came
to evict the settlers, a gunfight broke out at Mussel Slough near the town of
Hanford. Four settlers and one would-be purchaser at the new rates were killed.
Two other settlers later died from their wounds. Ultimately, the SP prevailed,
sending five ranchers to prison and evicting others from their homes. No rec-
ompense or even apology was made to the men and women whose lives had
been destroyed.

Three years later, in 1883, the public image of the SP took another downward turn. The widow of Collis P. Huntington's trusted associate David D.
Colton, in the course of suing the railroad over the disputed value of stocks she
had inherited from her husband's estate, made public hundreds of letters ex-
changed between Huntington and Colton between 1874 and 1878. The bulk
of these letters dealt with the delicate matter of bribing Washington congress-
men and Sacramento legislators to favor pro-railroad legislation. Colton was
supposed to have burned the correspondence.

The SP did not win any friends in Los Angeles either with its ten-year effort,
beginning in 1890, to impose on the City of the Angels an SP-owned port in
Santa Monica. Even the affluent oligarchy of Los Angeles, normally well disposed to the railroad, balked at Collis P. Huntington's plan, backed by his friends
in Washington, to organize the Port of Los Angeles as an SP monopoly. The
business community instantly realized what the future of Los Angeles as a shipping center would be with both the port and all rail access to the port exclusively in SP hands. At the height of the port controversy, Huntington had the
chutzpah to propose to Congress that the SP not be asked to pay back the $50
million due the federal government by 1899, when the thirty-year loan from
Congress with which the railroad was first financed came due. Huntington sought
instead a fifty-to-a-hundred-year delay in repayment, with the SP paying only
one-half of one percent interest on the principal. Otherwise, Huntington argued, the SP would be forced into bankruptcy. Few believed him. When Congress rejected Huntington's proposal in January 1897, Governor James H. Budd,
a Democrat, declared a public holiday.

Governor Budd, a University of California-trained engineer; Adolph Sutro,
the Prussian-born Populist party mayor of San Francisco (also an engineer by
profession); and *San Francisco Examiner* editor William Randolph Hearst openly
fought the SP through the last years of the nineteenth century. Their opposition prepared the way for the bold challenge in 1899 of the Ventura County
oilman and rancher Thomas Robert Bard. The fight against the SP had been
spearheaded in the 1890s by the short-lived Populist party. Bard, by contrast,
was no free-silver Populist, but a conservative, corporately oriented Republican, one of the creators of the Union Oil Company and its first president, angry at SP domination of his party and of his ranching, land development, and
oil interests. Over the years a conservatively oriented anti-SP faction of South-

ern Californian Republicans, most of them entrepreneurs fearful of the growing SP monopoly, had gathered around Bard, a somewhat aloof Pennsylvania-born patrician, surprisingly high-minded for having made such a success in the rough-and-tumble world of oil, land development, and ranching.

By 1899 this reform Republican faction had grown powerful enough in the legislature to deny election to the United States Senate to Colonel Daniel M. Burns of San Francisco, whom the SP was advancing as a candidate after the collapse of the candidacy of San Diego businessman Ulysses S. Grant, Jr., the son of the late president, who had desperately wished to return to Washington in triumph. A hearty hedonist with a checkered political past, mining interests in Mexico, and a taste for liquor, women, flashy clothes, and the race track, Colonel Burns was just the sort of United States senator the SP had in mind: a longtime political ally who, for a price, could be depended upon in Washington. Thomas Bard, however, believed that to send Burns to the Senate would constitute "a shame to our People and to Christian Civilization." Reluctantly at first, Bard yielded to the urging of the reform Republican leader, Dr. Chester Rowell of Fresno, and entered the Senate race. It took a year of wrangling and a special session of the legislature for the anti-railroad Republicans to get Bard elected. At one point in the contest Governor Henry Gage, a railroad man, met secretly with William F. Herrin of the SP Political Bureau in rooms rented under a fake name in the Palace Hotel in San Francisco to plot strategy. Bard's public reception in Sacramento following his election contrasted dramatically with what would undoubtedly have been a more robust affair for Colonel Burns. Only lemonade was served, a small string orchestra played, and no ladies of the demimonde were in evidence. Whether out of boredom or pique, pro-SP Governor Gage boycotted the affair.

Two years later the SP was further assaulted. Neither candidate to succeed Gage as governor—Republican George Pardee, mayor of Oakland, and Democrat Franklin Lane, city attorney of San Francisco—was out of the SP political stable. Had Lane won the election, an avowed SP enemy would have sat in the governor's chair, but the prospect of the independent-minded Lane as governor also frightened an ambitious Democrat by the name of William Randolph Hearst, by then based in New York, who did not want Lane, a brilliant journalist and lawyer, to threaten Hearst control of the Democratic party in California. At Hearst's behest the San Francisco Examiner failed to get behind Lane's candidacy. Defeated, Lane went on to Washington in 1906, appointed by President Theodore Roosevelt to the newly formed Interstate Commerce Commission. Lane probed the SP with a special vengeance, finding, among other things, that the SP favored 103 large California corporations and ranches and price-gouged the others.

The same year that Franklin Lane went to Washington, plans were underway at the SP to dump Governor Pardee, the Oakland oculist who had had the temerity to oppose the SP in certain right-of-way controversies. Fresh from its recent victory in denying Thomas Bard a second term in the United States Senate, the SP Republicans forgathered in Santa Cruz on 2 September 1906 for the state Republican convention, confident that they had the votes to deny Pardee renomination in favor of James N. Gillett, destined (as it turned out) to be the last of the SP governors of California. Friendly delegates rode to Santa Cruz from across the state on free railroad passes. Boss Parker brought the pro-SP Southern Californian delegation up in a specially chartered Pullman car, stocked liberally with food and drink. Parker also picked up the tab for the Southern California delegation's entire stay in Santa Cruz. Abe Ruef, the wily political boss of San Francisco, rode south to Santa Cruz with full confidence that he held the balance of power. For a consideration of $14,000 from William Herrin (one rumor claimed that the bribe was actually $20,000 in gold coin), Ruef had persuaded his protégé Eugene Schmitz, a onetime orchestra leader ("Handsome Gene") whom Ruef had installed in 1902 as mayor of San Francisco, to throw his support behind SP candidate Gillett. His reputation in good condition because of his admirable handling of the earthquake and fire that had leveled San Francisco that April, Mayor Schmitz was himself something of a dark horse candidate for the governorship. Ruef would have liked to have stolen the convention for Schmitz. Knowing this to be impossible, he had cut a deal—for cash. The support of Ruef and Schmitz insured Gillett's nomination.

On the evening of 6 September 1906, Mayor Frank Laughlin of Santa Cruz, former chairman of the Republican State Central Committee, invited the key players of the adjourned convention over to his house for dinner. For $40 Laughlin hired a photographer to take an after-dinner portrait of the assembled group. On 10 September 1906 the photograph—later captioned "The Shame of California"—mysteriously found its way into the editorial offices and thence into the pages of the San Francisco Call. It was a remarkable photograph, a tableau vivant of political bossism in the Ragtime era of back rooms and cigar smoke. Perusing it today—the walrus mustaches, the amply distended vests, the high starched collars, the smiles of men at their ease after wine and dinner, so pleased with themselves after having insured the election of the next governor of California—one can almost hear a background of Scott Joplin music. Prominent in the group are Walter Parker, the SP boss of Los Angeles, jowly and flesh-faced; and host Laughlin, delighted to have entertained such distinguished company. George Patton, chief SP lobbyist and father of the future general, has a look of well-bred amiability on his face appropriate to a Virginia-born gentleman. Justice Frederick W. Henshaw of the state supreme court stands to the left, and Congressman Joseph R. Knowland is on the right. In the center are Walter Herrin and the gubernatorial nominee, James Gillett. Nine of the gentlemen are standing in a semi-circle around two seated colleagues. The one seated in the center of the group, occupying the position of honor, is Abe Ruef.

Nominee Gillett has his hand on Ruef's shoulder, as if from a mixture of gratitude and a desire to assert at least a minimum of equality with the man who
had just—for a fee—given him the governorship. The photograph said everything: it had been Abe Ruef's convention from start to finish. Gillett went on
to beat the anti-SP Democrat Theodore A. Bell, who was hampered, as Franklin Lane had been in 1902, by Democratic disunity. One photograph in a San
Francisco newspaper was still a mere grain of sand in the well-oiled SP machine.

The last four years of the SP's control over California were the most flagrant.
Certainly the legislature of 1907 set new records for influence-peddling and
outright bribery. Abe Ruef, his coat pockets bristling with sheaves of legislation
he wanted passed, took to the floor of the senate and the assembly, although
he was not an elected member of either body, sitting here and there next to a
legislator for a moment of kibbitzing and quiet smiles.

Money power had built California (so money power believed), and whether
it be the SP or individual capitalists, money power was in no mood to abandon
the field to reform. The oligarchical Old Guard, moreover, was ably led: in
Los Angeles by such powers as Harrison Gray Otis of the *Times*, Jackson A.
Graves of the Farmers and Merchants National Bank, and Henry E. Huntington of the Pacific Electric Railroad, and in San Francisco by an interlocking
establishment of Christians and Jews reflecting the social ecumenicism that was
a special characteristic of that city's upper class.

Banker William Henry Crocker can be singled out (to borrow a description
accorded him by a contemporary) as the perfect type of the laissez-faire Bour-
bon of turn-of-the-century California, with a personal fortune based on wealth
made a generation earlier on the frontier and a determination not to surrender
an iota of prerogative. Both Crocker's lineage and fortune were, in California
terms, impressive. For all his ability to bellow up and down the line as Chinese
construction workers laid track, William Henry's father, Charles Crocker, was
of all the Big Four the one most self-consciously interested in establishing a
California dynasty that would be educated, diversified in fortune, well married,
and socially dominant. Crocker sent his son William Henry to Phillips Academy, Andover, and Yale. Returning to San Francisco in the early 1880s, William Henry—in adulthood a handsome, elegant man with a closely trimmed
beard and mustache—established himself as the young merchant prince of San
Francisco: a founder of the Crocker National Bank, later its president, a major
investor in securities and real estate, a developer of downtown buildings, a director of a half-dozen major enterprises (including Pacific Telegraph and Telephone, Metropolitan Life, Pacific Gas and Electric, and the Palace Hotel), and
the leading member of a score of civic committees. For more than fifty years
Crocker was the leading personage, public or private, of San Francisco. Among
other activities, he saw to the building of a magnificent Episcopal cathedral

atop Nob Hill, for which the Crocker family donated the land and contributed much of the money. Hospitals, opera, symphony, the University of California (he was a regent from 1908 to his death in 1937) all enjoyed his presence and financial support. In April 1906, when San Francisco lay in smoldering ruins, Crocker left for New York, where he personally spearheaded the multimillion-dollar refinancing of the destroyed city.

Such a man—in the second generation of a great fortune which he had ex-panded and diversified by his own enterprise, his dynastic ambitions gratified by his four children's marrying into major families (including a gratifying con-nection with the French aristocracy), a member of the major clubs of New York and San Francisco, an art collector and patron of scientific research—can nat-urally be expected, when it came to politics, to be on the right. In an age when political donations suffered neither ceiling nor scrutiny, Crocker and his kind dominated the Republican party which dominated California. They were not a ferocious, obscurantist right—far from it. By Atlantic Coast standards they were benevolent; but they wanted it played their way, all the time. They regarded California as a feudal fief which their parents' generation had seized through force of will and which they now held in fealty. Disinterested in politics as an art or a science, finding officeholding vulgar (with the exception of a United States senatorship), they were content to let lesser men, including a corrupt political boss or two, govern California, provided that California be governed to their advantage.

As is frequently the case with major second-generation wealth in America, the California establishment had a tendency to clannish snobbishness. Their breeding and gentility were in disconcerting contrast to their parents' more Ho-meric virtues, but they prized lineage and refinement, drawing themselves to-gether into a charmed circle. Titled foreigners, however, regardless of fortune, always had entrée; now and then a new American member, such as Patrick Calhoun, was allowed in, if his wealth and lineage were impressive enough. As the grandson of the great John C. Calhoun of South Carolina, Patrick Cal-houn's lineage was impressive enough, as was his record as a corporate attorney and financier with strong New York connections. Born to antebellum wealth (his father was reputed to be the largest cotton grower in the South), Patrick Calhoun rose on his own merits to become by the 1880s the most successful corporate attorney in the South. He was also a major investor in real estate, manufacturing, mining, cotton, lumber, and oil, and was instrumental in or-ganizing the Southern Railroad system in 1894 on behalf of J. P. Morgan and Company. Aside from deprovincializing Calhoun by providing an up-close look at the big money circles of New York, the experience of organizing the South-ern Railroad got Calhoun interested in municipal railway systems, which he proceeded to acquire and reorganize in Pittsburgh, Baltimore, and St. Louis. Acquiring street railway interests in San Francisco, Calhoun moved to that city in early 1906, serving as president of the amalgamated United Railroads of San Francisco.

Tall, florid, portly in the accepted style of the period, possessed of great wealth and superb social credentials, Patrick Calhoun found himself welcomed among the elite of San Francisco, who opened their homes and their clubs to this millionaire scion of the Old South. Calhoun was also introduced to Abraham Ruef, a gentleman definitely not in the *Social Register*. The elegant boss—his dark and delicate Semitic smallness, his subtlety and indirection in such contrast to Calhoun's florid assurance—sympathized totally with Calhoun's desire to get rights-of-way for overhead trolley wires throughout San Francisco, despite the fact that most San Franciscans favored an underground system. The Board of Supervisors of the City and County of San Francisco had final jurisdiction in the matter, Ruef instructed Calhoun. And the board could be persuaded. Over the next few years, Mr. Calhoun presented Mr. Ruef with a total of $200,000 in cash to help persuade the supervisors of San Francisco that overhead trolley wires were in the city's best interests.

II

Had a member of California's small but thriving Socialist community been privy to the dealings between Patrick Calhoun and Abraham Ruef, he or she would have been appalled, but not surprised. Turn-of-the-century California sustained an active Socialist minority whose disgust with the excesses and corruptions of the corporate hold on California politics fed directly into the Progressive reforms. "The moral and intellectual leverage," writes Richard Hofstadter in *The Age of Reform*, "exerted by the Socialist Party and Socialist ideas in the Progressive era has never been sufficiently recognized." Nowhere is this more true than in California, where a strong tradition of respectable middle-class Socialism, Fabian and Bellamyite, as opposed to the more proletarian and revolutionary varieties in vogue in Eastern industrial centers, helped make non-threatening, even respectable, such notions as the public ownership of utilities, prison and hospital reform, social welfare, public housing, workmen's compensation, and other social programs eventually enacted by the Progressives. *Looking Backward: 2000–1887*, Massachusetts newsman Edward Bellamy's novel of a future American cooperative utopia, first published in 1888, spurred the growth of the Nationalist movement throughout the United States. Composed mainly of middle-class intellectuals, Nationalist Clubs would meet in earnest sessions to discuss such Bellamyite ideas as state ownership of industry and utilities, social security, social welfare, women's suffrage, ballot reform, and free public education.

The California Nationalist Club organized itself in Los Angeles in May 1889. By 1890 sixty-two Bellamy Nationalist Clubs flourished in California, thirty-three of them in Los Angeles alone. Led by such colorful and articulate figures as Henry Gaylord Wilshire and William C. Owen, the India-born son of a brigadier of Bengal Lancers, the Nationalist movement, so the *Overland Monthly* reported in June 1890, "put a silk hat on socialism" by making socialist ideas acceptable to "people connected with literature and the professions." At club meetings and picnics, the thirty-five hundred members of the movement would meet for debates on such topics as public ownership of utilities (including railroads), women's suffrage, and ballot reform, or to listen attentively as such papers as "The Menace of Monopoly" or "The Meaning of Sociology" were read.

While Nationalism never became a potent political force in California, it did help to shape the California Populist party, which advanced the case against the SP through the 1890s. More importantly, it put into circulation as acceptable notions a number of bold social and political reforms, together with the entire question of public ownership. One important California Progressive, Charles Dwight Willard, directly traced his lifetime interest in reform to reading *Looking Backward*. In the case of other California Progressives, Nationalism, followed by Populism, created an ambience—in Southern California especially—in which a middle-class Protestant community which had come to California out of incipiently utopian motivations in the first place found it perfectly natural, once there, to dream of shaping a public polity that would more completely express its collective desire for a better life.

In 1890, in the course of one of their infrequent ventures into active electoral politics, Nationalist movement activists, meeting in state convention in Los Angeles, nominated Henry Gaylord Wilshire, president of the Fullerton and Anaheim Nationalist Clubs, to run for Congress in the sixth district. In his eccentricities and solid accomplishments, his paradoxical entrepreneurialism, his flirtation with quackery and his sound, even prophetic, notions of social reform—no Socialist Californian could have better exemplified the paradoxes of Socialism, Southern Californian style, than this young Fullerton rancher-entrepreneur. Born in 1861 into a wealthy Cincinnati family (his father, a banker, invested wisely in oil), Henry Gaylord Wilshire dropped out of Harvard after one year to return home and run a small mill. He failed miserably. Shamed before his father and his friends, Wilshire fled to California. There he pursued two seemingly contradictory ambitions—success and Socialism (to which he converted in 1887)—each intended to ease the pain of hometown failure. Making money in California, Wilshire might atone for his Cincinnati humiliation. Advancing Socialism, he might assert his lifelong contention that his mill had failed because he had come up against the corporate trusts. It had not really been his fault.

After a brief sojourn in San Francisco, where his father's connections, together with his own handsomeness and Harvardian manner, secured him social acceptance among the Crockers and the Tobins, Wilshire, joined by his brother, headed for Southern California, where the land boom was in full eruption, in 1886. The brothers Wilshire, helped along by some family money, speculated in Los Angeles, Santa Monica, Pasadena, Long Beach (they bought up the shorefront), and Orange County real estate, making money in each instance. Settling on a ranch near the city of Fullerton, which he helped to develop, Wilshire had transformed himself by 1890, the year the Nationalists nominated him for Congress, into a wealthy rancher-entrepreneur, growing walnuts and citrus on his property and pioneering the introduction of the grapefruit. Five years later the Wilshire brothers conceived the idea of developing a boulevard running from downtown Los Angeles to Santa Monica on the shore. Filing subdivision plans with the Los Angeles County Recorder's Office on 21 December 1895, the brothers embarked upon their dream. Ultimately, they would subdivide and develop the first four blocks west of Westlake Park of the boulevard that today bears their name.

H. Gaylord Wilshire (as he signed himself) was a promoter and a visionary in the style of Abbott Kinney of Venice and a number of other Southern California entrepreneurial eccentrics of this era: a visionary, and perhaps something of a quack, the Wizard of Oz behind the green curtain. Eventually, after his early success, Wilshire used up two inherited fortunes, his own and his wife's, while creating and dissipating a third, three million dollars in gold-mining stock which he had sold against enterprises in Kern County and British Guiana.

Wilshire's promotion of Socialism occurred on the same flamboyant level as his sale of stock or his pioneering of billboard advertising in Los Angeles in the early 1900s. In all instances, Wilshire dealt in superlatives. Like his personal hero George Bernard Shaw, whom he physically resembled, Wilshire made his mark as a scold and wag, but not as an elected official. After a vigorous, indeed brilliant speaking campaign, he received a mere eleven hundred votes in the congressional election of 1890, whereupon he shook the dust of California from his feet for five years, leaving for New York, where he ran for state attorney general (and was again defeated), and then moving on to London, where he toyed with the idea of changing his citizenship and running for Parliament. Returning to Los Angeles in the late 1890s, Wilshire made one more attempt at Congress in 1900, chalking up four thousand votes, the largest single vote thus far cast for a Socialist candidate in the United States—but still not enough to get him into Congress.

Meanwhile, beginning with his founding of the *Weekly Nationalist* in Los Angeles in 1889 and his discovery of his excellent debating and lecture-platform skills in the congressional election of 1890, Wilshire was trying out another role: that of Socialism's leading American journalist and platform provocateur, the Peck's Bad Boy of American Socialism. Befriending a still relatively obscure Anglo-Irish journalist and music critic by the name of George Bernard Shaw in London in the early 1890s, Wilshire found a lifetime role model. The brilliant Shaw, just on the verge of success but still having difficulties making ends meet, was not averse to having a wealthy American friend from California. Wilshire imitated Shaw's speaking and prose styles, his Mephistophelean beard (which enabled Wilshire to cover a scar on his cheek, the result of a horse-riding accident), and even Shaw's tweed suits, plus fours, Yorkshire jackets, and assertive cravats. Like Shaw, Wilshire was a showman and a snob, as well as a sincere ideologue. Called by a *Los Angeles Record* reporter "the very Beau Brummell of fashion" because of his habit of lecturing on Socialism in evening dress, Wilshire let it be known that he had dined and golfed with peers of England and knew London club life. He claimed that his social connections gave Socialism respectability. The very fact that Wilshire was of upper-class old American stock, he asserted, dispelled the notion that Socialism was the exclusive prerogative of scruffy, ill-educated foreigners. "Socialists," he asserted, "are the instructors of ignorant and immature humanity." One morning in November 1900, a specimen of ignorant humanity—a Los Angeles patrolman—arrested Wilshire for speaking in a public park. The judge dismissed the case, but Wilshire was so insulted that he moved back to New York.

Amusing as a platform debater, Wilshire was at his best as an editor and journalist. Leaving Los Angeles for New York, he took his magazine the *Challenge* with him. Founded the previous year in Los Angeles, the *Challenge* (a title he changed a few years later to *Wilshire's Magazine*) eventually soaked up over a million dollars of Wilshire's personal fortune. When *Wilshire's Magazine* was banned from the United States mails as subversive, Wilshire moved it to Toronto, where it was published with the rubric "Under the Protection of the British Crown" on its masthead, and from which city, by international agreement, it could be mailed into the United States. With such pioneering promotions as subscription prizes (in 1910 a young Socialist by the name of Thomas J. Mooney won a trip to the Socialist Congress in Copenhagen), Wilshire built the circulation of *Wilshire's Magazine* to an impressive 425,000 copies per issue. During the Progressive Era, *Wilshire's Magazine* was the most influential Socialist journal in the United States, and its subsidiary publishing house, the Wilshire Book Company (which also sponsored a Socialist Book Club), introduced a wide variety of Socialist authors, European and American, to American audiences.

Wilshire personally wrote a good part of every issue of *Wilshire's Magazine*: peppery, sometimes dyspeptic, but always lucid essays, later issued in book form, in which Wilshire scolded capitalism and the trusts roundly and argued for the Socialist alternative. During his London years, Wilshire had come under the influence of the Fabian Socialist Society, brilliantly led by George Bernard Shaw and Sidney Webb. It was Fabian Socialism, nonviolent, nonrevolutionary, non-Marxist, that Wilshire preached. From the vantage point of today, a half century after the New Deal, it is difficult to understand why *Wilshire's Magazine* was ever considered dangerous enough to be banished from the mails. Rejecting a Marxist theory of revolution and class struggle, the Fabians believed that modern industrial societies, unless repressed, would naturally evolve into more cooperative, socialized economic structures. As a writer and platform performer, Wilshire argued for the nationalization of railroads and utilities, the municipal ownership of water, gas, electricity, telephones and streetcar service, women's suffrage, public reclamation projects to put the unemployed to work, an eight-hour day, an end to child labor, free public schools (to include hot lunches and textbooks), unemployment insurance, a social security system, a national public highway trust—and other, similar ideas, few of them (with the exception of the nationalization of heavy industry) outside the mainstream of liberal American social thought through Progressivism and the New Deal.

Wilshire's broadly conceived, humanistic Socialism—nonviolent, nonrevolutionary, interdenominationally assimilative, nurtured on Fabianism and edging into Social Democracy—was typical of much of the upper-middle-class Socialism of Southern California; this sensibility, in turn, nurtured a species of pre-Progressivism at the turn of the century. For more than twenty years, a broad Socialist and non-Socialist left front, humus-like, flourished in Los Angeles: Nationalism giving way to Populism in 1892, Populism allying itself with Socialist-Labor in the election of 1892 on such issues as direct legislation and charter reform, Populism taking some of this Socialist-inspired fervor back to the Democratic party in 1896, the Social Democracy of America arriving in 1897 and allying itself with this already flourishing left. The Union Reform League, in turn, founded in 1898 by the Reverend William Dwight Porter Bliss, attracted many adherents from Socialist-Labor and Populism, thus forging a link between the left and the liberal elements in the Protestant church, a potent force in all of Southern California.

In October 1899 the Christian Socialist Economic League of Los Angeles, a monthly dinner club, formed itself under the leadership of the widely respected Dr. John Randolph Haynes, thus bringing Christian Socialism into the very core of the Los Angeles establishment. (H. Gaylord Wilshire was also a founding member.) Scion of old Philadelphia, Haynes, then in his mid-forties, had received both an M.D. and a Ph.D. degree in medical sciences from the University of Pennsylvania, practicing for thirteen years in Philadelphia before removing to Los Angeles in 1887 for his health. Converting to Socialism (he was a corresponding member of the English Fabian Society), this aristocratic, outgoing physician, a lover of wine and food and Oriental rugs, did not let his Socialist beliefs stand in the way of accumulating a fortune in real estate, banking, and insurance, or of carrying on a prosperous surgical practice. The initial appearance of the Christian Socialist Economic League of Los Angeles at a dinner round table was totally appropriate, for Dr. Haynes loved to advance his ideas in the setting of his sumptuous home, rich and warm with family antiques and paintings, after a first-rate meal prepared by the family chef, accompanied by judicious selections from Dr. Haynes's excellent wine cellar.

The Christian Socialist Club led to the formation of a Voters' League, which was not Socialist and certainly more action-oriented than the dinner club, but which nevertheless bore the stamp of Dr. Haynes's program. Haynes believed fervidly in more democracy ("The remedy for the evils of democracy is more democracy," he claimed), specifically the initiative, the referendum, and the recall, which he fought for as president of the Direct Legislation League of California. If voters could in an industrial democracy put their own legislation on the ballot, Dr. Haynes believed, or vote yea or nay on controversial measures, or recall corrupt officials, the resulting democratic atmosphere would yield naturally to Socialism. In 1907 many of Haynes's ideas were taken up by the reforming Republicans of the Lincoln-Roosevelt League, but he never formally joined the ranks of the young reformers. Aside from being a full two generations their senior, Dr. Haynes preferred to remain further out on the left than his Republican colleagues in reform.

In Pasadena, Fabian ideas tinkled among the teacups in the book-lined parlors of such affluent Pasadenans as Mrs. Thaddeus Lowe and Peter and Beatrice Goddard Gates. Passing through Pasadena, the Argentine writer Blasco Ibañez confessed himself astonished that so much Socialism should flourish in such gracious surroundings. The most fervid of the Pasadena Socialists was Kate Crane Gartz, a Chicago-born heiress. The daughter of an important iron and steel millionaire, Richard T. Crane, Kate Crane Gartz grew up in a world of paradox. Her father was a man of iron among iron men, yet possessed also of a philanthropic streak. He helped finance Jane Addams's Hull House, for instance, served on the Chicago Board of Education, and donated parks, playgrounds, and nurseries to the children of the Windy City. There was a strong streak of Presbyterian piety in the Crane household. Kate's brother Charles went into church-related education, eventually rising to the presidency of the Presbyterian-sponsored Roberts College in Constantinople. A prominent Progressive on the national scene, Charles was later sent by his good friend Woodrow Wilson, another Presbyterian, to China as American minister. As pious and philanthropic as the elder Crane might be, however, this iron-willed man was a capitalist of his age and class. At his factories he employed female workers of a very young age—although he did allow his daughter Kate to play with them; the youngsters made castles with the wet sand used to create channels for melted iron to run through. "Then the time came," Kate Crane Gartz later remembered, "when I was ashamed to face those girls who were making the wealth that kept me in luxury and ease."

As a young Chicago society matron, the mother of three small children, ensconced at the center of a select social circle revolving around Mrs. Potter Palmer, Mrs. Gartz had a second epiphany, this time with more lasting effect.

Leaving a downtown gathering late one evening on the arm of her husband, she saw a group of scrubwomen down on their knees. "I wondered if they had children at home," she wrote of this experience, "and thought how terrible it would be if I had to leave my babies and go out at night and scrub floors for men to walk on." Possessed through this incident of what she later described as a Tolstoyan insight into human suffering, Mrs. Gartz threw herself into volunteer work at Jane Addams's Hull House and began a serious reading of Tolstoy and Socialist literature. This is not to say that she ever left her class. When she and her husband moved to Pasadena for Mr. Gartz's health, they were welcomed with a lavish party at the Valley Hunt Club, which they soon joined. The couple moved into a vine-and-rose-covered mansion, the Cloister, at the corner of Mariposa Street and Santa Rosa Avenue in Altadena, where they entertained such visiting luminaries of the left as Floyd Dell and Max Eastman. Mrs. Gartz did what she could, meanwhile, to help the locals. She sent a young working girl with tuberculosis off to an Arizona sanitarium, rose early in the morning to meet bail for an arrested Wobbly, paid for the defense of a local Mexican-American whom she considered unjustly arrested, wrote a check for the burial expenses of a workman whose widow she supported. "I became a Socialist," she later said of her philosophy, "because I brooded over the tragic contrast of the sorrows of the poor and the luxuries of the rich. Those who had created everything had nothing while those who had everything created nothing—and as long as there is that widespread breach between rich and poor, we are not civilized." Eventually, after being herself widowed, she would be giving away an estimated 75 percent of her income (but not the principal!) to charities and Socialist causes.

Two Northern California Socialists, Edwin Markham and Jack London, lived daily with this paradox of Socialist affluence, of serving two masters. Markham learned to live with it. The paradox helped to destroy Jack London. Markham, headmaster of a special Oakland laboratory school associated with the University of California, burst into national prominence in 1899 with the publication on 15 January in the *San Francisco Examiner* of "The Man with the Hoe," a poem of social protest which one admirer described as "the battle cry of the next thousand years." Born in Oregon in 1852 into extremely troubled circumstances (his father did not believe that the baby was his), Markham was raised by his divorced mother on various marginal Oregon and Northern California ranches amidst poverty and that special sort of emotional cruelty that only a half-crazed mother—repudiated, fanatically religious, guilt-ridden—can inflict upon a son who by his very existence reminds her daily of her sin. Not surprisingly, the emotionally starved young Charles Edward Anson Markham (as he was known before he changed his name to Edwin as an adult, in an effort to escape the past) turned to books, although his mother forbade them, saying that reading kept him from his farm work. Young Markham became a voracious reader, educating himself well beyond his spotty schooling. Eventually obtaining a bachelor's degree from the small Christian College of Santa Rosa in Sonoma County, Markham embarked upon a twenty-year career as a country schoolmaster, teaching mainly in the sparsely settled El Dorado County in the Sierra foothills. A four-thousand-volume library provided him with companionship.

From this voracious reading and from his natural sympathy with the downtrodden and emotionally deprived (so reflective of his own condition), together with the Swedenborgian religious sympathies he had absorbed while attending college in Santa Rosa from Thomas Lake Harris, founder of the nearby Fountain Grove utopian cooperative, Markham evolved a vague species of Christian Socialism, literary and high-minded, nurtured on John Ruskin *(Fors Clavigera, The Crown of Wild Olive)*, Thomas Carlyle *(Past and Present)*, and the mysticism of Emanuel Swedenborg and Tolstoy: a yearning, somewhat vague belief that the cruelly exploitative industrial order could only be redeemed by a return to religious and communal values. Markham believed that somehow earnestness, personal culture, and good intentions might transform an unjust society. By 1886 he was writing poems of social protest on behalf of the exploited that were good enough to be accepted by William Morris in London for *Commonweal*.

That same year, Markham happened to see a reproduction in the March issue of *Scribner's Magazine* of Jean François Millet's painting of a French peasant gazing up stupidly from his labor. At the time Markham was also reading Charles Fourier, the early-nineteenth-century utopian socialist. Fourier's call for a redeemed agricultural economy and Millet's depiction of a brutalized peasant coalesced in Markham's mind, and he set some dozen lines of poetry in a notebook, verse dealing with the social injustices that had extinguished the spark of humanity in the peasant's eyes. Thirteen years later, Markham, now derusticated to the prosperity of a respectable university-associated headmastership, his loneliness assuaged by acceptance into Bay Area literary, social, and intellectual circles, happened upon the original of Millet's painting at a hardly Socialist Christmastime soiree at the San Francisco home of Mrs. William Crocker. Markham sat transfixed before the painting for two hours. Returning home, he retrieved the notebook put aside thirteen years earlier and resumed writing his poem.

When "The Man with the Hoe" appeared the next month in the *Examiner*, lavishly illustrated and set in special type, it caused a sensation. Markham's Oakland friend, the flamboyant poet Joaquin Miller, greeted it as "the whole Yosemite—the thunder, the might, the majesty." Markham's ultra-conservative friend Ambrose Bierce never spoke to him again. Collis P. Huntington of the Southern Pacific offered a $5,000 honorarium to any poet who might refute Markham's poem in equally effective verse. "The Man with the Hoe" eventually appeared in an estimated fifty thousand newspapers around the world and was translated into forty languages. With its depiction of a brutalized humanity, dehumanized by economic oppression, "The Man with the Hoe" sprang instantly before the world's attention as the Socialist poem of the century.

Markham's poem tapped something deep in the American psyche—some fear of loss, of being left out of the inner circle and the better life: the better schools, the accepting circle of fine friends, the secure place in the community. Is it too much to speculate that, beholding the figure of Millet's bent, brutalized peasant, Markham experienced a fearful image of his own inner dread of remaining unloved, of being a nobody? His legal father, after all, had repudiated him, and his crazed mother, divorced and cast on her own, could never forgive the boy for his illegitimacy. No punishment was too great: no school, no books, whippings, long days alone with the sheep in the hills of Suisun.

And yet this abused boy remained under this woman's spell well into adulthood—divorced his first wife, in fact, because he could not leave his mother's apron strings, then proceeded to marry and divorce once again when his second wife could not abide living with his mother in San Jose. "Oh, Elizabeth, Elizabeth," he once wrote one of the many women he turned to for comfort (although he never mailed this particular letter), "be a sweet mother to me—I never had a mother—I have always somehow felt as though she has died in tender infancy—My life has been so desolate." Desolate indeed the long lonely years of rural schoolmastering, the fear of never being discovered, never counting at all; and painful to note—and more than a little ugly as well—the reputation he gained in those years for using the schoolmaster's rod rather frequently, punishing the country children as his mother had once punished him. In Oakland, the Society for the Prevention of Cruelty to Children publicly cited Markham for one particularly offensive flogging: this benevolent Socialist reformer, so soon to be busy about a series of reform articles regarding child labor, the coauthor of *Children in Bondage*, a book that helped provide so much protective legislation. Snug with his third wife and many books in a Staten Island cottage (Markham left California in 1901); doing his best to strike a stance of Whitmanesque benevolence, the onetime country schoolmaster might very well play the Good Gray Poet for the rest of his life; but Millet's peasant, brutalized into insensitivity, looking bovinely out on the world with just the beginnings of avenging anger in his eyes, was a more accurate expression of Markham's inner life.

Eight years after the publication of "The Man with the Hoe," in 1907, another former Oakland Socialist by the name of Jack London published a Socialist novel, *The Iron Heel*, whose anger, revolutionary and programmatic, contrasted sharply with Markham's Christian Socialist optimism that all might one day be well. *The Iron Heel* is a bitter, hard-edged book, in bold contrast to Markham's yearning sympathies and blurred idealism. In the novel London predicted that a series of revolutions, countered by oligarchical repressions, would rack the United States in the twentieth century. As was also the case with Markham, however, Jack London could not make up his mind what side he would be on, if and when the proletariat at long last took to the streets. Like Markham, London was conceived and born under contested circumstances to an eccentric mother, capable of great harshness. A young man whose early social, cultural, and emotional deprivation paralleled Markham's point by point, although in urban circumstances, London found in Socialism a philosophy of life and a way out of poverty through self-education. London's tutors in Socialism—the enormously learned autodidact Frank Strawn-Hamilton, a workingman intellectual, and Austin Lewis, a teacher and law student—were the formative preceptors of his youth, tutors whom he would later depict in the autobiographical novel *Martin Eden* (1909). Through these radical polymaths, young London discovered the evolutionary theories of Herbert Spencer and absorbed fragments of the philosophy of Friedrich Wilhelm Nietzsche, whose work had not yet begun to appear in English. To suit his psychological and emotional needs, London fashioned a Socialism incorporating strong individualist and evolutionary strains.

Anna Strunsky—a young, dark-eyed, and very lovely Russian Jew then studying at Stanford University, whom London met on 1 December 1899 at a Socialist Labor party meeting in San Francisco—tried in vain in the course of their relationship to coax London to more orthodox Socialist thinking. London was fascinated by Anna's eyes, her bookishness, her knowledge of the European Socialist tradition. He even coauthored a book with her, *The Kempton-Wace Letters* (1903), an epistolary novel dealing, significantly enough, with what is today called sexual politics. Although Anna Strunsky (later to serve the international Socialist movement in Europe as an elected official) could refine London's thinking and challenge him as no other woman would ever do, she could not correct what she considered an arrogant individualism in London, a contempt for weaker peoples and an exultation in his own strength and will-to-prevail running contrary to Socialist orthodoxy.

Not that London did not know the poor. He did—from his own experience primarily, as he grew up in a series of shabby Bay Area farms and seedy Oakland houses. In 1902 he spent some time among the abjectly poor of London's East End, deliberately down and out, moving from flophouse to flophouse. His account of the experience, *The People of the Abyss* (1903), is a graphic depiction of urban poverty that boldly underscores the underclass being created by British industrialism: a class of stunted men and women and hollow-eyed children living within a few minutes' walk of great urban monuments to Empire. London also knew work. He himself had sailed before the mast, worked in a jute mill, shoveled coal into an unappeasable furnace until every muscle stiffened with pain. As an artist, he could write brilliantly from the proletarian point of view, a fact that made him enormously popular (and thoroughly approved of) in Soviet Russia, even to this day. On the one hand, London could say, as he did before a Los Angeles audience in 1905, that "it is the proletarian side of my life that I revere the most, and to which I will cling as long as I live." At the same time, however, London both feared and despised poverty and brute labor, wanted nothing to do with them, and justified his contempt with a Darwinian Nietzscheanism whose logical end was the exultation of the prevailing individual and of the "strong races" over the weak. Thus flawed in his orthodoxy, London took to the lecture circuit as a Socialist spokesman after two attempts at elective office, running for mayor of Oakland in 1901 (245 votes) and 1905 (981 votes). He became, in fact, the best-known Socialist in prewar America. Accompanied by his attentive Korean valet, London preached revolution across America in 1905, speaking to two thousand at Harvard, three thousand at Yale, bearding the plutocrats in their clubs in New York before entraining for the University of Chicago. London's Yale speech (later published as the essay "Revolution") was sensationally typical: London wearing a freshly valet-pressed red flannel shirt, galvanized his audience, then was carried off on the shoulders of cheering undergraduates.

In one very powerful scene, Ernest Everhard, revolutionary hero of *The Iron Heel*, confronts some of these Yalies, now having recovered their capitalist sobriety after forgetting all this Socialist nonsense and entering the family firm upon graduation. Considered one of the best Socialist novels, *The Iron Heel* chronicles from the vantage point of the future the four revolutions necessary to overthrow the stranglehold gained by the Oligarchy on the United States (later the world) in the early twentieth century. In his iron will to power, however, his domineering intellect and individualism, Ernest Everhard has a strange affinity with the very same Establishment which executes him in 1932, after the failure of the Second Revolt. That revolt, moreover, involves confrontations between the Oligarchy and the proletariat in which the people, machine-gunned down on the streets of Chicago, seem to be deserving what they get. Understandably, some of London's fellow Socialists were disturbed. They believed that the bleakness and violence of *The Iron Heel* would hurt Socialism at the polls.

After Jack London began seriously to develop his magnificent hilltop ranch in southern Sonoma County, his interest in Socialism waned. He replaced the imaginative ideal of Socialist America with the concrete goal of the agrarian utopia he was trying to create at Glen Ellen. Typically, he persuaded himself that it was the Socialists themselves, especially the Jews, who were out of step, and not he. "The Socialists," he told the *Western Comrade* in 1915, "the ghetto Socialists of the East, no longer believe in the strong, firm socialism of the early days. Mention confiscation in the ghetto of New York and the leaders will throw up their hands in holy terror." When the revolution came, London said, he would stay right on his ranch at Glen Ellen and let the revolution go to blazes. "I've done my part." In a letter dated 7 March 1916, written in Honolulu and sent to the Socialist local at Glen Ellen, London resigned from the party.

Out of all this Socialist ferment, little of an externally explicit Socialist nature was accomplished in California: a cooperative of Russian Jewish chicken farmers in Petaluma, the colony at Llano del Rio. On a subliminal psychological level, however, the flourishing of Socialist ideas and personalities in turn-of-the-century California helped to establish a disposition toward public ownership of utilities, increased regulation of industry, and the expansion of social programs and public services. As Hofstadter suggests, no definite cause-and-effect relationship between Socialism and Progressivism has yet been established. The flourishing of both Socialism and Progressivism among the California upper middle classes, however, does suggest a discernible circuitry of motivation and influence. Ideas and possibilities could flow from the far left to the reforming conservatives (which, as we shall see, was what California Progressivism was all about) because the barrier of class and class antagonism, which the California Progressives loathed and feared, was not present. Socialist left and reforming right belonged in a number of subtle but influential ways to the same California club.

III

Into this club, this expanding California, women sought further admittance and an expansion of opportunity. Their struggle—whether it be the right to practice medicine or to go before the bar, to vote and run for office or to work as staff reporters for William Randolph Hearst at the San Francisco Examiner, to dance (as in the case of Isadora Duncan) in a new expressive medium or (as in the case of the Dress Reform League at the newly established Stanford University) to walk free of imprisoning corsets—added to the cumulative reform sentiment gathering strength in California. As a frontier society, California had been short of white females. While the notion that women were revered in frontier California is a myth, they were paid special attention to, if only because of their scarcity. Young girls born into this woman-scarce California environment (the middle classes at least) were simultaneously pampered as scarce creatures and allowed a range of freedom and challenge unknown to women in more demographically balanced communities. On the level of social myth (the Girl of the Golden West) and quite frequently on the level of familial fact, a generation of California women, born on the frontier or brought to California as children, maturing in the late 1880s and early 1890s, reached adulthood at the turn of the century possessed of much innovative, frequently reforming energy. As the novels of William Dean Howells and Henry James bear out, this release of energy on the part of younger American women was no exclusively Californian phenomenon. It did, however, have its specifically Californian context and its Californian heroines, real or (as in the case of the novels of Gertrude Atherton) imagined.

Caroline Maria Seymour Severance of Los Angeles, for instance, was asked in 1911 at age ninety-one to be the first woman to register to vote after suffrage was enacted in California, because ever since her arrival in Los Angeles in 1875 this tireless feminist—whose reform lineage went back to her abolitionist involvement in Boston in the 1850s, whose friends and colleagues in the movement had been Elizabeth Cady Stanton, Susan B. Anthony, Lucy Stone, and Julia Ward Howe—epitomized to the reform women of California a continuity between their efforts and the reform traditions of the East. In Mrs. Severance the reforming women of California found a splendid survivor of the world of Stanton, Anthony, Stone, Howe, and such sympathetic male reformers as Ralph Waldo Emerson, Wendell Phillips, Theodore Parker, William Lloyd Garrison, Bronson Alcott, and John Greenleaf Whittier, with all of whom this Los Angeles Christian Socialist had been associated at one time or another in her long reform career.

Nor was San Francisco devoid of a comparable figure. Born in upstate New York, as was Severance, and like her also a product of the excellent female seminaries of that region (the famed Emma Willard was her girlhood teacher), Sarah Brown Ingersoll Cooper of San Francisco resembled her cousin, the agnostic controversialist Robert Ingersoll, in both force of intellect and power as a public speaker. Unlike her cousin, however, Sarah Cooper was devoutly Christian, although in 1881, unable to accept the doctrine of infant damnation, she left Presbyterianism for a doctrinally less exacting Congregationalism. Trained as a teacher, Sarah Cooper arrived in San Francisco in 1869, her health broken by overwork and the death of three of her four children. She and her husband, a minor federal official whom she had met while she was serving as a governess on a Georgia plantation, had spent the Civil War in Tennessee, he attending to his duties as an assessor of internal revenue, she teaching Bible classes, organizing relief for refugees from the battle zones, nursing her children as, one by one, they slipped from her grasp.

San Francisco revived her energies and her involvements. Of a literary persuasion, Sarah Cooper joined the *Overland Monthly* staff initially as a proofreader, and was later promoted to essayist and book reviewer. She wrote for the religious press as well and did field research and reports on education in California for the United States commissioner of education in Washington, D.C. Sarah Cooper taught a lively Bible class, first under Presbyterian auspices, then—after her heresy trial for rejecting infant damnation (how could she believe this, she who had lost three of her own children?)—moving her class to the First Congregational Church of San Francisco. As an 1871 *Overland* essay of hers shows ("Ideal Womanhood"), Sarah Cooper espoused a feminism energized by

Christian transcendentalist fervor. The specific question of suffrage was not, in her mind, a major issue; the question was, rather, could American women transform society through the sheer release of moral energies in a score of worthy causes? This attitude did not imply an avoidance of the women's movement. Through the 1890s Cooper organized a number of women's congresses in San Francisco. At Cooper's behest, Susan B. Anthony herself came out to San Francisco in 1895 to address a very successful Women's Congress which Cooper had organized. She also organized a Pacific Coast Women's Press Association, was active in The Century, San Francisco's first women's club, was elected treasurer of the World's Federation of Women's Clubs, and in 1893 served as one of the delegates to the feminist Pan-Republican Congress meeting at the Columbian Exposition in Chicago. In all these efforts, however, Cooper spoke—eloquently, as it turned out, her dignified demeanor and delicate beauty bringing a hush to the crowd—of the responsibilities for women to act primarily as agents of a moral uplift which would in turn animate social reform.

Unlike Severance, preaching a similar message in the Southland while supported in great comfort by her Boston banker husband (turned Southern California orange grower for his health), Sarah Cooper lived close to the margin in a few rented rooms. Her husband, despondent over his flagging career, took his own life. Having lost three children and a husband, Cooper turned to the care of Harriet, her increasingly melancholic sole surviving child, who served as her secretary-companion. Friends advised Cooper to have the young woman institutionalized after she had made a few botched suicide attempts, but Cooper refused. She went so far as to sleep in her daughter's room so as to keep an eye on her, before rising at four in the morning to handle her vast correspondence, which included exchanges with Clara Barton of the Red Cross, Elizabeth Peabody, Julia Ward Howe, and Susan B. Anthony—all this before the day's actual work began. On the morning of 11 December 1896, however, neither mother nor daughter awoke. Sometime in the night, as her mother slept, Harriet Cooper had crept from her bed and opened a gas jet, asphyxiating the last two members of the ill-fated Cooper family.

Caroline Severance and Sarah Cooper threw major energies into the kindergarten movement, which for them embodied everything that American women should be up and doing in an effort to prepare for a better California. The kindergarten movement embodied an amalgam of philosophical idealism, feminine nurture, and social reform that spoke directly to women reformers. Indeed, the links between early feminist reform and the kindergarten movement—beginning in Germany, then coming over to the United States—were pronounced and continuous. The German philosopher and educator Friedrich Froebel, himself the victim of a neglected childhood, founded the first kindergarten in Bad Blankenburg, Germany, in 1837. As a philosopher, Froebel taught the essential unity of all knowledge and the primacy of natural experience as a means to intellectual and spiritual fulfillment. As an educator and an educational theorist (his *Menschenerziehung* appeared in 1826 and was translated into English as *The Education of Man* in 1877) and, more importantly, as an educator of educators, Froebel taught that early childhood presented the crucial phase of the lifelong learning process; hence the kindergarten was as important as the graduate faculty or professional school for the ultimate health of a society. Among Froebel's disciples was an ardent German feminist named Emma Marwedel, who in 1865 helped form an association for the advancement of women, Germany's first. Converted to Froebel's theories, Marwedel devoted the rest of her life to two causes: the education of women in industrial arts and the kindergarten movement.

When the American feminist Elizabeth Palmer Peabody met Marwedel in Hamburg in 1867 she was heading a girls' industrial school. In 1870 Peabody brought Marwedel to New York to found kindergartens and schools that would prepare young women to become skilled industrial workers. These efforts met with mixed success. In 1876 Caroline Severance brought Marwedel to Los Angeles, where she founded the California Model Kindergarten and the attached Pacific Model Training School for Kindergartners, with Mrs. Severance paying the bills.

One of Emma Marwedel's teacher-trainees was Kate Douglas Smith, a Maine-raised Santa Barbaran of twenty whose stepfather had brought his family to Southern California in 1873 for his health, only to die three years later, leaving them in genteel poverty. Caroline Severance had sponsored the very bright and attractive young Kate Smith at Emma Marwedel's school, providing her room and board in the Severance household. Of a literary bent, Miss Smith paid some of her expenses by selling one of her stories for children to *St. Nicholas* magazine. In 1878 Emma Marwedel secured for Miss Smith a teaching position in what she considered an important social experiment being inaugurated in San Francisco—a free public kindergarten, intended for the working classes of that city, the first free kindergarten to be established in the United States. Visiting San Francisco in the summer of 1878, Felix Adler, an ardent American disciple of Froebel and the leader of the Ethical Culture educational movement in New York, had fanned enthusiasm for the kindergarten idea among local educators and social activists. Under the leadership of San Francisco educator John Swett, principal of Girls' High School and a pioneer in women's education in the West, a Public Kindergarten Society was organized upon Adler's departure, and two floors were rented in a building at 64 Silver Street in the working-class South of Market section of the city. The Silver Street Kindergarten, with Miss Kate Douglas Smith, formerly of Santa Barbara and Los Angeles, in attendance, opened its doors.

Certain favored late-nineteenth-century American women, possessed of beauty, radiance, willfulness, idealism, and persistent intelligence, corroborate the fictional heroines of Howells and James, with all their confident courage and ardent American aspiration. Kate Douglas Smith (known more universally by her married name, Kate Douglas Wiggin) was such a real-life counterpart of those heroines. For one thing, as Gertrude Atherton, another young aspiring San Francisco writer, would later remember her, young Miss Smith was a smashing social success, the bright center of the city's younger crowd along with Sibyl Sanderson (later a diva of the Paris Opera), given to parties, dances, and those amateur theatricals which kept alive her earlier ambition to go on the stage until, as she put it, God put her on a quieter, sometimes wearier path. In the course of her Silver Street career, both Dion Boucicault and Sir Henry Irving, whom she met at parties when their companies were playing San Francisco, offered the elegant young woman acting roles in their troupes. Lovely but not conceited, a blue stocking incapable of a pretentious judgment or a cutting remark, and just respectable enough in family background for socially anxious San Francisco, Kate Smith enjoyed a few years on the town (within the proprieties of the Victorian era) before her marriage on 28 December 1881 to Samuel Bradley Wiggin, a Boston lawyer and childhood friend who had followed her to San Francisco.

As a type, Kate Douglas Smith Wiggin prefigured the Junior League social activist of a later era, although it must also be observed that many major nineteenth-century American women reformers were of upper-class background. Miss Smith's social life, however, remained ever subordinate to her work. Joined by her sister Nora, with whom she later collaborated on the three-volume *The Republic of Childhood* (1895–1896), Kate Smith taught class after class of deprived children from the South of Market area, trying to awaken in them a capacity for curiosity which in so many cases poverty, disease, malnutrition, and a family life clouded by drunkenness and emotional and physical violence had stifled. She also trained over two hundred other young women in Froebelian theory and kindergarten arts, setting up a California Kindergarten Normal School for that purpose. As could be expected from an aspiring writer, her annual reports, filled with anecdote and novelistic detail, made delightful reading and were soon being distributed throughout the East Coast and Europe. ("Is a grasshopper a worm?" she reports one child as asking. "No, it's an insect; insects have wings," she corrected. "Oh, angels is insects, isn't they?" came the child's answer.)

In *The Story of Patsy* (1882) Kate Douglas Wiggin turned one very tragic San Francisco experience of hers into literature, telling in this children's classic the story of a small crippled boy from one of her classes who, after a grave illness, died in her arms as she sang to him the school hymn from Silver Street. Returned to the East and prematurely widowed in 1888, Wiggin turned to full-time writing for children as her primary means of support. *Rebecca of Sunnybrook Farm* (1904), a story based upon her Maine girlhood, would eventually sell three million copies, becoming one of the most popular children's stories of all times.

In the spring of 1879, in the first year of the Silver Street operation, Sarah Cooper visited the kindergarten at the invitation of John Swett. Within ten minutes of watching Miss Smith at work with her charges, Cooper found herself weeping. "Why did I not know of this work before?" she asked the younger woman. "Why did nobody tell me? It is the most beautiful thing I ever saw. Let me help you immediately." With the fervor born of her baffled longing for redemptive social work, Sarah Cooper—*Overland* essayist, feminist, Bible teacher, increasingly burdened with the care of a despondent husband and a troubled daughter—threw herself into assisting the kindergarten movement in the San Francisco Bay area and elsewhere in California and the nation. Cooper became, in fact, the movement's major theorist, organizer, and fundraiser on the Pacific Coast. As in the case of Elizabeth Peabody of Boston, who saw in each child "the possibility of the perfect man," Froebel's theories and their practical application in kindergarten training spoke directly to Sarah Cooper's Christian transcendentalism in search of social usefulness: her belief, that is, that great moral energies lay beneath the surface of American life, capable of transforming individuals and society. Kindergarten theory, after all, was based upon a confluence of two favorite American notions: the perfectibility of man and the establishment of a social environment conducive to individual perfection. Sarah Cooper believed that properly conducted kindergartens could create utopian environments in which children might tap into their inner creativity and spontaneity at a critical age. She was especially interested in the preventive aspects of the kindergarten experience among the poor. American cities, she wrote, were filling up with neglected children possessed of fatally bad habits—and hard, staring faces—by the age of six. The realities of urban-industrial life among the lower class were stifling the children of the poor into premature demoralization or, worse, channeling them into debauchery and crime. A free public kindergarten system removed young children from these corrupting influences, giving them the chance to consolidate a more creative personality from which a coping adult identity might develop.

Through the Golden Gate Kindergarten Association, incorporated in San Francisco in 1884, Sarah Cooper raised money to start schools in San Francisco and elsewhere. By 1895, 3,588 San Francisco children were enrolled in forty free kindergartens operated by the Golden Gate Association and underwritten by such California heiresses as Mary Crocker, Miranda Lux, Phoebe Apperson Hearst, and Jane Lathrop Stanford, the wife of Leland Stanford, Sarah Cooper's girlhood schoolmate from upstate New York. Then in the process of establishing a university as a memorial to their recently deceased fifteen-year-old son, the Stanfords gave the association grants totaling $40,000 by 1886, and in 1891 endowed a $100,000 trust fund. Some sixty-five thousand issues of the

Annual Report of the association were mailed out in 1892 alone, the year Mrs. Cooper was elected world president of the International Kindergarten Union. By 1894 it was estimated that 235 free public kindergartens had been established in the United States and abroad on the Golden Gate model.

IV

The kindergarten movement helped to focus the attention of Phoebe Apperson Hearst, widow of the outrageously rich silver and land baron and United States senator George Hearst, and mother of William Randolph Hearst, crusading publisher of the *San Francisco Examiner*, upon the question of education in general and the state-supported University of California in particular. Spurred by the example of what Mrs. Jane Stanford was accomplishing with her fledgling university down the peninsula in Palo Alto, Mrs. Hearst in the late 1890s let it be known to the authorities of the University of California at Berkeley that she, if properly received, would take an interest in the progress of California's state university, chartered in 1868 and struggling along with minimal state support ever since. Occurring on the other end of the educational spectrum from the kindergarten movement, the expansion, upgrading, and reform of the University of California nevertheless bristled with similar pre-Progressive energies.

Academic leadership in the grand late-nineteenth-century and turn-of-the-century style of Charles Eliot of Harvard, Andrew White of Cornell, Daniel Coit Gilman of Johns Hopkins, Woodrow Wilson of Princeton, and William Rainey Harper of the University of Chicago first came to California with the appointment of David Starr Jordan to the presidency of Stanford in 1891. Previously Daniel Coit Gilman, a member of the Yale faculty, had spent a miserable three years (1872–75) as the founding president of the reorganized University of California, battling the state legislature for adequate support before answering a call to the presidency of the newly established Johns Hopkins University in Baltimore. An educator and administrator of the first rank, Gilman made many friends among the intellectuals of the state; but California, then in the throes of a depression and the beginnings of an urban populist political revolt that would put the Workingmen's party in Sacramento, was in no mood to take much counsel from the former librarian of Yale College and professor of geography in the Sheffield School of Science.

With the arrival of David Starr Jordan in 1891, however, the situation improved. Great public interest had attached itself to the founding of Stanford University, the arches and quadrangles of which—sketched out by H. H. Richardson just before his death—were rising in a Santa Clara Valley wheat field as Jordan arrived. Stanford's founding endowment, approaching $20 million, made it the highest endowed private university in the United States at the time. Trained in medicine and natural history (the great Louis Agassiz was his teacher and lifelong model), widely published in scientific journals and the author of a steady stream of books on ichthyology (his specialty) and a half dozen other topics, Jordan—a tall, somewhat shambling man with a drooping walrus mustache— arrived at Stanford after a successful term as president of Indiana University. An extraordinarily skilled communicator in both speech and writing, President Jordan was by the end of the 1890s the single most influential intellectual in the state of California, North or South: a prophet in residence (so thought Charles Fletcher Lummis, who named his son after him) preaching a message of education, social uplift, eugenics (a lifelong interest), internationalism, and world peace.

An essay Jordan wrote for the November 1898 *Atlantic Monthly*, "California and the Californians" (later published as a booklet) must be considered a key statement of the pre-Progressive consciousness. Surveying his adopted state, Jordan saw much that was rich and beautiful and exuberant in the life around him. Yet the society of California lacked tone. Californians expected to get by too easily, Jordan argued, in politics, in government, in social institutions, in commerce and agriculture, because, in contrast to the East or the Midwest, it had all come too easily. This get-rich-quick syndrome—Jordan called it "the possibility of the unearned increment"—had introduced a certain baneful sloppiness into the California version of American civilization. The state needed reform and discipline in just about every one of its social and political institutions. Although he did not say so in this particular essay, Jordan wanted Stanford University to develop into an utopian statement of California possibilities, from which might radiate reforming energy in every direction. Stanford University, after all, drew its endowment, which enabled nearly all students to attend on scholarship, from frontier California itself, in the person of the Stanfords and their fortune. In every way possible—architecture, landscaping, student admission policies, curriculum, and campus life—Jordan encouraged Stanford University to embody the best of cosmopolitan culture and high thought (Jordan was a Unitarian, a pacifist, a teetotaler, a fitness fanatic), bringing the Stanford style to bear upon the celebration and reform of all aspects of California life.

Both Jordan and his philosophical counterpart at Berkeley, Professor Joseph Le Conte, believed that California, because of its physical grandeur and healthfulness, its abundant naturalism, offered a special opportunity to fuse science and ethics. Social evolutionary thinking had a powerful appeal for the late-nineteenth-century California mind. Evolution in the natural world, the equation ran, was nowhere more manifest than in California, where, as George Santayana would say at Berkeley in 1911, nature was the primary symbol for an emerging society. Believing themselves children of nature even more intensely than did other Americans, Californians welcomed evolutionary thought as having a special applicability to themselves. With nature so grand, the reasoning went, should not an equally impressive physical type and social community be evolving out of this natural basis? At the University of California at Berkeley, Joseph Le Conte—like Jordan a physician, a natural scientist, a student of Louis Agassiz—taught a course in the interaction of biology and ethics that helped attune generations of California undergraduates to this ethical evolutionary point of view, including novelist Frank Norris and Franklin K. Lane, Progressive secretary of the interior under Woodrow Wilson, who called Le Conte "the Sierra in my collegiate skyline." An ardent lover of mountaineering and horseback treks into the Sierra, a founding member of the Sierra Club (he died, in fact, in 1901 at age seventy-eight while trekking in the Yosemite with the Sierra Club), Le Conte taught a version of evolutionary theism based on the premise that "evolution is entirely consistent with a rational theism and with other fundamental religious beliefs." In nature, in human beings, and in human society, Le Conte taught, the higher builds itself upon the lower. In the case of social progress, the evils to be overcome—whether they be corrupt politics or inefficient administration—possessed perfect parallels in the transcended deficiencies so evident in natural evolution.

When one considers the fact that many of the Progressive leaders had taken Le Conte's course as University of California undergraduates in the 1880s and 1890s, a linkage suggests itself between Le Conte's pre-Progressive ethical evolutionism and the effort, one or two decades later, of college men from the University of California to bring California to its next evolutionary plateau of improvement.

Thanks to Phoebe Apperson Hearst, the university itself experienced an upgrading in the late 1890s and the early 1900s that anticipated the later reform of the state. In 1897 Mrs. Hearst volunteered to endow an international architectural competition calling for a master plan for the Berkeley campus, then a hilltop cluster of two major buildings and a few surrounding facilities. The next year Mrs. Hearst was given a seat on the board of regents by Governor James H. Budd. Budd, himself a California graduate in engineering, had made a very wise decision, for under Mrs. Hearst's patronage, Berkeley evolved from a neglected afterthought of the state legislature to an institution that had advanced itself by 1919, the year of Mrs. Hearst's death, into the first stages of national reputation. Mrs. Hearst gave money, first of all, of which she had an abundance. She spent $200,000 on the international architectural competition alone, won in 1898 by Henri Emile Bernard of Paris. She financed a mining building in honor of her late husband, together with the outdoor Greek Theater and a women's gymnasium and social center designed by Bernard Maybeck. She underwrote a university museum and paid for the establishment of a Department of Anthropology, for which she financed archeological and anthropological expeditions to Italy, Mexico, Russia, and Egypt, accompanying the Egyptian venture herself.

Like Mrs. Stanford, Mrs. Hearst had grown up in simple rural circumstances: in her case, on a Franklin County, Missouri, farm, where she walked miles every day to school and so loved culture that she taught herself French from a grammar book, having no idea whatsoever how the language was pronounced. By age seventeen she was teaching in a country school, which was where George Hearst, twenty-two years her senior, found her when he returned to his home county a very wealthy man after ten years in California and Nevada. He was smitten by the seventeen-year-old schoolteacher, whom he used to carry piggyback on his shoulders. Arriving in San Francisco as Mrs. Hearst in 1862, Phoebe Apperson discovered just how rich her husband was. With the exception of one troubled period when the Hearsts had to move into a boardinghouse, she spent the rest of her life sustained by the bounty of the Ophir Mine in Nevada, the Homestake Mine in South Dakota, and the Anaconda Mine in Montana, together with the income from vast landholdings in the San Joaquin Valley and around San Luis Obispo. Her love of art and culture, so slenderly maintained in rural Franklin County, now underwent a lifetime of amplification and gratification, including a passion for collecting objets d'art (her collection formed the basis of a museum later established in the Palace of Fine Arts in San Francisco) which her son William Randolph would later take to even further extremes. The advancement of the University of California appealed to Mrs. Hearst, then in her mid-fifties, as the culmination of her lifetime interest in education, especially women's education, from kindergarten through the secondary level (she endowed the National Cathedral School for Girls in Washington, D.C.) and onto undergraduate and graduate programs.

For the University of California to sustain its new momentum, however, it needed a president equal in academic prestige and public presence to Jordan of Stanford. In 1899 the regents found such a man in Benjamin Ide Wheeler of Cornell. A Brown undergraduate (1875) and a *summa cum laude* Ph.D. in classical philology from the University of Heidelberg (1885), a sportsman of distinction, and an academic administrator with a taste for Germanic efficiency, Wheeler carefully negotiated his authority with the regents before accepting the Berkeley presidency. He wanted strong authority over every aspect of the institution and the right to recruit new scholars, which they granted him. Wheeler's leverage in the negotiations consisted of his international reputation as a classicist with extensive publications, symbolized by his appointment for the 1895–96 academic year to the Chair of Greek Literature at the American School for Classical Studies in Athens; his field experience in the excavations at Corinth, leading to the revival of the Olympic Games; his brilliance as a teacher at Brown, Harvard, and Cornell; and—of equal importance—his political activism in Rhode Island and New York, which had resulted in an extensive network of political friendships, including warm relationships with former president Grover Cleveland and future president Theodore Roosevelt. (In 1909–10 Wheeler would hold the Theodore Roosevelt Professorship of the University of Berlin.) Athletic, assertive, academically and politically well connected, Wheeler, so the regents agreed, was just the man they needed to take the University of California into the twentieth century. After a mere year in office, Wheeler presented the regents with a fifteen-point program for proper growth. Nineteen years and twenty new departments later, he had accomplished all fifteen of his goals. Wheeler eventually came to grief because of his pro-German sympathies at the outbreak of World War I. In the interim, however, he brought to Berkeley a tone, a style, a sense of the wider world, and a capacity for assertive leadership that in every way paralleled the great work of Jordan at Stanford. Like Jordan, Wheeler spoke and wrote freely of both the promise and the backwardness of his adopted state. His influence, like Jordan's, must be seen as instrumental in developing reform sentiment in an entire generation.

V

Meanwhile the business community of California, and of Southern California especially, was doing its best to equal the academic community in building up pre-Progressive reform sentiment. The reform of California, it was perceived, would be good for business. As long as the railroad and a handful of oligarchs controlled the state, smaller entrepreneurs did not have a chance. Nowhere was this belief more widespread than in Southern California, where a handful of men—Harrison Gray Otis, Moses H. Sherman, Henry Edwards Huntington most conspicuously among them—seemed capable of manipulating the entire apparatus of politics and public opinion for their own enrichment. In the decade-long battle of Los Angeles businessmen to prevent the SP from imposing a monopolistic harbor on the city, anti-oligarchical sentiment gathered strength in the business community. Channeled through the chamber of commerce, this opposition to monopoly provided yet another psychological basis for reform a decade later. With all public transit in Henry Huntington's hands, moreover, the business community had before it another scandalous example of a monopolistic money machine. Otis's *Times* promoted water projects that brought water to suburbs serviced by Pacific Electric, the land itself being owned by syndicates in which Otis and Huntington each held major interests, all this making for a closed circle of profit. Not surprisingly, smaller businessmen, including garden-variety millionaires such as Dr. John Randolph Haynes, grew resentful. The inefficient public utilities of Los Angeles, moreover, seemingly accountable to no one, helped create sentiment for public ownership of water and power among even the most conservative members of the chamber of commerce.

For nearly two decades Charles Dwight Willard, the literary-minded executive secretary of the Los Angeles Chamber of Commerce, served as chief spokesman for reform as good business. As is the case with so many turn-of-the-century Southern Californians, Willard was an intriguing paradox: an initially reluctant Southern Californian, brought to the Southland in 1886 as a last resort in his struggle against tuberculosis (he literally had to be carried off the train on a stretcher when he arrived), who became in time the Southland's leading booster after Charles Fletcher Lummis. Fighting a lifelong battle against TB, Willard frequently used cocaine to offset fatigue and pain. The drug, in turn, induced in the otherwise proper Willard, a classics graduate from the University of Michigan (1883), a morbid state of mind, claustrophobic and death-obsessed, which Willard funneled into some fifty short stories he wrote in the early 1890s for publication in the *Argonaut* and the *Pacific Monthly*, two San Francisco-based literary magazines, as he was struggling to regain his health and to establish himself in his new surroundings.

Descended from distinguished New England ancestry on his father's side (two direct ancestors had served as presidents of Harvard) and from upstate New York Quaker stock on his mother's, Willard had been raised in an atmosphere of high thinking and serious moral purpose. At the time of Abraham Lincoln's assassination, Willard's father—a physician, professor of classics, and Unitarian minister, then serving as a surgeon in the Union Army—waited in line with his five-year-old son and lifted him up so that the boy might peer into the open casket of the slain Emancipator. Charles Dwight Willard never forgot this childhood vision of the dead president, an image fixing itself forever in his mind alongside his awareness of his own family's tradition of abolitionism and social reform. Arriving in Southern California from Chicago, where he was working as a newspaper reporter before his health collapsed completely, Willard initially felt little gratitude toward the Land of Sunshine. "It has no past," he observed the year of his arrival. "Its future reveals nothing but an ignominious scramble for dollars, its politics are odious and its population mongrel."

"What is there about California that makes me hate it?" Willard wrote his mother on 20 February 1887 from Santa Barbara, where he was recuperating. "I cannot tell why, but I despise this country—not the people exactly, for they are most of them easterners who live here under protest and pretend to be glad of it. . . . California is not for me." The next year, 1888, Willard had recovered sufficiently to move south to Los Angeles, resume his career as a reporter and editor—serving successively on the *Herald*, the *Times*, and the *Express*—and write short stories in his spare time. Between 1888 and 1891 Willard wavered between two identities: a morbid, introspective cocaine-ridden consumptive given to gloomy short stories in the mode of Edgar Allan Poe, Fedor Dostoevski, and Ambrose Bierce, and an up-and-about reformer-journalist, the child of abolitionist Quaker parents, concerned for the welfare of the community. In May 1891 Willard married Miss Mary McGregor of Sierra Madre. She, in turn, insisted that her new husband eat regularly (meals she prepared with great skill), get off cocaine, and stay away from long conversations with what she considered the morbid literary intellectuals her husband had befriended.

Rested, well fed, sexually satisfied, his nerves no longer frayed by cocaine, Charles Dwight Willard grew less and less interested in introspective literary gloom and more and more interested in the world about him. Abandoning his contemptuous attitude toward Southern California and Los Angeles, he grasped in a rush of intuition a heroic life's work unfolding before him: the reform and advancement of his immediate social environment. By 1895 Charles Dwight Willard, executive secretary of the Los Angeles Chamber of Commerce since 1892 (the year he gave up writing fiction), was at the center of Los Angeles booster and reform efforts. In 1893 he organized the seven-county Southern California delegation and exhibition to the Columbian World's Fair in Chicago. In 1894 he founded *Land of Sunshine*, a magazine promoting the Southern California lifestyle, selling it to Charles Fletcher Lummis a year later. In 1895 he founded and led the Free Harbor League, dedicated to thwarting SP plans to force Los Angeles to accept its port at Santa Monica. He organized a League for Better City Government in 1895. As secretary of the Municipal League of Los Angeles, founded in 1902 and the single most influential reform group (six hundred strong) in Los Angeles history, he helped prepare the way for a series of major charter and political reforms enacted in the ensuing ten years.

At his wife's insistence, Willard no longer hung out with morbid writers and intellectuals. He did, however, organize the Sunset Club of Los Angeles in 1895, the counterpart of the Bohemian Club of San Francisco. At gatherings of the Sunset, Willard met for dinner and discussion with such Establishment intellectuals as Senator Stephen Mallory White, entrepreneur Abbot Kinney, artist J. Bond Francisco, and writer Theodore S. Van Dyke in an ambience of responsible upper-class intellectualism and gentlemanly clubmanship totally devoid of the outsider morbidity Mrs. Willard so deplored.

The core of Willard's reform philosophy was business, the gospel of efficiency. As executive secretary of the Los Angeles Chamber of Commerce and later as executive secretary of the Jobbers' Association of Los Angeles, an organization of shippers and forwarders, Willard fought the stranglehold the SP had on the business life of Southern California, especially its tendency to favor San Francisco over Los Angeles in rates and shipping schedules. Willard believed that only when the SP was broken could the full creativity of the private sector be liberated and businesslike methods be brought to local and state government. Willard was himself an indifferent businessman, losing money in the few ventures he found time or had the courage for. He could, however, serve brilliantly as spokesman and tireless publicist for the civilizing influence of commerce and for the necessity of freeing the commerce of California from the SP.

Up in Northern California an eminently successful businessman, Amadeo Peter Giannini, was doing his best to prove one of Willard's key notions: namely, that a reformed and progressive private sector was capable of delivering up a

significantly improved quality of life to the people of California. As a boy growing up in the 1870s, Giannini experienced the frontier as it survived in California ranch life. His father, an industrious immigrant from the province of
Genoa, bought a forty-acre farm in the Santa Clara Valley near San Jose. Psy-
chohistorians make much of childhood traumas in the careers of the great. What,
then, might be construed from the fact that A. P. Giannini's father was brutally
murdered by one of his own ranch workmen in a quarrel over the paltry sum
of one dollar? No matter how much his mother may have shielded young
Giannini from the pain of this event, it must have seeped down into his psyche, affecting his character and attitudes. Is it too farfetched to see something
of a connection—the boy whose father is murdered in a dispute over a dollar
grows into the adult banker who makes it his life's work to insure the savings
and fiscal well-being of ordinary working men and women? Is there a connection between Giannini's adolescent realization of how hard his father had worked
to acquire those forty acres and how paltry the reason he had lost his life, and
the adult banker's determination to make available to small farmers and small
businessmen some sort of systematic handling of their finances? We can only
guess.

It cannot be emphasized too strongly how restrictive American banking was
before the opening of the Bank of Italy at nine o'clock, Monday morning, 17
October 1904, in a remodeled saloon near the intersection of Columbus and
Montgomery streets in San Francisco, or, concomitantly, how great was the
alienation felt by the majority of Americans toward banks, banking in general,
and bankers in particular. To read American fiction of the immediate post–
Civil War period, for instance, is again and again to encounter the banker as
the moral heir of Simon Legree. Hamlin Garland's short story "Under the Lion's
Paw"—the story of a returning Civil War veteran whose farm is foreclosed by
the local bank—is perhaps the apogee of such bitterness. To put it mildly, there
are no banker-heroes in the American literature of this period. Under Giannini's guidance the Bank of Italy struggled against this disaffinity by lowering interest rates, simplifying the loan process, including depositors in the ownership
of the bank, and educating its constituency regarding the benefits banks offered
individuals and society as a whole. A triumph of public education, this wooing
of the ordinary depositor—"the little fellow," as Giannini described him—reversed a century-old mistrust, and like many worthwhile things it took time.
Giannini himself would take the time to show a widow how to fill out a deposit
slip. Such patience paid off. By 1927 one out of every five Californians of all
ages was a depositor with the Bank of Italy.

It was Woodrow Wilson himself, the great Progressive standard-bearer among
Democrats, who stimulated Giannini's thinking about the possibilities of branch
banking as a means of democratizing banking services. "The banks of this
country," Giannini heard Wilson say in a speech given at Pasadena in May

1908, "are remote from the people, and the people regard them as not belonging to them, but as belonging to some power hostile to them." It is not known, of course, how many took Wilson's admonition to heart, but we do know that A. P. Giannini did. Inspired by Wilson's remarks, Giannini toured western Canada, studying those provinces' branch banking system. In 1909 the Bank of Italy established its first branch outside San Francisco—in San Jose. The San Mateo branch was opened in 1912. By 1918 the Bank of Italy had twenty-four branches in eighteen cities. By 1921 the total had grown to thirty-nine. By 1922, the Bank of Italy had a total of sixty-two branches extending from Chico to San Diego. Twenty-three new branches were added in 1922 alone.

As A. P. Giannini saw it, a good bank is simply a communal agency through which society maximizes the uses and effects of its available cash by allowing depositors an agency through which to pool their resources. By allowing loans against deposits a bank doubled, even tripled, the amount of work that money could do. Giannini deplored idle money: the cache of coins buried in a North Beach backyard in San Francisco, the unloaned assets (unloaned because of needlessly high interest rates or a needlessly defensive tight-money policy) sitting idle in a bank vault, doing no one any good. A bank, Giannini believed (and he practiced this belief), should energize capital by circulating it in ways that promoted new growth. In a very real sense, banks did not own their money. They merely managed it on behalf of their depositors. The Bank of Italy was not a property, but a public enterprise to be managed on behalf of society as one would manage a public trust. Capitalism, Giannini believed, thrives best under participatory conditions. At his insistence, shares in the Bank of Italy were sold to as many investors as possible, no one of them being allowed to acquire a dominating interest. By 1924 some 13,692 people owned shares in the Bank of Italy. Of some 175,000 shares outstanding, only 23,364 were in aggregates larger than 350. Giannini himself owned only 1,010 shares of the bank he had founded.

From its start the Bank of Italy was a loan-oriented institution. By 1906, two years after its foundation, the bank had a million dollars out in loans. Loans, in fact, exceeded deposits by some $200,000. The loan policy of the Bank of Italy was liberal and venturesome; it was not, however, foolish. The bank entered into very close relationships with its small business creditors. Its business extension department specialized in helping independent businessmen seek out opportunities, design programs, and then secure enabling loans. The Bank of Italy often acted as a consultant in the specifics of the enterprise or brought in outside experts to work with its business creditors. Giannini himself was not above teaching certain creditor farmers in the Santa Clara Valley how best to plant and harvest peas. The Bank of Italy reversed the prevailing notion that a bank loan was personal privilege. Insofar as possible, the Bank of Italy presumed that any sound business scheme was worthy of its backing, unless proven otherwise. Giannini had an unnerving habit of dropping in on his branch managers unannounced and asking to see the file of rejected loan applications. Case by case, he would review the manager's reasons for rejecting each loan. In certain instances, he would find that the loan officer had been too cautious, that with certain provisos and safeguards this or that loan should be made because the business enterprise in question—and most importantly, the applicant in question—seemed worthy of backing by the bank. State bank examiners sometimes did not agree with the venturesomeness of this or that Bank of Italy loan, yet defaults were rare.

Perhaps the most dramatic example of how the Bank of Italy served the California dream can be found in the area of home ownership. At the heart of the California dream was the prospect of individual home ownership. The first dramatic growth experienced by the Bank of Italy was energized by this homing instinct. Bringing back the records and assets of the Bank of Italy from San Mateo, where they had been taken in a horse-drawn wagon by Giannini himself as fire ravaged San Francisco on 19 and 20 April 1906, Giannini opened for business, using a plank laid across two barrels as his teller's cage. Within four months, 542 structures had been rebuilt in San Francisco's North Beach, a significant number of them financed on liberal terms by the Bank of Italy. The work of helping North Beach to rebuild itself also helped the Bank of Italy double its assets.

Nowhere was the California home-owning instinct more prevalent than in Southern California, where during these years hundreds of thousands of Easterners and Midwesterners were flocking in search of a better life. When the Bank of Italy began its expansion into the Southland in 1913, it associated itself with the home-building instinct. "The Bank of Italy," read an advertisement placed by the bank in the newspapers and magazines of Southern California in 1913, "has been, from its inception and is now, ready and anxious to make loans to people owning, or intending to build, their own homes—to the smaller mortgage borrowers who need $1,000 or less. The Bank of Italy has built up its present reputation, its present enormous resources, largely through catering to the small depositor—the wage earner, the producer, the small business man, the man who owns a small home or a piece of improved property, the man who is the bone and sinew of Southern California's progress."

By the time A. P. Giannini's Bank of Italy was on its way to becoming the Bank of America, the largest bank in the world by the end of the Second World War, the Progressive movement in California was running at high tide, thanks in great part to the pre-Progressives of an earlier era. Because they inaugurated the rethinking and restructuring of California institutions, the pre-Progressives established overall premises for the specific political and social reforms of the ensuing Progressive era. Politics, like music, art, theology, or even banking, does not function in a vacuum. The Progressive movement was destined to achieve so much in the reforming of California because the reformers of the first era had been so optimistic regarding the possibilities of California itself.

8

Progressivism and After

On the evening of 21 May 1907 a group of fifteen reform-minded young men, journalists and lawyers, nearly all of them Republicans, gathered for dinner at Levy's Cafe in downtown Los Angeles. They had been convened by Edward Dickson and Chester Rowell, two of the journalists among their number, just back from covering the horrors in Sacramento, and by Marshal Stimson and Russ Avery, two Los Angeles attorneys. At an earlier series of luncheon meetings at the University Club in Los Angeles, Dickson of the *Los Angeles Express*, Rowell's office-mate in the press room at the Capitol, had given the vivid details of the buying and selling of votes underway in the legislative session of 1907. Stimson and Avery had also attended these University Club meetings, where certain preliminary discussions had occurred concerning the formation of a reform league, a topic that Dickson and Rowell had already been discussing in Sacramento. Seated around the dinner table at Levy's that evening were Rowell, Dickson, Stimson, and Avery, the conveners of the meeting, together with Dr. John R. Haynes, the millionaire physician-reformer; attorneys Robert N. Bulla and Meyer Lissner of Los Angeles; oilman S. C. Graham; and Colonel Ed Fletcher, a San Diego businessman. The remaining six were journalists: T. C. Hocking, publisher of the *Modesto Herald*; G. B. Daniels, publisher of the *Oakland Enquirer*; Irving Martin publisher of the *Stockton Record*; Colonel E. A. Forbes, publisher of the *Sacramento Union*; A. J. Pillsbury, the *Sacramento Union* editor; and Harley W. Brundige, editor of the *Los Angeles Express*.

Talk during the meal revolved around the deplorable state of California politics, and when Dickson called the meeting to order over coffee and cigars, a more formal agenda of needed reforms was discussed: a direct primary system, so as to take the nomination of political candidates out of the control of the

SP-dominated party machines; an initiative provision in the state constitution and local charters as well, so that the public could have direct access to the lawmaking process or revoke laws that it did not like; a local and state referendum provision, allowing the public to express its opinion on bills in the process of being enacted into legislation; and lastly, a recall provision making it possible to remove corrupt or inept officials from public office. These four measures—the direct primary, the initiative, the referendum, and the recall—were of special interest to Dr. Haynes, founder of the Direct Legislation League of Los Angeles, but other measures were discussed as well: the regulation of public utilities; the conservation of forests; the outlawing of child labor, prostitution, and gambling; hospital and prison reform; women's suffrage and a minimum wage law for working women; the direct election of United States senators; the systemization of public finance; charter reform; public transportation. Overriding all issues, however, asserting itself as the beginning, the sine qua non of any reform program, was the necessity of curbing the Southern Pacific—what one dinner discussant at Levy's Cafe termed the "constructive destruction of the Southern Pacific machine."

From this meeting emerged a loose coalition of Tory reformers, Theodore Roosevelt Republicans to a man, who promised each other that they would not seek elective office personally but would band together to put independent, honest men into state and local office. Chester Rowell, Edward Dickson, Russ Avery, Meyer Lissner, and Marshal Stimson (the last three all young Los Angeles attorneys) constituted the inner core of leadership of what developed up and down the state through the spring and summer of 1907 into an informal affiliation of reform fraternities. By August, when the league gathered in Oakland for its first statewide meeting, there were about fifty activists involved, thirty-eight of whom were able to attend the meeting. At no time would the league exceed a hundred members. On 1 August 1907 the clubs formally adopted the name League of Lincoln-Roosevelt Republican Clubs to suggest the membership's dedication to a heritage of reforming conservatism which these young attorneys and journalists considered the best and most usable heritage of the Republican party.

Who were the men of the Lincoln-Roosevelt League, and who were their counterparts among the Progressive Democrats of California? They were young men, for one thing, the majority of them in their thirties, largely Protestant and small-town in origin, upper-middle-class, university-trained professionals, abhorrent of both the corporate oligarchy and labor unions, forward-looking and reform-minded, yet at the same time slightly nostalgic for a lost myth of American self-reliance and individualism that was, at bottom, the indispensable myth for their own continuing professional success. The majority of them were born elsewhere, especially in the Midwest, Wisconsin leading the list. (By 1910, in fact, a full 60 percent of California's entire population was Midwest-born.) There were exceptions to this Midwest rule. San Francisco City Attorney Franklin

Knight Lane was born in Canada (the only foreign-born California Progressive of note), and a few others were Eastern-born: Los Angeles attorney Marshal Stimson, for instance (Cambridge, Massachusetts), and San Francisco attorney Francis J. Heney (Lima, New York). There was one former Washingtonian, Russ Avery, born in Olympia, and even a few native sons, such as James Duval Phelan of San Francisco, and Hiram Johnson, Simon Julius Lubin, and Lincoln Steffens of Sacramento.

Most of the California Progressives, however, had been brought to California sufficiently early in their lives. They attended public, not private, schools, with Los Angeles High School having the most Progressive alumni, and then—with a few exceptions, such as Harvard undergradates S. J. Lubin and Marshal Stimson—went on to the University of California at Berkeley, which in later years, as the Progressive movement waned, became the repository of their Progressive hopes and aspirations. James Duval Phelan and John Francis Neylan were Irish Roman Catholics and S. J. Lubin was of Russian Jewish background; most Progressives, however, were of Protestant stock, with the New England-oriented denominations—Congregationalism, Unitarianism, Christian Science—appearing most frequently. Phelan and Lane were Democrats; most others, however, registered as Republicans. Nearly all were lawyers by training, if not in their day-to-day profession.

Only one key protagonist among the California Progressives might be said to have had firsthand experience of the waning Far West frontier: San Francisco attorney Francis J. Heney, who after his admittance to the bar in 1883 worked as a cattleman and Indian trader in the Arizona Territory before being named attorney general of Arizona in 1893. Hot-tempered and forceful, Heney had killed a man in self-defense during his Arizona days and had once successfully defended himself in court with a chair when an opposing attorney threatened violence. Heney was older than the rest of the Progressives, however, and never fully trusted by them, for they were post-frontier in their orientation and attitudes, city men, club men, a significant number of them born to affluent circumstances. Four of their number—Phelan, Lubin, Rudolph Spreckels, and William Kent—had been born to impressive wealth, and the majority of the rest were from comfortable backgrounds. Few self-made men, battle-scarred and tinged with the compromises of an unregulated marketplace, felt themselves inclined, or pure enough in heart, to join their band.

The working classes would have been equally out of place. The California Progressives pretended to abhor class consciousness, preferring to see their programs as intended for all the people, yet class feeling and self-interest on the part of labor and capital alike edged against the left and the right flanks of the Progressive movement. Labor, for instance, never fully liked or trusted Progressivism as a movement or the Progressives as individuals, with the exception of Franklin K. Lane, a lifelong union advocate, and Chester Rowell, a social philosopher who favored the labor cause. In the late 1880s Samuel Gompers had successfully steered the American labor movement away from obsessive ideological concerns and in the direction of bread-and-butter issues. The embattled trade unions of Southern California tended to avoid the many nationalist or Socialist organizations flourishing there, considering these groups to be dominated by upper-middle-class amateurs, social theorists with little contact with ordinary working men and women. In the case of the Teamsters' strike of 1901 in San Francisco, reform mayor James Duval Phelan clashed head-on with organized labor, led by Teamster Mike Casey and Father Peter Yorke, who bitterly upbraided Phelan for calling out special police, the National Guard, and strikebreakers. Phelan was, Father Yorke orated, a traitor to his fellow Irish Roman Catholics, proving himself loyal only to his class. The strike destroyed Phelan's political career for well over a decade and put the Union Labor party dominated by Boss Ruef in power, replacing Phelan's reform administration. The fact that Ruef was subsidized by the SP only reinforced the ironies of class conflict. In the long run, San Francisco labor preferred a machine subsidized by the SP to a reform Democratic administration dominated by millionaire Phelan and capable of ordering out the police to protect scabs.

The Teamsters' strike of 1901, pitting as it did reformers against labor, underscored an incompatibility that could never be overcome. Even Hiram Johnson, who had represented the Teamsters for eight years, was never truly popular with the working classes of San Francisco. When Johnson ran for vice-president alongside Theodore Roosevelt on the 1912 Progressive ticket, the South of Market San Francisco working classes voted overwhelmingly in favor of Democrat Woodrow Wilson. Johnson, for his part, never felt fully at home with his Teamster clients. Throughout his career as a labor lawyer, he managed to maintain impeccable ties with the San Francisco business establishment.

Johnson's attitude was typical of the California Progressives, whose legal and professional orientation gave them little in common with wage-earners. Themselves employed outside large structures, the Progressives of Southern California, where the movement had its greatest strength, had grown to maturity in an atmosphere of bitter labor-management strife, beginning in 1890 when Harrison Gray Otis—his face beet red, his neck veins bulging purple—had ordered all union typographers out of the *Times*. Throughout the long ensuing struggle, the Progressives tended to see both labor and large capital as equally at fault.

This labor-versus-Progressive dichotomy can be reformulated in Northern and Southern California ethnic and religious terms. In Northern California, especially in the Bay Area, foreign-born Roman Catholics dominated the population. In Southern California, most noticeably Los Angeles, the dominant population was Midwestern native-born Protestant. Fifty-six percent of Los Angeles was Protestant in 1906, and only 15 percent of San Francisco. In 1910, 68 percent of all San Franciscans were either children of the foreign-born or foreign-born themselves, while only 35 percent of the population of Los Angeles had such foreign ancestry. Progressivism drew its essential strength from the native-born Protestant Republicans of the Southland, not from the Catholic Democratic immigrants of the North. In the 1910 gubernatorial election, for instance, Hiram Johnson won every Southern Californian county but lost twenty-one of the forty-nine counties of the North. Johnson was elected governor, in fact, precisely because Los Angeles County gave him one-fifth of his statewide vote, hence his margin for victory. While Catholic immigrants and the children of immigrants in Northern California preferred to remain skeptical and defensive when it came to high-minded talk of reform, seeing in such proposals little that spoke to their social identity or self-interest, Protestants encountered in these very same proposals notions that spoke to their deepest identity. Progressivism, after all, sought to reform the body politic as Protestantism had sought to reform the Catholic Church. In the face of Catholic and Jewish immigration, furthermore, Progressivism also reasserted by implication (and occasionally by overt statement) an embattled conviction of the essentially Protestant nature of American society.

Fresno journalist Chester Harvey Rowell, the dominant intellectual among the California Progressives, epitomized the Protestant-flavored high-mindedness with which the Progressives sought to explain themselves as they seized control of the state—for its own good. Like Lincoln Steffens—a California-born journalist turned New Yorker, covering the national reform movement for *McClure's Magazine*—Chester Rowell had more than a passing interest in philosophy, which he first studied as an undergraduate and graduate student under George Sylvester Morris and John Dewey at the University of Michigan, before going on to Germany in 1892 to attend the Universities of Halle and Berlin. From Morris, an American Hegelian in the manner of Josiah Royce, Rowell absorbed a lifelong insight into the interaction of ideal and process in the evolution of human society. Ideals—ideas perceived from the point of view of their ethical content—provided the motor force behind social evolution, Morris taught; an important aspect of corrective work in the world therefore consisted of guiding the evolution of society with the stimulus of good ideas. Just as long as these ideas did not become dogmas, worried the younger philosopher John Dewey, another lifelong influence on Chester Rowell. For Dewey, then in the process of evolving his philosophy of instrumentalism, the solving of social problems was in itself a primary form of intellectual speculation. Ideas are not just imposed from above, Dewey taught. Ideas are discovered in action.

All his life, Chester Rowell, the student of Morris and Dewey, sought to respond to the twin imperatives of detached intellectual enquiry and active work in the world absorbed from his early apprenticeship to Hegel and Morris and to the roll-up-your-sleeves philosophy of young John Dewey. In Germany, for instance, Rowell studied philosophy and languages (he mastered German and French), but he also attended courses in public health, education, and the delivery of social services, then being pioneered by the German state's expanding program of social legislation. Widely traveled, multilingual, far more polished than his fellows, Rowell returned to the United States in 1894 and began an academic career. In 1898, however, faced with his wife's declining health, he resigned his position in the German department of the University of Illinois to accept his uncle's offer to become editor and general manager of the *Fresno Republican*.

The uncle, Dr. Chester A. Rowell, was a wealthy Fresno physician, publisher, and reform politician of great influence in the San Joaquin Valley and among the legislators of Sacramento. While teaching college, Chester Rowell had held his activist side in abeyance in favor of scholarly enquiry. Thrust unexpectedly into journalism, Rowell found within himself a capacity for a type of pragmatic work in the world that his undergraduate mentor John Dewey claimed America desperately needed: a work of engaged intellectual diagnosis in the service of social reform. For forty-nine years, until his retirement in 1947, Chester Rowell busied himself with serving (so he formulated it) the rise of California to community, to public good, through the upgrading of its collective public conscience. Loyalty to the public interest, Rowell believed, was the major standard of ethical evolution against which California should be judged.

As of 1898, community in California was unstable and the public interest ill-defined; hence loyalty to California as a public ideal was not overly strong. Sitting down to his desk in a vice-ridden, politically corrupt Fresno, set squarely in the midst of a great valley under the total dominion of the railroad, Chester Rowell beheld a true work of civilization: to encourage Californians through journalism and political action to glimpse an image of themselves as a community, as holding a life in common, and then to encourage them to serve this newly awakened public interest through reform. Cautious, latently conservative, believing in reformed republicanism rather than plebiscitary democracy, sensitive to the factor of class as a source of public action, Chester Rowell was neither a radical reformer nor a naive one. He was, however, a tireless producer of commentary and, in his active role—given the erratic, irascible nature of Hiram Johnson, who made so many enemies—the true effective leader of California Progressives.

A considerable number of the California Progressives turned to journalism as a full- or part-time occupation. If their intellectual leader was Chester Rowell of the *Fresno Republican*, their most dependable war-horse was Fremont Older, editor (since 1895) of the *San Francisco Bulletin*. Tall, mustachioed, having the air of the frontier about him, Older had decided upon a career in journalism at age thirteen in Wisconsin upon reading the biography of Horace Greeley. Leaving school, Older went to work on a small rural Wisconsin paper, setting type, correcting proof, writing notices in that species of literary and jour-nalistic apprenticeship that was so common in nineteenth-century America. Older's father had died in a Confederate prisoner-of-war camp, and a staggering total of six uncles had also fallen in the Union cause. Older's mother remarried in 1869, moving to Sacramento. Fremont lived with an aunt for a while before himself going to California in 1873, arriving at age seventeen and getting his first job as a typesetter on the *San Francisco Morning Call*, which he would later head as president and editor-in-chief. A decade of peripatetic printing and some reporting—Reno, Virginia City, Oakland, Santa Barbara, San Mateo, Redwood City—ensued before Older returned to San Francisco and established himself as the best investigative reporter in town.

Fiercely ambitious, Older angled for a major editorship, which came his way in 1895. For a self-educated man such as Older, journalism offered opportu-nity. The same thing became true, however, for the university-trained Progres-sives. For Fremont Older, journalism was a near-religion, which he had begun to master in its basic details as a boy acolyte. Older loved the feel of type, the smell of still-wet ink on the proof pages he insisted upon personally correcting, even as a senior editor, sitting in a glass-enclosed booth out in the city room for all his reporters to see, a constant cigar clamped aggressively between his teeth. Most Progressives, by contrast, regarded newspaper work merely as a convenient pulpit and a stage in their own struggle for success. Many Progres-sive journalists—beginning with Franklin Lane, who launched himself into anti-railroad investigative reporting in the late 1890s—were lawyers, for whom jour-nalism was a first step on the road to larger things, a way of getting noticed as well as doing some good. Not for them a lifetime of deadlines, late hours and endless cups of coffee, low wages, disillusionment, and a seedy alcoholic mid-dle age. Their reputations established, they left newspapering for wider oppor-tunities in business, law practice, or the bench. Those who remained in jour-nalism soon got into newspaper ownership, where the only real economic opportunities lay.

The case of Edward Augustus Dickson, one of the founders of the Lincoln-Roosevelt League, personifies this Progressive use of journalism as a way of get-ting started in the world by launching oneself as a reformer journalist. Dick-son's vehicle was the *Los Angeles Express*. Wisconsin-born (1879), as were so many of the California Progressives, and a 1901 graduate in law from the Uni-versity of California at Berkeley, Dickson was working as a political reporter on the *San Francisco Chronicle* in 1906 when his work came to the notice of Ed-win T. Earl, publisher of the *Los Angeles Express*, at the time the most reform-minded newspaper in California. Charles Dwight Willard had bought into the *Express* in 1897, becoming its editor as well. Willard hoped to improve his in-vestment by turning the *Express* into a well-respected, highly circulated reform newspaper. As usual, Willard succeeded as a reformer but lost out as a businessman. The *Express* succeeded as a reform journal but ran into cash-flow problems until it was bought out by Earl, a millionaire citrus shipper, in 1901. A neighbor of Harrison Gray Otis in Los Angeles who moved in the same social circles, Earl was determined to give the *Times* a run for its money. As associate editor of the *Express*, Dickson put it on the cutting edge of the reform movement in Los Angeles. During the 1907 legislative session, Dickson had a desk adjacent to Chester Rowell. Observing the chicanery of the railroad-dominated legislature, including the blatant behavior of Boss Ruef on the assembly and senate floors, the two editor-reporters, both Republicans, made plans for an organization, eventually known as the Lincoln-Roosevelt League, that would fight SP control of the state.

II

California's first major reform crusade was already underway in San Francisco. Reform had been on the minds of certain San Francisco gentlemen of wealth since the 1890s. Their leader was James Duval Phelan, a youngish (born 1861) Irish Roman Catholic millionaire, a reform Democrat, who after legal studies at Hastings College of the Law and European travel had established a reputation in San Francisco as a shrewd banker and real estate investor (he doubled the family fortune), a cultural leader, and a spokesman for reform sentiment. As an essayist and public speaker, Phelan—a smallish, dapper man, his beard kept well trimmed, his tailoring impeccable, a lifelong, very ardent and discreet wooer of the ladies—was fond of comparing and contrasting San Francisco to the great cities of Europe whose administrations he had studied after graduation from law school. Municipal administration, Phelan believed, citing Lord Bryce's remarks in *The American Commonwealth* (1888), was the weakest link in the American chain of government, a deficiency compounded in its bad effects as the United States made the transition from a rural to an urban nation.

In 1896 *Bulletin* editor Fremont Older persuaded Phelan to run—successfully—for mayor of San Francisco. With the help of Franklin K. Lane, another reform Democrat, whom Phelan appointed charter commissioner and who later ran successfully for city attorney, and the assistance of a Committee of One Hundred, Phelan gave San Francisco a new charter, approved by the voters on 26 May 1898, which among its other reforms surrounded the two areas of municipal government most attractive to graft—public works and public employment—with numerous safeguards.

Humiliated by his inability to negotiate a settlement in the Teamsters' strike of 1901, which forced twenty thousand out of work and tied up nearly two hundred ships in the harbor, Phelan retired from public office, forced to stand hopelessly by as Boss Ruef's handpicked Union Labor party candidate, orchestra leader Eugene "Handsome Gene" Schmitz, succeeded him in City Hall.

Shunted into political retirement, Phelan watched and waited for an opportunity for revenge.

With his mayor in City Hall (Schmitz was reelected in 1903 and 1905), the board of supervisors under his influence, the Southern Pacific and the unions solidly behind him, and a well-oiled political machine running smoothly, Abraham Ruef—whose university training, polished manners, good tailoring, and taste for the arts stood in such contrast to the prevailing image of a big-city political boss—played San Francisco as first violinist and concertmaster. Did certain utilities require franchises from the City and County of San Francisco? Then large amounts in cash, discreetly inserted into unmarked envelopes, found their way into Ruef's possession for distribution to the relevant officials, with Ruef's own expenses deducted off the top. Twenty thousand came in from the Pacific Gas and Electric Company, $125,000 from the Home Telephone Company, and $200,000 from the United Railroad Company, Patrick Calhoun president, so that overhead electrical trolley lines would not have to be placed underground at United Railroad's expense. It was later estimated that Ruef personally pocketed a half million dollars from such dealings.

Joined by a number of other reform-minded men of wealth, including Rudolph Spreckels, a young millionaire then in his early thirties, Phelan laid plans for a counterrevolution. With Spreckels financing the effort and Fremont Older thundering away in the *Bulletin*, the Phelan-Spreckels coterie formed a shadow government in San Francisco, dealing directly with the president himself. Upon being secretly visited in Washington by Fremont Older and apprised of the San Francisco situation, Roosevelt agreed to assign two of his best federal agents, detective William J. Burns and prosecuting attorney Francis J. Heney, to come to San Francisco as special agents working directly with the Phelan-Spreckels group to clean up the city. Arriving in San Francisco from Oregon, where he had been investigating timber fraud cases, Detective Burns, one of the most skilled investigators in American police history, set to work uncovering and documenting the network of bribery and corruption in San Francisco.

The destruction of most of downtown San Francisco by earthquake and fire in April 1906 delayed matters. During relief efforts, Roosevelt entrusted a million dollars in federal emergency relief directly to the Phelan group for distribution as an overt sign of his distrust of Mayor Schmitz—who, incidentally, had conducted himself with great skill and courage during the conflagration. By late 1906, however, District Attorney William L. Langdon, his staff augmented by Burns and Heney, was ready to take his case against Schmitz and Ruef and certain supervisors to the grand jury.

Abraham Ruef, however, was not without a plan of defense. He sent Mayor Schmitz to Europe for a vacation. Before leaving, Schmitz appointed board of supervisors chairman James L. Gallagher acting mayor. Acting Mayor Gallagher, in turn, accused District Attorney Langdon of misconduct, declared his office vacant, and appointed in his place none other than Abraham Ruef. This attempted coup d'état was Boss Ruef's greatest bit of chutzpah, his most daring ploy. Removed a few days later as district attorney by court order, Ruef spent the next few years vainly trying to stay out of San Quentin. In early November 1906 Francis J. Heney, acting as a special assistant district attorney of San Francisco, took to the grand jury the case assembled against Schmitz and Ruef by District Attorney Langdon and Detective Burns. Eight months later, as the first statewide convention of the newly formed League of Lincoln-Roosevelt Clubs met across the Bay in Oakland, Eugene Schmitz, convicted of bribery, was removed from office, and Abraham Ruef was facing a raft of charges.

The actual charge on which prosecutor Heney secured convictions against Schmitz and Ruef—the relatively harmless soliciting and receiving of bribes from French restaurants (a genuine restaurant on the first floor, rooms for sexual assignations on the floors above)—underscored that it was easier for Progressives to convict corrupt public officials for their relationship to organized vice than for their relationship to organized corporate bribery. Corporate corruption concealed itself much more skillfully. Investigations into corporate bribery, moreover, soon stumbled into very prominent names, thereby alienating the Establishment from the reform cause, whereas vice involved a sector of society possessed of less influence. The conviction of a public official such as Mayor Schmitz of a charge connected to vice did, however, remove the official from office, and warn corporate bribers that the Progressive reformers were sharpening their investigative and prosecutorial skills. And besides, the Progressives had a special dislike of gambling, liquor, and vice. They associated such pursuits with the vulgarity of an earlier California, for one thing, and for another, vice seemed associated generally with foreign elements. Chester Rowell, for instance, began his reform career by ridding Fresno of gambling and prostitution rings controlled by the Chinese tongs of San Francisco and catering to hordes of single male agricultural workers, many of them foreign-born, who flocked into Fresno on payday. Los Angeles Progressives were especially annoyed at the openness with which prostitution was carried on in their city, from red-light barracks on the Plaza to more elaborate uptown operations, such as Cora Phillips's establishment on Alameda Street, outside of which two great stone lions stood guard. Pearl Morton, Cora's chief rival for the carriage trade, ran a fancy house at 372 New High Street. Mrs. Morton used to take her ladies walking on off afternoons, in the company of the house's white bulldog, or for a ride in an open carriage. On these expeditions Mrs. Morton and her companions dressed in opulent finery, ostrich plumes flying from their oversized hats, parasols opened for protection against the Southern California sun.

It was liquor more than prostitution, however, that most affronted the Progressives' sense of social order. While prostitution and gambling were specialized enterprises, alcoholism was a broadly based social evil. To the Progressive mind the saloon, especially the urban saloon, epitomized the sort of society—class-conscious, foreign, corrupt—they loathed. Like an onion, the California Progressive anti-saloon movement can be peeled away to reveal layer after layer of objection and motivation. The outer layer of objection—the devastation wrought by alcohol among the working classes and the poor—is self-evident. Even a cursory examination of judicial and other records corroborates the Progressive contention that alcohol was destroying significant segments of the population. Among city dwellers, moreover, alcohol had attained the status of a social institution. In *John Barleycorn* (1913), the history of his own alcoholism, Jack London graphically portrayed how saloons provided the urban workers and the poor with their only club, their only place to go. Saloon keepers cashed checks, lent money, dispensed advice, passed on information, and generally acted as neighborhood arbiters. To the Progressive way of thinking, saloon keepers used whatever good they did do as a lure to ensnare their patrons in to drink. The legacy of the saloon, the Progressives believed (and with great justification), was spent paychecks, lost jobs, quarrels, violence, beaten wives and children, alcoholism, early death. Peeling the prohibitionist onion down further, one encounters an association between saloons and foreigners, specifically Roman Catholic foreigners. Even among more educated and hence presumably more tolerant Progressives such as David Starr Jordan, Chester Rowell, Franklin Lane, Marshal Stimson, and John Randolph Haynes, this equation of saloon and Roman Catholic subversion lingered in the mind as the legacy of an earlier, more hostile attitude.

Not surprisingly, then, the prohibitionist movement never really took hold in Northern California, which was Catholic, foreign, and labor-oriented. Only such Protestant-dominated Northern counties as Modoc, Humboldt, and Lake passed dry ordinances in the 1890s. By that time, San Francisco had the highest number of saloons per capita of any large city in the United States. An 1899 count revealed an astonishing 440 saloons in the sixty-four-square-block, largely Irish Catholic working-class South of Market district alone. In Protestant-dominated Southern California, many communities—Compton, Long Beach, and Ontario, among others—voted themselves dry, while others, most noticeably Pasadena, where the so-called Whiskey War had been in progress since 1888, made constant warfare against the saloon. The Anti-Saloon League of California, an association of Protestant churches organized in 1898 (Dr. John Haynes and Marshal Stimson served as officers) met with great success in Southern California. Largely through its efforts, Los Angeles passed a law in 1899 that limited the city to 200 saloons. As the gentlemen of the California Protective Association, an anti-prohibitionist lobby founded in 1896, looked on warily, saloon after saloon came under attack in the Southland.

By 1910, the year Hiram Johnson took office as governor, the Anti-Saloon League had virtually suppressed the saloon in Los Angeles County. Johnson himself chose as his running mate Los Angeles City Councilman Albert J. Wallace, a prosperous rancher and oilman, an ordained Methodist minister, and president of the Anti-Saloon League of California. For the United States Senate, the Progressives ran another Los Angeles city councilman, John D. Works, also a strong temperance advocate. The prohibitionist vote organized by the Anti-Saloon League brought in by Wallace and Works was crucial to the 1910 Progressive victory, including the election of reform candidate George Alexander, an avid dry, as mayor of Los Angeles. The very next year the Anti-Saloon League cashed in its winning chips with the Progressive-dominated legislature: the Wylie local option law, while not making California totally dry, constituted a tightening of controls that helped establish the psychological premise for California's backing of the postwar Volstead Act, which the Progressives, in alliance with the Protestant churches, helped put through Congress as a penultimate expression of their waning influence.

III

The suppression of saloons was but one aspect of an entire Progressive program for the reform of Los Angeles. The Progressives wanted nothing less than the restructuring of Los Angeles into an urban paradigm of the Protestant ethic, "a place of inspiration for nobler living," as minister Dana Bartlett described it in *The Better City* (1907), a book setting forth a complete program for the moral and organizational renewal of Los Angeles. Tall and fatherly in demeanor, a disciple of settlement house pioneers Jane Addams of Chicago and Jacob Riis of New York City, Maine-born Dana Bartlett conducted the Bethlehem Institute on Vignes Street, a social, educational, and social service center for working-class and immigrant people, including the city's many Mexicans. Bartlett's settlement house offered food, clothing, baths, classes in English, job placement, day care for working families, medical attention, counseling, library services, and whatever else working-class immigrants to Los Angeles might need to survive in their new environment. Involved in many phases of Los Angeles life, including its politics, Bartlett nurtured within his bosom an optimism, Emersonian and religious, regarding the human prospect as encountered in the City of the Angels, where he had arrived in 1896 after theological studies at Yale and Chicago and settlement work in St. Louis and Salt Lake City. Involved on a day-by-day basis with the struggling and the underprivileged, Bartlett nevertheless saw signs of impending justice and civility everywhere about him: school gardens, better housing, an improved sewage system, the rise of clubs, child labor laws, the growth of philanthropic and volunteer organizations, the rise of family camping in the Sierra Madre, the establishment of educational programs for the physically and mentally disadvantaged. After an era of plundering individualism, furthermore, the elite of Los Angeles (so he believed) was showing every sign of cooperating toward beneficial social and political ends.

Bartlett exulted in the fact that most of the "best citizens" of Los Angeles were American-born and that their American spirit was catching. Avoiding xenophobia, and living himself amidst immigrants, Bartlett took a refreshingly positive attitude toward the new peoples of Los Angeles. Yes, he admitted with a bland tolerance that is mildly amusing to present-day sensibilities, some Mexicans did get into knife fights after drinking red wine, and the Slavs or Greeks could be unnecessarily secretive; but once it was properly Americanized, the immigrant stock of Los Angeles—in which Bartlett included the Chinese and the Japanese, a noteworthy inclusion in that bitterly anti-Asian age—constituted the vigorous biological future of the city, a human reservoir which should be safeguarded through a systematic public health program emphasizing the prevention of tuberculosis and the teaching of good health habits. As naive and patronizing as Bartlett's remarks occasionally are, they stand in refreshing contrast to so much other contemporary commentary (such as that of David Starr Jordan), with its persistent undervaluing of immigrant capacities. Nor did Dana Bartlett share the anti-organized-labor bias of most Southland Progressives. The working man, he believed, had a dramatic chance for a better life in Los Angeles, with its good wages and sunny climate, its opportunities for home ownership.

A City Beautiful enthusiast, Bartlett pointed to Frederick Law Olmsted's work in Kansas City and Cleveland and to the urban master plan devised by Daniel Hudson Burnham for James Duval Phelan's Committee for the Adornment and Beautification of San Francisco as examples of how Los Angeles should seek to organize itself into a garden city, one million strong by 1920 and without a single slum. While promoting this vision of Los Angeles as an orchestration of parks, parkways, promenades, public squares, waterside boulevards, and noble architecture, Bartlett, the experienced settlement worker, also had some practical advice often ignored by City Beautiful planners—public comfort stations, for one thing, well designed and publicly maintained, as in European cities. As it was, most working men of Los Angeles, when away from their homes, had to drop in to the nearest saloon to use the toilet facilities. All too many stayed on for a drink or two. Public baths were another of Bartlett's causes. Community shower baths had been successfully introduced from Europe to Boston, New York, Philadelphia, and Baltimore, he pointed out, and had proven effective in suppressing disease and promoting self-respect among the less advantaged, including working-class families without extensive sanitation facilities in their homes: all too common in a society that gave immigrants no place to bathe, then called them dirty foreigners. Bartlett himself set up public showers at the corner of Vignes and Ducommon streets, where for a small fee working people and their children might clean themselves.

The Better City was partially a daydream. If James Duval Phelan to the north, with his considerably greater financial resources, was envisioning San Francisco as a neo-Mediterranean baroque city, the Reverend Dana Bartlett was sustaining a comparable but more Protestant vision of Los Angeles transformed into a mid-American urban utopia. The mere fact that Los Angeles could inspire such high-minded dreams, however, underscores the visionary and reformist energies at work in the City of the Angels in the early 1900s. As a utopianizer, Bartlett offered in *The Better City* an idealistic and idealized prescription for what, in the lesser and more compromised realm of reality, was actually beginning to occur. As early as 1887 a group of Los Angeles ministers had formed a loose association aimed at ridding Los Angeles of vice and political corruption. Lacking political skills, these ministers did little more than establish the evangelical tone and premises of political reform in Los Angeles. Their first effective successor, however, the League for Better City Government, organized by Charles Dwight Willard in 1896, addressed itself at once to the pressing problem of charter reform. Governing itself through a charter enacted in 1888, Los Angeles did not conduct its public business like a modern city, with a strong mayoral executive possessing the authority to appoint administrative commissions, a regular civil service, and a balance of power between the mayor and the elected legislative council. Instead it was organized as a small township, with a weak mayor and with all true power residing in the city council. As in the case of most small towns, moreover, the local oligarchy of Los Angeles stood in a proprietary relationship to city government. In the municipal election of 1897, Willard's League for Better City Government proposed to the voters of Los Angeles a new charter based upon a separation of powers, a strong mayor, a nonpolitical civil service and an influence-free board of public works. The proposed charter failed to get the necessary three-fifths ratification, and therefore the new mayor, Meredith P. Snyder, also backed by the league, could only make gestures in the direction of the cleanup of Los Angeles which so many considered the city's first step to maturity.

Organized vice, for one thing, was flourishing, largely because—so a Committee of Safety, formed in 1899, believed—too many Los Angeles police were on the take. The committee brought in its own Pinkerton detectives to uncover this network of payoffs, going so far as to purchase through a third party a notorious saloon bordello for use as a cover for its Pinkerton operatives. Aside from its moral ambiguity, this program of subsidized vigilantism drove the committee into bankruptcy by 1902, but not before an entire network of corruption tying the police department to organized vice had been revealed.

These revelations prompted the formation in 1902 of the Municipal League of Los Angeles (Charles Dwight Willard again serving as executive secretary), a federation of virtually every reform element in the city, paralleling Phelan's committee in San Francisco. Nourishing itself on the ideals and statistics relating to municipal reform being set forth nationally in such studies as Charles Mulford Robinson's *The Improvement of Towns and Cities* (1902), Charles Zueblin's *American Municipal Progress* (1902), Delos F. Wilcox's *The Ameri-*

can City (1904), and Frank J. Goodnow's City Government in the United States (1904), the Municipal League pushed for charter reform as the necessary first step for the reorganization of Los Angeles. At last, in the election of December 1902, the Municipal League succeeded in securing the necessary three-fifths vote for a new charter, which the state legislature ratified in January. Into this charter were funneled the reform ideas of a decade, together with the energies of such successive organizations as the Citizens' League (1893), the Direct Legislation League (1895), the League for Better City Government (1896), and, lastly, the board of freeholders elected in 1900 to consider the entire question of charter reform, a board containing such disparate members as Socialist H. Gaylord Wilshire, Social Democrat John R. Haynes, and Harrison Gray Otis and his son-in-law Harry Chandler, corporate oligarchs of the most conservative sort. Among other things, the new charter brought a modern concept of civil service to Los Angeles, gave expanded executive authority to the mayor, established the beginnings of a comprehensive social welfare program, and, thanks in large part to the lobbying efforts of Dr. Haynes's Direct Legislation League, put into the hands of voters the initiative, the referendum, and the recall.

By 1906, then, such young Los Angeles Progressives as Edward Dickson, Russ Avery, Marshal Stimson, and Meyer Lissner were in a position to try to break the hold of the SP on Los Angeles municipal government. Forming a Non-Partisan Committee of One Hundred, chaired by the conservative Republican attorney for the Times (the young reformers deliberately desired this symbol of a united front), the Non-Partisans captured twenty-one of the twenty-three local offices they sought in the municipal election of 1906—with the exception of the mayoralty, which their candidate, Lee C. Gates, lost to the SP and labor candidate George Harper, a conservative Democrat. The young Progressive reformers made this alliance with the oligarchs because they considered labor and the Southern Pacific a bigger threat to reform. The oligarchs, for their part, fearing both the Socialists and the railroad, agreed to an alliance with the Progressives. Labor, meanwhile, considering the Non-Partisans their biggest enemy, made common cause with the railroad, as it had already done in San Francisco through the Union Labor party, controlled by Boss Ruef and financed in part through railroad contributions. Ambitious young businessmen and professionals, the Progressives sought to hobble labor by forcing upon it an entangling railroad alliance and to divide the right against itself—the oligarchs aligned against the SP—and thus to put their own reforming center into power.

With more than twenty of their candidates in office, the Progressives reorganized themselves after the 1906 election into two organizations, the Good Government Group (derisively called the Goo-Goos by their enemies on the left and the right) and the City Club, which the Progressives envisioned developing into a political club of like-minded gentlemen in the manner of London's Carlton or Reform. Their goals were threefold: further charter reform, the banishment from political power of the SP, and the removal of Mayor George Harper from office. Harper did his best to make himself removable. A lax, genial, pleasure-loving playboy of upper-class background, his easy amiability among ordinary citizens paralleling that of Mayor Eugene Schmitz in San Francisco, Harper had been put into office by the SP machine and, as in the case of Schmitz and Ruef, had no problem taking guidance from Boss Parker. Whereas Schmitz was a devoted family man, however, Harper had a taste for the sporting life, as both business and pleasure. Harper and his police chief, Edward Kern, together with a third partner, whom Harper appointed to the police commission, were all on the take from a red-light syndicate. There is good evidence, moreover, that His Honor personally patronized the establishments under his protection. A photograph, in any event, of the mayor, an admiring circle of girls gathered around, was purportedly in the possession of Harrison Gray Otis, which is why Harper appointed Otis's good friend and fellow army general Adna R. Chaffee to the presidency of the board of public works, despite the fact that Otis had opposed Harper in the election. Charged with the construction of the Los Angeles aqueduct, the board of public works exercised primary control over the arrival and distribution of Owens Valley water in Los Angeles; and Otis, who had promoted the aqueduct in the *Times* while quietly buying up property in the San Fernando Valley that would be subdivided and developed once the water arrived, had a more than passing interest in aqueducts and hence in having his good friend General Chaffee at the helm of Public Works.

All of this perturbed the Progressives, none more so than Edwin T. Earl, the millionaire citrus shipper (he invented the refrigerator boxcar) turned newspaper publisher. As owner of the *Los Angeles Evening Express*, Earl was angered that his arch-rival in publishing and detested personal enemy Harrison Gray Otis, opposed to Harper in the election of 1906, now seemed so willing to go along with the Harper administration just as long as it served his land and water interests. In a manner similar to the investigations sponsored by Phelan and Spreckels in San Francisco, Earl, joined by *Express* associate editor Edward Dickson, private detective Paul T. Blair (whom Earl personally hired), and assistant prosecuting attorney Thomas L. Woolwine, began in 1909 to uncover and unravel the skein of payoffs, protection payments, stock fraud, and influence-peddling centered in the mayor's office, the police department, and the board of public works.

The Good Government Group, meanwhile, availing itself of provisions in the charter of 1906, gathered enough signatures to place Mayor Harper's recall on the ballot for 26 March 1909. Harper had further outraged the reformers by placing his police chief, Edward Kern, now resigned, on the board of public works and later dismissing prosecuting attorney Thomas L. Woolwine from the public payroll. The Kern appointment was especially galling. Did Harper intend to bring to the Owens Valley project, they asked themselves, an organized payoff system similar to that already in force among red-light interests? With the recall election drawing closer, however, Harper, confronted privately with the evidence gathered by detective Blair and prosecutor Woolwine, acknowledged defeat. The mayor resigned personally to Earl, a private citizen, on the promise that his numerous shady involvements would not be made public. The fact that Earl was agreeing to suppress evidence of criminal conspiracy does not seem to have bothered anyone. With Harper out of office, former police chief Kern resigned from the public works board. Shortly after, Chief Kern entered the State Hospital for Inebriates. A year later he committed suicide in a hotel room in Texas. Harper remained on in Los Angeles, as careless as ever, filing for bankruptcy in May 1912.

Just as the reformers of San Francisco, after removing Mayor Eugene Schmitz from office in June 1907, installed as mayor an Olympian patriarch, Edward Robeson Taylor—a seventy-year-old physician, lawyer, and poet then serving as the dean of Hastings College of the Law—so did the Los Angeles reformers turn to a similar reconciling father figure after the terrible ordeal of 1909. Appointed by the city council after Harper's resignation, the new mayor of Los Angeles, George Alexander, age seventy, could not have offered a more dramatic contrast to his playboy predecessor. Born (1839) in Scotland and brought to Chicago as a boy of twelve, George Alexander had sold newspapers on the streets of Chicago to help support his immigrant parents as they struggled for a foothold. When government land became available in Iowa in early 1856 the Alexander family moved to a farm, where young George worked equally hard through his teenaged years. The outbreak of the War Between the States found Alexander recently married and starting his own farm. An ardent Unionist, Alexander enlisted and saw fierce combat as a foot soldier at Vicksburg and the Shenandoah campaign. Returning to Iowa after the war, Alexander grew prosperous in the wholesale grain business. Along with thousands of his fellow Iowans, he moved back to Southern California during the boom of the eighties.

Arriving in Los Angeles in 1886, Alexander began a second career as a civil servant. Highly respected for his work as chief deputy recorder and, later, as a key superintendent in the building of new streets for the expanding city, Alexander made the transition from appointive office to elective politics, being elected to the county board of supervisors, which was where he was serving in 1909 when the reformers selected him as their candidate for mayor. Interestingly enough, the young Progressives chose a man of their grandparents' generation to take their movement to city hall. In doing this, they were speaking to that element of nostalgia for a former and better pre-industrial America that was ever at the psychological center of Progressivism. White-haired, chin-whiskered in the style of an earlier generation, given to Lincolnesque black frock coats, a

soldier who had served under Grant and Sheridan, George Alexander emanated competence and Republican rectitude, the best of Iowa translated to
Southern California.

This "wonderful old man" (to quote the Progressive weekly review *California
Outlook*) threw himself with remarkable energy into the work of reform. There
was a flurry of firings and appointments as Alexander cleaned out Harper appointees who had not had the sense or the decency to resign. Alexander rooted
out irregularities in the harbor and aqueduct projects and persuaded the voters
to set up a board of public utilities to regulate rates in an open, fair manner.
Not even the Los Angeles dog pound escaped his reforming notice. The new
mayor also told the new police chief to rid the city of prostitution. As the police
closed in upon previously protected establishments, Pearl Morton and her girls
boarded a train for San Francisco, which after a raft of sensational graft trials
was beginning to grow weary of virtue.

IV

In all these efforts, Mayor Alexander was assisted by the fact that in the election
of 1910 the Progressives, specifically the Lincoln-Roosevelt League under the
presidency of Chester Rowell, had captured political control of the state of California itself. During the legislative session of 1909, the Progressives lobbied
into law an all-important direct primary law. The voters, and not party conventions, now controlled the nomination of candidates. This single stroke ended
the ability of the SP to select candidates through the manipulation of party conventions. Now able to put their own candidates before the voters in primary
and general elections, the gentlemen of the Lincoln-Roosevelt League prepared
for the general election of November 1910. Rowell, Dickson, Stimson, Lissner, Avery, and the others of the inner circle had already chosen their candidate for governor, Hiram Warren Johnson, the forty-three-year-old prosecuting
attorney in the San Francisco graft trials.

A San Francisco lawyer who had never before held political office, Johnson
was thrust into the statewide limelight when he took over as special prosecutor
in the graft trials after chief prosecutor Francis Heney was shot down in the
courtroom by a prospective juror whose prior record as a convicted felon Heney
revealed in the course of cross-examination. While Heney, shot in the head,
hovered between life and death, Johnson brilliantly continued the trials. Now,
two years later, he impressed the Lincoln-Roosevelt League, which he served
as statewide vice-president, as the logical candidate for governor. Traveling up
to San Francisco in January 1910, Rowell, Dickson, and Stimson spent a Sunday evening dinner session in Johnson's home trying to convince him to run.
Johnson resisted. He hated his hometown of Sacramento, for one thing—and
for deeply personal reasons. As an anti-railroad candidate, moreover, he would

have to square off against his own father, Grove Johnson, a prominent pro-railroad Sacramento attorney and state legislator with whom son Hiram had never really gotten along—whom he had fled Sacramento, in fact, to escape. And besides, Francis Heney, now recovered from his head wound, wanted the job with a fierce and obvious ambition. Thrust accidentally into the limelight by Heney's misfortune, Johnson did not wish to seem to be pushing his accidental advantage over Heney even further. Then there was the matter of personal income. Johnson had labored long to build up his legal practice, which he was now being asked to abandon for the uncertainties of politics. She would rather die, Mrs. Johnson joined in, than have her husband run for the governorship.

That following fall, Hiram Johnson, the Progressive Republican candidate for governor of the great state of California, was touring California in an open-topped crimson Locomobile, promising that when he was elected he would "kick the Southern Pacific out of politics in California." Agreeing to run in February (his wife mollified by the promise of a senatorship for him and the brilliance of Washington, D.C., after a term or two in provincial Sacramento), Johnson had won the Republican primary in August and was now facing Theodore Bell, the Democratic nominee, a Napa attorney and former congressman, a Progressive himself in the manner of Woodrow Wilson and running an equally vociferous anti-SP campaign. Johnson and Bell were not so much running against each other, in fact, as running against the SP. Given Bell's record as an anti-railroad candidate (once before, in 1906, Bell had sought the governorship on an anti-SP platform), Hiram Johnson might seem to have entered the race at a disadvantage. But Johnson was conducting a more flamboyant campaign than Bell and had a more disciplined party apparatus, thoroughly under the control of the Lincoln-Roosevelt League. Pulling into town after town up and down California, Johnson would stand in his shirt sleeves in the open Locomobile after a crowd had been attracted (in smaller towns or more out-of-the-way places by the ringing of a cowbell) and let loose a torrent of orchidaceous oratory against the SP. A brilliant trial attorney, Hiram Johnson tapped his deepest powers as an orator when he was on the attack. And no prosecutor could wish for a more compelling defendant than the great SP octopus, now on the run before both the Democratic and the Republican nominees. Johnson's rhetoric, however, surpassed in metaphor and cleansing fire the more stately arguments being leveled by Bell. Even his mentors, Rowell, Stimson, Avery, Dickson, Lissner, and the others, confessed themselves astonished by Johnson's showmanship and energy. He ran one Locomobile into the ground and virtually used up another. Added to this, the infamous "Shame of California" photograph taken at Santa Cruz in 1906, showing Abe Ruef, now a convicted felon, with a congressman, a state supreme court justice, and assorted SP power brokers, was reproduced as a billboard and placed in hundreds of key locations throughout the state.

At the end of it all, Johnson won out over Bell, 177,000 to 155,000 votes. Three and a half years after meeting for dinner in Levy's Cafe in Los Angeles, the young men of the Lincoln-Roosevelt League had successfully seized the municipal government of Los Angeles and the state government in Sacramento. They had placed one of their number in the governor's chair and sent another, former state supreme court justice John D. Works, president of the Good Government League of Los Angeles, to the United States Senate.

Hiram Johnson's first term was a heady time, a Camelot, for the Progressives of California. With their wing of the Republican party in control of the governorship and the legislature, the opportunity existed for what during those exultant and accomplishment-filled years—1910, 1911, 1912, 1913—seemed like the very recreation of the political and social order of California, the state's second founding time. Although the major figures behind the Progressive coup d'état—Rowell, Dickson, Stimson, Lissner, Avery, Haynes—were not themselves in public office, they were constantly in Sacramento, advising Governor Johnson on important staff appointments or this or that piece of legislation, or drawing up briefing papers and memoranda and lobbying legislators. How pleasurable to be at last on the inside, in power, with an emerging state to set on its proper course!

"Give us a square deal for Christ's sake," the chaplain had implored the legislature in its 1911 opening session. Two years later, on 5 April 1913, Charles K. McClatchy, publisher of the *Sacramento Bee*, wrote, "The moneychangers—the legions of Mammon and of Satan—these have been lashed out of the temple of the people." McClatchy was not just referring to such Progressive anti-vice measures as the Red Light Abatement Law passed that year, or the other laws suppressing racetrack betting, gambling, and slot machines. He was referring to the breaking of the political power of the SP by such newly enacted political reforms as the direct primary, the secret Australian ballot, the popular election of United States senators, the nonpartisan election of judges (who previously were so amenable to making pro-railroad decisions), the initiative, the referendum, and the recall, these last three approved by the voters as a constitutional amendment in November 1911. Finally, in 1913, cross-filing was enacted. Candidates could now enter primaries as either Republicans or Democrats, or seek both nominations. For the next forty years, until the repeal of cross-filing, formal political party affiliation, hence party discipline and party machines, meant little in California.

Its political hold on California thrown off through these measures, the railroad itself now came under the regulation of the state it had itself regulated such a short time ago. The Stetson-Eshleman bill, passed in February 1911, empowered the state railroad commission to enforce as well as set fair rates. The following December an all-encompassing Public Utilities Act expanded the commission into an independent, quasi-judicial board with regulatory power

over railroads, gas, electricity, telephones, telegraph, water distribution systems, pipelines, and other common carriers. Also enacted were measures relating to flood control, harbor administration (previously an egregious pork barrel), the standardization of weights and measures, and the reform of water law.
In the field of education, new legislation called for pensions for teachers, free
textbooks for public school children, the establishment of a comprehensive curriculum, including mandatory kindergartens, and the abolition of partisan politics in school board elections. In the industrial field, child labor was severely
curtailed, an eight-hour day and a minimum wage were set for female industrial workers, and in 1913 the pioneering Workmen's Compensation, Insurance, and Safety Act was passed, setting up an Industrial Accident Commission, together with an all-important State Compensation Insurance Fund, which
for the first time removed some of the terrifying uncertainty of loss of work
through sickness or job-related accidents. Also created in the legislative session
of 1913: a Commission on Immigration and Housing, headed by Simon Julius
Lubin, a Harvard-educated Sacramento businessman with a background of settlement work in New England and New York, who threw himself headlong
into the effort to clean up the disgraceful conditions in the agricultural labor
camps of California, providing migrant workers with such elementary facilities
as water, toilets, shower baths, cooking stoves, and schools for their children.

In this last area, social welfare and services, the Progressives introduced reforms which, carried on and expanded over five decades, would eventually put
California among the most social-welfare-oriented states in the country. Two
Progressives, Arthur Judson Pillsbury and Simon Julius Lubin, concentrated their
best administrative and reformist energies in this area. Born in New Hampshire
and raised in Kansas, an attorney-journalist like so many of his colleagues, A.
J. Pillsbury worked for a number of California newspapers after qualifying for
the bar, but his compelling interest was the design and delivery of social programs. Betwen 1904 and 1907 Pillsbury served as executive secretary to the state
board of examiners, the commission with overall responsibility for monitoring
California's hospital, prison, and social welfare facilities. At the behest of Governor George C. Pardee, a pre-Progressive reformer, Pillsbury toured the United
States in the fall of 1905 inspecting over eighty public institutions in an effort
to bring back to California the best social service doctrine and practice. Pillsbury's final report, published in 1906 as *Institutional Life*, served the Progressives as a handbook for social service reform. Historians who see a connection
between Progressivism and the New Deal can find ample corroboration in Pillsbury's pre-liberal vision of government as the primary monitor and principal
deliverer of social programs and welfare services. Among many reforms rec-
ommended, Pillsbury called for the removal of the state board of charities and
corrections from partisan politics. The board, he wrote, deserved the support of
tax dollars but had to be removed from direct political influence if it were to

do its work—which was the continuation and acceleration of reform programs underway since the 1890s.

A review of related documentation corroborates Pillsbury's belief that, at least as far as budgets and facilities were concerned, California had in the 1890s and early 1900s been doing progressively better by its public charges: the deaf, the blind, the feebleminded, the orphaned, the wayward, the imprisoned. Retarded children, for instance, had been entitled to state care since 1885 at the Home for Feeble-Minded Children in Santa Clara County. On 24 November 1891 the home's 119 children were moved by special train to a new facility near Glen Ellen in Sonoma County, north of San Francisco Bay, where they found land-scaped grounds to walk in (beauty, one report read, has a way of soothing the children's spirits), a gymnasium for those with sufficient physical coordination, even a military drill program, complete with cadet uniforms, for the less se-verely handicapped boys. In *Institutional Life*, Pillsbury called on the state to discriminate more closely among its six-thousand-odd juvenile charges. Feeble-minded girls, for instance, often showed a capacity for self-support in laundry work or other forms of domestic occupation. They should, moreover, be pro-tected from sexual exploitation. All children under state care, whether handi-capped or not, deserved corrective medical and dental care—teeth straightened, crossed eyes uncrossed, crooked limbs reset—and a program of vocational train-ing leading, if at all possible, to their being able to support themselves. Pills-bury also argued that the mentally troubled deserved corrective programs which sorted out the criminally disposed from the nonviolently troubled, putting the former in special centers for the criminally insane and the latter into programs modeled upon those of McLean's Hospital, a private institution outside Boston.

By 1910 many of Pillsbury's recommendations had been enacted. New facil-ities were added, many of them in a stately Romanesque or Mission Revival style of architecture, and staffs were expanded. Trained psychiatrists attempted more sophisticated diagnoses than masturbation or sunstroke. Whenever possi-ble, patients were put to work, and new therapies—such as hydrotherapy—were introduced. "With our continuous baths, packs, massage, sprays, electric light and steam cabinets, under the care of graduate nurses," reported Stockton State Hospital superintendent Fred P. Clark in 1910, "the indigent insane receive the same treatment that is accorded the man of means at the most fashionable and expensive health resort."

Establishing a State Commission on Lunacy, Hiram Johnson—himself no stranger to mental torment—put himself personally behind the continued re-form of the state asylums according to Pillsbury's guidelines. Progress in prison reform was slower than in other areas, with the exception of the reform of court procedures and the establishment of a separate juvenile system. The records for San Quentin prison for 1889 reveal that in a population of 1,373 (839 native-born, 534 foreign-born) there were 72 seventeen-year-olds, 7 sixteen-year-olds,

5 fifteen-year-olds, 2 fourteen-year-olds, and a boy of twelve. This mixing of boys with the general prison population, lamented the official report for that year, was a disaster for all concerned. By 1910 San Quentin still housed a fourteen-year-old, a fifteen-year-old, 12 sixteen-year-olds, and 24 seventeen-year-olds, but these were cases which the courts had adjudged unassimilable to either the Preston School of Industry or the Whittier State School, correctional institutions for juveniles, including girls, operating on a cottage residential system with a full program of vocational training. In *Institutional Life* Pillsbury had argued that such juvenile institutions, practicing a blend of discipline and vocational training, could deter 85 percent of juvenile offenders from graduating to adult criminality. Behind this hope lay an awareness that California could not handle the prison population it already possessed. San Quentin, for instance, had 696 cells for 1,900 prisoners in 1910, and Folsom prison had 394 cells for 1,000 inmates. A three-prisoners-to-one-cell ratio, Pillsbury believed, made the prisons of California incapable of rehabilitation. At his urging, Governor Johnson sought funds for new prison construction.

Simon Julius Lubin, meanwhile, the young heir to the Weinstock, Lubin and Company department store established in Sacramento by his father, a Russian Jewish immigrant, was directing the newly established (1913) Commission on Immigration and Housing with passionate brilliance. At Harvard, Lubin had studied philosophy under former Californian Josiah Royce, together with economics. After graduating in 1903 he spent two years in settlement work in South Boston, followed by another two years in a settlement house in the Lower East Side of New York. All of this—the self-confidence that came with education and fortune (not to mention Lubin's commanding physical presence); a dose of Roycean idealism, with its emphasis upon redemptive work for community; a solid grounding in economics, including agricultural economics (an appropriate interest in this San Joaquin Valley man); and four years of exposure to life among the Irish poor of South Boston and the variegated population of the Lower East Side—preeminently fitted Lubin for the task of directing the Progressive effort to bring social services to the rural and inner-city poor of California.

Lubin first began discussions with Governor Johnson concerning the creation of the new Commission on Immigration and Housing in 1912, after learning of the disgraceful conditions endured by migrant workers in the field. In the broad and plenteous fields of California, Lubin discovered, was poverty and squalor equal to that in any Lower East Side tenement: shabby, filth-ridden shacks, no sanitation, no running water, no schools for the children, no medical care, no drinking water in the fields, no prescribed rest periods. It was conditions like these on a hop ranch near the town of Wheatland in Yuba County that gave rise to a riot on 13 August 1913 that left four dead (including the sheriff and district attorney of Yuba) and prompted Johnson to push through

Lubin's recommendation for a statewide assault on rural squalor. Lubin himself drafted the legislation and served as director without compensation for the first ten years of the commission's existence. No detail was too small for Lubin's corrective scrutiny (the foul habit of storing manure against the side of field workers' shacks, for instance), and no constituency too humble. He refused to regard the wandering men of California as a universal criminal class, to be hounded out of one community after another or peremptorily thrown into jails or workhouses on vagrancy charges. Vagrants, hobos, tramps, or homeless men in search of work—Lubin demanded that local authorities make distinctions. With his encouragement, various hostelries, public and privately supported, were established where wandering men could get a meal and clean themselves up so as to be able to follow up leads from the jobs-available list Lubin had each hostelry establish and keep posted. In this way they could avoid the threatened downward slide into vagrancy.

The rights of women also occupied a prominent position among Progressive priorities. 1911, the year of the *California Outlook's* greatest vitality, was the year California admitted women to the vote—just barely. The suffrage movement had a much longer lineage than Progressivism, which it began to align itself with in the early 1900s. California suffrage activist Hester Harland prided herself upon her personal friendship with Susan B. Anthony, seeing in this association a linkage between the suffrage movement in California and the long struggle in the East, led by some of the most impressive American women of the previous generation.

By the early 1900s, however, a new generation of activists was coming to the fore, in California and elsewhere. "Suffrage," wrote Chester Rowell in the *Fresno Morning Republican* on 25 April 1911, "became a serious issue when attractive well-dressed women took it up." However flip, Rowell's point was well taken. In the early years of the twentieth century the upper-middle-class women of California, many of them college-educated, threw themselves into the cause of women's rights with a passion: women such as Elisabeth Thacker Kent, the daughter of a Yale professor and the wife of Progressive congressman William Kent of Marin County. Mrs. Kent chaired the Equal Franchise League of Marin before going to Washington with her husband, where she played a prominent role in lobbying for the 19th Amendment. Another California activist, Maud Younger, fled from the social distractions of San Francisco to work in New York City as a waitress, becoming active in the just-forming Waitresses' Union of that city. Returning to San Francisco, where her father was a wealthy dentist and investor, Younger went to work in a local restaurant and began organizing for equal pay for waitresses. Fair wages, she argued, "do more to keep a girl 'respectable' than all the rescue missions in existence." In 1908 Maud Younger founded the Wage Earners' Equal Suffrage League in an effort to get working women behind the right to vote.

The California suffrage movement had its left-leaning adherents, such as Charlotte Anita Whitney, a graduate of Wellesley College and settlement work in New York, who was a Socialist, and even a right-wing adherent or two, such as novelist Gertrude Atherton (she described her politics as Hamiltonian), whose novel *Julia France and Her Times* (1912) matched up a liberated heroine with a character named Daniel Tay who was a San Francisco–based Progressive politician involved in the reform of California. Most of the suffrage leadership in California was Protestant, Republican, and solidly upper middle class. By 1910 the suffrage movement had aligned itself with the Lincoln-Roosevelt League, promising support in the election of 1910 in return for a constitutional amendment in 1911 giving women the vote.

The campaign the suffrage proponents waged in the months prior to the January 1911 special election included traditional techniques—rallies and speeches, a "Yellow Special" train touring the state (yellow was the suffrage color), and a traveling magic lantern show—together with such innovations as the direct mailing of nearly a million leaflets and brochures, an early example of this increasingly important mode of political advertising. The expected endorsements came in—Fremont Older, David Starr Jordan, Chester Rowell, Lieutenant Governor Albert J. Wallace—and a few unexpected ones, such as those of Jack London and Boss Abraham Ruef. But the suffrage leaders felt betrayed by Governor Hiram Johnson's refusal openly to endorse the amendment, which to his credit he did help get on the ballot. Reading the *Los Angeles Times*'s thundering editorials against suffrage as a threat to family life and, by implication, female chastity, Johnson perhaps knew how evenly divided the voting men of California were on this issue. It passed by a mere 3,587 votes.

The campaign did produce California's first important woman governmental official, Katherine Philips Edson, active in Southern California suffrage circles since 1896 and the dominant presence on the 1911 campaign's statewide steering committee. The wife of a rural Los Angeles County Antelope Valley rancher, Mrs. Edson joined the Hiram Johnson administration in 1912 as a special agent of the state's Bureau of Labor Statistics, where she prepared legislation regarding wages, benefits, and working conditions for women. After more than a decade of work as a state commissioner, an industrial mediator, a Republican party activist (one of eight women on the National Executive Committee), Edson was appointed executive director of the California Division of Industrial Welfare, the first woman to hold a major administrative post in state government.

V

The Asians of California, men or women, did not fare as well. Of all groups in California, including the working classes of San Francisco, the Progressives had the least sympathy for Asians. Far from participating in the general benefits of reform, the Asians of California experienced during the Progressive era their worst ordeal before the internments of 1941. The Progressives generally believed that Asians could never be successfully integrated into white American society. They also feared the growing military might of Japan. There were exceptions, of course. David Starr Jordan knew and respected Japanese culture from his travels there and fostered the coming of Japanese exchange students to Stanford. Having lived in Japan briefly after graduation from Berkeley, Edward Dickson never joined in the anti-Asian attitudes of his fellow Progressives, which could reach the intensity of the following editorial, taken from the Progressive *California Weekly.* "Our legislature," the editorial ran, "should limit Mongolian ownership of soil to a space four feet by six. A white population and a brown population, regardless of nationality or ideals, can never occupy the same soil together with advantage to either. Let us dwell apart and in amity, for we cannot dwell together that way."

Progressives such as James D. Phelan and Chester Rowell—each proponents of a strong Pacific Fleet—were convinced that Japan would one day launch an attack against the United States. The Japanese of California, they believed, constituted a growing fifth column for that inevitable invasion day. Homer Lea— a small, misshapen Los Angeleno, formerly lieutenant general in the Imperial Chinese Army and a founding member of the Lincoln-Roosevelt League—was the prophet and chief articulator of this ambivalent Asian awareness among the Progressives, with its mixture of admiration and fear. Deformed, plagued by headaches and eyestrain, nevertheless Lea by sheer force of will led a relatively normal life among his friends at Los Angeles High School, even accompanying them into the San Bernardino Mountains on rugged camping treks. He also devoured books on military history and strategy, and constructed a miniature battleground in his backyard, where he reenacted the great battles of history with scholarly precision, using standard military maps and models. Lea had dreams of one day leading an assault on a great fortress.

Entering Stanford University in 1896, he fell in with a secret group of right-wing pro-imperial Chinese students, the P. Wong Wui Society, dedicated to the overthrow of the dowager empress and the restoration of the rights of the boy emperor. Returning to Los Angeles after graduation, Lea—with the assistance of Ansel O'Banion, formerly sergeant in the Fourth U.S. Cavalry—formed a military company of pro-emperor Chinese cadets, whom he drilled and took on maneuvers and with whom he marched in the Tournament of Roses Parade. Shortly after, the Boxer Rebellion erupted and Homer Lea left for China, where (so he claimed—and there is little reason to doubt him) he was commissioned lieutenant general in the forces fighting to restore the young emperor. Lea and his fellow conspirators, including cadets from his own Los Angeles company, planned to kidnap the dowager empress, Tsi An, and place her stepson, Hong Hsui, on the imperial throne. During the relief of the besieged legation at Peking, Lea fought alongside another Los Angeles–based general, Adna Chaffee. With the defeat of his cause, Lea fled to Japan. There he encountered a martial society that at once attracted and frightened him. The Japanese army and navy, he was convinced, would one day be used against the United States.

Homer Lea's Asian attitudes, his obsession with the destined warfare between the United States and Japan, with California as the chief prize, was shared on a more prosaic level by most Progressives. In time, this phobia became a monstrous self-fulfilling prophecy that drove Japan into a state of paranoia regarding American intentions in the Pacific, and also engendered Japanese overconfidence regarding American vulnerability to attack. For the time being, however, this Asian phobia surfaced in the form of a Progressive legislative assault against Japanese immigrants. With Governor Johnson's encouragement, Francis J. Heney joined with another Progressive, Ulysses S. Webb, state attorney general, to prepare legislation that effectively barred some forty-five thousand Japanese non-citizen immigrants from owning land in California. The Japanese government protested so furiously to President Woodrow Wilson that he sent Secretary of State William Jennings Bryan out to Sacramento to lobby—in vain, as it turned out—against the measure. Once before, in 1906, Washington had been forced to deal directly with California because of Japanese protests: when the San Francisco school board ordered the city's ninety-three Japanese pupils to attend the Chinese public school, forbidding them to attend classes alongside whites. Rebuked by the Japanese government for this affront, President Roosevelt had been forced to invite Mayor Schmitz and the school board back to Washington to hammer out a face-saving compromise. Now the Alien Land Law, as it was called, was the latest in a series of restrictive measures, local and statewide, designed to exclude Asians from entering the mainstream of California life.

It was also, however, a contest of wills between Hiram Johnson and the man who had kept him from the vice-presidency, Woodrow Wilson. A relatively unknown attorney in 1907, governor of California by 1910, Johnson had in 1912 run alongside former president Theodore Roosevelt on a national Progressive ticket, the Bull Moose, and for the Progressives of California this precipitous entrance into the national limelight by their standard-bearer, and by themselves as well, had been a heady experience, leading to the formation of an autonomous California Progressive party. Californians held Theodore Roosevelt in special regard. Roosevelt's exuberant synthesis of brains and brawn, outdoorsiness and bookishness, spoke directly to the Californians' conception of themselves as Americans possessed at once of a special relationship to nature and the outdoors, and to civility. Charles Fletcher Lummis had been fanning the flames of this Roosevelt cult ever since the 1890s. TR had been a year ahead of Lummis at Harvard, where they had had a nodding acquaintance, based on

Roosevelt's approval of the way that freshman Lummis had stood up to a hazing by sophomores. Lummis saw his own experience reflected in TR's: a sickly Harvard man redeemed by the vigorous life of the West. "I owe everything to the West!" Roosevelt once exulted to Lummis. "It made me! I found myself there!" In each detail of Roosevelt's life and personality—his reforming conservativism, his intellectuality, his touch of Tory bohemianism, his great gusto and capacity for physical experience, his synthesis of Harvard and the West— Lummis beheld guidelines for the Californian as an emerging American type. Throughout 1897 and 1898 Lummis lobbied ceaselessly to have Roosevelt appointed to the presidency of the University of California, and when Roosevelt, having gone on to even bigger things, invited Lummis to lunch at the White House in December 1901 to discuss conservation and the Indian question, Don Carlos was ecstatic.

For the young Progressives of California—who, after all, had named their league in his and Abraham Lincoln's honor—Theodore Roosevelt embodied all that they aspired to be and to do. Franklin Lane admired Roosevelt so much that he ran for governor of California in 1902 as a Roosevelt Democrat. When Lane, then city attorney of San Francisco, appeared before the president and the Congress to argue for San Francisco's Hetch Hetchy water supply project, Roosevelt was so impressed with the young San Franciscan that he offered Lane the next available seat on the Interstate Commerce Commission. Appointed in 1905, Lane served eight years before becoming Wilson's secretary of the interior.

During the gubernatorial campaign of 1910, the former president wrote a letter to his son Theodore Roosevelt, Jr., then living in San Francisco, warmly endorsing Hiram Johnson's candidacy. The Progressives distributed a million reprints. Elected governor but not yet inaugurated, Johnson went east on a pilgrimage to Roosevelt at Oyster Bay, wishing to make perfectly clear to everyone the actual as well as symbolic connection between California Progressivism and the New Nationalism being advocated by Roosevelt, with its regulatory programs, and subtly rightward intent. Roosevelt, in turn, welcomed the support coming from the Pacific Coast. Generously, he said that the not-yet-inaugurated Johnson was a man of presidential timber. Johnson returned to Sacramento dreaming of one day attaining the presidency. More and more, he cast himself in a Rooseveltean mold, appropriating TR's podium gestures and saying "Bully!" whenever appropriate. In the spring of 1911 Roosevelt spent ten days visiting his son in San Francisco. Governor Johnson and the former president, who was anxious to be president once again, lost no opportunity to compliment each other in public. "California," Roosevelt said at one point, "has come mighty close to realizing my governmental ideals." By the time the Republican convention of 1912 drew near, it was assumed that Roosevelt would replace William Howard Taft on the ticket and that Hiram Johnson of California would most likely be TR's running mate.

So then: by late 1911, just four short years after their organizing dinner at Levy's Cafe, the inner core of the California Progressive leadership—Johnson, Rowell, Stimson, Lissner, Neylan, and the others—already in control of California, were positioning themselves to unseat an incumbent president, seize control of the national Republican party and transform it into a party of reform, then march on to reform the nation itself under the reelected Teddy Roosevelt and his good friend Hiram Johnson of California. The California Progressives, in fact, must be given major credit for persuading Roosevelt to attempt to unseat Taft, whom TR had put into the presidency in the first place. When that failed, when the Chicago convention renominated Taft on 22 June 1911, the California delegation was among the first to walk out and call for a separate Progressive ticket. Had the Progressives captured the national Republican party, a major realignment might have occurred in American politics. As it was, Progressivism was doomed to the inevitable failure awaiting third parties in America. Roosevelt and Johnson, nominated on 5 August 1912 at a hastily called Progressive Convention in Chicago, campaigned brilliantly on a "Hands across the Continent" ticket. Johnson stumped the United States as flamboyantly as he had California two years earlier, making more than five hundred speeches during the Bull Moose campaign. But when it was all over, only California, Washington, South Dakota, Michigan, and Pennsylvania voted Progressive, enough to keep Taft from a second term and put Woodrow Wilson into the White House with a landslide of 435 electoral college votes.

Back in California, the Progressives wrenched themselves once and for all out of regular party alignment. Having seized control of the Republican party apparatus through a successful primary, they kept Taft's name off the ballot entirely. The president of the United States was forced to campaign in California as a write-in candidate. Such unapologetically hardball politics isolated the Progressives once and for all from the Republican party regulars. This arrogant affront could never be forgiven. California Progressives thus drove a cleavage between themselves and the regular Republican conservatives who had lent them some measure of support. To complete this suicidal scenario, the Progressives withdrew from the Republican party entirely, regrouping themselves on 5 December 1913 as the California State Progressive party. Edward Dickson, Marshal Stimson, Senator John D. Works, and a few others opposed the move. Why surrender a party apparatus they had fought so long to seize control of? they asked. But the voices of Chester Rowell and the others favoring a separate party predominated. With the formation of the Progressive party, the ousted oligarchs of the right marched back into the inner Republican citadel, delighted by this unexpected return to power. With the collapse of the California

State Progressive party a few years later, the oligarchs found themselves once again in control of California.

VI

Angry, distrustful to the point of paranoia, bitter regarding his past, resentful of the intellectuals and college boys who had put him into power, Hiram Johnson was hardly the man to keep California Progressivism on a steady course. Eventually he quarreled with nearly everybody, and the movement, partly because of this, collapsed. On the surface of things the Sacramento-reared Johnson would seem to have enjoyed a model Progressive upbringing: born of Protestant stock, brought up in a town of just the right size (24,640 in 1870), publicly educated through Sacramento High School and the University of California, which he left in his junior year to marry his high school sweetheart and study for the bar as a law clerk in his father's firm. Lincoln Steffens, another California Progressive of sorts, would later write of an outwardly similar Sacramento upbringing in the idyllic "A Boy on Horseback" sequence of his *Autobiography*.

In reality, Johnson's home life was a torment. He loathed his domineering father, for one thing. Grove Laurence Johnson arrived in California in 1863, running ahead of both the Civil War and a minor fraud charge in Syracuse, New York. Prospering as a Sacramento attorney, the elder Johnson first sought political office as a Democrat. Failing this, he turned Republican, winning election to the state assembly, the state senate, and the U.S. House of Representatives. In season and out, Grove Johnson defended the Southern Pacific. As a member of the House Committee on Pacific Railroads in 1896, he favored the effort to have the SP debt refinanced for another eighty-five years. William Randolph Hearst of the *San Francisco Examiner* considered Grove Johnson one of the railroad's most important point men in Washington. Largely because of Hearst, Johnson went down to defeat in his bid for a second term in Congress, but returned shortly after to the state senate.

As a father, Grove Johnson—a forceful, often ornery man, a political infighter with an instinct for the jugular—made constant warfare against his two sons, Hiram and Albert, both of whom followed their father in the law. Hiram got angry. Albert got drunk. Loathing their father, both brothers joined the anti-railroad movement with a special vengeance, and struggled with their father for political control of Sacramento. As reform city attorney of Sacramento, Hiram openly and bitterly opposed his father the state senator at every possible turn. Grove Johnson, in turn, liked to say that he had two sons, "one, Hiram, full of egotism, and the other, Albert, full of booze." In 1902, Hiram and Albert, wearying of a series of brutal personal and political battles with their father, left Sacramento and opened a law office in San Francisco. Five years later Albert's liver gave out, and he died. When Hiram returned triumphantly to Sacramento as governor in 1910, his father resigned from the legislature.

By this time, however, anger and resentment had become a way of life for Hiram Johnson. Deformed by his difficulties with his father, Hiram Johnson nurtured another private, irreconcilable resentment: the fact that he had had to leave the university in his junior year to marry his two-and-a-half-months'-pregnant girlfriend, a student at Mills College in Oakland named Minerva (Minnie) Lucretia McNeal, the daughter of a prosperous Sacramento contractor. In later years Governor and then Senator Johnson, at least twice a serious contender for the presidency, put it about that he had talked Minnie into an early marriage before she could leave for voice training with Adelina Patti in Europe. Its gesture toward refinement gives the story unintended pathos. For the rest of their life together, Minnie Johnson guarded ferociously the respectability so terribly endangered by her illicit pregnancy. Hiram, in turn, was under a special burden of obligation to his wife, whose reputation he had endangered, but he was also resentful toward her for the fact that he was forced at age nineteen to give up his plans to attend college and law school in exchange for a job as a court reporter while studying law in his father's office. All this conflict might very well make a man dyspeptic as the years went on. Hiram Johnson developed a fiery temper; he was twice fined for punching opposing counsel in court. Believing that he lacked sufficient education, he became vain to the point of egomania in compensation. Usually he could carry the pose off, for he was possessed of quick intuition and electric rhetoric, albeit somewhat devoid of a capacity for abstract ideas. Nervous, moody, irritable, he had few, if any, male friends. In later years, the suppressed volcano within him erupted in a litany of physical ailments: headache, upset stomach, swollen colon, flatulence, insomnia, dizziness, depression, and general irritability, the ailments of a man whose guts are torn by an anger that almost knows no name. Throughout 1921, after the collapse of his second presidential bid, he suffered from suicidal fantasies.

Meanwhile, Hiram Johnson quarreled. First of all, he quarreled with Francis J. Heney, the chief prosecutor in the San Francisco graft trials who had given him his start in public life; and since Heney himself had a terrible temper (expelled from the University of California for brawling, later a fighter and a drinker), Heney fought back. Johnson, after all, had from Heney's point of view stolen the Lincoln-Roosevelt gubernatorial nomination from him in 1909, when the Progressives finally decided that the hard-drinking Irish-German Catholic Heney, whom they had first considered backing, was, with his terrible temper and ambiguous Arizona record, not exactly their sort of fellow. Four years later, when Heney wished to run for the United States Senate, Johnson wanted the nomination for himself. (Remember, Minnie Johnson hated Sacramento.) When

Heney prevailed, however, forcing Johnson into four more years as governor, the disappointed Johnson gave his rival only tepid support, and the Democratic nominee, James Duval Phelan, went on to Washington. Twice thwarted by Johnson in his attempts at high office, Heney hated Johnson, who returned the sentiment. The Heney-Johnson rivalry constituted an early disruption of Progressive solidarity. There were soon to be others.

Hiram Johnson was not, after all, a Progressive reformer by temperament or deep conviction. The Progressives were college men, intellectuals, while he was a man of action (so he believed) schooled by experience. Riding the wave of reform sentiment to the 1909 Progressive nomination, Johnson soon decided that the Lincoln-Roosevelt men, with their fifty candidates in the field, were also political amateurs with little sense of organization, and so he organized his gubernatorial campaign as a semi-independent enterprise. Installed in the governorship, he immediately put himself at a distance from the men who had given him his chance. Relishing power, Johnson began building his own machine, and as the Lincoln-Roosevelt men began to realize that they had installed a canny politician in Sacramento, they grew disenchanted. By 1913 Progressive politics in California had become a comic opera of quarrels, intrigues, and double cross. In the North, Heney was joined in anti-Johnson feelings by William Kent, opposed to Johnson because of the Alien Land Law, which Kent despised, and because Johnson refused to back the aristocratic Marinite for re-election to Congress. Fremont Older was angry because Johnson would not parole from San Quentin the convicted Abraham Ruef, whom Older now regarded as more a victim than a victimizer. In Los Angeles, Edward Dickson, who had never really liked Johnson in the first place, and Edwin Earl, publisher of the *Express*, quarreled with Johnson because the governor preferred to run Southern California through Chester Rowell and Meyer Lissner. After 1917 Johnson and Dickson ceased speaking to each other. Earlier, Dickson and Lissner, two of the original founders of the Lincoln-Roosevelt League, had also stopped speaking to each other because Marshal Stimson and Russ Avery had formed a clique with Lissner to launch themselves independently into Los Angeles politics. In 1919, when Johnson, now a United States senator, campaigned vociferously against American entrance into the League of Nations, even the faithful Chester Rowell, ever so patient over the years with Johnson's baiting anti-intellectualism, repudiated his chief, toward whom he had in fact always been ambivalent. Rowell joined Stimson and others in backing Johnson's greatest rival, Herbert Hoover, for the presidency.

While all this intrigue was underway throughout the state, San Francisco, left and right, capital and labor, was growing weary with its fling with virtue. The very event which thrust Hiram J. Johnson into the limelight—the attempted courtroom assassination of special prosecutor Francis Heney on 13 November 1907—had shrouded the entire graft investigation in an ambience of conspiracy that eventually cast doubt upon the proceedings. It was shocking enough for San Franciscans to have Heney shot down in an open courtroom by Morris Haas, an ex-convict; but then, as Heney lay between life and death, Haas put a bullet into his head in his jail cell, compounding the mystery. Who smuggled the pistol in to him? San Franciscans asked. Was Haas eliminated by the police, as some believed, because he knew too much about departmental corruption? When the police chief of San Francisco himself disappeared that November—mysteriously lost overboard from the police launch while crossing San Francisco Bay on a densely foggy night—San Franciscans were even more perturbed. Who was next? they asked. What sinister network controlled San Francisco?

At this point a recovered Heney made a dramatic announcement. Previously, he stated, he had gone after the bribe-takers—the petty politicians, the available local bureaucrats; henceforth he would prosecute the bribe-givers as well. The bribe-givers, unfortunately, included many prominent San Franciscans, and as such pillars of the community as John Martin, Eugene De Sabla, and Frank Drumm, all directors of Pacific Gas and Electric, came under indictment for slipping Boss Ruef envelopes of cash in exchange for favorable utility rates, a shocked silence began to pervade the marble corridors of the Pacific Union Club on Nob Hill. It was one thing to indict a supervisor or two or a labor official, or to try to remove a mayor (a former orchestra leader, after all) for taking a bribe from a French restaurant. It was another matter entirely to reach into the establishment and make common criminals of the city's leading citizens. Rudolph Spreckels, the financial underwriter of the graft investigations, was asked to resign from the Pacific Union Club, and down the hill at the Bohemian Club the members silently drifted away when Fremont Older stepped up to the bar. Shocked by the hostility of former friends, Older resigned from his club, and he and his beautiful wife, once at the very center of the city's fashionable set, found themselves cut from invitation lists. The indictment of United Rail Company president Patrick Calhoun on charges of bribery offered the final provocation. San Francisco found itself on the verge of open class warfare.

A series of strikes intensified the class-against-class atmosphere. Laundry workers went out in April, the metal trades in May. On 5 May 1907 the car men's union walked out on Patrick Calhoun's United Railroads, demanding wage increases and an eight-hour day. The walkout soon flared up into one of the bitterest and most violent strikes in Pacific Coast history. Fremont Older believed that Calhoun deliberately provoked the strike in order to distract San Franciscans from the graft investigations in general and his own indictment in particular, and to galvanize the establishment to look to its self-defense. If so, then Calhoun's plan worked brilliantly. The striking car men were provoked into violence by the importation of twelve hundred strikebreakers from outside the state. There were riots and barricades, and six deaths from gunshot wounds, and two hundred and fifty serious injuries. Throughout it all, Calhoun, surrounded by armed bodyguards, rode around San Francisco in an open automobile like a tsarist police commissioner suppressing Bolsheviks. To his own, Calhoun seemed a champion of the capitalist system, a true grandson of the Great Nullifier Calhoun, fighting as had his forebear on the barricades for the master class. To the strikers Calhoun epitomized the insufferable arrogance of ownership. To the reformers, he seemed a man willing to provoke civil insurrection in order to destroy the graft investigations and thus avoid a jail sentence. Calhoun suppressed the strike, and he also succeeded in turning the oligarchs totally against the graft trials, convincing them to see in the investigations an attack on private property. In time he beat his indictment, getting a hung jury after a protracted three-year court case. But before the final non-verdict was in, the prospect of actually going to the penitentiary took hold of Calhoun, so Fremont Older believed, and he grew desperate. Surrounding himself with armed guards, he employed a force of private detectives to seek out compromising material on Phelan, Spreckels, Heney, Older, and the other reformers, and once—again according to Older—he actually kidnapped Older off the streets of San Francisco, spiriting him by train to Santa Barbara. Only a last-minute failure of nerve by a hired assassin, Older claimed, saved him from summary execution.

By 1909 the oligarchy had had enough. When Heney, backed by Phelan and Spreckels, ran for district attorney, Calhoun's friends persuaded Charles Frickert, an accommodating former football star from Stanford, to run against him. Weary of the turmoil—the courtroom histrionics, the disappearence of the police chief, the bloody strike, the strained labor-management relations—and anxious to get on with the business of rebuilding San Francisco after the devastating earthquake and fire of April 1906, the voters ushered in Frickert, who, once in office, quashed the remaining indictments. The new mayor, moreover, James "Sunny Jim" Rolph, elected on a united Union Labor and Republican ticket, was just the sort of reconciling figure everyone wanted. A self-made millionaire, a member of the Pacific Union Club who lived in the working-class-dominated Mission District (the Brooklyn of San Francisco), Rolph had excellent connections with both camps. For the next twenty years, the genial, debonair Sunny Jim—resplendent in cutaway coat, striped pants, and Hamilton collar, a pearl stickpin in his cravat, a fresh boutonniere in his lapel—presided harmoniously over a city that had long since grown bone weary of the deeply divisive effort to pursue virtue.

Down in Los Angeles, the reformers were soon to experience a similar reversal. Fiercely believing, as ever, in charter reform, they put a Progressive-inspired charter before the voters in December 1912, calling for the establishment of a citizen commission system of government. It was defeated, and even more disastrously, the very capstone of Progressive reform, the referendum, was used by the opposition to call for a new municipal election in June 1913, thus effectively recalling the reform administration of Mayor George Alexander. As in the case of the San Francisco reformers, the Alexander group had become caught in the cross fire between left and right—precisely the sort of class warfare which the Progressives dreaded as most destructive to the reform cause. "When the spectre of class rule is raised," Chester Rowell lamented, "then all questions of truth, right, and policy disappear, and the contest is no longer over what shall be the government but wholly who shall be it."

The Socialists of Los Angeles, for one thing, still believed that they were the best candidates to be the government, and a surprisingly large number of Los Angeles voters agreed. In their first municipal victory, the 1909 election of George Alexander, the Progressives had encountered the strength of Los Angeles Socialism. For all his momentum, Progressive candidate Alexander defeated the Socialist candidate Fred Wheeler by a mere 1,678 votes. In the years that followed, the Progressives proved unable, or unwilling, to build a municipal machine, while the Socialists continued to consolidate their strength. Alexander's second Socialist challenger, attorney Job Harriman, showed every sign of becoming mayor of Los Angeles in 1910 until the dynamiting of the *Times* that October, followed by the confession of the McNamara brothers, fatally hurt the Socialist cause; otherwise, Los Angeles might very well have gone Socialist. Deeply shaken by the bombing, in which twenty workers had died, Alexander and the Progressives were forced to make an alliance with the right in order to win their second election. Both left and right, however, despised the Goo-Goos of the Good Government Group and the rest of the Progressive apparatus. The Socialist-oriented workers of Los Angeles, already indifferent to what they considered an anti-labor, anti-foreign, nativist upper-middle-class reform movement, grew even more hostile after their cause had been disgraced by the dynamiting of the *Times* by labor activists; the oligarchs, led by *Times* publisher Harrison Gray Otis, were equally contemptuous. The fact that Hiram Johnson had publicly excoriated Otis in a characteristic outburst of Johnsonian choler did not help matters either, nor did the fact that Otis loathed his publishing rival Edwin T. Earl of the *Express*, a major power in the Lincoln-Roosevelt League. The Progressives, for their part, although they feared Socialism more, felt totally ill at ease in their enforced alliance with the very oligarchy they had set out in 1907 to destroy. Caught thus between the still strong Socialists and the ever strong Los Angeles Merchants and Manufacturers Association, the Progressives possessed an uneasy hold on Los Angeles government. What Chester Rowell called "the menace of class rule" was dramatically reasserting itself.

Midway through Alexander's second term, Los Angeles city prosecutor Guy Eddie—a vigorous warrior against vice, gambling, and illegal liquor sales, a closer of salacious cabaret and vaudeville shows, and a leader in the Good Government Group—was himself arrested on a scandalous morals charge. Aside from the embarrassment involved, the Progressives were left without a successor to the aging Alexander. Desperate, they tried to convince city engineer William Mulholland, the popular head of the Los Angeles aqueduct project, to run, but the conservatives in the Progressive alliance insisted upon John W. Schenk, an attorney with close ties to Otis and the oligarchs. With Mulholland as their standard-bearer, the Progressives might have remained in power through the decade, given the fact that they had at least a working agreement with the Republican oligarchs and the conservative Democrats. (What they could have accomplished in such a compromising alliance, however, is another matter.) As it was, the Socialists and the more labor-oriented Democrats lined up solidly behind police judge Harry H. Rose, who ran on an explicitly anti-Progressive ticket. Rose attacked Meyer Lissner by name and called candidate Schenk a stooge of the Goo-Goos. Thoroughly compromised in their reluctant alliance with Otis, outmaneuvered and outnumbered by the Socialist-Democratic coalition, the Progressives went down to defeat in 1913 with candidate Schenk.

In six short years the Progressives had won and lost Los Angeles. A dispirited Russ Avery said that he was finished with politics for good. Meyer Lissner, the object of some nasty anti-Semitic attacks during the campaign, took his wife on a long trip to Europe. Upon their return, the Lissners moved to Pasadena, where they devoted their energies to ballroom dancing at the Hotel Maryland.

Between the Los Angeles defeat of 1913 and the presidential election of 1916 the Progressives of California lost their momentum as an organized political force. In the national elections of 1914 Progressive candidates lost all across the United States, including California senatorial candidate Francis J. Heney. Reelected to a second term as governor, Hiram Johnson proved a notable exception. As governor, Johnson nominally presided over the last reasonably functional independent Progressive state party in the country, but it was a party severely weakened by its Los Angeles defeat, its defeat in the Senate race, and its failed effort to persuade voters to pass a minimum wage law for working women. Some Lincoln-Roosevelt men, moreover, found themselves disenchanted by their titular leader Theodore Roosevelt's bellicose turn to the right after war broke out in Europe. Others, correctly sensing the conservative drift of the nation at large, were quietly drifting back to the regular Republican party.

The regular Republicans, however, were not overly eager to welcome the Progressives back into the fold. When the Progressives bolted in 1913 to form their own party, the ancien régime headed by William H. Crocker of San Francisco reestablished its hold on the Republican machinery, putting trusted attorney Francis V. Keesling in as state chairman. Neither Crocker, nor the SP nor Keesling, nor any of their sort for that matter, was now willing in 1916 to hand the regular Republican party back to Hiram Johnson and his friends, who had driven them from power in 1910. A titanic struggle for party power ensued between Johnson and the re-Republicanizing Progressives, on the one hand, and the old guard on the other, a quarrel which cost Charles Evans Hughes the presidency of the United States.

Somewhat out of touch with the realities of American politics, much less the California scene, after six years on the Supreme Court, Hughes was scheduled to swing through California between 17 and 22 August in his campaign against the severely embattled incumbent, Woodrow Wilson. Before his California visit, Chester Rowell, then a Republican national committeeman, wrote Hughes a long letter describing the efforts of the old guard Republicans to exclude the Progressives from the party. Rowell advised Hughes to associate with both Republican factions on his swing through California. He also asked Hughes to endorse Hiram Johnson's candidacy for the United States Senate. Governor Johnson, Rowell wrote, had already come out for Hughes. Hughes never did endorse Johnson, however, on the grounds that Johnson was running as a Progressive and not a regular Republican. In the course of his California visit, moreover, he associated himself exclusively with the Crocker-Keesling faction. "I come," Hughes told a San Francisco audience, "as the spokesman of a re-united Republican party, to talk to you of national issues. With local conditions I have no concern." At a large rally held in the newly completed Civic Auditorium in San Francisco, Hughes, passing over Governor Hiram Johnson, saluted William Henry Crocker as "San Francisco's favorite son." The next day Hughes appeared at a Commonwealth Club luncheon served by non-union waiters—this in the midst of a waiters' strike—despite the advice of some Republicans that he avoid the event. This Hughes refused to do, saying that it would show a lack of courage on his part. To complete this triduum of disaster, Hughes found himself in the Hotel Virginia in Long Beach the following evening, a mere four floors away from Hiram Johnson, who was en route between campaign appearances in Bakersfield and Redlands. Hughes's escorts, Crocker-Keesling men, did not inform the candidate of Governor Johnson's presence. Johnson, for his part, did not wish to humiliate himself by trying to penetrate the cordon sanitaire around the candidate. And so word went out that Charles Evans Hughes had snubbed the governor of California. This, together with his public praise of Crocker and the strike-breaking Commonwealth Club luncheon, fixed an image of Hughes as an impossibly ultramontane Easterner, rather contemptuous of California in general and California Progressive Republicans in particular.

Compounding Hughes's problems, Progressives won a number of top positions in the Republican party the following September. With an aggrieved Hiram Johnson's approval (and who could ever be more bitterly aggrieved than Hiram Johnson?) these Progressive Republicans, now back in regular party power, did as little as possible for the national nominee. In the November election President Woodrow Wilson won California, the swing state in the election. The night of the election, Hughes had gone to bed thinking that he would be president, only to awake to the shocking news of the California returns. Hughes later said of the Hotel Virginia incident, "If I had known that Johnson was in that hotel, I would have seen him if I had been obliged to kick the door down."

Loving revenge almost for its own sake, Hiram Johnson had taken colossal revenge on Charles Evans Hughes for the withheld endorsement, the praise of Crocker in San Francisco, the supposed snub in Long Beach. For offending Hiram Johnson, Hughes forfeited the greatest political prize the Republic has to offer. And yet Hiram Johnson, now heading for Washington and the United States Senate, was alone as never before. At a dinner held in the Palace Hotel in San Francisco on 8 July 1916, with Johnson himself presiding, the Progressive party of California ceremonially disestablished itself. Go back to being Republicans or Democrats, Johnson urged the audience of Progressive faithful; Progressivism is no longer an independent party, though it remains a strong influence in California and the nation. Johnson went to the Senate as a Republican—but also as the man who had caused the defeat of Charles Evans Hughes. Johnson trusted no one, and there were fewer and fewer who trusted him. Twenty-eight years in the Senate rendered Hiram Johnson a solitary, inaccessible figure, an anachronism in the frock coat and high celluloid collar of an earlier day—the days of the Progressives.

VII

Their party disbanded, their influence absorbed into regular party structures, the Progressives found themselves with more time on their hands than in their days of power and office. Many used this new freedom as an opportunity to prosper in the private sector. By background and temperament most Progressives were aspiring capitalists, watching their investments, joining the best clubs. The grandfather of the movement in Southern California, after all, Dr. John R. Haynes, was as passionate about real estate as he was about direct democracy. James Duval Phelan, paterfamilias of the movement in the North, was, as one critic phrased it, jealous of every nickel not his own. During the gubernatorial campaign of 1909, Hiram Johnson attacked the SP not in the name of anti-capitalist radical sentiment, but because the SP stranglehold on California was preventing the large landowners of California and the corporations from their proper growth and profits. It was the haves, not the have-nots, whom Johnson invited to kick the SP out of California politics. For the young men involved, moreover, Progressivism could be made to pay: not as directly as it did for Edwin Markham, perhaps, who made $250,000 off "The Man with a Hoe" (most of it squandered in bad investments), but as an enlargement of experience and connections, an apprenticeship in power that translated directly into the skills necessary for a business career. Precisely because he was so successful as an officeholder, Franklin K. Lane proved the great exception. After more than two decades in public office, Lane was forced by near bankruptcy to resign as secretary of the interior and accept a position in private industry. Friends had to lend him the money to pay his family's train fare back to the West Coast.

Others did not make the same mistake. Made confident by the role he was playing in shaping events as a journalist, Edward A. Dickson used his Progressive momentum to make the transition from the ranks of employees to the ownership class. In 1919 Dickson and a partner acquired the *Los Angeles Express*, whose circulation had been tripled by the Progressive excitement, and built it into a successful fifteen-newspaper chain. In 1931 Dickson sold out, to his great profit, then proceeded to build a second fortune as the president of a savings and loan association. John Francis Neylan also began life as a reporter and ended up a millionaire, thanks in great part to his early involvement in politics and government. Neylan was a twenty-four-year-old reporter on Fremont Older's *Bulletin* when Hiram Johnson, impressed by Neylan's investigative skills, invited the young New York City–born Seton Hall graduate up to Sacramento to direct the newly created California Board of Control, a fiscal watchdog agency with wide-ranging authority. When Neylan took over the finances of the state in 1911, California was a quarter of a million dollars in debt. Six years later, when Neylan left his post to begin a legal and business career in San Francisco, the state had a $4.5 million surplus. His management skills sharpened, Neylan prospered as an attorney and sometime editor for the Hearst Corporation, the president of a land and oil company, and a canny investor—while continuing to agitate for Progressive causes, especially public works projects, as an influential private citizen.

Appointive office, frequently connected with public works and education, kept many Progressives publicly involved long after their movement had spent itself as a force, which was one reason why Herbert Hoover, a preeminently successful appointive official from the private sector, took up the leadership of the California Progressives in the 1920s after Hiram Johnson had withdrawn into dyspeptic solitude. Appointive office, for one thing, bypassed the electorate, which had a way of rejecting Progressive candidates, with the exception, of course, of the *annus mirabilis* of 1909. Defeated in a 1901 campaign for mayor of Fresno and a 1914 campaign for the United States Senate, Chester Rowell exercised his authority as a Republican party official and newspaper columnist. Defeated in 1902 for governor of California and in 1903 for mayor of San Francisco, Franklin K. Lane went on to Washington as an appointed member of the newly created Interstate Commerce Commission under Roosevelt before being appointed secretary of the interior by Wilson. Dickson and Lissner gave a lifetime of appointive service on Los Angeles boards ranging from public utilities to the 1932 Olympic Games. As appointed officials, removed from the immediate sanctions of the electorate, Progressives could more easily give vent to their conception of government as a public trust almost beyond politics, a steward-ship of high-mindedness and efficiency in the public interest. For this reason, service connected with the University of California and public works became Progressive specialties. Such Progressives as Phelan, Rowells, Haynes, Lubin, Earl, Neylan, and Dickson all served as regents of the University of California during the university's formative years. Empowered by sixteen-year appoint-ments, these Progressive regents guided the evolution of the University of Cal-ifornia according to a mutually held Progressive vision of excellence, effi-ciency, and public service. The university was their Progressive dream come true, their vision of elite high-mindedness in the public interest translated into buildings and libraries, faculty and students, research and teaching programs. Appointed regents as young men at the height of the Progressive era, Rowell, Neylan, and Dickson served well into the 1940s and 1950s (Dickson alone served forty-three years as regent), providing a Progressive continuity that became, in effect, the formative philosophy of the university. Finding a haven at the Uni-versity of California, the Progressives kept their dreams alive for another half century.

In the creation of major water and power projects for Los Angeles and San Francisco, the Progressives afforded themselves the continuing satisfaction of wielding governmental power in the public interest. The belief that utilities should be publicly owned was one of the few points of uncontested agreement between the Progressives and the Socialists. Since both points of view flourished in Los Angeles, that city moved rather early in the direction of public ownership. The battle over Los Angeles Harbor, moreover, had biased the moderate center in favor of public ownership as well. Anything, the businessmen of Los Angeles believed, was better than an SP monopoly. In a special election held in Sep-tember 1905, Los Angeles committed itself to a municipally owned Owens Valley water project; the question of public versus private operation was left open. In 1909 Progressive leader Meyer Lissner became the first president of the newly created Los Angeles Public Utilities Commission. At the urging of Lissner and other Progressives, Los Angeles decided both to own and to operate its water and hydroelectric power project as a public enterprise.

So did San Francisco, largely through the Progressive leadership of Mayor James Duval Phelan and his city attorney, Franklin Knight Lane. The reform charter lobbied through by Phelan gave the municipal government of San Francisco the authority to acquire and develop utilities. At City Engineer Mi-chael O'Shaughnessy's suggestion, Phelan and Lane got behind the idea of damming the Tuolumne River on federal lands in the Sierra Nevada, filling the Hetch Hetchy Valley with Tuolumne water as a reservoir, then bringing the water by aqueduct to San Francisco, a plan exactly paralleling that of Los Angeles in the Owens Valley. In 1905 Gifford Pinchot, chief forester of the United States, gave his approval to the San Francisco plan, despite the fact that it would involve the irreparable loss of the Hetch Hetchy, a valley of great beauty near the Yosemite. In 1908 Secretary of the Interior James R. Garfield followed up Pinchot's approval with a formal authorization. By 1913, with Franklin K. Lane (who as city attorney of San Francisco had written the first supporting briefs for the Hetch Hetchy project) serving as secretary of the interior, the stage was set for the final element of Congressional approval. A bill was introduced by Representative John E. Raker of Alturas confirming the grant of Hetch Hetchy by the federal government to San Francisco. The battle over the Raker Act, violently opposed by John Muir and the Sierra Club, solidly arrayed the California Progressives behind a philosophy of massive public works to make possible the urbanization of California.

By the time Progressive John Francis Neylan was seeing the Hetch Hetchy project through its financing in the 1920s, California had become a solidly Republican state, remaining so until the late 1950s. Between 1910 and 1932 70 percent of all registered voters in California were Republicans—and so were most governors, state and federal legislators, and mayors of important cities. During this era a conservative political streak surfaced in California, Southern California in particular, that seemed to contradict the general innovativeness, often edging into eccentricity, of other aspects of California life. In certain cases— the vindictive imprisonment of Tom Mooney and Warren Billings in 1916, for instance, or the passage of a criminal syndicalism law in 1919—this conservatism expressed itself in a harsh, unjust, unconstitutional manner.

On 22 July 1916, little more than a month after Republican candidate Charles Evans Hughes visited San Francisco, a bomb exploded on Market Street in the course of a Preparedness Day parade, killing ten and wounding forty. Two Socialist activists with long histories of labor agitation, Tom Mooney and Warren Billings, were convicted on flimsy, most likely framed, evidence advanced by District Attorney Charles M. Fickert, the handpicked servant of the local oligarchy who back in 1909 had quashed the graft trials. The war in Europe had turned San Francisco to the right, as it had the rest of the nation, and the local oligarchy was quick to capitalize on this jingoistic drift to launch a major offensive against labor in the name of anti-radicalism. The conviction of the McNamara brothers in 1910 for the *Times* bombing had broken the back of labor in Los Angeles. The San Francisco oligarchy wanted a similar victory. After a rigged trial that could never have stood up under impartial judicial scrutiny, Billings was given life in prison and Mooney was sentenced to be hanged. Sensing the problematic nature of the conviction, Governor William D. Stephens commuted Mooney's sentence to life in 1918, just a few days before Mooney was to have been executed. For twenty-three years, until his pardon in 1939, imprisoned Tom Mooney—a headstrong, egotistical man, half in love with his martyr's role, although it was eating up his life—served as a rallying point for the left in California and around the world.

Hemmed in by a triumphant conservativism, harassed by a criminal syndicalism law passed by the state legislature in 1919 proscribing any organized activity on behalf of "a change in industrial ownership or control, or effecting a
political change," Socialism disappeared as a mainstream force in California.
Gaylord Wilshire, once the irrepressible spokesman for California's special brand
of Fabianism, devoted himself in the 1920s to promoting his "I-on-a-co" machine, an electrical device which Wilshire claimed could cure heart disease,
diabetes, cancer, goiter, varicose veins, dropsy, gallstones, and problems of the
prostate.

The California Progressives (or more correctly, the former Progressives) were
not exempt from this rightward drift. As governor, Hiram Johnson had remained quiet as an army of fifteen hundred out-of-work men had been dis-
persed by club-wielding police in Sacramento in the fall of 1913. The next year
he sent the National Guard in against the IWW during the Wheatland distur-
bances. But none of this was dramatic enough to foretell his future as a near-
paranoid conservative isolationist. As a senator, Johnson's rabid opposition to
American entrance into the League of Nations alienated him from such pro-
League Progressives as Stimson, Dickson, Haynes, and Rowell, who broke with
Johnson once and for all over this matter. Consumed by presidential fever,
Johnson hoped to use the League controversy as a springboard to the White
House. By 1919, in fact, Johnson had made peace with the conservative Republican oligarchy, including William Henry Crocker, who joined fellow Bay
Area banker Herbert Fleishhacker, *Chronicle* publisher Michael H. de Young,
and Congressman Joseph R. Knowland (whose last appearance in a Johnson
campaign had been as a face on the "Shame of California" billboard) as Johnson delegates to the Republican convention of 1920. Also solidly behind Johnson were San Franciscans I. W. Hellman of Union Trust Bank and J. A. Brit-
ton of Pacific Gas and Electric, two stalwart champions of monopoly. The
nominee, Warren Gamaliel Harding of Ohio, offered Johnson the vice-
presidential nomination, which Johnson refused, unwisely, as it turned out; for
a mere three years later Harding lay dead in the Palace Hotel in San Francisco,
and Hiram Johnson would have been president.

By that time, however, Herbert Hoover of Palo Alto had displaced Johnson
as head of Progressive Republicanism (as it now became) in California. An engineer, a self-made millionaire, a Stanford University graduate and trustee,
Herbert Hoover epitomized the Progressive virtues of self-reliance and business
efficiency in the public service, in the form these attributes survived into the
1920s. During the First World War, Hoover, already a millionaire from mining ventures in Australia and China, and some fellow Stanfordites had organized the Committee for Relief in Belgium, which literally fed that country
through the course of the war. President Wilson brought Hoover back to the

United States in 1917 to serve as food administrator, and Warren Harding made him secretary of commerce. Handsome, dignified, bookish, married to Lou Henry Hoover, one of the most beautiful and accomplished hostesses in the state (whose poised elegance, that of a Gibson Girl moving gracefully into middle age, stood in such contrast to Minnie Johnson's hypochondriacal frumpiness), Herbert Hoover had little trouble displacing Hiram Johnson as leader of California Progressive Republicanism, despite the fact that Hoover had never held elective office. Progressives favored appointive office, in any event, and the harmoniousness of Hoover's personality, together with the polished gentlemanliness he had acquired during his prewar residence in London, appealed to something snobbish deep in the California Progressives—their conception of themselves as gentlemen—which found no corroboration whatsoever in the neurotic, provincial angularity of the distressingly carminative Hiram Johnson. Calling himself a Progressive, Hoover argued for American entrance into the League of Nations throughout the 1919–20 controversy. Stimson, Dickson, Rowell, and even Democrat Franklin Lane, meanwhile, spent 1919 and 1920 creating a rather effective Hoover-for-President boomlet in opposition to the California oligarchy's advancement of Hiram Johnson, a campaign which thrust Hoover into the Harding cabinet. By 1922 the Progressive remnant was plotting ways to keep Hiram Johnson from returning to the United States Senate. Johnson prevailed, but his abortive effort to replace Calvin Coolidge in 1924 showed him once and for all to be a man who was nowhere more alone than in his home state, among those who had brought him to power in 1909. Adding insult to injury, Chester Rowell wrote an essay in the *New Republic* on 29 October 1924 entitled "Why I Shall Vote for Coolidge."

The New Deal found Hiram Johnson on the outer edge of the isolationist right, a senator unknown for a single piece of creative legislation but famous for his vitriolic attacks. FDR's New Deal, Johnson believed, had behind it a sinister combine of Wall Street, the Jews, and upper-class Ivy League WASPSs, all out to seize control of the country. Johnson fought the Lend-Lease program to embattled Great Britain as bitterly—but less effectively—as he had fought the League of Nations. He opposed American preparedness for entry into the Second World War as steps in the direction of domestic dictatorship. Three weeks before he died in 1945, Johnson cast one of three dissenting Senate votes against American entry into the United Nations. Johnson's anti-New Deal isolationism, while extreme and violently expressed, was not unique to his generation of California Progressives. As early as 1920–21, Marshal Stimson was pulling back from the Progressivist program of government regulation of business, warning that the Progressives had gone too far and that if trends continued some form of Socialism was imminent. Writing in the *Yale Review* for the spring of 1936, Chester Rowell, who by then had lost faith in political parties in general, described the New Deal as virtual revolution. Now working for William Randolph Hearst, John Francis Neylan almost equaled his one-time chief Hiram Johnson in anti–New Deal isolationist vitriol.

In his typically melodramatic style, idiosyncratic and yet representative also of his mass constituency, Neylan's boss, William Randolph Hearst, operating as ever from a unique place in American society that was powerful yet oddly removed from the secure center of the establishment, went through each phase of the Progressivist odyssey from reform to embattled isolationism. In Hearst's case, the withdrawal from the struggle took the form of a retreat into an actual castle and the lifting high behind him of the drawbridge. So powerful in the American popular imagination is this memory of Citizen Hearst in San Simeon—the hundred-and-fifty-room castle in the Santa Lucia Mountains on the San Luis Obispo seacoast, which Hearst began to develop in 1919, the year his mother died—that his earlier reputation as a reformer with strong ties to Progressivism is virtually forgotten, obscured by his later notoriety as the right-wing isolationist baron of mass media.

Presented the *San Francisco Examiner* in 1888 at his own request by his multimillionaire father, Senator George Hearst, in the hopes that the floundering newspaper might challenge his hitherto ne'r-do-well son (a St. Paul's and Harvard expellee) to make something of himself, the twenty-four-year-old William Randolph, still given to dressing in the over-bright colors of his Lampoon and Hasty Pudding Club days at Harvard, threw himself into newspapering with surprising vigor and perhaps equally surprising reformism, given the fact that young Willie, a playboy spendthrift who loved late-night suppers in the company of ladies of the chorus, was the scion of the very California capitalist class, with its deep foundations in mining, oil, land, and railroads, that he, once ensconced at the *Examiner*, proceeded to attack.

From the start of his legendary career, however, Hearst understood the first and last premise of a new species of American journalism: namely, that causes touched by populist resentment and vigorously advanced through crisp writing and bold headlines sold newspapers. Crusading against the railroad-dominated machine of Chris Buckley, Abe Ruef's predecessor as political boss of San Francisco, Hearst had the satisfaction of seeing Buckley flee to Canada in 1889, under indictment by a grand jury. Driving Boss Buckley out of town sold newspapers. So did baiting the Southern Pacific, especially when it was done with the acerbic brilliance mustered by Ambrose Bierce, a literary Hearstling of great talent. Hearst put columnist Bierce semi-permanently on the SP beat. Train wrecks were reported with ghoulish accuracy, and the railroad's passenger service constantly castigated. George Hearst's fellow United States senator from California, Leland Stanford, was not amused. When the Pacific Railroad Funding Bill came before Congress in 1896, Hearst went on a personal crusade to defeat the effort to forgive or at least postpone the Southern Pacific debt to the federal government.

Throughout the 1890s, under Hearst's direction, the Monarch of the Dailies, the first newspaper of what would eventually be a nationwide chain, also advocated such pre-Progressive notions as charter reform, publicly owned water and transit systems, public school reform, and the popular election of United States senators (a measure that would have forever precluded George Hearst's ascension to Washington). Looking back at these early *Examiner* years, Fremont Older, a reporter on Hearst's staff at the time, saw in them the first conditioning of Californians on a popular level to the reform idea in general and to specific Progressive programs.

Moving to New York in 1895 as the new owner of the *Journal*, young Hearst continued to attack such Olympians of the American capitalist establishment as J. P. Morgan, W. K. Vanderbilt, John D. Rockefeller, and Elihu Root, disclosing their networks of interest, their monopolies and deals, their bought-and-paid-for public officials. He advocated—under the rubric of the Hearst American Internal Policy—such notions as control of the trusts, public ownership of railroads and utilities, the direct election of senators, a graduated income tax, and universal public education.

As his influence grew, however, an element of right-wing populism, suppressed in California, which as yet was devoid of the lower-middle-class masses of the East, surfaced in Hearst. Something in their resentment—these urban wage earners, these shopmen and tradesmen and minor administrators hemmed in by the new immigrants on one side and an oppressive upper class on the other—spoke to Hearst's perception of himself as, ultimately, for all his California money, a person condemned ever to remain on the fringes of the Eastern establishment, and so he courted this new constituency as no newspaper had ever done before, in city after city, beginning in New York, where he vanquished Joseph Pulitzer's *World*.

In late 1906 Lincoln Steffens interviewed Hearst, then a Democratic congressman, on a train running from Chicago to New York. Steffens, like Hearst another Californian sojourning in the East, caught glimpses of something beyond the ambitions or abilities of ordinary American politicians, even those aspiring to the presidency (as Hearst was), something that Steffens half-consciously feared, and only half-consciously understood: the conjuncture of mass media ownership and ruthless political ambition. Hearst, Steffens saw apprehensively and almost overtly suggested, was capable of seizing the ax and fasces of the Republic into his own hands as Tribune of the People.

Between 1902 and 1908 Hearst won election to Congress but was defeated for the presidency, the mayoralty of New York City, and the governorship of New York. His outspoken opposition to American entry into World War I nearly severed his hold on his constituency, but after the war was over and the horror of it all stood revealed, his campaign against American entry into the League of Nations reconciled his newspapers once again with their lower-middle-class constituency, which was sick of foreign entanglements. Falling back upon his newspaper empire, Hearst contented himself with another sort of power, over public opinion, and with the amusements of a new American place, Hollywood, where the collective fantasy life of the nation was centering itself. The first year of the League of Nations battle, 1919, was a busy year for Hearst. He went into the movie-making business, for one thing, setting up the Hearst Cosmopolitan Movie Studio in New York City as a vehicle to promote the career of Marion Davies, a former Ziegfeld Follies showgirl with whom he had been associated since 1917. Hearst believed he could single-handedly make Davies the new Mary Pickford. Secondly, he began negotiations with his mother's architect, Julia Morgan, an engineering graduate of the University of California and the first woman to take a diploma in architecture from the prestigious École des Beaux Arts of Paris, regarding the development of the Hearst Ranch at San Simeon in San Luis Obispo County. Phoebe Apperson Hearst died from influenza shortly after these first conversations occurred.

Originally planned as a cluster of great bungalows, the San Simeon enterprise eventually developed into the most spectacular private building project of its era, or any other era, for that matter: a soaring hilltop castle, Casa Grande, designed by Morgan in the Spanish Revival Churrigueresque style made popular by Bertram Goodhue at the Panama-California International Exposition held in San Diego in 1915, surrounded by gardens, statuary, fountains, pools, guest and support buildings, and a private zoo. In its Hollywood aspects, Hearst Castle, as it came to be known, was a monument to the world associated with Marion Davies, the most lavish house of Hollywood's most lavish era. But insofar as it served as a repository for the books, paintings, furniture, tapestries, and statuary of Europe—upon which Hearst spent millions, pushing himself to the edge of bankruptcy by the late 1930s—Casa Grande was also a monument to his mother, Phoebe Apperson Hearst, a onetime frontier schoolteacher, in love with culture from her first days, teaching herself French from a grammar book back in Franklin County, Missouri, and dreaming of herself one far-off day seeing the castles and art galleries of Europe. Mother and mistress, Europe and Hollywood, each went into the making of Hearst Castle at San Simeon.

Hearst Castle was also an epic version of the retreat into wealth being pursued on a lesser scale by an entire generation of aging California Progressives, in whose ranks William Randolph Hearst ambiguously belongs. They also were finding for themselves castles of fact and castles of the mind where they might withdraw into baronial isolation. It was Hearst's prerogative, however, to find for himself a most spectacular mountaintop setting from which to survey an unreformed, resistant America. Working by telephone and telegram from San

Simeon, he helped secure Franklin Delano Roosevelt's nomination in 1932, on the specific promise that Roosevelt would avoid foreign entanglements, which was by then an item of rigid dogma among former Progressives. "I am definitely Progressive," he wrote in a signed editorial entitled "The Creed of a Progressive" for 15 August 1934, "but a practical Progressive like dear old Theodore." A half century before either the practice or the term came into usage, William Randolph Hearst led a bicoastal life, divided between New York City and San Simeon. Two former Progressive leaders, Fremont Older and John Francis Neylan, helped Hearst operate his West Coast enterprises. Neylan, whom Hearst called twice a day on the telephone, functioned as general counsel and overall editorial supervisor of Hearst's five West Coast newspapers, in addition to carrying on his own lucrative law practice. Progressively more conservative in his personal beliefs, Neylan saw to the success of the Hearst operation with the same acuity with which he had once monitored the finances of the state of California for Hiram Johnson. At Hearst's behest, Neylan played a key role in the breaking of the San Francisco general strike of 1934.

Fremont Older is an enigmatic figure in the story of the twilight era of California Progressivism. Unlike Neylan and the others, Older did not move to the right in his later years. He continued to champion a number of leftish causes, including a twenty-year effort to free Tom Mooney from San Quentin. Older's pro-Mooney position, in fact, lost him the editorship of the *Bulletin* after twenty-four brilliant years at the helm. William Randolph Hearst, wanting his left wing covered in San Francisco as well as his right, invited Older over to the *Call* in 1918, telling him to bring the Mooney case with him. In 1929 Hearst bought out the *Call* and installed Older as president and editor of the combined *Call-Bulletin*. Still sporting his drooping Western frontier mustache, still tireless as he pushed his reporters after a story or personally read proof, the ashes of his constant cigar spilling down on the ink-wet galleys, Fremont Older was also a curiously disillusioned man during these post-Progressive years of ascendant Babbitry followed by the Depression. With the help of a similarly chastened Lincoln Steffens, Older had come to understand the ambiguities and the resistance of the system—and the equally important personal realization that physicians must first heal themselves.

In 1911 San Francisco journalist Theodore Bonnet had first advanced these notions, eventually self-evident to Fremont Older, in an impassioned, scornful tract entitled *The Regenerators*, in which Bonnet indicted the entire San Francisco reform movement as "private animosity masquerading as public duty." Each of the key protagonists among the reformers, Fremont Older included, Bonnet argued, had his axe to grind, his own self-interest primarily in mind. Alas, Fremont Older confessed a few years later in *My Own Story* (1919), such charges of mixed motivation had more than a little validity.

Abraham Ruef, Older admitted with open irony, emerged from the entire

affair as the only unambiguous gentleman in the entire lot, reformers and pros-
ecuted alike. Perceived as the embodiment of political corruption before the
trials, Ruef was transformed retrospectively in Older's mind into just another
player in the comedy, just another victim of the system. Arrested, kept illegally
under guard in a private home, where he was interrogated day and night by
Detective Burns, cajoled and pressured by the reformers to plead guilty and to
name names on their promise of immunity, Abe Ruef had never groveled—
and had named no names. Gentlemen, when caught in a difficult situation,
Ruef believed, never tell stories and certainly never beg. Infuriated, the reformers secured for Ruef a fourteen-year sentence to San Quentin, a difficult place
indeed for a gentleman accustomed to the civilities of life. Would Ruef now
break? the reformers wondered. "The zebra," Ruef replied, "is one of the most
beautiful and graceful of animals. Why, therefore, should I cavil at my attire?"

No sooner had the gates of San Quentin closed on Ruef than Fremont Older
was having second thoughts. The bribe-givers, he realized, were safe in their
leather chairs in the Pacific Union Club. The bribe-takers were still in City
Hall. Where did that leave Abe Ruef? Taking the ferry across the Bay, Older
called on Ruef in San Quentin. Towering over Ruef physically, Fremont Older
nevertheless felt small as the onetime boss was brought in, wearing his convict's
stripes. "Is this success," he asked himself, "or is it failure? Is this a real victory
or an appalling defeat? After all the years of mad pursuit, is this the harvest?
The imprisonment and branding of one poor, miserable, helpless human being?"
And then Fremont Older begged Abraham Ruef's forgiveness. This encounter
between accuser and accused, righteous editor—his righteousness crumbling—
and convicted bribe-taker, was the beginning of a deep understanding between
them and a lifelong friendship. Older spent the next five years lobbying for Ruef's
release. Many Progressives were shocked by Older's sudden reversal, his Lincoln-
Steffens-esque contention that it was the system, not Ruef, that was at fault.
Had they not reformed the system? they challenged. Governor Hiram Johnson
refused Older's pleas for clemency. Ruef, meanwhile, asked Older, his onetime
persecutor, to serve as custodian of his estate while he served out his sentence
in gentlemanly silence. On the day of Ruef's release, after five years in prison,
Fremont Older was there to take him home.

9

Stories and Dreams:
The Movies Come to Southern California

On Sunday afternoons in the fall of 1887, Horace and Daeida Wilcot of Los Angeles were wont to take leisurely carriage rides out to the Cahuenga Valley. Having recently lost their only child, a boy of nineteen months, born to them in middle age, the Wilcots were grieving, and these Sunday afternoon excursions behind the two prize Arabian horses Horace Wilcot had brought with him from Topeka in 1883 when he migrated to Southern California helped distract the Wilcots from their grief. Crippled by typhoid fever as a teenager in Michigan, Horace Wilcot had prevailed over his handicaps to work his way through Adrian College as a cobbler and a janitor (pulling himself about on crutches) before moving on to Topeka, where he married, was widowed, then remarried, while growing wealthy in real estate.

Wilcot arrived in Los Angeles already a prosperous businessman, hoping like countless other Midwesterners of that era to find better weather and even greater prosperity in the Southland. Buying up large tracts of property, including the present site of UCLA, Wilcot subdivided and sold. The Wilcot home on Hill Street became a Los Angeles showplace. And then, the long-awaited son—followed so soon by bereavement.

Out driving one Sunday afternoon in late 1887, Horace Wilcot moved his Arabians through a sunny landscape of undeveloped fields broken intermittently by orange groves, peach, fig, and apricot orchards, and small farms leased by absentee owners to Chinese vegetable growers. In the immediate distance Horace and Daeida could see the Santa Monica Mountains, which sealed off the San Fernando Valley from the Los Angeles plain. The Cahuenga Valley through which they drove had as yet experienced only scattered settlement, despite its proximity to Los Angeles. It was, however, classic Southern California country, endowed with a mission (San Fernando and its tributary Cahuenga

Chapel), historical associations (General Andrés Pico had surrendered California to John C. Frémont at the Cahuenga Chapel on 13 January 1847), and a pattern of haphazard settlement throughout the American era. Water-scarce, the Cahuenga Valley never attracted great numbers of horticulturists. Sheep, however, capable of scrounging pasturage from even the barest of hills, had proven profitable, and as late as the mid-1880s, long after the sheep era had passed elsewhere in Southern California, large droves moved deliberately across the plains of Cahuenga and the Santa Monica foothills.

Pulling off the Cahuenga Road into an orchard of figs and apricots just beneath the Santa Monica foothills, Horace and Daeida Wilcot sensed between them a mood, an immediate conviction that this was a special place. What Horace Wilcot liked he usually bought. Within a reasonable time he had bought the orchard and the surrounding 160 acres and was soon filled with ambitious plans to acquire even more Cahuenga property, which he subdivided (on paper at least) into a city called Hollywood, a name chosen by Mrs. Wilcot. Despite the collapse of the land boom in 1888, Wilcot pushed on with his plans, crisscrossing his subdivision with as yet empty avenues, which he lined with pepper trees. Selling their Los Angeles home, the Wilcots moved out to a house on their Cahuenga property. Mrs. Wilcot planted two English holly bushes alongside their home. The holly bushes did poorly. Hollywood, as Horace and Daeida Wilcot envisioned their city-to-be, would be a model Southern Californian community: Christian, righteous, and very dry—no saloons, no liquor stores, with free land offered to Protestant churches locating within the city limits. Unfortunately, Hollywood grew too slowly for Horace Wilcot to get an adequate return on his investment. When he died in 1892, he was, like so many other residents of Southern California, land rich and cash poor.

Horace Wilcot had, however, established Hollywood as a destination point, if not a flourishing Protestant community. By 1899, when Hollywood had about five hundred residents, visitors were coming out by electric streetcar and tallyho to the Glen-Holly Hotel, a twenty-room, one-bath establishment at the corner of Ivan and Yucca, famed for its seventy-five-cent chicken dinners. At least one Southern Californian of distinction, the floral artist Paul De Longpre, decided to settle permanently in Hollywood. In 1901 De Longpre built himself a Moorish-style villa on the corner of Hollywood Boulevard and Cahuenga Avenue, surrounded by a garden filled with real-life versions of the flowers he so skillfully translated to canvas. De Longpre's house and garden soon became a destination point surpassing the Glen-Holly Hotel. Flower lovers from near and far would come out to Hollywood by electric trolley to stroll down the grand gallery of the French-born artist's Moorish mansion, comparing his paintings in the gallery with the abundant blooms outside. De Longpre's example created a civic style. By the early 1900s Hollywood was justifiably praised in the tourist literature of the period for its pepper-tree-lined avenues and its snug, flower-bedecked cottages.

The electric trolley which brought visitors from Los Angeles to De Longpre's home in Hollywood had been established by the all-powerful triumvirate of Moses Sherman, Eli P. Clark, and Harry Chandler, who were by then active in buying and subdividing Hollywood real estate and promoting the newly built thirty-three-room Hollywood Hotel, also in the Moorish style. By then Southern Methodist, Episcopal, and Methodist churches were flourishing in Hollywood, so at least something of Horace Wilcot's dream of a churchly utopia had come true. In 1903, the 166 eligible male voters of Hollywood voted to incorporate themselves as a city. An early ordinance prohibited the driving of more than two thousand sheep at any one time down any one Hollywood street. A high school was voted into existence in 1903, and in 1904 Sunset Boulevard—unimproved, empty, and dusty for most of its course—at last linked Los Angeles with Hollywood. Throughout the first decade of the twentieth century, in other words, Hollywood developed along lines and patterns totally similar to those of countless other small Southern California towns, as orchards gave way to house-lined streets, and churches, schools, and banks (the Bank of Hollywood, established in 1903) made their appearance. Then the "movies" (as early Hollywood residents called film folk, as well as the product they produced) arrived, beginning as early as 1907 or 1908, and Hollywood embarked upon another course, one that rendered it within the decade America's premier city of dreams.

II

Within months of Horace and Daeida Wilcot's first visit to the future site of Hollywood, in autumn 1887, Thomas Alva Edison and his associates at Edison Laboratories in West Orange, New Jersey, began tackling in a relatively haphazard way the problem of motion photography. Edison and his associates took up the problem where the English-born Californian photographer Eadweard Muybridge had left it after nearly two decades of experimentation. In 1872 Muybridge had been retained by Leland Stanford, the railroad magnate and former governor of California, to help Stanford win a wager. Stanford bred prize horses on his farm in Palo Alto south of San Francisco and had bet a friend $25,000 that all four hooves left the ground simultaneously when a horse was in full gallop. Rigging up a series of twelve cameras along the track, each tripped by a separate string, Muybridge obtained a series of photographs that proved Stanford's contention conclusively. The photographs also depicted motion as a series of separate photographs. By increasing the number of photographs from twelve to forty and projecting them onto a screen via a wheel and a magic lantern device which he called a zoopraxiscope, Muybridge accomplished the first major step in the technology of motion pictures.

The Edison Laboratories took the process one step further by substituting a single camera for Muybridge's clumsy multicamera approach. The Edison camera took a sequence of exposures on fifty feet of continuously running film, kept in

motion by sprocket wheels which drove the film via evenly staggered side per-
forations. The developed film was then rerun inside a cabinet called a Kinetoscope. Looking through a lense into the cabinet, a viewer experienced the illusion of motion.

Edison and his associates seemed to have had a playful, even ironic attitude
toward their new invention. The first film clips they made depicted a laboratory
assistant, Fred Ott, displaying his humorous specialty, a magnificent on-call
sneeze, for all ages to come. Viewers at the Chicago World's Fair of 1893 were
willing to pay a nickel to see Fred Ott sneeze, and so despite the fact that Edison never considered his Kinetoscope possessed of much commercial possibilities, a new American industry was born. By April of the next year a commercial Kinetoscope was in operation at 1155 Broadway in New York City.

The next step, soon taken, was to free Fred Ott and his successors from the
cabinet and, by conjoining the Kinetoscope with the magic lantern, to project
motion pictures onto a screen. Inventors in France, Great Britain, and the United
States went to work on the problem and within months of each other came up
with similar solutions. On 22 March 1895 the Lumière brothers of Lyon, France,
demonstrated their projection device in the basement of the Grand Café in Paris.
Guests at the event beheld workers leaving a factory, a baby being fed, and a
train arriving in a railroad station, all brought to life via images projected by
thirty-five-millimeter film running past a light lens at the rate of sixteen frames
per second. Showings of similar projection devices in New York City (April
1895), Washington, D.C. (June 1895), and London (October 1895) soon followed.

Initially, the new medium, like a child learning to walk, contented itself with
demonstrating that its simple trick could be done in the first place: that moving
images recreating reality could be filmed, then projected onto screens in darkened rooms. Fred Ott's sneeze was succeeded by Lumière's factory, baby, and
train, a man and woman kissing (this provoked condemnation in certain evangelical circles), Niagara Falls, and more trains, moving toward the audience
with such realism that people shrieked and ducked down in fear. These were
followed in 1897 by newsreel reports of such events as the Corbett-Fitzsimmons
fight in Carson City, Nevada, the funeral of Queen Victoria, the kaiser review-
ing his troops, the effects of the Galveston cyclone, and President McKinley's
funeral.

Eight years after the invention of motion pictures in 1895, the medium took
a quantum leap. In 1903 an Edison Company cameraman by the name of Edwin S. Porter produced and directed two films, *The Life of an American Fireman* and *The Great Train Robbery*. Each film told a simple story. A mother
and child are rescued from a burning building; a gang of robbers hold up a
train, flee, and are caught. American audiences reacted overwhelmingly to
Porter's story-films, discovering to their delight that film could be used as a ve-

hicle for narrative as well as for the already familiar scene viewing and rudimentary reportage. With the arrival of story, film secured for itself a direct and powerful relationship to the dream life, individual and collective, of the American people. Porter invited his audience not just to observe images, but to participate on the deepest levels of personal identification in the action of the story—the fireman racing to rescue mother and child, the bandits fleeing into the hills with their booty—and in that act of identification to intensify their relationship to experience in a process first described systematically by Aristotle in the fourth century B.C. Like audiences in an open-air amphitheater in ancient Greece, Americans gathering in darkened rooms were enabled by this new medium, now that Edwin S. Porter had conjoined it with the power of story, to enter into events either familiar or beyond their own lives' scope, but in both cases speaking directly to the inner life of fantasy and dreams. This capacity for story and dreams, for which it was uniquely suited, fixed film at the center of America's inner life, and out of this synergy between technology and dream would soon emerge Hollywood.

Story films could make money, as Harry Davis of Pittsburgh discovered in 1905 when he transformed his vaudeville house into a theater for the full-time showing of motion pictures, beginning with Porter's one-reel melodrama *The Great Train Robbery*, for which Davis charged a nickel. Davis's nickelodeon, as it was called, engendered similar establishments around the country. Three companies—Edison, Biograph, and Vitagraph—were soon producing films for the rapidly expanding nickelodeon market, using technology developed and patented initially by Edison Laboratories and later by other investors becoming active in the field. Faced with the commercial possibilities of the medium he had created, Edison had abandoned his indifferent attitude for a diametrically opposite approach. Followed in short order by others who were taking out patents in the new medium, Edison sought to control the emerging industry as a licensed monopoly in which only approved companies could produce films. In 1907 the Edison Company licensed eight production companies to use Edison technology. This arrangement was further formalized in January 1909 with the establishment of the Motion Pictures Patents Company, known more familiarly as the Trust, which sought no less than the all-encompassing regulation of the motion picture industry. The Trust devised a system based upon the payment of taxes for equipment used and royalties per foot of film reel either produced or exhibited. Even film directors would be paid upon the basis of the amount of footage they produced. For ten years the Trust sought to control the production and distribution of motion pictures in America, despite the creative subversion of independent filmmakers, underground distributors, and bootleg exhibitors. It would have been easier for Gutenberg to have controlled the printing and distribution of books after the invention of printing.

It was, to begin with, a decentralized industry. Essanay and Selig had their studios in Chicago; Lubin was in Philadelphia; Vitagraph, in Brooklyn; Biograph, in New York; Edison, in New Jersey. Kalem maintained a floating operation that included filming sojourns in Ireland and Palestine. In the winter of 1907 Selig director Francis Boggs and cameraman Thomas Persons, having finished all interior scenes for *The Count of Monte Cristo* in Chicago, found that weather conditions in the Windy City were too overcast for filming outdoor scenes. Needing good weather, Boggs and Persons entrained for Los Angeles, where they completed their one-reel melodrama, which was released on 30 January 1908. Hearing of the excellent weather conditions in Los Angeles and delighted that *The Count of Monte Cristo* had been brought in on schedule, Colonel William Selig established a permanent operation in Los Angeles in early 1908. Selig filmed *In the Sultan's Power* in a mansion at Eighth and Olive streets—the first complete film made in Los Angeles—and then used a nearby Classical Revival villa and gardens as background for *The Roman*. Selig's next production, *Carmen*, involved the building of a set depicting a small Spanish courtyard, the first movie set ever constructed in Los Angeles. Not only did Selig appreciate Los Angeles's weather, he also relished his distance from the subpoena servers constantly being dispatched by the lawyers hired by Edison Laboratories to initiate suits against producers such as Selig who were not always willing to pay what Edison considered its fair share of licensing and reel-footage fees. Between 1908 and 1909 a number of other independents equally reluctant to pay, together with a number of bootleg operations, came to Los Angeles for similar reasons. The New York Motion Picture Company, for instance, harassed by Trust thugs, moved its studio from Long Island to a former grocery store on the outskirts of Los Angeles. Initially the suburban village of Hollywood could not compete as a location against Los Angeles or Santa Monica and Santa Barbara, where American Film and the Bison Company were establishing themselves. After 1910, however, the distinction becomes moot, for that year Hollywood voted to surrender its charter and incorporate itself into the City of Los Angeles.

In 1908 Essanay of Chicago established its studio outside of Southern California altogether, in Niles Canyon outside of Oakland in the San Francisco Bay area. Three years later Essanay was joined in the Niles by the Flying A Company, which produced Westerns. Had this Niles venture taken hold, Anita Loos later speculated, the film industry would have developed—to everyone's benefit—in close contact with San Francisco's flourishing theatrical, literary, and artistic communities. A San Francisco–based film industry, Miss Loos believed, would have enjoyed California's excellent weather along with an urban sophistication lost when films migrated from the East. Yet the Los Angeles area had one major advantage during this tumultuous founding era, with its Trust-initiated lawsuits and violent sabotage. Los Angeles was closer to Mexico. San Francisco might out-compete Los Angeles County in scenic locations, might have more established actors available, might offer films the energizing and disciplining effects of urban culture; but San Francisco was also a legal town, with numerous law offices affiliated with Edison lawyers in the East, and hence a dangerous environment for independents, who, if operating in Southern California, were able to move their operations across the border into Mexico, which they occasionally did when harassed by Trust attorneys and thugs. History looks for deeper reasons for the location of the film industry in and around Los Angeles, and they are there and will soon be unfolded, but in those Keystone Comedy days there were also motivations as superficial as the desire to flee Trust detectives, subpoena servers, and confiscators of equipment by going across the border into Mexico.

In those first years, between late 1907 and 1913, no studio or important filmmaker seems to have made a commitment to a permanent Los Angeles location. Selig, Biograph, and the others maintained Eastern headquarters and studios and came to the Southland only for a winter-spring shooting schedule.

III

Of these temporary sojourners, none was of more importance than the Founder himself. In the winter of 1910, David Wark Griffith came to California already energized by regional and personal affinities. Griffith's father, Jacob Wark (later a colonel in the Confederacy), had traveled overland to California in 1850 while on duty with the United States army. Griffith himself had first come to California in the summer of 1904 as an actor in the Melbourne MacDowell Repertory Company. Because he despised acting and wanted ferociously to become a great playwright, Griffith used the stage name Lawrence Griffith, intending to revert to David Griffith only when his first masterpiece had been produced. Playing in San Francisco, where he stayed at the theatrically oriented Windsor Hotel at Fourth and Market streets, Griffith met one night at the Grand Opera House on Mission Street a stage-struck San Francisco native of Norwegian descent, Linda Arvidson, whose concert debut had been sponsored by Mayor James Duval Phelan himself, the Lorenzo de Medici of local arts. At the time she met Griffith, Arvidson had a bit part in a play running at the Alcazar, produced by David Belasco's brother Fred, who had remained behind when the great David had left San Francisco for New York. Falling in love, the two young actors courted that summer of 1904 in their off hours: strolling the picturesque streets of Chinatown and the Latin Quarter in the manner of the young lovers in Frank Norris's novel *Blix*, walking alongside the pounding surf at Ocean Beach, the magnetic, aquilinely handsome David keeping Linda spellbound with his sonorous recitations of Shakespeare in a stage voice softened by the accent of his native Kentucky, or telling her of the poems, plays, and stories he would one day write (so he hoped) with the passionate prodigality of Shakespeare himself.

Shakespearean the young Kentuckian would eventually become, but in a medium only being turned that very year by Edwin Porter to the purposes of story.

The Melbourne MacDowell Company folded in San Francisco, and when next we catch sight of Griffith our aspiring Shakespearean is picking hops in Ukiah in Northern California, an experience he later used as the basis for a perfectly awful play, *The Fool and The Girl* (1907), which opened and soon closed in Washington, D.C. In 1905 Griffith landed the role of the Indian Alessandro in a stage version of *Ramona* touring California. Linda Arvidson was acting in Los Angeles when *Ramona* reached that city. Reunited, the young actors continued their courtship in the City of the Angels, this time strolling together by moonlight past the cloisters of Mission San Gabriel, which five years later Griffith would return to and film with pioneering technique and sensitivity. Griffith loved the mission and the other suggestions of Old California which he and Linda encountered in their courtship strolling. Like the Confederacy which would ever haunt his imagination (and account for perhaps his greatest masterpiece), Spanish California spoke to the young Southerner a comparable tale of doomed chivalry, of ideals which had been brilliantly fought for and lost.

When earthquake and fire destroyed San Francisco in April 1906, Griffith wired Linda Arvidson a marriage proposal from Boston, where he was then playing. Drawing her life's savings from the temporary outdoor office of the German Savings Bank, Linda left for Boston on a train ticket supplied by the Red Cross, which had also provided her clothes. Shortly after her arrival, she and David were married at Old North Church.

David and Linda Griffith returned to California in January 1910, "deluxing" their way, as Linda described it, across the continent on the Twentieth Century Limited from New York City, where David had established himself since 1908 as Biograph's leading director, with 288 films to his credit. Griffith initially installed his Biograph troupe, including seventeen-year-old Mary Pickford, in the Alexandria Hotel, before moving them out to more permanent quarters in the Hollywood Inn on Hollywood Boulevard. Artist Paul De Longpre rented out a portion of his garden to Griffith for the setting of a film aptly entitled *Love Among the Roses*—although which came first, plot or garden, is uncertain, for Griffith never depended upon prepared scripts, preferring instead to develop his plots as scenes, actors, or momentary inspirations presented themselves. Widely read, gifted with truly Shakespearean profusion, Griffith possessed in his head a tumult of plots, many of them lifted—again in the Shakespearean manner— from literature. Remembered today for a half dozen lavish, highly crafted masterpieces, Griffith spent his early career cranking out one-reelers. He produced approximately four hundred films for Biograph alone. Many of these, their outdoor sequences especially, were filmed in Southern California during the Griffith troupe's 1910, 1911, 1912, and 1913 winter-spring Hollywood sojourns.

For his first studio Griffith rented a vacant lot ten minutes by trolley (seven minutes by automobile) from the Alexandria Hotel, and hired carpenters to build a fifty-square-foot stage and two platforms for tent dressing rooms. Interior scenes were filmed on this hastily constructed outdoor stage, with the Southern California sun for lighting. A nearby shed provided facilities for the developing and projection rooms and a dressing and makeup room for his actors, leaving the two tents for the exclusive use of Linda Arvidson, Mary Pickford, Mabel Normand, Blanche Sweet, Vivian Prescott, and the other actresses in the troupe. This shed was later supplemented by a rented loft at Spring and Second streets, where Griffith maintained a cutting and projection room together with his own personal headquarters. Dinner was taken at the Hollywood Inn or the other hotels and boardinghouses housing the troupe; breakfast and lunch were usually enjoyed at Hoffman's Restaurant near the loft. The Griffiths, joined by other members of the troupe, would sit on counter stools, enjoying the hearty fare of early-twentieth-century America. Thus Hollywood—as a concept, as an industry, as a mythic place—developed from an embryonic acting troupe pursuing its ancient bohemian lifestyle of itinerant performance, hostelry life, intrigue (sexual and otherwise), and improvisational creativity under the disciplining guidance of its troupe leader, in this case thirty-year-old David Wark Griffith, who, whether he knew it or not at the time, was setting in motion a process that would eventually bring the production of American film once and for all to Southern California.

Intriguingly, Griffith put his new medium rather immediately at the service of Southern California's own major effort at identity, the mission myth. For his first all-California film, Griffith moved his troupe out to Mission San Gabriel, where he and his wife had strolled five years earlier, and there filmed *The Thread of Destiny*, a story of Old California starring Mary Pickford. Film historians have long since recognized that the subtly lighted interior scenes, filmed by Griffith's great cameraman William Bitzer inside Mission San Gabriel itself, mark a major step forward in film technique. Griffith wanted a reverent mood to pervade these interior scenes, and Bitzer responded with the unselfconscious genius of that Ur-era. For a scene in which an old padre, played by Christie Miller, blesses his congregation, Griffith and Bitzer waited for just the right moment, when a slant of afternoon light fell directly across the pulpit. The resulting scene proved dramatically the capacity of indirect lighting to create an interplay between exterior effect and interior emotion.

Griffith also effected another departure. Instead of filming from scene to scene in the remorseless style of the one-reeler narrative, he used the details of Mission San Gabriel—the walls, altar, belfry, and garden—on a shot-by-shot, detail-by-detail basis so as to integrate architecture and setting into the symbolic center of his story. *The Thread of Destiny* proved that film was capable of narrative by means of visual symbol and association in a manner parallel to that of painting, but differing in that film images were reassembled shot by shot into a complex visual tapestry that was at once realistic, symbolic, and in motion. From the point of view of Southern California's development during this period, Griffith's use of an eighteenth-century mission reenergized by the early twentieth-century mission myth to explore and demonstrate the possibilities of a new art medium is in itself symbolic. From the point of view of scientific history, the mission myth was an illusion, a dream, but Southern California had used this illusion to activate itself. That film, being developed by Griffith into a medium capable of appealing so directly to dream life, could also find materials in this mission myth upon which to found its future as an art form linked Southern California and film together at a common point of symbolic beginning.

Finishing *The Thread of Destiny*, Griffith went on to film *In Old California* in the hills bordering Hollywood, then brought his company seventy miles out of Camulos in Ventura County to film the novel which had begun the mission myth in the first place, *Ramona*, starring Mary Pickford. Griffith had already secured the rights from Little, Brown before leaving New York. In *The Thread of Destiny* Griffith had concentrated upon close-up shots of architecture; in *Ramona* he stationed Bitzer's camera on vantage points allowing for panoramic views of Southern California's coastal mountain range, as well as following up the use of visual detail pioneered in *The Thread of Destiny* with highly articulated close-up scenes of sheepshearing. Linda Arvidson later wrote of this film, "Scenes in the little flower-covered outdoor chapel where Ramona's family and their faithful Indian servants worshipped; love scenes at Ramona's iron-barred window; scenes of heartache on the bleak mountain top but a few miles distant where Alessandero and Ramona bury their little baby, dead from the white man's persecutions; and finally the wedding scene of Ramona and Felipe amid the oranges and roses and grass pinks of the patio. Even bells that were cast in old Spain rang silently on the screen. The Biograph Company brought out a special folder with cuts and descriptive matter. The picture was Mr. Griffith's most artistic creation to date."

In the other films made so rapidly in this first winter-spring of 1910–11—*The Converts, The Way of the World, Over Silent Paths*—Griffith also utilized locations at Mission San Gabriel, Mission San Fernando, and Mission San Juan Capistrano. All in all, between 20 January and 6 April 1910, in little more than three months, Griffith made twenty-one films, almost all of them utilizing explicitly Southern Californian locations: the missions, most dramatically, but also the oil fields, the Santa Monica sea coast, Port Los Angeles, Pasadena, the Sierra Madre, Hollywood itself, together with scenes shot in the orchards, vineyards, citrus groves, and farms surrounding Los Angeles. On his second visit, January–February 1911, Griffith filmed on the Santa Monica seacoast America's first feature-length film, *Enoch Arden*, in two reels as opposed to the customary one. He returned with his Biograph players in January 1912 for five months of shooting and remained even longer in 1913, filming for editing in the Biograph studios in New York the most ambitious film attempted by an American to that date, the stunningly realized costume drama *Judith of Bethulia*.

Although personally ambivalent about Southern California for his entire life, one side of his nature preferring instead the urban excitement of New York, Griffith proved in film after film between 1910 and 1913 that, no matter how much of a head start the East possessed as a film center, Southern California— meaning Los Angeles, meaning Hollywood—possessed an affinity between medium and place that would soon attract the entire industry to it like a powerful magnet. Here, Griffith proved, was an environment, social and scenic, that was composed of fragments available for eclectic use. One began with the weather and the light, which were preeminently suitable, then progressed to a geography that gathered seacoast and desert, mountain and valley, forest land and prairie all within commuting distance of each other, as if for a director's convenience. Southern California supported an architecture of rich diversity for interior and exterior filming. In a very real sense the entire society was a stage set, a visualization of dream and illusion which was, like film, at once true and not true. New York City, upstate New York, suburban and rural New Jersey— Griffith's previous haunts—offered locations and scenery aplenty, but Southern California offered certain energizing affinities between art and location. Ambitious to create films that would become worlds in themselves, self-referencing and complete, Griffith felt himself attracted to a society comparably in search of eclectic self-definition, a place where dream and fact energized each other. Within a few short years this interaction between the medium of film and the society of Southern California would develop into a symbiosis called Hollywood that would be of major importance to both the region and the film industry.

Only Los Angeles proper seemed excluded from D. W. Griffith's early camera—but no matter, Griffith's disciple Mack Sennett more than made up for the master's neglect. Beginning his career as an actor with Biograph in New York, Sennett learned directing by being directed by Griffith. In March 1911 Sennett directed his first comedy, *Comrades*, for Biograph. He and a close associate, actress Mabel Normand, convinced that film had found its future in Los Angeles, returned there in the summer of 1912. Within thirty minutes after their arrival at the train station, Sennett was busy filming the first of the many comedies—called Keystone Comedies, after the company he soon founded— that today stand as a founding statement in the history of American film. Hiring English vaudevillian Charles Chaplin, then playing Los Angeles, in late

1913, Sennett established a lineage from Porter to Griffith (who had worked with Porter at Biograph) to Sennett to Chaplin that encompassed in direct succession the greatest film talents of the pre–World War I period.

A brash Irish-Canadian given enthusiastically to liquor, cigars, and women (tradition assigns him the invention of the casting couch), Mack Sennett exuberantly cast Los Angeles and its environs as the background of the countless Keystone Comedies produced between 1913 and 1916. No other American city had ever been celebrated through film as Sennett celebrated greater Los Angeles. Taking to the streets for innumerable chase scenes, Sennett caught Los Angeles in the process of becoming a major American city. Flickering behind Sennett's comedic cops in hot pursuit are images of fine homes adjoining empty lots awaiting development, and streetcars rolling through inner-city pastures. Signs of construction are everywhere. Viewing these comedies across the country, Americans caught glimpses of a city where everyone seemed to live in a bungalow on a broad avenue lined with palm, pepper, or eucalyptus trees, where there was never any snow on the ground or other evidence of bad weather. It is difficult to assess the public relations effect the Sennett imagery of sunny beaches, gardens, and homes had as it flickered before middle America in darkened movie halls, but Los Angeles was being announced subliminally by Mack Sennett as a new American place with its own ambience and visual signature, and Americans did emigrate there in droves, pushing the population to well over a million before the Keystone era was over.

IV

One such new arrival was Cecil Blount De Mille, the thirty-two-year-old scion of an already distinguished New York theatrical family. As in the case of D. W. Griffith, with whom he shares founder status (albeit with dramatically different significance), De Mille first saw Los Angeles as a traveling actor playing the Mason Opera House in June 1903. The winter of 1913 found De Mille looking for new opportunities after a decade of comparative success as an actor, playwright, and director of operettas and stage plays. Dining one evening at the Claridge Grill in New York with vaudeville producer Jesse Lasky, De Mille, depressed by the recent failure of a play he had directed, commiserated with Lasky, whose own enterprises were also ailing. "Let's make moving pictures," Lasky suggested to De Mille. Turning over a Claridge menu, the two sketched out an organizational table for the Jesse L. Lasky Feature Play Company, with Lasky as producer and chief financial backer and De Mille, who had never directed a film in his life, as director-in-chief. As they were talking Lasky's brother-in-law, Sam Goldfish (later Goldwyn), walked in. As it turned out, Goldfish's wholesale glove business was also in trouble. Hearing of Lasky and De Mille's plans to make movies, Goldfish (later responsible for the quintessential Hollywood phrase, "Include me out") said succinctly, "I'm in."

Selecting a script, *The Squaw Man*, on the grounds that it could be inexpensively filmed outdoors, De Mille, who had just squeezed in a crash course in directorial technique at the Edison Studios in the Bronx, headed West by train with his crew to Flagstaff, Arizona, where he intended to film. A dust storm in Flagstaff convinced him to continue on to Los Angeles, where, as had Griffith three years earlier, he ensconced himself and his crew in the Alexandria Hotel. De Mille went even further afield than Griffith, however, in selecting a studio—out to the sleepy village of Hollywood, where he located himself in an L-shaped barn abutting an orange grove on the corner of the dirt roads Selma and Vine. De Mille rented the barn from its owner, Jacob Stern, for the high price of $200 a week, with the proviso that Stern could still stable his horses and carriage in the building. De Mille had been led to the barn by L. L. Burns and Harry Revier, two photographers who maintained laboratories in another part of the structure. Nailing a sign over the barn door, "Jesse L. Lasky Feature Play Company Studio," De Mille put his crew and cast to work filming *The Squaw Man* on 29 December 1913. To cut down on expenses, he himself played the part of a faro dealer. Jesse Lasky came out from New York a few weeks later to inspect his company, staying with Cecil and Constance De Mille in their rented house in Cahuenga Canyon, where howling coyotes kept Lasky awake on his first night.

Lasky found the barn at Selma and Vine converted into processing facilities and offices, and an outdoor stage overhung with canvas light-diffusers set up in the nearby orange grove. De Mille, crew, and cast commuted to locations in a rented two-ton open-air Ford truck, which also bore the "Jesse L. Lasky Feature Play Company" logo emblazoned on its side. Whereas Griffith's Biograph crew, being temporary sojourners, dressed Eastern and maintained themselves in hotels or boardinghouses as quasi-tourists, De Mille and company, out in California to make a permanent go of it, threw themselves flamboyantly into a theatrical version of the local style. Attired in jodhpurs, De Mille scouted out locations by horseback and wore boots and leather puttees as protection against rattlesnakes. He also wore a six-shooter at his side as protection against the aforementioned rattlesnakes and against a possible second attack by the unknown party—sent out by the Trust, De Mille claimed—who had shot at him with a rifle as he rode home one late afternoon through Cahuenga Canyon. ("The first critic of a De Mille picture" was how CB described his assailant.) The entire filming of *The Squaw Man* was marred by threats to De Mille— anonymous letters, using words cut from newspapers—and the sabotage of the completed negative by an intruder (fortunately, De Mille had kept a second negative in another location), all testifying to the seriousness with which the

Trust and its agents viewed the threat posed by independent companies in far-off Southern California.

Although the Lasky Studio had agreed to pay the Trust the customary one-half cent per foot of reel for the right to film and distribute its product, *The Squaw Man*, scheduled for six reels, threatened the two-reel limit set by the Trust in an effort (so the Trust claimed) to save the American people from eye-strain. Actually the Trust feared the notion of longer, feature-length films such as were already being made in Italy. One- and two-reelers were inexpensive to make and fit conveniently into a controllable context of quick production, distribution, and turnover. More reels meant more half cents per foot. Longer films would be more expensive to produce and would involve a new system of marketing in which the Trust might lose out.

The success of *The Squaw Man*, the improbable story of a Wyoming cowboy who inherits an English earldom, fulfilled the worst fears of the Trust. Produced in a month on a minimal budget, processed in a converted barn studio, barely escaping destruction by a mysterious intruder, rushed by De Mille to the Philadelphia studio of Sigmund Lubin for resprocketing when the first negative was found deficient, *The Squaw Man* nevertheless grossed an amazing $244,700 after its release on 15 February 1914 in six reels. The Jesse Lasky Feature Play Company of Hollywood and New York was in business.

In the next few years, a profusion of films—*The Call of the North, The Virginian, The Trail of the Lonesome Pine, The Warrens of Virginia, The Rose of the Rancho*—were cranked out by De Mille in quick succession (it took seven days to film *The Wild Goose Chase*, starring Ina Claire) atop the raised platform in the orange grove next to the barn at Selma and Vine or out on the newly acquired Lasky Ranch in San Fernando Valley. The Hollywood of 1914, where these New Yorkers were busy establishing a permanent full-scale production facility, was, according to Cecil's brother William Churchill, who joined the staff as a scenario writer, an idyllic, sleepy Southern California town of sunny streets and comfortable homes and gardens, where life moved at a leisurely pace. Restaurant service consisted of two drugstore lunch counters a mile apart on Hollywood Boulevard; night life, two movie theaters closing at half past ten. "To the north," Cecil later wrote, "rose primitive, desert mountains, unchanged for centuries; green in February and March, but burning a russet brown through the arid summer heat. A few steps outside the town and you were in desert country. Sitting in the patio of your home after dinner you could hear the coyotes howl as they, too, felt the romance of the place." Less than six weeks after his arrival, William Churchill de Mille (only Cecil capitalized the D in the name) moved his family permanently out from New York. Like Cecil, he had decided to become a Southern Californian.

This choice on the part of Cecil B. De Mille to locate permanently in Hollywood, made in early 1914, must be considered both the actual and the symbolic founding of Hollywood as fact and myth. Unlike D. W. Griffith, CB liked Southern California and threw himself with ferocious energy into the task of shedding New York and putting on Southern California. A few months after his arrival he moved his wife and daughter out from the East, picking them up at the Los Angeles train station in an open touring car piled high with violets. The De Milles took up residence in a country house in the Cahuenga Pass between Hollywood and San Fernando Valley, set in a landscape of wild open country broken by a few vineyards. De Mille's mother joined them in 1916. When he arrived from New York, William Churchill de Mille noted that nine months of rugged outdoor life (fourteen films in 1914 alone) had bronzed and hardened Cecil, who seemed explosive with new energy. In contrast to the well-tailored habitué of the Lambs Club his brother had been, William discovered Cecil exuberantly playing a new role: the director as "Champion Driver," the term Cecil used to describe his persistent boyhood fantasy of himself as a hero on horseback, orchestrating the movements of great masses by sheer force of will. Whereas D. W. Griffith directed in a conventional business suit, with only his recherché headgear—a Chinese coolie hat, a Russian peasant cap, or a Mexican vaquero's sombrero—suggesting Art, Cecil B. De Mille evolved a Southern California–inspired costume of jodhpurs, leather boots and puttees, holster and pistol, military shirt, and flat cap worn in reverse (the better to peer through a camera lens) that remained the official Hollywood director's uniform long after it was no longer necessary to direct outdoors while standing in rattlesnake-infested chaparral.

Between 1913 and 1920 (by which time he was earning $260,000 a year), Cecil B. De Mille served as Champion Driver in the establishment of Hollywood as a subculture of Southern California and as a place of national significance. In each aspect of his personal style—his directorial costume, his military campaign demeanor on the set, his mansion in the Laughlin Park area of Hollywood on a street later named De Mille Drive, his ranch hideaway, Paradise, where De Mille provided his guests brightly colored Russian silk blouses and cummerbunds as mandatory dinner wear—Cecil B. De Mille created a reputation which became a legend and a legend which in turn became a founding myth. Like Griffith, De Mille maintained a troupe which was also an entourage. Some younger members of De Mille's troupe—Gloria Swanson, Ina Claire, Ramon Novarro, Wallace Beery, Mervyn LeRoy, Walt Disney—became themselves legends; others—opera diva Geraldine Farrar, most notably—came to De Mille with existing reputations. Cameraman Alvin Wyckoff worked closely with De Mille in much the same way as Billy Bitzer served Griffith. For years Anne Bauchens cut and edited all of CB's films. William Churchill, CB's brother, directed a staff of six scenarists who were constantly churning out scripts. One of them was Jeannie Macpherson, an astonishingly beautiful ex-actress who, like Anita Loos and Elinor Glyn, was destined to exert significant influence on the story content of the Hollywood cinema. Cecil and William invented the concept of in-house writing, carried on with team precision, a major premise of the studio system.

D. W. Griffith brought protean genius to Hollywood. Cecil B. De Mille brought the showmanship of New York. Personally and professionally, De Mille was a son of the New York stage. His father, Henry Churchill de Mille, was a respected New York actor, producer, and playwright who died at the height of his career when CB was only eleven. After her husband's death CB's mother continued to support her family as a theatrical agent, perhaps the first woman to become active in this field in American theater. From 1898 to 1900 Cecil studied at the American Academy of Dramatic Arts in New York City before going on stage in New York and in traveling companies. Musically adept, he sang at least one role in operetta. Like his father and his brother, Cecil wrote plays—*The Return of Peter Grimm, The Genius, After Eve, The Royal Mounted* (coauthored with brother William)—winning for himself, as his father had before him, election to the Lambs Club. It was at the Lambs that Cecil worked up the shooting script for *The Squaw Man.*

The stage had first brought De Mille into collaboration with Jesse Lasky, the two of them codirecting an operetta in 1912 entitled, significantly enough, *California*, with score by Robert Hood Bowers, lyrics by William Le Baron, and Fritz Sturmfels as lead tenor. Lavishly produced, *California* featured a railroad running past a mission and orange trees bearing real fruit, which the actors picked and ate in between musical numbers.

This last touch, the real oranges, was pure David Belasco. Given his start in the theater by the mighty Belasco himself and by Belasco's partner, Charles Frohman, who went down with the *Lusitania*, Cecil B. De Mille sustained with Belasco a relationship energized by boyhood association, lifelong affection, discipleship, and creative rivalry. Largely at De Mille's urging, Lasky bought ten plays from Belasco in 1914 for $100,000 for De Mille to direct, including two specifically California stories, *The Rose of the Rancho* and *The Girl of the Golden West.* When Belasco saw the rushes of *The Rose of the Rancho* in New York and wrote De Mille in praise of its dramatic action and fully realized California setting, an ecstatic De Mille had proof positive that he had managed to bring the best of the Belasco stage tradition to a new medium, film, and a new place, Hollywood.

Because Belasco had such a profound effect upon De Mille and because De Mille had such a profound effect on Hollywood, David Belasco must also be considered an honorary founder of early Hollywood. Few personalities before or since have exercised such a major influence on American entertainment as this Portuguese-Jewish Sephardic San Franciscan, raised alongside Josiah Royce in the South of Market district and educated, as was Royce, at the Lincoln Grammar School at Fifth and Mission. In the early 1860s, while in his late teens and early twenties, Belasco threw himself without reservation into the flourishing theatrical life of San Francisco as an actor, scenarist, director, manager, and impresario, transferring his activities to New York in the 1890s. Handsome and urbane, Belasco regarded life through flashing eyes set dramatically in a face worthy of the Italian Renaissance, at once sensual and spiritual, shrewd and exalted. Although Jewish—and not even an ordained rabbi at that!— Belasco affected a white clerical collar, in tribute, so he said, to a Roman Catholic priest who had befriended him in his youth. (Ushered into the great impresario's study in New York, young Mack Sennett, twenty years old and looking for work as an actor, felt himself in the presence of the Archbishop of Broadway.)

Tory bohemian to the core, the possessor of a massive, eclectic, and miscellaneous erudition, Belasco was also an excellent businessman, active in syndicating both plays and playhouses. On stage Belasco demanded realism, spectacle, and constant surprise and excitement. *Madame Butterfly*, produced in New York in 1900, set new standards for production values for the American stage. For the storm scene of *The Girl of the Golden West*, Belasco devised breathtaking effects to depict thunder, lightning, and falling snow. For *The Rose of the Rancho* (1906), which De Mille brought to the screen in 1914, Belasco worked with a crew of twenty-five electricians to effect shifting color variations suggestive of "the strong sunlight of my beloved California and the wonderful shades and tones of sunset, night, and dawn," and hung real oranges on the stage-set trees.

There were in David Belasco's stage work precursors of Hollywood and its later style: an obsession with lavish production values, a love of pageantry, and above all else, a belief that story, story, story must ever energize the production and move it forward. No wonder, then, that Belasco, who borrowed from everybody, found it so easy to borrow from film once this new genre had established itself, as he did when he hired Mary Pickford for the stage after seeing her in Griffith's *The New York Hat*. After all, he had helped create the genre. The circle became complete in 1914 when Jesse L. Lasky signed Belasco on as consulting dramaturge and coproducer for Lasky and De Mille's budding Hollywood enterprise.

Like Belasco, Cecil B. De Mille had a supreme showman's capacity to invest the ordinary with magic. Among other things, De Mille made a cult of the bedroom and the bathroom, investing these previously prosaic places with shimmering glamour by furnishing them with swan-shaped canopied beds and sunshine bathtubs that in their baroque grandeur often verged on the obsessive. Like Belasco, De Mille brought to his sets a hyperrealism that was frequently an end in itself. In *The Squaw Man*, De Mille insisted that the Indian girl be played by Red Wing, a young Indian woman with some acting ability. To depict the sinking of the *Lusitania* in *The Little American* (1917), De Mille rebuilt the entire deck of the stricken liner on San Pedro Harbor, with a mechanical tilting device that sent Mary Pickford and a crowd of extras splashing into the Pacific.

Like Belasco, De Mille experimented with music and color. Personally acquainted with many of the finest composers of the New York stage, including a friend from the Lambs Club, Victor Herbert, De Mille pioneered the commissioning of special scores to accompany his films. He experimented with color-tinting techniques two decades before color came even provisionally into use. The first of De Mille's color experiments, *Joan the Woman* (1916), a life of Joan of Arc starring opera diva Geraldine Farrar, inaugurated four decades of costume spectacles in which De Mille sought to outdo the master himself, which at long last he did in *The Ten Commandments* (1923). ("At last!" the master telegrammed De Mille on opening night, "a spectacle that out-Belascoes Belasco!") As early as 1915, De Mille was recreating on the primitive back lots adjacent to his studio barn elaborate sets depicting medieval France, Arabia, Montenegro (CB did two Montenegrin films in 1915 alone), soon to be followed by legendary recreations of ancient Egypt, Babylon, and the Holy Land. Each time De Mille remade *The Squaw Man* (in 1918 and 1931) he left the first version looking more and more impoverished. By the early 1920s the more discerning critics were admonishing De Mille for losing sight of his—or anyone else's—art in his obsessive use of costumes, sets, crowd scenes, orgies (a De Mille specialty), and excessive ritziness.

Film historian Paul Rotha blamed De Mille for almost single-handedly derailing American films into vulgar display and fantasy. Such De Mille films as *The Golden Bed* (1925), climaxed by a "Candy Ball" in which a candy manufacturer spends his fortune on an evening's entertainment, and *Madame Satan* (1930), in which the inevitable De Mille party is held on a dirigible which crashes (the more fortunate revelers are able to parachute to safety), certainly justify Rotha's harsh indictment. And yet De Mille knew his audience, as did David Belasco—knew that it demanded first of all to be entertained and only secondarily to be uplifted or instructed. Neither Belasco nor De Mille ever won unambiguous praise from highbrow critics. They took their consolation at the box office. Belasco's box office created modern Broadway, and De Mille's box office created Hollywood.

V

"He was the teacher of us all," De Mille later remarked of his fellow Hollywood founder D. W. Griffith. "Not a picture has been made since his time that does not bear some trace of his influence." Interestingly enough, Griffith was also called "the David Belasco of the screen" by critics searching for a pithy way to suggest his contribution during the early years of transition as the dominant popular American entertainment medium changed from stage to film. There was an element of rivalry between Griffith and De Mille. Jesse Lasky and Sam Goldfish had initially wanted Griffith, not De Mille, to serve as director-in-chief of Famous Players, but in the long run De Mille, and just about every other Hollywood director, could openly acknowledge Griffith's presiding genius without feeling any personal threat. By the 1930s, after all, Griffith was used up and finished, doomed to lonely hotel rooms, whiskey, and brooding resentment that the Hollywood he had founded had now cynically rejected him.

Today, nearly forty years after Griffith's death, his genius is universally recognized. Film historian Iris Barry believes that Griffith, along with Frank Lloyd Wright, is the greatest American artist since Walt Whitman. Even the acerbic Paul Rotha, who found so little to approve of in American film, was by the late 1920s enthusiastically acknowledging Griffith's primary role in establishing the syntax of film narration. Film critics and historians have all agreed that in pioneering such techniques as the close-up, the angle shot, the long shot, the crosscut, and the flashback, Griffith played a primary role in liberating the camera from its previous restriction to filming scene by scene, as in a stage play, and making it a new and distinct medium. The camera, Griffith asserted in both his remembered masterpieces and the more than four hundred quickies he cranked out for Biograph, was no slave to setting. The camera possessed its own power over time and space. Image by image, shot by shot, scene by scene, film was capable of reordering experience into new patterns of reality. These patterns, in turn, were capable of the highest modes of moral and imaginative statement. Borrowing plots from classic literature—Poe, Tennyson, Stevenson, Browning, even O. Henry and Jack London—Griffith worked virtually without a script, improvising from scene to scene. His dependency upon literary classics for plot lines, Paul Rotha asserts, underscores Griffith's ambivalence toward the medium he was pioneering. Personally he wanted to be a writer, not an actor or director. Even as he laid down the foundations of a new major art form, literature remained in Griffith's Victorian mind a higher form of statement.

As in a Griffith film, the scene now crosscuts briefly to Chatsworth Park, Los Angeles, June 1913, in the final months of Griffith's third Southern California sojourn. It will be another six months before De Mille even arrives in Southern California. A squadron of carpenters is busy constructing sets intended to recreate the walled city of Bethulia in ancient Samaria, scene of the biblical Book of Judith. When this work is done, hundreds of extras swarm onto the set, attired in biblical costumes meticulously researched for accuracy. Handsome, aloof, commandingly seated on a dais alongside his cameraman, Billy Bitzer, D. W. Griffith uses gesture and megaphone to rehearse a scene from his forthcoming *Judith of Bethulia*, which he will finish the following fall in the Biograph Studio in the Bronx. Released in early 1914, *Judith of Bethulia*, the story of the widow Judith and Holofernes, the Assyrian general whom she disguises herself to assassinate, will end Griffith's relationship to Biograph and send him back to Southern California on a more permanent basis.

The years 1912 and 1913 are pivotal in American film history. In July 1912 Adolph Zukor, a Hungarian-born furrier turned film exhibitor, joined with the great Daniel Frohman of Broadway to bring to New York Louis Mercanton's four-reel *Queen Elizabeth*, starring Sarah Bernhardt. Compared to the films that Griffith was then cranking out for Biograph, *Queen Elizabeth* was primitive. It was, in effect, a filmed play, shot in twelve separate scenes by an immobile center-stage camera. The actors even bowed to their unseen audience at the conclusion of the performance. Yet the success of *Queen Elizabeth* proved that American audiences would sit through feature-length films of serious intent. Seeing the eight-reel Italian spectacle *Quo Vadis?* in Europe in 1912, exhibitor George Kleine bought the American rights. *Quo Vadis?* opened at the Astor Theater on Broadway on 21 April 1913 and ran for twenty-two weeks, demonstrating that Americans were willing to pay one dollar to sit in a large theater and watch a two-hour feature film with lavish production values. *Quo Vadis?*, like *Queen Elizabeth* and the other European spectacles that soon followed—*The Last Days of Pompeii, Anthony and Cleopatra, Les Misérables*—encouraged D. W. Griffith to launch himself on an equally ambitious course. With the exception of *Queen Elizabeth*, Griffith had not even seen these films at the time he was putting *Judith of Bethulia* into production in Los Angeles. Yet generalized ambition to surpass the Italians and the French had already spurred him into action.

The result of this ambition, *Judith of Bethulia*, the first four-reeler ever made in the United States, is a landmark American film. Sumptuous, evocative, richly acted, and majestically paced, *Judith of Bethulia* proved unambiguously through what Edward Wagenknecht aptly describes as its "rich, brooding splendor of imagination" that the American cinema was capable of achievement of the highest order. In *Judith of Bethulia* Griffith simultaneously summarized his Biograph period and—in his crowd scenes, his cutting from mass action to individual event, the rich psychological interactions he suggested between Blanche Sweet (Judith) and Holofernes (Henry B. Walthall), his balletic orchestration of action and stasis, his symbolic imagery—anticipated the soon-to-be-achieved masterpieces *Birth of a Nation* and *Intolerance*. Unfortunately, *Judith of Bethulia* also demonstrated another Griffith characteristic: cost overruns. Budgeted for $18,000, the sets, costumes, and cast of *Judith of Bethulia* ran costs up to $36,000. Exasperated, Biograph kicked Griffith upstairs, making him a supervisor of other directors but with no specific films of his own.

Reluctant to continue on at Biograph as an administrator, Griffith resigned in the fall of 1914. Returning to Los Angeles, he began filming an epic story of the Civil War and Reconstruction based upon Thomas Dixon's pro-Confederate novel *The Clansman* (1905). It was first shown on the evening of

8 February 1915 at Clune's Auditorium in Los Angeles under its initial title, *The Clansman*. Today *The Birth of a Nation*, as it was soon called, is considered among the two or three finest films ever made. A twelve-reel epic of war and the aftermath of war, it was history written by lightning, as President Woodrow Wilson told Griffith when the film was shown in the White House. It has been analyzed and reanalyzed, scene by scene, shot by shot, for more than fifty years by those seeking to understand and appreciate Griffith's genius.

Obviously of supreme importance in the history of film as an art form, *The Birth of a Nation* is also of importance in tracing the history of Hollywood. While *Judith of Bethulia* was a Hollywood–New York production, *The Birth of a Nation* was purely Hollywood. During its filming in the second half of 1914, Griffith worked out of the Reliance-Majestic Studio and adjoining property at the corner of Sunset and Hollywood Boulevards. Battle scenes were filmed near Santa Monica. The agricultural region of Calexico provided Griffith with cotton fields and other plantation scenery. A mere six months, in other words, after Cecil B. De Mille had set up operations in a barn at Selma and Vine, Hollywood was supporting the production of a film masterpiece. Up until then Hollywood had been a Johnny-come-lately competitor against New York City and to a lesser extent Philadelphia and Chicago as a center of the American film industry. After the release of *The Birth of a Nation*, Hollywood attained a primary status it never surrendered. With *The Birth of a Nation*, the movies came permanently to Los Angeles.

In his next major production, *Intolerance* (1916), Griffith provided Hollywood with one of its most complex and enduring metaphors, Babylon, sumptuous city of ancient Mesopotamia, famed for its Hanging Gardens, its color, luxury, and sensual living, a city vanquishing its conquerors with the seductive force of its luxuriance and threatening to assimilate all newcomers, Jews and Gentiles alike, to permissive gods and easy ways. Although surviving as a primary metaphor (and until 1919 as an actual set), Babylon actually accounted for only one-fourth of the four-part plot of *Intolerance*. Stung by criticism that *The Birth of a Nation* was racist (it was), Griffith decided to fight back with what early film historian Terry Ramsaye called "the first and only film fugue": a four-plot depiction of intolerance in ancient Babylonia, Judea at the time of Christ, France on the eve of the Saint Bartholomew's Day Massacre of Huguenots in 1572, and contemporary America. Each story, Griffith declared, would "begin like four currents looked at from a hilltop. At first the four currents will flow apart, slowly and quietly. But as they flow, they grow nearer and nearer together, and faster and faster, until in the end, in the last act, they mingle in one mighty river of expressed emotion." To unify his "protest against despotism and injustice in every form," Griffith used the recurring image of Lillian Gish as a mother rocking a cradle, suggestive of Walt Whitman's "cradle endlessly rocking," and meaning (if anything) that each generation must in recurrent struggle in its own time and place combat the forces of intolerance and bigotry.

For his Babylon story, Griffith chose a storyline, developed as he went along, that concerned, among many other things, the courtship of King Belshazzar and the Princess Beloved (ever the Victorian, Griffith was addicted to saccharine names); Belshazzar's efforts to replace the worship of the love goddess Ishtar; the counterplotting of the priests of Baal; and the siege of the city by Assyrian hordes, let into the city by the treacherous priests of Baal. All this afforded Griffith the opportunity to mount and film a spectacle that even today, at the other end of the century, astonishes audiences by the grandeur of its sets, its balletic rhythms, its crowds, costumes, and architecture. As in the case of *Quo Vadis?* and *Judith of Bethulia* three years earlier, Griffith was again seeking to outperform an Italian cinema spectacle: *Cabiria*, a magnificently produced and filmed story of ancient Rome released in 1914 just as the First World War aborted the inventive Italian film industry. Not only did Griffith outperform *Cabiria* in the Babylonian sequences of *Intolerance*, he created in the empty back lots of Hollywood an *Ur*-epic of film spectacle that, Cecil B. De Mille admitted in the mid-1950s, had inspired, challenged, and ultimately defeated every producer and director of cinema spectacle in the years that followed. *Intolerance*, Paul Rotha lamented, helped wed American film to an equation between spectacle and art, expense and creativity, that in the long run doomed the industry to conspicuous mediocrity. At the same time, even Rotha confessed himself overwhelmed by such scenes as the Feast of Belshazzar and the attack against Babylon, scenes exhaustively researched by Griffith and his staff for historical accuracy. As Edward Wagenknecht points out, even Oxford's great Assyriologist, Archibald Henry Sayce, was thrilled by Griffith's recreation of ancient Babylon. "History," writes Iris Barry of these scenes, "seems to pour like a cataract across the screen."

At the center of Griffith's heroic inspiration was the set, Babylon itself, reconstructed on the corner of Sunset and Hollywood boulevards. Pennypinched by Biograph during the filming of *Judith of Bethulia*, Griffith vowed to spare no expense in the creation of what is today still the most ambitious and successful theatrical set ever designed and assembled. Inspired by the Tower of Jewels, center structure of the Panama-Pacific International Exposition in San Francisco, Griffith hired English stage designer Walter Hall (a squat, pugnacious Winston Churchill look-alike) to design and construct a set depicting the distilled essence of Babylon. When the hordes of carpenters, scene painters, and other craftsmen had completed their task, Hall presented Griffith with a three-hundred-foot-high theatrical-architectural masterpiece that was as breathtaking as it was expensive and ephemeral. Here indeed, in courtyards and staircases, columns and porticoes, statuary of exotic gods (including Ishtar nursing a man-sized infant at her breast) and mighty elephants trumpeting over all, was Hollywood's answer to San Francisco's Tower of Jewels: a fantasy creation intended for the moment, but also intended to express, if only evanescently, an inner dream, a metaphor of identity, that would last beyond its physical manifestation, continuing in memory to color and shape the culture around it.

Over this set David Wark Griffith literally soared, lord of his creation, borne aloft alongside cameraman Billy Bitzer atop a fifty-foot-high adjustable elevator platform that moved smoothly along on mining-car rail wheels. Six years earlier Griffith had been working with his itinerant troupe atop a simple wooden platform hastily constructed on an empty Los Angeles lot—and now this, the greatest theatrical set ever constructed, on which, for the Feast of Belshazzar scene, hundreds of beautiful, young, costumed female dancers were moving rhythmically in unison to the "Bacchanale" music from Saint-Saëns's *Samson and Delilah*. Never before in modern times, in Europe, Asia, or America, had such a purely aesthetic, nonutilitarian pageant been documented; thanks to Billy Bitzer's camera, it would last beyond the day it transpired beneath the sun of Southern California.

It was during this period, from *Judith of Bethulia* in 1913 through 1916 and the filming of *Intolerance*, that the legend of D. W. Griffith as founding Hollywood director took substance and form. Less flamboyant than the costumed De Mille, Griffith nevertheless established equal, if not surpassing, mastery on the set. Anita Loos remembered visiting Griffith on the set of *Judith of Bethulia* as a sixteen-year-old aspiring screenwriter in the company of her chaperoning mother. "Tall, bronzed, and rangy like a cowboy," Loos writes of this encounter, "Griffith was in his shirt sleeves and wore a battered straw sombrero tied under his chin with a black shoe string; the ridiculous get-up didn't detract one bit from his enormous distinction. Griffith must have been in his early thirties, but he had an authority that seemed to deny he had ever been young. His highly arched nose belonged on some Roman emperor; his pale eyes, in sharp contrast to the tan of his complexion, shone with a sort of archaic amusement, as if he were constantly saying to himself, 'What fools these mortals be!' "

Samuel Goldwyn had a similar impression. "His features are clean-cut," Goldwyn observed of Griffith on the set, "and to the suggestion of the eagle in his profile the clear blue eyes—eyes which you could never possibly mistake for gray even across a room—contribute a final authority. These eyes while he is at work, so people tell me, glow with enthusiasm, but during the chance interview they join with the mouth in a look of amused observation."

Authority, engagement, yet a certain mysterious detachment as well: Griffith played Gatsby on the set, the handsome stranger, seeming to spring from a Platonic conception of himself, in enigmatic control of his surroundings. Through the eyes of the camera and the reminiscences of his contemporaries, an image of Griffith is preserved that will forever haunt Hollywood with a remembered presence embodying all the emerging energies of a nascent art. We see Griffith in an aloof mood, lunching alone from a hamper prepared by the Alexandria

Hotel, or, more congenially, playing the benevolent headmaster to a crowd of local boys in the flat caps and collarless shirts of the era who have wandered onto the set from nearby neighborhoods to see what all these people in Babylonian costumes are up to. During a break in shooting, Griffith—a battered straw hat atop his head, his director's megaphone at his side—discourses to the aspiring film folk gathered around him regarding the special genius and assured future of the medium they are all pioneering together. One contemporary compared these impromptu outdoor sessions to the way philosophers offered instruction in ancient Greece. We see Griffith shadowboxing for exercise, singing operatic arias during interruptions on the set, bending over Blanche Sweet the better to suggest how he wanted a seduction scene played, dancing with Lillian Gish to the accompaniment of a wind-up Victrola.

Like F. Scott Fitzgerald's Gatsby, Griffith worshipped youth and beauty with a touchingly romantic reverence. Griffith believed that older actors and actresses could not withstand the exacting scrutiny of the close-up. Beginning with sixteen-year-old Mary Pickford, he brought a succession of youthful actresses to the screen. Separated from Linda Arvidson in 1911 but not divorced until 1936, Griffith moved constantly amidst troupes of young actresses, with whom he seems (so the evidence suggests) to have been contented to play the Platonic father-hero, whatever other liaison he might be pursuing at the time. Lillian Gish was Griffith's Daisy Buchanan (to continue the Gatsby analogy). He discovered her and her sister Dorothy for Biograph in June 1912 when the girls were still teenagers (as were most of Griffith's female discoveries) and forever after revered her with old-fashioned Southern chivalry as a pure and luminous womanly ideal. During love scenes Miss Gish's mother served as chaperone on the set, and young Lillian, at Griffith's insistence, was exempt from kissing on the mouth. Off screen, Griffith escorted Miss Gish to various Los Angeles social events with an air of distant chaperonage. "The two made an extremely romantic-looking pair," Anita Loos recalled. "I remember seeing them enter the grand ballroom of the old Alexandria Hotel in Los Angeles one night, when D. W. looked like one of his own Southern aristocrats of *The Birth of a Nation* and Lillian, in her pink ball gown and black lace mitts, was so breathtakingly beautiful that for a man not to be in love with her seemed inhuman. Astoundingly enough, D. W. seemed almost inhuman; he was of Welsh extraction, and the Welsh are a very peculiar breed, poetic, unpredictable, remote, and fiercely independent. For such a man to be in love must be terribly frustrating, because his deepest instinct is to be a loner."

Intolerance cost money—a quarter of a million dollars for the Feast of Belshazzar alone. Griffith's payroll averaged $12,000 a day. For the Fall of Babylon sequence, Griffith gathered together 15,000 extras and 250 horse-drawn chariots in the early morning hours of a shooting day chosen for its probable good weather. As the masses assembled under Griffith's direction, however, word reached the director that a fog bank was unexpectedly rolling in from the coast. Realizing that he could never again assemble such a crowd, or its payroll (15,000 separately issued salary checks), or even the 15,000 box lunches ordered and at the ready, Griffith plunged into the Fall of Babylon. Fortunately, the city fell just as the fog bank rolled in, stopping the cameras. All in all, Griffith spent $1.9 million to film 300,000 feet or seventy-five reels of negative, which he edited down to fourteen reels for the preview of *Intolerance* at Riverside on 6 August 1916, before opening at the Liberty Theatre in New York on 5 September.

The failure of *Intolerance* at the box office destroyed Griffith financially and—although not immediately—in other ways as well. Overwhelmed by the spectacle and by the effort to keep four plots straight, audiences found themselves in agreement with assistant cameraman Karl Brown's assessment: "There was so much about the picture that didn't hang together that I soon stopped trying to understand any of it." Among other things, *Intolerance* failed on the level of idea. The figure of Lillian Gish as the mother endlessly rocking her cradle was just not enough to hold four such disparate plots together. Griffith's pacifist intent, moreover, ran counter to growing war sentiment after the sinking of the *Lusitania*, and the film's occasional lapses into overwrought sentimentality so identified it with an earlier era that almost at once it seemed out of date. Forced to refinance *Intolerance* midway through its filming with profits from *The Birth of a Nation*, Griffith now watched eighteen months and $2 million evaporate at the box office. "I have always dated the beginning of his decline with *Intolerance*," Cecil B. De Mille later observed. De Mille was right.

After it was over, however—after the filming, and the commercial failure of what had been filmed at such heroic expense—Babylon endured on the corner of Sunset and Hollywood Boulevards. Almost immediately the Los Angeles Fire Department, unimpressed by things symbolic, demanded that the set be torn down as a fire hazard. Griffith resisted, using portions of the set as headquarters for his next film, like a defeated prince camping temporarily in his ruined city after sacking besiegers had departed.

Yet as much as the set bespoke the past—Babylon's past and, with the failure of *Intolerance*, Griffith's eventual and inevitable past as well—it was, like all successful festival architecture, a gesture in the direction of things to come. This Babylon wrought by Griffith and Walter L. Hall—this "make-believe mirage of Mesopotamia," in Kenneth Anger's phrase, "dropped down on the sleepy huddle of mission-style bungalows amid the orange groves"—stated unequivocally that by 1915 a new place and a new industry, Hollywood, had fully consolidated itself in less than three years. This Hollywood would be capable of extravagances of the highest order, such as the Feast of Belshazzar or the Fall of Babylon, provided that such extravagance served the collective dream life of the nation. Like the set, Hollywood was, and was not, a real place. What was real was wood, plaster, gypsum, painted canvas, papier-mâché molded into a thousand shapes, against the backdrop of which hundreds of girls danced and illusory Assyrians advanced on the city. These film illusions engendered dream upon dream in innumerable American places.

Not surprisingly, there were efforts to preserve the set as landmark festival architecture, like the Palace of Fine Arts in San Francisco, but its construction materials were too flimsy. The set, after all, despite its masterly design, was more illusion than architecture. Even as Griffith delayed its dismantlement, the set began to crumble. Soon weeds were growing in the palace of Belshazzar and Hall's mighty elephants were trumpeting over torn reliefs, collapsed stairs, damaged statues, walls where wood and cheap gypsum showed through a semblance of marble. By 1919 most of the set was dismantled. Portions of it, however—a portico, a pillar, a triumphant elephant or two—were stored and reused on the back lots of Hollywood for years to come, the *membra disjecta* of Griffith's dreams, serving, as did the legacy of his career, the ongoing work of Hollywood.

10

Hollywood, Mass Culture, and the Southern California Experience

By 1911, before the movies settled permanently in Hollywood, an estimated ten million Americans were regularly attending motion picture theaters. Between 1910 and 1912 that figure doubled. In Europe, especially after the First World War destroyed or bankrupted so many production facilities, the cinema developed as a highbrow avant-garde art. In the United States, by contrast, movies were mass entertainment. The very substitution of the popular designation *movies* for the earlier Greek- or Latin-inspired cognates incorporating *kinetos, cinema, vita,* or *bio* underscored (so film historian Benjamin B. Hampton was emphasizing as early as 1931) the underlying democratic structure of the American film industry, whose first great director, after all, Edwin S. Porter, was not an artist or even a theater man but a blue-collar mechanic who returned to working with his hands after his directing days were over. The all-time popular star of American movies, comedian Charlie Chaplin, was an itinerant vaudeville performer who had spent two years of his youth in a workhouse for the poor. "The cinema," Lenin is reported to have said after seeing *Intolerance*, "must and shall become the foremost cultural weapon of the proletariat."

Film historian Lewis Jacobs emphasizes that a full ten years before Lenin had this insight, American movies were already holding up a surprisingly encompassing mirror to ordinary American life. The one-reelers playing in the nickelodeons to which working people flocked, Jacobs points out, generally depicted not spectacles or costume dramas but the stories and situations, invariably comic, of everyday life. Crowded into nickelodeons, the working people of America at last had for their enjoyment an art form that told their story, depicted their tastes and values without judgment or condescension. Laughing at themselves, American audiences laughed together. Such highbrow cinema theorists as Professor Hugo Munsterberg of Harvard in his pioneering essay *The*

Photoplay (1916) and British psychologist Gerard Fort Buckle in *The Mind and the Film* (1926) emphasized that the enjoyment of motion pictures demanded no special literary abilities or preparation, and only a minimum of conscious attention. Films spoke directly to the cognitive and subconscious self with next to no dependence on the apparatus and language of formal culture. The movies, Vachel Lindsay emphasized in *The Art of the Moving Picture* (1915), were an appropriately American art form: accessible, democratic, capable of bringing stories and dreams to ordinary America.

Such also were the thoughts of William Churchill de Mille as he rode the train westward from New York in the summer of 1914 to join his brother Cecil in Hollywood. Like most New Yorkers, de Mille had always believed "that the United States was bounded by the Hudson, the East River, the Battery and the Bronx." Crossing the United States by train, however, de Mille encountered for the first time the breadth of the American continent, together with the variety and essential unity of the American people. The New York theater, de Mille realized, could never begin to reach the millions of Americans inhabiting this vast continent, but the screen could. But how? What kinds of stories could satisfy so diverse an audience? "I watched the changing scenes go by," de Mille recalled of that near-mystic train ride of 1914: "cities, towns, villages, then scattered farms, and finally little settlements and ranches with miles of desert around them. So many kinds of people, each looking at life through the problems of his own environment; and our job was to find stories which would reach them all; an appeal to any special class of people no matter how large would still fail to reach enough people. What did they all have in common? Only their emotions. Their ideas on most matters were different, even their gods were different; but love, hate, fear, ambition—these were basically the same in all of them." Motion pictures in America, de Mille believed, should strive for a new mode of mass appeal entertainment, one based upon common experience and emotion. Hollywood, which even then his brother Cecil was in the process of establishing, should base itself on the box office and not upon any elitist conception of art. "It was to the elemental, then, that we must appeal," de Mille concluded. "Style and art were interesting but not essential."

Sitting a week later in a darkened room in the Los Angeles suburb of Hollywood, watching rushes of *The Rose of the Rancho*, de Mille experienced further insights into the nature of his new calling. Feeling how the audience—including de Mille himself—was caught up in the drama as intensely as an audience watching a stage play, de Mille realized that motion pictures were "the first really new form of dramatic story-telling which had been invented for some five hundred years." In his mind's eye de Mille saw "a potential theater of the whole people: acted drama brought within the means of the poorest family, accessible all over the country, and beyond into foreign lands. It would be a new theater which the people themselves would control by sheer force of numbers, since dictatorship, while frequently controlling the intelligentsia in their patronage of the so-called 'higher arts,' has never been able to influence popular drama. I had always followed the spoken drama as the democrat of all arts, but here was an art being born infinitely more democratic; an art which might soon cause spoken drama to be considered merely as aristocratic entertainment for the few who could afford it."

Espousing such demotic ideals, William de Mille and his brother Cecil were nevertheless upper-middle-class New Yorkers through and through, sons of a distinguished family, graduates of good schools, members of Manhattan clubs. The men they worked for, however, the money men who soon controlled Hollywood, more closely approximated those de Mille had in mind when he predicted that through motion pictures the people would at long last have their say. A decade into the twentieth century a loosely affiliated group of young Jewish immigrants from New York's East Side, a number of them in the garment, glove, or fur business, got into the business of showing films in small arcades and theaters. Fur merchant Marcus Loew, who had begun life selling newspapers Horatio Alger style, was the first to get into this new venture. Loew was soon joined by another furrier, the Hungarian-born Adolph Zukor. Another East Side immigrant, William Fox, invested successfully in a theater, then left the garment business altogether. Three of these exhibitors—Zukor, Jesse Lasky, and Lasky's brother-in-law Samuel Goldfish—played immediate roles in the establishment of Hollywood.

For Lasky—rotund, balding, rabbi-like in his rimless spectacles—the move back to California was a homecoming. Born (1880) in San Francisco, Lasky had been raised in the Santa Clara Valley town of San Jose, the son of a semi-prosperous Jewish shoestore owner who wanted Jesse to study law at the newly established Stanford University in nearby Palo Alto. When his father died, so did Jesse's Stanford career. A skilled cornet player whose boyhood dream was to play with John Philip Sousa, Jesse was not without resources. After a brief stint as a reporter on the *San Francisco Post* and a sojourn in Alaska during the Gold Rush, Jesse Lasky went into music. The turn of the century found him in Honolulu, the only white musician in the Royal Hawaiian Band. When his sister Blanche grew proficient on the cornet as well, the two formed a brother-and-sister act, The Musical Laskys, and traveled around the country on the small-time vaudeville circuit with their mother. After three years of third-rate hotels and second-string houses, Jesse Lasky edged into the management of vaudeville acts. This new business prospered. By 1911 Lasky, then based in New York City, was commissioning and producing musical routines and one-act comedy sketches for the national vaudeville circuit. One of his writers was an aspiring young actor-playwright by the name of Cecil B. De Mille.

Blanche Lasky married Samuel Goldfish, a highly successful glove manufacturer born in the Warsaw ghetto (1882) and raised in Birmingham, England, where his parents ran a small antique business. Running away from home at the age of twelve or fourteen (reports vary), Goldfish worked his passage to the United States, then spent five years in a glove factory in Gloversville, New York, before persuading his company to send him on the road as a drummer. By the time he was thirty, Goldfish owned his own successful glove company in New York City, where he met Jesse Lasky, joined him as an investor in the vaudeville business, and married Jesse's sister Blanche. Muscular, compact, handsome in the rugged style of a prizefighter who has never lost his looks, Goldfish offered a physical contrast to his pudgy, bespectacled brother-in-law. It was Goldfish, moreover, who first—in early 1913—got interested in branching out from vaudeville into motion pictures. Seeing *Queen Elizabeth*, the first feature-length film to be shown in the United States, Goldfish grasped at once the future profitability of feature-length motion pictures. Restlessly he roamed New York City, ducking in and out of theaters, dreaming of getting into this new business.

The exhibitor who brought *Queen Elizabeth* to the United States, Adolph Zukor, had by 1913 already been in the motion picture theater business for a decade, since 1903, when Zukor joined two other furriers, Max Goldstein and Morris Kohn, to open a penny arcade on the southern side of Union Square in New York City. Hungarian-born (1873), Zukor had been intended by his parents for the rabbinate, a path which Adolph's brother eventually chose after Adolph had said good-bye to Hungary at age seventeen and booked steerage to America. Reaching New York in 1888, Zukor went to work in the garment factories of the Lower East Side before moving on to Chicago, where relatives from the old country had prospered in the fur business. By 1903 Zukor had returned to New York as the prosperous member of a furrier partnership. Pleased with his investment in the Union Square penny arcade, Zukor branched out into nickelodeons, travel films, and (in association with Marcus Loew) popular-priced film-and-vaudeville shows. There was in Adolph Zukor a mysteriousness, a reserve in speech and demeanor, that stood in direct contrast to Lasky's *haimish* amiability and Goldfish's rugged outspokenness. Lean, chiseled, polished in manners and tailoring, Adolph Zukor was at once silently cunning and a natural aristocrat. Whereas Lasky was a lower-middle-class American from San Jose, California, and Goldfish sprang from the Warsaw ghetto, Adolph Zukor came from the more established and secure Hungarian Jewry, from a family noted for producing generations of doctors and rabbis. In the long run (which came very swiftly) it would be Adolph Zukor who most conspicuously triumphed, drawing unto himself at Paramount (as his company would be called) control of a vast empire encompassing the production, distribution, and showing of motion pictures on a national basis—just as William Churchill de Mille predicted.

II

By 1915 Hollywood was an established fact; by 1926 it was the United States' fifth largest industry, grossing $1.5 billion a year and accounting for 90 percent of the world's films. Long gone by then were the old East Coast–based companies with their fussy Greek and Latin names. In their place had arisen Hollywood-based organizations—Paramount, First National, Fox, Universal, Metro, Goldwyn, United Artists, Warner Brothers—maintaining huge studios and linked to national distribution systems and theater chains. The studio system characterized Hollywood from the first. By 1915, for instance, Hollywood's founding company, the Jesse Lasky Feature Play Company, had grown to five directors, five cameramen, and eighty players located in a number of buildings on ten acres at Sunset and Vine, with outdoor operations on a large ranch in the San Fernando Valley. By then, C. B. De Mille—who was fond of quoting Sir Henry Irving's statement that theater "must be carried on as a business or it will fail as an art"—was busy bringing system and efficiency to his staff, even writing a memorandum that no company cars could be used for personal shopping. De Mille's counterpart, D. W. Griffith, also found himself mired (over his head, as it turned out) in the demands of running a business. The sheer magnitude of *The Birth of a Nation* and *Intolerance* demanded major studio facilities and financing. The business history of *The Birth of a Nation* is almost as complex as the film itself. Griffith began the film for Mutual, refinanced it under the auspices of the Epoch Film Corporation, then joined with Thomas Ince and Mack Sennett to form Triangle, whose trademark was Fine Arts Productions. For *Intolerance* Griffith formed another company, the Wark Producing Corporation, syndicated to some fifty investors, including Lillian Gish. Located at the intersection of Vermont and Sunset Boulevard, Griffith's Fine Arts Studio pioneered the concept of a full-service production facility, complete with a corps of on-site scenario writers presided over by veteran writer-publicist Frank Woods.

The momentum gathering behind the Hollywood studio system dramatically asserted itself that same year, 1915, the *annus mirabilis* of Hollywood's foundation, when more than twenty thousand spectators gathered on the 230-acre Taylor Ranch five miles north of Hollywood on the Los Angeles River for the opening of Universal City. Carl Laemmle, another European-born ex-clothier, had founded the Independent Motion Picture Company (IMP) in 1909, later reorganizing it as the Universal Film Manufacturing Company. Laemmle's magnificently equipped Universal City studio featured Hollywood's first artificially lighted stage, personally dedicated by no less than Henry Ford and Thomas Alva Edison. Within a year after its dedication, Universal City had already accounted for an astonishing 250 films. Against such an onslaught the Trust had no chance. Weakened by a series of lawsuits that began in 1912 with a successful action by William Fox against the Edison Company, the Trust companies faded away with the rise of Hollywood. By 1920 only one Trust company was still operating.

Forced out of Paramount in 1916, Sam Goldfish joined Edgar Selwyn to form Goldwyn Pictures Corporation. Liking the name Goldwyn, Sam went to court and dropped the slightly comic Goldfish in favor of this more dignified moniker. Griffith reentered the entrepreneurial scene in 1919, joining Charles Chaplin, Douglas Fairbanks, and Mary Pickford to form United Artists, a company owned and controlled by stars and directors. "So," mused Richard Rowland of Metro, "the lunatics have taken charge of the asylum." The next year, 1920, theater owner Marcus Loew acquired control of Metro Pictures. In 1924, Loew, Goldwyn, and Louis Burt Mayer, a Russian-born Jew who started his career with a nickelodeon in Haverhill, Massachusetts, joined together to form Metro-Goldwyn-Mayer, perhaps the single most successful studio company in Hollywood history.

Throughout this period of studio formation, the decade 1914–24, one figure, Adolph Zukor, emerges as Hollywood's preeminent business intelligence. A founder ranking with Griffith and De Mille in terms of vision and creative energy, Zukor also emerges ahead of his compatriots Lasky and Goldwyn in the drive to create a national entertainment industry based in Hollywood and financed by New York. Development by development, the rise of Hollywood occurred under Zukor's subtle but firm management. Joining Daniel Frohman to bring *Queen Elizabeth* to the United States in 1912, Zukor proved that American audiences would pay to attend feature-length photoplays. In association with Frohman (aside from David Belasco perhaps the best-known theatrical producer in the United States) Zukor went on to found the Manhattan-based Famous Players in Famous Plays Company, committed to the feature-length concept. Under the overall directorial supervision of Edwin S. Porter, Famous Players began producing a film a week in 1913, graded as Class A, B or C depending upon production values, starting with a Class A production (costing $20,000) of Anthony Hope's *The Prisoner of Zenda*, starring the well-known Broadway actor James K. Hackett.

Zukor had also been expanding his activities as an exhibitor and theater owner in partnership with Marcus Loew. Zukor's next venture, Paramount Pictures Corporation—which he founded in January 1914 in association with Lasky, Goldfish, and W. W. Hodkinson, a West Coast theater owner—bridged the worlds of production, distribution, and theater ownership. The system was simple. Starting with some 104 films a year, Paramount commissioned films from Famous Players, Lasky, Morosco, and Pallas—then distributed them nationally to contracted exhibitors who had already advanced money to Paramount. Within a few years, upwards of six thousand theaters across the country were booked into the Paramount system. Meanwhile, Zukor had forced Hodkinson out of power at Paramount and in 1916 had merged Lasky and Famous Players into the Famous Players–Lasky Corporation, thus assuring Paramount of a favored relationship with one of Hollywood's most important production studios.

Feeling himself edged out by Zukor's growing power, Samuel Goldfish parted company with Paramount and struck out on his own. Goldfish's brother-in-law Jesse Lasky remained on as Zukor's vice-president and manager of production. Thus by 1916 Adolph Zukor, as president and chief financial officer of Paramount, held power and significant ownership over the essential apparatus of the American film industry as it would function in the post-Trust era. Over the years, rivals surfaced to Paramount's power—most dramatically First National, formed by a hundred key theater owners in April 1917—but until the rise of Metro-Goldwyn-Mayer in the late 1920s Paramount and Adolph Zukor dominated the movie industry. By 1920 Paramount was releasing three to four films a week to some five thousand theaters. In 1926 Zukor built the thirty-story Paramount Building on Times Square, which also housed the luxuriant Paramount Theater, among the grandest of the 1920s picture palaces. From his office on Times Square, Zukor presided over a far-flung $150 million empire, which included the Public Theaters Corporation, a chain of some seven hundred theaters located in key cities and towns across the United States.

For so many figures from the same background—many of them knowing each other from the old clothing, fur, glove, vaudeville, and nickelodeon days in New York, others with regional and family affinities that went back to Europe—to seize exclusive power over the Hollywood-centered national entertainment industry created a situation that could not be ignored. Sometimes responses could be humorous. "Put that finger down," John Barrymore once cracked to a Hollywood magnate admonishing him for an indiscretion. "I remember when it had a thimble on it." Other times—as in the case of the national reaction to the Hollywood scandals of the early 1920s—responses could be openly anti-Semitic. Never before had so many Jewish Americans, most of them still speaking in the accents of the Central and Eastern European Pale, come as a visible group into so much economic and cultural power. When Marcus Loew, head of the Metro-Goldwyn Corporation, who had begun his working life as a newsboy on the Lower East Side, died in 1927, he left a personal fortune of $25 million. The non-Jewish majority might approve of such all-American rags-to-riches success, but such success could also be resented. There was also the more sinister suggestion, made in the pulpit and the press, that the entertainment industry, possessed of such overwhelming influence over the national majority, was dangerously under the control of a foreign-born, still largely alien minority. Resentments gathered. W. W. Hodkinson, the WASP who initially created the Paramount Distributing Company, lost control of it to Adolph Zukor, a Hungarian-born Jew. When Cecil B. De Mille, a New York–born Episcopalian, was forced out of Famous Players–Lasky in 1925, he was told (so he later claimed), "Cecil, you have never been one of us." De Mille went on to produce and direct the aggressively Christian *The King of Kings* in retaliation.

Ambivalences existed on both sides. Samuel Goldfish, the quintessence of the spottily educated, malaprop-prone Hollywood tycoon of the first immigrant generation, changed his last name to Goldwyn to soften its Jewish suggestions. Douglas Fairbanks and Erich von Stroheim each concealed their Jewish descent, Fairbanks behind Anglo-American preppiness, von Stroheim behind an almost parodic hyper-Prussianism.

A certain insecurity, in any event, would continue to hold Hollywood's leadership to its own peculiar conception of patriotism and American value. In part because of its minority immigrant origins, Hollywood would be ever eager to please in the matter of promoting what it understood to be the national culture. Ironically, this apprehension of what America was, slightly out of focus from the start, in turn helped shape the emerging twentieth-century American identity. Subtly (and often not so subtly) made to feel itself different, the Hollywood leadership set about to serve but also to enlarge the national myth. When the First World War came, Hollywood was ready: with Liberty Bond drives that astonished government officials with Hollywood's ability to raise money, with ferociously anti-German photoplays depicting the Hun at his worst, with a Home Guard unit organized by Cecil B. De Mille, whose propagandistic films led the way in unleashing an orgy of anti-German hatred throughout the United States. When the war was over anti-German films were a drug on the market. The day the Armistice was signed, American audiences, eager for a resumption of what President Warren G. Harding eventually described as normalcy, began to stay away in droves. But a relationship between Hollywood and the patriotic right had been established, and twentieth-century Southern California, as eager as Hollywood to prove itself before the eyes of more established American regions, would also evolve around this aggressively patriotic sensibility.

III

Adolph Zukor's decision to remain in New York underscored the fact that Hollywood depended upon Eastern banks for financing. Not until the rise of A. P. Giannini's Bank of Italy/America in the 1920s could Hollywood locally generate its necessary capital. With a few exceptions—Los Angeles businessman Frank C. Garbutt, for instance, who in 1914 financed the filming of Jack London's *The Sea Wolf*—Southern California investors avoided the movies in favor of oil and real estate, and so Hollywood turned to Wall Street. In 1919 Goldwyn Pictures became the first Hollywood studio to be listed on the New York Stock Exchange. By the early 1920s the Hollywood director, who in the first era had reigned supreme over his set, was replaced in authority by the producer representing investment interests. A. P. Giannini altered this system somewhat in the mid-1920s, as he acquired control of numerous Southern California banks. Making loans to smaller studios—including Cecil B. De Mille's own independent studio, established in 1925 after De Mille broke with Lasky and Zukor—Giannini brought a measure of localism to the financing of Hollywood. With Giannini's help, De Mille set out to challenge Famous Players–Lasky, First National, and Metro-Goldwyn-Mayer, and thus keep (so De Mille hoped) Hollywood in contact with independently creative personalities such as himself, Sennett, and Griffith.

By 1918 Hollywood was a major industry, financed and operated on the industrial model. It was also very soon a monopoly. Among themselves, Paramount, Loew's, First National, Fox, and Universal operated some twenty thousand theaters in the United States and Canada by 1927, together with forty-six film exchanges in all important cities. This massive distribution and exhibition capacity was linked via common ownership to virtually all major production facilities in Hollywood, where thousands of workers kept busy producing film after film, assembly-line style, for double features (often changed biweekly) at those twenty thousand theaters, attended by a hundred million Americans each week. Paramount, Cecil B. De Mille claimed, set such rigid quotas that he often found himself shooting the first scenes of a film for which there existed only a title and a sketchy story line. To preclude story shortfalls, producer-director Thomas Ince (destined to die under mysterious circumstances in 1924 aboard William Randolph Hearst's yacht) perfected an industrialized technique of story production in which staffs of well-trained writers cranked out plot after plot. Such techniques and such a system, Paul Rotha was claiming by 1929, could rarely, if ever, produce art. Only a few Hollywood artists, Rotha argued—Charles Chaplin, Douglas Fairbanks, Erich von Stroheim, King Vidor, and Henry King among them—managed to beat the system once the machine-made era took over the silents.

Questions of talent or art aside, industrial Hollywood created a new genre of Southern Californian, the Hollywood movie star, who in turn began to exercise enormous influence on the ways and means with which Americans defined their values and identities. Two of Hollywood's first stars, Geraldine Farrar and Theda Bara, provide contrasting case studies of how the star system built itself. Largely because of the persistence of Sam Goldwyn, the Lasky Studio signed opera diva Geraldine Farrar in the fall of 1915 to go to Hollywood for eight weeks and make three pictures—*Maria Rosa, Carmen,* and *Temptation.* Miss Farrar's fee ($20,000) was not excessive in comparison to her fees for an eight-week concert tour, but the reigning diva of American opera was, according to Sam Goldwyn, as shrewd at negotiating as she was talented at singing. In addition to the $20,000 fee, Farrar demanded that Goldwyn and Lasky provide her with a private railroad car to and from California, a fully staffed two-story house in Hollywood, a chauffeur-driven limousine, a bungalow-sized dressing studio equipped with a grand piano, all living expenses for herself and her staff, and an augmented orchestra to create the proper mood music on the set. When Farrar detrained from her private car in the Santa Fe Depot in Los Angeles, the mayor himself was on hand to escort her on a red carpet past a cheering crowd of five thousand. Schoolchildren strewed flowers in her path. "All Los Angeles," Samuel Goldwyn later remembered, "reminded you of a fiesta day in some Italian city." The following evening the Lasky studio threw a welcoming banquet for two hundred guests in the Hollywood Hotel.

Not only did Geraldine Farrar bring, as Goldwyn knew she would, class, real class, to motion pictures, she also turned out to be an excellent screen actress. Elegant, beautiful in a darkly Irish way, Farrar responded enthusiastically to director De Mille and turned in excellent performances in her three roles. On 1 October 1915 Lasky previewed *Carmen* in Symphony Hall, Boston, where Farrar had begun her career. The reviews were enthusiastic. Because of Farrar's starring role, Boston treated De Mille's version of *Carmen* as a serious artistic event. Two seasons later Geraldine Farrar returned to Hollywood, where De Mille directed her in *Joan the Woman* and *The Woman God Forgot*, in which Farrar played Tecza, daughter of Montezuma, last emperor of the Aztecs.

Geraldine Farrar came to Hollywood with the established prestige of grand opera. In the case of Theda Bara, Hollywood proved that it could create a reputation through sheer hype. Miss Bara made her film debut in *A Fool There Was* in 1915. This was also the year that a former newsman-turned-publicist by the name of Frank Woods, assisted by the pioneering public relations team of Bennie Ziedman, Willard Keefe, and Jack Lloyd, created a frenzy of prerelease anticipation for *The Birth of the Nation*. Thanks in part to Woods's brilliant press-agentry, an artistically distinguished film also made a killing at the box office. That year director Frank J. Powell cast an unknown actress, Miss Theodosia Goodman of Cincinnati, Ohio, to play the lead role in William Fox's production of *A Fool There Was*, based upon a stage play inspired by "The Vampire," a poem by Rudyard Kipling which had in turn been inspired by a painting by Sir Edward Burne-Jones. Painting, poem, play, and film all dealt in their various ways with the vampire theme: the destruction of a weak man by a femme fatale. While *A Fool There Was* was still in production, press agents Johnny Goldfrap and Al Selig got to work. Theodosia Goodman, a nice Jewish girl from Cincinnati, was transformed into Theda Bara (an anagram for Arab Death), the love child of a French artist and an Egyptian princess, conceived on the Nile and born in the shadow of the Sphinx. The press bought it, or at least pretended to. In Chicago Miss Bara, attended by Nubian footmen, gave a press conference in a crowded hotel room darkened with black velvet hangings and aromatic with burning incense. When the press left, she tore down the draperies and threw open the window, gasping, "Give me air!"

All in all, Miss Goodman Bara did some forty vamp movies for Fox between 1915 and 1919 before settling down as a Beverly Hills housewife. As silly as her promotion might seem today, the vamp figure Bara portrayed, together with her own industry-created stardom, dramatized for the first time Hollywood's ability to respond to and in turn shape social realities through the mediating figure of the movie star. For all the hype—the spurious ancestry, the bogus Nubian footmen, the incense and skulls—Theda Bara did assert that Americans were in a transitional state regarding their willingness overtly to acknowledge sexuality as a primary force in human affairs. Emerging midway between the Victorian heroine as interpreted by D. W. Griffith and the sexually threatening flapper a mere six or seven years away, Theda Bara, the vamp, for all the silliness of the role she played, embodied a significant aspect of American consciousness. In the matter of human sexuality, a shift of attitude was occurring, and Theodosia Goodman of Cincinnati, Ohio, and Beverly Hills, California, helped this new point of view articulate itself.

During his Biograph years, D. W. Griffith developed such talents as Mary Pickford, Lillian and Dorothy Gish, Blanche Sweet, Mack Sennett, and Lionel Barrymore. Many of Griffith's actors and actresses were unknowns whom he discovered and tutored in their new craft. In general Griffith preferred an ensemble, with no one player distinguished from the other in either billing or salary, but when Carl Laemmle of Independent Motion Pictures lured Florence Lawrence away from Biograph in 1910 with promises of more money and personal publicity, the ensemble ideal received its death blow. Among Griffith's actresses was a Toronto-born teenager, Gladys Smith, acting under the name Mary Pickford. Griffith had hired her at the rate of five dollars a day. With Florence Lawrence gone, Griffith developed the talents of Mary Pickford to the point that David Belasco cast her in his 1911 stage production of *The Good Little Devil*. Carl Laemmle of IMP stole Mary Pickford from Griffith with promises of increased salary and personal billing, which Griffith had refused to confer upon any of his troupe. Adolph Zukor, in turn, lured Mary Pickford to Famous Players in 1914 at the astronomical salary of $104,000 a year. Ensconced at the helm of Famous Players–Lasky and Paramount, Zukor decreed in 1916 that the star system, organized around Mary Pickford (whom he was then paying $10,000 a week), would flourish in his organization. A year later First National lured Miss Pickford away from Zukor with an offer of $1,050,000 for three pictures.

An obscure English vaudevillian, Charles Chaplin, experienced a similarly meteoric rise under the new system. In November 1913 Chaplin was appearing at the Empress Theatre in Los Angeles for less than $100 a week. Admiring the English comic's talent, Mack Sennett called on him backstage with an offer of $150 a week to appear in a series of Keystone comedies. The last of these, *Tillie's Punctured Romance*, won Chaplin a national reputation. In late 1914 Essanay offered him $1,250 a week. In 1915 Famous Players offered $10,000 a week, followed in 1916 by Mutual's offer of $670,000 a year. In 1918, a mere five years after playing the Empress Theatre in Los Angeles for peanuts, Charles Chaplin signed on with First National for $1 million a year. Zukor and his colleagues were willing to pay these astronomical sums, infinitely beyond the compensation schedule of any other American enterprise, because a radically new connection had been forged between film stars and the American mass audience that translated directly into equally astronomical profits at the box office. There was literally no precedent in American history for the capacity of Hollywood stars to speak directly to the dream life of the masses.

Once this connection was made, however, it took on a rigidity from which the star only rarely escaped. Mary Pickford, America's sweetheart, was forced to play adolescent roles (and to keep her adolescent curls) well into her thirties. When at long last she tried adult roles, the public rejected her, forcing her into retirement in 1933 at age forty. Charlie Chaplin's on-screen persona, the lovable tramp, was such a fixed part of his identity that Chaplin often appeared at off-screen press conferences in his universally recognized baggy trousers, frayed cutaway coat, derby hat, and cane, as if to acknowledge the superiority of the comic tramp who touched millions with his lovable simplicity over the English vaudevillian whose personal hauteur, political opinions, and scandalous sex life eventually earned him such opprobrium that he was forced to quit the United States.

For the first time in history, mere entertainers possessed a power over the masses that eventually surpassed the strongest political identifications. On screen and off, their looks, their clothes, each detail of their personal histories (true or concocted) linked Hollywood stars directly to the deepest aspirations of their mass audience. This dynamic connection transformed Hollywood into an emotionally and imaginatively energized American place, touched by magic and myth. Through its star system Hollywood took ordinary Americans—which by and large the stars themselves were, in terms of talent and frail humanity—and endowed them with a quality of transcendence that flattered star and audience alike. Remaining ordinary, the stars glorified the ordinariness of those whose adulation made their careers possible. They touched ordinariness with a glamour of appearances and possibilities for which each individual in the audience of millions secretly yearned, sitting in a movie theater of an evening or on a weekend afternoon in a respite from routine, dreaming of the someone or something that might await them in the day, the week, the month, the year ahead.

IV

As usual, Cecil Blount De Mille, showman extraordinaire in the Belasco tradition, understood these American yearnings perfectly. Just as D. W. Griffith dominated the prewar era with his late Victorian moral melodramas, so De Mille came into his own as a major Hollywood force in the late teens and early 1920s with a series of pictures that spoke directly to the prosperity, upward mobility, and erotic yearnings of the Jazz Age. Himself the offspring of the Northeast upper middle class, with strong social connections in New York, De Mille understood instinctively that postwar America was experiencing a revolution of expectations in which the prewar working classes (with whom American film had found its first major audience) were becoming middle class and the middle classes were aspiring to even higher levels of consumption and taste. In this process, De Mille intuited, Hollywood should serve as a national tutor in values and behavior.

And so in a series of parlor and boudoir comedies De Mille set out to teach upwardly mobile America how to dress, dine, decorate its homes, and make love. De Mille spent small fortunes importing major designers to Hollywood from Paris and New York to create new fashion lines for each new picture. Interior designers devised equally elegant sets, including the elaborate bathrooms with sunken bathtubs that became a De Mille trademark. No detail was too small for De Mille's attention: the veil on one of Gloria Swanson's hats, the proper Ivy League knot in Wallace Reid's necktie, the sequence of silverware used during a meal, the sequence of lingerie revealed in undressing, vases and floral arrangements, cigarette cases, how to take off an overcoat or step into a bath, the different ways men and women should hold their cigarettes, how to stand nonchalantly or come into a room just so, with a pause at the door before making an entrance. Depicting his characters playing golf, dancing at supper clubs, entertaining at parties, dressing and undressing with style, De Mille provided a parvenu postwar generation with rudimentary rituals of consumption which, if frequently vulgar and materialistic, nevertheless helped the expanding middle classes take the art of living a little more seriously.

Thanks mainly to Cecil B. De Mille, Hollywood emerged in the early 1920s as the major arbiter of taste in mid-America, a position it would hold securely for the next two decades. Thanks again to De Mille, Hollywood also took a leadership role in the postwar sexual revolution. While European moviemakers had dealt frankly with sexuality as a motivation in human life as early as 1906, American filmmakers had proceeded more cautiously. Not until 1913, with the release of *Traffic in Souls*, a film dealing with white slavery, did an American film deal explicitly with sexuality. Costing $5,700 to produce, *Traffic in Souls* grossed $450,000, thereby testifying unequivocally to the selling power of sex. Two years later Theda Bara debuted as the vamp, and swimming star Annette Kellerman appeared on screen semi-nude in *A Daughter of the Gods*, causing a sensation.

These films were superficial, however, in comparison to the bold, unexpected power of De Mille's *The Cheat* (1915), which to this day French critics consider a landmark in the evolution of cinema. Written by Hector Turnbull, drama critic of the *New York Tribune*, whom William de Mille had brought out to Hollywood as a staff writer for the Lasky studio, *The Cheat* starred Fanny Ward as a wife whose husband has embezzled $100,000 in charity funds. The wife goes to a wealthy financier, played brilliantly by Sessue Hayakawa, who promises to give her the money if she becomes his mistress. The wife agrees but is rescued at the last moment from fulfilling her part of the bargain when funds are obtained elsewhere. Furious with baffled lust, Hayakawa brands Ward on the shoulder with a red-hot poker. Her husband tries to kill him in revenge. On trial for attempted murder, the husband tells his story before a packed courtroom. Outraged, the spectators surge forward to tear Hayakawa apart. In *The Cheat* De Mille coaxed from Ward and Hayawaka an indirect, intensely psychological performance, backlit with mood-reinforcing chiaroscuro powerfully expressive of sexual shame and ambition. "*The Cheat*," a French critic raved, "is *La Tosca* of the cinema!"

Never before on film, and rarely before on the American stage outside of classic theater, had sexual obsession been treated with such openness. Released in December 1915, *The Cheat* anticipated De Mille's preoccupation from 1918 to the mid-1920s, once his wartime propaganda work was over, with marriage, divorce, and sexuality. In this effort De Mille was joined by his chief scenario writer, Jeannie Macpherson, a former screen actress of commanding presence and inventive mind who convinced De Mille that the Victorian and Edwardian constraints by which Hollywood had previously guided itself had become obsolete. Working closely with Macpherson, De Mille directed a series of sexual comedies—*Old Wives for New* (1918), *Male and Female* (1919), *Don't Change Your Husband* (1919), *For Better or Worse* (1919), *Why Change Your Wife?* (1920), *Forbidden Fruit* (1921), *The Affairs of Anatol* (1921), *Saturday Night* (1922), *Manslaughter* (1922), *Fool's Paradise* (1923), and *Adam's Rib* (1923)— which against a backdrop of glittering luxury celebrated a brand of sophisticated sexuality that included the options of divorce and extramarital sex, unthinkable in prewar Hollywood. In *Male and Female* and *Manslaughter*, moreover, De Mille availed himself of the flashback technique to depict sexual shenanigans amongst the ancients. These orgy scenes became standard De Mille fare for the rest of his career.

Only one of De Mille's erotic films—*The Affairs of Anatol*, (1921), a dark comedy of sexual intrigue adapted from a story by Arthur Schnitzler set in prewar Vienna—approached in artistic subtlety the murky and cynical sexual satires being concurrently directed by De Mille's lesser-known contemporary Erich von Stroheim. The Vienna-born son of a Jewish hatter, von Stroheim had migrated to the United States some time between 1906 and 1909, and drifted throughout the West as a day laborer before showing up in Hollywood in 1914 as a bit player, securing small parts in *The Birth of a Nation* and *Intolerance*. Von Stroheim claimed to be of noble Prussian descent and a graduate of Heidelberg University. He was neither. He was, however, a director of genius. With the securely established De Mille as his advance guard, Von Stroheim followed suit with a series of darkly psychological sexual satires and melodramas—*Blind Husbands* (1919); *Foolish Wives* (1922); the (1922–23) Hapsburg tetralogy *Merry-Go-Round, The Merry Widow, The Wedding March,* and *The Honeymoon; Greed* (1923–24), based on Frank Norris's novel *McTeague;* and the unfinished *Queen Kelly* (1928), which treated with even greater psychological intensity and directorial talent the themes first broached by De Mille. To De Mille's startling but generally superficial repertoire von Stroheim added brilliant, if frequently brutal, depictions of some of the gongorisms of human sexual behavior: cynical seduction, sadomasochism, fetishism, and other obsessions, often realized by von Stroheim against a background of Hapsburg power whose glittering extravagance marked the underlying decadence and cruelty that were the context and premise of erotic obsession.

As a result of such films by De Mille and von Stroheim, together with Rex Ingram's *The Four Horsemen of the Apocalypse* (1921), and George Melford's *The Sheik* (1921) (both starring Rudolph Valentino) and other films of similar intent, Hollywood itself became highly sexualized—which is to say that Hollywood emerged in the American consciousness as the major source of imagery and energy for the sexual revolution that was by then in full sway. "The Roaring Twenties did not come to Hollywood," actor-director Raoul Walsh later claimed. "They were born there."

In the beginning Hollywood tried hard to be decorous. In late 1915 Jesse Lasky gave an elegant white-tie-and-tails ball for Geraldine Farrar at the Hollywood Hotel that was a model of decorum. Miss Farrar and the great actor John Drew, then playing the Mason Opera House in downtown Los Angeles, opened the proceedings at the head of a thoroughly proper grand march. It was also a species of playacting, of dressing up and making pretend. But the real ambience at the hotel, as Anita Loos encountered it a year or two later, was raffishly bohemian, despite the efforts of its owner, Miss Hershey, to enforce an atmosphere of refinement. Actors and actresses, after all, had their own codes of social and sexual conduct, suited to their traditionally single, nondomestic lifestyle. In pursuit of pleasures sybaritic, Keystone's Mack Sennett and his entourage of player dependents—Fatty Arbuckle, Harold Lloyd, Charlie Chaplin, W. C. Fields, and of course a number of the Bathing Beauties (discovered on Sennett's tufted green leather casting couch)—disported themselves off-screen, especially at late-night parties at Sennett's twenty-room mansion, with a Rabelaisian gusto worthy of their on-screen performances. A devoted sensualist, Sennett conducted his personal life as a rollicking romp not that distinguishable from the on-screen mayhem that made him rich and famous. Sennett's entire company, Anita Loos claims, was once forced to relocate for six months in Tijuana, Mexico, when one of the Bathing Beauties, generous with her favors, was discovered to be under-age—thus putting a number of Keystoners, in Loos's deft phrase, within the shadow of San Quentin prison.

V

All this might seem harmless enough at first glance, actors and actresses being traditionally exempt from bourgeois morality, except for the fact that the film folk of Hollywood, thanks to the emergent mass medium which had created them, stood in a direct, public, and highly energized relationship to mid-America, and mid-America contained within itself a core of fundamentalist rectitude that had already outlawed liquor through Prohibition and could not be expected to condone overt sexual license in Hollywood. Even as De Mille and his followers titillated audiences with risqué comedies and sexual satires, resentment was building up in mid-America that was just as great as the approval so evident at the box office.

An opportunity to express this resentment came in the mid-1920s after a succession of scandals involving sex, liquor, drugs, suicide, and murder engendered an anti-Hollywood crusade. Already in 1918 the American public had proved that it could destroy as well as create a reputation. That year, movie star Francis X. Bushman, who the public thought was a bachelor, was sued for divorce by his Maryland wife on the grounds of Bushman's adultery with co-star Beverly Bayne. Despite the fact that less than two years later De Mille's divorce comedies would begin creating lines at the box office, Bushman's public was neither amused nor forgiving. For seven years—until he was given the role of Messala in *Ben Hur*—Francis X. Bushman was banished from the screen. A mere two years later, in March 1920, America's sweetheart, Mary Pickford, and her secret lover, Douglas Fairbanks, would each divorce their respective spouses and marry each other—enhancing both their careers.

On 10 September 1920 Mary Pickford's sister-in-law Olive Thomas, a former Ziegfeld showgirl whom artist Harrison Fisher had once called the most beautiful woman in the world, poisoned herself in her Paris hotel room. Only twenty at the time and a rising Hollywood actress, Olive had preceded her husband Jack Pickford, Mary's brother and a Hollywood star in his own right, to Paris, where the couple planned to enjoy a delayed honeymoon. In her brief career the extraordinarily beautiful Olive Thomas had managed to express perfectly as a show girl, actress, and fashion model the transition from the *belle epoque* of Evelyn Nesbit and the Ziegfeld Follies of New York to the era of Hollywood and of *The Flapper*, the title of Olive's first and last film success. Subsequent investigation by the Paris police into Olive Thomas's last days revealed that the radiant young actress, married to the ideal American boy (as Jack Pickford was promoted), had a taste for low life, including friends in the underworld, and probably a heroin habit. Despondency over her addiction and her husband's philandering, the police concluded, had most likely led to the suicidal depression during which she had ended her life. Stung by newspaper reports of his unfaithfulness, his wife's addiction, her association with underworld figures, and his own use of drugs, Jack Pickford, the boyish star of *Seventeen* and *The Little Shepherd of Kingdom Come*, retreated into a Los Angeles hospital with a case of nervous collapse, leaving it to his sister Mary to defend him to a scandalized public.

A year to the day after Olive Thomas's death, another Hollywood actress, Virginia Rappe, age twenty-five, died in a private hospital in San Francisco. The resulting scandal further weakened Hollywood's sagging reputation. Reluctantly starring in this sordid story was Roscoe "Fatty" Arbuckle, a 266-pound comedian second only to Charlie Chaplin in popularity. A former plumber's helper from Smith Center, Kansas, Arbuckle had first made his reputation with Mack Sennett, with whom Arbuckle shared a taste for liquor and wild parties. On screen and off, Roscoe Arbuckle delighted in a species of gross buffoonery that made little demand upon the imagination. Anita Loos reports that in his Keystone days Arbuckle would fling butter pats to the ceiling of the Hollywood Hotel dining room, considering this the height of wit. Gross, hard-drinking, likable in a sloppy good-old-boy sort of way, Arbuckle had already brushed against scandal in March 1917 when the press carried reports that he had played Master of the Revels at an early morning party in Brownie Kennedy's roadhouse in Woburn, Massachusetts. The bill for the affair, including for the services of certain ladies who later talked to the press, had come to $1,050. Even more embarrassing, producers Adolph Zukor, Jesse Lasky, and Joseph Schenck, coming under Arbuckle's spell after a dinner at the Copley Plaza in Boston, had attended the revels at Brownie Kennedy's, thereby threatening a scandal that would touch not just Hollywood but the New York leadership as well. Rumor had it that it cost Zukor and his associates $100,000 in assorted gratuities to persuade authorities not to prosecute.

This brush with the law no doubt put Zukor, Lasky, and Schenck on guard against Arbuckle as a late-night companion. Professionally, however, Arbuckle's slapstick (being fat, Anita Loos claimed, was Arbuckle's only claim to talent) met with the approval of the public. In early September 1921 Paramount signed Fatty to a three-year, $3 million contract. Piling a group of his cronies and attendant lady friends into his $25,000 custom-made Pierce Arrow and another car, Arbuckle led a merry caravan north to San Francisco for a Labor Day weekend of partying. Arriving at the St. Francis Hotel on Union Square late Saturday night, 3 September 1921, Arbuckle and his entourage rented three adjoining suites on the twelfth floor and commenced a three-day party, fueled by bootleg liquor.

Among the ladies in Fatty's company were Maude Delmont and Virginia Rappe. Mrs. Delmont made a specialty of providing young women for Hollywood parties, with whom she would then launch various shakedown schemes, such as soliciting payoffs by threatening charges of rape. That the aspiring actress Virginia Rappe was in Mrs. Delmont's company was in itself a sad situation, but inevitable, perhaps, given Rappe's evolution over the previous few years from promising actress smiling on the sheet-music cover of "Let Me Call You Sweetheart" to the party-girl starlet of shady reputation. Shortly after three o'clock on the afternoon of Monday, 5 September, Virginia Rappe was found on the bed in Suite 1221 of the St. Francis Hotel moaning in agony. Rushed to a private hospital on Pine Street, she slipped into a coma. Five days later she died. What exactly happened to her has never been made fully clear. There is a strong possibility that Virginia Rappe died of peritonitis following a mishandled abortion. Her condition could also have been exacerbated by drinking or by some form of sexual encounter with Arbuckle. What Maude Delmont told the district attorney, however, ignited a scandal. Arbuckle, Delmont claimed, had dragged Virginia Rappe into Suite 1221, torn her clothing to shreds, and violently raped her. Rappe's last words in the hotel room and at the hospital, Delmont testified, were that Arbuckle was responsible for her death.

Arbuckle was arrested on suspicion of murder. At some point in the investigation, the sordid rumor surfaced that an impotent Arbuckle had used a champagne or Coca-Cola bottle or a jagged piece of ice to violate Miss Rappe. William Randolph Hearst, anxious to establish his authority over Hollywood, gave orders to his *San Francisco Examiner* staff to play up the incident, including the suggestion of unnatural rape, in all its gross detail. In mid-November District Attorney Matthew Brady, who sensed political advantage in the affair, brought Arbuckle to trial on charges of first-degree murder. It took three separate trials for Arbuckle's lawyers to win acquittal. Not only did the third jury acquit Arbuckle, it also apologized. "Acquittal is not enough for Roscoe Arbuckle," the foreman told the court. "We feel a grave injustice has been done him and there was not the slightest proof to connect him in any way with the commission of any crime."

The damage, however—to Arbuckle and to Hollywood—was horrendous and irreversible. After his acquittal Fatty might very well tell the press that his innocence had been proven and that he would continue to devote his life "to the production of clean pictures for the happiness of children," but back in New York Adolph Zukor had other ideas. Arbuckle, Zukor realized, had come to symbolize to the American public that something was rotten in Hollywood. What had once been comic, Fatty's fatness, had worked against him in the course of the trial. California's top criminal lawyer, Earl Rogers, turned down an offer to defend Fatty, remarking that no jury could be expected to sympathize with a fat man—especially in these circumstances, when Arbuckle's weight might be brought in evidence against him. Fatty's fatness also provided the press with an easy symbol of the salary scale accorded top Hollywood stars. Admiration turned suddenly into resentment as the rags-to-riches story reversed itself. Even Hollywood joined the chorus of self-hatred. Fatty Arbuckle, claimed director Henry Lehrman, shows what happens when Hollywood made "idols and millionaires out of people that you take from the gutter." A hostile crowd mobbed Arbuckle in the Santa Fe Depot in Los Angles. Theater audiences threw refuse at the screen when his movies played, and in at least one instance an audience prevented the projectionist from showing an Arbuckle comedy. As press clips of these incidents, together with pulpit denunciations, piled up on his desk, Adolph Zukor decided to cut his losses. Impounding a million dollars' worth of Arbuckle comedies already filmed, Zukor ordered Arbuckle blacklisted from any further work.

Even while the Arbuckle scandal still raged however, Hollywood suffered another shock: the murder of director William Desmond Taylor on the night of 1 February 1922. Taylor's unsolved murder remains a classic in the annals of American criminal history. Detail by detail, the Taylor case reads like fiction— an archetypal Southern California detective story, anticipating in fact the subsequent fiction of Raymond Chandler and Ross MacDonald, with their themes of false identity, the buried past, and malevolent intentions masked by the glittering, sunny surface of Southern California. On the morning of 2 February 1922 Taylor's butler Henry Peavey, a very tall, effeminate black man with the voice of a cracked soprano, came to work at Taylor's bungalow court apartment at 404½ South Alvarado Street in the Westlake district of Los Angeles. Opening the door at approximately 7:30 A.M., Peavey discovered Taylor's corpse on the living room floor. The first doctor to arrive on the scene quickly examined Taylor's neatly dressed corpse and concluded that the director had died of a hemorrhage. There were no signs of struggle either on Taylor's body or in the undisturbed living room, decorated with affectionately inscribed photographs of movie stars. Subsequent examination by the coroner's office, however, determined that Taylor had been neatly dispatched as he held his hands up by a single shot from a .38; the bullet had entered Taylor's left side and lodged in the right side of his neck. The victim most likely knew his killer. Since nothing had been disturbed or taken, either from Taylor or from the house, robbery was ruled out as a motive.

Two days later the *New York Times* reported that the murdered forty-five-year-old Hollywood director William Desmond Taylor was actually William Cunningham Deane-Tanner, the Irish-born son of a British army colonel. After a career in London as an actor, Deane-Tanner had come to New York, where he set himself up in the antique business at 246 Fifth Avenue, between Twenty-seventh and Twenty-eighth streets. In 1908 he left his wife, actress Ethel Mae Harrison, and their daughter. Dapper, urbane, impeccable in accent and tailoring, Deane-Tanner disappeared from New York in 1912 after an afternoon watching the Vanderbilt Cup Races on Long Island. Four years later, Deane-

Tanner's brother Dennis, a former British officer also in the New York antique business, disappeared, leaving behind a wife and two children. By the late teens William Cunningham Deane-Tanner was doing business in Hollywood as director William Desmond Taylor. Edward F. Sands was serving as his butler. Returning from a European vacation, Taylor fired Sands for forging his name on certain checks. Sands disappeared, and Henry Peavey, who discovered Taylor's body, was hired in his place.

As the police investigation continued, the press found itself with an even better story than the Arbuckle case. The Taylor mystery seemed to write itself like detective fiction. An unnamed informant in Denver claimed that the fired (and now missing) butler Sands was actually Taylor's brother Dennis. Was Taylor shot by his own brother? One neighbor on South Alvarado reported hearing a shot on the evening of 1 February. His wife reported seeing a man in an overcoat and muffler leave Taylor's bungalow court apartment at approximately the same time. The witness also said that the man in the overcoat could have been a woman, judging from the way he or she was walking. It was further revealed that Taylor had been on a campaign against drug traffic in the studios. Had he been eliminated by drug dealers? Why did the keys on Taylor's key ring fit no known doors in his house or office? And then there was the matter of women, the many young actresses, including Mabel Normand and Mary Miles Minter, with whom the impossibly handsome, urbanely avuncular Taylor had formed various degrees of attachment. Both Minter and Normand had separately visited Taylor at his bungalow on the evening of his death, and an examination of Taylor's personal effects revealed a letter and an initialed handkerchief linking the forty-five-year-old Taylor with the twenty-one-year-old Mary Miles Minter. Minter compounded her involvement by creating an hysterical scene at Taylor's house the morning his body was discovered and fainting at his funeral before a crowd of ten thousand onlookers.

Neither Mabel Normand nor Mary Miles Minter ever came under formal suspicion in Taylor's death, but the press delighted in linking their names to the investigation whenever possible. As in the case of Arbuckle and the champagne bottle, the rumor that one of Minter's monogrammed pink negligees (never actually produced in evidence) was discovered in Taylor's bedroom bureau was reported as fact. Normand and Minter each became victims of the very publicity engines that had created their careers in the first place. America's leading comedienne at the time of William Desmond Taylor's death, Mabel Normand grew confused and distracted after the scandal, and perhaps even more dependent upon the cocaine Anita Loos claims she was using before the incident. She married a childhood friend in an effort to stabilize herself emotionally, but her career slid downhill rapidly. By age thirty-five Mabel Normand was dead from tuberculosis.

Her career in ruins, the once beautiful Mary Miles Minter began to eat com-

pulsively, ballooning into a caricature of her former self, and engaged in a series of nasty public quarrels over money with her mother, Mrs. Charlotte Shelby,
who was also linked romantically to Taylor. (Was Minter's mother the
man/woman in muffler and overcoat seen leaving Taylor's bungalow that evening? After the murder, Mrs. Shelby left for Europe without being questioned
by the police.) Only D. W. Griffith had the courage—and the old-fashioned
chivalry—to offer the blacklisted Mary Miles Minter work.

The paradox that Taylor, a past president of the Screen Directors Guild, could
have surfaced with such prominence in Hollywood without his New York identity coming to light testifies to the social superficiality of Hollywood in the year
1922. In the nine years since De Mille's arrival in 1913 the industry had grown
so quickly that major positions and reputations, such as Taylor's, involved minimal disclosure. So many Hollywoodites, after all, were fleeing former selves
from someplace else, or were caught like Taylor in harem-like involvements,
or, like Olive Thomas, Mabel Normand, and Wallace Reid, were secretly on
drugs. Given his start by De Mille in *Maria Rosa*, playing opposite Geraldine
Farrar, the ruggedly handsome six-foot-three Reid cultivated an image of Ivy
League polish. He was also a family man, married to actress Dorothy Davenport, and the devoted father of two small children with whom he was frequently photographed. Reid attained stardom in numerous all-American roles,
many of them involving automobile racing. In the course of filming a boxing
movie, *The World's Champion* (1922), Reid appeared pale and fatigued on the
set. At certain times he could barely remain on his feet. Committed by his wife
to a private sanitarium in March 1922, Wallace Reid died a miserable death
the next year at age thirty of complications relating to his addiction.

This time, however, Hollywood was prepared to manage the scandal. In the
final months of his ordeal Reid was staunchly defended by William Harrison
Hays, head of the newly established Motion Picture Producers and Distributors
of America Inc., more commonly called the Hays Office. Hays personally visited Reid at the Banksia Place Sanitarium and defended the stricken actor as a
sick man, not a criminal, who had initially taken morphine on doctor's orders
as relief against a painful neck injury. A Protestant Indiana Republican of impeccable middle-American credentials who had been serving as postmaster general in the Harding administration, Hays had been brought to Hollywood during the Arbuckle scandal to lead the industry's effort to reform itself. As the
Arbuckle scandal dragged on, Zukor, Lasky, Goldwyn, and the others knew
full well what was at stake should the hostility of mid-America to Hollywood
continue to grow. A hint of anti-Semitism was surfacing, moreover, in the anti-
Hollywood denunciations fulminating from the press and pulpit of middle
America: the ancient canard depicting the Jew as corruptor of the innocent.
What sort of moral degeneracy, it was asked, was being foisted on the Ameri-
can people by all those New York and Hollywood producers with foreign ac-

cents? Forming an industry-wide protective association, the Hollywood leadership gave Hays carte blanche to direct an emergency cleanup campaign.

The first thing that this "Cato of voluntary censorship" did upon his arrival from Washington in April 1922 was to banish the hapless Arbuckle from the industry. Playing Savonarola to Hollywood's Florence, Will Hays laid down the law: no more drugs, no more wild parties, no more sexual scandals of any sort. With Hays's encouragement, studios established spying systems which turned in to the front office the names of drinkers, dopers, extras who moonlighted as call girls, film folk living together outside wedlock. This reign of terror did not last long, but it did quickly convince the nation that Hollywood had returned itself to rectitude, as did two self-criticizing pictures: *The World's Applause* (1923), daringly based on the William Desmond Taylor case, and *Human Wreckage* (1923), in which Wallace Reid's widow Dorothy Davenport starred in a story depicting the horrors of drug use.

V

Thanks to Cecil B. De Mille, recently active as a director of risqué comedies, Hollywood also discovered religion. "Rediscovered" would be more accurate, for a mere two years after the projection of moving images had been perfected as a technique the Calvary crucifixion portions of the Oberammergau Passion Play were filmed for commercial release. The New York showing of this film in January 1898 caused a sensation, as did *The Life of Moses*, a five-reeler released by Vitagraph reel by reel in 1908–9. The next year Adolph Zukor successfully released a three-reel version of the Oberammergau pageant that helped prove that Americans were ready for feature-length films. *The Illumination* (1912) told the story of two couples, one Roman, the other Jewish, affected by the life of Christ. The last film of pioneering American director Edwin S. Porter, *The Eternal City* (1913), based on Hall Caine's novel of early Christianity, was filmed on location in Rome for Famous Players at the then astonishing cost of $100,000. As the receipts rolled in, producer Adolph Zukor said that Porter's budget was proving a bargain.

Filming the Kalem Company's five-reel *From the Manger to the Cross* (1912) seems to have engendered in certain members of the cast a genuine sense of religious purpose. Filmed on location in Egypt and Palestine, where Kalem built a pioneering studio facility in Jerusalem, *From the Manger to the Cross* was previewed on 30 October 1912 in Queen's Hall, London, before an audience of over a thousand clergymen. Handled by director Sidney Olcott in a straightforward narrative fashion, this life of Christ became an immediate classic. (As late as 1938 it was being reissued with sound.) In *From Manger to Cross: The Story of the World-Famous Films of the Life of Jesus* (1922) and his later autobiography *Actor-Soldier-Poet* (1939), R. Henderson-Bland, the actor-poet (and subsequent British war hero) who played the Christ, described how a strange transforming power entered him as he prepared for his role, which could only be approached, he soon concluded, with a conviction of religious mission. Only by achieving a profoundly religious identification with Jesus Christ, Henderson-Bland believed, could he play the part. Playing Jesus for the screen transformed his life.

When it became apparent by 1922 that scandal-ridden Hollywood had better get on the religious bandwagon once again to reestablish favor with the American public, Cecil B. De Mille was, as usual, on hand with his market-oriented showman's instincts. The same director who had inaugurated the postwar era of sophisticated sexual comedies that had partly accounted for Hollywood's troubles now became a directorial Moses in boots, jodhpurs, pistol belt, and pith helmet, leading the film industry back into favor with Christian America. There was even an element of sincerity in De Mille's career as a maker of religious films (as much sincerity as can ever be ascribed to this ultimate showman-promoter), for these films tapped into some of his deepest childhood memories and identifications. De Mille's ancestry combined two religious strains, with the dominant Episcopalianism made evangelical by the Dutch Reformed piety of the Flemish side of the family. De Mille's grandfather, an Episcopal clergyman in North Carolina, raised his son Henry de Mille on the Bible, Latin, and Greek. Initially intending to follow his father's vocation, Henry enrolled in Columbia University in 1871 on a scholarship granted by the Society of New York for the Promotion of Religion and Learning. Coming under the influence of the writings of Charles Kingsley, the English clergyman-novelist, Henry de Mille wavered between religion and the theater. Although he had prepared himself for the Episcopal priesthood, de Mille chose the theater instead—but even here the emphasis was evangelical, for de Mille began his acting career in 1882 in the church-sponsored Madison Square Theater run by the Reverend Doctor George S. Mallory, a prominent Episcopal priest and theatrical impresario. Prosperously associated with David Belasco as an actor, playwright, and producer, Henry de Mille raised his family in an atmosphere of Episcopalian piety enlivened by the Tory bohemianism of the New York stage. Among Cecil B. De Mille's earliest childhood memories was that of sitting at his father's feet in the family home in Pompton, New Jersey, as Henry de Mille read from the Bible or from the novels of Charles Kingsley. *"The King of Kings* and *The Ten Commandments,"* De Mille later wrote, "were born in those evenings. . . ."

However, in January 1893 the de Mille family suffered a terrible shock. Striken by typhoid, de Mille died at the height of his career. Just before his death, eleven-year-old Cecil and his brother were brought into their father's bedroom for a last painful farewell. After his death, Mrs. de Mille brought her sons before the open casket and bade them to follow in their father's footsteps as Christian gentlemen.

Whatever his failures in depth or taste, Cecil B. De Mille was not being merely pragmatic when he turned to the making of religious films in 1923. On the other hand, he was not being anyone's fool, either. *The Ten Commandments* returned over $14 million in gross receipts on a $1.5 million investment. Of equal importance, it helped Hollywood regain favor with mid-America. ("It wipes the slate clean of charges of an immoral influence against the screen," claimed *Photoplay* magazine.) And it revitalized De Mille's career after the failure of *Adam's Rib*, a confused flapper story with historical flashbacks, which had been panned by the critics. For all this, however, De Mille did manage to speak powerfully to the collective imagination of both Jewish and Christian America in the first part of this film, which made pioneering use of Technicolor to depict the sufferings of the Israelites in Egyptian bondage and their escape across the Red Sea. To add authenticity and valid emotion to these scenes, De Mille recruited members of the Orthodox Jewish community of Los Angeles to play the ancient Israelites on the sand dunes at Guadalupe outside Santa Maria. When these Orthodox extras rebelled at a ham dinner served them by the commissary, De Mille ordered that a kosher kitchen be set up for the duration of the filming. When they recreated the crossing of the Red Sea, De Mille claims, these Orthodox extras had real tears streaming down their faces. "They *were* the children of Israel. This was their Exodus, their liberation. They needed no direction from me to let their voices rise in ancient song and their wonderfully expressive faces shine with the holy light of freedom as they followed Moses toward the Promised Land."

The same intensity, De Mille asserted, albeit Christian in motivation, characterized the filming of *The King of Kings* in 1926. As a precaution, De Mille wrote into each of his leading actors' contracts a clause promising good behavior during production. (Two journalists, looking in vain for a scandal, secretly trailed actor H. B. Warner, who portrayed Jesus of Nazareth, hoping to catch Warner in an after-hours indiscretion.) Strict decorum was enforced on the set. Extras who joked or made sarcastic remarks regarding any aspect of the film were fired on the spot. De Mille asked all his leading actors to remain in character as much as possible throughout the working day. Warner took his meals alone in his tent, and when costumed as the Christ spoke only to De Mille. Each morning the workday began with religious worship conducted by one of De Mille's clerical advisors or by visiting clergymen. Among De Mille's favorite advisors was the Jesuit Daniel A. Lord, who celebrated mass each morning on the set. An informal religious service of five minutes of organ music and silent meditation followed the filming of the crucifixion scene on Christmas Eve 1926. The entire cast stood silently with bowed heads.

All this was a long way from Olive Thomas's suicide in Paris, Fatty Arbuckle's Labor Day party, William Desmond Taylor's murder, Wallace Reid's death from drug addiction, and the rest of the scandals that had cost Hollywood the confidence of churchgoing Americans. With this one stroke, for which the earlier *Ten Commandments* had been but a prologue, De Mille put Hollywood at the center of Christianity itself. For no vehicle, with the exception of the Bible itself, had presented the life of Jesus so extensively to so many people (an estimated eight hundred million viewers within De Mille's lifetime) and with such ability to cut across barriers of culture as this silent film did.

Even in this most sacred of stories, however, there were the usual De Mille touches. Rather than begin the Christ story with Bethlehem or with John the Baptist before Herod, as the evangelists do, De Mille opens with a banquet scene in the home of Mary Magdalene, a courtesan angry that her newest admirer, Judas Iscariot, has renounced her company in favor of following the rabbi Jesus of Nazareth. Actress Jacqueline Logan's version of Mary Magdalene is supremely De Mille, down to her pet leopard. From his first appearance on screen, however, H. B. Warner as Jesus Christ instantly establishes the film's authority. Warner's Jesus of Nazareth—tall, blond, Aryan—possesses no correspondence whatsoever to the undoubtedly Semitic appearance of the historical man from Nazareth. He is, rather, a Forest Lawn Jesus, a daydream of the Savior as a Northern European type, an image emanating from Hollywood in Southern California, where the American evangelical Protestant imagination had at long last arrived in force. Instinctively, De Mille knew that millions of Americans envisioned Jesus of Nazareth this way: tall, Hollywood handsome, Nordic. No wonder that so many American Jews felt uneasy about *The King of Kings*, or that so many of them openly protested. The very title of the film implied a reasserted Christian sovereignty that, given the rise of anti-Semitism in the United States and Europe in the 1920s, offered legitimate cause for anxiety.

De Mille's Jewish bosses in New York had almost abandoned him during the filming of *The Ten Commandments* for overspending, forcing him (with the help of A. P. Giannini) to raise a million dollars in safety collateral. Shortly after, in 1925, De Mille was forced out of Famous Players–Lasky with the remark from one New Yorker that he had "never been one of us." Now, bankrolled by evangelical banker Jeremiah Milbank, De Mille asserted his prerogatives (and took subtle revenge) in eighteen reels of primal Christian sentiment ("that essence of hypocritical nonsense," Paul Rotha called *The King of Kings*, ". . . propaganda for the Christian religion") that, paradoxically, was also winning back Christian America to Jewish Hollywood. In later years De Mille privately screened and rescreened *The King of Kings*, openly weeping at certain parts. He also had a cross erected on his Paradise Ranch property, beneath which he placed the tombstone of Stamford De Milles, one of his ancestors. De Mille claimed that he liked to come to this quiet spot for meditation. One wonders if he also brought along the aspiring actresses who were wont to keep him company on those weekends in Paradise.

VI

Whatever alienation may have erupted during the scandals of the early 1920s, Hollywood had by the same period emerged in the national imagination as one of the most intensely symbolic, emotionally valent landscapes in America. As a town, an industry, a state of mind, a self-actualizing myth, Hollywood had attained this status in seven short years, from 1913 to 1920, because it had used the medium of motion pictures to answer a need for dreams that was basic to America: dreams about mobility, an improved life, romantic love, a better home, a more creative occupation, travel, leisure, excitement of all sorts. Moralists at home or abroad might (correctly, in many cases) condemn these dreams as unreal, childish, superficial, even destructive and immoral, but Americans persisted in having them, and Hollywood persisted in meeting their needs with stories and imagery. Such primal activity could not help but have major social and cultural consequences for Southern California. From the start a land of dreams, a tabula rasa upon and through which fantasies and longings expressed themselves, Southern California found its function and identity further fixed by the presence of Hollywood, which by 1920 or so had become its leading social metaphor. By the mid-1920s myth and reality, dream gesture and landscape had so interpenetrated each other in an actual place—Hollywood and its attendant community of Beverly Hills, plus portions of Santa Monica and Los Angeles—that each aspect of architecture and lifestyle, social psychology and infrastructure bespoke an integrated condition based upon the Hollywood myth. This myth, in turn, as a matter of dream wish and behavior, affected the way Americans in other parts of the country viewed themselves and arranged their lives.

All this was a grave responsibility for a few Los Angeles suburbs whose origins had occurred only yesterday. By 1920 Hollywood had attained a population of only thirty-six thousand. Beverly Hills remained covered with lima bean fields until 1906, when the Rodeo Land and Water Company hired landscape architect Wilbur David Cook, Jr., formerly of Frederick Law Olmsted's office in New York, to devise a master plan for a community of suburban estates. In an effort to establish a destination point and sense of location amidst the lima beans, the Rodeo Company in 1911 promoted the construction of the Beverly Hills Hotel on Sunset Boulevard. Designed by Myron Hunt and Elmer Grey and managed by the supremely competent Mrs. Margaret Anderson, who was wooed away from the Hollywood Hotel, the neo-Spanish Beverly Hills Hotel immediately convinced Los Angelenos that there could be such a place as Beverly Hills.

As usual, Cecil B. De Mille set the pace. In the first years of Hollywood, actors and directors alike lived simply in rented rooms or studio apartments, as if Hollywood were an experiment that could with a minimum of notice be folded up and moved back to New York. In 1916, however, De Mille ensconced himself and his family in an elaborate Spanish-style mansion in the Laughlin Park subdivision of Hollywood on what later became De Mille Drive, and a trend was established. The Hollywood lifestyle involved an estate, the bigger the better. De Mille's fellow director-producer Thomas Ince soon followed suit with Dias Dorados, a Spanish Revival villa in Beverly Hills.

By the mid-1920s Hollywood and Beverly Hills along Sunset Boulevard or Benedict Canyon abounded in Mission, Spanish Revival, and Tudor mansions that were themselves stage sets, wherein such luminaries as Douglas Fairbanks and Mary Pickford, Rudolph Valentino, Gloria Swanson, Pola Negri, Tom Mix, Charles Chaplin, Wallace Beery, John Barrymore, Buster Keaton, Will Rogers, and Harold Lloyd lived private lives that were also public performances. Belle Vista, John Barrymore's Beverly Hills estate (it eventually grew to sixteen buildings on seven acres), featured such amenities as a swimming pool, a skeet shoot, a private zoo, and an aviary stocked with over three hundred rare birds. Greenacres, the twenty-two-acre Beverly Hills estate of comedian Harold Lloyd, encompassed a forty-room Italian Renaissance villa worthy of Lorenzo de Medici himself, twelve distinct formal gardens, and a miniature fairy-tale house for the children, complete with its own plumbing and electricity.

In his classic study *Hollywood: The Movie Colony, the Movie Makers* (1939), Leo Rosten, guided by the theories of Thorstein Veblen, succinctly described the social and psychological mechanisms that were at work during this era of lavish Hollywood expansion, as American culture charged Hollywood with the work of conspicuous display and consumption. In reverse compensation for the demands of the Protestant ethic, Americans asked the stars and leading producers and directors of Hollywood to live the life that every American would supposedly live if given the opportunity. Hollywood was a caste apart, fed, clothed and housed specially; allowed broad latitude in sexual conduct, marriage and divorce; required only to remain young, glamorous, and on view. Hollywood stars thus became an aristocracy, American style, a status made even more convincing in 1925 when Gloria Swanson, marrying a French marquis, became the Marquise de la Falaise, at whose Beverly Hills home each dinner guest was attended by a liveried footman. In later years director Raoul Walsh recalled a Beverly Hills party given in the mid-1920s by De Mille and Lasky for actress Pola Negri and attended by *le tout Hollywood*—Gloria Swanson, Alice Terry, Harold Lloyd, Marie Dressler, Rudolph Valentino, Greta Garbo, Douglas Fairbanks, Mary Pickford, Lionel Barrymore, Ronald Colman, Adolph Zukor, Thomas H. Ince, D. W. Griffith, the Warner brothers (Jack, Harry and Sam), Charles Chaplin, John Gilbert, Bebe Daniels, Adolphe Menjou, Samuel Goldwyn, William S. Hart, Tom Mix, and a very young Ida Lupino, just arrived in town—which remained fixed in Walsh's memory, especially the image of Rudolph Valentino guiding Gloria Swanson across the floor in a tango, as the distilled essence of this magic silent film era, when people out of nowhere suddenly found themselves responsible for a nation's dreams.

As a result of the scandals of the early 1920s, Hollywood made a series of self-conscious, self-promoting pictures, led off by James Cruze's *Hollywood* (1923). They all stressed a single point: the little guy or gal could make it in the industry. Film after film—*Hollywood* (1923), *Inez from Hollywood* (1924), *The Legend of Hollywood* (1926), *The Runaway* (1926)—each in its own way, emphasized that the glamour of Hollywood should not obscure its basic American decency and opportunities for upward mobility for people possessing talent and willing to work hard. Even when such films involved satire, for example the classic *Merton of the Movies* (1924), in their final scenes they asserted that in its heart of hearts Hollywood was mid-American in value, and mid-Americans would always be welcomed there. These films effectively did the post-scandal work of reconciliation so necessary for continuing profits at the box office, but they also served as internal warnings. The Hays Office specifically requested that James Cruze make *Hollywood*, which featured Fatty Arbuckle in his last on-screen role having the door of a casting office slammed shut in his face.

In the matter of social security, however, Hollywood (perhaps like mid-America itself) would always remain insecure. The Los Angeles establishment, William de Mille complained, never accepted film people into the better clubs, not even the brothers de Mille, with their impeccable New York connections. Jewish society, grouped around the Concordia Club, founded in 1891, was on guard against the Lower East Side immigrants who had risen to prominence in the movie industry. Exclusion threw even upper Hollywood, with its incomes in the millions, into a state of permanent defensiveness which was reflected in a muted but always motivating passion for respectability and acceptance. Take Pickfair, for example, the Beverly Hills home of Mary Pickford and Douglas Fairbanks, which functioned throughout the 1920s as the paradigm of Hollywood style. As an estate, a way of life, a Hollywood symbol, Pickfair embodied the formula of glamour in search of respectability that was the essence of 1920s Hollywood.

Even before the outbreak of the scandals of the early 1920s, Douglas Fairbanks and Mary Pickford had risked a major scandal of their own with their secret affair, which had begun during the Liberty Bond drives of World War I, when the two stars, each married to someone else, had found themselves constantly in each other's company. On 28 November 1920, after a double divorce (complicated in Pickford's case by a publicity-hungry Nevada official who claimed that she had failed to establish bona fide Nevada residence), the couple married—and waited. Would the very fans who had a few years earlier banished Francis X. Bushman for adultery and divorce now accept similar behavior from America's sweetheart and the dashing Fairbanks? The answer was a resounding yes! America had changed. The Pickford-Fairbanks honeymoon soon developed into a royal progress through Europe and the Far East. Crowds followed them everywhere. In London Pickford had to be carried out of a garden party by Fairbanks when shrieking fans threatened to tear her apart in their excitement. A photographer caught the look of terror in Pickford's eyes as she made her hasty exit on her husband's shoulders.

Returning to Southern California, Pickford and Fairbanks took up residence in Pickfair, their Beverly Hills hilltop estate, which soon became the White House of Hollywood, the very essense of glamour and respectability as envisioned in the movie kingdom. Sensing full well that both they and Hollywood were on trial, Fairbanks and Pickford conducted their married life publicly, released artfully to the press detail by detail—who came to dinner, who walked the dogs, what Doug gave Mary for her birthday—so as to create an impression of Average America raised to royal status. The royalty of Europe and the Far East cooperated by dropping by to visit, adding their luster to the likes of Albert Einstein and Babe Ruth, as if to verify Pickford's and Fairbanks's royal condition: the queen of Siam, King Alfonso XIII of Spain, the duke and duchess of Alba, the duke and duchess of Sutherland, the earl and countess of Lanesborough, a honeymooning Lord and Lady Mountbatten ("Edwina and Dickie"), and the duke of York, Prince George of England himself, the future King George VI, then serving in the Royal Navy. Each night the Pickfair dinner table was automatically set for fifteen, and it was usually filled, either by the famous on pilgrimage to Hollywood or by an assortment of Fairbanks's many cronies.

And yet, for all its glamour—the visiting royalty, the celebrities and garden-variety millionaires—Pickfair also manifested mid-American propriety and unevenness of taste. No liquor was served, at least in the early years, and dinner parties, followed invariably by a preview screening of an unreleased movie, ended precisely at ten so that Doug and Mary might arrive fresh at the studio the next morning at six. Avoiding expensive rugs, paintings, and antiques, Mary Pickford furnished Pickfair with solid department-store copies of European styles such as Babbitt himself might use to adorn his new house in the Midwest. Were Pickfair's department-store furnishings a parvenu lapse in taste on Doug and Mary's part—or a strategic decision to make Pickfair more comfortingly mid-American, a way of not moving too conspicuously beyond the taste of the millions of fans who also bought their clothing and furniture at department stores and went to bed early on week nights so as to be at work the next morning on time?

In any event, Doug and Mary established a deeply personal connection with millions of fans through their Pickfair life. Seeing how Doug and Mary did it—entertained, went for walks together, worked in the garden on weekends—millions of mid-Americans entering upon the prosperity of the 1920s were provided the imagery with which to conduct and evaluate their own lives. On screen and off, moreover, Douglas Fairbanks was establishing a new American type, an image of realized upper-middle-class American manhood that to this day pervades the pages of *Esquire, Gentlemen's Quarterly,* and *Playboy.* Part of this image was Hollywood sham, of course—specifically Fairbanks's Harvard connection. Graduating from Denver High School with extremely poor grades, Fairbanks had tried without success to enter Harvard College in 1900. He spent five months there, however, going to parties and palling around with like-minded gentlemen before heading for Europe. This informal experience was later magnified into a Harvard connection as a special student. Regardless of whether Fairbanks managed to pick up anything in the way of academic instruction at Harvard, he did possess himself of a vision of Anglo-American gentlemanliness which he later made his trademark as an actor and which, in turn, affected the way in which aspiring American gentlemen spoke, dressed, and generally disported themselves from the 1920s onwards. Ambivalent regarding his dark complexion, the result of half-Jewish ancestry on his father's side (his real name was Douglas Elton Ulman), Fairbanks made the suntan an American preoccupation. Superbly conditioned, he helped make tennis an upper-middle-class obsession. He also popularized tennis whites and the blue blazer.

Cast as a dapper light comedian in the pre-1920 period, Fairbanks turned to escapist costume spectacles in the 1920s, beginning with *The Mark of Zorro* (1920) and continuing through *The Three Musketeers* (1921), *Robin Hood* (1922), *The Thief of Bagdad* (1924), *Don Q, Son of Zorro* (1925), *The Black Pirate* (1926), *The Gaucho* (1927), and *The Iron Mask* (1929). In these vehicles Fairbanks expressed to the full his exuberant athleticism in innumerable sword fights, leaps, back flips, somersaults, rope swings, and equestrian stunts. These costume spectacles, together with such comparable efforts as *Ben Hur* (1926), involved elaborate sets that directly carried on the scenic traditions established by D. W. Griffith in *Intolerance.* The castle built on Santa Monica Boulevard for *Robin Hood,* in fact, exceeded the scale of Griffith's Babylon. When director Raoul Walsh first saw the Arabian Nights sets designed by William Cameron Menzies for *The Thief of Bagdad,* he gasped in awe at the architectural fantasy of domes and minarets rising on the back lots of Culver City.

Babylon, Bagdad, the Roman Colosseum (for *Ben Hur*), Nottingham Castle: these sets rose up and remained alongside a growing Los Angeles which, as Charles Lockwood has wittily shown, embraced an element of fantasy in its architecture and urban identity as well. By the late 1920s Los Angeles had developed into a cityscape wherein much prosaic architecture, together with some architecture of great merit, was enlivened by medieval castles, Hansel and Gretel cottages, Dutch windmills, Egyptian and Chinese movie palaces, and other fantasies that were directly inspired by the movies. The dominant imagery of the previous generation—epitomized in Charles Fletcher Lummis's vision of Southern California as the Spanish Southwest—now gave way to the more inclusive, eclectic imagery of Hollywood. A sustaining connection, however, between Southern California and the dream of better days had been preserved; and this, after all—the dream—had energized Southern California since the late eighteenth century, when Spanish pioneers had pushed north from Mexico in search of a better life.

Bibliographical Essay

Frequently used citations

American Quarterly (AQ)
California Historical Society Quarterly (CHSQ)
Huntington Library Quarterly (HLQ)
Land of Sunshine (LS)
Mississippi Valley Historical Review (MVHR)
The Overland Monthly (OvMo)
Pacific Historical Review (HR)
Southern California Quarterly (SCQ)

1

Charles Lewis Camp, *Earth Song, A Prologue to History* (1952) suggests the forces at work in the formation of Southern California. Valuable geographies include Clifford M. Zierer, editor, *California and the Southwest* (1956); Daivd L. Lantis, Rodney Steiner, and Arthur Karinen, *California, Land of Contrast* (1963); David N. Hartman, *California and Man* (1964); Robert W. Durrenberger, *California, The Last Frontier* (1969); and Gordon B. Oakesholt, *California's Changing Landscapes: A Guide to the Geology of the State* (1971). W. H. Hutchinson, *California: Two Centuries of Man, Land, and Growth in the Golden State* (1969), and Warren A. Beck and Ynez D. Haase, *Historical Atlas of California* (1973) are invaluable. See also Ruth Putnam and Herbert I. Priestley, "California the Name," *University of California Publications in History*, 4 (1917), 293–365.

For the climate, see Ernest L. Felton, *California's Many Climates* (1965) and Harry P. Bailey, *The Climate of Southern California* (1966). Charles Francis Saunders, *The Southern Sierras of California* (1923) is a classic, as are George Wharton James, *The Wonders of the Colorado Desert* (2 vols., 1906), Joseph Smeaton Chase, *California Desert Trails* (1919), and Edmund Carroll Jaeger, *The California Deserts, A Visitor's Handbook* (1933). See also Elna Bakker and Richard G. Lilland, *The Great Southwest: The Story of a Land and Its People* (1972).

The exuberant flora of Southern California has inspired a number of guides and studies. Consulted were Mary Elizabeth Parsons, *The Wildflowers of California* (1914); Charles Francis Saunders, *With the Flowers and Trees in California* (1914); Edmund Carroll Jaeger, *The Mountain Trees of Southern California* (1920); Willis Linn Jepson, *The Trees of California* (1923); Edith S. Clements, *Flowers of Coast and Sierra* (1928); Edmund C. Jaeger, *Desert Wild Flowers* (1940); Howard E. McMann, *An Illustrated Manual of California Shrubs* (1951) and *An Illustrated Manual of Pacific Coast Trees* (1956); Willis Linn Jepson, *A Manual of the Flowering Plants of California* (1963); E. Yale Dawson, *The Cacti of California* (1966); Peter V. Peterson, *Native Trees of Southern California* (1970); Peter H. Raven, *Native Shrubs of Southern California* (1970); W. S. Head, *The California Chaparral* (1972); Philip A. Munz, *A Flora of Southern California* (1974).

Regarding the fauna of the Southland, see Edmund C. Jaeger, *Denizens of the Desert* (1922); Lloyd Ingles, *Mammals of California and Its Coastal Waters* (1957); Ernest S. Booth, *Mammals of Southern California* (1968); Sam Hinton, *Seashore Life of Southern California* (1969); and Robert T. Orr, *Marine Mammals of California* (1972). William L. Dawson, *The Birds of California* (4 vols., 1921) is a most magnificent book.

Regarding the Indians of Southern California, see the *Standard Handbook of the Indians of California* (1925) by Alfred Louis Kroeber.

To date, nothing has replaced the seven-volume *History of California* (1886–90), issued by the Bancroft Company, as the most authoritative chronicle of Southern California before the Conquest. See also Hubert Howe Bancroft's other study, *California Pastoral, 1769–1848* (1888), together with Irving Berdine Richman, *California Under Spain and Mexico, 1535–1847* (1911) and C. Alan Hutchinson, *Frontier Settlement in Mexican California* (1969). Robert Glass Cleland's *The Cattle on a Thousand Hills* (1951) covers the first phase of the American era, while the troubles of Old Californians are narrated by Leonard Pitt in *The Decline of the Californios: A Social History of the Spanish-speaking Californios, 1846–1890* (1966).

Histories of Rancho El Tejón include Helen S. Giffen and Arthur Woodward, *The Story of El Tejon* (1942); Earle Crowe, *Men of El Tejon, Empire in the Tehachapis* (1957); and Frank F. Latta, *Saga of Rancho El Tejon* (1976). Regarding the extraordinary career of Tejón's founder, see Stephen Bonsal, *Edward Fitzgerald Beale: A Pioneer in the Path of Empire* (1912). See also F. F. Latta, *Alexis Godey in Kern County* (1939); Clarence Cullimore, *Old Adobes of Forgotten Fort Tejon* (1949); and Harlan D. Fowler, *Camels to California* (1950). For the story of Kit Carson and Beale, see *Kit Carson's Own Story of His Life*, edited by Blanche C. Grant (1926). Bishop William Ingraham Kip writes of the Tejón in *The Early Days of My Episcopate* (1892). Charles Nordhoff describes his visit in *California for Health, Pleasure and Residence* (1882).

2

Southern California as an American culture and civilization is best studied in Carey McWilliams, *Southern California Country* (1946), and Franklin Walker, *A Literary History of Southern California* (1950). The *California Historical Society Quarterly (CHSQ)* and the *Quarterly of the Historical Society of Southern California (SCQ)* contain scores of important articles on the development of Southern California in the early years. Also of importance are William H. Ellison, "The Movement for State Divison in California, 1849–1860," *Quarterly of the Texas State Historical Association* 17 (1913): 101–39 and Oscar O. Winther, "The Colony System of Southern California," *Agricultural History* 27 (1963): 94–103.

The overall history of early Los Angeles is best treated by Remi A. Nadeau in *City-*

Makers (1948) and by Robert M. Fogelson in *The Fragmented Metropolis: Los Angeles, 1850–1930* (1967). Also consulted were John Albert Wilson, *History of Los Angeles County* (1880); Charles Dwight Willard, *The Herald's History of Los Angeles City* (1901); Laurance L. Hill, *La Reina: Los Angeles in Three Centuries* (1931); Oscar O. Winther, "The Rise of Metropolitan Los Angeles, 1870–1900," *Huntington Library Quarterly (HLQ)* 10 (1947): 391–405; Shirley Bystrom, "Los Angeles, 1846–1860," M.A. thesis, University of California at Berkeley (1951); W. W. Robinson, *Los Angeles From the Days of the Pueblo* (1959); and Richard Barsness, "Los Angeles' Quest for Improved Transportation, 1846–1861," *CHSQ* 46 (1967): 291–306. Valuable for facts and figures are Joseph Gregg Layne, *Annals of Los Angeles, 1769–1861* (1935); *Census of the City and County of Los Angeles, California, for the Year 1850, Together with an Analysis and an Appendix*, edited by Maurice H. Newmark and Marco R. Newmark (1929); and *Los Angeles City and County Directory for the Year 1872*, with an introduction by Ward Ritchie (1963). William B. Rice, *The Los Angeles Star, 1851–1864: The Beginnings of Journalism in Southern California* (1947) is of importance.

Reverend Woods's experience is found in Lindley Bynum, editor, "Los Angeles in 1854–55, the Diary of Rev. James Woods," *SCQ* 25 (1941): 65–86. Regarding the massacre of the Chinese, see Paul M. De Falla, "Lantern in the Western Sky," *SCQ* 62 (1960): 57–88, 161–85; and William R. Locklear, "The Celestials and the Angeles," *SCQ* 62 (1960): 239–56.

Decade by decade, promotional material provides statistics and insights. For the 1870s: William McPherson, *Homes in Los Angeles City and County* (1873); A. T. Hawley, *The Present Condition, Growth, Progress and Advantages of Los Angeles City and County* (1876); the Southern California Horticultural Society, *Sketches of the Los Angeles Fair* (1878). For the 1880s: John M. Davies, compiler, *Los Angeles City and County, Resources, Climate, Progress and Outlook* (1885); George Butler Griffin, *Pocket Guide of Los Angeles* (1886); and Ward Brothers, *Winter Scenes in Los Angeles* (ca. 1889). The Los Angeles Chamber of Commerce issued many pamphlets. Among the most informative are *Facts and Figures concerning Southern California and Los Angeles City and County* (1888), and Harry Ellington Brook, *The City and County of Los Angeles*, which had a tenth edition in 1902.

The names on the land in Southern California can be traced through Nellie Sanchez, *Spanish and Indian Place Names of California* (1914); Gertrude Mott, *A Handbook For Californians* (1926); and the authoritative *California Place Names* (1949) by Erwin Gudde. Also valuable is Hero E. Rensch and Mildred Brooke Hoover, editors, *Historic Spots in California* (3 vols., 1932–37).

The ranchos of Southern California were studied in Robert Hornbeck, *Roubidoux's Ranch in the '70s* (1913); Anita M. Baldwin, *Santa Anita Rancho* (1916); William W. Morrow, *Spanish and Mexican Private Land Grants* (1923); Myrtle Garrison, *Romance and History of California Ranchos* (1935); W. W. Robinson, *Ranchos Become Cities* (1939); idem, *The Old Spanish and Mexican Ranchos of Orange County* (1950); Robert Granniss Cowan, *Ranchos of California: A List of Spanish Concessions and Mexican Grants* (1956); Ruth Waldo Newhall, *The Newhall Ranch* (1958); Harold S. Chase, *Hope Ranch* (1963); Philip S. Rush, *Some Old Ranchos and Adobes* (1965); Paul W. Gates, *California Ranchos and Farms, 1846–1862* (1967); and Esther Boulton Black, *Rancho Cucamonga and Dona Merced* (1975).

Robert Glass Cleland's *The Place Called Sespe: The History of a California Ranch* (1940) is a classic of California historical literature. See also Cleland's *The Irvine Ranch* (1962).

Regarding Benjamin Davis Wilson, see *American Biography, A New Cyclopedia* 40

(1930): 144–46 and John W. Caughey, "Don Benito Wilson," *HLQ* 2 (1939): 285–300. Wilson dictated his memoirs to Hubert Howe Bancroft just before his death. The Huntington Library also has a copy. Further light is shed on Wilson in *The Indians of Southern California in 1852: The B. D. Wilson Report*, edited by John Caughey (1952). Jonathan Trumbull Warner recalled his early career in "Reminiscences of Early California From 1831 to 1846," *Annual Publications of the Historical Society of Southern California* 7 (1909): 176–93. See also Joseph John Hill, *The History of Warner's Ranch and Its Environs* (1927); and Lorrin L. Morrison, *Warner, The Man and the Ranch* (1962). Aside from *Adobe Days* (1925), the developed Southern Californian sensibility of Sarah Bixby Smith is evident in her poetry. See *My Sagebrush Garden* (1924), *Pasear* (1926), *Wind upon My Face* (1929), and *The Bending Tree* (1933).

When it first appeared in 1916, Charles Fletcher Lummis justly described Harris Newmark's *Sixty Years in Southern California, 1853–1913* as the Pepys's diary of Los Angeles. A resident of Los Angeles since 1853, Newmark wrote out a series of autobiographical fragments in 1913, just before his death. Perry Worden, a trained scholar, amplified, annotated, and authenticated Newmark's recollections, which were put into further shape by two nephews, Maurice H. and Marco R. Newmark. The fourth edition (1970) was revised and augmented with an introduction and notes by W. W. Robinson.

Important promotional books dealing with Southern California as a whole are S. L. Welch, compiler, *Southern California Illustrated* (1886); Charles Frederick Holder, *Southern California* (1888); Walter Lindley and Joseph Widney, *California of the South* (1888); Charles Dudley Warner, *Our Italy* (1891); George Wharton James, *B. R. Baumgardt and Company's Guide Book to South California* (1895); and John Wesley Hanson, *The American Italy, Southern California* (1896).

For the impressions of visitors, see Ludwig Louis Salvator, Archduke of Austria, *Los Angeles in the Sunny Seventies*, translated by Marguerite Eyer Wilbur from the German edition of 1878 (1929); William Henry Bishop, *Old Mexico and Her Lost Provinces* (1883); Emma Hildreth Adams, *To and Fro in Southern California* (1887); Samuel Storey, *To the Golden Land* (1889); Katherine Abbott Sanborn, *A Truthful Woman in Southern California* (1893); Ratcliffe Hicks, *Southern California; or, The Land of the Afternoon* (1898); Frederick Hastings Rindge, *Happy Days in Southern California* (1898); and Henry James, *The American Scene* (1907).

Regarding the work of the railroads in promoting and settling Southern California, see Edna M. Parker, "The Southern Pacific Railroad and Settlement in Southern California," *Pacific Historical Review* (PHR) 6 (1937): 103–119 and James Marshall, *Santa Fe, the Railroad that Built an Empire* (1949). Jerome Madden, land agent for the Southern Pacific, issued *The Lands of the Southern Pacific* (1877), *Southern Pacific Sketch Book* (1887), and *California: Its Attractions for the Invalid, Tourist, Capitalist, and Homeseeker* (1892). The advertising efforts of the Santa Fe reached a high point in Charles Augustus Keeler, *Southern California*, illustrated by Louise M. Keeler (1898).

Glenn Dumke's *Boom of the Eighties in Southern California* (1944) documents the frenzy of the 1880s. Theodore Strong Van Dyke's *Millionaires of a Day* (1890) is a good contemporary account, while Frederick R. Sanford's *Bursting of a Boom* (1889) is a weak but sometimes informative novel. Earl S. Pomeroy illuminates some aspects of the rush to Southern California in *In Search of the Golden West: The Tourist in Western America* (1957). John Packard's "The Role of the Tourist Hotel in California Development to 1900," M.A. thesis, University of Southern California (1953) should have been published years ago. The Bancroft Library has a number of publicity pamphlets from the Hotel Del Coronado, 1890–1900. See also J. Harold Peterson, *The Coronado Story* (1954).

John E. Baur's *The Health Seekers of Southern California, 1870–1900* (1959) commands the topic. For contemporary claims, see L. M. Holt, *The Great Interior Fruit Belt and Sanitarium of Southern California: San Bernardino County . . .* (1885); Peter Charles Remondino, *The Mediterranean Shores of America* (1892); William A. Edwards and Beatrice Harraden, *Two Health-Seekers in Southern California* (1897); and F. C. S. Sanders, *California as a Health Resort* (1916). See also Oscar O. Winther, "The Use of Climate as a Means of Promoting Migration to Southern California," *Mississippi Valley Historical Review* (MVHR) 33 (1946): 411–24.

Horace Bell's *Reminiscences of a Ranger; or, Early Times in Southern California* appeared in 1881. In 1930 Lanier Bartlett issued further sketches by Bell under the title *On the Old West Coast*. The biography *Fortune Favors the Brave: The Life and Times of Horace Bell* (1953) by Benjamin S. Harrison is well researched. There is no biography by Benjamin Ignatius Hayes. See, however, *An Historical Sketch of Los Angeles County* (1876) by Hayes, J. J. Warner, and J. P. Widney, together with *Pioneer Notes from the Diaries of Judge Benjamin Hayes, 1849–1876*, edited by Marjorie Wolcott (1929). The 138 volumes of Hayes's *Scrapbooks* are in the Bancroft Library.

Benjamin Cummings Truman wrote about dueling, *The Field of Honor* (1884), and wine, *See How It Sparkles* (1896), as well as about California: *Homes and Happiness in the Golden State* (1883); *Tourists' Illustrated Guide to the Celebrated Summer and Winter Resorts of California* (1883); *From the Crescent City to the Golden Gate via the Sunset Route* (1886); *Southern California* (1903); and *The Missions of California* (1903). He also interviewed Vásquez in prison: *Life, Adventures and Capture of Tiburcio Vásquez, the Great California Bandit and Murderer* (1874).

The charming saga of the colony of Polish intellectuals can be traced in Helena Modjeska's own *Memories and Impressions* (1910), together with John S. Fox, "Modjeska's Home," typewritten MS, Works Project Administration Report, in the Bancroft Library (1936); Milton L. Kosberg, "The Polish Colony of California, 1876–1914," M.A. thesis, University of Southern California (1952); Antoni Gronowicz, *Modjeska: Her Life and Loves* (1956); Charles Morley, editor and translator, *Portrait of America: Letters of Henry Sienkiewicz* (1959); Theodore Payne, *Life on the Modjeska Ranch in the Gay Nineties* (1962); and Marion Coleman, *Fair Rosalind: The American Career of Helena Modjeska* (1969).

James Miller Guinn's *Historical Biographical Record of Southern California* (1902) is a standard source of early biographies. See also W. W. Robinson, *Lawyers of Los Angeles* (1959) and H. Brett Melendy and Benjamin F. Gilbert, *The Governors of California* (1965). In the mid-1950s Marco R. Newmark published an extensive series of "Historical Profiles" in the SCQ. Also of value is Henry D. Barrows, "Pío Pico," SCQ 3 (1894): 54–65.

Ramona appeared in 1884. Helen Hunt Jackson's other Southern California sketches are available in *Glimpses of Three Coasts* (1886). *Helen Hunt Jackson* by Ruth Odell (1939) is complete and well-written. The development of the Ramona myth can be traced through Charles Fletcher Lummis, *The Home of Ramona* (n.d.); Adam Clark Vroman and T. F. Barnes, *The Genesis of the Story of Ramona* (1899); George Wharton James, *Through Ramona's Country* (1908); and Carlyle Channing Davis, *The True Story of Ramona* (ca. 1914). The Bancroft Library has a file of articles, pamphlets, and other ephemera relating to the Ramona Pageant Play by Garnet Holme. In 1906 the Los Angeles Chamber of Commerce issued a catalogue of *Ramona*-related material, the *Antonio F. Coronel Collection*.

3

Any consideration of this period begins and ends with the invaluable bibliographical *vade mecum*, Doyce B. Nunis, Jr., editor, *Los Angeles and Its Environs in the Twen-*

tieth Century: A Bibliography of a Metropolis, Compiled under the Auspices of the Met-
ropolitan Los Angeles History Project (1973). Carey McWilliams's *Southern California*
Country, An Island on the Land (1946) is still the best overall study. See also Frank
Beach, "The Transformation of California, 1900–1920," Ph.D. dissertation, University
of California at Berkeley (1963). Recent histories of Los Angeles include Remi Nadeau,
Los Angeles, From Mission to Modern City (1960); the History Division of the Los An-
geles County Museum, *Los Angeles, 1900–1960* (1961); Robert M. Fogelson, *The Frag-*
mented Metropolis: Los Angeles, 1850–1930 (1967); and W. W. Robinson, *Los Angeles:*
A Profile (1968). Two specialized studies of relevance to this period are Spencer Crump,
Ride the Big Red Cars: How Trolleys Helped Build Southern California (1962) and Max
Vorspan and Lloyd P. Gartner, *History of the Jews of Los Angeles* (1970).

Turn-of-the-century historiography frequently edges into promotional writing, yet there
is much good information in James Miller Guinn, *History of Los Angeles City and County*
(1900), later expanded into *A History of California and an Extended History of Los An-*
geles and Environs (3 vols., 1915). Charles Dwight Willard's *The Herald's History of Los*
Angeles City (1901) is equally informative. Promotional writings and guides from this
era include R. B. Dickinson, *Los Angeles of Today Architecturally* (1896); *Los Angeles*
Then and Now (1897); Harry Ellington Brook, *The City and County of Los Angeles in*
Southern California (1898); *Newman's Directory and Guide of Los Angeles and Vicinity*
(1903); Benjamin C. Truman, *The Queen City of the Angels: Los Angeles* (1904); *Greater*
Los Angeles Illustrated: The Most Progressive Metropolis of the Twentieth Century (1907);
The Los Angeles Times, *Southern California's Standard Guide Book* (1910); Robert J.
Burdette, editor, *Greater Los Angeles and Southern California* (1910); *Los Angeles, The*
Old and the New (1911); and James Whitin Abbott, *Among Cities Los Angeles is the*
World's Greatest Wonder—Why? (ca. 1914). *Sunset* magazine kept up a lively coverage
of Los Angeles with Arthur M. Dole, "How Los Angeles Grows" 16(1905): 176–88;
Bertha H. Smith, "The Making of Los Angeles" 19(1907): 237–54; William Woodhead,
"Los Angeles: The Most Rapidly Growing City in America" 26(1911): 124; and Walter
V. Woehlke, "Los Angeles—Homeland" 26(1911): 3–16. See also Charles Mulford Ro-
binson, *The Call of the City* (1908), and Griffith J. Griffith, *Parks, Boulevards and*
Playgrounds (c1910). Of delightful antiquarian interest is the Ladies Aid Society of the
Fort Street Methodist Episcopal Church, *Los Angeles Cookery* (1881).

The best-known autobiography dealing with turn-of-the-century Los Angeles is the
classic *Sixty Years in Southern California, 1853–1913* (1916) by Harris Newmark. See
also Marco Ross Newmark, *Jottings in Southern California History* (1955). Other valuable reminiscences drawn heavily upon for background include Jackson Alpheus Graves,
My Seventy Years in California, 1857–1927 (1927); Rufus Landon Horton, *Philosophy*
of Modern Life: An Autobiography of a Lawyer (1929); and Robert C. Cowan, *A Back-*
ward Glance: Los Angeles, 1901–1915 (1969). Marshal Stimson's *Fun, Fights, and Fiestas*
in Old Los Angeles: An Autobiography (1966) is an informative delight.

Suggestions advanced regarding the attitudes and lifestyle of the Los Angeles Estab-
lishment were derived, in part, from such diverse but interrelated sources as Mark Sibley
Severance, *Hammersmith, His Harvard Days* (1877); "Clubs of Los Angeles," *Land of*
Sunshine (LS) 5(1896): 125–35; J. Torrey Connor, "La Fiesta de Los Angeles," *Sunset*
8(1902): 267; Harry B. Lummis, "Tennis at Santa Monica," *LS* 16(1902): 224–25; *As*
We See 'Em: A Volume of Cartoons and Caricatures of Los Angeles Citizens (1905);
Charles Fletcher Lummis, editor, *Out West: Los Angeles and Her Makers* (1909);
W. W. Robinson, *Lawyers of Los Angeles* (1959); and Michael Regan, *Mansions of Old*
Los Angeles (1965). Aside from *Happy Days in Southern California* (1898), Frederick
Hastings Rindge wrote *Meditations on Many Matters* (1890). See also Lawrence Clark
Powell, *Some Thoughts on the Republication of Frederick Hastings Rindge's "Happy Days*

in Southern California" (1972). Regarding California's first native-born senator, see Leroy
E. Mosher, *Stephen M. White: Californian, Citizen, Lawyer, Senator* (2 vols., 1903)
and Edith Dobie, *The Political Career of Stephen Mallory White* (1927). Pío Pico's obituary was published in the October 1894 *Land of Sunshine* 1(1894): 92–93. Ella Ludwig's *History of the Harbor District of Los Angeles* (1928) is a most useful—exhaustive
and exhausting!—study of Los Angeles's first major public works project. See also
W. W. Robinson, *San Pedro and Wilmington: A Calendar of Events in the Making of
the Two Cities and the Los Angeles Harbor* (ca. 1937); Franklin Hoyt, "Influence of the
Railroads in the Development of Los Angeles Harbor," *SCQ* 35(1933): 195–212; and
Richard W. Barsness, "Railroads and Los Angeles: The Quest for a Deepwater Port,"
SCQ 47(1965): 379–94.

The career of Harrison Gray Otis is admirably set forth in Richard Connelly Miller,
"Otis and His Times: The Career of Harrison Gray Otis of Los Angeles," Ph.D. disser-
tation, University of California at Berkeley (1961). Gray's boosterism is evident in his
"Los Angeles—A Sketch," *Sunset* 24(1910): 17–48. Regarding the saga of Otis versus
organized labor, see Lincoln Steffens, *Autobiography* (1931) and Justin Kaplan, *Lincoln
Steffens* (1974), together with Louis Adamic, *Dynamite: The Story of Class Violence in
America* (1935) and David F. Selvin, *Sky Full of Storm: A Brief History of California
Labor* (1975).

Edwin R. Bingham, *Charles F. Lummis, Editor of the Southwest* (1955), is the stan-
dard academic biography of Lummis. Dudley Gordon's *Charles F. Lummis: Crusader
in Corduroy* (1972) is a totally idiosyncratic study—hero-worshipful, disorganized, repetitive, yet also anecdotal and charming in the manner of medieval hagiography.
Scholarship needs more such eccentric works! Two of Lummis's offspring, Turbese
Lummis-Fiske and Keith Lummis, collaborated on *Charles F. Lummis, The Man and
His West* (1975). See also Marc Simmons, *Two Southwesterners: Charles Lummis and
Amado Chaves* (1968). Lummis edited *Land of Sunshine/Out West* from January 1895
to February 1903. From then until his resignation in November 1909, Lummis was
assisted by coeditor C. A. Moody. It would be impossible to cite any significant percentage of Lummis's volcanic outpouring of journalism in *Land of Sunshine.* Of special
relevance to this chapter, however, are the 1895 architectural pieces, "The Lesson of
the Adobe" 2(1895): 65–67; "The Patio" 3(1895): 12–16; "Something about the Adobe"
3(1894): 48–50; and "The Grand Veranda" 3(1895): 63–67; together with Lummis's Los
Angeles essays, "Los Angeles, Queen of the Southwest" 6(1896–97): 45–55; "A Magic
Growth" 10(1898–99), 99–100; and "The Making of Los Angeles," *Out West* 30(1909):
227–57. Between June 1902 and June 1903, Lummis serialized a long essay in *Out
West* entitled "The Right Hand of the Continent," in which he compared and contrasted Southern California with the rest of the United States. Lummis's archeological
imagination is evidenced in "The Southwest Society Archaeological Institute of America," *Out West* 20(1904): 369–73, and "Catching Our Archaeology Alive," *Out West*
22(1905): 35–45. In "T. R. Westerner," *Sunset* 42(1919): 17–19, 74–82, Lummis eulogized his fellow westernizing Harvardian and lifelong role model.

Charles Fletcher Lummis wrote most of his books in the 1890s, after which time he
directed his energies to public affairs and journalism. He began his literary career in
1879 with the private publication of *Birch Bark Poems* at Harvard (reprinted in 1969 by
Dawson's Bookshop, Los Angeles). In *A Tramp across the Continent* (1892) he described
his pedestrian pilgrimage to Southern California, which awakened in him that lifelong
love affair with the Southwest which received its best expression in *The Spanish Pioneers*
(1893) and such other collections as *A New Mexico David and Other Stories and Sketches
of the Southwest* (1891); *Some Strange Corners of Our Country: The Wonderland of the*

Southwest (1892); *The Land of Poco Tiempo* (1893); *The Man Who Married the Moon and Other Pueblo Indian Folk-Stories* (1894); *The Gold Fish of Gran Chimer* (1896); *The King of the Broncos and Other Stories of New Mexico* (1897); and *The Enchanted Burro* (1897). In *The Awakening of a Nation* (1898) Lummis eulogized the first ten years of the administration of President Porfirio Díaz of Mexico. After this ferocious outburst of bookmaking, Lummis's book production tapered off for twenty years. In *My Friend Will* (1911) he told the story of his willful recovery from stroke. He also produced *In Memory of Juan Rodríguez Cabrillo, Who Gave the World California* in 1913, and in 1916 he joined Frederick Webb Hodge to edit Mrs. Edward E. Ayer's translation of *The Memorial of Fray Alonso de Benavides, 1630*. In the last decade of his life, his health and eyesight deteriorating, his life's work accomplished, Lummis resumed the writing of books. Although he never completed his long-labored-on encyclopedia of the Spanish Southwest, he did manage to produce *Spanish Songs of Old California* (1923), to reedit and enlarge *Some Strange Corners of Our Country* into *Mesa, Canyon, and Pueblo: Our Wonderland of the Southwest* (1925), and to expand *The Spanish Pioneers* into *The Spanish Pioneers and the California Missions* (1929). He gathered his poetry into *A Bronco Pegasus* (1928) and the best of his journalism into *Flowers of Our Lost Romance* (1929). My impressions of Lummis are based upon an appreciative absorption of these books, together with a reading of the complete files of *Land of Sunshine/Out West*. Essential to an understanding of the influence of John Ruskin and his American disciple Charles Eliot Norton on young Lummis is Roger B. Stein, *John Ruskin and Aesthetic Thought in America, 1840–1900* (1967).

Grace Ellery Channing (later Grace Ellery Channing Stetson) explicated her Italian ideas for Los Angeles in "Italy and 'Our Italy'," *LS* 11(1899): 24–29, and "What We Can Learn From Rome," *Out West* 19(1903): 239–49, 357–68, 473–83, 605–16. Italian locales and constant Italianizing pervade her *Stories of Italy* (1894); *The Sister of a Saint and Other Stories* (1895); *Chap-Book Stories* (1896); and *The Fortune of a Day* (1900). For other examples of this imposition of Mediterranean metaphors on Southern California, see Elizabeth Bacon Custer [she was widowed at Little Big Horn], "Memories of Our Italy," *LS* 3(1895): 51–56 and Charles D. Tyng, "Lessons From the Alhambra," *LS* 4(1896): 214–21.

Regarding the life and career of Abbott Kinney, see *Out West* 30(1909): 371; and Guinn, *History of California* 2:121–24. Kinney outlined aspects of his own multifaceted utopian thinking in *Tasks by Twilight* (1893); *The Conquest of Death* (1893); *Eucalyptus* (1895); *Forest and Water* (1900); and "Sanitary Santa Monica," *Sunset* 4(1900): 98–102. Regarding the eucalyptus crusade, see Alfred J. McClatchie, "The Eucalyptus of the Southwest," *Out West* 20(1904): 336–46, 422–36. There is an undated planner's map, *Venice of America*, in the Huntington Library, San Marino. Also consulted: John B. Dame, "California's Venice," *Sunset* 16(1905): 32–36; Kate Greenleaf Locke, "[Venice] A Realized Ideal," *Sunset* 16(1905): 32–36; Kate Greenleaf Locke, "[Venice] A Realized Ideal," *Sunset* 16(1905): 36–38; Nancy Langley, "Venice in Beavers and Bustles," *Westways* 27(1935): 24–25; Roger Holmes, "Venice—Abbott Kinney's Dream City," *Westways* 49(1957): 6–7; and Patricia Adler, *A History of the Venice Area* (1969).

Regarding the genesis of the mission myth, see John Ogden Pohlmann, "California's Mission Myth," Ph.D. dissertation, University of California at Los Angeles (1974). There is a typewritten acting version of John Steven McGroarty's "The Mission Play, A Pageant Play in Three Acts" (1911) in the Huntington Library. See also *The Mission Play* (1923) and *The Mission Play Souvenir Book* (1930). The entire issue for 24 January 1920 of the periodical *California Life* was devoted to background studies of McGroarty and *The Mission Play*. Also consulted: Willard Huntington Wright, "The Mission Play,"

Sunset 29(1912): 98–100; and *John Steven McGroarty: In Memoriam, 1862–1944* (1944). From 1906 to 1914, McGroarty edited *The West Coast, An Illustrated Monthly*. He also wrote *Just California and Songs Along the Way* (1903); *Wander Songs* (1908); *The King's Highway* (1909); *California, Its History and Romance* (1911); *Five Wander Songs* (1918); "Old Missions of California," *California Life* 17(1920): 38–42; *Los Angeles from the Mountains to the Sea* (3 vols., 1921); *Mission Memories* (1929); *California of the South* (5 vols., 1933–35); and *Past Eighty* (1943). McGroarty edited a *History of Los Angeles County* in 1923 and *Little Flowers of St. Francis, Translated from the Italian* in 1932. My interpretation of McGroarty, his play, and the social uses of the mission myth is based upon a reading of this material. Regarding the Mission Inn, see Zona Gale, *Frank Miller of Mission Inn* (1938), and Tom Patterson, *A Colony for California: Riverside's First Hundred Years* (1971).

Charles Dudley Warner opened speculations regarding the possible cultural and eugenic effects of Southern California in "Race and Climate," *LS* 4(1896): 103–6. For biographical studies of Joseph Pomeroy Widney, see Carl W. Rand, *Joseph Pomeroy Widney, Physician and Mystic*, edited by Doris Sanders (1970), and the chapter "The Community Builders of Los Angeles—Dr. Joseph P. Widney" in Marco R. Newmark, *Jottings in Southern California History* (1955), 89–93. Widney began his writing career with *California of the South* (1888), which he coauthored with Walter Lindley. In the early 1900s he turned to racial and religious speculations: *The Way of Life* (1900); *Via Domini, Poems* (1903); *Race Life of the Aryan Peoples* (2 vols., 1907); *All-Fader* (1909); and *Ahasuerus, a Race Tragedy* (1915). During the 1930s, when he was in his nineties, he restated his theories in a series of privately published books which only a handful of scholars on grants (including myself) have ever been foolhardy enough to tackle. They include *The Lure of the Land: An Idyll of the Pacific* (1932); *The Genesis and Evolution of Islam and Judaeo-Christianity* (1932); *The Faith That Has Come to Me* (1932); *Whither Away? The Problem of Death and the Hereafter* (1934); *The Three Americas, Their Racial Past and the Dominant Racial Factors of Their Future* (1935); *Race Life and Race Religions* (1936); *To the Engle Peoples of the World* (1937); *Civilizations and Their Diseases and Rebuilding a Wrecked World-Civilization* (1937); *The Song of the Engle Men and an Appeal to the Widely-Scattered Engle Men of the World* (1937); *The Greater City of Los Angeles: A Plan for the Development of Los Angeles City as a Great World Health Center* (1938); and—at long last!—*Life and Its Problems as Viewed by a Blind Man at the Age of Ninety-Six*, edited by T. Cameron Taylor (ca. 1942). Given developments in Germany in the late 1930s, the titles of certain of Widney's books have chilling reverberations indeed. See also *Conversational Gems* compiled by Rebecca Davis Macartney (1935).

Jessie Benton Frémont published a poem in *Land of Sunshine*, "Dolores" 7(1897): 3–4, and an essay, "California and Frémont" 4(1895–1896): 3–14. Lummis eulogized her in *Out West* 18(1903): 90–95, as did his coeditor Charles Amadon Moody, in "Here Was a Woman," *Out West* 18(1903): 169–85. The Frémonts' daughter, Elizabeth Benton Frémont, published her *Recollections* in 1912, compiled by I. T. Martin. See also Catherine Coffin Phillips, *Jessie Benton Frémont* (1935) and Ferol Egan, *Frémont: Explorer for a Restless Nation* (1977). Between 1898 and 1899 Margaret Collier Graham wrote a column, "The Angle of Reflection," for *Land of Sunshine*. Her local color short stories were collected in *Stories of the Foothills* (1895) and *The Wizard's Daughter and Other Stories* (1905). Regarding Graham's feminist thinking, see *Do They Really Respect Us? and Other Essays* (1912) and *Gifts and Givers, a Sermon For all Seasons* (1906). See also Jane Apostol, "Margaret Collier Graham, First Lady of the Foothills," *SCQ* 63(1981): 348–73. Another Southern Californian feminist statement is Grace Ellery

Channing Stetson, "The Marriage Question," in William Dean Howells, editor, *Their Husband's Wives* (1906). Regarding the emergence of women's clubs, see "The Woman's Parliament of Southern California," *LS* 8(1897–98), 284–89, and, "The Woman's Club," *LS* 16(1902): 35–36. Caroline Maria Seymour Severance wrote *The Matter of Clubs* in 1906, edited by Ella Giles Ruddy. For the details of Severance's career, see Mary S. Gibson, *Caroline M. Severance, Pioneer* (1925). Background information regarding Severance, Charlotte Perkins Gilman Stetson, and other women active in Southern California at the turn of the century can be found in *Notable American Women, 1607–1950: A Biographical Dictionary* (3 vols., 1971). See also Doyce B. Nunis, Jr., "Kate Douglas Wiggin: Pioneer in California Kindergarten Education," *CHSQ* 41 (1962), 291–309.

Gilman's autobiography, *The Living of Charlotte Perkins Gilman* (1935), is a minor classic. For secondary material, see Floyd Dell, *Women as World Builders: Studies in Modern Feminism* (1913); Carl N. Degler, "Charlotte Perkins Gilman on the Theory and Practice of Feminism," *American Quarterly (AQ)* 8(1956): 21–39; and William T. Doyle, "Charlotte Perkins Gilman and the Cycle of Feminist Reform," Ph.D. dissertation, University of California at Berkeley (1960). For Gilman's response to the issue of race and climate, see "Beauty as an Educator," *LS* 3(1895): 193–94 and "The Superior Northerner," *LS* 3(1895): 209–11. While not of immediate applicability to her sojourn in Southern California, Gilman's novella *The Yellow Wall Paper* (1899) depicts the emotional stresses endured by women of a certain class and situation in late-nineteenth-century America. See also *In This Our World, and Other Poems* (1895); *What Diantha Did: A Novel* (1910); and *The Crux: A Novel* (1911). Central also to an understanding of this pioneer feminist's thinking are *The Labor Movement* (1892); *Women and Economics* (1899); *Concerning Children* (1901); *Human Work* (1904); *Women and Social Service* (1907); *The Home, Its Work and Influence* (1910); *The Man-Made World; or, Our Androcentric Culture* (1911); and, *His Religion and Hers: A Study of the Faith of Our Fathers and the Work of Our Mothers* (1923). Between 1909 and 1916, Gilman edited and was sole writer for *The Forerunner, a Monthly Magazine*.

4

Histories of Pasadena consulted include Hiram Alvin Reid, *History of Pasadena* (1895); John Windell Wood, *Pasadena, California, Historical and Personal* (1917); Harold Davis Carew, *History of Pasadena and the San Gabriel Valley* (3 vols., 1930); W. W. Robinson, *Pasadena: A Calendar of Events in the Making of a City* (1949); Henry Markham Page, *Pasadena: Its Early Years* (1964); and Manuel Pineda and E. Caswell Perry, *Pasadena Area History* (1972). Two memoirs of use are Lon F. Chapin, *Thirty Years in Pasadena* (1929) and Jennie Hollingsworth Giddings, *I Can Remember Early Pasadena* (ca. 1949). For descriptive and promotional writing, see: *Album of Pasadena* (188–?); Theodore Parker Lukens, *Pasadena, California, Illustrated and Described* (1886); *Pasadena, Crown of the Valley* (1892); Pasadena Board of Trade, *Illustrated Souvenir Book* (1897) and *Pasadena, California, The City Beautiful* (1901); D. C. Daggett, "Pasadena, the City of Homes," *LS* 14(1901): 345–60; Eleanor Gates, "Pasadena—Paradise Regained," *Sunset* 27(1911): 603–16; and Pasadena Board of Trade, *Pasadena, California, The Ideal Home City* (1913). For specialized insight, see *The Whiskey War in Pasadena* (1888); George Wharton James, *Scenes on the Line of the Pasadena Mountain Railway* (1893); Theon Cummings, M.D., *Climate, The Mother of Destiny . . . Pasadena* (1898); and *Pasadena Daily News, A Book of the Crown City and Its Tournament of Roses* (1907). Also consulted: the Pasadena High School literary magazine, *The Item* (1899–1910).

For Charles Frederick Holder's views, see *Pasadena, Its Climate, Homes, Resources* (1888); *All About Pasadena and Its Climate, Homes, Resources* (1888); *All About Pasadena and Its Vicinity* (1889); *The Highlands of Pasadena* (1889); and "Home Life in Southern California," *LS* 7(1897): 255–63. Regarding tourism in Pasadena, see "Pleasure Resorts of Los Angeles County," *LS* 8(1897–98): 147–55 and Ruth K. Wood, *The Tourists' California* (1914). The magazine *The Californian* (called at various times *Huntington Life, Maryland Life, Huntington Maryland Life,* and *California Life*) was issued in the early 1900s by the Hotels Maryland, Huntington, and Green. It is an invaluable guide to the tourist and hotel culture of Pasadena. The aesthetic responses of Olive Percival can be traced through her *Mexico City, an Idler's Note-Book* (1901); *Leaf-Shadows and Rose-Drift, Being Little Songs from a Los Angeles Garden* (1911); *Yellowing Ivy* (1946); and *Our Old-Fashioned Flowers* (1947). See also Kate Douglas Wiggin, *My Garden of Memory* (1923). Regarding the architecture and decorative arts of Pasadena, see *California Southland* (after 1929, *California Arts and Architecture*), a periodical issued between 1918 and 1929; *California Design 1910*, edited by Timothy J. Andersen, Eudorah M. Moore, and Robert W. Winter, photographed by Morley Baer (1974); and Randell L. Makinson, *Greene and Greene: Architecture as a Fine Art* (1977).

Isaac F. Marcosson's *A Little Known Master of Millions* (1914) is an early and adulatory study of Henry Edwards Huntington. For the saga of Arabella Huntington, see James T. Maher, *The Twilight of Splendor: Chronicles of the Age of American Palaces* (1975). Regarding the Huntingtons' collecting, see John E. Pomfret, *The Henry E. Huntington Library and Art Gallery* (1969) and James Thorpe, Robert R. Wark, and Ray Allen Billington, *The Founding of the Henry E. Huntington Library and Art Gallery* (1969). See also S. N. Behrman, *Duveen* (1972). Regarding the boyhood and adolescence of the Huntingtons' young neighbor, see Martin Blumenson, editor, *The Patton Papers, 1885–1940* (1972).

Regarding the Ur-era of Los Angeles letters, see Henry Winfred Splitter, "Literature in Los Angeles Before 1900," *Journal of the West* 5(1966): 91–104. Of special interest: Lizzie F. Baldy, *The California Pioneer and Other Poems* (1879). Four general surveys are of special importance to any consideration of the emergence of letters in the Southland. They are Franklin Walker's *A Literary History of Southern California* (1950) and Lawrence Clark Powell's three studies—*Books: West Southwest* (1957); *California Classics: The Creative Literature of the Golden State* (1971); and *Southwest Classics: The Creative Literature of the Arid Lands* (1974).

For background regarding the Arroyo School, see W. W. Robinson, *The Story of the Southwest Museum* (1960); Ruth Mahood, editor, *Photographer of the Southwest, Adam Clark Vroman, 1856–1916* (1961); *An Informal History of the California Institute of Technology* (1966); and Barry Sanders, editor, *The Craftsman, An Anthology* (1978). Horatio Nelson Rust's papers are in the Huntington Library. See especially Rust's "Scrapbook of Personal Articles."

Charles Fletcher Lummis set forth his hopes for literature in the Southland in "The New League for Literature and the West," *LS* 8(1898): 206–14, 260–66 and "Books in Harness," *Out West* 25(1906): 195–225. For Jack London's early appearances in *Out West*, see "The Master of Mystery" 17(1902): 330–39 and "The Sickness of Lone Chief" 17(1902): 468–75. Regarding Sharlot Hall, see Charles Franklin Parker, "Out of the West of Long Ago," *Arizona Highways* 19(1943): 6–11, 35. The literary career of another Lummis favorite, Gwendolen Overton, can be sampled in *The Heritage of Unrest* (1901); *The Golden Chain* (1903); *Anne Carmel* (1903); *The Captain's Daughter* (1903); and *Captains of the World* (1904). Regarding Robinson Jeffers, see Lawrence Clark Powell,

Robinson Jeffers: The Man and His Work (1940); Frederick I. Carpenter, *Robinson Jeffers* (1962); and Melba Berry Bennett, *The Stone Mason of Tor House* (1966).

Mary Austin's *Earth Horizon* (1932) touches scathingly upon her relationship with Lummis. See also T. M. Pearce, *The Beloved House* (1940); Donald P. Ringler, "Mary Austin: Kern County Days, 1888–1892," SCQ 45(1963); and T. M. Pearce, *Mary Hunter Austin* (1965). The emergence of Austin's remarkable talent during this period can be traced through *The Land of Little Rain*, illustrated by E. Boyd Smith (1903); *Isidro*, illustrated by Eric Pape (1905); *The Flock*, illustrated by E. Boyd Smith (1906); *Lost Borders* (1909); *California, the Land of the Sun*, paintings by Sutton Palmer (1914); and *Mother of Felipe and Other Early Stories*, edited by Franklin Walker (1950).

For a full-length study of George Wharton James, see Roger J. Bourdon, "George Wharton James, Interpreter of the Southwest," Ph.D. dissertation, University of California at Los Angeles (1966). The *Arroyo Craftsman* (October 1909) survived for one issue. See also James's article on rustic construction and landscaping in the Los Angeles area, "Fashioned By Nature," *Out West* 5(1913): 141–53. James's preoccupations, all of immediate relevance to an understanding of Arroyoan attitudes, can be traced through such published expressions of his prodigious energy—and lifetime habit of overwork!—as *Nature Sermons* (1894); *In and Around Grand Canyon* (1900); *Indian Basketry* (1901); *The Indians of the Painted Desert Region* (1903); *In and Out of the Old Missions of California* (1905); *The Wonders of the Colorado Desert* (2 vols., 1906); *What the White Race May Learn from the Indian* (1903); *Through Ramona's Country* (1908); *Heroes of California* (1910); *The Old Franciscan Missions of California* (1913); *California, Romantic and Beautiful* (1914); *The Lake of the Sky: Lake Tahoe* (1915); *Quit Your Worrying* (1916); *Living the Radiant Life* (1916); and *Singing Through Life with God* (1920). For a touching example of James's forgiveness of his persecutor (or was this a peace offering?), see "Charles F. Lummis: A Unique Literary Personage of Modern America," *National Magazine* 27(1912): 129–43.

A pioneering publication is Lou V. Chapin, *Art Work on Southern California* (1900). *The Dictionary of Art and Artists in Southern California before 1900* by Nancy Dustin Wall Moure, with research assistance by Lyn Wall Smith (1974), is an invaluable guide. See also Henry W. Splitter, "Art in Los Angeles Before 1900," SCQ 41(1959): 38–57, 117–38, 247–56.

For examples of Lummis's boosting of the art and artists of Southern California in *Land of Sunshine/Out West*, see "Borglum and His Work" 4(1895–96): 34–37; "Wachtel and His Work" 4(1895–96): 168–72; "L. Maynard Dixon and His Work" 10(1898): 4–11; "Alex F. Harmer and His Work," 12(1899–1900): 22–27; "The Ruskin Art Club" 16(1902): 87–88; "Old Art in California" 21(1904): 211–30; and "The Artists' Paradise" 29(1908): 173–91, 241–56. Regarding Francisco, Wachtel, Borglum, and Judson, see George Wharton James, "J. Bond Francisco, Musician and Painter," *Out West* (1913), 78–97; Anthony Anderson, *Elmer Wachtel: A Brief Biography* (1930); Willadene Price, *Gutzon Borglum, Artist and Patriot* (1961), and George Wharton James, "William Lees Judson, Painter," *Out West* 3(1913): 255–56. For personal statements, see John Gutzon Borglum, "An Artist's Paradise," *LS* 1(1894–95), 83; and William Lees Judson, "How I Became an Impressionist," *Overland Monthly* (*OvMo*), n.s. (1897), 417–22. Printed sources on Maynard Dixon include Grant Wallace, *Maynard Dixon: Painter and Poet of the Far West* (1937); *Maynard Dixon, Painter of the West*, introduction by Arthur Miller (1945); and Wesley M. Burnside, *Maynard Dixon, Artist of the West* (1974). See also Wilbur Hall, "The Art of Maynard Dixon," *Sunset* 46(1921): 44–45 and Ansel Adams, "Free Man in a Free Country: The West of Maynard Dixon," *American West*

6(1969): 41–47. A very limited collection of Dixon's own *Poems and Seven Drawings* was printed by Grabhorn Press in 1923. The Lummis-Dixon letters are in the Library of the Southwest Museum in Los Angeles. See also Edith Hamlin, "Maynard Dixon, Artist of the West," *CHSQ* 53(1974): 361–76 and *Rim-Rock and Sage: The Collected Poems of Maynard Dixon*, introduction by Kevin Starr (1977).

For contemporary response to the Dominguez Air Meet of 1910, see the "Aviation Number" of *Out West* (January 1910), especially Charlton L. Edholm, "The Noble Sport of Aviation," *Out West* 32(1910): 2–28. See also Charles K. Field, "On the Wings of Today," *Sunset* 34(1910): 245–52. Later accounts include Marco R. Newmark, "The Aviation Meet of 1910," *SCQ* 28(1946): 103–8; Remi Nadeau, "Gathering of the Early Birds," *Westways* 52(1960): 4–6; and J. Wesley Neal, "America's First International Air Meet," *SCQ* 43(1961): 369–414.

For general background regarding art nouveau and Craftsman influences, see Diane Chalmers Johnson, *American Art Nouveau* (1979); and Barry Sanders, editor, *The Craftsman, An Anthology* (1978). See also Carl E. Schorske's *Fin-de-Siècle Vienna: Politics and Culture* (1980).

5

The central, all-encompassing study of agriculture in California is the as yet unpublished history by Richard Steven Street, "Into a Good Land: The Emergence of California Agriculture, 1850–1920," which won the James D. Phelan Award in 1977. Dr. Street has generously made his manuscript available to me, and all dependencies of fact or interpretation upon this totally authoritative history are gratefully acknowledged. Other studies of California agriculture which proved of value include, in order of publication, California Development Association, *Problems of Agriculture in California* (1924); R. L. Adams, *Farm Management Notes* (1926); Robert Glass Cleland and Osgood Hardy, *The March of Industry* (1929); Osgood Hardy, "Agricultural Changes in California," *Proceedings of the Pacific Coast Branch of the American Historical Association* (1929); William S. Brown and S. B. Show, *California Rural Land Use and Management: A History of the Use and Occupancy of Rural Lands in California* (2 vols., 1944); Walton Bean, "James Warren and the Beginnings of Agricultural Institutions in California," *PHR* 13 (1944): 361–75; Paul S. Taylor, "Foundations of California Rural Society," *CHSQ* 24 (1945): 193–228; Claude B. Hutchinson, editor, *California Agriculture* (1946); William Wilcot Robinson, *Land in California* (1948); Robert Glass Cleland and Frank B. Putnam, *Isaiah W. Hellman and the Farmers and Merchants Bank*, edited by Mary Jane Bragg (1965); Paul W. Gates, *California Ranchos and Farms, 1846–1862* (1967); and John H. Davis and Ray A. Goldberg, *Agribusiness* (1967). General studies that contain much valuable California material include Joseph Schafer, *A Social History of American Agriculture* (1936); R. O. Cummings, *The American and His Food: A History of Food Habits in the United States* (1940); Fred A. Shannon, *The Farmer's Last Frontier: Agriculture, 1860–1897* (1945); Oscar E. Anderson, Jr., *Refrigeration in America: A History of a New Technology and Its Impact* (1953); Gilbert Fite, *The Farmer's Frontier, 1865–1900* (1966); John T. Schlebecker, *Whereby We Thrive: A History of American Farming, 1607–1972* (1975); Walter Ebeling, *The Fruited Plain: The Story of American Agriculture* (1979); Edward L. Schapsmeier and Frederick H. Schapsmeier, *Agriculture in the West* (1980). Periodicals consulted at various times and libraries include *California Crop Reports, California Cultivator, California Farmer, California Fruit Grower, Pacific Rural Press, Rural California, Southern California Rancher.*

Regarding specific crops, see Elizabeth M. Riley, "History of the Almond Industry in

California, 1850–1934," M.A. thesis, University of California at Berkeley (1948); Arthur Inkersley, "Celery-growing in the Peat Lands of California," *OvMo* 46 (1905): 101–6; E. Philpott Mumford, "Early History of Cotton Cultivation in California," *CHSQ* 6 (1926): 159–66; Colin Campbell Archibald, "History of Cotton Production in California," M.A. thesis, University of California at Berkeley (1950); Charles C. Cooley, "The California Date Growing Industry, 1890–1939," *SCQ* 49 (1967): 47–64, 167–91; Byron Martin Lelong, *The Olive in California* (1889); Jane Hedder, "The Story of the California Olive Industry," *OvMo* 65(1915): 574–75; Byron Martin Lelong, *California Prune Industry* (1892); Edith Catharine Meyer, "The Development of the Raisin Industry in Fresno County," M.A. thesis, University of California at Berkeley (1931); Rolf W. Ordal, "History of the California Walnut Industry," Ph.D. dissertation, University of California at Berkeley (1952); Horace Davis, "Wheat in California," *OvMo*, n.s., 32 (1898): 59–63. See also T. A. Kendo, *Treatise on Silk and Tea Culture and Other Asiatic Industries Adapted to the Soil and Culture of California* (1870), and John E. Baur, "California Crops that Failed," *CHSQ* 45 (1966): 41–68.

County histories, directories, and descriptive pamphlets, together with agriculturally related biographies and memoirs, proved invaluable in establishing the context and specifics of agriculture on a county-by-county basis, with a selective emphasis upon certain San Joaquin Valley counties, especially Kern, and the counties of San Bernardino and Riverside in the citrus belt. General studies of major use included Wallace Smith, *Garden in the Sun* (193); Joseph A. McGowan, *History of the Sacramento Valley* (3 vols., 1961); and Stuart Nixon, *Redwood Empire* (1966). See also Jerome J. Collins and Bentham Fabian, *The Agricultural Lands of California* (1869); *The Diary of Ensign Gabriel Moraga's Expedition of Discovery in the Sacramento Valley, 1808*, translated and edited by Donald C. Cutter (1957); Edward Francis Treadwell, *The Cattle King* (1931); and Sylvanus Griswold Morley, *The Covered Bridges of California* (1938). County-related material consulted included the following items, beginning with the northern counties and moving southwards: Leigh Hadley Irvine, *History of Humboldt County* (1915); Genevieve Yoell Parkhurst, *Lassen County* (1909); A. J. Wells, "Slicing the Great Ranchos [of Tehama County]," *Sunset* 23 (1909): 219–21; Bourdon Wilson, *Glenn County* (1910); Elizabeth Eubank, *Glenn County Directory [and History]* (1948); Nicholas Wilson Hanson, *As I remember* (1942), Lake and Colusa Counties; William Turner Ellis, *Memories: My Seventy-two Years in the Romantic County of Yuba, California* (1939); *The Autobiography of Lincoln Steffens* (1931), Sacramento County; V. Aubrey Neasham and James E. Henley, *The City of the Plain: Sacramento in the Nineteenth Century* (1970); Thomas J. Gregory, *History of Solano and Napa Counties* (1912); Arthur Quinn, *Broken Shore: The Marin Peninsula* (1981); Daniel H. Bradley, *California Farms, Orchards, Vineyards* (1915), issued by the Alameda County Board of Supervisors; M. B. Levick, *Madera County* (1911); Wallace W. Elliott, *History of Fresno County* (1882); A. J. Wells, "The Romance of the Fresno Ranch: An Old Time Principality Being Broken Up For Colonization," *Sunset* 22 (1909): 557–69; Lilbourne Alsys Winchell, *History of Fresno County and the San Joaquin Valley, Narrative and Biographical* (1933); Ben Randal Wallser, editor, *Fresno Community Book* (1946); Francis X. Singleton, *Cathedral in the Valley* (1952); William Wilcox Robinson, *The Story of Tulare County and Visalia* (1952); Robert R. Brown and J. E. Richmond, *History of Kings County* (1940); Willie Arthur Chalfant, *The Story of Inyo* (1922); Myron Angel, *History of San Luis Obispo County* (1883); Andrew Jackson Wells, *San Luis Obispo County* (1910); William Wilcox Robinson, *The Story of San Luis Obispo County* (1957); Juan Francisco Dana, *The Blond Ranchero: Memories of Juan Francisco Dana*, as told to Rocky Dana and Marie Harrington (1960); Frank Sands, *A Pastoral Prince: The History and*

Reminiscences of J. W. Cooper (1893), Santa Barbara County; Grace Lyons Davison, *The Gates of Memory: Recollections of Early Santa Ynez Valley* (1955); William Wilcox Robinson, *The Story of Ventura County* (1955); Mrs. J. E. Pleasants, *History of Orange County* (1902); John Raymond Gabbert, *History of Riverside City and County* (1935); Tom Patterson, *Landmarks of Riverside and the Stories Behind Them* (1964); Patterson, *A Colony for California: Riverside's First Hundred Years*, foreword by John G. Galbert (1971); Edgar F. Howe and Wilbur J. Hall, *The Story of the First Decade in Imperial Valley* (1910). Between 1914 and 1915, the Los Angeles Chamber of Commerce issued a valuable series of promotional pamphlets regarding the agricultural possibilities of Los Angeles County and environs. Of special interest are *Alfalfa, A Few Notes on Its Culture in Southern California; Dairying in Southern California; Live Stock in Southern California; Onions, How to Grow Them in Southern California; Orange Culture in Southern California; Poultry in California;* and *Vegetable Culture in Southern California.* See also F. R. Maulsby, *Antelope Valley* (1913), and C. B. Glasscock, *Lucky Baldwin: The Story of an Unconventional Success* (1933). Kern County histories include: W. M. Morgan, *History of Kern County* (1914); Thelma Miller, *History of Kern County* (2 vols., 1929); Herbert G. Comfort, *Where Rolls the Kern* (1934); William Wilcox Robinson, *The Story of Kern County* (1961); William H. Boyd, *California Middle Border: The Kern River Country, 1772–1880* (1972). The Bancroft Library has an extensive collection of Kern County promotional pamphlets from this period. See also Bakersfield, California, *Homeseekers and Development Number* (1910); George Wo Wear, *Pioneer Days and Kebo Club Nights* (1932); Arthur S. Crites, *Pioneer Days in Kern County* (1951); Norman Berg, *A History of Kern County Land Company.* Regarding the all-important (for this study) San Bernardino County, see *Ontario, A New Fruit Colony, Located in San Bernardino County* (1883); John Brown, Jr., and James Boyd, *History of San Bernardino and Riverside Counties* (3 vols., 1922); and William Wilcox Robinson, *The Story of San Bernardino County* (1958). The Bancroft Library has an extensive collection of pamphlets on San Bernardino County and Redlands and related topics. See also Henry L. Graham, *Redlands: A Perfect Climate, the Finest Orange Groves in the State, Beautiful Parks and Fine Residences* (1904); Roger W. Tresdail, *Redlands 'Twixt Mountain, Desert, and the Sea* (1927); and Lawrence Emerson Nelson, *Only One Redlands: Changing Patterns in a Southern California Town* (1963). Of special interest is R. Louis Gentilcore, "Ontario, California, and the Agricultural Boom of the 1880s," *Agricultural History* 34 (1960): 77–87.

Aside from the *Pacific Rural Handbook* (1879), Charles Howard Shinn also wrote *Intensive Horticulture in California* (1901). Ezra Slocum Carr, author of *The Patrons of Husbandry on the Pacific Coast* (1875), is also responsible for *An Address Before the State Agricultural Society at Sacramento on Wednesday Evening, Sept. 22, 1875* (1875). Luther Burbank's career can be traced through his *The Harvest of the Years* (1927), with Wilbur Hall; Ken and Pat Kraft, *Luther Burbank, The Wizard and the Man* (1967); and Peter Dreyer, *A Gardner Touched with Genius* (1975). Edward James Wickson's many publications include *The California Fruits and How to Grow Them* (1889); *Luther Burbank: Man, Methods and Achievements* (1902); *The California Vegetables in Garden and Field* (1913); *One Thousand Questions in California Agriculture Answered* (1914); *California Garden—Flowers, Shrubs, Trees and Vines* (1915); *Second Thousand Answered Questions in California Agriculture* (1916); *California Nurserymen and the Plant Industry, 1850–1910* (1921); *Farming in California* (1923), with R. E. Hodges; and *Rural California* (1923). See also *In Memoriam, Edward James Wickson* (1924), in the Bancroft Library.

Carey McWilliams's *Factories in the Field* (1939) is the classic account of farm labor in California. See also Lloyd H. Fisher, *The Harvest Labor Market in California* (1953), and Varden Fuller, "The Supply of Agricultural Labor as a Factor in the Evolution of Farm Organization in California," Ph.D. dissertation, University of California at Berkeley (1939). Also of interest are E. M. H., *Ranch Life in California* (1886); Morrison I. Swift, *What a Tramp Learns in California* (1896) and Nels Anderson, *The Hobo: The Sociology of the Homeless Man* (1923). Regarding specific groups, see Paul Taylor, *Mexican Labor in the Imperial Valley* (1928); Gabriel Davidson, *Our Jewish Farmers and the Story of the Jewish Agricultural Society* (1943); Hans C. Palmer, "Italian Immigration and the Development of California Agriculture," Ph.D. dissertation, University of California at Berkeley (1965). The saga of the Japanese in California can be traced through H. A. Millis, *The Japanese Problem in the United States* (1915); John P. Irish, *Japanese Farms in California* (1919); Wallace Irwin, *Seed of the Sun* (1921); Jean Pajus, *The Real Japanese California* (1937); Floyd W. Matson, "The Anti-Japanese Movement in California, 1890–1942," M.A. thesis, University of California at Berkeley, (1950); and Emil T. H. Bunje, *The Story of Japanese Farming in California* (1957).

Regarding women in agriculture, see Bertha H. Smith, "What Women Are Doing in the West," *Sunset* 26 (1911): 640–47 and "A Daughter of the Vine," *Sunset* 30 (1913): 95–98.

Leon D. Adams's informative and well-written *The Wines of America*, second edition revised (1978), is the closest we have to a systematic history of wine in America. See also Guy J. Guttadauro, *A List of References for the History of Grapes, Wines, and Raisins in America* (1976). M. A. Amerine and V. L. Singleton, *Wine: An Introduction for Americans* (1965) is a comprehensive introduction to the technicalities of wine. Regarding Jefferson's ideas, see R. de Treville Lawrence, editor, *Jefferson and Wine* (1976). Histories of wine in California include Herbert Boynton Leggett, "The Early History of Wine Production in California," M.A. thesis, University of California at Berkeley (1939); Vincent Phillip Carosso, *The California Wine Industry, 1830–1895: A Study of the Formative Years* (1951); M. F. K. Fisher, *The Story of Wine in California* (1962); and Robert Lawrence Balzer, *Wines of California*, edited by Darlene Geis (1978). See also Maynard A. Amerine, "Hilgard and California Viticulture," *Hilgardia* 33 (1962): 1–23; Charles L. Sullivan, "A Viticultural Mystery Solved: The Historical Origins of Zinfandel in California," *California History* 57 (1978): 114–29; Theodore Schoenman, editor, *Father of California Wine, Agoston Haraszthy*, foreword by Robert L. Balzer (1979). Useful descriptive travelogues include Idwal Jones, *Vines in the Sun: A Journey through the California Vineyards* (1949); Bob Thompson, *California Wine: A Sunset Pictorial* (1973); Earl Roberge, *Napa Wine Country* (1975); Michael Topolos and Betty Dopson, *Napa Valley* (1975); and Patricia Latimer, *Sonoma and Mendocino Wine Book* (1979). Wine country novels, useful for determining the myth of California wine, include Frona Eunice Wait Colburn, *In Old Vintage Days* (1937); Idwal Jones, *The Vineyard* (1942); and Alice Tisdale Hobart, *The Cup and the Sword* (1942). See also Sara Bard Field, *The Vintage Festival, a Play Pageant and Festivities Celebrating the Vine in the Autumn at St. Helena, Napa Valley* (1920). Information regarding specific winemakers and wineries is available in *History of the Organization and Progress of the Italian-Swiss Colony, Asti, Sonoma County, California* (1903); Lloyd Eric Reeve, *Gift of the Grape, Based on Paul Masson Vineyards*, with photographs by Ansel Adams and Pirkle Jones (1959); Robert Balzer, *Uncommon Heritage: The Paul Masson Story* (1970); Francis L. Gould, *Charles Krug Winery, 1861–1961* (1961); Janet Newton, *Cresta Blanca and Charles A. Wetmore, a Founder of the California Wine Industry* (1974); Leo J. Friis, *John Frohling: Vintner and City Founder* (1976); William Andrew Spalding, *Los Angeles Newspaperman: An Autobiographical Account*, edited with an introduction by Robert

V. Hine (1961); and Leonard John Rose, L. J. Rose of Sunny Slope, 1827–1899: California Pioneer, Fruit Grower, Wine Maker, Horse Breeder (1959). For listings of winemakers, see Ernest P. Peninon and Sidney S. Greenleaf, A Directory of California Wine Growers and Wine Makers in 1860 (1967); California Board of State Viticultural Commissioners, Directory of Grape Growers, Wine Makers, and Distillers of California (1891).

Maynard L. Amerine, "Some Early Books about the California Wine Industry," Quarterly News Letter of the Book Club of California 16 (1951): 51–56 provides an excellent introduction to the historical literature. Of pertinence to this chapter are the following nineteenth- and early-twentieth-century items: T. Hart Hyatt, Hyatt's Hand-Book of Grape Culture (1867); Emmet H. Rixford, The Wine Press and the Cellar: A Manual for the Wine-Maker and the Cellar-Man (1883); George Husmann, Grape Culture and Wine-Making in California (1888); Frona Eunice Wait, Wines and Vines of California; or, A Treatise on the Ethics of Wine Drinking [1889], facsimile edition, with introduction by Maynard A. Amerine (1973). See also Agnes Manney Tenney and Marian Sutherland Miller, "A Biographical Sketch of Mrs. Frona Eunice Wait Colburn," OvMo, n.s., 84 (1926): 46–47, 56. Arpad Haraszthy's 1871–72 Overland Monthly series, "Wine Making in California," was reprinted in 1978 with an introduction by Ruth Teiser and Catherine Harroun. See also California Wines and Vines (1883) and the jointly published pamphlet, California Grapes and Wine by Arpad Haraszthy, President, State Board of Viticulture, and The Vine Land of the West, or Champagne and Its Manufacture, by David W. C. Nesfield (1883). Eugene W. Hilgard's Report of the Viticultural Work During the Seasons 1883–4, 1884–5, 1885–6 appeared in 1886. See also Hilgard's Soils: Their Formation, Composition and Relations to Climate and Plant Growth (1906). Andrea Sbarboro took his fight for wine as an agent of temperance through The Fight for True Temperance (1908) and Temperance vs. Prohibition: Important Letters and Data From Our American Consuls, the Clergy and Other Eminent Men (1909). Important early statements of connoisseurship include John I. Bleasdale, The Report of a Jury of Experts on a Brandy Made by Gen. Henry M. Naglee at San Jose . . . To Which is Added a Short Essay upon It and Other Spirits (1879); John Thomas Doyle, The Truth about California Wines (1892); Giacomo Grazzi-Sancini, Wine—Classification, Wine Tasting, Qualities and Defects, Appendix E to the Biennial Report of the Board of State Viticultural Commissioners for 1891–1892; Charles Furley Oldham, Paper on California Wines Read Before the Society of Arts on January 31, 1894 (1894); and Benjamin Cummings Truman, See How It Sparkles (1896).

L. M. Holt, The Great Interior Fruit Belt and Sanitarium of Southern California: San Bernardino County . . . (1885) is an important statement in the evolution of California's citrus culture. See also Conte Giogio Gallesio, Orange Culture: Treatise on the Citrus Family, Translated from the French Expressly for "The Florida Agriculturist" (1876); Thomas A. Garey, Orange Culture in California (1882); T. W. Moore, Treatise and Hand-Book of Orange Culture in Florida, Louisiana and California (1884); William Andrew Spalding, The Orange, Its Culture in California, with a Brief Discussion of the Lemon, Lime, and Other Citrus Fruits (1885); Byron Martin Lelong, A Treatise on Citrus Culture in California (1888) and New Varieties of Citrus Fruits (1891). The Los Angeles Chamber of Commerce issued Orange Culture in Southern California in 1915. Consulted also were various issues of the California Citrograph and S. M. Kennedy, "The Orange at Home," LS 9 (1898), 181–85. Historical investigations include Jessie Edna Boyd, "Historical Import of the Orange Industry in Southern California," M.A. thesis, University of California at Berkeley (1922); Minnie Tibbets Mills, "Luther Calvin Tibbets, Founder of the Navel Orange Industry of California," SCQ 25 (1943): 126–61; Leon D. Batchelor and Herbert Webber, editors, The Citrus Industry (1946); Edward M. Ainsworth, *Journey with the Sun: The Story of Citrus in its Western Pilgrimage* (1968); Esther Klotz, Harry W. Lawton, and John H. Hall, *A History of Citrus in the Riverside Area* (1969). Of interest is the novel by Sidney Herbert Burchell, *Jacob Peek, Orange Grower: A Tale of Southern California* (1915). Regarding the lemon industry, see G. W. Garcelon, *Fifteen Years with the Lemon* (1891); G. H. Powell, *The California Lemon Industry* (1913); Charles Collins Teague, *Fifty Years a Rancher* (1944); Michael R. Belknap, "The Era of the Lemon: A History of Santa Paula, California," *CHSQ* 47 (1968): 113–40. The June 1905 issue of *Sunset* magazine has three relevant articles: Heatherwick Kirk, "A Lemon Propaganda"; Elizabeth A. Ward, "Lemon Growing in California"; and Maude W. Glasby, "The Largest Lemon Ranch." Numerous broadsides, programs, and guides to various citrus fairs and festivals were also consulted. Among them: *Annual Citrus Fair of the San Gabriel Valley* (1885); *California Valencia Orange Show, Offical Souvenir and Program, May 23 to 30, 1922* (1922); Anaheim Chamber of Commerce, *Anaheim in the Heart of the Famous Valencia Orange District* (1922). In her 1966 UCLA doctoral dissertation, "Sunkist Advertising," Josephine Kingsbury Jacobs tells the fascinating story of the selling of the California orange. See also A. H. Naftzger, "Marketing California Oranges and Lemons," *LS*, 14 (1901): 247–58, and Charles Collins Teague, *Ten Talks on Citrus Marketing* (1939). John Sallsin and Laurie Gordon's *Orange Crate Arts* (1976) is a sheer delight.

Regarding the theme of rural life and community, so important to this chapter, see Robert V. Hines's humane study *Community on the American Frontier* (1980). See also Hines's *California's Utopian Colonies* (1953); Bernhard Marks, *Small Scale Farming in California: The Colonization System of the Great Valley of the San Joaquin in Central California* (1890); Virginia E. Thickens, "Pioneer Agricultural Societies of Fresno County," *CHSQ* 25 (1946): 17–39, 169–78; H. E. Erdman, "The Development and Significance of California Cooperatives, 1900–1915," *American History* 32 (1958): 179–84. Regarding Llano del Rio, see Abe Hoffman, "A Look at Llano: Experiment in Economic Socialism," *CHSQ* 40 (1961): 215–36; Aldous Huxley, "Ozymandias, The Utopia That Failed," *CHSQ* 51 (1972): 118–30; Paul Kagan, "Portrait of a California Utopia," *CHSQ* 51 (1972): 131–54. The Bancroft Library has an extensive correspondence and pamphlet collection regarding the California Land Settlement Board (1917–21) and its Durham and Delhi colonies. Of special interest are Walter V. Woehlke, *Food First: How One Western State Is Staking the Farmers* (1920), reprinted from the October 1920 *Sunset* magazine, and Robert Welles Ritchie, *Rural Democracy at Delhi* (1920), reprinted from the 27 November 1920 *Country Gentleman*. Elwood Mead's *Helping Men Own Farms* appeared in 1920. Regarding cooperative marketing, see Rahno Mabel MacCurdy, *The History of the California Fruit Growers Exchange* (1925); Henry Ernest Erdman and Erich Otto Kraemer, *History of Cooperation in Marketing California Fresh Deciduous Fruits* (1933); Kelsey B. Gardner and A. W. McKay, *The California Fruit Growers Exchange System* (1950). See also Grace H. Larson and Henry E. Erdman, "Aaron Sapiro: Genius of Farm Cooperative Promotion," *MVHR* 49 (1962): 242–68 and Dave Laren, "The Raisin Maiden Today," Sunday Punch section of the Sunday *San Francisco Examiner/Chronicle*, 15 August 1982, p. 4.

6

The Library of the California Historical Society possesses a two-volume *Scrapbook* of newspaper and magazine notices and reviews concerning Arthur Page Brown and his work, most likely compiled by Brown's widow. The *Scrapbook* is invaluable in recreating the previously unknown career of the architect of the Ferry Building. The *Wave* for

Christmas 1982 ran a brief biographical sketch. Obituary notices have also been consulted, specifically the *San Francisco Bulletin* for 21 January 1896, the *San Francisco Post* for 21 January 1896, the *San Francisco Examiner* for 22 January 1896, and the *California Architect and Building News* for 8 February 1896. Brown elaborated his ideas regarding the architectural features of San Francisco in an article entitled "Architecture of California", published in the *San Francisco Chronicle* for Sunday, 30 December 1894.

Richard W. Longstreth's *On the Edge of the World: Four Architects in San Francisco at the Turn of the Century* (1983) is a work of brilliant, encompassing scholarship. Generously made available to me in manuscript, Professor Longstreth's study of Coxhead, Polk, Schweinfurth, and Maybeck contains also the most solid, comprehensive information thus far regarding Brown's California career. The interpretive influence, and certainly all matters of documentation, that this chapter owes to Longstreth's monumental study are both self-evident and freely acknowledged. Other descriptions of Brown's extant work are available in Roger Olmsted, T. H. Watkins, and Morley Baer, *Here Today: San Francisco's Architectural Heritage* (1968); David Gebhard and others, *A Guide to Architecture in San Francisco and Northern California* (1973); Gladys Hansen, editor, *San Francisco: The Bay and Its Cities* (1973); Leslie Mandelson Freudenheim and Elisabeth Sussman, *Building With Nature: Roots of the San Francisco Bay Region Tradition* (1974); Phyllis Filberti Butler, *The Valley of Santa Clara: Historic Buildings, 1792–1920* (1974); and Charles Hall Page and Associates, *Splendid Survivors: San Francisco's Downtown Architectural Heritage* (1979). See also Joseph Armstrong Baird, *Time's Wondrous Changes: San Francisco Architecture, 1776–1915* (1963); Harold Kirker, *California's Architectural Frontier: Style and Tradition in the Nineteenth Century* (rev. ed., 1973); and Randolph Delehanty, *San Francisco* (1980).

There is a *Scrapbook* of Ferry Building clippings from the 1890s in the San Francisco History Room of the Main Library. Regarding other Brown buildings, see also Alex F. Oakey, "A Word to the Wise," *OvMo*, n.s. (August 1891), 132–43; *Twenty-Five Hundred and Seven Pine* (pamphlet, 1932); Othmar Tobisch, *The Garden Church of San Francisco: A Church of the New Jerusalem, Swedenborgian* (pamphlet, 1964); and the relevant Junior League files in the San Francisco History Room. The entire issue of the *Messenger of the Young Men's Christian Association of San Francisco* for 1 April 1893 is devoted to Brown's YMCA building at Mason and Ellis. This issue also contains the only photograph of Brown that I have been able to locate. Regarding the Towne residence, see Alonzo Phelps, *Contemporary Biography of California's Representative Men* (1881) for a biography of Albon Nelson Towne and *Our Society Blue Book: The Fashionable Private Addresses Directory* (1894) for a discussion of the house itself. Regarding the 1893 Columbian Exposition in Chicago and Brown's California State Building, see *American Architect and Building News* for 19 March 1892 and *Final Report of the California World's Fair Commission* (1893). Information regarding the Midwinter Fair and Brown's role as Fair architect was gleaned from Arthur H. Barendt, "Midwinter Exposition Buildings," *The Wave*, 9 September 1893; *The Official Guide to the California Midwinter Exposition* (1894); *The Official Catalogue of the California Midwinter International Exposition* (1894); *The Official History of the California Midwinter International Exposition* (1894); and *Midwinter Fair and the Golden State: Colored Art Views* (1894). Of great usefulness is Raymond H. Clary, *The Making of Golden Gate Park: The Early Years, 1865–1906* (1980). Willis Polk discussed Brown's work in "Our Colonial Craze," *San Francisco Examiner*, 13 September 1891 and, "Artistic Work in Buildings," *San Francisco Examiner*, 27 November 1892. Regarding Polk and the Giralda Tower, see Harold Gilliam, *The San Francisco Experience* (1972). Kenneth H. Cardwell, *Bernard Maybeck: Artisan, Architect, Artist* (1977) has much interesting information regarding Maybeck's relationship with Brown and the Maybeck stamp on certain Brown projects. See also Richard Longstreth, A *Matter of Taste: Willis Polk's Writings on Architecture in the "Wave"* (1979).

Regarding the earthquake and fire of 1906 and Brown's buildings, see Louis J. Stellmann, *The Vanished Ruin Era* (1910); Arnold Genthe, *As I Remember* (1936); and William Bronson, *The Earth Shook, the Sky Burned* (1959). The disposition of Brown's estate can be traced through a legal brief dated June 1898: "In the Supreme Court of the State of California. In the Matter of the Estate of A. Page Brown, Deceased. Lucy P. Brown, Appellant."

The general ambience and ethos of Brown's formative New York years can be surmised from a perusal of Richard Guy Wilson et al., *The American Renaissance, 1876–1917* (1980). Regarding Brown's chief patron in San Francisco, see David Warren Ryder, *"Great Citizen": A Biography of William H. Crocker* (1962). For the background to the Burnham plan, see chapter 6 of Mel Scott, *The San Francisco Bay Area: A Metropolis in Perspective* (1959) and Judd Kahn, *Imperial San Francisco: Politics and Planning in an American City, 1897–1906* (1979). Regarding the abundant creativity of San Francisco during the fin-de-siècle, see Oscar Lewis, *Bay Window Bohemia* (1956).

7

Richard Hofstadter, *The Age of Reform: From Bryan to FDR* (1955) and George E. Mowry, *The Era of Theodore Roosevelt, 1900–1912* (1958) are two studies of fundamental importance to this and the following chapter, as also are Robert Glass Cleland, *California In Our Time, 1900–1940* (1947) and Carey McWilliams, *Southern California Country: An Island on the Land* (1946). George E. Mowry, *The California Progressives* (1951) is the classic account of the California chapters of the Progressive story. See also Royce D. Delmatier, Clarence F. McIntosh, and Earl G. Waters, editors, *The Rumble of California Politics, 1848–1970* (1970) and Spencer C. Olin, Jr., *California Politics, 1846–1920: The Emerging Corporate State* (1981). Regarding the rise of the Southern Pacific, see Oscar Lewis, *The Big Four* (1938) and Stuart Daggett, *Chapters on the History of the Southern Pacific* (1922).

Pre-Progressive figures emphasized in this chapter include David Starr Jordan, Joseph Le Conte, Benjamin Ide Wheeler, and A. P. Giannini. Jordan's *California and the Californians* (1899) is an early call for reform. See also his abundant autobiography *The Days of a Man* (2 vols., 1922). *The Autobiography of Joseph Le Conte*, edited by William Dallam Armes (1903), is a classic. See also Le Conte, *Evolution and Its Relation to Religious Thought* (1899), and A *Journal of Ramblings through the High Sierra of California by the University Excursion Party* (1875), reprinted by the Sierra Club (1930). Monroe E. Deutsch collected Wheeler's speeches and essays in *The Abundant Life* (1926). Regarding Giannini, see Julian Dana, *A. P. Giannini, Giant in the West* (1947), and Marquis and Bessie Rowland James, *Biography of a Bank: The Story of Bank of America* (1954). Located in San Francisco, the Archives of the Bank of America contain some relevant folders regarding the early history of the parent Bank of Italy.

Howard H. Quint, *The Forging of American Socialism* (1953) is the best general study of this topic. See also Ira B. Cross, A *History of the Labor Movement in California* (1935); Robert V. Hine, *California's Utopian Colonies* (1953); and David Selvin, *Sky Full of Storm* (1966). In "Nationalism in California," *OvMo*, n.s., 15 (1890): 659–61, F. I. Vassault made a pioneering report on the Nationalist Clubs of Southern California. See also George B. Benham, *Patriotism and Socialism* (1895). Regarding the author of *The Man with the Hoe, and Other Poems* (1899) and *Lincoln and Other Poems*

(1901), see William Le Roy Stidger, *Edwin Markham* (1933), and the psychoanalyti-
cally astute *The Unknown Edwin Markham: His Mystery and Significance*, by Louis
Filler (1966). Information regarding the fascinating Henry Gaylord Wilshire can be found
in *Men of California* (1901); Ralph Hancock, *Fabulous Boulevard* (1949); and Howard
H. Quint, "Gaylord Wilshire and Socialism's First Congressional Campaign," *PHR* 26
(1957): 327–40. Wilshire's own writings include *Fabian Essays in Socialism* (1891); *Liquid Air Perpetual Motion at Last: A Lecture before the Southern California Academy of
Sciences* (1899); *Wilshire Editorials* (1906); and *Socialism Inevitable* (1907).

Two central collections of Jack London's Socialist writings are *London's Essays of Re-
volt*, edited and with an introduction by Leonard D. Abbott (1926), and Philip S. Foner,
*Jack London, American Rebel: A Collection of His Social Writings, together with an
Extensive Study of the Man and His Times* (1947). *Letters From Jack London*, edited by
King Hendricks and Irving Shepard (1965), contains much pertinent commentary by
London on Socialism and related issues. See also London's caveman allegory of Social-
ism, *The Strength of the Strong* (1912). The long and vocal Socialist odyssey of Kate
Crane Gartz can be traced through *The Parlor Provocateur; or, From Salon to Soap-Box:
The Letters of Kate Crane Gartz*, with an introduction by Mary Craig Sinclair (1923);
Letters of Protest (1925); *More Letters of Protest* (1927); *A Woman and War* (1928); *Still
More Letters* (1930); *Prophetic Letters* (1937); *Dear Mr. President* (1946); and *My Philosophy* (1947). Edward Francis Adams, *A Critique of Socialism Read before the Ruskin
Club of Oakland* (1905) testifies to the social acceptability of Socialism in California
during this period, even among its critics. The Southern novelist Thomas Dixon, Jr.,
was not so kind, however. Dixon's novel *Comrades: A Story of Social Adventure in California* (1909) traces the degeneration of a Socialist cooperative into a fierce dictatorship.

Information regarding Sarah Cooper's early California career can be found in Ella
Sterling Cummins, *The Story of the Files* (1893), pp. 163–66. Anna M. Stovall, who
succeeded Cooper as head of the Golden Gate Kindergarten Association of San Francisco, wrote her predecessor's biography in *Pioneers of the Kindergarten Movement* (1924).
See also Cooper's "Ideal Womanhood," *OvMo* 6 (1871): 453–60. Commissioned by
William Randolph Hearst after his mother's death and privately printed by master book
designer and printer John Henry Nash, Winifred Sweet Black Bonfils's *The Life and
Personality of Phoebe Apperson Hearst* (1928) is written in the rushed, incipiently hysterical style favored by the leading sob sister columnist of the Hearst newspapers. It contains, however, fascinating material regarding Mrs. Hearst's culture-hungry rural girlhood and her closeness to her only child, William Randolph. As evidence of Mrs. Hearst's
passion as a collector, see *Catalogue of Mrs. Phoebe A. Hearst Loan Collection, Issued
by the San Francisco Art Association* (1917). See also *The International Competition for
the Phoebe Hearst Architectural Plan for the University of California* (1899).

The early kindergarten movement is treated in International Kindergarten Union, *Pioneers of the Kindergarten in America* (1924). Regarding Kate Douglas Wiggin, see Wig-
gin, *My Garden of Memory: An Autobiography* (1923); Nora Archibald Smith, *Kate
Douglas Wiggin as Her Sister Knew Her* (1925); Doyce B. Nunis, Jr., "Kate Douglas
Wiggin: Pioneer in California Kindergarten Education," *CHSQ* 41 (1962); and Lois
Rather, *Miss Kate: Kate Douglas Wiggin in San Francisco* (1980). Wiggin herself wrote
extensively about her work in San Francisco and the kindergarten movement in general.
Much of this material has been collected in the Bancroft Library as the pamphlet col-
lection *Free Kindergarten Work of the Pacific Coast* (5 vols., 1878–1915). See especially
Wiggin, "The Relation of the Kindergarten to Social Reform" (1889) and her "The Re-
lation of the Kindergarten to the Public School" (1891). See also Sarah B. Cooper, "The
Kindergarten in its Bearing upon Crime, Pauperism, and Insanity," *California Review*

(1893), 1–7. The Bancroft Library also maintains a file of *Annual Reports of the Golden Gate Kindergarten Association of San Francisco* (1879–1979). Regarding the suffrage movement, see Donald Walker Rodes, "The California Woman Suffrage Campaign of 1911" M.A. dissertation, California State University at Hayward (1974). Of special interest to the question of equal pay is Maud Younger, "Taking Orders: A Day as a Waitress in a San Francisco Restaurant," *Sunset* 21 (1908): 518–22. Regarding prohibitionism, see Gilman M. Ostrander, *The Prohibition Movement in California, 1848–1933* (1957). Regarding life in the opposite camp, see David Warren Ryder, *"Great Citizen": A Biography of William H. Crocker* (1962).

<h1 style="text-align:center">8</h1>

Biographical information regarding the many personalities discussed in this chapter comes from such standard reference sources as *Appleton's Cyclopaedia of American Biography; Dictionary of American Biography; Notable American Women, 1607–1950; Who Was Who in America*, and *Who Was Who in American Politics*. The extremely useful *Historical Biographical Dictionaries Master Index*, edited by Barbara McNeil and Miranda C. Herbert (1980), is an invaluable guide to these standard reference sources. California sources for biographical information include Willoughby Rodman, *History of the Bench and Bar of Southern California* (1909); J. C. Bates, *History of the Bench and Bar of California* (1912); *Press Reference Library* (2 vols., 1913); Rockwell D. Hunt, *California and Californians* (5 vols., 1926); and *California's Stately Hall of Fame* (1950). Biographical material regarding individual California Progressives is diverse. The following has proven of especial value: Edward Augustus Dickson (1879–1956): *University of California at Los Angeles: Its Origins and Formative Years* (1955) and *Memorial Addresses Honoring E. A. Dickson* (1956). John Randolph Haynes (1853–1937): Marco R. Newmark, "Historical Profiles: John R. Haynes," *SCQ* 37 (1955): 84–86. Hiram Warren Johnson (1866–1945): Irving McKee, "The Background and Early Career of Hiram Warren Johnson, 1866–1910," *PHR* 19 (1950): 17–30; Spencer C. Olin, Jr., *California's Prodigal Sons: Hiram Johnson and the Progressives* (1968); John James Fitzpatrick, "Senator Hiram W. Johnson, A Life History, 1866–1945," Ph.D. dissertation, University of California at Berkeley (1975). Franklin Knight Lane (1864–1921): Anne Wintermute Lane and Louise Herrick Wall, eds., *The Letters of Franklin K. Lane, Personal and Political* (1922); Keith W. Olson, *Biography of a Progressive, Franklin K. Lane* (1979) and Lane's own *A Brief in the Matter of Reservoir Rights of Way for a Domestic and Municipal Water Supply for the City and County of San Francisco* (1907). Homer Lea (1876–1912): Obituary, *Los Angeles Times*, 2 November 1912; Marshal Stimson, "A Los Angeles Jeremiah: Homer Lea, Military Genius and Prophet," *SCQ* 24 (1942): 5–13; Clare Boothe Luce, "Ever Hear of Homer Lea?" *Saturday Evening Post* 214 (7 March 1942): 12–13, 69–72, continued on 14 March 1942, 27, 38–40, 42; Marco R. Newmark, "Historical Profiles: Homer Lea," *SCQ* 37 (1955): 177–84. Simon Julius Lubin (1876–1936): *Addresses in Memoriam* (1936). John Francis Neylan (1885–1960): *Addresses and Writings*, the Bancroft Library; Richard Dillon, "John Francis Neylan, An Appreciation," in *Some Outstanding Books from the Library of John Francis Neylan* (1963); Roger W. Lotchin, "John Francis Neylan: San Francisco Irish Progressive," in *The San Francisco Irish, 1850–1976*, edited by James P. Walsh (1978). Fremont Older (1856–1935): *My Own Story* (1919); *The Romance of San Francisco Journalism* (1930); *Growing Up* (1931); Evelyn Wells, *Fremont Older* (1936); Robert Luther Duffus, *The Tower of Jewels* (1960); Christopher Lasch, *The New Radicalism in America, 1889–1963: The Intellectual as a Social Type* (1965). James Duval Phelan (1861–1930): Robert E. Hennings,

"James D. Phelan and the Wilson Progressives of California," Ph.D. dissertation, University of California at Berkeley (1961). Arthur Judson Pillsbury (1854–1937): Obituary, *Berkeley Gazette*, 2 April 1937; *Scrapbooks* (15 vols., 1898–1911), the Bancroft Library. Chester Harvey Rowell (1867–1948): *Papers*, the Bancroft Library (see especially "Orientophobia: A Western Editor's Views on the White Frontier," from *Colliers*, 6 February 1909); Miles C. Everett, "Chester Harvey Rowell, Pragmatic Humanist and California Progressive," Ph.D. dissertation, University of California at Berkeley (1966). Rudolph Spreckels (1872–1958): Joseph Lincoln Steffens, "Rudolph Spreckels, a Business Reformer," in *Upbuilders*, introduction by Earl Pomeroy (1968). Joseph Lincoln Steffens (1866–1936): *The Autobiography of Lincoln Steffens* (1931); *The Letters of Lincoln Steffens*, edited by Ella Winter and Granville Hicks with a memorandum by Carl Sandburg (2 vols., 1938); Justin Kaplan, *Lincoln Steffens: A Biography* (1974); Patrick F. Palermo, *Lincoln Steffens* (1978). Marshal Stimson (1876–1951): *Papers* (including the Homer Lea *Scrapbook*), the Huntington Library. Charles Dwight Willard (1860–1914): *Papers*, the Huntington Library; Donald Ray Culton, "Charles Dwight Willard: Los Angeles City Booster and Professional Reformer, 1888–1914," Ph.D. dissertation, University of Southern California (1971).

For valuable studies of specific aspects of the Progressive movement in California, see F. M. Davenport, "Did Hughes Snub Johnson?—An Inside Story," *American Political Science Review* 4 (1949): 321–32; James C. Findley, "Cross-filing and the Progressive Movement in California Politics," *Western Political Quarterly* 12 (1959): 699–711; Franklin Hichborn, "The Party, the Machine, and the Vote: The Story of Cross-filing in California Politics," *CHSQ* 38(1949): 349–57 and 39 (1960): 19–34; W. H. Hutchinson, "Prologue to Reform: The California Anti-Railroad Republicans, 1899–1905," *SCQ* 44 (1962): 175–218; Ashbrook Lincoln, "Theodore Roosevelt, Hiram Johnson, and the Vice-Presidential Nomination of 1912," *PHR* 28 (1959): 267–84; Spencer C. Olin, Jr., "Hiram Johnson, the California Progressives, and the Hughes Campaign of 1916," *PHR* 31 (1962): 403–12; and "Hiram Johnson, the Lincoln-Roosevelt League, and the Election of 1910," *CHSQ* 45 (1966): 225–40; Jackson K. Putnam, "The Persistence of Progressivism in the 1920s: The Case of California," *PHR* 35 (1965): 395–411; and Michael Rogin, "Progressivism and the California Electorate," *Journal of American History* 55 (1968): 297–314. In the late 1930s Stanford doctoral candidate Alice M. Rose assembled a magnificent archive of the papers and correspondence of the California Progressives, now in the Stanford University Library. See also Rose's essential monograph, "The Rise of California Insurgency: Origins of the League of Lincoln-Roosevelt Republican Clubs, 1900–1907," Ph.D. dissertation, Stanford University (1942). For an important eyewitness account of this era, see Joseph Gregg Layne, *The Lincoln-Roosevelt League, Its Origins and Accomplishments* (1943). The Bancroft Library has files of the *California Weekly* (1908–10) and the *California Outlook* (1911–12), two important Progressive journals.

Walton Bean's *Boss Ruef's San Francisco* (1952) is a classic account of the San Francisco graft trials. For a revisionist perspective, see James P. Walsh, "Abe Ruef Was No Boss: Machine Politics, Reform, and San Francisco," *CHSQ* 51 (1972): 3–16. For a look into an earlier era of bossism by the Bay, see William A. Bullough, *The Blind Boss and His City: Christopher Augustine Buckley and Nineteenth-Century San Francisco* (1979). For James Duval Phelan's early ideas regarding reform, see his "Municipal Conditions and the New Charter," *OvMo*, n.s., 28 (1896): 104–11. For opposing points of view regarding the trials, see Arno Dosch, "The Uplift in San Francisco," *Pacific Monthly* 18 (1907): 374–380, and Theodore Bonnet, *The Regenerators* (1911). Of great value is

Alexander Saxton, "San Francisco Labor and the Populist and Progressive Insurgencies," *PHR* 34 (1965): 422–38.

Albert Howard Clodius's "The Quest for Good Government in Los Angeles, 1890–1910," Ph.D. dissertation, Claremont Graduate School (1953) commands the field. See also Grace H. Stimson, *Rise of the Labor Movement in Los Angeles* (1955) and Martin J. Schiesl, "Progressive Reform in Los Angeles under Mayor Alexander, 1909–1913," *CHQ* 54 (1975): 37–56. Methodist minister Charles Edward Locke inveighed against prostitution in *White Slavery in Los Angeles* (ca. 1913). For a more genial consideration, see William W. Robinson, *Tarnished Angels: Paradisiacal Turpitude in Los Angeles* (1964). Regarding the author of *The Better City* (1907) and *The Brush Aflame* (1923), see Mary E. Stilson, "Dana Bartlett, The Modern Mission Father," *Out West*, n.s., 3 (1912): 222–26.

Reporter Franklin Hichborn chronicled the reform sessions of the California legislature in a continuing series entitled *The Story of the Session of the California Legislature*, issued for the sessions of 1909, 1911, 1913, and 1915. See also Hichborn's *The System* (1915) and "First Biennial Message of Governor Hiram W. Johnson, January 6, 1913," in *Appendix to the Journals of the Senate and Assembly of the Fortieth Session of the Legislature of the State of California* (1913). *The California Progressive Campaign Book* (1914) outlines the high points of Progressive achievement in the first Johnson administration. The annual reports of all state hospitals, prisons, and social service agencies for this and the previous era are found in the *Appendix to the Journals of the Senate and Assembly* issued each year by the state of California. Adelaide R. Hasse, *Index of Economic Material in Documents of the States of the United States: California, 1849–1904* (1908) provides a partial breakdown of this complex material. See also Arthur Judson Pillsbury, *Institutional Life, Its Relations to the State and to the Wards of the State* (1906) and Simon Julius Lubin, *Report on Relief of Destitute Unemployed, 1914–1915, to His Excellency, Governor Hiram W. Johnson* (1915).

Of relevance to the rightward turn of Progressivism in decline is Richard D. Batman, "The Road to the Presidency: Hoover, Johnson, and the California Republican Party, 1920–1924," Ph.D. dissertation, University of Southern California (1965). Of value also are George Washington Kirchivey, *A Survey of the Workings of the Criminal Syndicalism Law of California* (1926) and Richard Hindman Frost, *The Mooney Case* (1968). Two contemporary statements of interest are Chester Rowell, "Why I Shall Vote for Coolidge," *New Republic* 40 (1924): 220 and John Francis Neylan, "The Politician, The Enemy of Mankind," a speech delivered at the San Francisco Bond Club Luncheon, Tuesday, 12 April 1938, at the Palace Hotel (a pamphlet in the Bancroft Library). Lincoln Steffens's interview with William Randolph Hearst appears in "Hearst, the Man of Mystery," *American Magazine* 63 (1906): 3–22. Hearst's selected editorials are gathered in *William Randolph Hearst: A Portrait in His Own Words*, edited by Edmond D. Coblentz (1952). Hearst's other utterances appear in *Selections from the Writings and Speeches of William Randolph Hearst*, edited by E. F. Tompkins (1948). For evolving variations on the Hearst theme, see Edward T. O'Loughlin, *Hearst and His Enemies* (ca. 1919, reprinted 1970); Cora Miranda Older (Mrs. Fremont Older), *William Randolph Hearst, American*, with a foreword by Fremont Older (1936); John Kennedy Winkler, *William Randolph Hearst: A New Appraisal* (1955); and W. A. Swanberg, *Citizen Hearst* (1961). See also Fremont Older and Cora Miranda Baggerly Older, *George Hearst, California Pioneer* (1933), and Thomas R. Aidala and Curtis Bruce, *Hearst Castle, San Simeon* (1981).

9 AND 10

Of writing about Hollywood there is no end. For those in doubt, see *Motion Pictures: A Catalog of Books, Periodicals, Screen Plays and Production Stills. Theater Arts Library*, UCLA (2 vols., 1972); Frances Mary Christeson, *A Guide to the Literature of the Motion Picture* (1938); Mel Schuster, *Motion Picture Performers: A Bibliography of Magazine Periodical Articles, 1900–1969* (1971); and idem, *Motion Picture Directors: A Bibliography of Magazine and Periodical Articles, 1900–1972* (1973). Useful general histories of film and the rise of Hollywood include Richard Griffith, *The Movies: The Sixty-Year Story of the World of Hollywood and its Effect on America* (1957); Arthur Knight, *The Liveliest Art: A Panoramic History of the Movies* (1957); Albert R. Fulton, *Motion Pctures: The Development of an Art from Silent Films to the Age of Television* (1960); Gerald Mast, *A Short History of the Movies* (1976); and Jack C. Ellis, *A History of Film* (1979). As an historian and critic, Lewis Jacobs is in a class by himself. See his *The Rise of the American Film: A Critical History* (1939), reissued in 1968 together with the essay "Experimental Cinema in America, 1921–1947"; *Introduction to the Art of the Movies: An Anthology of Ideas on the Nature of Movie Art* (1960); *The Emergence of Film Art* (1969); and *The Movies as a Medium* (1970).

In 1920 Terry Ramsaye, a movie critic on the staff of the *Chicago Tribune*, was commissioned by *Photoplay* magazine to write a history of American film. Running in 36 installments in *Photoplay* over three years and published in two volumes in 1926, Ramsaye's *A Million and One Nights: A History of the Motion Picture* is, in my opinion, the *Magnalia Christi Americana* of American film, a capacious, anecdotal compendium of fact and heightened narrative that—like all such classics of reportage and memory—appeared in the last days of the silent film era it so exuberantly describes. Five years later, pioneering Hollywood producer and publicist Benjamin Bowles Hampton produced a second and similar classic, *History of the Movies* (1931), reissued in 1970 as *History of the American Film Industry from its Beginnings to 1931, with a New Introduction by Richard Griffith*. As diverse as they were in background and scholarship, Jacobs, Ramsaye, and Hampton each understood, without a suggestion of snobbery, the importance of film as a medium of mass entertainment and instruction, together with its possibilities and achievements as a form of democratic art. Other important studies of early Hollywood include Edward E. Wagenknecht, *The Movies in the Age of Innocence* (1962); David Robinson, *Hollywood in the Twenties* (1968) and *The Great Funnies, a History of Film Comedy* (1969); Jack Spears, *Hollywood: The Golden Era* (1971); Anthony Slide, *Early American Cinema* (1970) and *Aspects of American Film History Prior to 1920* (1978); and Kevin Brownlow and John Kobal, *Hollywood: The Pioneers* (1979). For an intriguing French perspective, see Maurice Bardeche and Robert Brassillach, *The History of Motion Pictures*, translated and edited by Iris Barry (1938).

Specialized histories and commentaries include Raymond Moley, *The Hays Office* (1945); Gordon Hendricks, *The Kinetoscope* (1966); and Alex Barris, *Hollywood According to Hollywood: How the Cinema World Has Seen Itself in Its Films* (1978). For brilliant analysis, see Sumiko Higashi, *Virgins, Vamps, and Flappers: The American Silent Movie Heroine* (1978). Charles Lockwood's *Dream Palaces: Hollywood at Home* (1981) is a thoroughly informative, elegantly written study. In his docudramatic novel *Promised Land: Notes for a History* (1938), English observer Cedric Belfrage included much fascinating reportage regarding the high life and low life of early Hollywood; so did Ezra Goodman in *The Fifty-Year Decline and Fall of Hollywood* (1961); and so—even more so!—did Kenneth Anger in *Hollywood Babylon* (1975), a minor classic of valuable information (some of which can be believed) and disturbingly appealing bad taste.

Among useful local histories are Mary E. Croswell, *Story of Hollywood* (1905); Frank Weber Benton, *Hollywood, California, All the Year* (1922); the Hollywood Branch of the Security Trust and Savings Bank, *The Story of Hollywood* (1922); Emily Barker Carter, comp., *Hollywood: The Story of the Cahuengas* (1926); Pierce E. Benedict, ed., *History of Beverly Hills* (1934); and Fred E. Basten, *Beverly Hills, Portrait of a Fabled City* (1975).

Vachel Lindsay's *The Art of the Moving Picture* (1915) and Hugo Munsterberg's *The Photoplay: A Psychological Study* (1916) are two major early studies. See also Gilbert Seldes, *The Seven Lively Arts* (1924) and Gerard Fort Buckle, *The Mind and the Film* (1926). Among many reactions to the scandals of the early 1920s are Laurance Hill and Silas Snyder, *Can Anything Good Come Out of Hollywood?* (1923); Tarnar Lane, *What's Wrong with the Movies?* (1923); and William M. Seabury, *The Public and the Motion-Picture Industry* (1926). Two entertaining perspectives can be found in Aldous Huxley, "Where Are the Movies Moving?" *Essays New and Old* (1927) and H. L. Mencken, "Appendix from Moronia," *Prejudices, Sixth Series* (1927). Paul Rotha's *The Film till Now: A Survey of World Cinema* (1930) is considered a classic, which I suppose it is— despite its almost hysterical anti-American or at least anti-Hollywood bias. Important later surveys include Leo C. Rosten, *Hollywood: The Movie Colony, the Movie Makers* (1939); Margaret Farrand Thorp, *America at the Movies* (1939); and Hortense Powder-maker, *Hollywood: The Dream Factory* (1950).

For the life and art of the legendary David Wark Griffith, see Linda Arvidson, *When the Movies Were Young* (1925); Iris Barry, *D. W. Griffith, American Film Master* (1940), reissued in 1965 with *An Annotated List of Films* by Eileen Bowser; Homer Croy, *Star Maker: The Story of D. W. Griffith* (1959); Robert M. Henderson, *D. W. Griffith: The Years at Biograph* (1970); Paul O'Dell (with the assistance of Anthony Slide), *Griffith and the Rise of Hollywood*; and Karl Brown, *Adventures with D. W. Griffith* (1973). *The Autobiography of Cecil B. De Mille*, edited by Donald Hayne, (1959) is obviously crucial to these two chapters, as is Gene Ringfold and De Witt Bodeen, *The Films of Cecil B. De Mille* (1969). See also William Churchill de Mille, *Hollywood Saga* (1939) and Agnes George de Mille, *Dance to the Piper* (1952). Regarding Adolph Zukor, see William H. Irwin, *The House that Shadows Built* (1928) and *The Public Is Never Wrong: The Autobiography of Adolph Zukor*, in collaboration with Dale Kramer (1953). Jesse L. Lasky's autobiography is *I Blow My Own Horn* (1957). Mack Sennett told his story to Cameron Shipp in *King of Comedy* (1954), which is suprisingly detailed regarding the Taylor murder case. See also Gene Fowler, *Father Goose: The Story of Mack Sennett* (1934). Regarding founder Samuel Goldfish/Goldwyn, see Samuel Goldwyn, *Behind the Screen* (1923); Alva Johnston, *The Great Goldwyn* (1937); Carol Easton, *The Search for Sam Goldwyn: A Biography of the Man Behind the Myth* (1976); and Lawrence J. Epstein, *Samuel Goldwyn* (1981). William Winter's *The Life of David Belasco* (2 vols., 1918) is a delightfully dated instance of old-fashioned fact-filled hagiography. Autobiographies of relevance to these chapters include John Barrymore, *Confessions of an Actor* (1926); Geraldine Farrar, *Such Sweet Compulsion* (1938); Lionel Barrymore, *We Barrymores*, as told to Cameron Shipp (1951); Frank Capra, *The Name above the Title* (1971); and Raoul Walsh, *Each Man in His Own Time: The Life Story of a Director* (1974). The Pickford-Fairbanks saga can be gleaned from Ralph Hancock, *Douglas Fairbanks: The Fourth Musketeer* (1953); Mary Pickford, *Sunshine and Shadow* (1955); and Booten Herndon, *Mary Pickford and Douglas Fairbanks, The Most Popular Couple the World*

Has Ever Known (1977). Constantly amusing and even informative is pioneering scriptwriter Anita Loos in *A Girl Like I* (1966), *Kiss Hollywood Goodbye* (1974), and *Cast of Thousands* (1977). *The Memoirs of Will H. Hays* are informative but dull. In *The Day the Laughter Stopped* (1976), David Yallop thoroughly discredits the loathsome charges leveled against Roscoe "Fatty" Arbuckle.

Acknowledgments

In my research I have enjoyed the resources and professional services of the Huntington Library at San Marino, the Bancroft Library of the University of California at Berkeley, the California State Library of Sacramento, the Public Library of San Francisco, the Library of the California Historical Society of San Francisco, the Library of the Society of California Pioneers in San Francisco, and the Mechanics' Institute Library of San Francisco. In each of these institutions I have benefited by those standards of service that are rightly among the glories of American librarianship. I wish particularly to acknowledge the kind assistance of Noelle Jackson, Kathy Martin, Virginia Renner, Doris Smedes, and Mary Wright at the Huntington; Gladys Hansen and Rhona Klein at San Francisco Public; and Irene Moran at the Bancroft. I would also like to thank the John Simon Guggenheim Memorial Foundation, the Huntington Library, and the National Endowment for the Humanities for assistance in the preparation of this study and—it is hoped—the ensuing volumes of the Americans and the California Dream series. James Raimes and Sheldon Meyer of Oxford University Press, New York, deserve special thanks for encouraging me to return to Californian studies amidst my other involvements. President John LoSchiavo, SJ, Dean David A. Harnett, and Dean Kathleen E. Dubs of the University of San Francisco, and Donald Winks, senior vice president of the San Francisco office of Hill and Knowlton, Inc., have been especially supportive. I owe special thanks to Marjorie Blackwell and Donald A. Plansky for help in reading galleys and to Patrick McCarthy, who proved of invaluable assistance in researching photographs of turn-of-the-century Southern California. Azita Adle and Linda E. Woodrich helped in the typing of the final draft. Tessa DeCarlo of Oxford University Press worked wonders with a bulky detail-laden manuscript and provided invaluable help with the index.

I wish to thank the following organizations which have kindly permitted reproduction of photographs: the Bancroft Library, University of California, Berkeley; Bison Archives, Los Angeles; California Historical Society, San Francisco; California Historical Society/Ticor Title Insurance, Los Angeles; the Huntington Library, San Marino; the *Los Angeles Times*; San Francisco Archives; the San Francisco Public Library; the Security Pacific National Bank Collection/Los Angeles Public Library; the Southwest Museum, Los Angeles; and the University of California Department of Special Collections, University Research Library, Los Angeles.

California studies are a movable feast, enlisting individuals active in a variety of other pursuits. Over the years the following individuals have helped along my ongoing dialogue with the California past: Gunther Barth, the late Walton Bean, Hugh Berryman, the late Ray Billington, R. A. Burchell, Michael Bush, Francis Carney, Robert Judson Clark, Randolph Delehanty, Richard Dillon, Stephen Fender, Charles Fracchia, Herb Garcia, Lois Gordon, Robert Gordon, M.D., James D. Hart, Therese Heyman, J. S. Holliday, the late Warren Howell, Andrew Jameson, Claudia Jurmain, William Kahrl, Harold Kirker, Gary Kurutz, Eugene Lee, Nina Lobonov, Oscar Lewis, Richard Longstreth, Robert Middlekauff, Doris Muscatine, Peter O'Malley Pierson, Lawrence Clark Powell, Pamela Prince, James Rawls, Dmitri Shipounoff, Albert Shumate, M.D., the late Claude Simpson, Gibbs Smith, Edward Staniford, Stanley Stewart, Richard Stevens Street, the late Franklin Walker, James P. Walsh, and T. H. Watkins.

Sheila, Marian, and Jessica Starr remain my continuing sources of pleasure and encouragement.

San Francisco, September 1984

Index

369

15, 38; consolidation of, 15, 39-40, 164; in *Ramona*, 62; Malibu Rancho, 15; Rancho Alamos, 16; Rancho Camulos, 21, 23, 56, 57, 60, 62; Rancho Cañada de los Alisos, 16; Rancho Cañada Larga y Verde, 16; Rancho El Tejón, 21, 29, 164 (*See also* Téjon, the); Rancho Heurta de Cuati, 38; Rancho La Ballona, 80; Rancho La Jurupa, 19, 38, 144; Rancho Los Alamitos, 15, 17, 39, 40; Rancho Los Cerritos, 15, 39, 40; Rancho Los Coyotes, 19; Rancho Los Flores, 19; Rancho Los Feliz, 65; Rancho Los Palos Verdes, 15, 39; Rancho Paso de Bartolo Viejo, 15, 19; Rancho Rodeo de las Aguas, 15; Rancho San Justo, 39-40; Rancho San José, 15; Rancho San José de Buenos Aires, 38; Rancho San Pasqual, 15, 53, 99; Rancho San Pedro, 15; Rancho Santa Ana, 38, 39; Rancho Santa Anita, 38, 39; Rancho Santa Gertrudis, 52; Rancho Santa Margarita, 19; Rancho San Vicente y Santa Monica, 15; Rancho Topanga Malibu y Sequit, 69; Ranchos de la Positas y la Calera, Los, 38
Ransome, Ernest L., 195
Rappe, Virginia, 325-27
Rebecca of Sunnybrook Farm (Wiggin), 222-23
Reid, Wallace, 321, 329, 330, 332
Religion: and Christian Socialism, 211-12, 219; in old Los Angeles, 14, 15, 42; and movies, 330-34; and Hollywood as Protestant myth, 284-85, 316, 332-33, 338. *See also* Catholicism; Episcopalianism; Progressivism in California; Prohibitionism
Reminiscences of a Ranger, The (Bell), 31; military metaphor in, 32-33
Report on Grapes and Wines in California (Haraszthy), 148
Republican party, 53, 70, 74; and California elite, 206, 263-64; and decline of Progressivism, 270-72, 275; reform faction of, 202-3, 212, 235, 237, 242, 253, 263; and Southern Pacific, 200, 201, 204; and suffrage leadership, 259
Rhodes, Eugene Manlove, 113
Richardson, H. H., 177, 181
Ridley, Alonzo, 23
Rindge, Frederick Hastings, 68-69
Riverside, 86, 87; as quintessential citrus town, 144-47
Roosevelt, Franklin Delano, 277, 278, 281
Roosevelt, Theodore, 121, 203, 227, 243,

270; and Hiram Johnson, 199, 238, 261; *See also* Lummis, Charles Fletcher; Parent navel oranges
Rowell, Chester, 203, 234-36, 242, 245, 258, 259, 269, 276; and C. E. Hughes, 271; on Japan and Japanese, 260; and labor, 237-38; post-Progressive career of, 273, 274, 277-78; and Progressive campaigns, 252-53, 254, 263
Royce, Josiah, 32, 95, 298
Ruef, Abraham, 201, 238, 242, 249, 250, 259, 278; and Patrick Calhoun, 207, 243; in prison, 281-82; and San Francisco graft trials, 243-44; and "The Shame of San Francisco," 204-5, 253
Ruiz, Francisco, 21
Rust, Horatio Nelson, 108

Sánchez, Francisco de Jesús, 56-57, 60
Saint Vibiana's Cathedral (Los Angeles), 42
San Francisco, 12, 31, 73, 193-94; and agriculture, 128, 130-31, 140; "Easternism" and, 181-82, 185, 205; elite of, 205-7, 223; labor in, 238, 281; and Market Street bombing of 1916, 275; and Mediterraneanism, 183, 187-88; and early movie industry, 288-89. *See also* Architecture; Brown, Arthur Page; Education; Progressivism
San Francisco Chronicle, 182, 196, 241
San Francisco Examiner, 154, 202, 203, 264, 325; and Maynard Dixon, 123, 124. *See also* "Man with the Hoe, The,"
San Francisco Morning Call, 123; and Fremont Older, 241
San Pasqual, battle of, 16, 18, 22, 23, 24; bravery of Californios at, 16; First U.S. Dragoons in, 24
San Simeon, 280-81
Santa Catalina island, 52, 108; developed as resort, 66
Santa Fe Railroad, 40, 41, 49; and citrus culture, 141, 146
Saunders, William, 141
Sbarboro, Andrea, 166, 167; on wine as a temperance agent, 157
Schmitz, Eugene, 204, 242, 243, 244, 250, 251
Schneider, Rev. F., 141
Schram, Jacob, 150
Schweinfurth, A. C., 187; as A.P. Brown's chief designer, 179-82; and Sainte Claire Club, 190; and Ferry Building, 194